CROWDS

CRO

Stanford University Press

Stanford, California

2006

Edited by Jeffrey T. Schnapp and Matthew Tiews

Stanford University Press
Stanford, California

This book has been published with the assistance of
the Stanford Humanities Lab and The Seaver Institute.

Printed in the United States of America on acid-free,
archival-quality paper

Library of Congress Cataloging-in-Publication Data

Crowds / edited by Jeffrey T. Schnapp and Matthew
Tiews.

    p.   cm.
    Includes bibliographical references and index.
    ISBN 0-8047-5479-9 (cloth : alk. paper)
    ISBN 0-8047-5480-2 (pbk. : alk. paper)
    1. Crowds.   2. Collective behavior.   I. Schnapp,
Jeffrey T. (Jeffrey Thompson), 1954–   II. Tiews,
Matthew.
  HM871.C76   2006
  302.3'3—DC22   2005026558

Designed by Tim Roberts
Typeset in Helvetica Black and Adobe Garamond

Contents

Introduction: A Book of Crowds

Jeffrey T. Schnapp and Matthew Tiews

IN HIS FOREWORD TO A 1987 publication on *The Crowd in Contemporary Britain,* the eminent judge Leslie George Scarman declared that "it is high time that a properly researched and scientific study should be published of the crowd in contemporary Britain."[1] Although Scarman's statement reflects his own recent role as leader of a government inquiry into the 1981 Brixton riots, it also unconsciously echoes the urgent sense of timeliness underlying Gustave Le Bon's justification for his 1895 best-seller on crowd psychology: "Organized crowds have always played an important part in the life of peoples, but this part has never been of such moment as at present."[2] Crowds, it appears, are an idea whose time has not infrequently come, particularly during the past two and a half centuries of world history. That this should be the case is perhaps unsurprising: as Lord Scarman also points out, "The crowd is nothing new in human society."[3] Indeed, accounts of collective behavior span western history from Plato's worries about mob rule in *The Republic* to the Gospel descriptions of the crowd that cried for Christ's death, from concerned reports of peasant revolts in the early modern era to newspaper headlines about the riots of the post–World War II era, Watts to Brixton to Seattle and Genoa.[4] Yet Le Bon struck a powerful and enduring chord with his ominous pronouncement that "the age we are about to enter will in truth be the ERA OF CROWDS" (*C,* xv).

Le Bon isn't known for understatement, and the popular success of his *Psychologie des foules* is attributable more to his way with aphorism than to rigorous sociological analysis. Rigorous or not, Le Bon's formulations caught on because of their ability to sum up a conviction that had been in the air since the American and French revolutions. It was shared with nineteenth-century predecessors such as Gabriel Tarde, Hippolyte Taine, Enrico Ferri, and Scipio Sighele,[5] and with twentieth-century successors such as Sigmund Freud, Robert Park, José Ortega y

Gasset, and Elias Canetti, not to mention with the leading artists, writers, commentators, historians, and politicians of both centuries.[6] The conviction in question held that even if "the crowd is nothing new in human history," a quantitative and qualitative difference distinguishes modern crowds from their premodern counterparts. In some deep and essential sense, crowds *are* modernity. Modern times are crowded times. Modern man is the man of the crowd.

By providing a readable and provocative synthesis, Le Bon's treatise both inaugurated and popularized the subdiscipline of collective psychology. It has been continuously in print since its first publication, translated into every major language and many minor ones—a Latvian version appeared in 1929—and has gone through innumerable editions. "While all our ancient beliefs are tottering and disappearing, while the old pillars of society are giving way one by one," the work goes on to argue in a prefatory passage alluded to in several essays in the present volume, "the power of the crowd is the only force that nothing menaces, and of which the prestige is continually on the increase" (*C*, xiv–xv). Despite their purported ties to a primal scene associated with premodern and even prehistoric predecessors, modern crowds are not reducible to updated tribes or clans. Heterogeneous and unstable, they arise as the result of the promiscuous intermingling and physical massing of social classes, age groups, races, nationalities, and genders along the boulevards of the industrial metropolis. They can no longer be conceived of as the passive subjects of history: as unruly hordes—or, better, herds—tamed and disciplined by some higher order of beings, be they priests, nobles, monarchs, or philosophers. Rather, the tumultuous events of 1776 and 1789 have recast the once reviled multitudes in the role of history's protagonists. The *res publica*, or "public thing," is now firmly in their hands: the state, economic production, communications, culture, the law. Theirs is the power to make and unmake all forms of government. Theirs is the new language of political action based on electoral campaigns, popular assemblies, and symbolic protest marches performed in city streets and squares. Theirs are the new media of mass persuasion from broadsheets to newspapers to posters to radio and television. In the era of crowds, the cornerstone of the state is popular sovereignty, not the inherited privilege of monarchs.

Le Bon's apocalypticism is hyperbolic and conveys the mixed sense of panic and expectation that animated public debates regarding the rise of mass-based civilizations and market-based economies at the turn-of-the-twentieth-century mark. As contemporary critics such as Tarde were quick to point out, his analysis is also crude, confusing as it does the vast realm of opinion or "mental" forms of assembly with that much smaller and intermittent realm of "psychic connections produced by physical contacts."[7] There can nonetheless be little disagreement regarding the accuracy of Le Bon's claims regarding the leading role assumed by mass assemblies in the political, economic, and cultural life of the industrial era. But to what degree has that leading role carried over to the postindustrial world? Do we still inhabit an era of crowds in any meaningful sense? Have modern models of political action been supplanted by more recent models that, instead of being based on the literal physical massing of bodies in public places, are based instead on spectacular gestures shaped by and for electronic media, representations that erase the boundary line between public and private space and that rely on virtual and asynchronous forms of presence and participation? If so, what are the implications for democracy, culture, and society?

Starting in 2000, the Stanford Humanities Lab (SHL) Crowds project undertook the task of tracing a cultural and social history of the rise and fall of the modern crowd—particularly the political crowd—between the great revolutions of the eighteenth century and the present. From the outset, the project's working hypotheses were as follows:

1. The era of popular sovereignty, industrialization, and ur-

banization saw the rise of a constellation of new forms of mass assembly and collective social action that reached their apogee in the first half of the twentieth century.

2. These forms began to attenuate gradually in the second half of the century, particularly in the wake of the protest movements of the 1960s and 1970s, as a result of the proliferation and ever-increasing prevalence of virtual or media-based forms of "assembly" over physical assemblies in postindustrial societies, as well as to long-term trends promoting economic decentralization, suburban sprawl, increased mobility, and political disengagement.

3. This shift, rather than abolishing the equation between crowds and modernity, has reshaped it, channeling experiences of crowding in postindustrial societies into certain limited domains of civic and electoral ritual, entertainment, and leisure, while assigning to large-scale mass political actions a fallback function restricted to times of exception (war, acute social conflicts, and the like).

The thesis was thus less one of rupture than of a process of specialization whose ultimate outcome is a progressive reduction of the role of physical crowds to that of an icon that circulates within a political economy characterized by the coexistence of media aggregation and bodily disaggregation. The icon in question is subject to a variety of uses and appropriations; its currency is sustained by contemporary resurgences of the history of marches, rallies, riots, and assemblies. It tends, however, to appear under an ever-deepening patina of otherness and anachronism: "otherness" inasmuch as the face of contemporary multitudes has increasingly become a foreign face associated with conflicts in Asia, the Middle East, and Africa relayed into first world living rooms and bedrooms via electronic media; "anachronism" to the degree that, even in the developing world, contemporary mass actions appear to have become ever more "citational"—they quote, sometimes in a nostalgic key, from a previous, now irrecuperable heroic era of

crowds—or designed for media audiences in remote locations—hence the prevalence of banners in English in non-Anglophone settings. The result is a decoupling of Le Bon's equation between crowds and contemporaneity.

As explained at greater length in the second half of the introduction, this volume represents one of three interconnected outputs of the SHL Crowds project. None of the three could have been realized without the generous support of the Seaver Institute, and of its director Victoria Seaver Dean, whose willingness to underwrite this experiment has been at once courageous and exemplary. Like the exhibition Revolutionary Tides: The Art of the Political Poster 1914–1989, to which it is tied, and the Web site (http://crowds.stanford.edu/) that serves as a bridge between exhibition and book, *Crowds* explores, nuances, and challenges the above working hypotheses by means of a sustained engagement with key aspects of the history of modern crowds. Its overall ambitions are to provide a reconstruction of the corpus of images and fictions of the collectivity that artists and writers elaborated between the eighteenth century and the present; to explore literature and art's complex dialogue with the new media-saturated public sphere that emerged in tandem with the new politics founded on principles of popular sovereignty; and to examine the interplay between these cultural products and the emergence of crowd-centered discourses in social sciences such as psychology, anthropology, sociology, and economics. A comprehensive cultural history of modern crowds can only be written by bringing together this multitude of facets in the service of a multiperspective, multilayered portrait.

The centrality of crowds and crowd-related phenomena to modern life has long been acknowledged to the point of becoming a mere commonplace, readily absorbed into larger, more encompassing labels like "mass culture." It has remained marginally visible in most post–World War II scholarship either as a result of the ubiquity of the phenomena in question (which have become naturalized over the course of two centuries) or because it has been approached in piecemeal fashion within the framework of a single discipline. An inherently expansive question requiring expertise from a diversity of disciplines and specializations within them, modern crowds are precisely the sort of large-scale topic that the SHL was established to address. SHL (http://shl.stanford.edu), founded in 2000 with seed monies from Stanford's then-president, Gerhard Casper, offers the opportunity for scholars and students in humanities disciplines to undertake the sort of large-scale, long-term, team-based, technology- and resource-intensive research projects that have traditionally been the domain of the laboratory sciences. Humanists have typically worked in isolation, performing their research and their writing much like traditional artisans, training their graduate and undergraduate students accordingly, and relying on the medium of print for the presentation and dissemination of their research results. Much as in the sciences and social sciences, disciplinary and institutional pressures have led to increasing hyperspecialization in humanities disciplines over the course of the post–World War II period and have often contributed to a narrowing of research agendas. On the positive side, the result has been a higher degree of rigor and expertise in individual fields and subfields, and the emergence of an expanded archipelago of domains of expert knowledge; on the negative side, fundamental questions can find themselves overlooked in favor of a myriad of mostly centripetal conversations limited to specific subdisciplines, with the result being a widening gulf between university-based research and potential interlocutors both within the university (students, curators, librarians) and outside (members of the educated public, media, museums, corporations). The SHL was founded on the belief that major opportunities for collaboration and innovation, not to mention for imaginative uses of information technologies and digital media, are lost as a result of the limitations imposed by this conventional approach to the production and presentation of humanities research.

The SHL has put in place a new model for humanities research and hands-on humanities training at all levels, from undergraduate to postdoctoral, that is project-based and collaborative in nature. Teams of faculty, students, and other on- and off-campus collaborators work under the leadership of a principal investigator in a true laboratory setting on undertakings whose scope and ambition render them high impact, high visibility, and multidisciplinary in a true (that is, nonornamental) sense. Project outputs typically experiment with hybrid models of scholarly "publishing," involve the multipurposing or repurposing of both new and traditional forms of scholarship, and cast students in the role of researchers and project leaders. SHL projects envisage themselves as "big humanities" projects—the analogy with "big science" is intentional—built on expert knowledge, but with an outreach dimension that often involves partnerships with public institutions such as museums, contemporary arts centers, and libraries, as well as innovative uses of social software, collaborative authoring tools, and new media technologies. The lab operates as an incubator: it provides physical facilities, financial and technical support, and expertise in project design and implementation while serving as a matchmaker with intramural and extramural partners once projects reach a mature phase of development.

The Crowds project was one of the flagship projects dating back to the time of the SHL's creation. During the course of the five years of its development, it has involved over fifty undergraduates, several dozen graduate students, and faculty at Stanford, the University of California, Berkeley, and numerous other institutions. An ongoing reading group and three seminars have played a key role in its unfolding with many of the elements that make up the *Crowds* book, as well as the Crowds Web site (http://crowds.stanford.edu/), prepared as course assignments within a seminar setting. The book itself is an experimental hybrid whose contours deliberately overlap those of the project Web site and the Revolutionary Tides exhibition. This book, the product of a complex gestational process that deviated from standard models for putting together multiauthor volumes, assumed its shape as an unabashedly *crowded* volume, with conventional essays interwoven with semantic histories and testimonials—the result of sustained interaction and teamwork involving a core project team made up of faculty and graduate students.

❋

When Victor Hugo describes a fifteenth-century Feast of Fools in *The Hunchback of Notre Dame* (1831), he famously compares the gathered multitude to a body of water: "To the spectators at the windows, the palace yard crowded with people looked like a sea, into which five or six streets, like the mouths of so many rivers, disgorged their living streams. The waves of this sea, incessantly swelled by new arrivals, broke against the corners of the houses."[8] Like Hugo's living streams, scholarship on crowds has itself come in waves over the past century—indeed, often in direct or oblique response to waves of crowd activity. If Le Bon and company attempted to define and analyze the menace of crowd behavior in the turbulent years after the Paris Commune and during Third Republic industrial strikes and post-Risorgimento uprisings, World War I proved an inspiration to the Anglo-Saxon sociological tradition for studies of collective activity in the military and in wartime civilian populations.[9] The next great wave of crowd studies, inspired by a Marxism running the gamut from mild to militant, concentrated on crowds in history, eschewing two fundamental principles of its predecessors: the idea that there exists a single psychology of the crowd—indeed, that there exists something like *the* crowd at all—and the concern with control over collective behavior. Following Georges Lefebvre's lead, George Rudé's classic study of the *Crowd in the French Revolution* (1959) examines crowd events "from below," an-

alyzing the varied demographic makeup of different Revolutionary multitudes and emphasizing the motivated and purposeful nature of crowd behavior.[10] Rudé's study finds its analogue in a body of work by leftist historians, including Lefebvre, Eric Hobsbawm, and E. P. Thompson—studies redescribing the Revolutionary and labor mobs that so concerned Taine and Le Bon as collections of discrete individuals engaged in a long tradition of protests against food shortages and political injustice.[11] The American school of social psychology, having reached a somewhat similar conclusion regarding the agency of collectivities from Neil Smelser's *Theory of Collective Behavior* (1962),[12] found itself poised to react to the mass demonstrations of the 1960s and 1970s with a mixture of political sympathy and scientific curiosity: typical is Sam Wright's *Crowds and Riots: A Study in Social Organization* (1978)—number 4 in the series Sociological Observations along with *The Nude Beach* (number 1) and *Seeking Spiritual Meaning* (number 2). "This is a book," Wright begins, "based on my observations of crowds and riots. . . . over a three-year period, I took notes while sitting, walking, and running about in situations of collective behavior."[13]

Neither the running about of activist social psychology nor the meticulously reconstructed riot demographics of the Rudé school of social history were much in evidence, however, when literary and cultural historians began revisiting the crowd. Instead, turn-of-the-century crowd theorists made a comeback as a series of studies devoted to reconstructing the intellectual and historical context of Le Bon and his peers began to appear: Robert Nye's *The Origins of Crowd Psychology* (1975); Serge Moscovici's *The Age of the Crowd* (1981; English edition 1985), which rehabilitates largely uncritically turn-of-the-century crowd writings; Susanna Barrows's *Distorting Mirrors: Visions of the Crowd in Late Nineteenth-Century France* (1981), which attempts to limn the gap between empirical evidence of uprisings in the late nineteenth century and the rhetoric of the crowd psychologists; Jaap van Ginneken's *Crowds, Psychology, and Politics* (1992), which extends and refines the foregoing studies.[14] The disciplinary marginality of these inquiries is amply demonstrated by the series designation of Barrows's book: Yale Historical Publications, Miscellany. The topic continues to be addressed to this day, but only in monodisciplinary and monographic studies: studies focusing on specific food riots in preindustrial Europe, examining the image of the crowd in the French nineteenth-century naturalist novel, tracing the demographic rise of industrial cities, analyzing group portraiture as practiced by this or that modern artist, charting the emergence of mass revivalist movements or mass entertainment forms.[15] But to date, there has been nothing approaching a comprehensive study of the cultural or historical importance of crowds and crowding, not to mention a study that intertwines humanities and social science perspectives.[16] To echo Lord Scarman, it is high time that such an enterprise be undertaken.

The present volume provides a deliberately crowded, multilayered look at modern multitudes by weaving together three types of contributions: full-length essays that slice their object of study in a number of ways; short essays that assume the form of "testimonies" regarding firsthand experiences of crowd behavior; and microhistories that track the shifting semantic fields of key vocabulary concerning collectivities. More extensive sets of both the testimonies and semantic histories figure on the Crowds project Web site, alongside a searchable database of rare but important social science writings on crowds from 1850 to 1920 in England, France, Germany, Italy, Spain, and the United States. The main sector of the Web site also features iconographic resources, reference materials on crowd theorists, and arrays of virtual galleries concerning topics such as theater riots, subway crowds, and crowd photography, and the history of techniques for calculating the size of crowds. In short, although the *Crowds* book is designed to function as a free-standing, self-sufficient artifact, its true identity is that of a print/digital hybrid that blurs the line between compo-

nents that are static and dynamic, definitively "built," infinitely buildable. Its cover provides shelter not only to paper pages but also to flickering pixels and digital sound files.

The backbone of the volume, however, consists in essays written from a multitude of disciplinary perspectives. Some track the history of a particular type of crowd: Susanna Elm describes the collective activity associated with pilgrims and martyrs; Allen Guttmann provides a historical overview of sports crowds; Urs Stäheli analyzes the behavior of crowds in financial markets. Other essays focus on problems of representing mass phenomena in different media: Jeffrey T. Schnapp uses the medium of photography as a lens through which to investigate the modernity of crowds in "Mob Porn"; Christine Poggi surveys "Art in the Age of the Crowd"; Andrew V. Uroskie discusses "The Spatial Rhetoric of Mass Representation"; John Plotz analyzes the vexed issue of the crowd as represented in American sociology; Anton Kaes explores the interplay between film's mass audience and its portrayal of urban crowds. Some of the contributions provide theses on the historical rise of certain aspects of the modern crowd: Joy Connolly interrogates the American interest in Roman crowd rhetoric; William Egginton outlines the shift from audience to crowd on the basis of the dynamic interplay of intimacy and anonymity in early modern theater audiences; Stefan Jonsson provides an overview of "The Invention of the Masses" in nineteenth-century France; Joan Ramon Resina discusses the rhetoric of medicalization in twentieth-century Spanish crowd theory. Other articles investigate crowd dynamics in specific contexts: Jessica Burstein's "Agoraphobia" riffs on the psychodynamics of externality and collectivity; Charles Tilly's "WUNC" provides a set of criteria for evaluating the effectiveness of collective action; Haun Saussy in "Crowds, Number, and Mass in China" examines the interaction between Asian and western imaginations of crowd behavior; Jobst Welge outlines the idealization of solitude that provides the counterpoint to modern descriptions of the multitude. Abstracts of each contribution appear following the table of contents to the book.

The essays are accompanied by an array of personal testimonies in which writers, scholars, artists, social activists, and ordinary witnesses reflect on their participation in major and minor moments of the post–World War II history of multitudes and on the impact that such events have had on their lives. The purpose of these contributions is to provide an experiential counterpart to the historical essays, with an eye to tracking continuities and discontinuities between the present era and that of Le Bon. Variable in character and tone, they address this issue as *an open question*, whereas the essays tend to position themselves on one side or another of the project's working hypotheses.

Interspersed among the essays and testimonies are a sampling of microhistories that explore the shifting semantic fields of terms associated with multitudes in such languages as English, Russian, Chinese, ancient Greek, Latin, Sanskrit, Spanish, French, and Italian. Like the visual conventions for representing crowds elaborated by artists, words powerfully shape the very debates and conversations within which they circulate as a common coin. Much rides on the distinctions of meaning, nuance, or implication between terms like *crowd, multitude, mob, mass, people*, and *collectivity*. Microhistories of these and other keywords provide a tightly focused framework for reconstructing the history of mentalities and ideas in ways that complement the arguments elaborated in the full-length essays. A more exhaustive set of semantic histories is available on the Crowds Web site. (Readers of this volume are encouraged to submit additional semantic histories and testimonies, as well as virtual galleries, via the contact e-mail addresses listed on the Web site.)

As noted above, one of the SHL's core goals is to expand the audience for high-level humanistic research by means of partnerships with public institutions. To that end, this book is being published concurrently with a major exhibi-

tion, Revolutionary Tides, which runs from September 14 through December 31, 2005, at the Iris & B. Gerald Cantor Center for Visual Arts at Stanford University and reopens at the Wolfsonian-Florida International University in Miami Beach, where it will be on display between February 24 and July 25, 2006.

Revolutionary Tides has a narrower focus than the *Crowds* book. It examines the artistic consequences of the triumph of popular sovereignty as a political ideal more than a century after the French Revolution. The exhibition and accompanying catalog (published in Milan by Skira in English, French, and Italian) track the changing face of revolution from World War I through the year of the fall of the Berlin wall by means of more than a hundred political posters as well as a number of related sculptures and objects from twenty countries, drawn from the collections of the Hoover Institution Archives and the Wolfsonian-Florida International University. Whereas the conventional approach to poster art emphasizes classifications based on artist, period, and nationality, or the development of specific technical practices, Revolutionary Tides is instead concerned with the emergence of a common graphic vernacular for depicting multitudes as political actors on a worldwide scale and in a multiplicity of only loosely interconnected artistic, political, and historical settings.

The show proposes a macrohistory of the political poster, with microhistorical texture provided by highly detailed captions gathered together in the Revolutionary Tides section of the Crowds project Web site, one "wing" of which serves as a virtual counterpart to the physical exhibition. It is organized into narrative units, each of which explores a particular graphic convention, iconographic element, or theme related to political crowds. Each unit blends together works by such celebrated artists as John Heartfield, Gustav Klucis, Valentina Kulagina, Norman Rockwell, and Xanti Schawinsky with works whose authors are long forgotten.

How to represent the people as the cornerstone of the

legitimacy of modern nation-states, their institutions, and laws? How to translate the abstract notion of the popular will into concrete visual terms? How to portray the decisive role played by mass movements in effecting social change? How to depict the modern mass leader with respect to the multitudes and vice versa? How to transform the mass medium that is the political poster into an effective tool of mass persuasion and mobilization? These are the sorts of questions that the artists represented in Revolutionary Tides set out to answer, however divergent their artistic stances, political beliefs, or the historical context to which they belonged.

✳

When our project team first set to work in 2000, it was easy enough to see the signs that Le Bon's *era of crowds* was nearing its end, at least in the world's leading industrial/postindustrial nations. The signs were both direct and indirect, short term and long term. Mass conscription armies were rapidly becoming a thing of the past. Organized labor was on the decline, and the organization of work was becoming increasingly flexible and atomized. Voting patterns continued to drift toward nonparticipation. Although urban agglomerations continued to expand in developing countries, suburban development was the driving force in their wealthy counterparts. On the American scene, the marches on Washington of the late 1990s seemed pale echoes of their Civil Rights era predecessors. "Crowds" of twenty individuals packed into the lens of a television camera had replaced the masses of demonstrators of an earlier era, and even the 1999 Seattle WTO protests seemed cast in the mold more of anarchist skirmishes than of classical mass actions. The defining collectivities of the new millennium seemed to be

the online masses in chat rooms, connected only by fiber optics and a shared passion for collectibles, gossip, or massively networked multiplayer games; or drivers, each hermetically sealed into an automobile container, gridlocked in roving bumper-to-bumper assemblies; or pedestrians milling about each in a solipsistic entertainment cocoon of his or her own devising.

These and other features of contemporary life point to a fundamental shift in the nature of multitudes. But do they truly dictate the crowd's obituary—or at least the obituary of crowds as literal physical assemblies? Probably not, as attested to by a recent upsurge in optimistic ruminations on the present and future of crowds found in works of economic analysis (James Surowiecki's *The Wisdom of Crowds*), technological foresight (Howard Rheingold's *Smart Mobs*) and even political theory (Tony Negri and Michael Hardt's *Multitudes*). So any obituary would be premature.[17] Various pasts continually inhabit every historical present, even in the era of globalization. History remains forever capable of high degrees of simultaneity, complexity, and contradiction. Even at its leading edge, brief fads like that for "flash mobs"—crowds of the underemployed and overconnected who contact each other by e-mail and wireless devices in order to assemble for the simultaneous performance of quirky gestures—confess the enduring lure of collective action, however ironically. And the millions worldwide who marched against the war in Iraq, the hundreds of thousands who continue to bring down regime after regime in the former Soviet bloc, the oceanic multitudes who participate in mass acts of mourning like the funeral ceremonies of Pope John Paul II, the legions of fans who regularly fill athletic stadiums, argue against any rush to declare the crowd at its end. Whether those who comprise such crowds belong to the past or to the present, this book is their book.

Abstracts

In "Mob Porn," Jeffrey T. Schnapp traces a speculative history of large-scale group portraiture in western art by means of a reconstruction of the broader setting within which panoramic photographs of human multitudes became graphic highlights of 1930s illustrated magazines. The essay identifies two dominant (and sometimes intertwined) modes for imag(in)ing the formation of the body politic: the *emblematic*, associated with the emergence of symbolic forms out of masses of individuals, and the *oceanic*, associated instead with moments of collective fusion within the framework of the political sublime. The latter informs the practice of panoramic crowd photography whose emergence, evolution, and technical practices are tracked with particular attention to the case of fascist Italy.

Stefan Jonsson's essay, "The Invention of the Masses: The Crowd in French Culture from the Revolution to the Commune," provides a detailed examination of a crucial era in the modern history of crowds. From the French Revolution and its earliest critics such as Edmund Burke, through the celebration of the modern urban crowd in Poe and Baudelaire, to the devastating critical attacks on the masses in the wake of the bloody Commune of Paris in 1871, Jonsson traces the shaping of the notion of the crowd in the era of popular sovereignty. Commenting on seminal political, artistic, and literary representations of the masses, Jonsson also notes the importance of the burgeoning social sciences, particularly statistics, in defining this new entity.

Joy Connolly takes the movie *Ben Hur* as the starting point for "Crowd Politics: The Myth of the *Populus Romanus*." Why is twentieth-century American cinema so fascinated with the Roman crowd? Looking at Roman representations of the populus, Connolly explores the ways Roman texts describe these collectivities as not-crowds: as homogeneous, unified, and obedient to their leaders. This is, she argues, a crucial part of the availability of the notion of "the People" for modern theorists of popular sovereignty who seek inspiration in the Roman republic.

William Egginton shows, in "Intimacy and Anonymity, or How the Audience Became a Crowd," the historical importance of the theatrical audience to the modern notion of the crowd. Examining theatrical institutions from the medieval period to the nineteenth century, primarily in Spain and France, he argues that early modern playhouses, responding to anxieties about unruly spectators, shaped their audiences into the kind of entity that came to worry nineteenth-century crowd theorists. This occurs, for Egginton, along the fault line between intimacy and anonymity. As he writes, "Precisely, in other words, as the rabble (*vulgo*) coalesce and are relegated to a certain negative collectivity, a distance is espoused between the realm of that collectivity (publicity) and an interiority whose depths are theorized as being both constructible and potentially infinite."

"Sports Crowds," Allen Guttmann's contribution to the volume, traces sports spectatorship through the centuries, from Greek and Roman games to modern mass athletic spectacles. A distinguishing feature of sports audiences is that the spectators are usually sports *fans*. "They see themselves," Guttmann notes, "as active participants, inspiring the home team with their cheers and demoralizing the visiting team with their taunts." Guttmann explores the ramifications of this psychological identification, showing how collectivities are built on shared affinities, and how this often leads to aggressivity. Although he argues against the idea that such aggression is ultimately cathartic, Guttmann notes the importance of such ritual in experiencing the excitement of agonistic contest without running entirely amok.

In "Captive Crowds: Pilgrims and Martyrs," Susanna Elm provides an outline of the history of religious crowds in western culture, beginning with pilgrimages to Jerusalem in the fourth century, and touching on the Crusades on the way to an analysis of the nineteenth-century apotheosis of Lourdes as a pilgrimage site. What began as an individual pursuit becomes, Elm shows, a collective phenomenon in the modern era. Pilgrimages are important for crowd theory as they become intertwined with media of communication and reliant on a tension between the modernity of mass mobilization and the ancient lure of the miraculous.

Anton Kaes devotes most of "Movies and Masses" to an analysis of Fritz Lang's *Metropolis*. Placing the film in the context of mass uprisings in Vienna, a rise in industrial mass production, and a new culture of mass entertainment, Kaes shows that the movie does not just depict crowds, it also creates the community of moviegoers—heterogeneous and unstable, to the difference of theater audiences—as itself a mass. "Only in the mass medium of film," he writes, "do the masses become visible to themselves—as spectators."

The role of the crowd in modern artistic production is outlined by Christine Poggi in "Mass, Pack, and Mob: Art in the Age of the Crowd." Beginning with a discussion of military painting and early nineteenth-century panoramas, Poggi traces the representation of masses through Manet and Seurat, the avant-gardes of the early twentieth century, and post World War II artists such as Joseph Beuys and John Baldessari. Woven through this story is an account of the importance of media—media of artistic production as well as media of communication—in the creation and representation of the crowd in art.

John Plotz's lively contribution to this volume, "The Return of the Blob, or How Sociology Decided to Stop Worrying and Love the Crowd," traces twentieth-century American sociology's conflicted relationship to the multitude. David Riesman's *The Lonely Crowd* and William Whyte's *The Organization Man* define 1950s social science as a denunciation of the seductive power of "the social" and its avatar, "the crowd." How then should we read the success of the recent return to the social in such critics as Robert Putnam? Plotz's essay responds with a lucid account of the sometimes strained interaction between sociological theory and cultural movements.

Joan Ramon Resina focuses, in "From Crowd Psychology to Racial Hygiene: The Medicalization of Reaction and the New Spain," on two major figures in Spanish crowd theory from the 1930s and 1940s: José Ortega y Gasset and Antonio Vallejo Nágera. If Ortega's *Revolt of the Masses* famously depicts the masses as a quantitative accumulation uncomfortably (and perhaps illegitimately) sharing space with traditional sources of authority, Vallejo relies on medicalized theories of degeneration to paint the masses as the embodiment of a pathological society. Ultimately, Resina argues, "To Ortega's bleak vision of an empire of the masses, fascism opposed a Hispanic empire. . . . The Hispanic doctrine thus became an alternative to the abhorred philosophical snares born of the Industrial Revolution, each, in its own way, proclaiming the triumph of the masses."

In "Crowds, Number, and Mass in China," Haun Saussy outlines some of the major issues in the discussion of crowds in Asia, whose populousness has long been described by westerners as "a mere plurality without individuality, a passive reservoir of labor power awaiting orders from an imperial throne—in short, a crowd of the 'defective' kind." While parsing this western response to Asian crowds, Saussy also offers a nuanced reading of several moments in Chinese imperial history where popular action is described with particular attention to its agency. Throughout, he highlights the importance of linguistic representation of crowds in the creation of a "crowd phenomenon": "The nominalism that would make *crowd* a mere designation in the mind links with the verbal magic that 'does things with words,' for to describe a crowd is, in a more than phantasmatic way, to summon it."

Urs Stäheli's "Market Crowds" explores the use of crowd theory in discussions of financial markets. Beginning with Charles Mackay's prototheoretical crowd treatise, *Extraordinary Popular Delusions and the Madness of Crowds* (first published in 1852), Stäheli shows how explanations of mass behavior have been used and abused to predict market actions. Stäheli's paper shows why the semantics of the crowd proves to be so attractive for describing financial speculation. If Mackay sees crowd behavior as a crucial element of modern market speculation, he does not address the question of how to deal with the crowd. Stäheli shows how the investment philosophy of the *Contrarians* benefited from crowd psychology. It is here, he argues, that crowd psychology becomes a tool for constructing the ideal speculator.

Charles Tilly's enigmatically titled contribution to the volume, "WUNC," outlines a general theory for the effectiveness of political demonstrations. Participants, observers, and opponents measure demonstrations against an implicit scorecard, he argues, a scorecard that measures WUNC: worthiness, unity, numbers, and commitment. These elements, in varying combinations, have characterized effective crowd behavior in the modern era. Tilly's essay traces the origin of these values in eighteenth-century social movements and argues for their applicability to demonstrations to this day.

In his essay, "Far Above the Madding Crowd: The Spatial Rhetoric of Mass Representation," Andrew V. Uroskie provides a far-ranging account of the tradition which sees the crowd as a *specific* problem of visual representation, and the way in which this particular question of representing the masses comes to stand in for a more general question of mass representation as such within twentieth-century visual culture. Uroskie examines crowd counting techniques, Soviet constructivism, and popular movies such as King Vidor's *The Crowd*. Ultimately, he concludes that the representation of collectivities within the visual rhetoric and discourses of artistic modernism was never a secure practice, but rather a difficult and ever-changing terrain of investigation.

Jobst Welge engages with the modernist dynamic of the individual versus the masses in "Far from the Crowd: Individuation, Solitude, and 'Society' in the Western Imagination." Noting the disdain of certain modernist writers for the masses, Welge traces the evolution of such anticrowd sentiments, the public, literary performance of solitude, and the perception and representation of crowds from an "individualist" perspective. Welge's trajectory from Petrarch to Peter Sloterdijk, through Rousseau, Poe, Nietzsche, and Rilke, provides a detailed analysis of the relation between individuated observers and formations of the crowd. Welge shows here that there is a long tradition of western lit-erature, both modern and early modern, which expresses the conflicted relationship between the individual and the crowd.

In "Agoraphobia: An Alphabet," Jessica Burstein's abecedarian exploration of the psychological ramifications of modern crowds in popular and academic culture, connections are nothing if not unexpected. Allegory, for instance, is defined as Etymologically, wandering outside of narrative. Experientially, talking without being understood by one's fellow citizens. See *Tenure*." Burstein's playful axioms nonetheless reveal the very great extent to which twentieth-century life is saturated with the rhetoric of the crowd, from movies ("H is for *High Anxiety*") to psychiatry ("D is for *DSM IV*"). Each entry resonates with the fear and attraction produced by public places filled with the multitudes.

CROWDS

1 Mob Porn

Jeffrey T. Schnapp

The sea has a *voice*, which is very changeable and almost always audible. It is a voice
which sounds like a thousand voices, and
much has been attributed to it: patience,
pain, and anger. But what is most impressive about it is its persistence. The sea never
sleeps; by day and by night it makes itself
heard, throughout the years and decades
and centuries. In its impetus and its rage it
brings to mind the one entity which shares
these attributes in the same degree: that is,
the crowd.

—ELIAS CANETTI, *Crowds and Power* (1981)

THE *Rivista Illustrata del Popolo d'Italia* was the lavish mass distribution monthly
to which readers of Italian fascism's official daily could turn for photographs and
articles on current events much like Americans could turn to *Life* magazine, Russians to *Ogonek*, and the Chinese to *China Reconstructs*. Starting in the mid-1920s,
the *Rivista* underwent a graphic makeover; among the changes introduced was the
inclusion of large-format foldouts—panoramic photographs, typically two to six
times wider than the standard page size. Foldouts were not uncommon in period
magazines and, as with 1960s foldouts of *Playboy* bunnies, they were understood
as graphic highlights detachable for purposes of display in the home or workplace.
What first drew my attention to the *Rivista*'s foldouts, however, was the object of
desire draped across the picture plane: teeming, seemingly infinite multitudes rallying around a visible or invisible leader, tightly packed into architectural settings
representative of the great historical cities of the Italian peninsula. The political
rally as source of vicarious photo- or pornographic thrill: such was the graphic
principle that would inform the next fifteen years of the *Rivista Illustrata*'s practice—years during which wave upon wave of innovative artists and graphic designers laid out its pages, among them Bruno Munari, Mario Sironi, Fortunato Dep-
ero, Giò Ponti, and Xanti Schawinsky. The graphic environment shifted with each
successive wave, but not the foldouts. Mass rally after mass rally unfolded in every
number, right up to the collapse of the fascist regime.

The obvious explanation for this persistence was the foldout's propaganda value. The *Rivista* was more than an Italian *Life* magazine. It was a semiofficial party organ, a material conduit between the legions of citizens wedged into squares
and Italian public opinion, whose aim was to promote the image of fascist Italy

as a perpetually mobilized modern nation under the rule of a perpetually mobile modern leader. Yet the notion of propaganda raises more questions than it answers ("propaganda" being the label assigned to forms of mass persuasion to which one is averse). It tells one next to nothing about the nature of the images placed in circulation or about the contours of the sociopolitical imaginary that they hoped to tap into and shape. Nor does it address the larger question of where and how photographic panoramas of the masses fit into the broader stream of crowd images that arises in European culture in the wake of the American and French revolutions, a topic first broached by interwar culture critics such as Siegfried Kracauer and Walter Benjamin, and by postwar art historians such as Wolfgang Kemp, but still acutely in need of the sort of in-depth analysis provided by the present volume and by its companion exhibition and catalog, *Revolutionary Tides*.[1] Last but not least, the invocation of a propagandistic function doesn't help one to understand how and why panoramic representations of political multitudes became intertwined with experimental typography and the art of photomontage and, with slight although significant variations, circulated not only in interwar Italy, Germany, the United States, Brazil, Mexico, and the Soviet Union, but also in the postwar period from the Chinese Cultural Revolution to the protest movements of the 1960s through the 1990s.

So the topic of this essay (as well as of *Revolutionary Tides*) is that literal specter of the Enlightenment known as the revolutionary crowd, hovering between reason and hallucination, between the emancipatory dreams of 1789 and the terror of 1792. It addresses the question of how revolutionary crowds were translated into graphic elements in a media landscape transformed by the spread of inexpensive industrial photolithography, the electronic transmission of photographic images to press agencies, the rise of live media such as radio, and the emergence of visual-verbal hybrids such as photojournalism and newsreels. The process

of translation is not reducible to a single story line. Viewed from the standpoint of artistic technique, it is the tale of an evolving repertory of illustrational, painterly, photographic, and photojournalistic practices that gradually reshaped the once text- and print-based public sphere. Viewed from an art-historical standpoint, it is the story of a complex of differentiated but overlapping iconographies of the crowd and of their place within the history of panoramic modes of representation. Viewed from an intellectual-historical standpoint, it is the story of how these practices and iconographies were influenced by millennium-long habits of metaphorizing, gendering, and abstracting human crowds, central to political philosophy at least as early as Aristotle and as late as Elias Canetti. Viewed from a sociopolitical standpoint, the story is that of the rise of a politics founded on principles of popular sovereignty and of the consequent need for new images and mythologies of the collectivity as well as models of political action and agency based on the physical massing of bodies in public spaces or the performance of symbolic marches and mobilizations in real space and time.[2] It is a multilayered tale, in short, as difficult to contain within the bounds of a single essay as are the oceanic masses enframed within the foldouts of the *Rivista Illustrata,* here woven together into four narrative units bearing the subtitles "Tides," "Types," "Tiles," and "Spillways." "Tides" concerns the oceanic metaphor as applied to crowds. "Types" sketches out the history of what will be referred to as "emblematic" crowd images. "Tiles" describes the development of "oceanic" human panoramas with respect to the prior emblematic tradition. "Spillways" deals with the transformation of "oceanic" fragments back into geometrical emblems in the context of modernist photomontage. The essay concludes with some reflections on the contemporary roles assumed by multitudes: on the one hand, their enduring function as sources of experiences of ecstasy and thrill in the domains of leisure and entertainment; and on the other, their increasing eclipse by virtual counterparts in the politic conflicts of postindustrial societies.

Tides

The phrase *la folla oceanica* (the oceanic mass) was the label applied by both viewers and producers to the *Rivista Illustrata* foldouts. The phrase is ubiquitous in early twentieth-century Italian political discourse, and nowhere more so than in fascist oratory, where it served to enforce fascism's claim that it alone knew how to catalyze and to channel the mighty and mysterious forces that characterized the era of crowds. The "era of crowds" was the definition of modernity proposed in Gustave Le Bon's 1895 classic *Psychologie des foules* and in the works of crowd psychology that influenced it by authors such as Hippolyte Taine and Gabriel Tarde, as well as by members of the Italian Positivist school (Enrico Ferri, Cesare Lombroso, Scipio Sighele, Pasquale Rossi).[3] "While all our ancient beliefs are tottering and disappearing, while the old pillars of society are giving way one by one," Le Bon affirmed with apocalyptic intent, "the power of the crowd is the only force that nothing menaces, and of which the prestige is continually on the increase."[4] Premodern multitudes had long been imagined as elemental hordes to be shaped and subjugated from on high; modern multitudes were instead the volatile protagonists of a volatile era, leaders themselves as well as breeding grounds for new forms of leadership and individualism. Nothing menaced their power because of an inherent heterogeneity and instability. They were the result of the promiscuous intermingling and physical massing of social classes, age groups, races, nationalities, and genders along the great boulevards of the industrial metropolis. Their prestige was continually on the increase because everything modern was potentially at their beck and call: political authority, the state, commerce, communications, culture, economic production. Brought

into being thanks to the loss of conscious personality that was purported to occur when human bodies agglomerate, the modern crowd is not reducible to the average of the individuals that make it up. Rather, it sets off a chain reaction like those that fascinated Le Bon in his writings on atomic particles: "just as in chemistry certain elements, when brought into contact—bases and acids, for example—combine to form a new body possessing properties quite different from those of the bodies that have served to form it," so it is with the crowd.[5] His socialist counterpart Ferri shared the same thought:

Collective psychology concerns not the simple mixing of individual elements, but rather their chemical combination. This means that the resulting psychic collective is not equal to the sum of its individual psychic parts (and this is the case both on the plane of feelings and that of ideas). On the contrary, it is always different, either for the better or for the worse, in precisely the same manner as a chemical combination of two or more substances confers on the final mass a temperature that is higher or lower than that of the bodies that make it up.[6]

The properties in question are the result of multiple liquids combined in a single test tube always with an uncertain outcome: an explosion, a surge of energy, instantaneous decay, new fermentations.

In *Psychologie des foules* Le Bon rarely assimilates the modern mob to tides, open seas, or ocean storms because he didn't need to.[7] The association was firmly established in the western sociopolitical imagination long before the *Rivista Illustra* foldouts were routinely imagined as portraits of human oceans, and long before Scipio Sighele probed the criminal crowd as a "perilous sea . . . whose surfaces are whipped up by every psychological wind."[8] This is attested to in a wide array of nineteenth-century literary sources. Early instances are William Wordsworth's perception of London, in *The Prelude or the Growth of a Poet's Mind*, as a

                                    perpetual flow
Of trivial objects, melted and reduced
To one identity by differences
That have no law, no meaning, and no end,

and Thomas De Quincey's hallucinatory vision of the London cityscape as an ocean "paved with innumerable faces, upturned to the heavens: faces, imploring, wrathful, despairing, surg[ing] upwards by the thousands, by myriads, by generations, by centuries."[9] Other accounts are less nightmarish, like "the tumultuous sea of human heads" that fills the narrator of Edgar Allan Poe's short story "The Man of the Crowd" with "a delicious novelty of emotion," and Charles Baudelaire's seminal writings on the industrial metropolis, where modern individualism is made to hinge on a dandy-bather navigating his way through aquatic multitudes.[10] The metaphor has become a constant by the end of the nineteenth century, shaping everything from Emile Zola's and J.-K. Huysmans's evocations of spectral urban (Paris) and rural (Lourdes) crowds, to Guy de Maupassant's elitist reflections in *Sur l'eau* (*On the Face of the Water*) on how individual wills blend with the common will like "a drop of water is blended with and lost in a river," to the promise lodged at the climax of the 1909 Founding Manifesto of Futurism that futurists will "sing the multicolored and polyphonic tidal waves of revolution in modern capitals."[11]

The "oceanic crowd" is, in point of fact, far more ancient, traceable at least as far back as the long-standing conflation in Greco-Roman culture of *turbulence,* whether maritime, meteorological, or political, with the *turba* (τυρвн), which is to say, the mob. The pairing animates much of ancient political theory as, for example, the characteristic passage in Cicero's *De re publica,* where he asserts that "there is no sea so hard to calm and no fire so hard to check as the vengeance of the unrestrained mob."[12] (Better, accordingly, to build cities destined for permanence and imperial might, like Athens and Rome, at a slight remove from the ocean and its proletarian tides.[13]) The figure recurs in a celebrated

simile from the opening book of Virgil's *Aeneid*:

And just as, often, when a crowd of people
Is rocked by a rebellion, and the rabble [*ignobile vulgus*]
Rage in their minds, and firebrands and stones
Fly fast—for fury finds its weapons—if,
By chance, they see a man remarkable
For righteousness and service, they are silent
And stand attentively; and he controls
Their passion by his words and cools their spirits:
So all the clamor of the sea subsided. (*Aeneid* I, vv. 149–55)[14]

In ancient thought, the man "remarkable for righteousness and service" (pietate gravem ac meritis si forte virum), the queller of revolutionary tumults and navigator of stormy seas, the *gubernator,* is radically unlike, radically "other" to, the always feminized rabble. He is a godlike being like the goddess-born hero of Virgil's epic, *pius Aeneas;* a subduer of his passions and the passions of others, not a fomenter. Le Bon and his Italian counterparts are well aware that what changes in the era of industry is less the volatility of the crowd or a newly favorable characterization of this volatility than the lineage of this superior being. No longer the monarch, the aristocrat, or the godlike man; no longer the tyrant imagined as the rabble's monstrous counterpart; he is the man of the crowd, at once immanent and transcendent, at once an insider and an outsider, at once Everyman and the exceptional individual who provides the masses with a singular identity, a singular face, a mirror image of a sovereign collectivity that never sleeps. Fully swept up in the multicolored and polyphonic waves of modern revolution, he is able to channel their tidal fury toward higher and nobler ends: national sovereignty, liberty, empire, progress.

An early name of his is Leviathan, as famously figured in the 1651 frontispiece illustrating the Hobbesian principle of contractual political representation according to which the sovereign is simultaneously understood as the power that forces individual citizens into a single body politic and as the expression of their collective will (fig. 1.1).[15]

The body of citizens that composes Leviathan's body, what Herbert Spencer referred to as the *macanthrope,* is made up of the natural motions of individual minds whose interaction gives rise to an ideal collective motion signaled by a reciprocal exchange of gazes. The multitude faces its own visage and vice versa in an act of mirroring that allows for no fundamental ontological gap between leader and led. This orderly model of the formation of the body politic will provide one of the richest veins for panoramic representations of the type that I will subsequently refer to as the *emblematic.*

The emblematic mass so pervades the history of western group portraiture until the modern era that exceptions are usually limited to battlefield scenes (from ancient Greek red-figure vases to Paolo Uccello's *Battle of San Romano*) or to representations of the unruly damned being herded by infernal taskmasters (Luca Signorelli's Orvieto frescos of the *Last Judgment*). What prevails instead are the geometrically arrayed choirs that surround the Redeemer in vast tableaux of total order like Fra Angelico's *Christ Glorified in the Court of Heaven* and Giotto's Arena Chapel *Last Judgment,* along with secular avatars. Liquidity is a secondary feature of the emblematic mass. It is present to the degree required for individuals to lose their contours in order to regain them within the confines of a single corporate body. It serves as a vehicle less for the loss of boundaries between individuals than for the triumph of (collective) Form: symbolic in premodern cultures—the mobs of the blessed in Last Judgment scenes form spheres, ladders, and celestial trees; abstract, mechanical, or "ornamental" (as Kracauer would have it) in the modern era.[16] The emblematic mass is but the tradition-bound, dry-land counterpart of the *oceanic* mass, and to set sail on the latter, a more dynamic cognitive model is required that would allow the sovereign individual to emerge while being immersed in the mob, to control while being controlled. The model in question is provided by theorizations of the sublime.

Figure 1.1 Frontispiece to Hobbes's *Leviathan.*

Oceanic imagery proliferates in treatises on the sublime no less than it does in ancient political theory. Already in Longinus, the *Iliad* was sublime because of "the flood [προχυσιν] of moving incidents in quick succession, the versatile rapidity and actuality, brimful of images drawn from real life," whereas in the less sublime *Odyssey,* it is as if

Figure 1.2 Arthur S. Mole, the Reverend John Alexander Dowie.

"the ocean ['Ωκανοῦ] had shrunk into its lair and lay becalmed within its own confines."[17] In Addison, Burke, and Kant, the ocean is the horizontal counterpart to the vertical mountainscapes that precipitate in the viewer a simultaneous sense of vertigo and of its overcoming, of control and loss of control, of thrill and an expanded sense of selfhood. Addison writes:

of all Objects that I have ever seen, there is none which affects my Imagination so much as the Sea or Ocean. I cannot see the Heavings of this prodigious Bulk of Waters, even in a Calm, with-

out a very pleasing Astonishment; but when it is worked up in a Tempest, so that the Horizon on every side is nothing but foaming Billows and floating Mountains, it is impossible to describe the agreeable Horror that rises from such a Prospect. A troubled Ocean, to a Man who sails upon it, is, I think, the biggest Object that he can see in motion, and consequently gives his Imagination one of the highest kinds of Pleasure that can arise from Greatness. . . . Such an Object naturally raises in my Thoughts the Idea of an Almighty Being, and convinces me of his Existence as much as a metaphysical Demonstration. The Imagination prompts the Understanding, and by the Greatness of the sensible Object, produces in it the Idea of a Being who is neither circumscribed by Time nor Space.[18]

Kant concurs, although without immediately identifying such "agreeable horror" with the experience of the divine. In the contemplation of vast, seemingly infinite objects in nature, a mental movement is initiated, Kant adds, that allows us "to see sublimity in the ocean, regarding it, as the poets do, according to what the impression upon the eye reveals, as let us say, in its calm, a clear mirror of water bounded only by the heavens, or, be it disturbed, as threatening to overwhelm and engulf everything."[19] The scene's excess with respect to the imagination's ability to comprehend the whole renders a plunge into the abyss inevitable: "the boundless ocean rising with rebellious force, the high waterfall of some mighty river and the like, make our power of resistance of trifling moment in comparison with their might." Yet the plunge is productive because it is controlled: "provided our own position is secure, their aspect is all the more attractive for its fearfulness" (*CJ,* 110).

Kant's proviso regarding the need for a secure perch as a precondition for experiencing the sublime will come under increasing pressure in the course of nineteenth century as models of sublimity built instead on experiences of immersion, shock, and somatic risk assume central importance. But the key point here remains the convergence between the Ciceronian-Virgilian revolutionary *turba* and a new theorization of land- and seascapes in the western world.[20]

Nineteenth-century culture will turn out large numbers of panoramic images of natural landscapes. It will turn out large numbers of calm and disturbed seascapes. Last but not least, it will also give rise to a new iconography of human oceanscapes within the framework of the political sublime. Initially an ill-defined notion embedded within historical debates over events such as the French revolution and the Paris Commune, the political sublime achieves a full secular conceptualization at the century's end in accounts like Freud's, in *Civilization and Its Discontents*, of humanity's enduring longing for "oceanic" experiences, whether of nature or human multitudes. Bounded by the self, alienated from peers as a result of the demise of traditional forms of group identity formation, committed to rationality and the scientific method, the modern self dreams of a regression to boundaryless narcissism: a state in which all the suppressed values of religious belief—the eternal, the absolute, the authentic, the divine—return, albeit in the form of a momentary mystical communion with the (sociopolitical) universe represented by modern crowds.[21]

Types

As already indicated, the field of modern mass panoramas is split between emblematic and oceanic representations. My case study for the former will be the photographic tableaux of the turn-of-the-century American evangelical/military photographer Arthur S. Mole; my case study for the latter will be the *Rivista Illustrata* foldouts.

Mole, born in 1889, was a follower of the faith healer John Alexander Dowie, founder of the Christian Catholic Church, whose fiery brand of evangelism informed a number of early mass photographic experiments extending back to the time of the founding in 1901 of Zion, Illinois.[22] Zion was established as a Christian utopia, combining revivalism with millenarianism, industry with piety, proselytizing

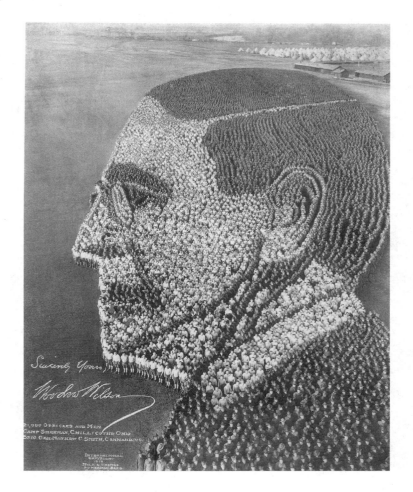

Figure 1.3 Arthur S. Mole, portrait of Woodrow Wilson.

via the media with the elaboration of mass spectacles. The city included the Zion Lace Factory, baking and candy factories, a printing and publishing house, and later, a radio station. Like everything else in Zion, all were owned by the church.[23] Within the setting of this evangelical community, panoramic photography of human multitudes assumed a role right from the start, to judge by the fact that in July 1904 the noted Chicago panoramicist George R. Lawrence was hired to document a series of parades, prayer meetings, and consecrations.[24]

Figure 1.4 László Moholy-Nagy,
Dream of the Boarding School Girls.

Mole's work built on Lawrence's legacy. His earliest photographic experiments were collective portraits bearing titles like "The Cross and the Crown" or spelling out biblical quotations, staged with members of the congregation during the years preceding the outbreak of World War I.[25] The resulting photographs were published in the church's illustrated review *Leaves of Healing* and sold to visitors, with profits going to the church. Two characteristic examples of Mole's work are "The Nine O'Clock Hour of Prayer or the Living Clock" (1915) and "The Reverend John Alexander Dowie" (1921) (fig. 1.2). The first marks the Christian Catholics' practice, inspired by Roman Catholic monastic practice, of interrupting the day at dawn and dusk with a minute of prayer. The clock is "living" thus not only inasmuch as a mechanical artifact is brought to life by being embodied by the members of the congregation, but also inasmuch as time is sacralized by the hour of prayer, transformed into the time well spent that leads to salvation. The second celebrates the twenty-first anniversary of the consecration of the Christian Catholic Church's tabernacle and city (Zion) by means of a "living" portrait that combines human bodies with stage props.[26] In between these pious compositions, Mole turned to military photography, working in collaboration with John D. Thomas, the leader of the Zion White Robed Choir, who became his crowd manager and producer. Together, they turned out dozens of photographs, most commissioned by specific battalions, such as "The Living American Flag" (1917; ten thousand sitters), "The Living Liberty Bell" (1918; twenty-five thousand sitters), "The Living Uncle Sam" (1919; nineteen thousand sitters), "The Human U.S. Shield" (1918; thirty thousand sitters), and their famous portrait of Woodrow Wilson (1918; twenty-one thousand sitters) (fig. 1.3). By the end of the war, Mole and Thomas's success was such that they nearly persuaded the American armed services to permit them to cross the Atlantic so as to shoot the most massive living portrait ever assembled: a clock marking the eleventh hour, portrayed by the entirety of the American armed forces stationed in Europe.

The technique developed by Mole for the purposes of these mass compositions was based on aerial surveying practices. A seventy- to eighty-foot tower was rigged up out of two-by-fours and steadied by means of cables. Once he was atop the tower, armed with an oversized eleven-by-fourteen-inch view camera mounted to the tower's flank, Mole would superimpose a transparency bearing an image over the camera's ground glass plate—inverting the drafting process used with camerae obscurae—and then proceed to bark out orders via a megaphone to a ground crew, directed by Thomas, whose job it was to mark out the image across the landscape. When the distances involved were beyond the megaphone's range, a white flag was used for signaling. The tableau was to appear undistorted, as if level with the picture plane, which meant both extreme, anamorphic-type distortions on the ground and visual torsion between the receding landscape in the backdrop. (In the case of the Wilson portrait, a mere hundred soldiers were required for the president's shoulder region, in contrast with the several thousand who make up the top of his head.) Up to a week of preparatory work was required to survey the landscape, trace sitter positions, and make calculations regarding the exact number of soldiers required and their distribution according to hat and uniform types. The actual shoot consisted in a close-order military drill, requiring long periods of standing at attention in precise formation.

Mole's technique may have been novel, but his compositions were not. Branches of the armed services and members of veterans groups had already been composing living flags and symbols in athletic stadiums and on marching grounds in the late decades of the nineteenth century. Other photographers, like Eugene Goldbeck, also found a highly profitable niche market in battalion portraiture. Nor were such compositions original in the deeper sense that, like Bosse's *Leviathan* frontispiece, they tap into a millennium of prior images—political, metaphysical, theologi-

Figure 1.5 El Lissitzsky, photogram of Lenin (1931).

cal—fusing the many and the one. This vast image bank of idealized crowds composed of angels, saints, and martyrs arrayed as signs encompasses to varying degrees pattern poetry from Porphyry to Rabanus Maurus to George Herbert to Renaissance hieroglyphs; figurations of celestial choirs in Last Judgment scenes; and the Christian chiliastic imaginary with its last signs and emblems of the faithful becoming one with/in the body of Christ. A case in point is Dante's *Paradise*, with its kinetic skywriting and succession of symbols formed by the blessed—circles, cross, eagle, and ladder—that lead the way to a face-to-face vision of God and of the Holy Jerusalem.

The jump from holy to secular athletes, martyrs to soldiers, angels to Tiller Girls, formations in heaven to military parades, political rallies, or football half-time shows, is easy to accomplish. However seemingly distant from the scene of the modern era of crowds, the same transcendental imaginary continues to shape secular utopias. Consider the case of someone aesthetically distant from the Mole's "living" clocks: László Moholy-Nagy, Bauhaus professor and the author in 1925 both of conventional photojournalistic oceanic crowd scenes like "Up with the United Front," shot in order to celebrate a Berlin Factory Workers Association demonstration, as well as of the "Dream of the Boarding School Girls" (fig. 1.4). The latter photomontage shows how, in the spirit of Emile Jaques Dalcroze's eurhythmics and various other group sports-hygiene-biomechanics movements, the bodies of dancers and athletes are released from the laws of gravitation, and this release is placed along the path of a group of schoolgirls, arrayed in a receding H formation. The dreamed-of passage from one geometry, a more restrictive one associated with the regime of acquiring literacy, to another, associated with enticing new erotic-machinic geometries, is not out line with Arthur Mole's twenty-one thousand soldiers cast in the image of Woodrow Wilson. Certainly no more so than are El Lissitzky's 1931 photogram of Lenin and its fascist twin, the 1934 One

Figure 1.6 1934 fascist poster, "One Heart Alone."

Heart Alone referendum poster in which the mob provides a receding ground for Mussolini's profile (figs. 1.5 and 1.6). The same would go for fascist, communist, and liberal-democratic experiments with everything from mass gymnastic exhibitions to "living writing" to stadium flip-card shows to the mass dance drills of Busby Berkeley. The Holy Jerusalem may be located in Leningrad, Rome, Beijing, Hollywood, or Zion, Illinois, but the formal principle as well as its ideological underpinnings remain analogous: out of the multitude emerges the face of the leader, the logo, the hieroglyph, the crux, in what is at once an allegory of collective transcendence and a transcultural form of play.

To underscore the continuities between premodern and modern emblematic representations of the crowd is not to overlook obvious divergences, like the increasing interest among post-1789 artists in panoramic modes of representation; shifts in perspective, medium, and scale; variations in the semiological status of emblems themselves of the sort called attention to by Kracauer in "The Mass Ornament." My aim, rather, has been to establish the simultaneous existence of old emblematic practices with the new oceanic ones, so as to suggest that the one interpenetrates the other. For all their formal divergences and differences in use, procedure, and location, for all the seeming absence of emblematic artifice in oceanic crowd scenes, both the emblematic and the oceanic are reducible, in the end, to allegories of crowd control. They serve as dialectical counterparts of one another, the first emphasizing the moment of transcendence when the one emerges out of the many; and the second emphasizing the more volatile moment of immanence in which the one taps into the tidal power of the multitudes (and vice versa).

Tiles

But if these are images of crowd control, what is the nature and degree of the control in question? What are the precise techniques by means of which a head is placed on the otherwise headless mob? And what are the formal, technological, and ideological variables involved? In the case of the *Rivista Illustrata* foldouts, an adequate answer requires a look back at the earlier history of panoramas. Understood in the strictest sense, the word *panorama* refers to 360-degree representations. The term and device were patented by their inventor, the Irishman Robert Barker, to promote an "IMPROVEMENT ON PAINTING, Which relieves that sublime Art from a Restraint it has ever labored under."[27] Such relief began its transformation into a mass phenomenon with the opening in London on March 14, 1789, of "Mr. Barker's Interesting and Novel View of the City and Castle of Edinburgh, and the Whole Adjacent and Surrounding Country." The show, which was enormously successful both with elite and popular audiences, quickly gave rise to imitations. Within a few years, similar panoramas were touring France, Germany, and the United States; within decades, they would span the world. Barker's original patent meticulously details the various lighting techniques, ventilation systems, and pictorial techniques that are required in order to make the viewer feel "as if he is really on the very spot."[28] The illusion was enforced by restricting the viewer's body position and movement to the center of the rotunda and screening his view of the upper and lower edges. Barker had little to say about the elaboration of the circular image, but subsequent documentation shows that it was based on segmentation or "tiling." A camera obscura or similar framing device would be positioned at a fixed location and rotated such that drawings could be generated one frame at a time. The resulting frames would then have to be stitched together by the artist so as to create an illusion of a seamless whole, with adjustments made so as to project straight lines from frame to frame along the curved surface of the canvas.

A few points need to be highlighted regarding the panorama's history because they carry over directly to panoramic photography. The panorama, intended as a method for emancipating painting—read "early photography"—by way of rendering it an even more sublime art, set out to wed an unbounded new sort of sublimity with an unbound-

Figure 1.7 Mass Rally in Sicily, *Rivista Illustrata*, September 1937.

ed new sort of realism. Through the combination of the two, the spectator was to find himself transported directly to "the very spot" of observation, which usually meant somewhere else, somewhere other, somewhere novel—like Edinburgh seen from on high viewed in downtown London, or London itself viewed from some astounding new angle. The spot in question, in other words, was precisely the sort of elevated, dislocated perch that Kant would have demanded for secure experiences of the vertigo, terror, and excitement that accompany the viewing of seemingly formless, infinite, overpowering, and overwhelming natural objects. Early panoramas rose to the double challenge of infusing what the era understood as hyperrealism with sensations of thrill and transport through recourse to vertiginous bird's-eye perspectives, whether of cityscapes, as in Joshua Atkinson's 1807 view of Saint Petersburg and an anonymous 1845 anamorphic view of London, or of mountainscapes like that of Loch Lomond, Scotland, painted for exhibition in London by John Knox in 1810. Cityscapes and mountainscapes would long remain the standard panoramic fare, but they were soon joined by scenes of exotic landscapes, fires, explosions, and disasters at sea as well as by the great land and sea battles of world history: Aboukir, Ostende, Agincourt, Moscow, and Waterloo (illustrated in Louis Dumoulin's immense turn-of-the-twentieth-century

Panorame de la bataille de Waterloo).[29]

Tourism, flight and fright; hallucination; the promise or threat of accident; oscillation between a sense of expanded selfhood made available through access to an all-encompassing gaze and a sense of endangered selfhood due to the sense of being encircled and engulfed; illusory participation in history's most dramatic events; estrangement of the familiar: panoramas traded in these pleasures and others, only to be overrun by a medium that represented yet another "improvement on painting": photography. The very fact that panoramas were built up out of segmented frames drawn up by turning about a fixed axis made the shift to photography a natural. Yet there were obstacles. Standard daguerreotype plate formats remained too small to achieve effects "sublime beyond description." And there was the question of how to smooth out transitions between frames due to the distortions introduced by the camera lens, particularly toward the edges of wide-angle images. The solution lay in the use of oversize cameras and in a modified tiling or montage procedure.[30] One early pioneer was George N. Bernard, who produced panoramic surveys of battlefields for the Union army during the American Civil War, making use of multiple wet-plate glass negatives, assembled into single images in his studio by means of cropping and trimming.[31] Another innovator, as in so many other do-

Figure 1.8 *Rivista Illustrata*, Man with a camera.

mains, was Eadweard Muybridge. In 1877 Muybridge carried an enormous custom camera up to the top of California Street Hill and shot the second expanded version of his famous 360-degree *Panorama of San Francisco,* composed of thirteen panels, each 20.5" x 16" in size, adding up to a total length of seventeen feet.[32] Muybridge's practice was to shoot his images with enough overlap so that, by means of cropping an inch and a half vertically and two inches horizontally, distortions could be limited and the individual panels could be bled into one another so as to seem more or less continuous.

When I first became intrigued by the *Rivista Illustrata del Popolo d'Italia* foldouts, I assumed that these painterly and photographic precedents, from Barker to Muybridge, had been largely superseded by the development and commercial production at the end of the nineteenth century of swing-lens cameras (like the Al-Vista, whose lens wheeled around 180 degrees while the film and camera body were held still) and rotational cameras (like the Cirkut, in which the entire camera wheeled in one direction while the film turned in another).[33] Such panoramic images, which were

devised to feed the public's seemingly unlimited hunger for Alpine scenes, city views, battle scenes and pictures of military assemblies, were a favorite for stereopticons and similar optical devices. So it seemed reasonable to assume that fascist-era photojournalists had simply embraced these new tools, shifting the content from sublime mountainscapes to sublime multitudes. This seemed to explain why, like stereopticon photos, their output was rarely panoramic in the strict 360-degree sense and why the images themselves were so meticulously turned out that an untrained eye struggles in vain to locate crop marks or distortions of the sort that abound in Bernard and Muybridge.

Close study of the actual photographs and a visit to the Luce Archive in Rome revealed these assumptions to be false. On the contrary, I discovered that there exists a direct genealogical link between the painted panoramas of the nineteenth century and the mass panoramic foldouts. Far from representing just an urban counterpart to rural landscape photography, the latter are actually works of what is perhaps best labeled "documentarist photomontage": photomontage deployed in the service of enhancing the reality effect, which means the thrill effect, that can be achieved by means of conventional press photography. Just as panoramic painting sought to relieve the art of painting of certain restraints seemingly inherent to painting as a medium, so mass panoramic photography seeks to relieve photojournalism of certain prosaic obligations and sets out to transport the viewer right to the very event. In the process of doing so, it deploys a battery of techniques to structure a particular experience of the event and to characterize the event itself as providing an opportunity to experience oceanic feelings. Mass panoramic photographs, in short, are trick "realist" photographs, tiled and smoothed together just like their nineteenth-century ancestors, but juiced up by means of photomontage and other forms of visual sleight of hand.[34]

The earliest of the *Rivista Illustrata* photographs dates from November 1926. Some hint at their ancestry, like the stadium scene of a fascist rally in Bologna, which bears this legend: "The photograph represents only *one* sector of the Lictorial stadium as is evident when you consider the stadium's elliptical form." This extends an invitation for the spectator to imagine the image as if it followed the curvature of the stands, potentially all the way around the entire ellipse. Later images, like a September 1937 six-panel image of a rally in Sicily, play on the very same sense of curvature to intensify the sense of grandeur and boundless space (fig. 1.7). The dictator is thrust out into the picture plane on a prowlike geometrical podium coursing across a seemingly infinite human ocean that gives way, in turn, to a literal sea. Nested in the image is the dictator's double, the cameraman.

The man with a camera is a standard feature of Italian mass panoramas (fig. 1.8). The cameraman's immersion in the mob, rendering him a literal man of the crowd, represents a guarantee of closeness and susceptibility to its tidal surges. But he is also always already high on the podium, hovering above. His is a hybrid perspective merging a god's-eye, overhead perspective with the view from the ground—which is to say that the cameraman must also be understood as a catalyst of revolutionary surges. He does not simply reproduce tidal flows, but rather *produces* them in the industrial and cinematic senses of the verb. Like the dictator-

Figure 1.9 Mass rally in Milan, *Rivista Illustrata*, June 1930.

Figure 1.10 Hitler's visit to Naples, May 1938, photomosaic, *Rivista Illustrata*.

Figure 1.11 Hitler's visit to Naples, May 1938, photomosaic, *Rivista Illustrata*.

demiurge who is at once immanent and transcendent with respect to the masses, the cameraman manufactures mobilizing "myths": images in and of movement that, in turn, must move if they are to succeed. It matters little whether these assume the form of live amplified words or trick photographs electrically relayed onto the pages of mass circulation magazines. Their intent is to electrify. Their enemy is the void: the gap in the crowd that threatens to break the circuit of feelings of mass communion and contagion; the pocket of silence that harbors indifference, skepticism, resistance, even opposition. Their remedy to this abiding *horror vacui* is a rhetoric of saturation and plenitude.

The productive (as contrasted with the *re*-productive) work of the photographer begins with the choice of an elevated orthogonal perspective like that long before perfected by panorama painters, a case in point being the June 1930 eight-panel foldout of a mass rally in Milan (fig. 1.9). Here one is dealing with a true example of an ocean-type image, not only tiled together in the conventional manner, but also composed like a photomosaic, in the which the masses appear everywhere and the leader nowhere. As anyone who as ever visited Milan's Piazza del Duomo can readily attest, the perspective that the foldout offers is a highly artificial construction, closer to a Byzantine than a single-point perspectival scheme. The square has been wedged open, transformed into a trapezoid, splayed so as to create the illusion of a vaster architectural setting, and therefore of a vaster human ocean: an illusion not of *enhanced* but of *compressed* depth inasmuch as the buildings have been ro-

tated off the central pictorial axis in the process of expanding the horizon line, and the entire backdrop of the image has been pulled forward toward the surface of the picture plane. The ultimate effect of the visual splay is paradoxical in a way that typifies the genre. On the one hand, it creates a sense of closeness and impending encroachment, as if the cityscape were opening up to enfold the viewer within the crowd's surge. On the other, it raises the viewer above and beyond the crowd, to an elevated perch, perhaps so elevated as to identify the panoramic camera eye with the gaze of il Duce.

This precise repertory of perspectival and editing tech-

Figure 1.12 Hitler's visit to Naples, May 1938, photomosaic, *Rivista Illustrata.*

Figure 1.13 Hitler's visit to Naples, May 1938, photomosaic, *Rivista Illustrata.*

Figure 1.14 Hitler's visit to Naples, May 1938, photomosaic, *Rivista Illustrata*.

niques—tiling, cropping, cutting, pasting, masking, even airbrushing—was refined over the course of the next decade. It in no way preempted recourse to other sorts of sublime crowd imagery, whether to diagonally angled Soviet-style single frames, emblematic mass sporting scenes,

parading soldiers disappearing into sunbursts, mass images of specific subcrowds—mass accordionists, mass sportsmen and -women, mass regional groups dressed in traditional folk costumes. But its most characteristic products remain panoramas like the photomosaic of Hitler's May 1938 visit to Naples: a composite image of the Piazza del Plebiscito fabricated out of at least five separate photographs (figs. 1.10–1.14). As revealed by a close inspection of the component "tiles," what has been edited out of the image are a series of "distractions": gaps in the crowd, electrical cables rising up to the top of the various lighting and loudspeaker towers, military groups parading at opposite ends of the piazza, a fleet of destroyers shrouded in the mist of the Bay of Naples.[35] The square itself has once again been pried open so as to strengthen the feeling of density and sprawl, while pulling the horizon line forward. Every graphic feature of the image has been manipulated to enhance the exclusive focus on the masses, on their energy, their power and potential heroism, their sense of expectation. But expectation of what? Or to frame the question otherwise, what is it that ensures that this particular oceanic mass provides a sublime rather than nightmarish viewing experience, or that the masses in question will be recognized as potential agents of national redemption rather than as a lawless destructive horde? The question might well be asked of every one of the *Rivista Illustrata* foldouts. The answer involves not only

Figure 1.15 Mass rally in Padua, September 1938, photomosaic, *Rivista Illustrata.*

the careful juggling of visual proximity and distance, horizontality and verticality, played out by means of camera placement and cropping practices that identify the camera eye itself with or as an external ordering agent, as a kind of deus ex machina, like the leader himself; but also two other factors: first, a set of internal "content controls"; and second, a set of strategies of contextualization.

In the case of the first, the internal "content" controls, the crowds depicted in the *Rivista* foldouts are tightly choreographed—not as tightly choreographed as the Rockettes or as Mole's Christian Catholic congregations, but spontaneous only in part. They typically brought together ordinary citizens with elements from the fascist youth, afterwork and trade groups, bused in from the throughout the provinces so as to ensure a full and enthusiastic house. In their midst circulated preprinted placards and rally coordinators ready to cheerlead a preestablished repertoire of chants at the appropriate cue. In their midst also circulated members of the secret police, invisible agents of surveillance and control paired with more visible agents like the Luce cameramen. But the frequent presence of uniformed members of the militia, army, and National Fascist Party is perhaps more significant because it calls attention to the intimate connection between emblematic and oceanic crowd

Figure 1.16 *Rivista Illustrata* foldout.

images. In many images, these disciplined crowds within the crowd, arrayed in the form of rectangles, squares, and fascist ax blades, interpenetrate the oceanic mass so as to hint at the translatability of the one into the other. Perhaps it's just a matter of time before everyone joins a formation and wears a uniform; perhaps it's simply a matter of differing degrees of mobilization and ideological commitment. Whatever the case may be, there is an emblem buried in every oceanic representation. Sometimes it floats to the surface, as in the case of a September 1938 photomosaic from Padua (fig. 1.15). Sometimes it is buried so deeply that its contours merge with those of the picture itself.

In the specific case of fascist mass panoramas, the emblem in question, whether a buried hatchet or the visage of il Duce, is characterized by the fact that the mass choreographies rarely occur on a naked stage. Architectural settings—Roman ruins, Renaissance and Baroque palaces, squares from the Risorgimento period—remind the viewer that the crowd portrayed is not the timeless, placeless, faceless socialist crowd rallying around abstract principles, but rather a *national* crowd, shaped by a national sense of place and tradition, and rallying around principles delimited by time and space. These architectures from the past are brought into the present by means of banners. On the occasion of the Naples 1938 rally, the banners, flags, towers—indeed, the mass rally itself—all bespeak of the imminent appearance of two leaders, planned for nightfall, at which time the Piazza del Plebiscito was transformed into a fascist phantasmagoria.

Earlier allusion was made to "strategies of contextualization," and it is to these that I now turn inasmuch as they represent perhaps the single most innovative development vis-à-vis the panoramic tradition and the one of the greatest potential interest for the history of photomontage and the documentarist aesthetic of the 1920s and 1930s. The panoramas of the previous century were meant to be experienced as autonomous artifacts, hyperreal in their effect but spatially and temporally dislocated from and dislocat-

ing of their viewing context. The *Rivista Illustrata* foldouts, on the contrary, find themselves increasingly woven into a thickly layered, "crowded" graphic environment where crowd imagery interacts with images of the leader, experimental typography, photomontages, drawings, and cartoons, always in meticulously assembled sequences. On the one hand, this graphic thickness has a symbolic purpose: that of casting the image of the masses in the image of the leader and/or the state and vice versa, as if the former, like Baudelaire's dandy, were "a mirror as vast as the crowd itself"[36] (fig. 1.16). By means of a sustained visual dialogue, the one is constantly presented as the inevitable counterpart of the other. On the other hand, the layering introduces a new dimension to panoramic representations, removing yet another "restraint" on their potential sublime effect. That dimension is *temporality*, in the double sense of narrative sequence and simultaneity. Mass panoramas, like period newsreels, are increasingly framed as the climax that follows a step-by-step process of regional and/or national mobilization—a process that by definition involves simultaneous motion from a multiplicity of locations toward a single site, the site of the rally: a motion charted in photomontages and image sequences that, as if the tiles out of which the eventual photomosaic will be composed, are first presented serially, and then combined in a final triumphal vision in which all of these images and moments are seamlessly folded into the totality that is the mass panorama itself—a totality presumably meant to enfold the viewer in the moment of viewing. In other cases, the mass panorama appears earlier or even at the beginning of the sequence, as if it were its graphic hub or source.

I will now take the reader very quickly through two of the latter sorts of sequences. The first dates from October 1932 and crosscuts the celebrations of the tenth anniversary of the March on Rome with statistical data in a succession of images that leads from Fascism's past to its future. The purpose of the sequence, introduced by a one-page article

(text continues on p. 30)

Figure 1.17 "Doveroso ricordo," *Rivista Illustrata*, October 1932.

Figure 1.18 "Doveroso ricordo," *Rivista Illustrata*, October 1932.

Figure 1.19 "Doveroso ricordo," *Rivista Illustrata*, October 1932.

MILIZIA VOLONTARIA
PER LA SICUREZZA NAZIONALE

374.144 militi e 25.313 ufficiali, di cui 1336 ufficiali
e 4914 militi in servizio permanente attivo

Milizia Ferroviaria 20.000; Milizia Portuaria 1000;
Milizia Stradale 500; Milizia Forestale 4000;
Reparti Postelegrafici 700; Legioni Libiche 2000.

Figure 1.20 "Doveroso ricordo,"
Rivista Illustrata, October 1932.

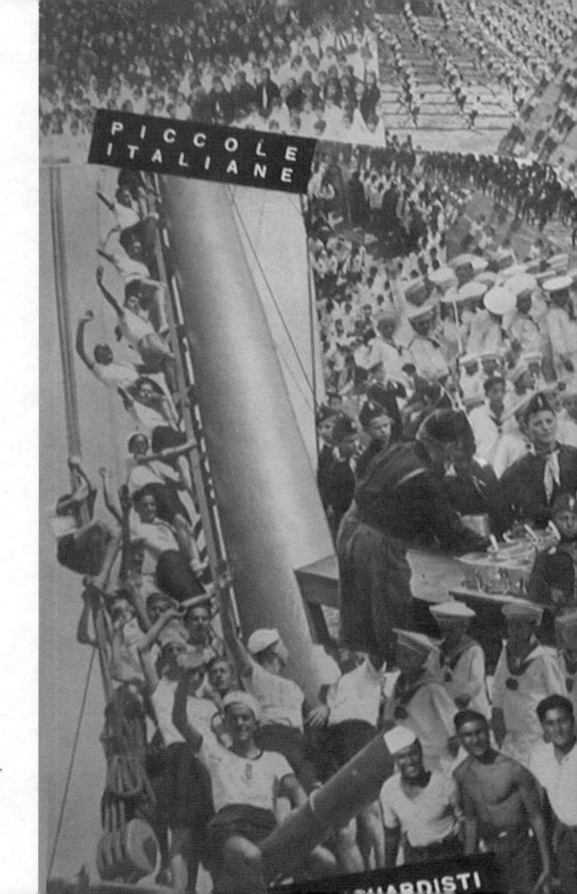

Figure 1.21 "Doveroso ricordo," *Rivista Illustrata*, October 1932.

GRUPPI UNIVERSIT...
FASCISTI: 56.63

BALILLA

GIOVANI
ITALIANE

O. N. B.
3 mili...

1A 'Turba': Latin

Alexandra Katherina T. Sofroniew

Turba, one of the Latin words for "crowd," comes from the Sanskrit verb *turami* meaning "to hasten," and the ancient Greek words τυρβαζω (a verb meaning "to trouble, to stir up") and τυρβη (the corresponding noun meaning "disorder," "confusion," or "tumult"). These origins reveal the negative connotations of the Roman conceptualization of a crowd as being the cause, or the scene, of commotion and turmoil. In addition, *turba* referred to civil disorder and the confusion that resulted from uncertainties in government and rule, and hence came to denote the disorderly mass of people—that is, the crowd, which gathered at times of protest and change.

Turba also represented natural disorder, and through the link to violent natural forces (an association that has come down to us in the word *turbulence*), the word evoked a state of movement. A crowd, as defined by *turba*, was not a static entity, but a driving force, one that needed to be channeled and controlled. In populous Rome, a large crowd of men was viewed as such an unpredictable and potentially hostile force that the Roman army was forbidden from marching into the city.

The association of the word *turba* with movement, and subsequently disorder, made it distinct from other Latin words for crowd such as *multitudo* (which had a numeric connotation) and *vulgus* (which was a definition based on class). Interestingly, these words were frequently used in conjunction with each other to flesh out crowd

Figure 1.22 "Doveroso ricordo," *Rivista Illustrata*, October 1932.

(continued from p. 20)

on the origins of *Il Popolo d'Italia* entitled "Doveroso ricordo" ("Duly Remembered"), is to serve as the springboard for a special issue devoted to surveying Fascism's achievements in a wide array of domains, from health services to science to sports.[37] The sequence runs as follows.

1. The celebration of Fascism's Milanese origins and of its martyrs on October 16, 1932 (fig. 1.17).

2. A panoramic representation of Fascism's present in the form of a mass rally in Rome's Piazza Venezia, under the aegis of Mussolini (who has been cropped out of the upper middle portion of the picture) (fig. 1.18).

3. The growth of the National Fascist Party, as marked by its 1.7 million members on the march (fig. 1.19).

4. The formation and growth of the fascist militia (Voluntary Militia for National Security), the mechanism by means of which Mussolini brought discipline to and regimented the most militant squadrist elements (fig. 1.20).

5. The nationwide proliferation of fascist youth groups (Piccole Italiane, Avanguardisti, Giovani Italiane, Balilla, GUF, and ONB) as a consecration of Fascism's glorious destiny (fig. 1.21).

Figure 1.23 *Rivista Illustrata*, March 1941.

descriptions and draw attention to different aspects of the social makeup of the crowd and the characteristics of its behavior. For example: "in quo admiratio magna *vulgi* atque *turbae*" (and on that day the mob and the crowd were greatly impressed). Here, Cicero uses *vulgus* and *turba* to indicate that there were crowds of both high-class and low-class people watching a public spectacle, and thus to remark on the diversity of the audience and the improbability of both groups enjoying the same event.

Turba's negative connotations are also exemplified by its common use in conjunction with *rixa*, a Latin word meaning "altercation" or "brawl." For example: "Ecce autem nova *turba* atque *rixa*" (At once there was fresh trouble and disputation).

Justinian, a Roman emperor in the sixth century ad, uses the word *turba* to signify a tumult in his legal definition of the difference between a tumult and a brawl that occurs in his *Digest of Roman Law*. *Multitudo* is used in this case in a purely numerical capacity, in apposition to *duorum*, meaning "two:" "namque *turbam* multitudinis hominum esse turbationem et coetum, *rixam* etiam duorum" (for a tumult is of a crowd of men who gather and make a commotion, but a brawl is between two).[1]

For the Roman elite (whose writings survive to us and are thus our major source of information despite their self-assigned position outside of the crowd), a crowd was never orderly or passive. In fact, certain Roman intellectuals viewed crowds as dangerous, both because of their overwhelming physical presence and because they thought that being in a crowd made one more susceptible to vice. Thus Seneca writes a letter "On Crowds" in which he states: "Quid tibi vitandum praecipue existimes, quaeris? Turbam. Nondum illi tuto com-

6. Fascism's success at bringing the working masses within the fold of the state through its after-work organizations and labor unions (fig. 1.22).

Here the narrative is drawn in conventional fashion. Fascism begins as a small outlaw movement; its transformation into a mass movement hinges on Mussolini, the founder of the party and of the various prolongations that discipline outlaw Fascism and build a bridge between the Italian populace and the party and militia, bearing fruit in the form of a fully fascistized mass society. In the process, it descends from Milan to Rome, then from Rome marches outward toward the expanding border of a renewed empire.

A second sequence, dating from March 1941, is more daring. It alternates pages filtered through the colors that make up the Italian flag with crowd scenes and banner headlines.[38] It begins with a tricolor typographical composition, cast in the usual romanized Futura typeface and preceded by a title in block red caps: "IL DU- CE'S SPEECH" (fig. 1.23). Then the following appears:

1. A full-page black and white image of Mussolini facing the green/black continuation of the transcript of the speech (fig. 1.24).

2. Two opposing green/black text pages with a vertical seam of an abstracted mass, bearing the tag "Naples," running between them (fig. 1.25).

Figure 1.24 *Rivista Illustrata*, March 1941.

Ecco perchè avremmo preferito, e fu pubblicamente dichiarato nel dicembre del '39, che se a una resa dei conti si doveva venire tra i due mondi irriducibilmente antagonisti, questa fosse ritardata di quanto era necessario per reintegrare tutto ciò che era stato da noi consumato o ceduto. Ma agli sviluppi, talora accelerati, della storia, non si può dire, come al faustiano attimo fuggente: fermati! La storia vi prende alla gola e vi costringe alla decisione. Non è la prima volta che ciò è accaduto nella storia d'Italia! Se fossimo stati pronti al cento per cento, saremmo scesi in campo nel settembre del 1939, non nel giugno del 1940. Durante questo breve lasso di tempo abbiamo affrontato e superato difficoltà eccezionali. Le fulminee schiaccianti vittorie della Germania ad occidente eliminavano l'eventualità di una lunga guerra continentale. Da allora la guerra terrestre nel continente è finita, non può riaccendersi, ed è finita con la vittoria della Germania, facilitata dalla non belligeranza dell'Italia che immobilizzò ingenti forze navali, aeree, terrestri del blocco franco-inglese. Taluni, che oggi affettano di pensare essere stato l'intervento dell'Italia prematuro, sono probabilmente gli stessi che allora lo ritenevano tardivo. In realtà il momento fu tempestivo, poichè se è vero che un nemico era in via di liquidazione, restava l'altro, il maggiore, il più potente, il numero "uno", contro il quale abbiamo impegnato e condurremo la lotta "sino all'ultimo sangue". Liquidati definitivamente gli eserciti della Gran Bretagna sul continente europeo, la guerra non poteva assumere che un carattere navale, aereo e, per noi, anche coloniale. E' nell'ordine geografico e storico delle cose che all'Italia siano riservati i teatri di guerra più lontani e difficili: guerra d'oltremare e guerra nel deserto. I nostri fronti si allungano per migliaia di chilometri e sono distanti migliaia di chilometri. Taluni acidi e ignoranti commentatori stranieri dovrebbero tenerne conto. Comunque durante i primi quattro mesi di guerra fummo in grado di infliggere gravi colpi navali, aerei, terrestri alle forze dell'Impero britannico. Sino dal 1935 l'attenzione dei nostri Stati Maggiori fu portata sulla Libia. Tutta l'opera dei governatori che si avvicendarono in Libia fu diretta a potenziare economicamente, demograficamente, militarmente quella vasta regione, trasformando zone predesertiche o desertiche in terre feconde. Miracoli! Questa è la parola che può riassumere quanto fu fatto laggiù.

Con l'aggravarsi della tensione europea e dopo gli eventi del 1935-36, la Libia, riconquistata dal Fascismo, venne considerata uno dei punti più delicati del nostro generale dispositivo strategico, in quanto poteva essere attaccata su due fronti. Lo sforzo compiuto per potenziare militarmente la Libia risulta da queste cifre: Solo nel periodo che va dal 1° ottobre 1937 al 31 gennaio 1941 sono stati mandati in Libia 14 mila ufficiali e 396 mila 358 soldati e costituite due armate: la V e la X. Questa contava dieci Divisioni fra nazionali e libiche. Nello stesso periodo di tempo sono stati mandati 1924 cannoni di tutti i calibri e molti di essi di costruzione e modello recente; 15 mila 386 mitragliatrici; 11 milioni di colpi di artiglieria, un miliardo 344 milioni 287 mila 265 colpi per le armi portatili; 127 mila 877 tonnellate di materiali del genio; 24 mila tonnellate di vestiario ed equipaggiamento; 779 carri armati con una certa aliquota di pesanti; 9 mila 584 automezzi vari; 4 mila 809 motomezzi. Queste cifre dimostrano che alla "preparazione" della difesa della Libia era stato dedicato uno sforzo che si può chiamare imponente.

Altrettanto può dirsi per quanto riguarda l'Africa Orientale, che abbiamo preparato a resistere malgrado le distanze e l'isolamento totale, che esalta la volontà e il coraggio dei nostri soldati. I soldati che si battono nell'Impero — senza speranza di aiuti — sono i più lontani, ma perciò i più vicini ai nostri cuori. Comandati da un soldato di razza, quale il Vicerè, e da un gruppo di generali di alto valore, i nostri soldati nazionali e indigeni daranno molto filo da torcere alle masse nemiche.

Fu tra l'ottobre ed il novembre che la Gran Bretagna radunò e schierò contro di noi il complesso delle sue forze imperiali reclutate in tre continenti e armate dal quarto, concentrò in Egitto quindici divisioni ed una massa considerevole di mezzi corazzati e li scagliò contro il nostro schieramento in Marmarica, che aveva in prima linea le Divisioni libiche, valorose e fedeli, ma non molto idonee a sostenere l'urto delle macchine "mitteris" (Do you ask me what you should regard as especially to be avoided? I say crowds; for as yet you cannot trust yourself to them with safety).[2] The leaders of Rome, both during the Republic and throughout the Empire, knew that a crowd could possess great power, especially under the canny leadership of a demagogue, and thus were forced to cater to the demands of the people or divert their attention elsewhere through the games and circuses that would become famous example of crowd manipulation. The word *turba* captured the unpredictable and tumultuous nature of the crowd in Roman times, when a commotion was created simply by people gathering together in the few open spaces of the densely populated city of Rome.[3]

Figure 1.25 *Rivista Illustrata*, March 1941.

3. A full-page red-filtered crowd, tagged "Turin," juxtaposed with a continuation of the same text in alternating green and black typefaces (fig. 1.26).

4. A split-screen photomontage of mass rallies: civilian rallies in the lower portion, tagged Milan, Catania, Genoa, and Bari; a military rally in the two-panel panorama that spans the upper portion, tagged Rome (fig. 1.27).

5. A black-and-white full page made up of seven images (one, tagged Bologna, running the full length of the page, the others half-page) of mass rallies in various cities, juxtaposed with the conclusion of the text in the form of a red banner headline reading "VICTORY, ITALY, PEACE WITH JUSTICE AMONG PEOPLES" (fig. 1.28).

The image of the masses binds the entire sequence together vertically or horizontally, fluttering through the pages along with the colors of the Italian flag and the transcription of a speech given by Mussolini in Naples calling on the populace to rise up and triumph against Italy's enemies. Here the mass panorama is at once everywhere and nowhere. It figures both as an irreducible whole out of which radiate other images of mass mobilization and as an autonomous graphic element that can be "cited" as the synecdoche of a totality encompassing the dictator and the nation. It is an orderly totality because the dictator's commanding presence is predicated on the no less commanding presence of the man with a camera, airbrush, scissors, glue, inks, and fonts. The latter shapes individual frames in which voids have been systematically edited out so as to evoke a perpetually mobilized nation-state, a nation-state bursting at the seams with energy. He then freely weaves these individual frames into a graphic environment that is saturated with words, statistics, colors, and images of surging revolutionary tides, yet remains geometrically austere. All this to done to create the illusion that under Fascism, oceanic feelings have become an integral feature of everyday life, but a constructive and controlled fact of life, reconcilable with the values of hierarchy and discipline.

Whether freestanding or not, mass panoramas are as much about unleashing revolutionary tides as they are about stilling and channeling them, as much about infinite oceans as about the absolute finitude of the frame, the grid, the geometry of the page, the edit and cut. The crowd, politically disciplined by the leader, is pictorially disciplined through photomontage.

Figure 1.26 *Rivista Illustrata*, March 1941.

1B Bathing in the Multitude

Michael Hardt

Have you ever noticed that at the great political demonstrations love is in the air? I don't mean the erotic charge of seeing so many beautiful people out together in the streets—although that is also a component of the experience. I mean primarily a properly political feeling of love. We recognize together what we can share in common, what power we have together, what we can do with each other.

This is the feeling I've had, for example, at the two sessions of the World Social Forum I attended in 2002 and 2003. They were not really demonstrations, I suppose, but rather encounters among people who spend their lives at demonstrations. Activists and intellectuals from all over the world came to Porto Alegre, Brazil, to confront the problems and promises of the contemporary forms of globalization. There were discussions, debates, and official pronouncements, of course, but the experience was primarily defined simply by being together with the nearly one hundred thousand people who had come. We could see in each other the possibilities of a new and better world. We could see in each other a new power. This is exactly Spinoza's definition of love.

One shouldn't forget also the feeling of love that arises perversely at many demonstrations from conflict and adversity. The first time you smell tear gas or come into physical conflict with the police or find yourself arrested at a demonstration can be a transformative experience. For me, the experiences at the World Bank–IMF protests in Washington

ROMA

MILANO

GENO

CATANIA

Figure 1.27 *Rivista Illustrata*, March 1941.

in April 2001 and the antiwar protests in New York in February 2003 come to mind. In both cases, the police seemed bent on posing obstacles and creating conflict at every turn. Such experiences inspire hatred and rage, of course, but they also create an intense solidarity and desire among those demonstrating together. I don't mean to suggest we should seek out confrontation with police and create conflict at demonstrations. On the contrary, I argue against such tactics every chance I get at political planning meetings before demonstrations. But sometimes that conflict comes whether we want it or not. And there is no denying the power of the experience of being so many together like that and suffering the assault of the police. That too is a kind of love, I suppose, a love born of adversity.

I should point out that when I describe this experience of love arising from seeing our common power in each other, I am not suggesting that we are recognizing some common faculty or characteristic or quality that preexists in all of us, some notion like "our common humanity." That would be a notion of recognition something along the lines of classic German idealism, posing this recognition as a revelation of our common authentic selves against alienation. No, I have in mind something closer to Walt Whitman's love for a stranger. What Whitman recognizes is really the possibility of camaraderie—not some common quality that we have always shared, but a common experience and a common power that we can create. One important distinction between the two notions lies in the temporality of the common. The notion of the common that interests me is not pregiven but points toward the future, as a possibility. That means that the preexisting notion of the common

Figure 1.28 Magneti Marelli ad, *Rivista Illustrata*, June 1935.

Spillways

The growing importance of strategies of contextualization bespeaks of the impact of film on contemporary graphics and photography—which is to say, of a growing sense that mass panoramicists were still laboring under too-great restraints to their sublime art. It attests to the increasing pursuit of effects of "liveness," "closeness" to the event, and simultaneity in the hierarchy of values pursued by photojournalists. The convergence between the photographic and the cinematic is considerable, but it lies beyond the scope of this essay. So I would like to conclude instead with some reflections on the broader impact of panoramas of human multitudes within modernist graphic culture, and then with an analysis of one post–World War II spillover. What interests me here is the emergence of and the ubiquity of abstracted images of the masses as visual quotations—quotations of the very "oceanic" conventions whose history has been reconstructed in the Italian context; quotations that translate the oceanic mass back into abstract geometrical emblems of a distinctive sort. Photomontage is often viewed as a formal method rooted in abstractionism, at odds with the aims of documentarism or reportage. But as Margarita Tupitsyn has emphasized in her work on Gustav Klucis, photomontage

Figure 1.29 *Rivista Illustrata*, March 1941.

also provided artists with a powerful new instrument of mass persuasion based on the manipulation of social realia, from statistics to slogans to photographs, which helps to explain why its path of development intersects that of the Italian mass panorama.[39] Both are arts of imagistic and informational crowding devoted to crowd shaping and crowd control. Both share the same agitatory ambitions, the same impatience with conventional forms of realism, the same desire to forge—whether in the metallurgical or counterfeiting sense—anticipatory images of society as it ought to be (but isn't yet).

The degree to which, for my present purposes, the Italian case may be considered normative, is, of course, an open question. Ideological frameworks make a difference, although sometimes more of shading than of substance. I have hinted all along at some of the distinctively fascist characteristics of the *Rivista Illustrata* foldouts. A case history of Soviet mass iconography, for instance, would have found a comparable panoramic imagination at work in such images as El Lissitzky's *The Current is Switched On* (1932) or Rodchenko and Stepanova's *USSR in*

(our common humanity, for instance) is fundamentally passive, whereas the other is active and creative: the common we share is something we create. More importantly, the preexisting notion tends to set aside or even ignore the differences among us by highlighting the common in greater relief. When we create the common, in contrast, we remain singularities; our differences remain different, yet we can work together and create a common power.

This is one reason why Toni Negri and I prefer the concept of multitude to the notions of the crowd, the masses, and the mob. On the one hand, this has to do with the nature of the multiplicity involved. One might say that all these concepts designate social multiplicities, but really, the apparent differences in the crowd and the masses easily fade to indifference. Too often the apparent multiplicity turns out to be merely an indifferent unity. The concept of the multitude, in contrast, is meant to name a set of singularities—that is, differences that remain different. On the other hand, this distinction of the multitude has to do with the passivity of the crowd, masses, and mob, which is closely related to their indifference. The mob, of course, along with the crowd and the masses, can do things, sometimes horrible things, but it is nonetheless fundamentally passive in the sense that it needs to be led and cannot act of its own accord, autonomously. That is why manipulation is such an important theme with regard to mobs and crowds. They cannot lead themselves; they must be led. In fact, all the classic discussions of manipulation, panic, and imitation from Le Bon and Tarde to Canetti and Kracauer rest on these twin characteristics of indifference and passivity. The multitude, in contrast, must be an active subject, capable of acting autonomous: a multiplicity of singularities that are able to act in common.

This multitude has been emerging in the political demonstrations of the "network movements" or the "movement of movements" that first appeared perhaps in Seattle in 1999 or in Chiapas in 1994. The distributed network is good image for an initial understanding of the functioning of this multitude because each of the nodes remains separate but potentially connects to all the others through an unlimited variety of relations. And such a network is open in the sense that new nodes can always be added with new relations to the existing network. Maybe we should think of the love in the air at the great political demonstrations these days as a kind of network love—the love that results when a multiplicity of singularities act in common and feel their power.

I'm reminded of the opening of a poem in prose by Charles Baudelaire: "Not everyone can bathe in the multitudes" ("Crowds," *Paris Spleen*). Such an immersion in the multitude is a beautiful image, and an adequate one as long as we understand that in the process of immersion, the bather does not remain a separate individual but becomes the bath—a becoming-multitude. But really this experience is not such an exclusive privilege as Baudelaire imagines. (That is the open nature of the network.) We all have an open invitation to bathe in the multitude.

Figure 1.30 Source for Magneti Marelli ad, *Rivista Illustrata*, June 1935.

Construction photo tableaux (1938), the former woven into a sequence visually coupling electrification with collectivization, the latter juxtaposing rallying workers with textile patterns. But this imagination, in keeping with the values of communist internationalism, emphasizes abstract representations of the crowd and/or the crowd's relation to industrial machinery, while deemphasizing place names, architectural settings, and images featuring regional or historical particulars. It also tends to place such images, constructed according the same elevated orthogonal perspective as their fascist counterparts, more emphatically in dialogue with the sorts of heroic ground-up diagonal perspective shots of worker heroes that abound in the films of Dovchenko and Eisenstein (although the latter left a powerful mark as well in fascist and liberal-democratic political art).

Likewise, a case history of American photography of crowds would have found overlaps with Italian and Soviet practice (self-evident in explicitly political works like Arthur Siegel's 1941 photograph "The Right of Assembly"), but overlaps within a setting where what prevails instead are compositions like Weegee's Coney Island suite built around a foreground in which individuals are visible in all their particularity as members of family or sentimental units. As in the crowd foldouts featured on the pages of *Life* magazine, collectivization in North America is typically associated with leisure activities or individual self-betterment, less with nation-building than with participation in the secular religion of work rewarded by affluence and fun. Rather than the loss of individuality in the oceanic multitude,

Figure 1.31 Pirelli ad, *Rivista Illustrata*, March 1938.

American photomontages tend to emphasize self-multiplication.[40] Case studies of Nazi Germany, Getulio's Brazil, and Maoist China would have yielded additional convergences and divergences of a similar sort. Yet for all these differences, what seem particularly striking are the continuities: technical/technological/graphic continuities and continuities also of a cultural-historical and perhaps even anthropological sort.

Certainly there can be no doubt that Italian industrial

groups knew exactly what it meant to "quote" the oceanic multitudes when they placed ads in the *Rivista Illustrata*. A first example, from Magneti Marelli, dates from June 1935 and reworks the conventions that this essay has been analyzing (figs. 1.29 and 1.30)—explicitly so because it pries apart a circular inset and mass panorama from an earlier photomontage celebrating the founding of the Italian national radio, inserting under the leader, in the guise of his podium, a massive amplifier, and between the inset and panorama, a bank of loudspeakers whose power of amplification is revealed as the force that binds together leader and mass. In a second advertisement, published in March 1938 for the Pirelli tire company, the masses have taken over the circular inset, recast as a wheel riding atop the prolongation of the capital P in the name *Pirelli* (fig. 1.31). Within the wheel and resting on them is the diagram of a factory; looming behind is a military star and a fasces composed of military, industrial, and civilian vehicles—trucks, tractors, autos, airplanes, and motorcycles—all shod with Pirelli tires. The composition is geometrical, but to designate it as such is not to say that it is contentless, neutral, or purely ornamental, for the star, the fasces, and the circle of workers figure as emblems of a fascist modernity defined by national mobilization and accelerated movement. This suggests that worker circles are ultimately no less emblematic than are Arthur Mole's living clocks; it is simply that they function within a context where traditional symbols have lost their value unless, like the fasces, they have been infused with industrial content.

But what, then, of images such as Moholy-Nagy's 1930 photomontage *Verantworte!* (*Be Responsible!*), in which the masses are transformed into panoramic decorative stripes (fig. 1.32)? A recent catalog description notes of *Verantworte!* that "the crowd scenes suggest demonstrations; the woman's mouth may represent the importance of speaking out, although it appears oddly glamorous." The montage is "a call to action, although the cause is not yet iden-

Figure 1.32 László Moholy-Nagy, Verantworte! photomontage 1930.

tified."[41] Far from standing for a desire to speak out, the "oddly glamorous" female visage is spliced into the oceanic mass so as to posit a fundamental equivalency. Both are volatile objects of modern masculine desires; both are to be approached with a mix of anticipation and anxiety. Italian advertisements for 78 rpm recordings of Mussolini's speeches rehearse a similar graphic convention. The leader's word radiates outward from his body, at once shaping the masses into concentric rings and piercing these very rings along a diagonal vector anchored in the doubly ringed title DUCE. Is the latter a microphone rising up from his podium, or a second upraised fist? Or is it the switch by means of which the crowd's electrical current is turned on, or the lever driving the engines that drive ship of state? It little matters. The oceanic multitude seduces and thrills, and in so doing poses a threat to individuality; but its blandishments may be at once accepted and overcome through recourse to geometrical discipline. Moholy's call to action may well be far more cautionary than the call issued by the Italian state record company to purchase copies of Mussolini's electrifying speeches, but, cautionary or not, it remains illegible outside of the framework of panoramic representations of the masses.

The final word will have to go to Andy Warhol, whose work from the early 1960s both traffics in panoramic imagery of human multitudes and lays bare the latter's central graphic trope. Warhol was only a decade away from what may perhaps rightly be viewed as the beginning of the end of Le Bon's era of crowds, found in contemporary mass politics, particularly as refracted through the rose-tinted lens of communist Chinese propaganda, the mirror image of the society of spectacle that he was already celebrating in

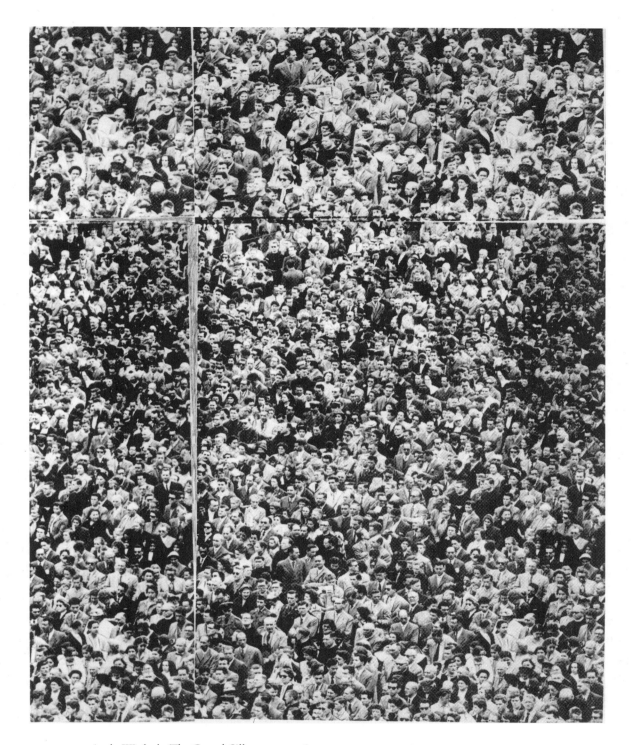

Figure 1.33 Andy Warhol, *The Crowd*. Silk screen, 1963.

his serial images of Hollywood celebrities. So to his serial portraits of Marilyn and Mao, he added his own contribution to the lineage of panoramas of human multitudes that I have retraced in this essay. These pictures, entitled *The Crowd*, tap into the same image bank of black-and-white throwaway press photos on which Warhol relied for the Death in America series (fig. 1.33). Like their car-crash counterparts, they refer to temporally dislocated events, current events whose currency is at once obvious and in doubt: "obvious" because, at first glance they might seem to refer to contemporary mass protest movements—1963 was the year of Martin Luther King's March on Washington; "in doubt" because, strictly speaking, they don't.[42] (The ambiguity is telling inasmuch as Warhol's 1963–1964 Race Riot series is based on "fresh" photojournalistic sources.)

The Crowd exists in two versions from 1963. Both appear to have been elaborated in tandem with the *Thirteen Most Wanted Men* panels for the New York State pavilion of the 1964 New York World's Fair (censored by the pavilion overseers). Both derive from a single black-and-white United Press International source photo, dated April 11, 1955, on the back of which Warhol penciled in a sketch of a woman's face. The photograph bore this legend: "Rome. Saint Peter and the Crowd: The huge statue of Saint Peter seems to look down benignly on the crowd in Saint Peter's Square that gathered to hear the Pope's blessing on Easter Sunday. It was impossible to estimate the tremendous throng accurately, but guesses range from 300,000 to 500,000."[43] No trace of Peter or the pope carries over into the Pop version of Mole's Christian Catholic multitudes (although a close inspection reveals recurring clusters of priests and nuns). Rather, the works assume the form of large and grainy silkscreen prints of abstracted masses, built up, like the star and crash images, out of a single visual block that is repeated, shifted right or left, flipped on its head, and cropped.[44] The resulting scene might well have been oceanic were it not for the fact that here the tiles have come apart. The seams

are showing and are crudely "covered up" by pencil marks. The repetitions are rudimentary. The squares have come unhinged (as has the implicit photojournalistic pact that links live events to their timely representation). The overall texture of the photographic image has become clotted as if printed on a sheet of tawdry newsprint—all of which makes any potential sense of vastness, power, and sublimity seem more than a little dated, more than little trumped up.

The Crowd was crafted as a hundred thousand voices of patience, pain, and anger echoed through the streets of Washington, with those of anti–Vietnam War protesters soon to follow. Yet the Pope of Pop anticipated the coming of an era in which Le Bon's volatile chemistry would cease to work: an era in which, in national settings where modernization has run its full course, a model of politics based on the physical massing of bodies in public places or the performance of symbolic marches in real time and space would be superseded by a politics of gestures that relies on virtual, indirect, and asynchronous forms of presence, organization, and participation. Predictions of just such a shift were long ago present in Gabriel Tarde's insistence that the crowd, understood as a finite "collection of psychic connections produced by physical contacts," was an atavism, "the social group of the past," while public opinion, understood as a potentially infinite "dispersion of individuals who are physically separated and whose cohesion is entirely mental," was the "social group of the future."[45]

The discontinuity is, of course, a matter of emphasis. All modes of political action, from negotiation to symbolic actions (including strikes and mass demonstrations) to acts of collective violence are fated to remain synchronous. Just as handwriting continued as a key instrument of communication under the regime of typewriting, and just as typewriting now continues to play a role under the regime of digital writing and printing, a fundamental simultaneity is to be expected. Where Tarde's intuition and Warhol's ironization prove prescient is that, just as handwritten documents look fundamentally *different* and function in a fundamentally *different* way within a setting where machine writing is the norm, so the once heroic image of the oceanic crowd now flickers live on LCD television screens under a growing patina of anachronism (an anachronism consciously embraced by mass choreographies like the Million Man March that seek to repeat and, by means of repetition, to appropriate the image of the civil rights marches of the 1960s). With their power and prestige mostly restricted to the domains of entertainment, sports, mediatized religion, and forms of recreation such as raves, the multicolored and polyphonic tidal waves of revolution in modern capitals now loom at a certain distance, as if brought back to life from earlier phases in history, as if material from the now sealed vault of modernity. The era of crowds is still very much with us, particularly in times of political turmoil and in the developing world. But in a deeper sense, perhaps it has passed.

2 The Invention of the Masses: The Crowd in French Culture from the Revolution to the Commune

Stefan Jonsson

THEY ARE MANY. THE FIGURES in Jacques-Louis David's *The Tennis Court Oath* (*Le Serment du Jeu de Paume*) are spread out, lined up, piled on top of each other, cramped together, their bodies suggesting sheer quantity (fig. 2.1). The ones who wave and peek through the large windows high on the walls extend the assembly beyond the depicted hall. It is impossible to tell where this human aggregation begins or ends. The national assembly of France spills over the frame and flows out across the entire field of vision.

The additive force that expands the aggregation outward is countered by vectors pointing in the opposite direction, symbolized by the innumerable arms stretching toward the center. The central figure, the scientist Jean-Sylvain Bailly, slightly elevated above the others as he stands on a table in the middle, solemnly swears that those gathered will not separate until they have agreed upon a new constitution. After Bailly, all the others will pronounce the same oath in unison.

It is an event both dignified and rebellious; it is history in the making. The oath sworn by the National Assembly on June 20, 1789, marks the beginning of the French Revolution. David recognized the gravity of the moment and the enthusiasm it released. Faces and bodies are frozen in an instant of emotional intensity. The persons are possessed by a common mission, which consists precisely in preserving their newly won unity.

The Tennis Court Oath is at once expansion and contraction, infinite numbers and complete accord. Language is at a loss, it appears, when trying to capture David's visualization of unity in quantity. Yet is it not this peculiar synthesis of number and union that is invoked each time the masses are summoned to give history a push forward? I will return to that question and to David's unfinished painting of the revolution.

Figure 2.1 Jacques Louis David (1748–1825). *The Oath of the Tennis Court,* June 20th 1789. Pen and wash with brown ink, heightened with white, on paper, 1791. MV 8409; INV Dessins. Photo: Gérard Blot. Photo Credit: Réunion des Musées Nationaux / Art Resource, NY. Chateaux de Versailles et de Trianon, Versailles, France. Used with the permission of Réunion des Musées Nationaux /Art Resource NY.

This essay will sketch the French beginnings of the discourse on the masses. The invention of the mass as a sociological category is inseparably linked to the emergence of democracy, particularly to the conflicts about how the new democratic sovereign, the people, ought to be represented—not only politically, but also, and above all, ideologically and culturally. I will try to demonstrate how the discursive object in question—"the mass"—gradually congeals through a process of terminological clarification and ideological consolidation that contains four stages, each of which adds a new layer of meaning to the term. In the first phase, "the mass" appears as numbers. In the second phase, "the masses" are what Victor Hugo called *les Misérables*. In a third stage, "the masses" refer to the organized workers' movements. Finally, "the mass" will come to express a certain political sickness, mass insanity, which is diagnosed in such a way that it envelops the majority of the population. In this fourth phase, "the masses" are literally the mad.

In *The Making of the English Working Class*, E. P. Thompson begins by discussing the founding document of the London Corresponding Society, an organization founded in 1792 by "Tradesmen, Shopkeepers, and Mechanics" to promote parliamentary reforms that would extend voting rights to the common people. Thompson quotes the first of the rules that Thomas Hardy, secretary of the society and a shoemaker by profession, set down in print: "That the number of our Members be unlimited."[1]

Today, such a rule may appear as an empty statute. Not so in England of 1792, where political rights were reserved for certain persons by virtue of their property or ancestry. By inviting "unlimited numbers" to further its political goal, the London Corresponding Society rejected a system where political rights were tied to rank, wealth, or name. This was a revolutionary challenge to the status quo, and Hardy was promptly sentenced on charges of high treason. As Thompson explains, the first rule of the London Corresponding Society is "one of the hinges upon which history turns."[2]

History turns: from a world in which politics was handled by an exclusive elite to a world in which political participation is open to all. History turns: from a system where political representation was based upon the inherited social identities of certain members of society to one in which political representation is founded upon the principle of equality of all citizens, regardless of their identities. History also turns toward abstraction: whereas the sovereign formerly manifested himself in regal symbols and spoke through ornamented ceremonials, the new sovereign of the people is a phantom without qualities, speaking through the bare fact of numbers.

The reason for this turn lies in the modern concept of democracy, which requires that the social body be broken down into numeric units. Popular sovereignty extends political rights to each member of the people. These rights are derived from no other source than the bare fact of inclusion into the polity; therefore, no member of the people can have greater or lesser political rights than any other. This is democracy's principle of equality. Such a principle invites an abstract view of the human being. Differences of class, wealth, talent, conviction, and identity no longer carry political weight. Deprived of substance, the individual is posited as a pure political subject. Correspondingly, society is desubstantialized, freed from the ties of traditions and organic communities which once gave it shape and weight. It is a strange turn of history. At the very moment when sovereignty is transferred to the people, the people loses its "essence." Its character as an organically living community of human beings evaporates, and the people appears as a series of abstract units measured according to arithmetic principles.[3]

The connection between numbers and democracy has never been as strong as during the French Revolution. To the political explosion was paired an eruption of counting, an enthusiasm for numbers, which in retrospect has struck many as bizarre. The best-known case is the invention of a new way to count time, the revolutionary calendar in which the week had ten days, the months were renamed, and human history made a clean break and started anew from Year 1. Another instance is the initial plan for an administrative reform of France, submitted to the National Assembly in September 1789, which divided France into eighty-one identically square *départements*, each of which was divided into nine equally square cantons.[4] The revolution was a period of "statistical imperialism," the historian Louis Chevalier states. He relates the following story from Year 9. A mayor in the provinces is asked if he can provide all the statistical data demanded by the government. "I will carry it out, and I would carry it out ten times more if I was ordered to," the mayor answers. "If the government asked me about the number of birds that every year fly over the surface of my region, I would tell them on the spot that I would not err on a single lark."[5]

When confronted with the problems of representing history and society, the *lumières* and *idéologues* of the late eighteenth century tended to seek mathematical solutions. "Political arithmetic" was the designation for inquiries into the relationship between demographic facts and other social facts.[6] Buffon, for one, had sought to subject the fluctuations of harvests, the rates of births and deaths, and human life in general to a "moral arithmetic."[7] Condorcet envisioned a "social mathematics," believing that the conflicting interests of society could be perfectly represented and managed through an adequate calculation of statistical data and laws of probability.[8] Emmanuel Sieyès, in his influential pamphlet *What Is the Third Estate?* (*Qu'est-ce que le tiers état*), relied on numeric evidence to prove that the third estate represented the general interest of the French nation as a whole, thus showing that the estates of the nobility and the clergy represented 200,000 persons combined, while the remaining people amounted to 25 million.[9]

A generation later, such exercises in counting and calculating social data were refined by Adolphe Quételet, the founder of population statistics in the modern sense. It is to Quételet that we owe the famous notion of *l'homme moyen*, average man. By computing all relevant demographic and biometric data of a given population, by subsequently establishing the average of each parameter, and by finally adding these averages together, Quételet discovered the "normal" human being: the "average" around which all the individuals of a given population are statistically distributed. Quételet thought he had discovered a human model valid at all times and in all places.[10]

Quételet's conception of the average man is highly relevant in our context for two reasons, both central to the history of the crowd and the masses. First, the average man is Quételet's solution to the problem of representing the people. Average man is a mirror in which the people may contemplate an ideal statistical reflection of itself, purged of individual aberrations and signs of social and regional origin. Average man therefore establishes a certain position of generality in society, a universal norm, which may be used by any particular class or party that seeks to establish itself as the rightful representative of the popular will. The class or party that is able to seize the universal standard can then reject other groups by accusing them of deviating from the universal norm and average. In this view, a failure to conform to the average man becomes a stigma, an evidence of nonbelonging. As we shall see, this political mechanism of inclusion and exclusion structures the history of the conception of the masses.

The second thing to bear in mind about Quételet's theory of *l'homme moyen* is that it is the first definition of the notorious man in the crowd—the evasive creature that populates the world of modernity, the person who never stands out but disappears into the background. The average man is also a man of the crowd in the sense that he is produced by a social imagination that presupposes a radical abstraction of society. For, in order to construct the average man, the concrete population of men and women of different identities, professions, and qualities must be decomposed into smaller units that can be measured and compared, and finally transposed into numeric entries in statistical calculations, from which there emerges, through a mysterious act of regeneration, the Average Man. The social imagination at work here is essentially similar to the democratic imagination of the revolution, which decomposed an allegedly natural order, leveling social hierarchies and abolishing feudal privileges, in order to redefine the human being as a free individual equipped with inalienable rights, and to define the people anew as a community of equals.

It is plausible, I think, to interpret the appearance of number in political treatises and in the social imagination more generally around the end of the eighteenth century as a paradigmatic change, one of the results of which is the modern discourse on the masses.[11] Just a light tuning of the terms is needed—Edmund Burke is the first one to carry it out—to move from the idea that democratic society is ruled by unlimited numbers to the view that it is ruled by the many, the multitude, and the mass. At the time of the French Revolution, these terms belonged primarily to the numeric and mathematical domain. The English word *mass*, like the French *masse*, denoted a large unspecified quantity of any substance. With the advent of democratic aspirations, these mathematical words were used by the social observer or political theorist to acknowledge the existence of the unlimited numbers of people that suddenly must be taken into account.

Or, to put the matter in correct historical sequence: democracy became an issue at this time because innumerable people asserted their presence in society. As industrialization and capitalism eroded the guild system and transformed rural patterns of life, uprooting peasants, artisans, and laborers, and releasing the great migration from country to city, a handful of European cities became urban and industrial centers, their inhabitants living in dense concentrations and their social classes so closely juxtaposed that wealthier citizens could not evade the sights, noises, and smells of the populous working classes.

I am running ahead of my argument, however, for here we have already arrived in the archetypical universe of modernity: the metropolis with its collisions of events, classes, dialects, professions, and lifestyles, which is a major source of the culture of modernism as such, famously registered and affirmed by Charles Baudelaire: "The pleasure of being in a crowd is a mysterious expression of sensual joy in the multiplication of Number. *All* is Number. Number is in *all*. Number is in the individual. Ecstasy is a number"[12]; and at the same time abhorred by Gustave Flaubert: "one element prevails to the detriment of all the rest: *Number* dominates over mind, education, race, and money itself—and even *that* is preferable to *Number*."[13]

Yet at the time Baudelaire and Flaubert wrote these lines, the crowd was already far more than a question of number. The mass had long lost its neutral mathematical denomination and become linked to other terms ("mob," "crowd," "populace," "foule") to the effect that it evoked all the dangers that intruded upon the social order. The masses were violence, criminality, and insurrection. The masses were irresponsibility, illiteracy, and disobedience. The masses were alcoholism, prostitution, and madness. For the masses, too, represent one of the hinges upon which history turns.

Edmund Burke's *Reflections on the Revolution in France* was published in November 1790. The book, which was an immediate success, stirred an intense debate in England, provoking rebuttals from Thomas Paine and Mary Wollstonecraft, among others. The pamphlet's primary accomplishment, if it can be called such, was to relate the order of numbers to disorder and violence. The effort of the new French constitution to represent society according to rational, arithmetic, or even geometric principles invited barbarism, Burke maintained.

Burke argued that the revolution tore apart the social fabric by violating its sacred institutions: king, church, and property. These institutions were natural because inherited: "derived to us from our forefathers, and to be transmitted to our posterity."[14] Subjection of the common people was a natural part of this sacred order, Burke wrote:

Good order is the foundation of all good things. To be enabled to acquire, the people, without being servile, must be tractable and obedient. The magistrate must have his reverence, the laws their authority. The body of the people must not find the principles of natural subordination by art rooted out of their minds. They must respect that property of which they cannot partake. They must labour to obtain what by labour can be obtained; and when they find, as they commonly do, the success disproportioned to the endeavour, they must be taught their consolation in the final properties of eternal justice. (*RRF*, 246)

Today such a view strikes us as inconceivable and inhuman. Burke, however, found it reasonable to compare the divisions within humankind to the differences between animal species—"for each kind an appropriate food, care, and employment": to treat "sheep, horses, and oxen" as if they were one and the same species, "to abstract and equalize them all into animals," was madness (*RRF*, 185). Yet such was precisely the madness of revolutionary France, its new leaders having "attempted to confound all sorts of citizens, as well as they could, into one homogeneous mass" (*RRF*, 186). By inducing common people to think themselves equal to their masters, the democratic politicians of France were "authorizing treasons, robberies, rapes, assassinations, slaughters, and burnings throughout their harassed land" (*RRF*, 40).

Burke's reflections move on two levels. He presents a theoretical argument concerning the dangers of putting abstract notions of liberty and equality in the stead of inherited institutions. He also describes current events in France, displaying a melodramatic taste for episodes of public confusion and violence. In Burke's exposition, these two strands merge and bifurcate according to a logic of their own. Sometimes, the shift from deliberation to instinctual reaction occurs from one sentence to the next: "It is said, that twenty-four millions ought to prevail over two hundred thousand. True; if the constitution of a kingdom be a problem of arithmetic. This sort of discourse does well enough with the lamp-post for its second: to men who *may* reason calmly, it is ridiculous" (*RRF*, 52). In this way, Burke discredits Sieyès's statistical argument for democracy by associating it with the rare cases of the summer of 1789, when Paris crowds hanged one or two officials from lampposts.

Each time Burke approaches the current situation in France, a rhetoric of fear and disgust takes over. It culminates in his account of October 6, 1789, when Paris women accompanied by the National Guard marched to Versailles to force the king and queen to return to the capital. It was passages like the following one, where almost everything is incorrect, that caused Burke's book to be dismissed as caricature by many of his contemporaries:

Instantly he [the sentinel guarding the queen's quarters] was cut down. A band of cruel ruffians and assassins, reeking with his blood, rushed into the chamber of the queen, and pierced with an hundred strokes of bayonets and poinards the bed, from whence this persecuted woman had but just time to fly almost naked, and through ways unknown to the murderers had escaped to seek refuge at the feet of a king and husband, not secure of his own life for a moment. This king, to say no more of him, and his queen, and their infant children (who once would have been the pride and hope of a great and generous people) were then forced to abandon the sanctuary of the most splendid palace of the world, which they left swimming in blood, polluted by massacre, and strewed with scattered limbs and carcasses. (*RRF*, 71)[15]

The word *crowd* is not to be found in Burke's pamphlet, but *mobs* are frequent. He also does not speak of *the masses* in its modern pejorative sense. In Burke, *mass* and *masses* are neutral designations of quantities of people and goods. Rather, Burke renders the acts of the people in a vocabulary that is baroque and premodern, at once sinister and condescending, conjuring up images now of savage beasts, now of ignorant children. The one canonized expression is "the swinish multitude."

Still, Burke should be counted among the first modern analysts of mass politics and crowd behavior. By connecting the rule of number, of mass, to political violence and disorder, *Reflections* lays the foundation for the conception of the masses that will be gradually modified and refined throughout the nineteenth century, until, in the 1890s, it crystallizes into a purportedly scientific theory called mass psychology. In this first incarnation, the masses name the result of the new principles of democracy and equality that transform a hierarchic society into a level field of atomized and exchangeable individuals, free to aggregate into larger units. Thus, individual and mass are no opposites, but related to each other as the singular to the plural. This issue will return as a dominating concern in Alexis de Tocqueville's *De la démocratie en Amerique* (*Democracy in America,* published in two parts in 1835 and 1840), in which the emergence of the masses and the rise of individualism are seen as one and the same process of abstraction: democracy breaks the "long chain from peasant to king" and "separates each link from the others."[16] If Tocqueville weighed the pros and cons of this development, Burke abhorred it, stressing that democratic ideas were to blame for the collective violence that followed in the wake of the revolution.

After Burke, *the mass* is no longer a simple designation of quantity but will signify in two directions at once. On the one hand, the mass implies the presence of numberless collectives within politics; on the other, the mass evokes instability and violence as the result of the political action of the lower classes. These two phenomena—political collectives and social instability—were sealed together by Burke, and ever since then, they will refuse to come apart. They will not uncouple, because there emerges with Burke a discourse that will insist that the two are intrinsically related. In Tocqueville, for instance, great numbers and violence are connected under the rubric "the tyranny of the majority," and he exemplifies this tyranny by mentioning mobs and riots.[17] Through its dual signification, the category of the mass guarantees that the relation between the two phenomena—numbers unlimited and violence—is never lost to the public. Indeed, from Burke onward, this will be the primary function of the discourse of the masses: to ensure that the presence of collectives within politics calls up the specter of violence, and that the presence of internal violence calls forth proposals to restrict democracy.

Who are the masses? We do not know, because those concealed behind that word have left few self-declarations. Who stormed the Bastille? What did they think? Why did they act? No documentary traces testify to their motives. To be sure, through archival research, historians have been able to find out who those men and women were that constituted the revolutionary crowds. But those historians have sunk deep into thick descriptions of how men, women, clubs, and societies reacted to historical events and political issues, and since these reactions, like human affairs in general, are determined by multiple pressures and concerns, the result is that the thing itself—the mass—dissolves and stands revealed as the great simplification it always was.[18] In *The French Revolution*, published in 1837, Thomas Carlyle reflects on this misfit of general categories to history's raw material:

With the working people, again, it is not so well. Unlucky! For there are from twenty to twenty-five millions of them. Whom, however, we lump together into a kind of dim compendious unity, monstrous but dim, far off, as the *canaille*; or, more humanely, as "the masses." Masses indeed: and yet, singular to say, if, with an effort of imagination, thou follow them, over broad France, into their clay hovels, into their garrets and hutches, the masses consist all of units. Every unit of whom has his own heart and sorrows; stands covered there with his own skin, and if you prick him, he will bleed. . . . —what a thought: that every unit of these masses is a miraculous Man.[19]

Carlyle's book originally had the subtitle "A History of Sansculottism," indicating an ambition to let the common people, *les sans-culottes,* enter front stage. The book is less a history of the revolution than an allegorical epic, however. The revolution provides the occasion to develop a cosmogonical vision of history as a struggle between the elements. In this epic, the 20 million working people of France play the major role, to be sure, but only in the disguise of a force called "Sansculottism." Carlyle draws a straight line from the fact of uncountable numbers to phantasmatic powers such as the Uncontrollable, the Immeasurable, and the Anarchic, which operate as independent agents in his epic and which effectively prevents the real historical actors from coming into view.

Carlyle describes the political action of the masses as a force of destruction, which dissolves society into a storm of numbers. But in contrast to Burke and Tocqueville, who judged the destructive force of the people as a violation of natural rights, Carlyle interprets the "destructive wrath" of Sansculottism as a primordial force:

[The] French Revolution means here the open violent Rebellion, and Victory, of disimprisoned Anarchy against corrupt worn-out Authority: how Anarchy breaks prison; bursts up from the infinite Deep, and rages uncontrollable, immeasurable, enveloping a world; in phasis after phasis of fever-frenzy;—till the frenzy burning itself out, and what elements of new Order it held (since all Force hold such) developing themselves, the Uncontrollable be got, if not reimprisoned, yet harnessed, and its mad forces made to work towards their object as sane regulated ones.[20]

For Carlyle, Sansculottism is a "World-Phoenix," rising in fire and consummating itself together with the old regime in fire, so that a new order is possible.[21]

In David's image of the revolution, the figures are leveled along a horizontal axis. It is an axis of equality: except for Bailly, who presides over the National Assembly and dictates the oath, no one rises above the rest. By pressing as many persons as possible into the visual plane, David suggests that the emerging democratic system is based on numeric might. By rendering the precise moment when everybody's attention is directed toward Bailly, the artist also turns the multitude of heads and figures into one body, thereby inventing a visual equivalent of the concept of democratic sovereignty, which stipulates that the many are turned into one single constitutive power.

If we take a closer look at the painting, we can identify some of the iconographic oppositions and political contradictions that David juggles to create the impression of great quantity in magnanimous union. First, the image is composed according to the neoclassicist formula of the ideal body, manifested through expression, gesture, shape, and volume, yet at the same time it attempts to record an actual historical event made up by real, historical persons. This stylistic tension between idealist principle and realist intention is superimposed by an opposition in the manifest content of the image. This is the tension between, on the one hand, the general will as a contractual matter reached through rational deliberation, and, on the other hand, the spontaneous manifestation of patriotism as a result of deep political passions. In turn, the image's combination of rationalism and passion is the result of a formal opposition in the image: the figures are inserted into a firmly organized space, structured by distinct lines of perspective, a clear division of back—and foreground, and with several subdivisions and compartments up front, all of which suggest a geometric matrix in which each figure is assigned a certain position and function; yet through physiognomies and gestures the image renders a collective that is about to explode in a moment of immense passion: cries of enthusiasm, gaping mouths, eyes brimming with tears, bodies embracing and hands holding each other, faces possessed by epiphanies and revelations: this does not suggest an assembly ruled by reason alone, but rather a collective acting on impulse.

The moment rendered by David is thus a strange equilibrium or conversion: a well-organized assembly and a raging mob are crossed with each other. This opposition reveals an ultimate contradiction, which has been emphasized by Antoine de Baecque, who argues that the image can be traced back to two distinct iconographic conventions.[22] The first convention is that of the idealized political body. The collective is figured as harmonious, unified, concentrated, gracefully resting in movement. It is a body at once potent and beautiful, according to the principles of neoclassicist style. The second model is that of the many-headed hydra, which at this time flourished in caricatures and popular prints that ridiculed the evil nature of the aristocracy and monarchic despotism. At the time when David prepared *The Tennis Court Oath,* he was also projecting a painting for the city of Nantes which was to include "the hydra of despotism." De Baecque convincingly argues that the idea of the many-headed hydra is absorbed and inverted in the image of the National Assembly. As a shadow existence, the monster of innumerable heads that shake and rattle in fits of madness injects a wild and chaotic element into the majestic beauty of the regenerated political body of France. Hence, the depicted event is shown from two sides simultaneously, and the view varies accordingly: one of enduring fraternity, one of dangerous subversion.

De Baecque's observations help explain why the image has retained its worth as a visual equivalent of the revolution. By incorporating the ideal political body *and* the hydra of despotism into one and the same image, the painter translates into visual form the dialectic of the revolutionary process itself, as it veers from enlightened rationalism to terror, from the scientific calculation of numbers to the mystic cult of the Supreme Being, from popular egalitarianism to despotism.

As I have mentioned, *The Tennis Court Oath* is also a visual representation of the people as the political sovereign. The notion of the people will therefore be inflected according to the same ambiguous pattern as the revolution. David's people is portrayed as an embodied union and as a loose aggregate of heads and figures; it is sovereign reason and a contest of passions. In this sense, the image also mirrors the contradiction that inheres in the modern conception of the people. For this is a term that always refers to two distinct concepts: in political theory and constitutional law, *the people* denotes a unified agent in which sovereignty is invested; sociologically, however, *the people* denotes a heterogeneous population that can only be grasped as number. It is as though the people always had two bodies, states the French historian Pierre Rosanvallon. The people-as-sovereign is well defined, dense and energized by the principle of unity that it both expresses and confirms. The people-as-society, by contrast, are evasive, abstract, and formless, pure number and seriality.[23]

Strangely, however, David manages to compress both concepts of the people into his image. The National Assembly renders the people both as ideal and as reality, both as sovereign principle and as historical reality. This in itself is evidence of the image's accomplishment as a representation of the French Revolution, for the revolution is characterized precisely by the fact that the two bodies of the people merge. The heterogeneous, many-headed people is unified into one political agent by the historical circumstances themselves, in order to institute "the people" as a principle of sovereignty. To use Rosanvallon's terms, the people-as-sovereign and the people-as-society fuse into the people-as-event.

This also is the ultimate horizon of David's image—the reason for its success, and the explanation of its failure. It is a success in the sense that *The Tennis Court Oath* is one of the few existing images of the people-as-event. David catches a transient historical moment in which the people is identical with itself, its reality embodying its ideal, its multitude fusing into union, its political passions confirming democratic sovereignty. But it is also a failure in the

2A 'Mass': English (French, German)

Marisa Galvez

Although it is impossible to determine when the word *mass* and its cognates (French *masse*, German *maß*) acquired their meaning as a political collective, historical events during the period 1787–1798 significantly shaped the meaning of the French cognate in this direction. Borrowed from the Latin word *massa*, meaning "lump, bulk, parcel of land, dough" (OED), the primary definition of the French *masse* from medieval times to the present is "a dense aggregate of objects having the appearance of a single body" (as in a large number of beings [eleventh century], or "metal ingot" [1309] [OED]).[1] Although retaining these physical connotations, the word is applied to moral and philosophical contexts from the early modern period onward. For example, the Castilian poet Gómez Manrique uses the Spanish cognate *masa* in the fifteenth century to invoke the commonplace of humanity coming from and returning to one substance: "Todos somos de una masa/a la cual nos tornaremos." Perhaps this flexible application of *mass* to human relations has to do with the perception of a mass as a single continuous body with its particular elements as less distinct (as in *en masse* as "bodily, as a whole," and uses of mass to mean "a great quantity of money" or "a formation of troops" [OED]). By the eighteenth century, *mass* extends into abstract and scientific representation in art, music, architecture, and physics ("en Peinture . . . En peignant des arbres, on doit moins s'attacher

sense that, once the revolutionary event passes, the two bodies separate. The people as a principle of sovereignty no longer finds any correspondence in reality; and the people as a sociological reality recedes back into invisibility, into numbers.

David was in fact unable to complete the great oil of the revolution. The historical situation unmade the self-identity of the people that he had made visible. Within a couple of years, the sworn unity of the Versailles assembly dissolved as many of the depicted persons fell into disrepute, were detained, executed, or became enemies. *The Tennis Court Oath* never went beyond preparatory drawings and sketches.

The aesthetic representations of the people were transformed accordingly, and David's artistic career testifies to this change. His next representations of the people were strictly allegorical. This aesthetic choice is understandable against the background of a historical situation in which the people as a sovereign principle no longer had any tangible equivalent in social reality. As director of the revolutionary festivities in Paris, David invented majestic carriages and solemn parades to celebrate the people. In one of these, the people is personified by a Herculean figure enthroned on a chariot pulled by two oxen, Egalité and Fraternité, who crush the ancien régime under their massive hooves. The allegory is ambiguous, however: when popular sovereignty is personified by a single figure, it is impossible to distinguish it from the despotic sovereignty of the monarch. It is easy to imagine the same image—but with Caligula, Louis XVI, or Napoleon on the throne. This problem was resolved by David and others by placing a female symbol on the throne. As woman, she did not disturb the equality among the male citizens. As fantasy, she did not intervene into the machinations of power. As symbol, she was nonetheless a rallying point, a unifying force. The feminized allegory of the people thus became a *corpus mysticum* that sanctioned the male citizens' *corpus politicum*. A bit into the nineteenth century, this visualization of the people-as-nation and the people-as-sovereign settles into a firm mold: Marianne with the Phrygian cap carrying the tricolor.[24]

Meanwhile, *The Tennis Court Oath* indicates what will happen to the people once it no longer incarnates the nation, democracy, or sovereignty. In the geometric matrix that organizes the assembled collective, one line of division is stronger than the others—the walls of the building itself constitute it. At the historical moment rendered by David, the force of the unified people floods the walls. Common men and women confirm the historical oath through their own presence. Once this moment has passed, however, these figures disappear from view, receding behind the walls of the building, which divides not only the room itself or the visual plane of the painting, but also the people as a political body. Thus, once a system of representative democracy is instituted, a new division establishes itself between the elected representatives, who embody the people as a political ideal, and those who make up the people as a social reality.[25]

Sieyès's *What Is the Third Estate* elucidates this aspect of David's image. According to Sieyès, the people was by definition identical with the third estate. He posited the bourgeoisie as the universal class of France, thus dissolving the distinctions between the estates, but at the same time instituting a new social division. On the one hand, there are now the universal citizens of the third estate who represent the interest of the people. On the other hand, there is the majority of the people, *le menu peuple*, who, because of their poverty and ignorance, cannot conceivably participate in those political decisions that are made in their name. Shut out by the division established by the system of political representation, the people becomes anonymous and invisible, its political voices muted and replaced by the discourse in the assembly.

This discourse will by definition justify itself as the voice of the people. However, the voice of the people that is implied in this context is far more refined and pure than the brute argot heard in the fields and the factories. Throughout the nineteenth century, the citizens who see themselves as the representatives of the people will insist on and defend this distinction. While their own ideas and actions are axiomatically in concord with the people, the people's ideas and actions are seen as expressions of immaturity and base instincts.

This is to say that the people's needs are exclusively registered through the lenses of its political and cultural representatives, the custodians of the general interest. Jules Michelet in 1846 explains the nature of these lenses: "You go hunting in the gutters with a magnifying glass, and when you find some dirty, filthy thing, you bring it to us exclaiming, 'Triumph! Triumph! We have found the people!'"[26] As the century passes, the people becomes an increasingly appalling entity for the upper classes: "this people so brutish, so ignorant, so vain, so disagreeable to brush against, so disgusting to see up close" (ce peuple si brute, si ignorant, si vaniteux, si désagréable à frayer, si dégoûtant à voir de près), writes Flora Tristan in 1843.[27] In order to account for this entity, politicians, social scientists, and writers establish a manner of speaking and a set of terms that purport to represent the nature of the people. It is against this horizon that the meaning of *the masses* gradually consolidates itself: the word will evoke the disgust and fear expressed by Flora Tristan, but it will also serve to exclude and control those who are seen as the source of that fear. It is a paradoxical and contradictory discourse: as masses, the people en-

aux détails qu'aux masses. —Académie Française 1762" [in painting trees, one should pay attention less to the details than to the masses]). To perceive and qualify mass, to inquire into the nature of mass itself, constitutes a subjective and often poetic act, the act of becoming (Weisze blasen seh ich springen;/wohl! die massen sind im flusz. [Schiller, *Das Lied von der Glocke*, 1799 — Grimm *Wörterbuch*). In a similar vein, Jean-François Féraud, including a *remarque* in his *Dictionaire Critique de la langue française (Marseille, Mossy 1787–1788)*, discusses the perception of masses:

REM. *Masse*, dans son sens le plus naturel, est un terme à la mode. "Le vulgaire ne voit que *des masses*: les détails de la natûre sont un spectâcle réservé pour nous" (dit le soi-disant Philosophe.) Marm.

[*Mass,* in its most natural sense, is a fashionable term. "The vulgar only sees *masses:* the details of nature are a spectacle reserved for us" (says the so-called Philosopher).]

We find this *remarque* (using a quote from the works of the eighteenth-century French writer Jean-Francois Marmontel, a member of the Academie Française) in a comprehensive guide to the authorized and proper usage of French for people from the remote regions of France. The "Philosophe" perceives the spectacle of nature in a particular way: seeing masses in nature is an act of *le vulgaire*. In 1798, the year before the end of the French Revolution, a new meaning of *masse* evolves in a new configuration of subjectivity, class, and perception in the *Dictionnaire de l'Academie de Francaise*, 5th edition:

* MASSE (EN). phr. adv. Collectivement, Tous ensemble. Il s'est dit principalement en Révolution. *Aller, se porter en masse. L'assemblée s'est portée*

Figure 2.2 Eugène Delacroix (1798–1863). *Liberty Leading the People*, July 28, 1830. Painted 1830. Oil on canvas, 260 x 325 cm. Photo: Hervé Lewandowski. Photo Credit: Réunion des Musées Nationaux / Art Resource, NY. Louvre, Paris, France. Used with the permission of Réunion des Musées Nationaux /Art Resource NY.

dangers the political order, which at the same time is founded in the name of the people.[28]

In the first half of the nineteenth century, David's horizontal representation of a French society of equals found its opposite in narratives and prints that viewed society as a hierarchy. In fiction and journalism allegories of height and depth were elaborated in astonishing detail. These descriptions still convey a sense of adventure today, as though the writers competed in a race to map the emerging urban world.[29] Here is Michelet: "It is the same with nationality as with geology—the heat is below. Descend, and you will find it increases. In the lower strata it is burning hot."[30] And here is Balzac, whose narrator spirals downward through Paris society until he reaches the blasting furnaces operated by the God of fire and lightning; it is the world of the proletarian: "Is not Vulcan, with his ugliness and strength, the emblem of this strong and ugly race of men, superb in its mechanical skill, patient so long as it chooses to be so, terrible one day in every century, as explosive as gunpowder, primed with brandy to the point of revolutionary incendiarism." The population living in this underworld, Balzac approximates, "amounts to three hundred thousand souls. Would not the government be overturned every Tuesday were it not for the taverns?"[31]

Energy, numbers, crime, and insurrection: these characteristics are tied together by Balzac; they return in Eugène Sue's *Les Mystères de Paris;* and they are further magnified in Victor Hugo's view of the underworld:

All human societies have what is known to the theatre as an "under-stage." The social earth is everywhere mined and tunnelled, for better or for worse. There are higher and lower galleries, upper and lower strata in that subsoil which sometimes collapse under the weight of civilization, and which in our ignorance and indifference we thread underfoot. . . . The volcano is filled with darkness capable of bursting into flame; lava at the start is black. . . . The deeper one goes the more unpredictable are the workers. At the level which social philosophy can recognize, good work is done; at a lower level it becomes doubtful, of questionable value; at the lowest level it is fearsome. There are depths to which the spirit of civilization cannot penetrate, a limit beyond which the air is not breathable by men; and it is here that monsters may be born. . . . Anarchy lurks in that void. The wild figures, half-animal, almost ghosts, that prowl in the darkness have no concern with universal progress, neither the thought nor the word is known to them, nothing is known to them but the fulfillment of their individual cravings. They are scarcely conscious, having within them a terrifying emptiness. They have two mothers, two foster-mothers, ignorance and poverty, a single guiding principle, that of necessity, and a single appetite, for all the satisfactions of the flesh. They are brutishly and fiercely voracious, not in the manner of a tyrant but of a

en masse. Levée en masse des Citoyens, et par extension, *des habitans d'un Pays.*

[Collectively, all together. It is said principally in Revolution. To go en masse. The assembly moved en masse. The rising en masse of the citizens, and by extension, of the inhabitants of a country.]

The events of the French Revolution inform this new meaning of *masse* as a political collective as they did words such as *revolution* and *Citizen:* here, the noun *masse* with the preposition *en* conjures up a moving spectacle of the *peuple.* During the French Revolution, the *Citoyens* forge a new political vernacular amidst the fall of the ancien régime: people became a mass *en masse.* Whereas before one evaluated social classes or intellect based on a perception of masses, in 1798 the masses themselves are a class subject and political actors on a world stage. It would take the rise of nineteenth-century urbanism and twentieth-century mass movements for the *mass* to emerge in all its visual force as a figurative spectacle that joins fragmentary viewpoints: a new magical cohesiveness that invokes symbolic, ritualistic meaning in the midst of changing historical consciousness. The narrative of French dictionaries, however, gives us a glimpse of how the historical rise of the modern political collective influenced the potential meaning of *mass.*

2B Ceremony

Michel Serres

It had been a long time since I had been present at a ceremony. Now that burials are not followed by funeral processions, now that we try to escape the boredom of official receptions, who enjoys such occasions? But yesterday, the French Academy gave a last homage to Léopold Sédar Senghor, who died in Normandy and was interred in Dakar; since my election to the Academy, I had known him, we had conversed, I had liked him. Beneath the nave of Saint-Germain-des-Prés, the cardinal officiated before the president and the prime minister of France, accompanied by their wives, all four seated at the balustrade of the chancel. I had been unable to convince myself to put on, like my colleagues, the green costume of the Academy.

As a Christian, a graduate of the École Normale Supérieure, and a Latinist, the deceased had asked for a Gregorian mass; as a Senegalese, he had a right to be remembered with Wolof chants and the tam-tam of his village; as a member of the Academy, a poet, and a statesman, he was treated to the obligatory morsels of literary and political elegance, probably heard by his departed soul. The church was full, so the sidewalks were overrun with rubberneckers.

Origin

Catholic pageantry often carries on rituals that come from ancient Rome. Thus yesterday, the

tiger. By an inevitable process, by the fateful logic of darkness, the child nurtured in misery grows up to be a criminal, and what arises out of that lowest level of society is not the confused search for an Absolute but an affirmation of matter itself.[32]

Hugo's allegory is elaborated with such phantasmatic creativity that it takes precedence over reality. *Les Misérables* (1862) is set in France during the Restoration and culminates with the republican insurrection of 1832. Like Thomas Carlyle's history of the French Revolution, Hugo's novel reads like a myth, in which all conflicts turn around a pole rooted in the dark void, and in which all characters are judged by the positions they occupy on the vertical axis. The keyword in the passage above is *misère*. Hugo construes a causal link between *misère* and criminality: "by an inevitable process . . . the child nurtured in misery grows up to be a criminal."

As Louis Chevalier has shown, *misère* was at first a fairly circumscribed term used to explain the criminal inclinations of the so-called dangerous classes. Gradually, it became a general term for the wretched condition of the working classes as a whole, to the extent that the working classes became synonymous with the dangerous classes. *Misère* was used as an umbrella term for all the symptoms of the material and mental destitution suffered by the Paris majority: crime, poverty, unemployment, homelessness, hunger, suicide, infanticide, prostitution, alcoholism, illiteracy, and all other conceivable evils and misfortunes. *Misère* did not denote any one of these phenomena in particular but suggested that they were connected, so that the presence of one—say, hunger—implied moral defects such as dishonesty and criminality.[33]

The problems discussed under the rubric *misère* were roughly the same ones as the organized labor movement would later bring up as *la question sociale*, the social question. However, by the mid-nineteenth century, and, as we shall see, in some circles until much later, it was not clear that misery was a social issue. More often, working-class misery was attributed to moral degeneration, or it was seen as an inevitable fact of nature. Malthus's population theory, predicting a ruthless social struggle for diminishing resources, was a constant reference in this milieu, as were the ideas of Cabanis, Lavater, and Gall concerning biologically determined—and physiognomically detectable—inequalities between different social groups.

Rarely were the groups in question seriously defined. Novelists, journalists, and social scientists could apparently take their readers' understanding for granted when they spelled words such as *les misérables*, the working classes, *la populace*, the multitude, *la foule*, the masses. Although most accounts began by pitying the masses, they typically went on to show why they were undeserving or incapable of exercising political rights; and in case the masses tried to obtain such rights by force, this only proved that they were violent and dangerous. Honoré-Antoine Frégier's account of the dangerous classes is an instructive case in point because it imperceptibly links poverty to vice, and vice to social danger: "The poor and criminal classes have always been and will always be the most productive nursery for all sorts of wrongdoers: we will designate them more particularly as the dangerous classes, for even when vice is not accompanied by perversity, by the simple fact that it is allied with poverty in the same individual, society should rightly fear him; he is dangerous" (Les classes pauvres et vicieuses ont toujours été et seront toujours la pépenière la plus productive des toutes les sortes de malfaiteurs; ce sont elles que nous désignerons plus particulièrement sous le titre de classes dangereuses; car, lors même que la vice n'est pas accompagné de la perversité, par celà qu'il s'allie à la pauvreté dans la même individu, il est un juste sujet de crainte pour la société, il est dangereux).[34] Frégier moves in circles. Certain classes are dangerous because they are feared; and they are feared because their vice and poverty make them dangerous. Such circular arguments are the rule in mainstream political discourse of nineteenth-century France. Once the rhetorical cover is stripped off, this discourse typically comes down to an assertion of the bare fact of exclusion.

For a long time planned under the title *Les misères*, Victor Hugo's novel is the great summa of the social maladies in mid-nineteenth-century France. Hugo occupies an ambiguous position in this context. To be sure, the working classes are described as dangerous and unreliable throughout *Les Misérables*. Yet they are also endowed with the potential to realize the universal ideals:

It is above all in the back streets, let us be clear about this, that the real Parisian race is to be found, the pure stock, the true face; in the places where men work and suffer, for work and suffering are the two faces of man. There, in that ant-heap of humble and unknown, the strangest types exist, from the stevedore of La Rapée to the horse-butcher of Montfaucon. *Fex Urbis*, "the lees of the city," Cicero called them, and "mob" was the word. Burke used mob, masses, crowd, public . . . the words are easily said. But what does that matter? What does it matter if they go barefoot, or if they cannot read? . . . Cannot light penetrate to the masses? Light! Let us repeat it again and again—Light and more Light . . . And then, who knows, opacity may be found to be transparent. Are not revolutions transformations? Let the philosophers continue to teach and enlighten, to think high and speak loud, . . . dispense the alphabet, assert men's rights, sing the Marseillaise . . . The crowd can be made sublime. (*M*, 508–9/632)

For Hugo, the masses constitute the raw material of humanity, not yet refined by education and literacy. If the ideal is injected into the masses, they cease being masses and become the sublime entity called the people, the ultimate sovereign

Euro-African space rebuilt in music was hollowed out by a temporal pocket that Senghor himself had sewn by claiming—was he right?—that plainchant came from the recitative chant of *Négritude*. But neither white Rome nor the Christianity of black Africa can pride itself on having invented the idea or the word *ceremony*. This term, of Etruscan invention and thus stolen by the Latin armies that assassinated this people—a people whose genius taught the Mediterranean the delicacy of art, an original approach to death, and the color of a piety that the people of neighboring cultures inherited—was taken up everywhere without anyone's really remembering what it had signified for those who first practiced it.

What lost sense does this atemporal music express? From what somber unspecified grave does it spring? Do those who know understand as little as the ignorant, and those who believe, as little as the impious?

Face to Face

Those present gather in memory of the deceased. There, all confront a ghost. Do they kneel before the God in whom Senghor believed, in order to pray to Him? All, here, in His presence? Does this single or double absence unite this crowd? On the contrary, does it divide into two parts, so that the majority can ogle the masters? The passersby peep at—ah!—the president and the prime minister, the chasubles and the green robes. Or is it split into three parts, so that those in the middle, decorated or noted writers, can be admired by the low who see them exhibited in the company of the high?

In the first hypothesis, transcendence assures the cohesion of the assembled collective. Sociology shows, in the second, what ceremonies serve

Figure 2.3 Ernest-Meissonier (1815–1891). *The Barricade, rue de la Mortellerie, June 1848*, also called "Souvenir of the Civil War." Oil on canvas. Photo Credit: Réunion des Musées Nationaux / Art Resource, NY. Louvre, Paris, France. Used with the permission of Réunion des Musées Nationaux /Art Resource NY.

of France. The French Revolution encapsulates this transfiguration. Interestingly, this view allows Hugo to distinguish between righteous and criminal uses of collective violence:

In any matter of collective sovereignty, the war of the whole against the part is an insurrection, and the war of the part against the whole is a form of mutiny: the Tuileries may be justly or unjustly assailed according to whether they harbor the King or the Assembly. The guns turned on the mob were wrong on 10 August and right on 14 Vendémiaire. It looks the same, but the basis is different: the Swiss guards were defending an unrighteous cause, Bonaparte a righteous one. What has been done in the free exercise of its sovereign powers by universal suffrage cannot be undone by an uprising in the street. The same is true of matters of pure civilization: the instinct of the crowd, which yesterday was clear-sighted, may tomorrow be befogged. (*M*, 886/1099–100)

For all its pedantry, Hugo's taxonomy of the various species of collective violence has the advantage of indicating the exact function of "the masses" in the social discourse of his era. "The mob [*la foule*] betrays the people," he states (*M*, 887/1101). "The war of the part against the whole is a form of mutiny," he also states. In Hugo's discourse, "the whole" is always synonymous with "the people," "the nation," and "the Republic." "The mass," or *la foule*, by contrast, is "the part." It either betrays "the whole" and so remains a blind mob; or "the mass" supports the whole and is then ennobled and become one with the people—the insurrection and the revolution being the rite of passage by which the mass becomes sovereign people. In Hugo, then, "the masses" names precisely that *part* of the population that has yet to realize the people as ideal, and hence is excluded from the polity that presents itself as the embodiment of that ideal.

We are now in a better position to understand the true nature of *les misérables*, and the political implications of *la misère* as a sweeping description of the conditions of the working classes. As we have seen, *misère* means both a material and a spiritual deprivation. The *misérables* are poor, which has the political implication that they do not pay taxes and hence, according to a general opinion of the nineteenth century, do not contribute to the general wealth of the nation. The *misérables* are also illiterate and ignorant, guided by their instinctual drives rather than by rational deliberation, which implies that they do not understand their own true interests, not to speak of the general interest.

Misère thus signals the absence of the two properties that at this time were used as criteria to qualify for political rights. The first criterion was motivated by liberal ideas of a social contract: only individuals who contributed to the public treasury would have a say in public affairs. The French constitution of 1830 stated that

for: coherence results from exchanged gazes. More dynamic, the third hypothesis describes preferment: the anonymous are assured that such a democracy opens passages by which they could, possibly, make a name for themselves.

In the three cases considered above, someone or several someones, absent or present, unique, rare, or numerous, turn to face the crowd. We are accustomed to these about-faces. The officiant prays, his face toward us. The reader leaves the assembly, ascends to the podium, and reads the Gospel, which we hear leave his lips. The perpetual secretary, and then the president, evoke, before the people, the memory of the deceased. We know these heads; we often give them a name, except that transcendence, unnamable, does not show its face. We live together by confronting these bodies, turned toward these entreaties. Collective equals face to face.

The Sole Ceremony

But we have changed all that, which dates back to the beginnings of human cultures and which ethno- and anthropologists can attest to at all latitudes. From now on, in the sanctuary, braving archaic interdictions, a handful of operators, whose faces no one notices although they too turn toward us, sport television cameras and headsets, high-fidelity microphones, booms with dazzling lights, on their shoulders, in their hands, or on their heads, dragging cables in whose loops, knots, and twists in which officials, like everyone else, entangle their feet. Tomorrow, on the screens of the region, the nation, or the world, depending on the importance of the ceremony, tens of thousands or millions of spectators will watch the same rite, retransmitted. From that moment, not only do those in the middle have less interest in being seen by the anonymous, whose numbers are unimpressive although they are crammed all along the street; but even the high try to show themselves to the lens of these machines that, facing everyone, make it so that everyone, high, middle, and low, will no longer exist together except in front of them.

Roman, Christian, or from Africa, Etruscan, forgotten, archaic, and for that very reason effective . . . ceremony now ends before it begins, having lost its function and utility: for what good is the eloquence of great organs and mysterious choirs, if those who manipulate the images will certainly suppress the plainchant, Couperin, the tam-tam and the Wolof recitatives, the voices (too long), the sublime (too profound), the vaults and the pillars (too wide and high), to show only, for one minute, the hesitant steps of old men coming out of the church, cruelly elbowing each other to show off—no longer to the curious amassed below the porch, whose importance is thereby diminished; but to the hole that, this evening or tomorrow, will unite the grand mass, virtual and invisible, the only social reality? Unnamable and absent, does transcendence turn back to rejoin the collective immanence? Who, then, to call great, if not the one who will shortly cut the feet or the neck of former high personages, so that their image passes muster?

Farewell Etruria; ceremony unfolds today only before these machines. And this is why I have been missing occasions for so long. In the sanctuary, the true officiants sport neither chasuble nor green robes, but the light boom at the end of their arm.

Glory

These machines make the real ceremony virtual. The flat image replaces, they say, corporeal presence. But as far as I know, ceremony itself has

only men who paid more than 500 francs could vote and campaign for a seat in the assembly. For the leading circles of society, it was self-evident that the laboring people were so preoccupied with survival and bread-winning that they, as Locke maintained, had "neither time nor ability to direct their thoughts at anything else." In this view, *misère* and political rights mutually exclude each other, and private property becomes the criterion for separating citizens from masses.

The exclusion of *les misérables* from the polity was also justified from an educational point of view. Hugo follows Immanuel Kant's conviction that education is the royal path toward man's emancipation "from his self-incurred tutelage." Unlike Hugo, however, Kant doubted that the majority would ever be able to take this step. They were so bent on immediate needs that they must remain in tutelage. The masses occupied a lower stage of evolution, comparable to that of savages who seek instant gratification of every desire. Only persons who had learned to suppress their passions, or who had channeled them into profitable economic activity, deserved the rights as citizens to act as representatives of the people.[35] The distinction between those guided by reason and those guided by passions thus served to confirm the distinction between those pretending to represent the general will and those who were excluded from the public arena.

Throughout the nineteenth century, these two discourses, one about the distribution of political power on economic grounds, the other about the distribution of power on cultural grounds, mutually reinforce each other. The synchronized operations of these two systems of representation determine the content given to the category of the masses. The first system is political and determines which persons have the right to be citizens and to represent "the people," and here the masses emerge as those who are deprived of such rights. The second system of representation is ideological and cultural; here the masses emerge as a social phenomenon governed by irrational passions that threaten civilized norms. Thus, the masses not only refer to the laboring classes that are set apart from the political body; they also epitomize the instincts from which society must purge itself, in order to constitute itself as a sovereign polity working for the general good. In these two forms, the masses constitute the haunting shadow of bourgeois society and the repressed supplement of the effort to represent "the people" as a unified political body.[36]

This explains why Hugo frequently sounds like a tutor to *les misérables*. The author represents the cultivated mind that alone is able to grasp the meaning of democratic sovereignty. He urges the masses to pull themselves out of misery, get educated, and become worthy citizens. He nourishes the dream that Eugène Delacroix visualized in his painting of the 1830 revolution, *Liberty Leading the People*

(*Liberté guidant le peuple*, fig. 2.2). Délacroix depicts the people as event. The worker and the bourgeois march in step across the barricade with Marianne, the spirit of freedom, spurring them forward.

The revolution of 1830 and the following insurrection of 1832 were clear-cut cases, however. These were revolts against a restored monarchy. By Hugo's standard, anyone who joined the insurrection was representing the people. Once this moment had passed, however, the path of the people again bifurcated. After 1832, the bourgeoisie, protected by the constitutional monarchy of Louis-Philippe, remained the sole representative of the French society, whereas the worker disappeared into the faceless multitude.

The next time they met on level ground, they would stand on opposing sides of the barricade, not as the halves of one people and one nation, but as two people hostile toward one another. "They form a nation within the nation," Daniel Stern said about the working classes after 1848.[37] They are the barbarians, Eugène Sue said in the preface of *The Mysteries of Paris*—"just as much outside civilisation as the savage tribes so well depicted by Cooper. But the barbarians of whom we speak are in the midst of us."[38] What if they attack us? Eugène Buret asked in 1840:

The workers are just as free of obligations toward their masters as the latter ones are toward them; they consider them as men of a different class, opposed and even hostile. Isolated from the nation, placed outside the social and political community, alone with their concerns and their misery, they are acting in order to leave that terrible solitude, and, just like the barbarians with whom they are often compared, they perhaps contemplate an invasion.[39]

In June 1848, the barbarians tried to take Paris, in what Hugo called "the biggest street war in history" (*M*, 987/1217). Hugo had great sympathies for the masses that rose in 1848, first and successfully in February to dethrone Louis-Philippe, and then again in June, in a failed attempt to protect the social reforms that had just been instituted to improve the condition of the working poor. In June 1848, the spirit of democracy was at least partly on the side of the rebels, Hugo admitted. Yet democratic sovereignty resided with the government, for it was democratically elected. The revolt therefore "had to be combated," he said. June 1848 was "mobocracy rebelling against *demos*."

Yet June 1848 obviously undermined the distinction between "mass" and "people" that Hugo wanted to uphold, just as it messed up his taxonomy of collective violence. If France was now irrevocably divided between two incompatible ideas of "the people" (Hugo himself distinguished between "La République rouge" and

always produced the virtual: the Etruscans probably invented it for this purpose. The exchange of gazes is already a passing of images. Certain pedants sometimes prefer the word *symbolic*, and for good reason, since the symbol originally reunited two pieces of baked earth previously severed by two mutual visitors, in order to remind them of their reciprocal debt of hospitality: yes, the collective was split in order to be better unified, the low enjoying contemplating the high—before killing them sometimes—and the high enjoying showing themselves to the low in their ephemeral glory.

This exchange of images confers glory on the parts of the symbol. If the participants dispute it or share it, they remain in the immanent glue of the social; if, on the contrary, it is given to God alone, transcendence unites the pious. Informational, negentropic, virtual, or symbolic, this vanity-glue can be transubstantiated one day into forces on the entropic scale, devastating, destroying lives and villages in passing, but it appears for a long time potential, anodyne, and inoffensive. But above all: we did not know who withholds, who gives, who will receive—God, our masters, you, me . . . ?—this illustriousness, this renown, this celebrity, this fame . . . blind in any event, to how long this light will remain virtual and to when it will be transubstantiated into a terrifying cyclone.

We have changed all that. We have constructed tools out of real glass and plastic materials, made for fashioning that virtual: society-making machines that withhold, draw in, and distribute—images, certainly, but also, by their intermediary, glory. Glory dazzles us with the light that the operators lit yesterday, at their whim, facing us in the chancel. Their machines transubstantiate a virtual social of three hundred people into another of 30 million; they have the power, immense and new, of changing scale and thus of transforming virtual symbols into gargantuan energies. If a man, already powerful, speaks in them, with them, and through them, he ignites the world.

There is now only one ceremony: the one produced by these machines, showing everywhere, replaces all the others. There is now only a single officiant in the chancel: the hole that we call the lens (*l'objectif*), probably by antiphrasis, because it has only subjective and collective functions. This is why, once again, we were lacking other occasions: we are now only watching one ceremony, but this one every day.

Religion

At the mass yesterday in memory of Léopold Sédar Senghor and his faith, believers gathered together in front of the mystery of the Eucharist. In the sanctuary stood the priests, facing us and leaning, eyes closed, over that transcendental transubstantiation. In the same sanctuary, cameras produced a series of those immanent transubstantiations, dazzling us with lights.

Are we changing religions? There is only one, television: universal, it kills all the others. It has a monopoly on ceremonies. At noon and in the evening, we turn on the set to make our prayer to the presenter, whose face is turned toward us as we are virtually assembled. Catholic pageantry was succeeded by the Protestant service, where the pastor allows some of those present to speak, one by one; this rite serves as a model for all the talk shows. It is certainly a question of ceremony—and of a religious one: the cardinal and the officiants bear witness, here, at Saint-Germain-des-Prés, to the absence of God; the television operators bear witness to the absence of all. Each one of them,

"La République de l'Idéal") the question as to the legitimacy of insurrectionary violence became undecidable, or rather, it could be decided only by taking sides. Hugo concluded that June 1848 was an "event which history finds it almost impossible to classify" (*M*, 988/1217).

Writing about the events in France of 1848, Karl Marx observed that the liberal ideal of freedom and equal rights that in 1789 had unified the people were in 1848 a force of disunion.[40] In this perspective, June 1848 appears as the liquidation of the revolutionary heritage. Neither of the struggling parts embodied the republican ideal of the people. Hugo could not conceive of an event like this, because his historical analysis presupposes the eternal viability of the 1789 ideal of a people united, without divisions of class, consisting of citizens that are all equal representatives of the people. Hence his twisted descriptions of 1848: "a revolt of the populace against itself," he states in *Les Misérables* (*M*, 988/1218). "On the one side the desperation of the people, on the other the desperation of society," he notes in his journal.[41] Describing the great barricade in Faubourg Saint-Antoine, Hugo captures the chaotic nature of a society that by 1848 was worn-out and broken:

The sight of the barricade alone conveyed a sense of intolerable distress which had reached the point where suffering becomes disaster. Of what was it built? Of the material of three six-storey houses demolished for the purpose, some people said. Of the phenomenon of overwhelming anger, said others. It bore the lamentable aspect of all things built by hatred —a look of destruction. One might ask, "Who built all that?"; but one might equally ask, "Who destroyed all that?" Everything had gone into it, doors, grilles, screens, bedroom furniture, wrecked cocking-stoves and pots and pans, piled up haphazard, the whole a composite of paving-stones and rubble, timbers, iron bars, broken window-panes, seatless chairs, rags, odds and ends of every kind—and curses. It was great and it was trivial, a chaotic parody of emptiness, a mingling of debris. Sisyphus had cast his rock upon it and Job his potsherd. In short it was terrible, an Acropolis of the destitute. (*M*, 988–89/1219)

Hugo continues his description of the barricade over several pages, naming the unnamable—a barricade at once sublime and monstrous, "beyond reason," just like the people itself. "The spirit of revolution cast its shadow over that mound, resonant with the voice of the people, which resembles the voice of God: a strange nobility emanated from it. It was a pile of garbage, and it was Sinai." Swinging from awe to disgust, Hugo admits his inability to understand the barricade. The huge mass resists comparison with past events. The pile of old scrap has an absolute newness to it, for which words have yet to been invented. "As we have said, it was raised in the name of the Revolution. But what was it fighting? It was fighting the Revolution. That barricade, which was chance, disorder, terror, misunderstanding and the unknown, was at war with the Constituent Assembly, the sovereignty of the people, universal suffrage, the nation and the Republic. It was the 'Caramagnole' defying the 'Marseillaise.' An insane but heroic defiance, for that ancient faubourg is a hero."

The ideals of 1789 turned into rubbish: the barricade of the Faubourg Saint-Antoine comes across as the burial mound for the deceased body of the people-as-one. The barricade, a symbol of a society that has exhausted its symbols and consumed its ideals, appears to be the work of the collective force that Carlyle called the wrath of Sansculottism, a chaos from which a new order would be regenerated. What kind of order? The barricade is the sphinx of the masses. Not even Hugo, a friend of the people, can solve its riddle, but keeps gaping in awe and terror.

The Saint-Antoine barricade is also mentioned in Gustave Flaubert's *Sentimental Education* (1869; *L'Education sentimentale*), but without the pathos or symbolism of Hugo. Flaubert's novel describes both the revolution in February and the failed insurrection of workers in the following summer. Contrary to most other accounts of this violent year, Flaubert's narrative lacks emotional investment. Where other observers detected the workings of historical forces and collective agents struggling to represent the grand ideal of France, Flaubert saw the 1848 revolution as a clash between delusions. Frédéric Moreau, the main character, toys with the idea of writing a comedy based on episodes from the French Revolution.[42] In a similar vein, *Sentimental Education* may be seen as an attempt to write a farce about the 1848 revolution.[43] It is easy to see why Flaubert derided it. In his view, 1848 demonstrated the same misfit between reality and ideal that is typical of the genre of comedy. The novel generates numerous comical effects by depicting the revolutionary crowds of Paris as filthy street children and drunkards and by subsequently contrasting their behavior with the solemn ideals of democracy and republicanism that are put forth in the name of the people. Consider Flaubert's account of the triumphant moment of the February Revolution, when popular crowds broke into the royal apartments of the Tuileries. Hierarchies are turned upside down as the servants try on the clothes and mimic the manners of their lords. Flaubert has but scorn for the pretentious new sovereign, "His Majesty the People":

Pushed along in spite of themselves, they entered a room in which a red velvet canopy was stretched across the ceiling. On the throne underneath sat a worker with a black beard, his shirt half-open, grinning like a stupid ape. Others clambered on to the platform to sit in his place.

"What a myth!" said Hussonet. "There's the sovereign people for you!"

present, represents the absence of the two all-powerful. Are these two priests in the same chancel opposed to each other? Should we choose between the absent transcendence to which all glory is given: *Gloria in excelsis Deo* . . . and the groaning of the world given over to violence to make that glory, acquire it, and keep it? We bow either before the merciful impotence of the former or before our own omnipotence without forgiveness.

Even better: because the two pastors are corporally distinguishable, before our eyes, in the sanctuary and by the objects that they manipulate, we can no longer mistake social religion for belief in God. Finally, here is a great day: because no one is deceiving us, we can no longer deceive ourselves. Yesterday, we celebrated together, once more, the great separation of the Church and politics, of divine mysticism and collective rites: the end of the sociologies of religions.

Two Critiques of Pure Religion

Beginning in the era of the Enlightenment, experimental science progressively but completely removed from religion all the geneses of the stars, the earth, and living beings. Celestial mechanics, astrophysics, geology, chemistry, natural history, and biology . . . these all took over the explanation of the world from religion. What is more, there were machines attached to these sciences whose effectiveness was an improvement on the recipes or rare miracles alleged in these traditions. This decisive critique, which almost killed them, resulted, however, in a reprieve: faith no longer has any relation to the predictions and causes described in its great narratives. Interpreters still attached to the letter of these texts are losing their time, their credit, and the match: the others pray to God without worrying about scientific rationality; sometimes they even practice it.

The second critique came from the human sciences, which cheerfully reduced the religious and its rites to collective functions: the gods unite the city, their myths form the human soul. More devastating than the first critique, this even succeeded in converting many pastors to the point that they became psychologists or sociologists at the risk of their faith.

But had I ever really noted the existence and the function of these new, informational machines that maintain the same relation with the social sciences as the tools functioning on the entropic scale have with the hard sciences? Do we understand that certain technologies function as *society-making machines*? A winch at work supports weight; the energy of a motor can carry men beyond the horizon; the tools of communication fashion the collective, its numbers and its own energies.

Thus television, as I have said, sucks in all ceremonies. The virtual union of everyone is accomplished facing the presenter, who is not present. Everything that proceeded or resulted from the social, that represented it, actualized it, heated it, transformed it, even studied it: religion, sport, theater, cinema, books, teaching, judicial trials, political assemblies, meetings of all sorts . . . now passes through television, no longer exists except by television, is recycled through television . . . which transubstantiates everything from someones into everyone. It appropriates *everything that concerns everyone and, first of all, existence in the presence of everyone*, which, for many, comes down to the same as existence itself, as well as *the very existence of everyone*. Socially speaking nothing exists without it, not even, finally, society itself. It does not reflect the opinions of society so

The throne was picked up and passed unsteadily from hand to hand across the room. "Good Lord! Look how it's pitching! The ship of state is being tossed on a stormy sea! It's dancing a can-can! It's dancing a can-can!"

It was taken to a window and thrown out, to the accompaniment of hisses and boos.

"Poor old thing!" Hussonet said, as he watched it fall into the garden, where it was quickly picked up to be taken to the Bastille and then burnt.[44]

The people are pathetically unable to represent the elevated ideals—democracy, republicanism, popular sovereignty—that are promoted in their name. Or worse, the people turn these ideals into their opposites: "In the entrance-hall, standing on a pile of clothes, a prostitute was posing as a statue of Liberty, motionless and terrifying, with her eyes wide open."[45]

Because words such as *the people, the Republic*, and *Liberty* lack correspondence in reality, they become vacuous slogans that can be grabbed by anyone to seize power. Flaubert ridicules not only the working classes who pose as nobility for a day, but he also is just as merciless toward conservatives and intellectuals who become good republicans overnight and pay just enough lip service to the popular will to retain their offices under the new majoritarian regime. Flaubert effectively liquidates "the people" as a credible political ideal. The people do not exist as a constitutive political power and not as an embodiment of the nation, but only as a cover-up for the pursuit of private ambitions and collective delusions. This explains why Flaubert's representation of 1848 lacks the pathos of Hugo, Stern, Michelet, Proudhon, or Marx. For the latter, history was a creation of a collective subject called the people—hence the excitement and seriousness with which they treated 1848. For Flaubert, there is no subject of history, and strictly speaking, no people either. There are only numbers unlimited, crowds driven here and there depending on the hour of the day: "The drums beat the charge. Shrill cries arose, and shouts of triumph. The crowd surged backwards and forwards. Frédéric, caught between two dense masses, did not budge; in any case, he was fascinated and enjoying himself tremendously. The wounded falling to the ground, and the dead lying stretched out, did not look as if they were really wounded or dead. He felt as if he were watching a play."[46]

Flaubert describes the masses as theatrical and grotesque. No sense of unity or commonality is found in the chaos. People slip in the mud on clothes and weapons. Frédéric, in the midst of it, steps on the soft hand of a sergeant lying facedown in the gutter. The firing is fierce, but people take breaks to have a pipe or a beer at the wine merchant's shop, which remains open. A stray dog howls. "This raised a laugh," concludes Flaubert about the spectacle.[47]

Gisèle Séginger has observed that Flaubert's mass is the opposite of any emancipatory historical force. No collective idea or common rationality is manifested through the actions of Flaubert's crowds. What is historically constant is not the emancipation of the people but the alienation of the masses. The mass is naturally alienated from society because collectives are favorable of the reproduction of prejudices, standard beliefs, or what Flaubert named *idées reçues*.[48] To Flaubert, then, the masses signal neither danger nor promise; they cause neither alarm nor pity. It is futile to search in his writings for the strong emotions that *les misérables* produce in other writers. Flaubert is relentless in his elitism, which in his view is the only warrant for impartiality. In a letter to George Sand that I already quoted, he expressed the matter clearly: "I believe that the crowd, the mass, the herd, will always be detestable."[49] In Flaubert, ultimately, the category of the people as a political agent is emptied of content. The people are always and ever the masses; and the masses are always and ever detestable.

If the people cannot realize itself as a unified political subject, however, the masses may still be unified in a quite different sense. The aestheticizing gaze of the author turns the variegated multitudes into a whole, much in the same way as the landscape painter forms trees, hills, fields, and streams into a landscape. In Flaubert, we find the first consciously aestheticizing representation of the masses. Watching the revolution unfold, Frédéric and his friend Hussonet evaluate it as an aesthetic spectacle—as play, drama, and image. "They spent the afternoon watching the people in the street from their window," the novel states at one point, confirming the transformation of the masses from a political subject into an object of aesthetic contemplation.[50] *Sentimental Education* inaugurates a manner of representing the masses that will recur as a standard figure in modernist narratives and that culminates with the cinematic city-symphonies of Dziga Vertov and Walther Ruttman in the late 1920s. Indeed, what Siegfried Kracauer in 1927 identified as the "mass ornament" is already half-developed in Flaubert. The crowd offers itself to a detached observer as an aesthetic adventure, an explosion of changing forms and shapes in swift movement: "from a distance the dense crowd looked like a field of black corn swaying to and fro"; "A vague mass of people swarming about below; here and there in its midst bayonets gleamed white against the dark background"; "a bewildering flood of bare heads, helmets, red caps, bayonets, and shoulders, surging forward so violently that people disappeared in the swarming mass as it went up and up, like a spring-tide pushing back a river, driven by an irresistible impulse and giving a continuous roar."[51]

Such descriptions can be produced only by someone who is separated from

much as create them: it does not mirror society so much as model it. It becomes society. As the latter has most often only virtual existence, even at the risk of actualizing it from time to time, by violence, warlike or other, these virtuality machines fashion it on all sides.

Whence the implacable hatred that they arouse in intellectuals educated in the social sciences: the machines take their area of specialization, multiplying it to a grandiose aura. They become an indefinitely resounding sociology in action. They give a portion of it to everyone.

Thus if someone or some thing remains, independent of these new machines, and can exist without them, then that thing or that person clearly takes on a function other than social. *They truly leave society.* Solitary meditation and detailed comprehension of a difficult question; the hard and rare work of language; the secret passing of the cultural torch; a private gesture where justice and humanity overabound; the climbing of a wall by a party of friends. . . . Can we, for a moment, suppose that television would show the hours of research of a mathematician concentrating for a long time; the silent day, spent in prayer, of a Trappist monk; the interminable promenade along the Loire of lovers alone in the world?

Everything that applies to ceremony in general is shown on television. We can no longer be mistaken: the rest cannot pass for ceremony.

Whence the second reprieve: these machines thus filter the religious from the collective and make a nonsocializable residue appear. Consequently, a transcendence appears that from now on no one can suspect of having a decisive role in groups and their unanimity. Next to the booms bathing the spectators with light, the priest officiates. For whom? The headsets and cameras officiate for everyone. And the priest for whom, other than everyone? For those most rare people who, outside of this union of solid interest, suffer from the absence of the Other and pray to him.

Thanks to their critique, the hard sciences relieve religions of their responsibility to explain the world; the new virtual symbol machines relieve them of the social weight with which the human sciences overwhelm them in order to critique them. These two filters purify religion.

What does it show? A direct experience that no mystic has described as irrational.

January 30–February 1, 2002
Translated from the French by Matthew Tiews

what he sees and enjoys from afar. Only in this sense does Flaubert attribute value to the actions of the revolutionary masses: they stimulate the senses. Frédéric feels his Gallic blood stirring. "The magnetism of the enthusiastic masses had caught him."[52] The emotional excitement is caused by the fact that he experiences the revolution by *looking at it* in the way one experiences a sublime artwork. As for the historical causes and political results of the upheaval, Frédéric Moreau is utterly indifferent.

The aestheticizing strategy of the intellectual individual in relation to a society of masses corresponds to the perspective of the political leader, for whom the people and society appear as distant masses below his own elevated position. *Sentimental Education* shows that in order to represent people as a mass, they must first be deprived of political agency, rational interests, and human subjectivity, so as to emerge as an object to be shaped by a writer's perspective or commanded by the political leader. Ultimately, the representation of people as a mass derives from a vision that dehumanizes the social field. As the most self-conscious of writers, Flaubert is aware that the aesthetic pleasure in the revolution presupposes an indifference as to its consequences: "For there are situations in which the kindest of men is so detached from his fellows that he would watch the whole human race perish without batting an eyelid."[53]

Compared to the stylistic exuberance of Flaubert's comedy of 1848 and to Hugo's romantic rendering of the same event, Ernest Meissonier's visual representation is calm and empty. Meissonier's *The Barricade*, a grisly companion piece to *Les Misérables* and *Sentimental Education*, focuses relentlessly on what Flaubert and Hugo turn away from (fig. 2.3). The workers that participated in the insurrection lie like trash in the gutters, with the remnant of the barricade they held scarcely visible in the background.

Meissonier was himself present on the scene in June 1848. As a captain of artillery in the National Guard, he belonged to the force of law and order that conquered the barricade in rue de la Mortellerie: "I saw the defenders shot down, hurled out of windows, the ground strewn with corpses, the earth red with blood it had not yet drunk. 'Were all these men guilty?' said Marrast to the officer in command. . . . 'I can assure you, *M. le Maire*, that not more than a quarter of them were innocent.'"[54]

In executing *The Barricade,* Meissonier intended to depict civil war in a way that would serve as a warning to future rebels. Yet like all true artists, he created a work that exceeds his intention. *The Barricade* is no simple object lesson. When the painting was first exhibited in 1851, one critic regretted that it lacked drama and artistic energy. In order to really see the painting, one must move close and scrutinize the fine details, but then it gives a much too agonizing impression. *The Barricade,* this critic complained, is nothing but an *omelette d'hommes*—a human omelet. Meissonier paints the bodies in the same nuance as the cobblestones from the razed barricade. The heads have the shapes of the rocks. The workers who a few hours before this moment held rue de la Mortellerie are here reduced to a raw, inorganic mass.

In a debate in the National Assembly 1850, Adolphe Thiers explained why it was necessary to restrict voting rights. He made a firm distinction between the people and the masses. "It is the masses, not the people, that we want to exclude; it's that disorganized mass, that mass of vagabonds that one cannot locate anywhere, that could not create a substantial shelter for their family: it is that mass that the law intends to banish" (C'est la multitude, c'est n'est pas le peuple que nous voulons exclure, c'est cette multitude confuse, cette multitude de vagabonds dont on ne peut la saisir nulle part, qui n'ont pas su créer pour leur famille un asile appréciable: c'est cette multitude que la loi a pour but d'éloigner).[55] Meissonier's painting shows the grim consequences of this logic of exclusion. Thiers himself was to realize the same policy in May 1871, when he ruthlessly suppressed the Paris Commune and ordered the execution of tens of thousands of communards.

In Meissonier's painting, the dead workers in the street are like a hostile substance—*la vile multitude*—repelled and ejected by the body politic. T. J. Clark has observed that Meissonier's painting renders the true anonymity of the people—an anonymity that cannot be traced back to the people themselves, but only to the dehumanizing violence to which they are exposed: "This is the real anonymity of the People, a *created* sameness, the result of violence and not a 'natural' fact."[56] To look at the people as a mass, or to depict it as a mass, is the first step toward transforming it into a mass.

This essay could end here. With Flaubert's aestheticization of the mass and his dehumanization of the people, with Thiers's assertion of the need to exclude the multitude from political life, with Meissonier's agonizing picture of the killed workers, "the masses" have been fully invented in the modern sense. The decades after 1848 will only repeat the same elements—dehumanization, exclusion, renewed insurrection—but amplified by an increasing polarization between the bourgeoisie and the working-class majority. Two things need to be added to complete the account of the invention of the modern discourse on the masses, however. The first is the formation of the labor movement as an organized force. The second is the formation of mass psychology in the proper sense.

The 1848 revolution was decisive for the formation of an organized labor movement in France. It made Sieyès's notion of the third estate as the universal class representing the French as a unity of equals seem like a joke. An alternative solution was to constitute the proletariat as a relatively independent political force. Hence Daniel Stern's impression that already by 1848 the working classes constituted a nation within the nation. Boissy, one of the insurrectionary workers, asked his comrades to separate from society: "Leave, leave this society for which you do everything and which does nothing for you, this society where those who do everything have nothing, where those who do nothing own everything" (Quittez, quittez, cette société pour qui vous faites tout et qui ne fait rien pour vous, cette société où ceux qui font tout n'ont rien; où ceux qui ne font rien possèdent tout).[57] Boissy's exhortation is an early instance of what Pierre Rosanvallon calls "the era of working-class separation" (le temps de la séparation ouvrière). Alongside the third estate, and as its main political competitor, "the fourth estate" constituted itself by means of an increasing number of parties, societies, and labor unions. Just as Sieyès argued in 1789 concerning the third estate, the representatives of the fourth estate claimed that it was suppressed by the privileged classes. The political concept of equality, it was argued, was a mere mirage as long as the political system tolerated stark inequalities of material wealth. As for the revolutionary notion of liberty, it had become an ideology to protect the property of the wealthy.

In 1864, sixty workers published a manifesto that immediately caught wide attention because it apparently confirmed the working classes' secession from the ideals of 1789. It is one of the founding documents of the French labor movement: "It has been repeated over and again that there are no longer any classes and that since 1789 all the French are equal before the law. But for us who have no property other than our arms, who are subject every day to the legitimate or arbitrary conditions of capital . . . it is very difficult to believe that statement" (On a répété à satiété qu'il n'y a plus de classes et que depuis 1789 tous les Français sont égaux devant la loi. Mais nous qui n'avons d'autre propriété que nos bras, nous qui subissons tous les jours les conditions légitimes ou arbitraires du capital . . . il nous est bien difficile de croire à cette affirmation).[58] The "manifesto of the sixty" amounted to an effort on the part of the working classes to dissociate itself from the system of political representation that used property and education as criteria to distinguish the most worthy representatives of the people. The labor movement also rejected what until then had been considered the superior way of representing the will of the people: by confiding the public interest to advocates—often lawyers by profession—who would serve as impartial deputies of public sovereignty. The labor movement suggested a contrary model of the representative: the comrade who shared the proletarian life and could voice its concerns in parliament. In this way, the separation of labor amounted to a dismissal of the idea that the political representative should be a neutral spokesperson for the people as a whole, and instead suggested that he—women were not citizens at this time—should represent the interests of the social class that had elected him. Such proposals were expressions of an emergent proletarian class consciousness, according to which the modern French nation was irremediably divided into classes that often had contradictory interests.

Throughout the latter half of the nineteenth century, the workers' movement became an increasingly powerful political force that contested the restricted democracy instituted as liberal parliamentarism. The organized efforts to address the social question (by means of higher wages, shorter work days, and improved safety measures) as well as the struggle for universal suffrage amplified the widespread fear of the masses among the upper classes. By the time of the Paris Commune in 1871, the masses no longer primarily referred to *les misérables*, and also no longer elicited compassion and pity. Although "the masses" certainly still evoked a state of destitution, the term by this time designated the organized collective actions and manifestations of the working classes: protest marches, labor unions, strikes, and socialist agitation.[59] Toward the end of the nineteenth century, the masses were seen as a collective agent directly threatening to oust the bourgeois classes from power.

A year after the Commune, a book appeared called *La Vie: Physiologie humaine appliquée à l'hygiène et à la médecine*. Its author was Gustave Le Bon, a medical doctor and one of the most influential intellectuals of the third republic. In this book, we find the usual stereotypes of the mass, but we also find the first attempt to *explain* crowd behavior in rigorously psychological terms: "Hallucination is a phenomenon which, by imitation or under the influence of identical excitations acting simultaneously on a great number of individuals in the same state of mind, is able to become collective. These collective hallucinations are veritable mental epidemics very common in history."[60] For Le Bon and others, the Commune was an example of just such an epidemic, a pathological phenomenon comparable to other medical and biological abnormalities.

Gustave Le Bon held the scientistic convictions of his age and joined those who sought to put the study of history and culture on the same positivistic footing as the natural sciences. Theorists like Théodule Ribot and Hippolyte Taine, influenced by the theories of Darwin and Spencer, argued that human behavior is primarily guided by hereditary dispositions. The major part of these dispositions constitutes a substratum of unconscious instincts that secure survival and reproduction. Higher qualities of intelligence and active memory, which alone constitute conscious individuality, form a thin layer of civilization that has developed recently and is unevenly distributed both among peoples and among the various individuals of a single people. Hereditary dispositions are ineluctable and dominate the conscious personality, these thinkers maintained. It is wishful thinking, they argued, to try to reform and improve individuals whose behavior reveals that they act under the influence of their subconscious passions and instincts. The brute nature of the majority of humankind must instead be soberly and scientifically disciplined.

For Gustave Flaubert, the Commune proved that governance had become too lax. Democratic ideals had brought France into a period of decline, for the simple reason that the majority of the French people were biologically unfit to take charge over public affairs. "The *people* never come of age, and they will always be the bottom rung of the social scale because they represent number, mass, the limitless," he stated after the communards had felled the Vendôme column.[61] Le Bon shared this opinion, and in his subsequent writings, he added a host of symptoms of this decline: the democratization of the access to education, the institution of the lay jury, urban congestion, and workers' strikes. In such collective situations, Le Bon claimed, the individual loses his reason and regresses to the level of the collective. In order to explain this leveling of individual consciousness, Le Bon introduced the notion of a "crowd soul," modeled on the widespread idea of a "racial soul"; and in order to explore how the crowd soul functioned, he turned to his colleagues in psychology. The result was Le

Bon's *La Psychologie des foules* (1895), regarded as the synthetic summation of French mass psychology.

As Robert Nye has noted, late nineteenth-century French psychology was entirely based on the study of mental pathologies. Le Bon and other mass psychologists built their theory of human collectives on these diagnoses of insanity, developed by Charcot, Esquirol, and Bichat, among others. Suggestibility, hypnosis, and mental contagion are the categories that form the discursive architecture of Le Bon's mass psychology. All of them are appropriated from the practice and analysis developed at the asylums of Salpétrière and Bicêtre. As regards mental contagion, Le Bon's use of the term had two sources. The first is Herbert Spencer's conception of primitive learning as an act of *imitation,* an idea later developed by the sociologists Gabriel Tarde and Emile Durkheim to account for similarities of behavior that make societies cohere. The second source is the clinical psychologist Prosper Despiné, who introduced the term contagion to explain how identical symptoms of mental illness could spread from a diseased individual to a healthy one, a phenomenon that was later popularized as *folie à deux* (*OCP*, 68). Le Bon collapsed these distinct ideas into one, establishing that "ideas, sentiments, emotions and beliefs possess in crowds a contagious power as intense as that of microbes. . . . Cerebral disorders, like madness, are contagious (the classical folie à deux)."[62] By transferring the universal claim of the sociological theory of imitation to the specific case of mental contagion, LeBon could conclude that humans are susceptible to brain disorders whenever they gather in groups.

All the varieties of mass psychology developed in the 1880s and 1890s—not only by Le Bon but also by Tarde, Sighele, Rossi, Duprat, Auguste Marie, and Charles Blondell—relied on a model of hypnotic suggestion that presumed a predisposition to madness in the hypnotized patient (*OCP*, 71). The hypnosis that induced hallucinations in a mad patient was seen as analogous to the alleged collective hallucinations induced by the agitator of the crowd. In order to explain how these hallucinations could spread to a mass of people, the mass psychologists appropriated the diagnostic term *contagion* to establish that collective behavior was an epidemic case of *folie à deux*. In *La Psychologie des foules*, Le Bon described how persons in a crowd are spellbound by hypnotic suggestion, which deprives them of their individual identities and instills in them whatever idea or emotion the leader wants. The idea or emotion then captures the entire group through a process of mental contagion, to the effect that everyone behaves in the same way, forming one collective social animal. The man of the masses "is no longer himself, but has become an automaton who has ceased to be guided by his will," Le Bon asserted.[63]

I began this essay by discussing how the mass emerged as a designation of a political system—democracy—that is ruled by numbers. I went on to show how the term became linked to the destitute condition of the working classes, *les misérables*, and particularly to their criminal and rebellious potential, and I then indicated how "the masses" in the second half of the nineteenth century evoked the workers' movement as such. What remains constant throughout these semantic transformations is the marginalizing function of the term. "The mass" is a scar in the political body. The scar reminds us that the people rarely corresponds to its own image of a unified sovereign. Under normal circumstances, the people is divided between those who are included in politics because they claim to represent the people, and those who are excluded from politics because they are represented by others; that is, they can be excluded because they are somehow already included through intermediaries. It is in this context that the notion of the masses acquires its meaning after 1789. In the spectrum of meanings associated with "the people," "the masses" come to signify the majority that is excluded from politics and that must nevertheless be evoked as its legitimation. "The mass-

es" are that part of the population whose exclusion founds the city of men.[64] It follows that "the mass" is no objective designation of those who are excluded from the polity. On the contrary, by conjuring up fantasies of violence, disorder, and barbaric instincts, the term itself operates as a mechanism of exclusion while at the same time justifying the exclusion that it performs.

Through yet a fourth redefinition of the masses, executed by the mass-psychological theories of Gustave Le Bon, Scipio Sighele, and Gabriel Tarde, the exclusion of the majority of the people from the polity is made permanent and is scientifically grounded. In this context, "the mass" is transformed from a social category into a psychopathological one. Mass behavior is clinically diagnosed as madness.

In *Madness and Civilization*, Michel Foucault describes how in the middle of the seventeenth century those who were considered mad were grouped with the idlers, the poor, and the vagabonds, and excluded from society on account of their *moral and social* inferiority. Foucault calls it the Great Internment.[65] With the emergence of mass psychology at the end of the nineteenth century, the scenario is reversed. Now those who were considered morally and socially inferior, and who organized collectively to redress their lot, were grouped with the insane, and excluded on account of their *mental* inferiority.

With the theory of mass psychology, all grounds for defending collective action were cut away from mainstream cultural and political vocabulary. Meanwhile, it also became possible to rewrite history. Lucien Nass, for example, described the Paris Commune as a "revolutionary neurosis" manifesting a "morbid psychology."[66] Another ambitious application of mass psychology was made by Alexandre Calerre, who classified all the major revolutions and rebellions in the history of France—David's 1789, Hugo's 1832, Meissonier's and Flaubert's 1848—with the aid of the vocabulary of contagion and suggestibility. Calerre also coined some collective diseases of his own, such as "contagious hysterodemonopathy" and "hallucinatory psychosis of a depressive order."[67] Le Bon, for his part, applied his theory in *La Psychologie du socialisme* of 1898, a book that clarifies the deeper political rationale of mass psychology. The problem at stake for Gustave Le Bon in 1898 is the same problem that was at stake in 1790 for Edmund Burke: how should society be represented, and by whom? Le Bon dismissed the labor movement's struggle for universal suffrage and social justice as a pathological delusion. "We must not forget," he wrote, "that the exact hour that definite decadence began in the Roman Empire was when Rome gave the rights of citizens to the barbarians."[68]

3　Crowd Politics: The Myth of the 'Populus Romanus'

Joy Connolly

The Roman Crowd on Film

An iconic moment in the history of film representations of the Roman crowd provides a useful visual analogue for my exploration of representations of crowd politics in ancient Rome. Picture the following cinematic scene, based on the popular novel published in 1880 by the Union General Lew Wallace. Among a turbulent mass of horses and men, Charlton Heston stands in a chariot drawn by four white horses: he wears a metallic Star of David in his brown leather tunic, complemented by an over-the-shoulder swath of fabric the color of the blue on the Israeli flag. Heston plays the Jewish noble Judah Ben-Hur, whose rival Stephen Boyd (Messala), along with his ebony team, is draped in Roman purple and gold. The two men exchange burning glances, and on cue, we see the masses cheering for Heston. Frank Thring, an urbane, world-weary Pontius Pilate, drops his handkerchief to start the race; the horses leap from the gate; and the camera pans the shouting, jostling, sweaty, robed, bearded, and veiled crowd gone wild.

The classic chariot race that is the climax of William Wyler's 1959 *Ben Hur*—a piece of "glorious trash," as its cowriter Gore Vidal justly calls it—is a crowd scene. As such, it is typical of major twentieth-century American films with a Roman theme: among the best known are D. W. Griffiths's silent *Intolerance* (1916), Henry Koster's *The Robe* (1953), Stanley Kubrick's *Spartacus* (1960), Rouben Mamoulian's *Cleopatra* (1963), Anthony Mann's *The Fall of the Roman Empire* (1964), and Ridley Scott's *Gladiator* (2000). Roman crowds in American movies are especially apt surrogates of the modern film audience. Mirroring the viewers sitting in the cinema, they gape at the games, parades, and other spectacles that signify the pagan decadence or imperial majesty of the Roman Empire—and by extension, of course, the consumerist decadence and capitalist majesty of American spectatorial culture.

The surge in the production of Roman themed films in the late 1950s and early 1960s can be attributed to a number of factors. Among them are Technicolor and other advances in film technology; the quest for grand narratives that would enact the epic conflict of the cold war; Hollywood's appeal to Christian religiosity, in an effort to rub out its long-standing prejudicial associations with Judaism and communism; and the crumbling of legal and social constraints on the baring of erotically appealing bodies in film.[1] Add to this the tendency throughout the twentieth century for works of social theory and their popular counterparts in the press to compare the rise of American mass culture in the welfare state with Rome's fall into mob politics and moral decay—a theme ripe for cultural imaginings of crowds, in all their heterogeneous, chaotic poverty.[2]

Movies like *Ben Hur* speak the language of Bernard of Clairvaux's *Apologia*, which condemns the beautiful statues and rich ornaments in Catholic churches in language that titillates the imagination as much as it frightens the soul. Their Roman crowds embody the appeal of the forbidden—miscegenation, heterodox religious practices, sexual freedom, and outrageous levels of material consumption. But if these things are "forbidden," they are also dynamic forces at the heart of stories of American exceptionalism and success: its minimal class structure, its politics of race and gender reform, its capitalist energy. By virtue of their otherness in time, space, and culture, the Roman crowds of Hollywood exorcise American viewers' fearful glimpses of the consequences of democracy, from mob rule to the contagions of multiculturalism, while enabling them to simultaneously exult in identification with a triumphant imperial populism.[3]

Politically speaking, the cinematic Roman crowd serves a second, and more insidious, function. Since its founding, the United States has named itself part of the legacy of Rome, and particularly Roman republican political thought and practice. Hollywood's Roman crowd is a symptom of the American fantasy of popular republican will—a fantasy in which obedience to the law is enacted in the muddled spontaneity and unpredictability of the mass experience. Visibly "foreign" in many ways—berobed, bearded, swarthy, and culturally heterogeneous—the crowd is an ideally universalized, sensuous, embodied mass; but it is a mass inscribed and contained within a subtly oppressive order. Through devices of plot and camera work, the multiplicity and diversity that characterizes the crowd at first glance yields to an impression of unity, manifested in costuming and the extras' close attention to the Romans' charismatic authority. The camera dwells on their mass expression of emotion: cries and sighs are emitted together. The earth- and jewel-toned robes, tunics, beards, and veils resemble uniforms; everyone appears to speak the same language; and most importantly, and prominently in several scenes in *Ben Hur*, the crowd swiftly obeys the smallest gesture of authority from governor or emperor.[4] Fans of Messala the Roman and the Jewish prince of Hur bow together under the supercilious gaze of the Roman governor.

Part of this is cinematic self-advertisement: the crowds of extras are signs of the massive and successful organization of the film industry. Until the advent of computer-generated backgrounds, part of the notoriety of the Roman film was the statistics it generated, the "cast of thousands." Working in tandem is a political script that writes the crowd as a unity, responsive to, even eager for rule, whether because of the compulsive appeal of Christianity (as attested by the awed crowds in *Ben Hur*, *Quo Vadis?*, *The Robe* and others), by majestic displays of wealth and power (*Ben Hur*, *Cleopatra*), by the pseudorepublican oligarchic authority of Maximus in *Gladiator*, or some mixture of the three. In its visible readiness to be ruled, the crowd enacts Cicero's claim in his late dialogue *On Law*, that the well-lived life is one in which one learns to obey the law *sua sponte*, of one's own will. Its uniformity is enthusiastic and spontaneous; its obedience is absolute.

I described *Ben Hur* as a useful analogue to the representation of crowds in Roman texts, and I should admit from the start that my contribution to a book on the crowd phenomenon is rather anomalous. For the most part, I will explore the ways Roman crowds are represented in Roman texts as not-crowds: as homogeneous, unified, and obedient to their leaders; and when they are violent, this too serves elite interests. But the Roman story is part of the history of crowds in western culture: and it is a crucial part, I think, of the availability of the notion of "the People" for theorists of popular sovereignty who seek inspiration in the Roman republic.

Why Rome? From Arendt to Canetti

Of the many images conjured in modernity by the conjunction of the words *crowd* and *politics*, July, 14, 1789, looms large. That evening the Duc de La Rochefoucauld-Liancourt informed Louis XVI of his royal troops' surrender to a Parisian crowd at the Bastille. "C'est une révolte," the king is supposed to have said. "Non, Sire, c'est une révolution," Liancourt famously replied. Behind their conversation, Hannah Arendt wrote,

we still can see and hear the multitude on the march, how they burst into the streets of Paris, which then still was the capital not merely of France but of the entire civilized world—the upheaval of the populace of the great cities inextricably mixed with the uprising of the people for freedom, both together irresistible in the sheer force of their number. And this multitude, appearing for the first time in broad daylight, was actually the multitude of the poor and the downtrodden, who every century before had hidden in darkness and shame.[5]

Arendt argues that the fateful distinction between the American and French republican revolutions lies in the difference between their leaders' views of the masses. Rousseau's was the guiding vision of the French revolutionaries, of a multitude only in the numerical sense, a mass driven by material necessity and moving with a single will. The American founders, by contrast, resisted viewing the population of the new United States as a singular entity: for them, the word *people* retained "the meaning of manyness," of "the endless variety of a multitude whose majesty rested in its very plurality" (*OR*, 93). But postrevolutionary power came into being on both side of the Atlantic through public associations and compacts resting on reciprocity and trust—an exceedingly thin basis for political stability and growth. Republican laws owe their existence to the power of the people, but the people is a mutable, unpredictable, unstable entity: consequently, "*il faudrait des dieux*, one actually would need gods," a source of authority above and apart from the people themselves (*OR*, 184).

Rome's value for modernity in Arendt's *On Revolution* rests in its invention of a performative constitution, that is, a constitution that never takes written form or appeals to absolutes like God or natural law.[6] The Romans solved the problem of legitimacy by grounding the people's sovereignty in "the old Roman trinity of religion, tradition, and authority"—which, crucially, is not an absolute; it is material power given visual form in reiterated performance, and performance is always contingent. The dynamic energy of these performances manifests itself in imperial expansion, which ties traditional authority together with growth and conservation. "The Roman Senate, the *patres* or fathers of the Roman republic, held their authority because they represented, or rather reincarnated, the ancestors whose only claim to authority in the body politic was precisely that they had founded it."[7] Arendt's account captures the essence of Roman thought about politics and performance, manifested in the central place held by rhetoric and oratory in Roman education. At every stage, however, it is obvious that Arendt sees this performative project as espoused and embodied not by the masses, but by the senatorial class. Although it plays a pivotal role in contemporary histories, letters, and speeches, the crowd is irrelevant to Arendt's account of republican politics. To what degree this is true of historical Rome is one of the questions I will try to answer.

First, it is worth explaining what an essay on Rome is doing in a book otherwise focused on modernity, Gustave Le Bon's true "era of crowds." We find ourselves today in what might justly be called a Roman moment. The American founders are enjoying a resurgence of popularity that is tied to the sweep of the pendulum of popular opinion toward greater respect for, or fear of, executive authority. Some in the United States and Great Britain publicly contemplate Rome as a model for empire; others echo Arendt's attack on the ignorant passivity of the republican citizenry—modernity's distortion of her vision of the virtuous habit of mass obedience at Rome. Philosophers revive Roman and neo-Roman notions of freedom and patriotism; theorists invoke Rome's name as they contemplate a new global "republican utopianism" whose goal is the self-government of the pluralistic multitude.[8] It's a fitting time to reexamine the multitude in Europe's first republic.

My aim is to define the crowd's place in the perpetual performances of oratory, elections, and legislation that constitute republican politics—specifically, in the informal mass meetings called *contiones* where crowds gathered to hear speeches from elected magistrates, in the period for which the most evidence is available: the middle of the first century BCE, during the last few decades before the republican government gave way to Julio-Claudian autocracy. In particular, I will focus on the issue of representation raised by the scene of Wyler's *Ben Hur*: the oscillation between notions of the crowd as multiplicity and the crowd as singularity, an oscillation that (I will show) effectively places the crowd outside the boundaries of what counts as legitimate politics in the late Roman republic—a development that reverberates in the crowd politics of modern democratic republics as well.

As moderns, we subscribe to a highly individualistic notion of citizenship that is a partial legacy of Roman law and its development of the legal concept of the person, buttressed by the dominance of Anglo-American liberal individualism and consumer capitalism in the wealthy nations of the West. At the same time, to say in a meaningful way "I believe in democracy" is surely to imply "I believe that others believe in democracy": citizenship, the source and sustainer of political agency, is ultimately a communal experience, and the modern rhetoric of citizenship reiterates the central concept of popular sovereignty, what we might now call popular ideological hegemony. The national community is the single grammatical subject of the famous opening declaration "We the People . . . do ordain and establish this Constitution for the United States of America."[9] The two vectors of citizen consciousness, self and community, exist in an uneasy balance: *e pluribus unus*, as Virgil originally put it in his poem *Moretum*, about a country dish resembling salad. According to the founding documents and material culture of the United States, which invoke Rome as a model with phrases like Virgil's, the republic is government of the people, by the people, for the people. What image is summoned up by the phrase "the people" if not a mass, a crowd?

But the crowds that give political communities their visible, lived form are also suspect things, in antiquity as in modernity—evocative of uncontrollable heterogeneity, disease, and unpredictable violence. Individuality is the armature of western civilization: crowds call this into question, and in doing so they unsettle civilization itself. Many intellectual and aesthetic traditions in antiquity reflect this view. There is the preoccupation of Greek and Roman historians with singularity: specifically, with *res gestae*, the deeds of great men, instead of popular movements; and there is the visual backdrop of ancient art, where artists paint and carve images of crowds with recognizable common identities (soldiers, priests, workers, and so on) instead of diverse assortments of individuals.[10] Here is the Stoic thinker Seneca, writing about half a century after the establishment of autocracy by Augustus:

> Just as it is in the case of sick men, who are so weakened by long illness that they cannot be carried out into the open without injury to themselves—so it is for us, whose souls are in a state of recovery from a long-lasting disease. Mixing with the many [*multorum*] is dangerous; there is not one of them who does not either commend some vice to us, or stamp vice upon us, or taint us, innocent as we are. (*Moral Epistles*, 7.1–2)

Seneca is part of an ancient philosophical tradition that defines the crowd as a single-minded tyranny that develops precisely as an intolerant response to its own internal diversity, its natural inequalities of wealth and talent. That he writes his philosophical letters in the middle of the first century CE under the autocracy of Nero is important, for his work is symptomatic of a turn in imperial literary representation by which the political legitimacy of the republican crowd is strategically forgotten. Once the legislative powers of the Roman assembly were arrogated by the emperor Augustus and his dynastic successors, writings like Seneca's begin to replace the old aristocratic narrative of the crowd as the site of public unrest with new high-culture images of the crowd as carrier of personal corruption.

Part of the moral impact of the image of the decadent imperial mob intent on bread and circuses is that it is a deformed version of the republican crowd which, if it is not consistently virtuous in fact, is associated with the virtue of strong civic participation. This is one of Gibbon's iconic images of imperial decline: from the habit of "public courage," the Roman crowds eventually "demanded only bread and public shows; and were supplied with both by the liberal hand of Augustus."[11] From the intertwined development of European humanism and republicanism in early modernity, to the appropriation of Roman symbols, names, and institutions during the American War of Independence and the French Revolution, the vision of Rome as an ideal balance between popular and aristocratic government has helped shape the landscape of modern politics.

Rome is not Greece; and here has lain its virtue. Niccolò Machiavelli considered Rome the exemplary model, Athens a dazzling failure; Thomas More and James Harrington appropriated Greek names and titles into their utopian political tracts, and little else. Thomas Paine criticized the unruly uproar of Athenian assemblies. Not a single purely Greek institution was incorporated into the American or French constitutions of the late 1700s. What the Roman republic offered was a model system of checks and balances, exempla of martial and domestic virtue, and a vision of unity bound by cultural sameness. As a political fantasy, Rome bridges the conceptual gap that Elias Canetti describes in *Crowds and Power*, by which the crowd is strictly separated from the military unit.[12] As Montesquieu says in 1734:

> After this [the Social War that opened Roman citizenship to inhabitants of the peninsula], Rome was no longer a city whose people had but a single spirit, a single love of liberty, a single hatred of tyranny. . . . Once the peoples of Italy became its citizens, each city brought to Rome its genius, its particular interests, and its dependence on some great protector. The distracted city no longer formed a complete whole. And since citizens were such only by a kind of fiction, since they no longer had the same magistrates, the same walls, the same gods, the same temples, and the same graves, they no longer saw Rome with the same eyes, no longer had the same love of country, and Roman sentiments were no more. The ambitious brought entire cities and nations to Rome to disturb the voting or get themselves elected. . . . The people's authority, their laws and even the people themselves became chimerical things, and the anarchy was such that it was no longer possible to know whether the people had or had not adopted an ordinance.[13]

Rome was viewed as a virtuous foil to Athens and its radical democratic crowd politics until the work of George Grote and John Stuart Mill replaced it with a virtuous Athens that could function as a tenable model for modern democracy.[14] But if the Roman republic is a model of civic practice from the Renaissance to the Enlightenment, and if it has become available as such a model again today, it is because the tradition of political thought in the West upholds a strategic misrepresentation of the Roman crowd. That misrepresentation finds its origin in acts of crowd control in Roman politics, acts designed to sustain elite domination of Rome and elite appropriation of political discourse as its own conceptual property while ensuring the people's assent. The words "The Roman People," we will see, comprise an impossible act of representation: the phrase is not quite an empty signifier, but an eternally inadequate one.[15] The crowd—always larger and more diverse than any act of representation can allow—seems to cancel out the possibility of its own hegemony.

I move now to crowd politics proper, especially the mass political meeting known as the *contio* and its extralegal counterparts in street violence in the late republic. I will explain how the crowd's ideological structuration in the *contio*—its physical setting and its patterns of hailing, persuasion, and mutual observation—enact the republican myth of the sovereign mass. In texts written by elite hands (our only available evidence), the turmoil of the crowd, real or imagined, turns out to be an essential element in the myth. It will quickly become clear that historians and orators of the late republic represent the violent crowd as a singularity properly subject to elite dominance. But the crowd as multiplicity—its dynamism, violence, unknowability, and difference—also plays a central role in elite Rome's encounter with the crowd.[16] Reminders that the crowd attending a political speech has turned violent in the past, and might turn violent again, not only instill elite beliefs in the necessity of crowd control; what is more interesting, they also appear to reinforce popular habits of submission to elite mastery by presenting the possibility of violence as a symptom of the *unrealizability* of popular identity and action. The rhetorical valorization of the turbulence of crowd politics is territory just as vulnerable to elite cooptation as is the language of consensus and obedience. The rhetoric of civil conflict and unrealizability fortifies abject habits of mass compliance analogous in effect to what Judith Butler has called the "pessimism" lurking behind poststructuralism's critique of unity and teleology.[17] But—to recall my Arendtian starting point—this does not mean that the crowd is irrelevant to the landscape of republican politics. On the contrary: as I will explain in the last section, its role goes further than to provide applause for elite leaders.

The Political Backdrop

Much has been written over the last thirty years about the central importance of identity formation in the creation and upholding of political legitimacy. Those studying classical antiquity, mainly for reasons of surviving evidence, have focused on aristocratic identity, and the structures of social logic that hail elites as dominant subjects.[18] These structures shape the Roman educational treatise—for one, whose curriculum of rhetoric and oratory gives the student mental and physical training in moving, persuading, and mastering the world. The wealthy, well-born Roman man stands straight, walks with a firm tread, speaks with authority, and moves with unstudied grace: never arrogant, always confident, both entitled to power and embracing its obligations, he broadcasts his status to the eyes of the world in every word and look. Such is the ideal elite political subject shaped by the original *liberales artes,* the arts appropriate to the free man.

What of the people, the second half of the ruling dyad Senatus Populusque Romanus, the SPQR proclaimed on coins and military standards? If the rhetorical education of the elite Roman may fairly be said to transmit elite *habitus*, the posture, gestures, expressions, and sense-making habits of thought that shape the individual field of action, it is the crowd experience that hails the Roman people as such. Being part of a crowd in the Roman Forum was a varied and unpredictable experience: sweating in the crush at a speech given by a powerful politician at a moment of crisis, like Cicero's orations against the conspirator Catiline; standing amid skeptical observers at the Rostra in times of relative peace; stoning elected officials when grain prices rise and famine threatens; cheering or shouting down speeches; watching public executions; witnessing oath-takings; assembling for elections and votes on legislation; spectating at games. "I put on beast-hunts of African beasts in my own name or in that of my sons and grandsons in the Circus, or in the Forum, or the amphitheater twenty-six times, at which about 3500 wild beasts were killed," proclaims the emperor Augustus (*Res Gestae*, 22). The first permanent stone theater was not permitted to be built in the city of Rome until 55 BCE: games, plays, mimes, and gladiatorial combats were held in many of the same public spaces as political speeches and judicial trials in the late republic. Overlapping geographies of theater performance, the games, and the mass political meeting perpetually reinforced habits of crowd spectatorship and is likely to have blurred distinctions between events.

Here Rome's contrast with Athens is instructive. A model has been proposed for popular hegemony in classical Athens, one historian asks, so why not in Rome?[19] Democratic Athens was precisely government by the people, the citizen *demos* (exclusively free adult men of Athenian parentage), who governed themselves in mass meetings held at least once a month. The city held 40 to 60 thousand citizens by the end of the fifth century BCE, perhaps 30 thousand in the fourth century as a result of war and plague. Virtually all of them lived in the city or close by in the small settlements of the region of Attica. Juries were made up more than 400 to 1,500 members, who were paid for their services, and the mass assemblies that passed laws normally consisted of at least five thousand to six thousand men, a significant percentage of the citizen population. Inscriptions name the enactors of Athenian law not "the city of Athens" but *hoi Athenaioi*, "the men of Athens." The Athenian multitude, all men, all ethnically homogeneous, understood itself as maintaining a direct, immediate relation with political action. The *demos* literally was the *polis*, the city-state.

Roman crowd politics operated under very different conditions. What the Romans called the free *res publica* (as opposed to the post-Caesarian autocracy established by Augustus by the mid-20s BCE) saw nearly eight decades of intermittent civil war in the first century BCE, during which Rome experienced a revolution in urban growth, imperial expansion, and regime change. The census of male citizens, already ten times as large as Athens at its height, shot up from approximately 400,000 in 115 to 1.5 million by 28 BCE.[20] Most of these new citizens were Italians, added to the rolls after the social wars of 91–90 BCE, and a percentage of them migrated to Rome: by the 50s, the city alone held approximately three-quarters of a million people.[21] Urban culture was immigrant-poor, largely unemployed, and polyglot, speaking Latin, Greek, and a variety of regional Italic, Celtic, and Semitic dialects.

Cicero notes that whereas the Athenians sat down to hear policy debate and then immediately held the vote, in a process that never lasted more than a single day, the Romans stood to listen to speeches arguing for and against legislation, voting only "after the people had been sent to their divisions and organized by tribe and century according to their rank, class, and age, after the advocates had been heard and the law had been posted for many days" (*For Flaccus*, 15). Athenian democratic debate revolved around spectatorship too, but active audience participation was not only legal; it was requested at the start of every assembly, where any Athenian citizen could stand up and offer his opinion. In Rome, mass meetings (*contiones*) were held in advance of voting or elections, usually in the Forum or another open-air space, but only elected magistrates and their chosen invitees (virtually always of senatorial rank) were legally permitted to speak there. Before the vote, as Cicero reports, the presiding magistrate would adjourn the *contio*, and the crowd reassembled into a quasimilitary, official formation divided in groups according to tribal identity, age, or socioeconomic status (earlier determined by the census). These were the formal voting or legislative assemblies known as the *comitia*. Although there is no evidence that they were officially dismissed, any women, slaves, children, and noncitizen men in attendance at the *contio* had no place to stand in the *comitium*, in keeping with their nonrole on the political stage.

Although the *comitium* possessed the legal authority to make laws, it could exercise its sovereignty only in limited ways. Most importantly, because it possessed no powers corresponding to the line-item veto, it could vote only for or against any initiative presented to it by an elected tribune—a man who met the high property qualifications that barred the nonrich from holding any public office in Rome.[22] By contrast, the *contio* was an impromptu gathering: lawmaking and elections were beyond its legal purview. At the *contio*, politicians presented arguments for and against upcoming legislation, decrees of the senate were proclaimed, important news was announced, current policies were defended and attacked, officers of the government were sworn in and released from service, new magistrates discussed plans for their year in office, triumphal speeches were given by victorious generals, and other events of general importance to the public took place, from funerals to executions.[23] Speakers at *contiones* tended to adopt a political stance the senatorial elite called "popular" (*popularis*), a word that carries overtones of demagoguery. But as several recent studies have noted, this stance should not be mistak-

en as a sign of ideological adherence to a true "people's politics." Even politicians like Cicero, whose careers were built on winning cases in the lawcourt and weaving influential alliances in the senate, and who voiced little sympathy with the material challenges faced by the populace or the demands for aid that they occasionally voiced in spontaneous protests, could stand before a mass meeting and speak its popular language with authority and plausibility.

What emerges from this picture is the difficulty of assessing the role of popular politics at Rome. Like crowds of other times and places, the crowds of the Roman republic engage in political demonstrations both peaceful and violent. They attend military triumphs and ceremonial sacrifices; they riot; they drag the dead bodies of hated public figures through the street, and mark their leaders' murders with impromptu funerals. One thing sharply distinguishes this crowd from its modern counterparts. Crowds are physical necessities of republican politics. Gathered together in assembly and addressed as *Quirites*, or "Romans," the crowd becomes the *populus*, the owners of the *res* that is the state.[24] "It is the People who bestow offices who those who deserve them," noted the second century BCE Greek historian Polybius in a controversial passage; "the People have the power to approve or reject laws, and most important of all, they deliberate and decide on questions of peace and war," so "from this point of view, one could reasonably argue that the People have the greatest share of power in the government" (6.14). Polybius could adopt this view, despite his knowledge that a small number of noble families dominated elections and made policy in Rome, because the People did meet in regular mass assemblies where they listened to public speakers, chose magistrates from slates of noble candidates, and passed legislation. The Senate proclaimed official advisory decrees, and magistrates called praetors issued legally binding judicial edicts, but the people made law.[25] This is the conflicting evidence historians face when they attempt to place the republic on the spectrum of oligarchy and democracy—the resolution of which Arendt attempted with her account of Roman authority's perpetual reconstitution of itself through the performance of authority, a performance that revives the historical memory of past acts of authority and the structures that support them.

The claim that the popular sovereignty of the Roman republic was merely a rhetorical screen for the rule of the few, and the counterclaim, that we have good reason to speak of democratic elements in Roman government, are two sides of a debate that is as ancient as the republic. Like Arendt, they ignore the existence of the Roman crowd as a lived, visible experience, one that leaves an undeniable mark on elite Roman culture. I will argue now that the crowd itself, despite itself, functions as a prop for republican stability, and that it does so precisely because it poses a fundamental problem of representation. When Roman historians and orators stage the crowd in eternal conflict with its elite leaders, in a pattern that is visible in the speeches they deliver at mass meetings, they seek to legitimize the unequal distribution of political power by casting elite-mass relations as a violent drama of uncertainty caught up in a permanently and naturally unfinalizable state. They construct a contradictory, double fantasy of the crowd as the essential participant in republican politics and as the site of violence and imminent collapse.

What do I mean by the "double fantasy" of the Roman crowd? If the crowd at the mass meeting is the physical manifestation—the visible reenactment—of popular sovereignty, the city's legends sketch out a folk history of the crowd, to which the contional speeches repeatedly refer, where the crowd is the site of murder and mayhem—which is to say, the site of Rome's earliest foundation. For the historian Livy, writing during the reign of the first emperor, Augustus, and drawing on the tradition of earlier historians and poets, Rome comes into existence in a series of lawless crowd actions. First Romulus murders his brother Remus in the middle of a crowd (*turba*), in a bid to establish him-self as sole king of his eponymous city; next, in need of citizens to fill his new city, he opens the city to a motley collection of bandits and fugitives (again, *turba*). Lacking the means to produce the next generation, the bandit crowd plots a mass rape and kidnapping from the neighboring town of the Sabines (*multitudo*). In a pivotal battle between Rome and the Sabines, Romulus prays to Jupiter to stop his frenzied troops from fleeing in a rabble (*turba*, in its third and last appearance in book 1), but the violence only ends when the raped women enter the field, place their bodies between the two sides, and take the blame for the struggle. Their plea for peace moves both the *multitudo* and its leaders, and "they made not only peace, but one body politic (*una civitas*) from two."

After the reign of the seven legendary kings of Rome, the monarchy is overthrown and the republic established in a sudden revolt of the *multitudo* sparked by another rape, this one of Lucretia by the king's son, ending in her suicide.[26] In later books, during the ongoing conflict between the patricians and the plebeians known as "the struggle of the orders," the crowd grows increasingly violent, unpredictable, and heterogeneous, as more conquered peoples are assimilated into the *civitas*. Eventually, *multitudo* and *turba* emerge as virtual synonyms for the class label *plebs,* and early Roman history climaxes with the angry secession of the *plebs* from the state, in protest against their lack of political rights. Only when the nobles' spokesman, Menenius Agrippa, tells a parable in which the state is reduced to a singularity represented as a human body, with the patricians as the belly and the plebeians as the limbs, do the plebeians agree to rejoin the city, on the condition that the patricians agree to establish a political office representing the people's interest (2.32–33). During the temporary split of the *civitas* into two, the people agree to become one, so long as their split is memorialized in the establishment, via the distance of informal representation, of a voice of political alterity.[27]

Livy's early Roman crowd is the setting for a cycle of murder, rape, desertion, and secession. The crowd seems clearly to belong in the dark category of *foeda,* the rottenness Livy has earlier announced that history is designed to cure. As Michel Serres insightfully remarks of Remus' death and the subsequent pattern of violent crowd scenes in Livy's first five books: "the crowd forms a ring; it breaks open; the people flee; the crowd forms again. . . . Rome has no unity; it is a collection. It is only a pack of repentant brigands in the wood of asylum or, along the banks of the Tiber, of she-wolves from lupanars: a mixture of outsiders . . . a multiplicity, a melange."[28] Yet Livy gives the crowd a central, violent role in Rome's founding as a monarchy and its reconstitution (repeated in the wake of several crises) as a republic. And we will see that late republican popular oratory repeatedly invokes this vision: the fact that the crowd represents the memory of secession and general license anchors its capacity to represent popular liberty and legitimacy.

Crowd Control

When I arrived at this match, coming straight from a day of working in an office, my head busy with office thoughts and concerns that were distinctly my own, I was not, and could not imagine becoming, "one" with any crowd. It was windy and cold and that biting easterly weather was felt by *me* personally—in *my* bones. I was, in what I was sensing and thinking, completely intact as an individual. And it was *me,* an individual, who was then crushed on all sides by strangers, noticing their features, their peculiarities, their smells—except that, as the match began, something changed. . . . I was becoming a different person from the one who had entered the ground: I was ceasing to be me.[29]

The sense of self-destruction Bill Buford experiences when he attends English football matches (in the course of his research on a book about hooliganism) derives in part from the physical sensations of human proximity he describes in this passage. Equally important, however, is his awareness of

being observed—by police officers, those seated above the hooligans' favored standing-room-only terraces, and most of all, by the media, patiently waiting for violent acts to capture on film. Where Buford calls the fans "supporters" or "lads," the police and the press call them "thugs," "hooligans," and "animals" who belong in the locked "pens" and "cages" of the stadium terraces, and these acts of observation and naming have immense power. They enable the police to view the supporters as a less than fully human herd; and they bestow on the supporters themselves (by Buford's account) a spirit of angry, bestial unity. Buford's experience is a useful place to start as we consider how the Roman crowd at the *contio* was observed and named, and encouraged to observe and name itself, by members of the socioeconomic elite. These are acts of labeling whose insistent, ritualized repetition invokes the crowd as a singularity, and at the same time, makes that singularity the basis on which its political legitimacy necessarily rests—a two-step of misnaming the crowd as *Populus Romanus.* Cicero calls the *contio* a *scaena,* a stage: the political role the elite orator designs for the crowd is the first step toward controlling it (*On Friendship,* 26.97).

When the Roman crowd gathers in the *contio* at the summons of a magistrate, it hears itself named by a special political label for Romans: *Quirites.* This word appears near the beginning (normally the first sentence) of all nine surviving contional orations by the politician Cicero and the three incorporated into Sallust's *Histories,* the most important contemporary sources available for mass meetings in the late republic. "I think that you have heard, Quirites, what has been enacted in the Senate," Cicero says at the beginning of a speech attacking the policies of Mark Antony (*Philippic,* 6.1). "I prayed to Jupiter Best and Greatest and to the rest of the immortal gods, Quirites," is more typical of the inflated tone of contional oratory (*After His Return,* 1). The repetitive use of the label, invoked at emotional climaxes, at important turns in the argument, and at the end of the speech, makes naming into a ritual. Who actually made up the crowd at the *contio* remains an open question, limited, probably permanently, by the state of the evidence. That evidence implies a range of possible audiences: the urban proletariat (those too poor to provide anything to the state except offspring, *proles*); the propertied classes, who had other purposes for being in the city's public spaces, especially business and court cases; rural Italians and foreigners. The point is that the composition of the crowd, an unknown quantity to us, was a point of uncertainty for elite orators as well; and yet they always address the crowd as *Quirites.*

Roland Barthes isolates a type of speech that is defined by its intention ("I am a grammatical example") more than by its literal meaning ("my name is lion"), and he points out that its intention is "somehow frozen, purified, eternalized," placed beyond the reach of rational critique: this speech he calls myth.[30] Mythic reference thickens and vitrifies into eternal reference meant polemically to establish as natural and innocent what are in fact profoundly nonneutral ideas and images. "On the surface of language something has stopped moving. . . . "[31] Originally, according to the legendary history of early Rome, Quirites were inhabitants of a Sabine town known as Cures; after the rape of the Sabine women that marked the beginning of the Roman community, the Sabines were incorporated into Rome, and the Romans assumed their name to refer to themselves in a civil capacity. When the orator at the mass meeting hails the crowd as *Quirites*, a label that none of them naturally possesses, it is the first step that tugs them away from their quotidian individuality and self-conceptions into a mythic unified collectivity. The name itself crystallizes the history of Rome as a multiplicity-become-one in an act of violence.

The crowd, summoned as a unity with its ancient name, listens to the magistrate who has called the meeting. The speeches that survive in contemporary accounts reveal a common tendency to intertwine the conflicting themes of liberty and dependence. Take as an example the historian Sallust's version of Gaius Memmius' speech of 111 BCE, at the height of a political crisis during the Jugurthine War, when it was widely believed at Rome that the North African king Jugurtha had bribed the current consul in order to escape Roman retaliation for his usurpation of the monarchy. Memmius's summons of the crowd names it as part of the republic even as he underscores its incapacity to care for itself. Masquerading as the oratorical tactic the Romans called *captatio benevolentiae*, the plea for the audience's goodwill, Memmius's opening lines remind the crowd that he speaks not only to the people but for them—necessarily, because they exist in a state of hopeless abjection:

Many things would discourage me from speaking to you, Quirites, if my enthusiasm for the republic did not overthrow everything else: the power of faction, your patient compliance, the absence of law, the fact that integrity has become more dangerous than honorable. I'm ashamed to say this: how for fifteen years you have been the plaything of an arrogant oligarchy [*superbiae paucorum*], how your defenders have been killed, appallingly, unavenged; how your spirit is so rotted with cowardice and sloth, that even when your enemies are in your power, you fail to rise up [*exsurgitis*], and you continue to fear men who should fear you. (Sallust, *Jugurthine War*, 31.1–4)

Memmius' speech places the crowd in a double bind. To recover their liberty, they must "rise up" against the few who seek to enslave them, but they must resist violence: "I am not calling upon you to take up arms, which your forefathers often did; there is no need for violent force or secession" (31.6). Yet violence, and specifically, the violent split of secession, is the historical memory that Memmius summons. The only acceptable alternative is for the crowd to agitate for its enemies to be summoned to the lawcourt.

Your forefathers, to assert their rights and establish their status, twice, through secession, occupied the Aventine Hill under arms.

3A 'People': English

Marisa Galvez

The word *people* derives from the Latin *populus*, meaning generally "a human community, a nation," the people "as transcending the individuals composing it," or "the state," and "the general public, populace, multitude" (*Oxford Latin Dictionary* [*OLD*]). As the standard of the Roman republic, Senatus Populusque Romanus (SPQR), suggests, *populus* was essential to the concept of a nation and of the sovereign power of Rome. Distinct from the Latin *gens*, meaning "a race, nation, or the rest of the world apart from Romans or Italians" (*OLD*), *populus* lacks the strong attachment to blood relations, class, or to the race of a person; similar to *gens* however, *populus* often carries political connotations. From *populus*—and more directly from Anglo-Norman words such as *puple*, *peple*, or Old/Middle French *pueple*, *pople* meaning "inhabitants of a country," "mankind" (twelfth century), or "common people" (thirteenth century)—come a family of English words such as *populace* (the common people), *populism* (the beliefs of members of a political party that claims to represent ordinary people), and *populous* (full of people or inhabitants) (*OED*).

In medieval English literature, the word "peple" becomes particularly charged after the Black Death, a period which sees increasing tensions between the governing classes and unrepresented individuals and communities. Ambivalence toward a growing plebeian resistance to established authority is reflected in the writings of William Langland, John Gower, and Geoffrey Chaucer. In their

On behalf of your liberty, which you received from them, will you not exert yourself to the utmost? And will you not do this all the more ardently [*vehementius*], because it is much more shameful to lose what you have achieved than never to have achieved it at all? I hear someone saying, "What do you advise?" Let vengeance be taken against those who have betrayed the republic. Not by your own hands, nor by violence [*non manu neque vi*], which are unworthy of you, but by the courts. (31.17–8)

Memmius demands that crowd at once rouse itself with the memory of the ancient acts of crowd violence that made Rome free and turn aside from that memory, refusing to reenact the authority that is traditionally theirs from the moment of Rome's foundation as a republic. He treats the Arendtian dynamic of republican performance as the crowd's responsibility, but they face an exceedingly limited scope of action. Their only choice is to admit responsibility for assenting to their own enslavement and to assent again, this time to the elite authority of the judiciary. The pattern is visible in other contional speeches. Sallust puts this oration in the mouth of the popular tribune Licinius Macer in 73 BCE: "Quirites! . . . for you I could recall what injuries, and how often the armed plebs seceded from the Senate, and how they established the tribunes of the plebs as the defenders of all the laws . . . but it remains only to exhort you, and to go first down the road on which I think liberty is to be seized!" (*Histories*, 3.48.1).

Like Memmius, Macer links current threats to popular liberty with reminders of the violent struggle for liberty fought by the Roman people in the past. "Yes, Quirites, long ago, you found safety as individual citizens in the many [*in pluribus*]," Macer declares, but he too both invokes and disbars the specter of civil disunity and violence, warning the crowd to resort to "neither arms nor secession" (3.48.24, 17).

The freedom of the Roman people, *libertas populi Romani*, is often described as the slogan of the "popular" politician, the *popularis*—those who worked the Roman political scene with appeals to the people from the Rostra in the open Forum rather than in the closed senatorial networks of the Curia. But as I have already said, this rhetoric is not limited to the ambitious *popularis* politician. Cicero is its unacknowledged master.[32] Cicero uses a favorite word of Memmius and Macer, *pauci*, "the few," in his argument in the Senate that the aim of a new proposal to distribute public land to the people (a typical popular tactic) was to pool power under the tyranny of the few (*On the Agrarian Law*, 3.13). The word *libertas* appears twenty-two times in his second speech against the agrarian law. In that speech, just as Memmius and Macer do, Cicero reminds the crowd of their forefathers' fight for freedom, won by "sweat and blood" (*sudore et sanguine*) and handed down to the present crowd "due to no effort on your part" (nullo vestro labore, 2.16). Cicero's remaining contional speeches, the speech on behalf of Pompey's command, the Catilinarian orations, and the fourth and sixth Philippics, begin and end with a call for *libertas*. "Liberty is the special property of the Roman people," he says (populi Romani est propria libertas; *Philippic*, 6.19). "Your ancestors refused to tolerate the slightest restriction on the liberty of Roman citizens" (*On the Manilian Law*, 4.11). Mob violence is repeatedly described as the crowd's unique political capacity and excluded as inappropriate for contemporary politics. "Is there any one of you inclined to violence, to crime, to murder? No one" (*On the Agrarian Law*, 3.16).

In several ways, then, speeches of Cicero, Memmius, and Macer distort the conditions on which the crowd may perform its political authority. Most simply, they enact a fantasy of aristocratic mastery: the elite speaker dominant. Second, the crowd is exhorted to recall a memory of past civic virtue: their forefathers' fight for liberty. But this is a hollow exemplum that is summoned up only to be set aside, for the crowd is simultaneously commanded—in a reversal of conventional aristocratic efforts—to mime their ancestors on the battlefield and in the forum, not to imitate the greatness of the past. The logic of exemplarity is brutally undone. Mass political action in defense of popular liberty is defined in terms of violence even as violence is barred as a legitimate option for politics. These speeches construct crowd action in terms of a choice so stark as to depart the realm of politics: violence or assent to elite leadership.

These speeches also hail the crowd as the free Roman people, the *populus Romanus*. This, too, as others have noted, leads to paradox.[33] Naming the crowd at the mass meeting as *Quirites* and *populus Romanus* as though these were natural names dismisses the fact (complained of by Cicero in other, private contexts) that the crowds attending *contiones* might be composed of noncitizens: Greeks, Asians, Italians. They might be women or slaves, because the *contio*, like the Forum itself, was technically open to all. More problematic is the essentially synecdochic identity of the Roman crowd as a political entity. However it comes into being, through accident or intention, the crowd of individuals that happens to attend the *contio* or *comitium* literally and legally constitutes the Roman people. Even those who "wear the mask of the polity," as Cicero says of elected magistrates, do not seek to represent the mass of Roman citizens, but rather act with the authority of the people that has been entrusted to them.[34] But the crowd present in the Roman Forum (among other venues) for a contional speech or a legislative assembly is *in fact* supposed to represent the people. Of course no crowd, however large,

works the "peple," represented as a heterogeneous community of different voices, possess an inherent moral legitimacy as the common voice of God (Gower's "Vox populi cum voce dei concordat," *Vox Clamantis*, 3:1267) but carry the danger of breaking down into cacophony and anarchic violence (Chaucer's "the noyse of peple," *Troilus and Criseyde*, 4:183–96).

The classical association of *people* with a nation, combined with the English sense of the word as a common voice, perhaps explains how it gains powerful implications as a speech act. Distinct from *crowd* or *multitude*, the "voice of the people" or *vox populi* has variously come to signify civil enfranchisement, a popular voice against established institutions, or the subversiveness of the rabble.

We see this range of meanings in legal, political, and colloquial uses of the word from the fifteenth century onward. A strong example of contractual language are the opening words of the Preamble to the 1787 Constitution of the United States, a voice on behalf of a nation of *people*: "We the People of the United States . . . do ordain and establish this Constitution for the United States of America." The contract of the nation is between the people and its representative government, as Thomas Jefferson makes clear in 1820: "I know no safe depository of the ultimate powers of the society but the people themselves" (*Letter to William Jarvis*). Today *people* figures predominantly in the conventional legal language of state prosecution formalized in the early nineteenth century: "The People vs. . . . "

On the other end of this institutional discourse of *people* is the often ironic usage of *vox populi* as general opinion or rumor. General W. T. Sherman writes "Vox populi, vox humbug" in a 1863 letter to his wife, expressing his curt dismissal of received opinion. With the rise of mass media and technology in the twentieth century enters the possibility of exploiting and manipulating the people's voice. The colloquial use of *vox pop* as a term for uninformed opinion appears in the 1950s/1960s British vogue for "vox pops," which were "street interviews with passersby presenting views on issues of the day which, with luck, were amusingly expressed and—for reasons of balance—effectively cancelled each other out" (Nigel Rees, *Bloomsbury Dictionary of Phrase and Allusion* [1991], 331).

After the Second World War, the qualifier "People's" as applied to a nation or organization explicitly of, belonging to, or for the people in the terminology of communism and socialism (People's Democracy, People's Republic of China) colors the western imagination of the word. During the counterculture movement of the 1960s however, *people* gains a new valence, as in the slogan of the Black Panther movement "Power To The People," accompanied by a raised clenched fist, or John Lennon's 1971 song "Power to the People (Right On!)." The "People Power" slogan represents youth culture rebelling against the repressed, conformist society of its parents, extolling sexual freedom, the use of recreational drugs, and rock and roll. This new voice of the people speaks out against the U.S. involvement in Vietnam and for the need to include previously excluded groups—women, blacks—while embracing new explorations in art and culture. Eldridge Cleaver summarizes the new power of the word when he says: "All power to the people—Black Power for Black People, White Power for White People, Brown Power for Brown People, Red Power for Red People and X Power for any group we've left out" (Rees, 264). In the language of mass movements, we see the latent power of *people* as both making and challenging institutional discourse.

may carry out this literally impossible task. Insofar as the Roman crowd may be said to perform in a political realm, then, it performs in the realm of fiction, of the imaginary and the false. The structure of the *contio* and *comitium* means that Roman crowd was eternally unable to realize itself as a collective political agent, despite the persistent labeling of crowd gatherings as "the Roman people." The crowd is not only an experiential event in finite time; it is also a complex symbol of the impossibility of representation that itself limits the horizons of the possible. The people are an entity founded in the imaginary and the false, the unrealizable, and the nonsensical.

A fiction, then, underlies and undermines the crowd's legal performances of authority. In his 1767 *Essay on the History of Civil Society*, a response to work by Adam Smith and Hume, Adam Ferguson suggestively places popular hegemony firmly in the realm of pretense and imagination. He writes of Rome:

> Even where the collective body is sovereign, they are assembled only occasionally: and though on such occasions they determine every question relative to their rights and their interests as a people, and can assert their freedom with irresistible force; yet they do not think themselves, nor are they in reality, safe, without a more constant and more uniform power operating in their favour. The multitude is everywhere strong; but requires, for the safety of its members, when separate as well as when assembled, a head to direct and employ its strength. . . . Though all have equal pretensions to power, yet the state is actually governed by a few. The majority of people, even in their capacity of sovereign, only pretend to employ their senses; to feel, when pressed by national inconveniences, or threatened by public dangers; and with the ardour which is apt to arise in crouded assemblies, to urge the pursuits in which they are engaged.[35]

Ferguson's assertion is not a simple valorization of singularity in the form of the so-called Iron Law of Oligarchy, the assumption that oligarchies rule primitive societies. If it were, he could not say that the people are free and in possession of the power "to determine every question relative to their rights and interests." He is thinking within a subtler frame that treats mass belief, even when it is based on a fiction, as a meaningful force in politics.[36] The logic of his declaration is paradox. "Though all have equal pretensions to power, yet the state is actually governed by a few": the people must believe in their pretensions, or else, Ferguson declares in another passage, the state will fall. Yet the operations of deceit that presumably enable republican government (as he describes it) are never specified. They rest in a cloudy region of ideology and self-imagining.

The rhetoric and reality of popular unrealizability functions in a context that, as Arendt rightly recognizes, grants vast privilege to the traditional authority of the senate. Representations of the contional crowd reveal a predominant pattern of respect for tradition, a pattern elite orators manipulate with dramatic symbols and gestures. A few anecdotes reveal the pattern. In the second century BCE, for example, when a tribune summoned the senator and general Scipio Aemilianus to trial in the Forum soon after his decisive victory over Carthage, Scipio had himself escorted there by a huge crowd. He mounted the Rostra with a triumphal wreath on his head, and exhorted the people to come with him to the temple of Jupiter to give thanks for the recent triumph. "The upshot," Valerius Maximus writes, "was that the tribune made his plea before the People without any people [apud populum sine populo]; deserted, he stayed alone in the Forum" (*Memorable Doings and Sayings*, 3.7.1g). According to the historian Diodorus Siculus, when the tribunes "dragged all the senators" to the Forum to account for the murder of the popular reformer Tiberius Gracchus in 133 BCE, the senatorial ringleader Scipio Nasica was the only man to admit to taking part. Such was the effect of "the *gravitas* and honest speech of the man," Diodorus writes, that "though they were still angry, the people nonetheless fell silent" (34/5.33.7). The same Scipio was hauled up on another occasion by a tribune to explain the senate's plans to deal with a looming grain shortage. Hoots and catcalls punctuated his speech, and finally he shouted: "Silence, please, citizens! For I know better than you what is good for the republic" (tacete, quaeso, Quirites! plus ego enim quam vos quid rei publicae expediat intellego; *Memorable Doings and Sayings*, 3.7.3). "When his voice was heard," Valerius Maximus writes, unconsciously echoing Diodorus, "all fell reverently silent, paying more heed to his *auctoritas* than to their own means of sustenance." A similar situation arose in 90 BCE, when a prominent elder senator was summoned by the tribune Quintus Varius to answer the accusation that he had had a hand in starting the Social War. "Quintus Varius of Sucro [in Spain] says that Aemilius Scaurus was corrupted by a king's bribery and betrayed the Roman people," the senator said, speaking of himself in the third person, "Aemilius Scaurus denies any connection to the charge. Whom do you believe?" (Asconius 22C; *Memorable Doings and Sayings*, 3.7.8). This was the typical choice faced by the crowd at the mass meeting: not what to think, but whom to believe.

The physical setting of most mass meetings, the Roman Forum, similarly functioned as a reminder of the unequal relationship between the wealthy senators and the popular masses. The shelf of marble called the Rostra, from which orators addressed the crowd in the Forum, towered at least 2.5 meters above ground level. Situated between the public Forum and the closed Curia, the normal meeting place of the Senate and one of the very few civic spaces in the city of Rome

3B Compactings and Loosenings

Susan Buck-Morss

My first experience of the crowd was in a sports stadium in New York City. It was a game of American football that the home team won, unleashing a euphoria among the spectators that I did not share psychically but was forced to share physically, as the tide of fans streamed down to the field and stormed the goalposts to unhinge them and carry them off.

Mine was not the abstract, metaphysical fear of submersion of the individual or loss of autonomy. It was a simple, visceral awareness: Run with the crowd or be trampled. This apparently innocuous event, culturally coded as entertainment, frightened me beyond any comparable experience. The ocean waves that in the child's eye rise menacingly before crashing on the seashore harbor a secret calm. You have only to dive under the threatening curl of their crest to enter their sanctuary, as the foam churns past overhead.

Not nature in its sublimity, but mechanical inexorability is the analogy for my experience of the crowd: the tight and uniform event that is set in motion by human intention, but runs out of human control. The crowd can be used as an instrument of terror because its unpredictability is precisely predictable. Walter Benjamin compared this "compact" mass with the "relaxed" (*locker*) crowd form of the revolutionary class, an observation that Theodor W. Adorno described in a letter to Benjamin as the most insightful words he had read on the subject since Lenin's *State and Revolution*. Benjamin wrote:

"The class-conscious proletariat forms a compact mass only from the outside, in the minds of its oppressors. At the moment when it takes up its struggle for liberation, this apparently compact mass has actually already begun to loosen. It ceases to be governed by mere reactions; it makes the transition to action. The loosening of the proletarian masses is the work of solidarity. In the solidarity of the proletarian class struggle, the dead, undialectical opposition between individual and mass is abolished; for the comrade, it does not exist. . . . The mass as an impenetrable, compact entity, which Le Bon and others have made the subject of their "mass psychology," is that of the petty bourgeoisie. The petty bourgeoisie is not a class; it is in fact only a mass. . . . Demonstrations by the compact mass thus always have a panicked quality—whether they give vent to war fever, hatred of Jews, or the instinct of self-preservation."[1]

The difference between the reactionary crowd and the progressive one can be physically sensed: The feeling of panic is replaced by the feeling of solidarity. I learned this during the antiwar demonstrations in Washington, D.C., in the late 1960s and early 1970s, when the crowd of hundreds of thousands, even millions, was present with a common purpose, a "collective *ratio*," as Benjamin describes it. Strangers share food and protection. Even as the marching crowd presses forward, its center remains calm, as safe as a seabed. Leaders merge with the crowd rather than manipulating them. Interaction takes the place of reaction. The experience of solidarity outlasts such events, giving confidence to future actions of individuals

that possessed a roof and four walls, the Rostra was the pivot of communication between the Roman Senate and the Roman People. Its ornaments commemorated the achievements of the senatorial elite, featuring statues of statesmen and generals interspersed with war booty, notably the prows of battleships taken in war. A few symbols of popular ideology interrupted the string of expensive statues proclaiming elite dominance: a statue of Marsyas, probably representing the banning of debt slavery; and the archaic Roman law code, the Twelve Tables, engraved in bronze, reminders of the Roman citizens' equality under the law.[37] The tensions expressed in the Rostra's art display reflect the tensions expressed in elite attitudes to the confrontation between crowd and speaker staged in every *contio*—the ease with which popular power could transmogrify into lawlessness and hysteria (ad furorem multitudinis licentiamque conversam; Cicero, *De Rep.* I.44).

For violence always lurked on the horizons of the possible when crowds assembled in the city's public spaces. Politicians addressing the crowd were forced to step down from the Rostra or the steps of temples habitually used for *contiones*.[38] Mob violence interrupted the games and processions of elected magistrates. Cicero and other elite sources normally represent these actions as led by demagogues, but this was not always the case: in times of famine and high food prices, crowds could riot in the absence of visible popular leadership.[39] Fear of mob violence occasionally forced the Senate to leave its regular meeting place in the Forum.[40] A mid-first-century CE commentator on Cicero reports the attempted stoning of a consul in 67 BCE; in 52, the mob killed anyone they met wearing fine clothing or gold rings, the mark of the senatorial class.[41] Three times in the 50s alone, elections were canceled as a result of crowd actions that were interpreted by the senators as signifying broad popular unrest. An enormous crowd held an unruly public funeral for Julius Caesar in 44, and ripped a poet named Helvius Cinna limb from limb, mistaking him for a praetor of the same name who had participated in the conspiracy to assassinate Caesar. From the beginning of the century there had been a string of riots over food prices and rents, including one in 75 where the consuls were attacked on the street, another in 67 when crowds stormed the senate house, and another in 47, leading to the death of 800 rioters at the hands of Caesar's soldiers. Crowds sacked Cicero's city house and country villa and forced politicians as powerful as Pompey to seek refuge in their homes. In 52, on the day after the assassination of a popular politician, Publius Clodius Pulcher, speeches by two tribunes so inflamed the crowd that it burned the senate house and its neighboring basilica, looted the homes of senators, and presented the *fasces*, insignia of elected office, to men of their own choice.[42]

For Roman politicians accustomed to working in the exclusive context of the senate or the smaller-scale conditions of trials by jury, the mass meeting offered opportunity and anxiety in roughly equal measure. As Cicero remarks in a speech in defense of a provincial governor accused of extortion, in the middle of the first century BCE:

Recall again the rashness of the multitude [temeritas multitudinis], their fickleness, typical of Greeks, and the great power of a seditious speech at the *contio*. Here, in this most dignified and restrained polity, where the Forum is full of lawcourts, full of magistrates, full of excellent men and citizens, where the senate house, the avenger of rashness and the controller or loyalty, looks over and guards the Rostra—nonetheless, how great are the waves that you can see being whipped up at *contiones*! (*Pro Flacco*, 24.57).

I have already noted that the speeches performed for the contional crowd are preserved exclusively by elite hands. In keeping with elite interests, they show that, for all its gestures toward popular participation, the *contio* perpetuates the traditional domination of the nobles and the exclusion of the crowd from Roman politics. Like the stormy seas with which Cicero compares it (followed by Virgil and Elias Canetti, among others), the crowd at the *contio* embodied a violent unpredictability that serves the interests of the dominant order. Staging the possibility of violence or resistance, even when it remains only a possibility, emerges as an opportunity for elite political theater. The act of facing down and controlling the mob manifests elite mastery in a powerful, memorable, visible form. If a united crowd, especially one that threatened violence, implicitly demanded accountability, even their demand operates within the context of elite performance and on elite terms. If the *contio* was always a potential site of explosive violence, a staging of the never fully realized dominance of the elite, that staging itself plays a crucial role in sustaining elite hegemony.

The available evidence is, of course, only a fraction of the lived experience of the Roman crowd. But it is the evidence that survives to shape perceptions of Rome in the history of the West. What it reveals is the early history by which the multitude is admitted into politics only as a singularity: the People. This is the essential illogic of crowd politics: that to enter the realm of the political, the crowd must either deny its crowd-ness, by assenting to its will being spoken in a single voice and in the name of singularity, or it must deny politics, by overturning the conditions of normality on which politics conventionally relies. Robespierre, a famous enthusiast of Rome, exploits the former condition in a report he made to the assembly shortly before the Terror began. In a move to eradicate his rivals,

in the name of the society to come, "a society in which neither the objective nor the subjective conditions for the formation of masses will exist any longer."[2]

Demonstrations that are productive of solidarity remain a part of our time. The millions of Spanish citizens who came out on March 14, 2004, in the wake of the Madrid bombings and on the eve of the national elections were a "relaxed crowd," as were the million women who marched for women's rights in Washington, D.C., later that spring. The astounding global demonstration for peace on February 15, 2003, to protest against George W. Bush's immanent invasion of Iraq, preserved in photographic record at http://www.punchdown.org/rvb/F15, is a harbinger of the tremendous possibilities of political solidarity in this new century.

Positioned against these progressive crowds we again see the compact masses, this time as riot police—paramilitary special forces wearing black armor and pressed tightly together, their faces immobile or masked to hide an inner panic, ready to react with a violence motivated at best by the instinct of self-preservation. The terms *proletarian* and *petit bourgeois* are not in use today. With regard to the crowd, however, the social reality that they describe has not disappeared.

he declared that all political clubs except his Jacobins were banned by the authority of "the great popular Society of the whole French people."[43] Popular politics, he claimed, were in fact working against the People's interest. Robespierre's declaration treats the People as an active agent with a sense of its own will, shared beliefs, and sense of common good. But it is also a passive entity that lacks a voice until Robespierre himself speaks. That Robespierre could plausibly speak of and for the People in this fashion was possible in part because by the eighteenth century, "the People" signified an idea of mass political will constituted, paradoxically, through a peculiarly qualified exclusion of the image-repertoire of the living crowd: diversity, unpredictability, and disorder. There is an ironic dimension to Robespierre's language, given the nature of his own tactics, which operate under the second condition of crowd politics, the destruction of politics as usual through social disruption and pure violence. His report is part of the strategy that Michael Hardt and Antonio Negri describe as the tautology of popular sovereignty, by which a dominant person or group constructs from the multitude a single subject that in turn makes legitimate its own power.[44]

Almost two thousand years before Robespierre, in 46 BCE, the Roman politician and intellectual Cicero anticipated him with these questions: "What is the body politic? Every gathering [*conventus*], even one of wild savages? Every multitude [*multitudo*] of fugitives and criminals who flock together in one place? No, you would say, of course not" (*Stoic Paradoxes*, 4.27). Cicero's chaotic *multitudo* connotes what Arendt calls "manyness"; his true *civitas*, which I am translating as "body politic," is a commonwealth bound by shared notions of justice, the common good, "chains of law, and equality before the law." Years earlier, in his philosophical dialogue *On the Republic*, Cicero had defined the republic (*res publica*, or public affairs) as the *res populi*, the property of the collective People, whose best option for government is to entrust themselves to the best men (1.39,

51). This definition, a thinly disguised elite idealization of the Roman republic, embodies Cicero's favorite political themes, the conservation of ancestral values (*mos maiorum*) and the harmony of the social order (*concordia rerum*) under the guidance of the senate. It rests on the assumption, characteristic of classical political thought, that the polity is an intelligible entity, subject to representation and available to rational analysis. Whereas the Roman *populus*, like its partner, the senate, is a theoretical singularity, a multitude united in one body, the *multitudo* is a shorthand sign of the impurity of political practice—a "leech" thriving in "urban filth and dregs," Cicero observes in a private letter about crowds in the Forum—that defines and helps sanitize the body politic in normative theory.[45] This is what I am calling the "myth" of the Roman people—a myth predicated on the rewriting of the crowd (*multitudo*, *frequentia*, *turba*) as a unified singularity, the *populus Romanus*.

Crowd Dynamics

In recent years, several historians of republican Rome have viewed the conditions I have sketched here as evidence that the people of Rome remained excluded, by any meaningful standards, from the political process; the *contio* was a masquerade, a stage play, a ritualized performance that sustained and reenacted elite authority.[46] Others have introduced models of dynamic negotiation through persuasion, arguing that "the popular will of the Roman people found expression in the context, and only in the context, of divisions within the oligarchy," or that the ideological function of contional discourse "reflected and continually justified the political hegemony of the Roman elite."[47]

So far I have argued, developing this line of thought, that the Roman crowd, whether obedient or violent, fulfills an elite fantasy of controllable popular liberty. From the first-century speeches of Cicero to modern cinema, the rhetorical techniques of crowd control show the sophisticated and effective ways in which the crowd—even in its violence and unpredictability—may be harnessed as proof and justification for the dominant order. The crowd represents noble fantasies, inscribed in particular in the physical layout of the Forum, of aristocratic domination; it represents, synecdochically, the People to themselves, reinscribing their turbulent multitudinousness as a single *populus*, demanding their enforced assent to the statement of Paul facing the soldier with the whip: *sum civis Romanus.* The fact that the Roman crowd could not realize themselves as a collective political agent—despite the persistent labeling of series of crowd gatherings as the "People"—lends Roman politics an unfinalizability that may, ultimately, explain its stability over centuries. In Michel Serres's reading of the restless fluctuation of a gathered multitude as an antilogic that defies rational signification, the crowd emerges as its own political enemy, the agent of its own invisibility.[48] Multiple, mutable, dynamic, crowds represent the limits of the theoretical imagination; they signify interpretation made impossible—not only making an uncomfortable fit with politics as usual, but revealing the crowd's vulnerability to exploitation and erasure at the hands of its elite masters.

Was this the crowd's only role?

In conclusion, I suggest that there is another way to read the fluctuating, unpredictable, sometimes violent dynamic it brings to republican politics, a dynamic of indeterminacy that is at once stabilizing and destabilizing. Crowd politics in Roman political imagination (and in politics on the ground, in particular, in violent gang warfare) is necessarily impossible to represent. The crowd represents the dynamism of Rome, its changeableness, its ever-expanding identity as an *imperium*. In Livy's account of the founding of Rome, we remember, the crowd is both essential to the city's beginnings and a herald of the violence that will eternally characterize its history. The crowd is the pivot of history, where it plays a role both in making the republic and in threatening its end. His crowd scenes reenact the violent crowds of the civil wars, repeatedly inviting the reader to experience the crowd in two modes: the righteous fury of men battling oppression and the terror of unpredictable, irrational mob violence. As invitations to identification, his crowds speak both hope and fear: they are both a model for republican citizenship and a reminder that popular action is dangerous: a goad to action and a restraint on it. As a model of virtue, the unified crowd deflects the nightmare of mobhood, but the bestiality of mob violence is also necessary in order to preserve popular liberty. Livy's text also entertains the recognition of the limits of authority and legitimacy. His crowd functions as a sign of stability and disturbance: the communal gathering reifies the republic while it provides an opportunity for revolution. And this is also the vitality of the state as Machiavelli sees it, famously expressed in his chapter "That the Discord Between the Plebs and the Senate of Rome Made This Republic Both Free and Powerful" (*Discourses*, 1.4).[49]

Thomas Jefferson wrote the Declaration of Independence with an eye toward public proclamation in a modern version of the *contio*; the French revolutionaries designed spectacle after civic spectacle for public participation. Their attention to spectacle and performance indicates that republics are established and reestablished precisely in the moment of their citizens' mutual recognition in the mass gathering. The crowd, impossible to analyze in its fluctuating, unpredictable opacity, places the republic beyond the reach of teleological politics. It sets up the republic as an unfinished project, a project of performativity.

The crowd expresses a violent energy. As Machiavelli and Arendt see it, the crowd embodies the restiveness and unpredictability that fueled Roman expansion and, theoretically, enabled Roman response to changing conditions of geopolitics. It was a sign of dynamic conflict that they view, in company with Livy, as proof of Rome's imperial destiny. Now the crowd is still multiple; it shifts and flows; people are present who should not be there, speaking languages that are not Latin, wearing clothing that is not appropriate for Roman public life. But this too is part of the logic of the Roman crowd in Roman republican politics. Signs of imperfection and unfinalizability are essential to politics that thematize popular consent.[50]

When one takes part in or personally witnesses a crowd, as the testimonials in this collection show, it's difficult to forget the experience. But once the crowd has dissipated, memories of it fade, and the very architectural space it once inhabited seems to defy the possibility of reoccupation. In Rome and the modern cities of western Europe and America (and increasingly around the globe), the tendency toward forgetfulness of the crowd's immanent presence is intensified by the look and feel of civic architecture. Areas set aside for government buildings are designed to stand alone as empty spaces in their own aesthetic right, so that the individual visitor is transformed into an observer on the sidelines, asking "intruders" to get out of their touristic picture frames, and closed off from any view of the business of the state. Iron fences, the clean gray lines of marble buildings, and geometric patterns of grass and fountain offer a visual analogue to the kinds of human bodies that are welcome there: clean, discrete, ordered subjects. The tumultuous masses of bodies that might fracture the borders of garden, street, and stairway present a threat to the purity of the design.

Roman anxieties help explain the way crowds have become uneasy intruders in our republican public space, and in the republican imagination, by examining some strands in the relationship public oratory creates between the crowd and "the people" as we have historically understood it as a political singularity. The Roman crowd is not simply a piece of history, the legal lawmaking body of an ancient city. Transcending its historical moment, it haunts the West's invention of political order based in popular sovereignty. Understanding the Roman crowd, and the role it plays in forming the myth of the *populus Romanus*, is a crucial step toward understanding the West's myth of itself as an assembly of governments by, for, and of the People.

4 Intimacy and Anonymity, or How the Audience Became a Crowd

William Egginton

IF WE ARE TO GRANT credibility to the notion, advanced by Le Bon and other crowd psychologists of the turn of the twentieth century, that the notion *crowd* is profoundly historical and that its historicity must be located in the period of high modernity,[1] then it becomes germane to pose the question of this concept's origins: if an assembly of individuals did not always have the characteristics of a crowd in the modern sense, what sorts of cultural practices might have led to the emergence of this specific sort of mass phenomenon? The thesis I would like to present here is that a powerful crucible for the transformation of generic assemblies into modern crowds is to be found in the audiences of early modern European playhouses. This is not to say that an equivalence can be established between the terms audience and crowd. Indeed, I am in full agreement with Gabriel Tarde that an audience is not a crowd,[2] that, to be more specific, essential characteristics of crowds as defined by the crowd psychologists are absent from early modern theater audiences. Rather, what must be underscored is how the theatrical establishments of early modern Europe, in responding to distinct social and political anxieties provoked by assemblies of large numbers of people in limited spaces, worked to bring about the very sort of social formation that would spark anxieties among political theorists in high modernity. To put it simply, if the early modern state, its functionaries, and its theoreticians were concerned with the chaotic potential of individuals when they came together as masses, the primary concern of nineteenth- and twentieth-century political theorists is with the possibility of crowds acting nonchaotically, as a unified force. The danger implicit in the democratic diffusion of political power was, according to the latter theorists, precisely that the people would *lose* their ability to reason individually and to act en masse. Needless to say, the same fear emerged as a desideratum of political movements on both the left and the right that saw in people the source of their revolutionary strength. The irony is trenchant: fearing the "horizontal and vertical mobility" of a newly formed urban society, the early modern state coopted its theatrical institutions to the end of "guiding" the theatergoing masses toward a more unified form of behavior via homogenized models of identification;[3] by the late nineteenth century, the societies whose theoretical fabric is woven of the same homogenized models of identification are haunted by the specter of that very unified behavior the theater had sought to instill.

I begin this essay by sketching out what the assemblies of spectators at late medieval dramatic events might have been, if they were neither, as I will argue, audiences nor crowds in the modern sense. From there, I go on to describe the emergence of early modern theatrical institutions and their mechanisms for the control and guidance of audiences, whose primary threat was that of being disorderly and of imposing through sheer number and volume cultural forms deriving from their own lack of taste. Underlying this concern with public disorder, there emerges at the conceptual level a distillation of experientiae whose extremes can be located along the axis spanning the concepts of *anonymity* and *intimacy*. Precisely, in other words, as the rabble (*vulgo*) coalesce and are associated with a certain negative collectivity, a distance is espoused between the realm of that collectivity (publicity) and an interiority whose depths are theorized as being both constructible and potentially infinite.[4] If seventeenth-century texts evince an anxiety mixed with disdain for the disorderly nature of the crowd and advance the theater as the ultimate institution for crowd control, eighteenth-century texts, and in the case of Spain most spectacularly the writings on public spectacle of Gaspar Melchor de Jovellanos, seem split between demonstrating an intensification of this anxiety and

holding out the image of an ideal public as shaped by appropriate theater policy. The crowd as a unity of individuals, conformable to models of decorum and enlightened behavior, is deemed the ultimate goal of public administration. This progression can be seen as achieving its apogee in Mesonero Romanos's descriptions of theater audiences in 1840s Madrid, assemblies operating as crowds in the strictest sense of a group of individuals responding harmoniously to shared affective situations: the same crowds, so congenial to bourgeois commerce,[5] that will haunt the manifestos, barricades, and theater halls of the late nineteenth century. The key, it will be shown, to understanding the power of the crowd lies in this historical analysis of intimacy and anonymity: for in the modernity that arises at the crux of the opposition between these concepts, the crowd is that entity that precipitates in the zone of their loss of distinctness.

Origins of the Audience/the Public (El Público)

When a multitude of the faithful crush together at the moment of the raising of the host during a celebration of the Eucharist in a cathedral in Worms in the fourteenth century (1316),[6] is it anachronistic to postulate that their behavior is identical to that analyzed under the rubric of "crowd psychology" in the late nineteenth and twentieth centuries, describable, for instance, in terms of "the predominance of unconscious personality," or the "possession of a collective mind"?[7] An admittedly tentative answer to this question would have to be affirmative for the following reason: modern descriptions of crowd phenomena depend on the unification of experientiae via a conceptual schema that is inadequate for describing medieval group behavior. Whereas modern descriptions presuppose the experiential primacy of an individual core of *intimacy*, which, upon joining in sufficient number with other individuals, melts away into or abandons itself to the often ecstatic and contagious *anonymity* of the crowd, it can be argued that the medieval experience described above works according to different principles.[8]

It should be clear that intimacy and anonymity form a conceptual coupling: without a contrasting experience of anonymity, there is no such thing as an experience of an intimate sphere whose secret life is precisely what remains unknown to the anonymous one, whose members' own intimacy stays reciprocally beyond our ken. Likewise, the feelings, both positive and negatively connoted, of anonymity so often invoked in the context of urban settings (Baudelaire, Benjamin, Mesonero Romanos) are only conceivable in opposition to the sphere of intimate knowledge that anonymity negates. And yet anonymity, irrespective of whether it corresponds to the comforting invisibility of the flaneur or to Chaplin's alienating vision of urbanity in *Modern Times*, seems to be inextricably tied to the particularly modern experience of the industrial metropolis. As Engels writes, "The greater the number of people that are packed into a tiny space, the more repulsive and offensive becomes the brutal indifference, the unfeeling concentration of each person in his private affairs."[9] How can we expect a similar notion to arise in a culture whose sense of space was so deeply rooted in place and in a profound familiarity not only with one's physical surrounding but with one's fellows as well?[10]

Historical records indicate a powerful tradition of collective participation in religious and profane festivals, spectacles, and other group events in the late Middle Ages, enough to warrant Hans Ulrich Gumbrecht's assessment of medieval culture as a culture of performance.[11] In fact, one could go so far as to stipulate that the primary focus of medieval existence was local community: the life of community participates in the individual's existence as well as in the existence of the universe in micro- and macrocosmic

ways, as is exemplified by the festivals celebrating seasonal change in which an individual family's sustenance was connected to the community's performance of rites intended to influence climatic change.[12] Spectacle, whether we classify it as religious or profane, thus enacted the same set of relations: those gathering to watch were indistinguishable from those performing and vice versa, and the "subject matter" of the performance was as inseparable from the place of its presentation (hence the superimposition of church architecture onto the exterior playing space of, for instance, a town square)[13] as it was from the eternal truths of history or faith that its words and gestures repeated. In such a context, there is no conceivable role for the movement back and forth between intimacy and anonymity that prevails in modernity's descriptions of its crowds.

Such an account of collective interaction in the Middle Ages contrasts sharply with that which emerges from an analysis of assemblies and the anxieties they provoked starting in the fifteenth century. As José-Antonio Maravall's famous thesis states, the baroque is characterized by a concerted effort on the part of entrenched interests to assert control in the face of what he terms a crisis resulting from an "expansive movement unleashed at the end of the fifteenth and reinforced in the sixteenth century."[14] This expansion—vertical (loosening of the embeddedness of estate identification) and horizontal (geographical movement of bodies, exploration, expansion of national borders)—threatened the underpinnings of the medieval caste system and prompted the implicit formation of a monarchical-seigniorial alliance whose interests clearly lay in resisting and constraining these expansive tendencies. Although I part ways with the functionalist assumptions inherent in Maravall's hypothesis, what cannot be refuted is the development, in the new urban settings of the seventeenth century, of a consciousness of mass identities and the open theorization of the possibility and desirability of controlling or "guiding" masses of individuals through the manipulation of popular cultural institutions. As the first and most obvious institutional setting for the gathering of large numbers of individuals—and in this respect it becomes the preeminent social metaphor of the seventeenth century—the theater becomes the testing ground for the implementation of certain mechanisms of control.[15]

Although the details of such implementation are in themselves of interest, what is of primary importance here is that the descriptions of such measures always project a particular image of the collectivity they are intended to control, and moreover evince traces of a general cultural anxiety concerning the nature of the collectivity represented by the *público*. As suggested by the wording of this petition, presented by the city of Seville in 1647 so as to have its theaters reopened, "se evitan muchos alborotos que ocasiona la jente de la armada por recojerse el ynvierno en esta ciud., don[d]e no aviendo comedias suseden muchas desgracias por no tener entretenimiento en que divertirse y particularmente los días de fiesta" (one avoids the many disturbances occasioned by the people of the armed forces who are lodged in the city during the winter, where, having no *comedias,* many unfortunate incidences occur as a result of the lack of entertainments with which to divert themselves, particularly on holidays).[16] Accordingly, the fear of outbreaks of violence was influential in determining public policy as regards the theater, including the organization of seating within public theaters,[17] as well as the very rate of production of theatrical spectacles, because fear of violence fed the urgency officials felt to put on at least two new productions a week.[18]

What is crucial to grasp is that the threat of violence—of *alboroto*, as the Seville petition describes it—is emphatically not of the sort we would associate with that posed by a unified, angry crowd. The potential and undesirable disturbance posed by the *vulgo* was of an explosive, uncoordinated nature, and the closest audiences came to acting in concert were the joined voices of displeasure, so greatly feared by an *autor de comedias*, sparked by those ancestors of the modern theater critic, the *mosqueteros*.[19] The greatest danger from the standpoint of the literary elite was that the theater gave the *vulgo* the unprecedented opportunity to turn the tables on established literary taste. As Cervantes famously grouses through the character of the canon in *Don Quijote*, "estas [comedias] que se usan . . . todas o las más son conocidos disparates y cosas que no llevan pies ni cabeza, y, con todo eso, el vulgo las oye con gusto . . . y los autores que las componen y los actors que las representaban dicen que así han de ser, porque así las quiere el vulgo, y no de otra manera" (these *comedias* of today . . . are all or most of all known to be absurdities and things that can't tell up from down, and, with all that, the *vulgo* hears them with pleasure . . . and the authors who compose them and the actors who represented them say that this is how they have to be, because that's how the *vulgo* wants them, and not in any other way).[20] Insofar as the *vulgo* existed as a unified concept, in other words, the object of this unity referred not so much to the people composing the *vulgo* as to the inherent vulgarity of their taste, a taste they were likely to impose on educated culture via a kind of collective economic power: "y que a ellos les está major ganar de comer con los muchos, que no opinión con los pocos" (and that it is better for them to earn food with the many than reputation with the few).[21]

Although public theaters were consistently organized with the goal of reinforcing class and gender boundaries, it is just as clear that they were a place where those boundaries were continually under attack. Despite the endeavors, sustained into the eighteenth century, of Spanish authorities to mandate the strict separation of the sexes in public theaters, the borders of the *cazuela* (stewpot, as the section for women was called) were fabled opportunities for clandestine trysts, as were the backstage areas themselves, where gentlemen often ventured in search of those women who, unlike in Britain's early modern theater, did grace the Spanish stage.[22] As concerns the anxiety provoked by the threatening of class boundaries, this description of the parterre of the Parisian public theater the Hôtel de Bourgogne comes down to us from the seventeenth-century writer Charles Sorel: "The parterre is very difficult because of the pressed in crowd: in the space are a thousand roughnecks mixed in with honest citizens at whom from time to time the low types hurl insults. A quarrel arises out of nothing, swords are put to hand, and the whole comedy is interrupted. In their most perfect repose these rascals never stop talking, yelling, and whistling."[23]

Just as the stage itself became modernity's most prevalent metaphor for questions of truth and knowledge,[24] the anxiety provoked by the image of the theatergoing public became nothing short of a generalized cultural motif for thinking about the dangers of collectivities in seventeenth-century thought, as evidenced by Baltasar Gracián's choice of titles for his chapter dealing with this topic in *El criticón*: "Plaça del populacho y corral del Vulgo" (Plaza of the masses and theater of the *Vulgo*). As is clear from any one of a number of examples, Gracián's principal concern in dealing with large assemblies of people is the threat posed by an accumulation of stupidity and its likelihood of overwhelming the *discreción* (discernment or judgment; German *Urteilskraft*)[25] of the few. The fact of the sheer multiplicity of those lacking *discreción* leads Gracián to the paradoxical, as he himself understands it, admission that what demonstrates true understanding is not to wish to be respected by "los varones sabios y prudentes" (wise and prudent men), but rather to be successful among "los ignorantes y necios" (the ignorant and fools): "Mirá, los sabios son pocos, no hay cuatro en una ciudad; ¡que digo cuatro!, ni dos en todo un reino. Los ignorantes son los muchos, los necios los infinitos; y assí, el que los tuviere a ellos de su parte, ésse será señor de un mundo entero" (Look! The wise are few, there aren't four in a city; what am I saying four! There aren't two in a whole kingdom. The ignorant are the many, fools infi-

nite; and in this way he who had them on his side would be lord of an entire world).[26] Granted, the ability of the crowd to be swayed, its tendency not to reason individually, is also a specific concern of the modern crowd theorists: "in the collective mind the intellectual aptitudes of the individuals, and in consequence their individuality, are weakened."[27] Nevertheless, what stands out in Gracián's case is that his *vulgo* is not made stupid by way of their collective commingling, but are congenitally stupid. If anything, they *should* be brought together in crowds, if only because then there might be some shadow of a hope that someone with real understanding would come to be influential in their eyes.

Even when speaking directly about the dangers of political revolt, Gracián spins the issue away from the threat posed by concerted action and instead emphasizes that the danger of power falling into the hands of the masses is that individuals with no natural capacity for leadership might take it upon themselves to lead, with disastrous consequences for themselves as well as for society at large. Thus he makes four specific references to leaders of revolts, identifying them by their practicing a particular trade and hence more broadly by their lack of nobility, education, or distinction (*C,* 385). As with the mix of people in the parterre of the Parisian public theaters, Gracián's *vulgo* poses a threat of confusion, of impurity, of throwing into imbalance the organizing principles of the world: "los letrados era cosa graciosa verles pelear, manejar las armas, dar assaltos y tomar plaças; el labrador hablando de los tratos y contratos, el mercader de la agricultura; el estudiante de los exércitos, y el soldado de las escuelas" (it was amusing to see the scholars fighting, wielding weapons, going on the attack, taking plazas; the workman speaking of treaties and contracts, the merchant of farming; the student of armies, and the soldier of schools) (*C,* 386–87). In the final analysis, the greatest damage is that done by the ignorant, in their multitudes, to the hard-won taste of the discriminating, "que lo muy bueno es de pocos, y el que agrada al vulgo, por consiguiente, ha de desgradar a los pocos, que son los entendidos" (since the very good is of the few, and he who pleases the *vulgo* must consequently displease the few, who are the intelligent) (*C*, 396).

The Extrusion of Intimacy

Gracián's world is the world that Maravall described as being the first to host the entity called society, an agglomerate of individuals unhinged—and indeed *trastornado* (overturned) and *al revés* (backward) are among Gracián's preferred descriptors for this world—from the social structures that grounded existence in medieval culture.[28] Nevertheless, the anonymous multitude that forms the negative backdrop for Gracián's moralizing tales and self-help manuals has as its essential counterpart an intimate core extruded, as it were, from the relentless publicization of social life. This intimate core is a treasure to be protected, to be sure, but it is also a powerful tool to be used in navigating the perilous public world, and in controlling its weak-minded denizens. Gracián's word for this core is *caudal*, and if there were a leitmotiv among his strategies for how to get ahead in the dog-eat-dog world of early modern society, it would be best expressed in the motto *incomprensibilidad de caudal*, or incomprehensibility of capital. This has nothing to do with actually having infinite resources at one's command. The point is rather that the depths of one's resources should never be made known to others. What others do not know about your hidden resources, they will respect and desire, and the result will be more power for you. The most powerful person in any society is the one who manages to convince all others that his inner resources are the most unfathomable, and hence infinite in terms of social capacity: "mayores afectos de veneración causa la opinión y duda de adonde llega el caudal de cada uno que la evidencia de él, por grande que fuera" (greater affects of venera-

tion are inspired by public opinion and doubt as to how deep one's resources go, than by evidence of them, as great as they may be).[29]

It should be clear that this image is theatrical. We only have *caudal* insofar as we present ourselves socially in the person of a character. Or, to put it in another way, a *persona*—which, as is well known, derives from the Greek word for mask—is Gracián's chosen word for the ultimate goal of personal development,[30] all the while implicitly importing into that figure all the trappings of the stage. What distinguishes the *persona* is his ability to stay within character, to convince the greatest number of people possible that his character is his character *all the way down*, that there is no other self, or actor, behind it to ground it in the world and limit the eternal sounding of its resources: "Hombre con fondos, tanto tiene de persona" (As much depth as a man has, so much is he a person).[31] *Persona* is externalized spirit; it is intimacy extruded from public anonymity and worn on an actor's sleeve; it is the secret self that we strive to represent in public, and that we desire to know and ultimately to be like when—as public, as audience—we momentarily extinguish our own characters in order to better take in those of the stage.

Anonymity and Public Power

The rise of what we can call *publicity*[32]—or, with Richard Sennett, *public man*[33]—as the condition of possibility of those forms of social organization associated with the modern state depends in large measure on the relation between intimacy and anonymity.[34] The relationality typical of feudal power must be characterized along an imaginary axis: each link in the power hierarchy was established across bonds of familiarity, mutual dependence, and personal coercion.[35] The power structures necessitated by the massive bureaucratic state apparatuses that emerged in the seventeenth century could not sustain such imaginary relationality across the distances and among the numbers of citizens entailed by state and imperial borders. Symbolic power, in which the sovereign could be represented in his absence as an entity embodying the national identity, became the norm for the modern state, and in many ways it still remains the norm, although the normative sovereignty of the state system shows signs of being superseded.[36] The relationality entailed by symbolic power assumes a complex play of intimacy and anonymity, and takes its model from the stage.

For an individual to conceive of him- or herself as belonging to an extracommunal entity such as a nation requires a double process of distantiation from a communal matrix and reidentification with a larger, abstract entity. It demands a process like that described above as the extrusion of the intimate, if only in order for the intimate core to find its home in conformity with a greater whole, a people, or even a general will whose concerted action provides the legislative (first as merely subject, then as author) body of the nation. This model is theatrical in that the force of such desired conformity follows precisely the pattern traced above of identification with a core of intimacy posited as being withheld by the character on the stage. But it is also theatrical in a much more concrete sense, in that theorists of state policy both took advantage of theatrical models and turned to the institution of the theater itself as a potential tool for habituating agglomerates of individuals to the basic elements of group identification.

One overriding concern of Gaspar de Jovellanos's generously titled "Memoria para el arreglo de la policía de los espectáculos y diversiones públicas, y sobre su orígen en España" (Memo for the improvement of behavior at spectacles and public diversions, and on their origin in Spain) is to criticize the decay of Spain's contemporary theater scene, to vituperate the license and liberality of its writers, while at the same time proposing in the strongest possible terms

a defense of the theater as an institution, provided the government adopt appropriate public policies concerning its management. Jovellanos's assessment of his contemporary theater scene is reminiscent of that of a theater snob like Cervantes speaking about the undue influence of the *vulgo* in his day; but now it is not mere taste that is at risk but public morals in general. In other words, the *vulgo* who once threatened the integrity of art has now been replaced by a vulgar art that threatens society's integrity:

¿Se cree, por ventura, que la inocente puericia, la ardiente juventud, la ociosa y regalada nobleza, el ignorante vulgo, pueden ver sin peligro tantos ejemplos de impudencia y grosería, de ufanía y necio pundonor, de desacato a la justicia y a las leyes, de infidelidad a las obligaciones públicas y domesticas, puestos en acción, pintados con los colores más vivos, y animados con el encanto de la illusion y con las gracias de la poesía y de la música? Confesémoslo de buena fe: un teatro tal es una peste pública, y el gobierno no tiene más alternativa que reformarle o proscribirle para siempre.

Shall we believe, perchance, that innocent childhood, that ardent youth, that leisurely and dainty nobility, that the ignorant *vulgo*, can see without danger so many examples of impudence and ill-breeding, of conceit and foolish honor, of disobedience to justice and the laws, of infidelity to public and domestic obligations, put into action, painted in the most lively colors, and animated with the charm of illusion and the grace of poetry and music? Let us confess in good faith: such a theater is a public nuisance, and the government has no other alternative than to reform it or proscribe it for ever.[37]

Because proscribing public diversions amounts to either at best an impossibility and at worst a public catastrophe, reform is the only answer. But it is precisely in the specific nature of his recommendations for reform that we glimpse the emergent outline of that entity whose cultivation Jovellanos sees as essential for the construction of a malleable body politic.

In all of Jovellanos's description of social life, the nega-

4A 'Crowd': English

Marisa Galvez

According to the *Oxford English Dictionary*, the word *crowd* seems to have first gained its meaning as a "large number of persons gathered closely together as to press upon or impede each other; a throng, a dense multitude" during the late sixteenth century. The revival of classicism during the Renaissance may have offered the impetus for the emergence of the word in the English language within a distinctive social discourse. In his *Odes* Horace often refers to large gatherings of people in public spaces as a negative everyday feature of Roman society. With Sir Thomas Drant's 1567 translation of Horace's epistle to Numitius, "Who will, and dare retche forthe his hande,/And man the throughe the croude," there appeared an English word for a multitude of people objectively seen, rather than referring to an action upon something, as implied in the verbs *press* (thirteenth century) or *crowd* (tenth century and after). Although still retaining physical connotations of crowding, the classical context of the noun *crowd* served as a springboard for writers to reflect upon the changing status of the individual during a key transitional period in English history.

The plays of Shakespeare amply demonstrate the application of classical notions of *crowd* to contemporary discussions of England's social structure. In *Coriolanus* (1608) Shakespeare portrays a body politic in crisis informed by the ongoing anxieties of interdependency across different social classes. In *Henry VIII* (1613) the royal

tive and undesirable is depicted in terms of disunity and unpredictable movement—"la pereza y falta de unión y movimiento que se nota en todas partes" (the laziness and lack of unity and movement that is noticed all over)—whereas the desirable takes the form of unity, tranquility, and stability:[38] "El estado de libertad es una situación de paz, de comodidad y de alegría; el de sujeción lo es de agitación, de violencia ye de disgusto; por consiguiente, el primero es durable, el segundo expuesto a mudanzas" (The state of freedom is a situation of peace, of comfort, and of happiness; that of subjection is one of agitation, of violence, and of displeasure; consequently, the first is durable, the second likely to undergo perturbations) (*OEJ*, 175). The obvious means, then, of bringing about a happy, peaceful body politic is through the facilitation of stable unity and the discouragement of disruption and unnecessary movement: "Por el contrario, unos hombres frecuentemente congregados a solazase y divertirse en común formarán siempre un pueblo unido y afectuoso; conocerán un interés general, y estarán más distantes de sacrificarle a su interés particular" (on the other hand, men who congregate frequently to enjoy themselves and have fun together will always form a united and affectionate people; they will know a general interest, and will be less likely to sacrifice it to their private interest) (*OEJ*, 176). It is worth noting that affect is conceived of here as a group attribute, both effective and consequential insofar as it is a kind of affect that helps create communal bonds ("a solazarse y divertirse en común") as well as the affect of union that results from this congregation. Furthermore, it is precisely this affective union that constitutes the body politic that Jovellanos describes, in almost proto-Rousseauian terms, as a general interest that outweighs or overrules private interest.[39] Finally, this investment in the general body politic is described ethically in quasi-Kantian terms as being the condition of possibility of freedom, "porque serán más libres."[40]

If the making of the perfect crowd is the recipe for a successful and enlightened body politic, the theater is the place for its confection: "el Gobierno no debe considerar el teatro solamente como una diversión pública, sino como un espéctaculo capaz de in[s]truir o extraviar el espíritu, y de perfeccionar o corromper el corazón de los ciudadanos" (the government should not consider the theater only as a public diversion, but rather as a spectacle capable of instructing the spirit or leading it astray, of perfecting or corrupting the hearts of citizens) (*OEJ*, 183). Indeed, if the model of everything undesirable and deserving of censure in modern society is the unruly crowd and that of everything desirable and deserving of promotion a stable unified one, then this is the ultimate justification for a strict policy of public intervention in all aspects of theater life, because it is the very nature and quality of the spectacle that determines the constitution of its attendant crowd:

¿quién no ve que este desorden proviene de la calidad misma de los espectáculos? ¡Qué diferencia tan grande entre la atención y quietud con que se oye la representación de *Atalía* o la del *Diablo predicador*! ¡Qué diferencia entre los espectáculos de los corrales de la Cruz y el Príncipe, y los del coliseo de los Caños, aun cuando sean unos mismos!

Who does not see that this disorder comes from the quality of the spectacles itself? What a great difference between the attention and quiet with which one hears a performance of *Atalía* or of the *Diablo predicador*! What a difference between the spectacles in the *corrales de la Cruz* and *el Príncipe* from those of the Coliseum of *Los Caños*, even if they are one and the same! (*OEJ*, 192)

Precisely because for Jovellanos the human being is so vibrantly reflective of his or her physical and social environment, the form and content of a theater piece as well as the organization and decoration of a theatrical establishment are essential for determining the ultimate nature of a crowd. Moreover, what ultimately fixates and hence liberates the crowd from the slavery of individual excess and violence could be described, in the terms I am advancing here, as the capture of intimacy. For those other souls that surround us provide us with a screen of anonymity against which to act out and hence fall slave to our most irrational impulses; but in a well-lit, comfortable theater space, there I and my fellow spectators may be seated in such a way that we both see the stage and each other (and are seen by each other): "Siéntense todos, y la confusion ceserá; cada uno será conocido, y tendrá a su lado, frente y espalda cuatro testigos que le observen, y que sean interesados en que guarde silencio y circumspección" (Let all be seated and the confusion will cease; each will be known, and will have at his side, front, and back four witnesses who will observe him, and who will be interested in his keeping silent and circumspect) (*OEJ*, 193). If this last description reminds us of Foucault's theorization—on the basis of Jeremy Bentham's influential design for the panoptic prison—of the disciplinary society, we should not be too surprised.[41] What reins in our individual behavior, and hence what sets us free to act for the greater good, is the danger that we be known—that, in other words, what our fellow strangers can see against the backdrop of a greater anonymity are our most intimate hearts, worn on our sleeves, no less public, than the stage in whose shadow we are gathered.

The Age of Crowds

"Baudelaire loved solitude; but he wanted it in the crowd" (Baudelaire liebte die Einsamkeit; aber er wollte sie in der Menge), Benjamin wrote,[42] and perhaps the

court fears popular unrest ("loud rebellion" [1.2.29]) and in scenes of pageantry, the crowd is ambivalently portrayed as at once a potentially uncontrollable multitude and an increasingly important moral arbiter upon which the history of the Elizabethan Protestant succession depends. At Anne Boleyn's coronation, a man recounts the popular energy and density "Among the crowd i' th' Abbey, where a finger / Could not be wedg'd in more" (4.1.57), and men could not distinguish their wives in the crowd, as "all were woven / So strangely in one piece" (4.1.79–80). Here the image of the crowd, gendered and intimately linked to Henry's sexual appetite and desire for a male heir, suggests procreation ("a finger / Could not be wedg'd in more" and "the great bellied women" [4.1.76]) and the costs of dynastic succession. Anne is a providential character as mother of the future Queen Elizabeth (she has "beauty and honor" and is an "angel" [2.3.76], [4.1.44]), but as the audience knows, coronation crowds also anticipate the unruly crowds of public executions. This representation of the multitude reflects England's state of flux and the emergence of the crowd as a phenomenon oscillating between two poles: on one end, an energizing, fascinating physical union of people that represents a procreative force and successful balance of the state and monarchy, and on the other, a dangerous mass inciting anarchy and the threat of popular instability.

In depicting *vulgus* and *greges* as threats to Roman state stability, Horace describes Cleopatra as "girt with her foul emasculate throng" (*contaminato cum grege turpium*, *Ode* 1:37). The classical notion of a dangerous woman who emasculates a crowd resonates in the context of Queen Elizabeth I's need to distinguish herself from figures such as Dido and Cleopatra—crowd-making women who in inciting sexual anarchy represent moral degeneracy as a threat to a successful patriarchal state. Elizabeth would confront the threat posed by the crowd by associating her body with the state in a traditional way, as she declares to her troops at Tilbury on the eve of the anticipated invasion of the Spanish Armada: "I know I have the body but of a weak and feeble woman; but I have the heart and stomach of a king, and of a king of England too . . ." (1588). Elizabeth instills balance in her body politic by explicitly referring to her virtues that transcend gender. To her, the "heart and stomach of a king" implies a solid moral compact between her and her subjects, and she strengthens this union by invoking the common enemies of England. As a Virgin Queen however, she "mans" the crowd by de-gendering the crowd phenomenon as an androgynous state, thereby allying herself with her crowd without being subsumed by it. Thus one sees in Elizabeth's rhetorical strategy an attempt to redefine the crowd by distancing herself from disharmony between social classes, or between the "head" and "stomach" of the body politic. Her rhetoric acknowledges an understanding of leadership as both in and outside the crowd, and a savvy recognition of a crowd discourse informed by both antiquity and contemporary social and political contexts. Even in today's world, the success of a leader depends on the extent to which he or she can imbue a people's phenomenological experience of a crowd—individualized and disparate—with the perspective of the common good.

same could be said of others in the nineteenth century who, when not endowed with a Nietzschean distaste for herds,[43] found in the figure of the crowd what we might call the fulfillment of that dream of unity and peace proposed by Jovellanos's public theater policy. A strange sort of solitude it was, however. Rather than consisting of a detachment from others, this solitude emerges from a general dispersal of otherness per se. The many, among whom one might feel the warmth of companionship or the oppressive nearness of their unwanted touch, have become the crowd, in which the one is absorbed into blissful solitude. Let us be clear, however, that such loss of self is in no way akin to a return to the structure of such prior collectivities as we have discussed in the case of the late Middle Ages. The phenomenon of absorption in crowds to which the modern world so copiously bears witness must be understood within the experiential scope of intimacy and anonymity: namely, the phenomenon of absorption is produced by the expansion of the sphere of intimacy out to the horizon of anonymity. Other people, what Heidegger referred to as *das Man*, are relieved of the resistance, or distantiality [*Abständigkeit*], to my intimacy that their status as anonymous others has granted them,[44] at the same time as my intimate reserve is shattered. The resultant experience does not undo the coupling of intimacy and anonymity, but rather produces a remarkable and ephemeral hybrid: the crowd remains fundamentally and at the same time an intimate and an anonymous entity. The recognition of this characteristic of the crowd is, it seems to me, essential for understanding both the importance of the crowd in modern political movements and the relation the crowd has to the historical development of theater audiences.[45]

As we have seen from the preceding historical analyses, the particular audience structure capable of producing the effect of a "collective mind" was not present in theater audiences through the eighteenth century, although Jovellanos's writings reveal the desirability of such a structure as a public policy instrument for engineering a free, enlightened society. Although an attribution of any kind of direct causality would be out of the question, it may certainly be claimed that in the European theater culture of the nineteenth century at least some central aspects of Jovellanos's vision do begin to become a reality; which is to say, popular thinking about crowds and theater audiences in particular begin to acquire precisely those attributes that were lacking but desired in Jovellanos's vision: *unity of identity in the form of shared affective response*. Nevertheless, whereas for Jovellanos, as for later proponents of revolutionary politics, such unity would ultimately lead to the ability to place the general good over the individual good, and hence to the possibility of freedom, modern times would reveal a dark side to this vision, concern for which was clearly at the forefront of the crowd psychologists' considerations.[46]

The first thing one notices about audience descriptions from this period is the abundance of organic and fluid metaphors. Mesonero Romanos, one of the great documenters of Spanish customs in the nineteenth century, describes the theater without people as a "cuerpo sin vida, un cadaver yerto e inanimado" (body without life, rigid and inanimate cadaver).[47] Although Mesonero is quick to focus his painterly eye on individual disturbances, making of them fodder for his sarcastic caricatures, he nevertheless more often than not allows individual actions, whether intrusive or not, to be registered in harmonious interaction with others, such that women, so often criticized in the misogynist tradition for their garrulousness, become here the source of an undifferentiated roar: "mil y mil voces, si quier gangosas y displicentes, si quier melífluas y atipladas, se confunden naturalmente en armónico diapasón, y más de una vez sobresalen por entre los diálogos de los actors o sobre los *crescendos* de la orquesta" (thousands and thousands of voices, perhaps nasal and disagreeable, perhaps mellifluous and shrill, are naturally confused in a harmonious tuning fork, and more than once leap out from among the dialogues of the actors or over the crescendos of the orchestra) (*RMR*, 139). The audience can even be expected to respond in kind and on cue, albeit according to the dictates of a leader: namely, of that section of the audience occupied by the theater intelligentsia, of whom he says, "los unos y otros esperan con atención la muestras inequívocas de su sentencia, y aplauden si aplaude, y silban por simpatía cuando escuchan a la inteligencia silbar" (one and all wait with attention for the unequivocal show of their sentence, and applaud if they applaud, and whistle in sympathy when they hear the intelligentsia whistle) (*RMR*, 141). Finally, the overall impression one is left with of this "theater from the outside," as he calls it, is the *simétrica variedad* of the audience, an extraordinary uniformity of behavior that transcends class and gender distinctions to form out of conspicuous individuals a fluid, if momentary, whole. Even as he separates groups out according to their social identity and the place they occupy in the theater, this paradoxically symmetrical variety remains common to all: "Los demás compartimentos de la planta baja son ocupados en simétrica variedad por aquella parte del *respectable público*, que en el diccionario moderno solemos llamar *las masas*" (the other compartments of the first floor are occupied in symmetrical variety by that part of the *respectable public* that in the modern dictionary we tend to call *the masses*) (*RMR*, 141). These masses, as he says with a withering condescension that Jovellanos probably would have been unable to grasp, are all here to "divertirse con la mayor fe del mundo, y pillar de paso, si

4B The Crowd Laughs

T. J. Clark

It may be true that when a mass of people is put in a dangerous situation, or just senses the power that comes from numbers, the gathering can take on an identity of its own, and that the caution, or inhibition, or even decency of some of its individual members may be overtaken by the dynamic of a body on the move. But my memories of crowds in the late 1960s—which is the only time in my life when some form of radical disobedience by the many seemed on the agenda—make me doubtful about how far such dissolution goes. Even in a moment of pervasive social uncertainty (it does not matter, in my view, if we end up calling the moment in question "revolutionary," because the decades of misrepresentation that have followed are testimony enough to the moment's unacceptable, inescapable force) crowds are class-divided, and the motor of *ressentiment* that may partly drive them is impeded, all the time, at every point of potential conflict or freeing of energies, by the brake of anxiety, unpreparedness, and ordinary (profound) bourgeois awkwardness with the body in action.

I remember the poet Edward Dorn saying to me in 1968, at the height of an occupation of the university I was teaching in at the time (he said it kindly, and I did not take the advice, then or later, as condescending, even though I knew that the "they" he referred to included myself) that I ought not to hope for too much from what was happening all round me, or from the panoply of 1968 worldwide. "Never forget these are middle-class children. They will not be able to do what they dream of." A friend said to me after the clashes in Grosvenor Square later the same year that he had glimpsed me only once in the melee, running backward from a line of policemen but still facing them—and laughing maniacally. I was in two minds, two bodies. I was laughing at the cops, at the dumb choreography of the "demonstration," and most of all at my own inability to strike.

Of course what I am reminiscing about is a conflict that lacked—or had too rarely and ambivalently—the "nothing to lose" support of a proletariat. This was Dorn's archaizing point. And how much, at the time, middle-class children appeared to fear that "nothing to lose," as if sensing that the mere shadow of it in the space they occupied would mean the game was up. How endless the hours of gloomy anticipation of provocateurs before each march began, and how insistently public (and private) discussion of what to do in advance turned on "the question of the violent fringe"—almost to the exclusion of any other kind of tactical thinking, it seems to me in retrospect. As if there could have been, or should have been, a way of dissociating ourselves from those to whom society had done most harm. As if there were not more urgent things to discuss—ways to make use of the space-time opened by the action of the crowd—which actually lay, for a moment, within the purview of the middle-class possible.

Crowds in the 1960s were divided by class, and they were also politically at odds with themselves. This last was a hopeful thing. Naturally they had their quota of armbands and megaphones and Nuremberg chanting of "Ho Chi Min." But I remember also the insubordination of the mass:

pueden, una leccioncita moral" (to have fun with the greatest faith in the world, and to grab in passing, if they can, a little moral lesson) (*RMR,* 141). The greater irony, of course, is that while Mesonero scoffs at the moral lessons these theatergoers are likely to bring home with them, the audience he describes is precisely the kind that Jovellanos dreamed of affecting.

Nine years before Mesonero penned this portrait of the theater in Madrid, Victor Hugo published a novel that opens with some of the most memorable descriptions of crowds ever written—a crowd that waits in ever growing impatience for the opening of a theatrical spectacle. He writes, "La foule s'épaississait à tout moment, et, comme une eau qui dépasse son niveau, commençait a monter lelong des murs" (The crowd grew denser by the moment, and, like a water that surpasses its level, began to rise along the walls).[48] Note how Hugo the poet captures the waves of people in the waves of assonance in these lines, "comme une eau qui dépasse son niveau, commençait a monter." As they are made to wait later into the day, "the temper of the crowd began to rise. A storm, which was yet only a rumble, was ruffling at the surface of that human sea."[49] Yet for all the apparent powers of nature at its disposal, the crowd is remarkably malleable, for when the curtain is raised "to make way for a personage, the mere sight of whom arrested the crowd, . . . as if by magic, [it] changed their anger into curiosity."[50] Nevertheless, the volatility and power of the crowd is never far from sight.

Biographically speaking, there is some logic to having this magical effect on an oceanic crowd take place inside a theater. Victor Hugo was, after all, in addition to the acclaimed author of *Notre-Dame de Paris,* the defamed author of *Hernani*: the play that put such a violent end to the dominance of neoclassical rules in the French theater. *Hernani* played in the face of vicious and desperate opposition for forty-eight nights, bringing in each night, as Hugo writes in his journal, five thousand francs.[51] And yet if Hugo has the audience to fear, there is another crowd, properly speaking, forming, and coming to his defense. If *Hernani* plays on, it is because "for forty-eight performances, ever-renewed by new blood, the romantic army kept up the fight. Inside the theater, outside in street and parlor, in the papers, the battle went on, throwing the young men of the Latin Quarter into a frenzy. In Toulouse, a young man died in a duel over *Hernani*" (*B,* 25). A culture war, certainly, the force of whose advent is announced by Hugo, by his followers, and by "his romantic army" with the prophetic conviction of an insatiable crowd. "Why bother to hiss Hernani?" Hugo asks. "Can one stop a tree from greening by crushing one of its buds?" (*B,* 27). The implication is clear; the place may have been merely the theater, but *Hernani* was no longer alone. This audience had become a crowd.

The Crowd on the Streets of the World

February 17, 2003. The *New York Times* begins one of its lead articles stating that the world knows two superpowers: the United States, shrill in its insistence on pursuing war with Iraq, on the one hand, and on the other, public opinion, expressing its dissent worldwide in the form of crowds taking to the streets as they have apparently never done before. Even if we can explain away the numbers by pointing out that there are approximately a billion more people on the planet now than there were thirty years ago, the growth is not attributable to those western societies that have been hosting this dramatic performance of popular discontent. This is curious because if Le Bon and others predicted that the twentieth century would be the era of crowds, in recent times, voices whose own political progenitors would have embraced this motto as their own have issued a sober dismissal:

CAE [Critical Art Ensemble] has said it before, and we will say it again: as far as power is concerned, the streets are dead capital! Nothing of value to the power elite can be found on the streets, nor does this class need control over the streets to efficiently run and maintain state institutions. For CD [civil disobedience] to have any meaningful effect, the resisters must appropriate something of value to the state. Once they have an object of value, the resisters have a platform from which they may bargain for (or perhaps demand) change.

At one time, control over the street was valued. In nineteenth-century Paris, the streets were the conduits for the mobility of power, whether economic or military in nature. If the streets were blocked and key political fortresses were occupied, the state became inert, in some cases collapsing under its own weight. This method of resistance continued to prove useful up through the 1960s, but since the end of the nineteenth century, it has yielded diminishing returns and has drifted from being a radical practice to a liberal one. This strategy assumes the necessity of centralizing capital within cities; as capital has become increasingly decentralized, moving freely across national boundaries and abandoning the cities, street action has become increasingly useless.[52]

The streets are dead, in other words. In the age of digital commerce and multinational capital, the appropriate form of resistance is thought not to involve the slow, brute numbers of massive crowds, but surges in the flow of information so vital to capital itself. Even if large crowds gather to disrupt the meetings of those shepherds of the new world order, analysis of oppositional strategies emphasizes the quick and fluid organization that the use of digital technology enables, rather than the sheer force of numbers.

the counterchant of "Ho Ho Ho Chi Min" which modulated into a Disney dwarf staccato of "Ho ho, Ho ho, ho ho ho ho . . . "; the great banner in Oxford Street proposing that we "Storm the Reality Studios" rather than the American Embassy; the graffiti replying to Trotskyist pieties with fragments from Donne and MacDiarmid and Randolph Bourne; the gales of laughter each time Vanessa Redgrave or Tariq Ali rose to speak. Crowds are insolent and unserious. They give license to the disrespectful. If we accept, as I think we must, that when crowds next fill the streets of the late capitalist world with insurgency in mind, they are even less likely than thirty years ago to be powered by proletarian revenge or exultation, then perhaps we would do well to look again at the distinctive feature of politics in the 1960s—its controlled unseriousness, the constant cackle within it of laughter in retreat—somewhat more closely, more hopefully. Our world is still a manifold of murders, suppressions, hungers, terror raining from thirty thousand feet. But it is also, necessarily, a texture of images put in place of that real. Its citizens are more and more expected to sign on to—fully to internalize and act upon—a pathetic virtual life. That dim visuality is the state's Achilles heel. Middle-class children may not be able to do what they dream of. But what they deride and disbelieve in (if they manage to go on improvising adequate forms for the depth of their derision) may someday lose its will—its brutal, expansive, so far unstoppable determination—to cover the world with lies.

But perhaps we are too quick to write the obituary of the crowd. If Richard Sennett's thesis may be taken for granted, that what was to be the age of crowds quickly degenerated into the fall of public man, perhaps as an understandable result of the excesses of crowd politics in the first half of the twentieth century in particular, this "fall" nurtured the rise of an obsessive individualism that proved fertile ground for the consumerist passions in the postindustrialized world.[53] As the character Will, played by Hugh Grant, in *About a Boy* puts it in response to a quote from that infamous line of Donne's, "In my opinion, all men are islands. And what's more, now's the time to be one. This is an island age. A hundred years ago, for instance, you had to depend on other people. No one had TV, or CDs, or DVDs, or videos, or home espresso makers. As a matter of fact, they didn't have anything cool. Whereas now, you see, you can make yourself a little island paradise." The obvious backdrop to his solipsistic consumerist identity would appear to be the intimate life of family he has forsaken and will manage to recuperate through the course of the film; but his solipsism is merely the epitome of modern intimacy itself. Such intimacy can be shared with a chosen few but might just as well be kept to oneself, in private, at home. It sees the world through a TV screen, or a computer screen, but always as a representation.[54] The true antonym for this intimacy is not, then, family, but rather the lost anonymity of public man. It is this fact, it seems to me, above all others that would explain why, at a time when the streets are supposed to be dead, they could come alive again to such effect. Perhaps CAE is premature in its dismissal of the streets because it identifies the power of the streets with the street as a place, as a physical rather than a virtual geography.[55] The power of a crowd, however, might mean more than merely the ability to occupy something of value. The power of the crowd, the embodiment of that anonymous sphere within which the intimate soul was born, is also the aporetic power of a kind of freedom from freedom itself. Freedom, the Enlightenment thinker asserts, is the freedom to transcend your individual desires and act for the benefit of the general good; freedom, the liberal capitalist asserts, is the freedom to fulfill your individual desires over and against the dictates of what others hold to be the general good. But the crowd has a way of confounding both credos: it haunts the general good of universal reason with the terror of unified unreason; it haunts the freedom of individual desire as the desire for something more, for shared affect, for community, for a greater good. That is why, even today—especially today—when a hegemony of screens creates the illusion of intimacy with a billion other souls, the crowds that walk the streets of the world present a power that, win or lose on any given day, cannot be ignored.

5 Sports Crowds

Allen Guttmann

Introductory Remarks

Sports spectatorship is a complex phenomenon that varies, within certain boundaries, from time to time and from place to place. It can be the solitary mediated experience of a single person quietly watching his or her television screen. It can also be the immediate collective experience of a hundred thousand shouting, screaming men and women—a sports crowd—packed into a domed stadium. Sports crowds sometimes gather on the spur of the moment, as they did when an American professor and his German students played a game of Sunday softball in a park in Tübingen, but sports crowds are more typically found in set places at set times, according to a schedule published well in advance of the event. In this sense, in situ sports spectators resemble people who subscribe to a series of monthly concerts or theatrical performances. A major difference is that in situ sports spectators are usually sports *fans*. They see themselves as active participants, inspiring the home team with their cheers and demoralizing the visiting team with their taunts. Sports crowds are partisan and almost always have been, which is why they are frequently disorderly and sometimes violent. Ancient moralists said that sports fans were intoxicated or insane; modern Italian slang calls them *tifosi*—that is, those who are stricken with typhoid fever.

An exception to this dour generalization about partisanship comes immediately to mind. Well-behaved Victorian and Edwardian sports spectators schooled themselves to express a nonpartisan admiration for athletic prowess. When Eton's cricketers took to the field against a team from Harrow or Winchester, a good play by one's opponents deserved as much hearty applause as a good play by one's own team. Historically, however, this code of behavior was an anomaly. Sociologically, it was class specific. The internalization of the ethos of nonpartisan good sportsmanship was never as complete among working-class sports fans as among spectators from the middle and upper classes. Gender also made a difference. In Victorian and Edwardian sports crowds, female spectators—who have almost always in every era been outnumbered by male spectators—were usually less partisan (and much less prone to verbal or physical violence). Many contemporary observers who commented with disdain on the unruly behavior of working-class fans noted with admiration the exemplary behavior of the ladies at Wimbledon or at Lord's. Some observers remarked on a less obvious phenomenon. Spectators who play the game they watch behave differently from those who have never tried their hand (or foot) at it. The niceties of strategy appeal to the aficionado, and sensational action attracts those who don't know the difference between the third-strike dropped-ball rule and the leg-before-wicket rule.

The nonpartisan Victorian code of good sportsmanship has more or less vanished (along with the class-bound amateur ethos with which it was closely related), and in situ spectators tend to behave today as they have through most of recorded history. As the anthropologist Christian Bromberger noted in his exemplary study of French and Italian soccer fans, "A passion for football cannot be nourished by the pleasure of pure contemplation."[1] Sports crowds identify emotionally with athletes whom they feel to be their representatives. And they let the world know it. There are many other things that now need to be said about sports crowds, but this chord—partisanship and disorder—will be the loudest.

The Past

Modern illusions about the dignity and decorum of Greek sports spectators should be dispelled along with Johann Joachim Winckelmann's romantic notion that Greek art was a manifestation of calmness and serenity. Spectators are hardly mentioned in the account of the funeral games for Patroclus in book 23 of the *Iliad,* but Homer does indicate that they were numerous and that they applauded loudly and "thundered approval." On a fragment from a sixth-century BC vase by Sophilos, we can see (and all but hear) Homer's heroes as they watch a chariot race. The tiny figures leap to their feet, wave their arms, and shout themselves hoarse.[2] It is an oddly familiar sight.

Olympian detachment and disinterested curiosity were no more evident at Olympia than on the plains of Ilium. During the games, the isolated site was crowded with visitors from the entire Greek world, which extended eastward to the far shores of the Black Sea and westward to the Mediterranean coast of Spain. The site was (and still is) fearfully hot and dry in midsummer, when the sacred games took place at the time of the second or third full moon after the summer solstice. In the fourth century BC, the Leonidaion was constructed to house wealthy or politically important visitors to the games, but most of the spectators had to be satisfied with sleeping in tents or with spending their nights under the stars. As late as the first century AD, after Roman benefactions had provided some minimal comforts, the philosopher Epictetus reminded his readers that Olympic crowds had to be stoical: "Do you not swelter? Are you not cramped and crowded? Do you not bathe badly? Are you not drenched whenever it rains? Do you not have your fill of tumult and shouting?"[3]

There is abundant evidence for this "tumult and shouting." The nineteenth-century scholar Johann Heinrich Krause, who is still the best modern source on Greek spectators, drawing not only on Epictetus but also on Pindar,

Isocrates, Philostratus, Polybius, Pausanias, and many other ancient sources, wrote vividly of the conduct of the crowd: "With what an indescribable enthusiasm those present dedicated themselves to the spectacle, with what a lively sense of participation did they share the athletes' feats and enact the outcome of the contests, how their spirits were excited by what they saw! They were impelled unconsciously to move their hands, to raise their voices, to jump from their seats, now with the greatest joy, now with the deepest pain."[4] The joy and the pain were the correlates of partisanship. Looking back, the modern Italian historian Roberto Patrucco concludes that the spectators behaved with the uninhibited "human passion" of modern sports spectators.[5] M. I. Finley and H. W. Pleket agree that Greek crowds were "as partisan, as volatile, and as excitable as at any other period of time."[6]

Intense partisanship meant, then as now, the potential for disorder. Enter the Hellanodikai, the officials who were in charge of the management of the Olympic games, and their assistants, who did the hard work of keeping the athletes and the spectators under control. The names of these assistants, *mastigophoroi* (whip bearers) and *rabdouchoi* (truncheon bearers), imply the crowd's reluctance to exercise self-restraint. (At Delphi's Pythian games, sacred to Apollo, the spectators were more Dionysian than Apollonian; their drunkenness was such a problem that they were forbidden to carry wine into the stadium.)

Whatever minimal decorum the Hellanodikai managed to impose at Olympia seems to have vanished completely during the chariot races in Hellenistic Alexandria, where the historian Dio Chrysostom condemned the outrageous behavior of the crowd:

When they enter the stadium, it is as though they had found a cache of drugs; they forget themselves completely, and shamelessly say and do the first thing that occurs to them. . . . At the games you are under the influence of some maniacal drug; it is as if you could not watch the proceedings in a civilized fashion. . . . When

you enter the stadium, who could describe the yells and uproar, the frenzy, the switches of color and expression in your faces, and all the curses you give vent to?[7]

Dio's repugnance matched that of modern journalists excoriating the "mindless" behavior of "football hooligans."

The Greeks of the *Iliad* were content that the funeral games in honor of fallen warriors terminated in symbolic death—that is, in athletic defeat—but the Romans celebrated funeral games in which the dead were honored by additional deaths. The first gladiatorial games, known in the plural as *munera*, were held in 246 BC by Marcus and Decius Brutus in honor of their deceased father. The *munera* consisted of three duels (six gladiators) and were held in the cattle market. One can assume that the number of spectators was fairly small and that there was no reference to unruly behavior. In the centuries that followed, there was an apparently irreversible tendency toward ludic inflation. The number of gladiators continually increased. The emperor Trajan, for instance, is said to have celebrated his victories over the Dacians, at the end of the first century AD, with combats among ten thousand gladiators, an extravagance surpassed by the naval battle staged by Claudius in AD 52 with nineteen thousand combatants.[8]

The crowds that gathered to experience this sanguine delight were immense and the arenas needed to contain them were huge. Because temporary arenas built of wood sometimes collapsed, killing large numbers of spectators and terrifying the rest, they were eventually replaced by monumental stone structures erected throughout the empire. The most famous of them was, of course, the Colosseum, more accurately referred to as the Flavian amphitheater because it was erected by the Flavian emperors Vespasian and his son Titus. This gigantic construction, finished in AD 80, seated fifty thousand. Despite their immensity, Roman arenas provided comforts unknown to Greek sports spectators. When we read that the arena at Pompeii provided the spectators with *vela et sparsiones* (awnings and perfumed sprays), we are apt to think of the luxury boxes of the domed stadia of modern American cities.

That the spectators preferred the gladiators to be free men rather than slaves or condemned criminals is clear from the remarks of Echion, a character in the *Satyricon* of Petronius, who speaks excitedly of an imminent show with skilled fighters, "and . . . not a slave in the batch."[9] Michael Grant's explanation for this preference is simple: "Free fighters were more sought after than slaves, presumably because they showed greater enthusiasm."[10] Georges Ville added that "the public preferred a free gladiator to a slave and a knight or a senator to an ordinary citizen."[11] Ressentiment also played a role. Nothing pleased the plebeian spectators more than the humbling of the high and mighty by the lowly. It was clearly a thrill to see one's rulers exposed for once to risks and hazards comparable to those encountered by ordinary mortals in their struggle to survive.

At the gladiatorial games, social hierarchy took spatial forms. In the amphitheaters at Arles, Nîmes, and probably in those of Rome as well, different "tribes" were seated in different *cunei* (wedges) of the stadium. Augustus had definite ideas about social rank and seating. Everyone, from senator to slave, had his assigned place. Armed guards reminded the spectators that external controls were ready to enforce order if internal restraint failed.

The poor had their place. Although most spectators paid for their seats, the *plebs frumentaria* (that is, those on the dole) had free tickets.[12] Neither poverty nor servile status was a bar to enthusiastic fandom. A funerary inscription for the slave Crescens informed posterity that he was keen on the Thracian style of gladiatorial combat.[13] The slave Davus, owned by the poet Horace, appears in the *Second Satire* as a fan who marvels "at the posters of athletes straining their muscles in combat."[14]

The *populus* that crowded the arena collected works of art that recalled for them their experiences at the *munera*. A common archeological find at Roman sites is an inexpensive clay lamp with gladiatorial motifs. Wealthy Romans bought bronze statuettes or commissioned murals and mosaics with images from the arena. In the *Satyricon*, Trimalchio has his favorite gladiator pictured on silverware.

Christians were not immune to the appeals of fandom. Augustine's disciple Alypius suffered a dramatic setback when he ventured into the amphitheater and was overcome: "For so soon as he saw that blood, he therewith drunk down savageness; nor turned away, but fixed his eye, drinking in frenzy, unawares, and was delighted with that guilty fight, and intoxicated with the bloody pastime."[15] Augustine's metaphors—drunkenness, intoxication—resonate from his age to ours. The spectators reacted to the sight of blood as if they were drugged or in an alcoholic frenzy.

Although many must have appreciated the skills of the highly trained combatants, others cared only for the outcome of the struggle, on which they often wagered considerable sums of money, or for the pleasure of deciding with a gesture—thumbs up or thumbs down—whether a wounded fighter lived or died.[16] Over time, the *munera* became increasingly sensationalistic and perverse:

> Soon bloodthirsty combats and magnificent scenery failed to excite the dulled nerves of the mob, aristocratic or vulgar; only things absolutely exotic, unnatural, nonsensical, tickled their jaded senses.[17]

Among the exotic treats were female gladiators. Two of them are depicted on a stele from Halicarnassus in Asia Minor.[18] The poet Juvenal—from whom we have the phrase "bread and circuses" (panem et circenses)—was, as expected, satirical about the (imaginary) spectacle of "women, breasts Amazon-naked," facing "wild boars at the games."[19] Less moralistic Romans were obviously excited by the sights of armed women. In the *Satyricon*, one of Trimalchio's guests complains of a poor gladiatorial show and anticipates a better one with "a girl who fights from a chariot."[20] When women fought, bare-breasted or not, an erotic frisson must have rippled through the crowd.

There was very little opposition to the gladiatorial games on the part of pagan moralists. Most educated Roman spectators seemed untroubled by the deaths of men and beasts. The philosopher-dramatist Seneca was among the handful of pagan writers who expressed the kind of horror that many twentieth-century critics feel at sports that are far less violent than the *munera*. For Seneca, the arena was the site of cruel and inhuman combats. His comment on the crowd was devastatingly succinct: "Mane leonibus et ursis homines, meridie spectatoribus suis obiciuntur" (In the morning they throw men to the lions and the bears; at noon, they throw them to the spectators).[21] Seneca's revulsion was exceptional; most Romans shared Cicero's conviction that the *munera* provided the spectators with an exemplary image of manly fortitude.[22] The poet Ovid was also upbeat about bloodshed, urging women to display their physical charms in the stadium, "where the sands are sprinkled with crimson."[23]

Christian moralists were, not surprisingly, sustained and vehement in their denunciations of the games. Tertullian's second-century tract, *De Spectaculis*, set the pattern for subsequent generations of patristic invective and protest. His objections were partly to the violence in the amphitheater and partly to the appalling hysteria of the spectators. "Look at the populace coming to the show—mad already. . . . One frenzy, one voice!"[24] Christian moralists were also horrified by the idolatry of the games. Fallen gladiators were jabbed with hot irons by a slave dressed as the god Mercury (to be certain that death was not feigned). Another slave, in the garb of Dis Pater, dragged the corpse away, after which the dead man's blood was offered to Jupiter Latiaris by the priest who served that deity. Small wonder, then, that Christian philosophers expressed fear for the spectator's soul. Novitian exclaimed, "Idolatria . . . ludorum omnium mater est!" (Idolatry is the mother of all these games!)[25]

Considering the level of violence of gladiatorial combat and the spectators' powder keg of religious, racial, ethnic, and class differences, one marvels that the Roman arena did not explode into disorderly riot. At least once, it did. The name "Pompeii" evokes visions of volcanic catastrophe, but the wealthy town was also the scene of a disaster that the inhabitants brought on themselves. The historian Tacitus reports that tumults erupted there during the *munera*, after which the town was for a decade deprived of its right to stage gladiatorial games. This singular episode of spectator violence was, however, very unusual. There was, in fact, an "almost total absence of documented riots."[26]

Paradoxically, the relatively nonviolent chariot races provoked spectator violence that rose to levels unknown among the fans of the *munera*. Like modern football hooligans, the Byzantine Empire's "circus factions" were organized groups of fanatically partisan fans. The factions—the "Blues" and the "Greens"—were a menace to civil society and even to the Byzantine state. In Constantinople, the rioting factions set fire to the city's wooden hippodromes so often—in 491, 498, 507, and 532—that the authorities finally rebuilt them in stone.[27] Many times during the fifth and sixth centuries, spectator violence increased to the point where troops were repeatedly called on to restore order. In 507, for example, after a victory by the immensely popular charioteer Porphyrius, the jubilant Greens ran wild and, in the course of the riot, burned Antioch's synagogue, a quite typical instance of ancillary anti-Semitism.[28]

The worst of these outbreaks occurred during the reign of Justinian. On January 13, 532, supporters of the Blues and Greens joined forces to prevent executions that were about to take place in Constantinople's hippodrome. On January 14, the emperor acceded to demands that he dismiss John of Cappodocia and other unpopular officials. On January 18, the mob proclaimed a new emperor to whom a number of panicky senators paid hasty homage. Fortunately for Justinian, his most capable general, Belisarius, arrived in time to quell the disturbance—at the cost of an estimated thirty thousand lives.[29] In comparison with this bloodbath, the worst episodes of modern sports-related violence seem relatively innocuous.

Confronted with the plain fact that the factions in the hippodrome were far more disorderly and destructive than the spectators in the arena, no one can plausibly contend that the violence of the sport determines the violence of the crowd. The size of the crowd must be a factor, but the difference in capacity between the Colosseum and the Circus Maximus was surely not great enough to explain the radically different behavior of the spectators. There is no reason to believe that the number of soldiers posted to keep order varied significantly from one site to the other. The solution to the puzzle may be that sports fans identify more intensely, bond more tightly, with teams than with individuals. Eric Hobsbawm, thinking of Benedict Arnold's famous definition of nationhood and referring specifically to soccer football, expressed this thought succinctly: "The imagined community of millions seems more real as a team of eleven named people."[30]

Representational sport of the kind referred to by Hobsbawm was understood by Pliny the Younger. In a letter, he condemned the "childish passion" of ignorant fans who cheered mindlessly for the Blues or the Greens but cared little for "the speed of the horses or the drivers' skill." Indeed, commented Pliny, "if the colors were to be exchanged in mid-course during a race, [the fans] would transfer their favor and enthusiasm and rapidly desert the famous drivers and horses whose names they shout. . . . Such is the popularity and importance of a worthless shirt."[31]

Although medieval sports spectators were an unruly lot, their disorders never approached the level of tumult and rampage exhibited by Byzantine circus factions. The main reason for this lower level of violence was the much smaller scale of medieval sports. The grandest tournaments were diminutive affairs compared with the races in the Circus Maximus or in the hippodromes of Constantinople and Alexandria. The two thousand persons attending the tournament at Sandricourt near Pontoise in 1493 were a mere 1 percent of the Roman crowd that cheered for the Blues and the Greens.[32]

In medieval times, most of the sports-related violence was perpetrated by the participants rather than by the onlookers. The explanation is simple. For the medieval knight, the line between tournament and battlefield, between mock and real warfare, was thin and easily transgressed. "Games resembled war and war resembled games," writes the French scholar-diplomat Jean Jusserand. "The union of warfare and games was so close that it is frequently difficult to decide if a given activity ought to be classified under one rubric or the other."[33] Frequently, one merged into the other. At a tournament held at Chalons in 1274, for example, when Edward I of England was illegally seized by the Comte de Chalons, whom he had challenged, a brawl broke out in which several people were killed.[34] When a group of squires held a tournament at Boston Fair in 1288, the fact that one side dressed as monks and the other costumed itself as canons of the church failed to prevent a riot. The fair was sacked and part of the town burned.[35] It is impossible to say exactly how much of the mayhem at Rochester, Chalons, Boston, and elsewhere can be attributed to the spectators rather than to the combatants because medieval chroniclers were seldom interested in the former. We can infer a good deal, however, from the fact that German towns were compelled to recruit hundreds of armed men to keep order while tournaments were in progress. Augsburg was said, in 1442, to have hired two thousand men to keep the peace.[36] And we do have at least one instance of a rampage by a mostly *bürgerlich* crowd in fourteenth-century Basel. A bloody tumult broke out after a number of citizens were trampled by mounted noblemen. Several knights were killed.[37]

In time, as the "civilizing process" brilliantly analyzed by Norbert Elias[38] transformed medieval violence into the relatively pacific behavior of the Renaissance, as knights in armor became courtiers dressed in silk and satin, tournaments evolved from ludic warfare into elaborately allegorical pageants within which armed combat played a very minor role. The perfection of military prowess became secondary, and the tournament became a theatrical production in which fitness to rule was associated with fineness of sensibility.

Typical of the Renaissance tournament was the famous Pas de la Bergère that René d'Anjou staged at Tarascon in 1449. The knights who performed at this tournament were costumed as shepherds, and the mise-en-scène included a thatched cottage occupied by a "shepherdess." Elaborate decor was as important as courtly deportment. Chivalric combat was "entirely absorbed into the fanciful disguisings originally designed as an adornment to it."[39] René described the event in his *Traictié de la Forme et Devis d'ung Tournoy,* a compulsively detailed etiquette book regulating exits and entrances, proper verbal formulas, and appropriate attire. Little is said of the clash of weapons. Jean Verdon, a modern authority on medieval leisure, comments that "René, who adored sumptuous festivals, was essentially interested in ceremony and costume; he regulated the minutest detail; but he did not indicate how the jousts were to be carried out."[40] When the Duke of Buckingham staged a grand tournament at Westminster in 1501, the focus of attention was on the pageant cars. They were a phantasmagoria of dwarves, giants, wild men, and allegorical animals (including a unicorn that followed the rule book for mythic behavior and laid its head upon a virgin's lap). And the jousts? They were "inept."[41]

At these events, which were more folderol than sports contests, lords and ladies performed and lords and ladies were the principal spectators, but they were not the only ones. The tournament functioned most impressively as a theater of privilege and power when the ruled were present to observe, admire, and be awed by their rulers. The crowd was segregated, just as it was in the Roman arena, but it was composed of men and women from every social class. When Antoine, the Bastard of Burgundy, accepted the challenge of Anthony Woodville, Lord Scales, the entire city of London seems to have been as excited as a modern metropolis hosting the Olympic Games or soccer football's World Cup Finals. When the tournament began, at Smithfield in the spring of 1467, a public holiday was proclaimed, and thousands made their way to the site. Below the king's box were three tiers for knights and squires. Across from them was a stage for the Lord Mayor and his aldermen. Commoners unable to shove their way into the enclosure climbed nearby trees to catch a glimpse of the jousts, which were disappointing, and the pageantry, which was marvelous.[42] When a tournament was held in a treeless urban square, which was often the case in the fifteenth and sixteenth centuries, city dwellers crowded into windows overlooking the site. The more adventurous among them clambered to the rooftops of adjacent buildings. The stands, windows, and roofs are carefully delineated in a print, dated 1570, which commemorates the 1559 tournament at which Henri II of France was fatally wounded.[43] At a tournament held in 1501 to celebrate the birth of Prince Arthur, son of Henry VII, there was a charge for admission, but Londoners cannot have been deterred by the expense. A contemporary chronicler reported that the throng was so thick that there "was no thynge to the yee but oonly visages and faces, without apperans of their bodies."[44]

The nascent bourgeoisie, excluded from active participation in knightly tournaments, staged archery matches. As archery guilds spread from Artois, Brabant, Flanders, and Picardy to northern France and to all of German-speaking central Europe, their annual meets, the Schützenfeste, evolved into major urban festivals combining a number of different sports with pageants, banquets, dances, drunkenness, buffoonery, and the pleasures of illicit sex.[45] At the grand archery matches held in Augsburg in 1509 on the occasion of a visit by Holy Roman Emperor Maximilian I, the entertainments included footraces for male and female attendants and servants, ninepin contests, horse races, and a tournament for mounted knights.[46] Footraces held in conjunction with archery meets were widely accepted as ways for young women to display their athleticism for the male spectators' admiration or mockery.[47]

Inevitably, the excitement of a holiday, intensified by the consumption of alcohol, meant a good deal of rowdy behavior. In German-speaking central Europe there was usually a Pritschenkönig (king of the whip) who combined the roles of police chief and poet laureate. He was expected to keep order and to provide festive verses.[48] He was not always equal to the task. Quarrels that began at a meet in Konstanz, in 1458, culminated in a war against the nearby city of Zurich.[49] There were, however, relatively few incidents of this sort. Good-natured interaction seems to have been the rule rather than the exception. When too many Nürnbergers crowded about the stand from which the winners were to receive their prizes, the affable donors simply passed the prizes over their heads to the proud victors. Cheers then drowned out the laudatory remarks intended to accompany the awards.[50]

Medieval peasants played a rough-and-tumble game from which, centuries later, all the modern "codes" of football evolved. Research into the crowds that gathered to watch a game of football is pointless because there were no crowds. When village met village to celebrate the vernal equinox with a lively match, everyone got into the game—men and women, adults and children, clergy and laity. Everyone was a participant. As a contemporary commented, "Neyther maye there be anye looker on at this game, but all must be actours." And if someone came simply to watch, "being in the middest of the troupe, [he] is made a player."[51]

It is common knowledge that the spectators who attend an equestrian competition like dressage are not members of the same social set as the sports fans who prefer NASCAR races or snooker contests. In contrast, the sports spectacles of ancient Rome seem to have been equally attractive to men and women of every social class. There were doubtless some differences. Greek-style athletics were probably more popular with the wealthy than with the plebeians, but there were no ancient sociologists to collect the data from which to connect the dots. At some point—during the Renaissance? in early modern times?—sports spectators began to experience the ludic equivalent of the division of labor. The crowd that gathered to bet on the outcome of a cockfight in the slums of London was obviously different in its social composition from the Restoration courtiers who rode out of town with Charles II to wager on the races at Newmarket.

It was at this time that divergence on the basis of social class became too obvious to overlook. Although Joseph Strutt asserted, early in the nineteenth century, that "blood sports" attracted only "the lowest and most despicable part of the [English] people,"[52] there is ample evidence that, as late as Tudor times, cockfights, bearbaiting, and bullbaiting were as popular among the elite as among the common folk. Henry VIII was fond enough of cockfights to add a pit to Whitehall, and his daughter, Elizabeth I, prohibited theaters from opening on Thursdays because they interfered with "the game of bear-baiting, and like pastimes, which are maintained for her Majesty's pleasure."[53] A century later, middle-class Englishmen like Samuel Pepys and John Evelyn felt differently. After observing a bearbaiting, on August 14, 1666, Pepys wrote that it was "a very rude and nasty pleasure."[54] Evelyn's dislike of animal sports was equally evident. He wrote on June 16, 1670, he was "forc'd to accompanie some friends to the Bear-garden . . . Where was Cock *fighting*, *Dog-fighting*, Beare and *Bull baiting*, it being a famous day for all these butcherly Sports, or rather barbarous cruelties."[55] As early as 1737, the *Gentleman's Magazine* condemned "the rude Exercises of Cock-Throwing, Bull-baiting, Prize-fighting, and the like Bear-garden Diversions (not to mention the more genteel Entertainment of Cock-fighting)." The editors, sounding very much like a modern critic of televised violence, went on to say that brutal sports inspired "the Minds of Children and young People with a savage Disposition and Ferity of Temper highly pleased with Acts of Barbarity and Cruelty."[56] It was still possible in Hogarth's day to find respectable men at a cockfight, but the currents of middle-class opinion, strongly influenced by evangelical religion, ran strongly against animal sports.

The social composition of the "fancy" who crowded around the prize ring was a bimodal mix of titled aristocrats and the urban mob. The Tex Rickards and Don Kings who promote twentieth-century boxing matches have often risen from the same social class as the men they pit against one another, but eighteenth-century fights were likely to be arranged by noble patrons of lower-class pugilists. The Duke of Cumberland, for example, was known for his sponsorship of John Broughton, considered to be England's champion. When Broughton lost his title in 1750, his patron, having backed him with an excess of confidence, was poorer by several thousand pounds.[57]

Turn-of-the-century observers often insisted that everyone joined the crowds that followed the fights. Pierce Egan, the first great sportswriter, described the crowd of thirty thousand gathered in 1824 for the Tom Spring-John Langan bout as "a union of all ranks, from the *brilliant* of the highest class . . . down to the *Dusty Bob* graduation in society; and even a *shade* or two below that. Lots of the UPPER HOUSE, THE LOWER house, and the *flash* house."[58] The American writer Washington Irving agreed: "What is the Fancy itself, but a chain of easy communication, extending down from the peer to the pick-pocket, through the medium of which a man of rank may find he has shaken hands at three removes, with the murderer on the gibbet."[59] If there was a chain, its middle links were missing. During the Regency, members of Parliament did appear at many fights, just as a number of American celebrities appear at

ringside for the monthly "fight of the century," but middle-class men were nowhere to be seen, and the members of Parliament were greatly outnumbered by those whom Egan described as cockneys or as "yokels" whose faces "exhibited *gape-seed* enough to have filled a corn-chandler's shop."[60]

Fight crowds included a number of disreputable women. The German traveler Zacharias Conrad von Uffenbach encountered one of them, whom he described as "rather vociferous." She proudly assured him "that two years ago she had fought another female in this place without stays and in nothing but a shift."[61] In one of Thomas Rowlandson's finest prints, *The Prize Fight* (1787), a few tubby females cavort among the generally nondescript spectators. On the whole, however, fight fans were and still are overwhelmingly male.

Were they violent? Far less often than might have been expected. If they were like dogs baying for the taste of blood, which is how moralists have characterized them, their bark was far worse than their bite. The typical transgression was a surge forward to disrupt a bout in which the favorite was about to be beaten.

Pugilism flourished on the margins of respectable society, condemned by the reformist middle classes, for whom the sight of a disorderly crowd was tantamount to an image of anarchy. Cricket crowds were quite another matter. They embodied the imagined community. By the late eighteenth century, cricket had become the archetypical English game. Nostalgia played a role. As England became increasingly urban and industrial, cricket—a game with ineradicable pastoral connotations—became increasingly important as an assertion of reassuring continuity. The industrial workers of Manchester, whose misery Friedrich Engels documented, had little in common with their employers, but it was a comfort to the comfortable to think that country squires still bowled for cricket teams that included their servants, the village wheelwright, and an assortment of other rural worthies.

Our Village, Mary Russell Mitford's evocation of English life in the early nineteenth century, includes a famous account of a cricket match. "I doubt," wrote Mitford, "if there be any scene in the world more animating or delightful than a cricket match." The spectators were "retired cricketers, veterans of the green, the careful mothers, the girls, and all the boys of two parishes. . . . There was not a ten-years-old urchin, or a septuagenary woman in the parish, who did not feel an additional importance, a reflected consequence, in speaking of 'our side.'"[62] John Nyron, the first great chronicler of the game, matched Mitford's fictionalized description with his own versions of the pastoral. In his books, whole counties turn out to watch their representatives. They never interfere with the play, not even when the ball is hit into their midst. "Like true Englishmen, they . . . give an enemy fair play."[63]

Mitford and Nyren romanticized. There were frequent disorders at eighteenth-century cricket matches. In 1744, nobles and gentlemen complained of unruly crowds at games at London's Artillery Ground. When Leicester met Coventry in 1787, there was "a pitched battle in the streets of Hinckley." Five years later, Westminster boys broke windows on their way to a game, and an irate citizen was taken to court for firing shots over their heads. The answer to the threats of riot was to fence the grounds and charge admission.[64]

By the middle of the next century, however, cricket crowds had become less fractious. They were patient, a necessary virtue when cricket matches lasted for days. They were partisan, which was inevitable when teams represented towns or counties, but they were—for the most part—orderly and well behaved. Although the Marylebone Cricket Club, the sport's governing body, enlarged the stands at Lord's to hold as many as thirty thousand spectators, historians agree that crowd control was not a problem. "Victorian cricket crowds behaved very well indeed."[65] Disorder was "generally verbal rather than physical."[66]

Although sentimental historians have claimed that cricket crowds were socially inclusive and that men and women from all ranks "jostled one another happily,"[67] the spectators' "civilized" behavior was largely a consequence of social exclusion. It was possible for anyone to pause on the way to a pub in order to observe a few minutes of cricket as it was played on the town common, but county cricket and international tests occurred in fenced grounds open only to those affluent enough to pay subscription costs or entrance fees. The ruffians whom one might have cautioned ("That's not cricket!") were absent. The game, opined a haughty leader of the Marylebone Cricket Club, was "none the worse for their absence."[68]

The decisive role of social class can be observed in the contrast between English and Australian cricket. Australia was, quite self-consciously, a much more egalitarian society. The Melbourne Cricket Club went against the grain of Australia's egalitarian culture and attempted to block lower-class spectators by charging a shilling for entrance to the grounds, approximately one-sixth of a worker's daily wages. For admission to the first test against England, in 1877, the club charged a prohibitive four shillings. The elitists' effort to keep the game to themselves was, however, doomed. As cricket grew increasingly popular, as it came to be perceived as a manifestation of Australian identity, working-class Australians played and watched. The "larrikins" (rough young men) among the spectators began to invade the pitch and cause delays in the game. On February 8, 1879, some two thousand of them stormed the grounds of the Sydney Cricket Club and attacked the visiting English team. Although middle-class fans strove to preserve the English tradition of polite applause for both sides, working-class Aussies developed a lusty countertradition of "barracking" friend and foe alike. Newspapers complained about the "unmanly behavior" of the "roughs" who jeered to unsettle the players, but working-class fans had a different notion of masculinity. They reveled in the fine (and sometimes gross) art of comic insult and clever invective. The stentorian wit of the most famous Australian cricket fan earned him a place in the *Australian Dictionary of Biography*.[69]

There was a time when cricket seemed destined to be as central to American culture as it was to Australian. The game flourished in the posh residential areas of Philadelphia and Germantown. Most of the players were ethnically English, and nearly all of them were middle-class in behavior if not in income.[70] It was baseball, however, not cricket, that became America's archetypical summer game. Baseball, which evolved from the English children's game of rounders, began as a sport for middle-class gentlemen. Historians now agree that New York's Knickerbockers were "the first properly organized baseball club"[71] and that the team played a baseball game on October 6, 1845. There are references in the *New York Herald* to earlier bat-and-ball clubs,[72] but the Knickerbocker rules were probably different enough from earlier rules to credit the club with the invention of baseball. At any rate, on June 19, 1846, they played an historic game against the New York Nine, which the hapless Knickerbockers lost by a score of 23 to 1.[73] The lopsided score may be explained by the fact that the Knickerbockers were a distinctively middle-class club, "more expert with the knife and fork at post-game banquets than with bat and ball on the diamond."[74]

No matter that baseball's founding fathers turn out to have been gourmets and that the Knickerbockers were soon overshadowed by other teams. Their version of the game spread quickly. The Gothams (1850) were followed by the Excelsiors (1854) and a number of other middle-class teams. The first viable plebeian clubs seem to have been the Eckfords of Greenpoint and the Atlantics of Jamaica, both founded in 1856. It was they—the dockworkers, teamsters, bricklayers, and carpenters, not the merchants and young professionals—who became the sport's typical players and typical fans.

Despite its claim to be the "national game," despite its hold on an extraordinary number of poets and novelists, baseball charmed the masses rather than the classes. During the Gay Nineties, factory workers and office clerks sang "Take Me Out to the Ball Game" and clambered aboard the newly manufactured trolley cars that did exactly that.

In the post–Civil War period, baseball's appeal was especially strong among working-class Irish Americans. From their ranks came the game's most popular player, Michael Kelly, known (and admired) as "a free spender, a fancy dresser, and an avid pursuer of night life." He was a womanizer, a gambler, a resourceful cheater, and an idol of the "Hibernian" fans. They sang his praises, literally, in "Slide, Kelly, Slide."[75]

Nineteenth-century baseball fans of every ethnic group were notably violent in verbal if not in physical behavior. C. L. R. James, the West Indian historian, remarks on this in *Beyond a Boundary* (1963). As a child in Trinidad, he had internalized the ethos of cricket. Visiting the United States, expecting that American baseball fans shared his commitment to the code of fair play, he was astonished and dismayed at the lack of sportsmanship he witnessed. Americans bragged of baseball fans whose hearts were "full of fraternity and good will,"[76] but James "heard the howls of anger and range and denunciation . . . hurled at the players as a matter of course."[77]

In 1883, the *Boston Globe* commented that "every class, every station, every color and every nationality will be found at a baseball match."[78] Albert G. Spalding made an even more extravagant claim, asserting that Chicago's churches and theaters had "no finer class of people" than the fans of his White Stockings. Baseball fans were, in fact, "the best class of people in Chicago."[79] The reality was quite otherwise. It was precisely because the urban elite was *not* singing "Take Me Out to the Ball Game" that Spalding and other baseball entrepreneurs worked as hard as they did to improve the public image of the game's players and its "cranks" (as the fans were then known).

One way to do this was to raise the price of the tickets until they were the equivalent of roughly a fifth of a workman's daily wages.[80] Another way was to lure female spectators through the newly invented turnstiles and into the grandstands. Hoping to replace rough urban men with refined urbane women, the owners instituted "Ladies' Days." The custom was to admit women free if accompanied by a "gentleman" (defined as any male with the price of a ticket). Ladies' Days had the enthusiastic support of the press. The *New York Chronicle* opined that "the presence of an assemblage of ladies purifies the moral atmosphere" and represses "all the outburst of intemperate language which the excitement of the contest so frequently induces."[81] The *Sporting News* also noted that men were "more choice in the selection of adjectives" when the women were present.[82] In the absence of statistical data, no one can say precisely what percentage of the nineteenth-century baseball crowd was made up of women, but the impressionistic evidence indicates that the spectators remained overwhelmingly male. A September 1897 excursion photograph of Boston's Royal Rooters, for example, shows not a single female fan bold enough to accompany her male relatives to Baltimore.[83]

By this time, soccer football had eclipsed cricket as England's most popular sport. In terms of social class, football's trajectory was remarkably similar to baseball's. The game began as a middle-class pastime, a nineteenth-century adaptation of folk football (which survived, in some parts of England and Scotland, well into the twentieth century). The game was initially codified by fourteen English collegians in 1848 on the basis of the various rules for a number of different games they had played at Eton and other public schools.[84] The first football club for adults was founded in Sheffield in 1857.[85] Initially, Sheffield FC and Sheffield Wednesday FC played their home games at the Yorkshire County Cricket Ground at Bramall Lane.[86] Cricket clubs everywhere midwifed football clubs and were then dwarfed by them.

The name *soccer* (from "Association") derives from the fact that the sport was nationally organized by the Football Association, founded on October 26, 1863, a day that scholars agree was "the most important date in the modern history of football."[87] The London-based founders, mostly graduates of Oxford and Cambridge, thoughtfully limited the duration of the football season (September 1 to April 30) so that it did not conflict with cricket's.[88] The game spread with astonishing rapidity. Birmingham had one club in 1874, twenty in 1876, one hundred fifty-five in 1880.[89] Liverpool had two in 1878 and over one hundred fifty in 1886.[90] The "old boys" wanted to keep the game for themselves, but the game was quickly diffused downward through the social strata. Aston Villa FC and the Bolton Wanderers, both founded in 1874, were typical of the many clubs that recruited their first members from the congregations of churches and chapels. Within a few years, other clubs destined to figure grandly in the annals of English sports were organized by the employees of industrial enterprises. Manchester United began as Newton Heath FC, founded in 1880 by railroad workers, and Coventry City FC had its start as a club organized by the workers at Singer's bicycle factory. In 1895, laborers at the Thames Iron Works founded a team that became West Ham United FC. The competitive balance tipped in 1883 when a team of Lancashire workmen—Blackburn Olympic Football Club—defeated the Old Etonians to win the Football Association's annual Cup Final. Blackburn's team included three weavers, a spinner, a cotton operator, an iron worker, a plumber, and a dental assistant.[91]

Between 1875 and 1884, a time when most fans were probably white-collar employees or skilled craftsmen, average attendance at the Cup Final was less than five thousand. Between 1905 and 1914, when soccer had become "the people's game," average attendance was nearly eighty thousand.[92] By that time, most of the fans were definitely working-class men. Indeed, the connection between soccer and the working class was so strong, and the feelings for the game were so intense, that "it was no exaggeration for some to describe football . . . as a 'religion.' The football grounds of England were the Labour Party at prayer."[93] The religious metaphor was also applied to the increasingly capacious stadia erected in the early twentieth century; they were dubbed "modernity's cathedrals." Such language became even more appropriate in 1927 when the Anglican hymn "Abide with Me" was introduced into the Cup Final program.[94]

The habitus of working-class spectators was often offensive to middle-class sensibilities. "The multitude flock to the field," wrote Charles Edwardes, "in their workaday dirt, and with their workaday adjectives very loose on their tongues."[95] It was not just the adjectives that offended men like Edwardes. Working-class spectators were seldom restrained by the canons of good sportsmanship that mandated applause for a jolly good play by the opposing team. Fans cheered for their home team and shouted insults at the visitors (a sorry lot, no doubt). Rough play on the field or a bad call by an official was occasionally followed by a barrage of rocks and bottles or by a pitch invasion. "Earth, small stones, rubbish of all sorts . . . began flying about our heads," wrote a spectator caught in an attack by Aston Villa fans who had been angered by a 5–1 loss to Preston North End. "Thicker and faster came the stones, showers of spittle covered us; we were struck at over the side [of our van] with sticks and umbrellas."[96] Were scenes of this sort common? As usual, the authorities disagree.[97] Disorder worried proper Victorians, but there was no need for a "moral panic." Although the average crowd for the Football Association's Cup Finals in the decade before World War I was 79,300, there were very few disturbances of any magnitude. Indeed, for all Football League games between 1895 and 1914, the average number of reported physical assaults came to little more than one a week, hardly a sign of a descent into anarchy.[98]

The Present

Between the 1890s and the 1950s, crowd disorders at football matches became less frequent as most working-class sports fans internalized middle-class notions of proper decorum. In the 1920s and 1930s, crowds were once again as large as they had been in Roman times. One hundred thousand or more spectators attended matches at London's Wembley Stadium, constructed in 1923, and they displayed remarkable self-restraint. The diminution of expressive (in contrast to) instrumental violence was a dramatic instance of the "civilizing process" described by Norbert Elias and his followers.

The curve of violence inflected upward during the last third of the twentieth century. Most of it consisted of hateful words and threatening gestures. In the United States, where the fans' repertory of invective has always included racial slurs, verbal assaults often became unutterably vile. To unnerve a basketball player whose father had been assassinated in Beirut, students at Arizona State University taunted him with chants of "PLO! PLO!"[99] When American fans regressed from verbal to physical violence, it was often in the form of a celebratory riot in which goalposts were torn down, shop windows smashed, and automobiles torched. In the wake of a championship, cities like Chicago or Detroit were liable to experience alcohol-abetted rampages by "feral packs of kids and criminals who loot, shoot and leave their hometowns awash in blood, bullets and broken glass."[100] In college towns, civil authorities came to expect postgame riots. The police learned to stand aside—far from the madding crowd's ignoble strife—and to contain rather than halt the mayhem.

The worst episodes of physical violence were probably those that erupted at high school football games where racial tensions aggravated traditional rivalries. When Washington's public and mostly black Eastern High School met private and mostly white St. John's High School in football,

5A 'Multitude': English

Susan Schuyler

Although the word *multitude* has shifted in its history to refer more frequently to people (particularly in reference to the body politic), its definition has nonetheless remained fairly intact since its introduction into Middle English from Old French, which in turn derived from the Latin *multitudo*, a derivation of the Latin root *multus*, meaning "much" or "many." Since its early history, the emphasis contained within the word refers more to quantity than quality or character. It therefore lacks some of the implied pejorative meanings of similar words such as *crowd, mass,* or *mob.* In Middle English, *multitude,* generally followed by the preposition *of,* meant: "(a) a large number of persons or things . . . (b) a large amount, abundance, greatness; mass; (c) a crowd, host, army, mob, flock; a great progeny; (d) a sum, size, total number (not necessarily large); plurality, multiplicity" (Middle English Dictionary).

In Middle and Renaissance English, *multitude* was frequently used to refer to abstract or uncountable objects or feelings. Some attempts seem to have been made to add a level of precision to the term. John Lydgate's *Serpent of Division* (1422) somewhat confusingly measures the multitude of a cohort: "To declare þe number and þe multitude of a Cohorte . . . þer be two maner Cohortes, þe more and þe lasse, & þe more . . . conteynyth fyve hunderid." Judging by Lambarde's note in *Eiren* (1581) on "Three or more in one companie (which the law properly calleth a multitude),"

on November 22, 1962, there was sporadic violence throughout the game among the fifty thousand spectators. When the game ended with St. John's ahead by a score of 20 to 7, an estimated two thousand black youths attacked the white spectators, whom they punched, kicked, and struck with bottles. Five hundred people were injured.[101] Violence of this sort—black on white or white on black—occurred so frequently in the 1960s and 1970s that some cities and towns refused to allow the traditional Friday night football game or permitted it only with the proviso that spectators be banned.

Violence committed by sports fans may or may not be a much greater problem in the United Kingdom than in the United States, but it is unquestionably more salient, more frequently covered by the mass media, and far more frequently analyzed by government commissions and academic researchers. The incidence of "football hooliganism" is probably greater in the UK than elsewhere. And it is probably more political.

Although Ian Taylor has argued in his early work that England's "football hooligans" were engaged in a "proletarian resistance movement,"[102] the rhetoric of hooliganism comes more often from the political right than from the political left. In the 1980s, hooligan supporters of Leeds United adopted the Nazi salute and "the terrace supporters of West Ham, Chelsea, Brentford, and Millwall [were] notorious for their pathological displays of fascist regalia."[103] Tottenham Hotspur FC, a club that was thought to have considerable support among London's Jews, was the target of anti-Semitic scurrility. Crystal City supporters chanted, "Spurs are on the way to Belsen, Hitler's gonna gas 'em."[104] Chelsea fans had a choral variant:

Spurs are on the way to Auschwitz
Hitler's gonna gas 'em again. . . .
The yids from Tottenham,
The yids from White Hart Lane.[105]

When English football clubs began to recruit black players, supporters were ready to substitute racism for anti-Semitism. John Barnes took the field for Liverpool in 1988 and Everton fans greeted him with cries of "Niggerpool! Niggerpool!"[106] The permutations of racism were, however, more complex than those of anti-Semitism because—contrary to the National Socialists' crazed ethnology—it is easier to identify a black person than it is to recognize a Jew. After calling Birmingham's John Fashanu a "fucking nigger," one of Millwall's fans turned to a black Millwall supporter and explained, "Sorry mate, no offence. I am talking to that black bastard on the pitch!"[107] Tony Witter, who played for Millwall, recalled a similar moment when Millwall fans shouting racist obscenities assured him that *he,* Witter, was "all right." Witter concluded, "I think they just see a blue shirt when they look at me. But with Ian Wright they see a red shirt, then they see a black face. But do they see my colour?"[108] Apparently, they did not. They were like those circus factions whom Pliny the Younger described as fanatically loyal to "a worthless shirt." In Witter's case, the shirt was a sign of identity—Millwall player—that trumped his racial identity, just as, for most Britons, nationalism trumps racism when athletes like Daley Thompson and Tessa Sanderson receive Olympic gold medals to the stirring sound of "God Save the Queen."

During the final decades of the twentieth century, football hooliganism went global. Bands of young men on the European continent or in Latin America consciously imitated English "hard ones." The Austrian *Terrorszene* and the (mostly verbal) violence of Italian "ultras," for instance, both seem to be direct consequences of cultural diffusion from the United Kingdom.[109] For many young Belgians who have left school for dead-end jobs or no jobs at all, a sense of self was acquired at football games and the opportunity they afford for verbal and physical violence. Among these youths, the exchange of Nazi symbols was common.[110] Similarly, German hooligans were part of a youth culture that defined itself against *das Bürgerliche* by provocation, that is, by "smoking, drinking, wearing make-up, fucking [*Bumsen*], riding public transport without paying, and stealing."[111] Especially prominent among German hooligans were the "Ossies" from what was once the misnamed *Deutsche Demokratische Republik*. They were characterized as "skinheads who use football matches to scream their hatred of the world, brandishing swastikas and reviving memories of the pogroms."[112] Like their English counterparts, the German hooligans discovered that Nazi slogans—"Send Schalke [fans] to Auschwitz!"—upset respectable middle-class fans. It hardly mattered that the youths who shouted the slogans had very little idea of what happened at Auschwitz.[113] The young, working-class male hooligans from Bologna, a city with a strong communist tradition, showed the same predilection for fascist and Nazi symbols.[114] Yugoslav fans had a similar reputation for horrendous behavior.[115] In fact, some have argued that the epidemic of "virulent ethnic hatred" that ravaged Croatia, Bosnia, Serbia, and Kosova "appeared first among soccer fans."[116]

Argentine fans favored sexual taunts. The *barras bravas* (die-hard fans) were known for racist and homophobic chants in which they characterized Brazilian fans as "all niggers" and "all queer."[117] Among the chants of Boca supporters was one that went like this:

Hinchada, hinchada, hinchada—hay una sola
Hinchada es la de Boca que le rompe el culo a todas.

the word may have played a part in legal vocabulary. In general, however, *multitude* seems most applicable to the abstract. The phrase "multitude of synnes" originates in the Bible and appears throughout (primarily theological) writing of the Middle Ages. First Peter 4:8 of the Wycliffite Bible (early version ca. 1384) reads, "Charite couerith the multitude of synnes." This phrase is repeated in *Book to a Mother* (1400): "In charite, þat heleþ, as Seynt Ieme seyþ, multitude of synnes," and still enjoyed currency a century later, as seen in this passage from Alain Chartier's *Le Quadrilogue Invectif* (1500): "But and ther be enythinge þat puttith you vndir them it is nothinge ellis but the multude of your synnys."

Throughout its history, the term *multitude* has referred to crowds of various characters. Middle English Bibles use the word to describe heavenly or religious crowds as well as menacing crowds (such as "þe multitude of oure enymes" in the Prose version of the New Testament, ca. 1400, and the stone-wielding multitude of the Wycliffite translation of Ezekiel 16:40). Outside early religious literature, the term retains this semantic elasticity. The frequency with which the word was used in religious literature lent it an appropriate ring of spirituality in similar contexts. For example, Christopher Wordsworth's hymn "Hark the Sound of Holy Voices" (1862) includes the line, "Multitude, which none can number/Like the stars, in glory stands." Negative meanings often associated with crowds also proliferate in the use of the word, as in Shaftesbury's command in *Character* (1708): "To affect a superiority over the Vulgar, and to despise the Multitude," and Cowper's observation, "Books are . . . spells,/By which the magic art of shrewder wits/Holds an unthinking multitude enthrall'd"

(1784). At other times, the term remains strictly neutral. Oliver Goldsmith writes in *Natural History* (1776), "Our horses would scarcely, in this manner . . . continue their speed, without a rider, through the midst of a multitude."

The most significant change in the word's development is the usage of *the multitude* to refer not to a specific crowd of people located in a defined physical space, but the crowd of people (a more dispersed or figurative body) that compose the state. The use of *multitude* in reference to the physical body could help to explain the shift in meaning first, from the generic "many" to "many people," and then more specifically to the body politic. In Guy de Chauliac's *Grand Chirurgie* (ca. 1425), *multitude* acquires a technical sense (in direct opposition to the use of the term to measure abstract quanitities); Chauliac names in his surgery manual "multitude of veines," "multitude of teres," and "multitude of spirites." The use of *multitude* as a technical word to describe the inner workings of the body does not seem to be particular to Chauliac; the *Medical Works* in Glasgow (1425) also cites a "multitude of teres" as a medical symptom.

From the sixteenth century onward, *multitude*—or, more specifically, *the multitude*—appears in the English language as a reference to the body politic. In this usage, the connotations of the word align with the speaker or author's conception of *the people*. In *Henry VI* (First Folio,1623), Shakespeare includes the line, "Thou art not King: Not fit to gouerne and rule multitudes," an early example of the use of the word to identify the people of a state. Hobbes also refers to "a multitude of men" in the *Leviathan* (1651). Elsewhere, Shakespeare uses *the multitude* as a derogatory term, referring to "the rude multitude" in *Love's Labour's Lost*

Fans, fans, fans—the only real fan is
Boca's, who tears the assholes of all the others.[118]

When the verbal violence of late twentieth-century fans turned physical, hundreds, perhaps thousands, died. Analyses of the violent deaths that occurred at football matches must discriminate, however, between the accidental and the intentional.

The textbook cases of accidental death occurred at Glagow's Ibrox Park and at Sheffield's Hillsborough Stadium. The Ibrox disaster happened on April 5, 1902, during a match between England and Scotland. The collapse of a wooden stand plunged twenty-five people to their deaths and injured over five hundred others.[119] The Hillsborough disaster happened on April 15, 1989, in the course of a game between Liverpool FC and Nottingham Forest FC. Ninety-six Liverpool fans died. The deaths occurred when the police opened a gate and allowed hundreds of fans to rush into a fenced pen that was already overcrowded. Exits were locked, as a measure of crowd control, and people were crushed to death against a restraining fence, also installed to control the crowd.[120] Accidental tragedies of this sort are generic rather than sport-specific because they happen at rock concerts, nightclubs, and other venues where hundreds or thousands of people gather in an unsafe environment.

Most sport-specific catastrophes are the result of intentional violence that spirals out of control. In 1964, for instance, a Uruguayan referee disallowed a Peruvian goal that tied the score in a home game against Argentina. Peruvian fans rushed to the steel-link, barbed-wire-topped fence that blocked their way to the field of play. They smashed through the fence and set fire to the stadium. The police responded, not very helpfully, by firing tear gas into the crowd. The panicky fans then struggled to escape through the stadium's underground exits, but three of the seven exits were locked. Hundreds of people were crushed to death.[121]

The best known example of the unanticipated deadly consequences of intentional violence on the part of sports fans is the disaster that occurred on May 29, 1985, in Brussels's Heysel Stadium. During a European Cup Final (Liverpool FC versus Juventus of Turin), a gang of English hooligans charged a group of Juventus supporters and pushed them against a brick wall. The wall collapsed, and thirty-nine Italian fans were killed.[122] This incident did more than any other to propagate the image of English soccer fans as a deadly menace. In fact, since the Heysel catastrophe, the mere mention of "football hooliganism" calls to mind images of drunken skinheads waving the Union Jack, chanting obscenities, and assaulting fans whose main offense was that they were not English. Some scholars have attempted to counter this stereotype by calling attention to the prevalence of ritualized aggression in the form of taunts and gestures and to the determination of most hooligans to keep the violence verbal,[123] but there was more than enough physical assault to justify public concern and sociological investigation.[124]

Not all football fans are working-class hooligans enflamed by xenophobia and a bonfire of other irrational hatreds. Italian "Ultras" are drawn from *un univers hétérogène*.[125] Despite extremes of invective, Italian fans have generally acted with more restraint than British football hooligans. Equipped with drums, witty songs, gigantic banners, and color-coded scarves, the Ultras are noted more for their cynical humor than for a propensity to assault one another. Ridicule of one's opponent can be wonderfully imaginative. In a culture where relics of the saints are cherished, Italian fans offer to sell relics of a rival team's owner—along with a certificate of *in*authenticity.[126] The mix of sacred and secular is part of the fun. At the game, banners adorned with images of the local saint are likely to wave next to placards inscribed with obscenities in the local dialect.[127]

In still greater contrast to skinhead hooligans, Scotland's Tartan Army and Denmark's Danske Roligans (*rolig*, "peaceful") are ventures in the propagation of a jolly carnivalesque form of spectatorship.[128] Norwegian followers of British football have banded together in the Supporterunion for Britisk Fotball (1985) in bold repudiation of chauvinistic fandom.[129] There is even some evidence that British hooligans are less hooligan than they used to be. Media pundits and academic analysts agree that there really was less mayhem in 2000 than there had been in the previous decade. The tabloid press, which had always exaggerated the level of violence, had fewer occasions to predict the imminent end of western civilization. Along with the decline in the level of sports-related violence came a return of in situ spectators to football grounds. There had been a decline in attendance from 40 million spectators in 1949 to 16.5 million in 1985. By 1998, attendance was approaching 25 million.[130] Various explanations for the decline in hooliganism and the return of the spectators have been put forth. Supporters' clubs and fanzines called for civility. There was an increase in the number of security personnel and in the quickness of their response to disorder. On the plausible assumption that it is harder to be a real nutter while seated, the government recommended—and the Football Association agreed—that stadia should have seats for all spectators. Whatever the reason—moral suasion, the perception of greater safety, the reality of greater comfort—the incidence of football hooliganism diminished.

(First Folio,1623). Ben Jonson echoes this designation with "the beast, the multitude" (1640). Milton further injects pejorative connotations into the phrase "the multitude" in these lines from *Samson Agonistes* (1671): "The unjust tribunals, under change of times,/And condemnation of the ingrateful Multitude." This pejorative sense does not seem to be present in this excerpt from the *Junius Letters* (1769): "The multitude, in all countries, are patient to a certain point." As perceptions of "the people" shift following the revolutions of the late eighteenth and nineteenth centuries, the term *the multitude* assumes, at times, a more positive sense. For example, Ruskin states in *Question of Air* (1869), "The strength of the nation is in its multitude, not in its territory," and purports a more egalitarian theory of art in *Modern Painters*, "The multitude is the only proper judge of those arts whose end is to move the multitude." It is perhaps the elasticity of this word which has kept its meanings relatively stable, but also which dictates its less frequent usage in comparison to *crowd, masses*, or *mob*.[1]

5B Rolling Stones Play Free Concert at Altamont Speedway, December 6, 1969

Greil Marcus

I had seen the naked woman perhaps a dozen times during the day. Again and again she would run toward a man and rub her body against his. The man would offer some version of "Let's fuck" and the woman would begin to scream and run blindly back into the crowd. After a few minutes she would start all over again.

But now, in the dark, behind the stage, with only a little yellow light filtering through to where I was standing, waiting for the Rolling Stones to begin their first song, the woman looked different. As she passed by, her head on her chest, I realized her body was covered with dried blood. Her face was almost black with it. Someone had given her a blanket; she held it as if she'd simply forgotten to throw it away, and it dragged behind her as she walked.

Then I saw the fat man. Hours before—it seemed like days—he had leaped to his feet to dance naked to Santana, the first band of the day. Those sitting near the stage, as I was, noticed that he used the excuse of the music to stomp and trample the people around him. A squad of Hell's Angels, whom the Rolling Stones had hired for crowd control, came off the stage swinging weighted pool cues and beat the fat man to the ground. People pushed back against each other to get out of the way, then stopped and made peace signs. The fat man didn't understand what was

Some Explanatory Thoughts: Who They Are and Why They Do It

At the University of Leicester, Eric Dunning and a number of other Norbert Elias–influenced sociologists have applied "figurational sociology" to the analysis of British football hooliganism. The results of their research, and that of European scholars like Germany's Gunter A. Pilz, are clear. Of course there are a few young working-class women "among the thugs," and even a few young professional men, but they are as rare as blue-collar workers in luxury boxes. The typical "football hooligan" is a young, unskilled, unemployed or underemployed working-class man. Soccer pitches are a site where they are able to indulge in "aggro" (aggression) and let the world know that they are not at all happy with their lot in life. The socially acceptable agonistic polarities of a football game—it's by definition "us against them"—provide society's outsiders with a pretext for the expression of their frustrations, disappointments, alienation, and anger. That corporate managers and mass-media experts have robbed them of what was once felt to be "the people's game" is only one reason for their resentment. The soccer pitch and its surround are a highly visible stage upon which the marginalized can act out a generalized sense of deprivation and grievance.[131]

It is important to note that the ubiquity of television in the modern world has transformed the composition of in situ sports crowds. As older men, and women of all ages, opted for the domestic comforts of mediated spectatorship, young men became an increasingly large percentage of the sports crowd. We should also bear in mind the economic plight of the working class under Margaret Thatcher and her European and North American admirers. If the unemployed are significantly more likely than the employed to express their frustrations in the form of football hooliganism, which is indeed the case, football hooliganism is bound to fluctuate with the rise and fall of the rate of unemployment.

To have said this much is to have begun the task of explanation. It is also, unfortunately, to encourage the misguided attempt to justify verbal and physical violence as a socially useful catharsis. It is the cherished belief of many sportswriters that spectatorship is a relatively harmless way for us to rechannel and release our innate and our culturally induced aggressiveness. Spectator sports are allegedly a safety valve, a way for the frustrated to blow off steam. Although this popular theory, fashioned by Freudian analysts from materials provided by Aristotle's theory of tragedy, has an impressive genealogy, empirical research has thoroughly disconfirmed it. It is worth some time to attempt, yet again, to cut the neck of the theoretical hydra.

Apropos of the alleged catharsis experienced by sports spectators, there is a rare consensus among non-Freudian social psychologists. This consensus derives from two types of experiment. In the first type, sports spectators are tested by pencil-and-paper or projective techniques before and after they attend sports events. In one such study conducted in the United States, obliging football fans submitted to interviewers who asked them thirty-six questions from the Buss-Durkee Hostility Inventory. The authors used the same technique to test spectators at a gymnastics meet. They concluded that there was no support whatsoever for the catharsis theory. Indeed, the scores demonstrated increased rather than decreased aggressiveness after the sports event. This was the case even when the fan's favored team won, which provides additional evidence against the theory that aggression is the result of frustration.[132] A replication with Canadian spectators who filled out the questionnaires before and after contests in wrestling, ice hockey, and swimming also called into question the assumption that sports events foster "goodwill and warm interpersonal relations."[133]

Similar results were obtained from paper-and-pencil studies that used the Thematic Apperception Test (TAT) and sentence-completion techniques to investigate the aggressiveness of football, basketball, and wrestling spectators. Analyzing the data gathered by these projective techniques, Edward Thomas Turner concluded austerely, "The results . . . do not support the cathartic or purge theory of aggression. Actually, the significant increase in the number of aggressive words after the football and basketball contests seem [sic] to support the contention that the viewing of violent or aggressive acts tends to increase the aggressiveness of the viewer."[134]

The second type of test involves a comparison of responses of subjects to violent and nonviolent films. For instance, the subjects of the experiment see either a travelogue or a filmed boxing match. They are then tested for their willingness to act aggressively against another person. This willingness is measured by the amount of electric shock the subjects *think* they administer to another person in what they are told is an experiment to test the effects of punishment on learning. (No shock is delivered, but naive subjects are unaware of this happy fact.) Twenty-five years of laboratory experiments conducted by Leonard Berkowitz and his students demonstrated conclusively that subjects who observe the boxing film are significantly more willing to administer a dangerously high level of electric shock than are subjects who see films of a travelogue (or a track meet, a tennis match, a baseball game, and so on).[135] A logical inference from this series of experiments is that the alleged catharsis achieved by watching violent sports does not occur. Indeed,

happening. Again and again he got up and was beaten down. Finally the Angels dragged him behind the stage.

The fat man too was now dark with blood. His teeth had been knocked out, and his mouth still bled. He wandered around the enclosure, waiting, like me, for the music.

As the Rolling Stones began to play, the mood tensed and the half-light took on a lurid cast. The stage was jammed with technicians, bikers, writers, hangers-on. Teenagers began to climb the enormous sound trucks that ringed the back of the stage, and men threw them off. Some fell fifteen feet to the ground; others landed on smaller trucks. I climbed to the top of a VW bus, where I had a slight view of the band. Several other people clambered up with me, waving tape-recorder mikes. Every few minutes, it seemed, the music was broken up by waves of terrified screams, wild ululations that went on for thirty, forty seconds at a time. We couldn't see the people screaming, but with every outburst of sound, the packed mass on the stage would cringe backward, shoving the last line of people off the stage and into the dirt. As people climbed back up, others would push them back down.

It was impossible to know what the screams meant. That a young black man from Berkeley, Meredith Hunter, would be killed in front of the stage by the Hell's Angels as the Rolling Stones played "Under My Thumb"—attacked, then chased into the crowd, where he pulled a gun and was stabbed, then beaten to death—would be the fact; from the sound the crowd made, such an incident could have been happening every time the band began another song.

All day long people had speculated on who the

Angels would kill. It was a gray day, and the Northern California hills were bare, cold, and dead. A sense of fatalism had settled over the event. From the start, the crowd had been inexplicably hateful, blindly resentful, selfish, snarling. People held their space. Someone had thrown a full beer bottle into the crowd, hitting a woman on the head, nearly killing her, and even then, people guarded the ground they sat on. Periodically, the Angels attacked people in the crowd or musicians who dared to challenge them, and when people tried to get away from the beatings, the rest of the crowd made no room for them.

From behind the stage I could hear Keith Richard of the Rolling Stones cut off the music and demand that the Angels stop attacking the crowd. I heard an Angel seize the mike from Richard. The screams were almost constant. Two more people climbed onto the VW bus, and the roof caved in. Some of those who fell off proceeded to punch in the windows with their bare hands.

With all this, the music picked up force. I turned my back to the stage and began to walk the half-mile or so to my car. Heading up the hill in the darkness, I tripped and fell headfirst into the dirt. I lay there, listening to the sound of feet passing me on either side and to the sound the band was making. The Rolling Stones were playing "Gimme Shelter." I tried to remember when I'd heard anything so powerful.

the implications are rather the opposite: aggression can be learned, and watching sports is one way to learn it.[136] As a German scholar concluded after studying over two hundred soccer fans, "Latent tension is neither repressed [*gebunden*] nor channeled but rather intensified and activated."[137]

Common sense confirms the results of pencil-and-paper tests and laboratory experiments. Very little sports-related spectator violence occurs before the game, when the fan is supposedly, according to the catharsis theory, at his most aggressive. The mayhem usually begins in medias res and climaxes after the final whistle has been blown. Wise Londoners avoid the Underground if Liverpool or Leeds has come to town and lost.

Given the persuasive evidence that sports spectatorship increases rather than decreases aggressiveness, we can turn the catharsis theory on its head and conjecture that spectators desire, consciously or unconsciously, to experience an intensification of aggressiveness. If people really do seek "excitatory homeostasis," as Jennings Bryant and Dolf Zillmann suggest, then the vicarious violence of sports spectatorship is one way to overcome boredom.[138] The social-psychological argument does not depend on the common experience of fandom (although it might have), but rather on laboratory experiments in which, for instance, subjects reported that rough-and-tumble football plays are more fun to watch than less violent ones. "Within the rules of the game, the rougher and more violent, the better—as far as the sports spectators employed in this study were concerned."[139] Gordon Russell has reported experiments that suggest, on the contrary, that sports violence is not as attractive to ice-hockey fans as the owners of the National Hockey League think it is, but the evidence at the box office seems in general to support Bryant and Zillmann.[140]

In an influential speculative essay entitled "The Quest for Excitement in Unexciting Societies," Norbert Elias and Eric Dunning theorized that there is a direct relationship between the routinization of daily life in modern industrial society and the prevalence of rough spectator sports like soccer, rugby, ice hockey, and American football. "In the more advanced industrial societies of our time," they wrote, "occasions for strong excitement openly expressed have become rarer."[141] Elias and Dunning emphasized that sports grounds have become a principal venue for the active expression of a variety of otherwise inhibited emotions. If we accept Elias's theory about "the civilizing process," then it is obvious that a propensity to commit acts of interpersonal expressive violence is precisely what modern society most strongly inhibits and what sports spectatorship most gratifyingly permits—either directly, in the case of fans who run amok, or vicariously, in the case of fans who merely empathize with and take pleasure in the violence they witness. In other words, sports are an especially attractive opportunity for uninhibited self-expression. It is doubtful that the vicarious sensations experienced by the sports spectator can be as thrilling or as satisfying as those experienced by the athletes, but the importance of these vicarious sensations should not be underestimated.

Sports spectacles are clearly not the only occasions for this kind of self-expression and vicarious sensation seeking—rock concerts come immediately to mind as another venue—but sports events are an especially attractive vehicle for the more or less culturally legitimate indulgence in and expression of strong emotion. One simple reason for this is that sports contests are almost always characterized by suspense, which is not the case with the predictable fare offered by most popular entertainment. The suspense is contained within a framework of predictability provided by the rules of the game and by the rationalized structure of league or tournament competition. Within the structural framework of a sport's rules and regulations, individual contests are relatively unpredictable, but they are reassuringly repeatable in that there can always be another contest, a new season, a repetition of the unexpected outcome within the familiar format.

This brings us back to where we began—to partisanship, identification, and representation. Suspense is a tepid sensation if one is not emotionally involved enough to care what happens next. Although sports spectators are unquestionably moved by a variety of motivations, ranging from a disinterested aesthetic appreciation of the athlete's prowess to the crass desire to win a bet, the most avidly, most intensively involved sports fans are those who move beyond empathy to identify with the athletes. The psychological term *identification* has been criticized because the vast majority of spectators are perfectly aware of the difference between themselves and the athletes, but empathy seems too weak a term to characterize the psychological dynamics of what

I have called *representational sports*.[142] For whatever reason, there is an almost irresistible impulse for sports spectators to feel that the athletes on the field represent them.

Whenever Glasgow's Celtics outscore Glasgow's Rangers in a soccer match, Roman Catholics rejoice. Whenever a baseball team wins the World Series, the streets of the city they represent—staid Toronto as well as volatile New York—are filled with shouting, screaming, drinking celebrants. When a team of young Americans defeated the Soviet Union's favored ice hockey players at the 1980 Olympic Games, the celebrants included not only dedicated fans but also first-time spectators who didn't know the difference between a slap shot and a mug shot. In short, sports spectators feel intensely that *their* race, religion, ethnic group, school, hometown, or nation is represented in an immensely important competition against some similarly represented rival. In all of these cases, the individual self tends to become one with a collectivity of identically represented selves.

A great deal of the research on the dynamics of identification on the part of contemporary sports fans has been done by Daniel L. Wann and his students. Their studies explore an array of factors that impinge on identification, such as its intensity and duration, and they leave no doubt whatsoever that—in most cases—the fans' identification with their representative teams is the magnet that draws them to the stadium and excites their passions once they are in their seats (or leaping out of them).[143] The psychodynamics of collective behavior ensures that each fan's individual sense of identification will be greatly intensified by his or her awareness that thousands of others, all around him, are experiencing the same sense of identification.

In the psychodynamics of representational sports, identification implies partisanship, a crucial component of the emotional equation. In sports contests, more than in most social situations, the collective self is clearly defined against the collective other. This fact helps to explain why "sport generates fanship that is more intense, more obtrusive, and more enduring than it is for other forms of entertaining social activities."[144] It is the intrinsically agonistic character of spectator sports that has always, from antiquity to modern times, made them especially suitable for their representational function. For sports fans, the appeal of the contest is that those who represent *us* block, tackle, kick, punch, pummel, or pin *them,* whoever they are. And because it is "just a game," we can reassure ourselves, once we have calmed down, that our emotional binges are harmless.

The problem is that the binges—the intense identifications—are *not* harmless. They increase the fans' propensity to behave aggressively. There is always the danger that partisanship will become hostility and that hostility will take physically violent forms. The historical record demonstrates that the danger is not trivial. The draconian solution to the problem of sports-induced or sports-intensified violence is to eliminate sports spectatorship, but no one—not even the most pessimistic analyst of sports crowds—is ready to suggest that we do this. That leaves us with Norbert Elias and the hope that sports crowds have internalized civilized codes of behavior to the point where they can experience the excitement of the contest without running amok. The Victorian-Edwardian code of fair play and good sportsmanship is dead and gone, but the vast majority of fans *do* manage to resist the move from vocal partisanship to felonious assault. It is too soon to despair.

6 Captive Crowds: Pilgrims and Martyrs

Susanna Elm

RELIGIONS ARE BY DEFINITION INTRICATELY interwoven with masses, crowds, and occasionally mobs or "leveling crowds," by the simple fact that most of them perform, to a greater or lesser degree, a continuing and delicate dance between individual and community, visions of selfhood and collective that may or may not be at odds with the "secular" world. That religion or religious motivation draws enormous crowds is evident—according to CNN, eight million people participated in the Kumbh-Mela ceremony in Allahabad in 2001; Saudi authorities restrict the number of annual pilgrims to Mecca to two million; in 2001 over six million faithful traveled to Lourdes; and from August 11 to 15, 2000, an estimated 2.5 million youths gathered in Rome for the *World Youth Rally*. Many more such figures could be cited.[1] Yet such religiously motivated crowds are only a part, although often a constitutive one, of "religion," and even as temporarily gathered crowds, they exhibit some distinct characteristics: although conforming to most crowd criteria, by gathering for example temporarily like-minded persons densely packed in delineated spaces, religious crowds differ markedly already through their cachet—their very religiosity, which sits uneasily with the frequently negative value judgment of "crowds."[2] Most crowd psychologists or scientists of mass behavior accord religiously motivated crowd phenomena a position slightly apart, more often than not by proffering an uneasy truce between their assessment of the mass and that of religion, which for many of them is in essence synonymous with Catholicism. Thus, the religiously motivated crowd phenomenon of central interest for most crowd psychologists is, not surprisingly, pilgrimage, sparked by the first mass armed pilgrimage, the Crusades. Pilgrimage stands paradigmatically for the relation between religion and the masses because it perfectly represents the ten-

133

sion between the crowd's ephemeral nature and the religion's archaism and *longue durée*, between the "modernity" of mass mobilization and the ancient lure of the miraculous.[3] Pilgrimage, its relation to mass mobilization, and its individual focal points, or "crystals," to use Elias Canetti's terminology, will thus form the backbone of the following. By tracing these phenomena back to their roots in Greco-Roman antiquity—I will concentrate my remarks on their western, Christian forms—it will become evident that pilgrimage en masse is in many ways an entirely modern phenomenon. Indeed, it emerged precisely during the period that was so formative for the new science of mass behavior as represented by Gustave Le Bon and others in late nineteenth-century France. Christian pilgrimage began as an individual pursuit, and this remained the case even after the sole exception, the Crusades.

Conversely, the individual crystals, or catalysts that attracted pilgrimage, especially the form of pilgrimage that was not focused on great urban centers like Rome or Jerusalem but on the individuals called saints and their guardians and epigones, the ascetics and monastics, originated in the context of the one religious mass phenomenon of the ancient world that we can grasp historically: the religious games, which included gladiatorial games, and martyrdom. Interestingly, however, precisely the mass mobilization of pilgrims today—millions every year visit Lourdes, Guadalupe in Mexico, Portuguese Fatima, Aparecida in Brazil, or the tomb of Francis Xavier in Goa—represents in one specific sense a return to the very origins of pilgrimage. Whereas until very recently the hardship of the journey itself was a transformative moment of pilgrimage, modern means of mass tourism, planes, buses, cars, and their relative comforts, now—and once again—place the crowd, the intense, dense community at the destination, center stage and thus grant it a transformative moment. However, despite their manifold transformations, what unites both ancient and modern religious crowds are two things: the

manner in which the individual's experience of a religiously motivated crowd is represented as shaped by the most advanced media of the time; and each participant's enduring human need to communicate with the otherworldly in the hope to obtain, as an individual supported by a collective, healing, salvation, and grace.

Religion and the Crowd Psychologist: Trajectory of a Certain Dilemma

Gustave Le Bon, the controversial father of crowd psychology, quite explicitly excluded from his study religious sects and castes like the church as being constitutive elements of what he termed *homogeneous* crowds. Rather, the crowd that preoccupied him was the *heterogeneous* crowd, which was temporary, mentally inferior, submissive, feminine, barbaric, like a wild beast, and no more likely to be tamed by a superannuated God and "préoccupations de l'au-delà" (preoccupations with the beyond) than a river's return to its source.[4] Yet for him, the crowd as such was itself also a deeply religious phenomenon. Goaded by transcendental images and magic formulas such as democracy, socialism, and equality, and characterized by intolerant, obedient followers worshipping their equally intolerant leaders, Le Bon's crowds embody all the destructive forces inherent in beliefs not properly tamed into a church (*PF*, 60–63, 98). And needless to say, he intended his study to be nothing less than a handbook that would enable capable men to do just that: to tame the crowd and thus to convert it once more into a church, albeit a new and different one, in which superior individuals would once more appropriately channel the crowd's ferocious powers.[5]

Freud's response to Le Bon exhibits a similarly distinct role for crowds under the influence of religion. In his morphology, such crowds are artificial ones. Organized and durable, their internal leadership combined with an external *Zwang* (compulsion) prevents them from exhibiting a central characteristic of the "natural crowd," its short *durée* and rapid dissolution.[6] The Catholic Church, Freud's example, is held together by the *Vorspiegelung* (illusion) of a leader who loves all equally: Christ. The individual's connectedness to that love is also the bond that unites him with the other members of the crowd, the *Massenindividuen.* What prevents the dissolution of such a crowd—and here Freud echoes Le Bon—is its inherent intolerance against all who are not bound by that love—that is, outsiders. An interesting tension emerges. For Le Bon and Freud, crowds are a priori negative forces, yet religion, at least in its organized form—and that means for both primarily the Catholic Church as they understand it—represents almost the opposite: it is an organization governed by elites; it is durable; and it is at least periodically a civilizing factor. Yet it simultaneously remains deeply implicated in the notion of a crowd in all its leveling potential.

Elias Canetti, too, sets religion apart. He states explicitly that his *Masse und Macht* (*Crowds and Power*) is not the place where he sought to explicate religion; that was to be the subject of a different opus. Even so, religion permeates *Masse und Macht,* and Canetti's observations capture sharply the tensions also inherent in Le Bon and Freud's description, between a religion's long *durée* versus its inherent potential to attract temporary crowds, between stability and organization versus momentary exaltation and frenzy, essential homogeneity yet temporary heterogeneity. According to Canetti, precisely this tension generates religion. "The dynamics of packs, and the particular kind of interplay between them, explain the rise of the world religions" (Aus der Dynamik der Meuten und der besonderen Art, wie sie ineinander spielen, erklärt sich der Aufstieg der Weltreligionen); "a sense of the treacherousness of the crowd, is, so to speak, in the blood of all the historical world religions" (ein Gefühl für die Tücken der Massen liegt den historischen Weltreligionen sozusagen im Blut).[7] The dynamism here alluded to is the continual interplay between an open and a closed mass. At the beginning stages of most world religions, Canetti poses an open, spontaneously growing crowd intent on embracing all equally. Then such an open mass "seeks to close in on itself" and is thus tamed into an institution, out of which, over time, new movements cause eruption into a (re)opened mass. At the very heart of institutionalized religion, Canetti locates the agent provocateur for the *Umschlag* (transition) from one type of crowd into another: the *Massenkristalle,* small, consistent groups of select individuals who function as crowd catalysts, such as saints and monks, of which the Catholic Church, in his assessment, possesses legions.

The masterful mise-en-scène of the interplay between openness, enclosure, crystallization, slowness, and fast re-eruption is the essence of world religions, indeed the basis for their survival (*MM,* 144, 22; 14–15, 18–20, 22–24, 29, 40–42). Catholicism is for him the undisputed master player, precisely because its age has given it both a deep distrust of undisciplined crowds and their power to level hierarchical distinction as well as the tools for their capture and taming. "There has never been a state on earth capable of defending itself in so many ways against the crowd. Compared with the Church all other rulers seem poor amateurs" (Es hat bisher keinen Staat auf der Erde gegeben, der sich auf so mannigfaltige Weise gegen die Masse zu wehren verstand. An der Kirche gemessen, erscheinen alle Machthaber wie traurige Stümper) (*CP,* 155, *MM,* 176). The Church, according to Canetti, owes its crowd-taming supremacy precisely to crowd formations, specifically the slow-moving masses of procession and pilgrimage. Both, unlike non-religious crowds, are here directed toward goals that are distant: heaven, and the *loca sancta* of martyrs, saints, and monks (*MM,* 175–79).

Before following the lines thus offered by the crowd psychologists as foils for a deeper analysis of some case studies, both ancient and modern, an important counterpoint is worth mentioning, Emile Durkheim's *Les formes élémentaires de la vie religieuse* (*The Elementary Forms of Religious Life*) published in 1912. The work also thematizes the deep interconnectedness between religion, the individual, and crowds, and although he did not directly cite any one, Durkheim "was doubtless affected by the crop of studies in crowd psychology that had appeared at the end of the nineteenth century, by Scipio Sighele, Gustave Le Bon, and, indeed, Gabriel Tarde among others." But Durkheim's evaluation of crowds and religion did not require a "setting apart," nor exhibit difficulties in reconciling "positive" aspects of religion with "negative" views of the crowd for the simple reason that he did not see crowd behavior as pathological and undesirable, and an argument against democracy. On the contrary, he argued that it was "out of this effervescence [of the crowds that] the religious idea seems to be born," that after "a collective effervescence men believe themselves transported into an entirely different world from the one that they have before their eyes." Moreover, "the only way of renewing the collective *représentations* which relate to sacred beings is to retemper them in the very source of the religious life, that is to say, in the assembled groups."[8]

Durkheim's assessment of religion's essential link to crowds echoes that of the crowd psychologists in form but differs in interpretation: unlike Le Bon, Freud, and Canetti, he does not view the collective aspect of religion as a destructive, destabilizing, or degenerative element in need of taming, but as the positive force generating sacred sentiments, which celebrate social solidarity and integration. That is, Durkheim's assessment may offer us a positive avenue even into the modern mass phenomena mentioned at the outset, drawing millions to specific places at specific times, usually with the help of modern means of mass transportation as well as mass media, but guided by ancient sentiments deriving from the fact that men are social

beings. Through the "effervescence" of crowds, "men become different. The passions moving them are of such intensity that they cannot be satisfied except by violent and unrestrained actions, actions of superhuman heroism or of bloody barbarism. This is what explains the Crusades."[9]

Pilgrimage—Crowds on the Move?

Gustave Le Bon and his immediate precursors, whose concepts he so effectively popularized, were deeply influenced by their own historical context—the violent upheavals and popular protests of the third republic—as well as the emergence of a number of scientific disciplines, such as sociology, psychiatry, and criminal anthropology, that sought to grapple with the new phenomena of popular protest and their underlying social crisis. Thus they saw crowds as a "set of mirrors" ("distorting mirrors," in Susanna Barrow's words) refracting their time—that is, late-nineteenth-century France.[10] The same period—a period that confidently announced the dawn of a new scientific age during which religious belief would be swept away like dust—also witnessed the emergence of one of the most potent sites of modern pilgrimage, also in France: Lourdes. As a brief summary of the emergence of Lourdes into mass consciousness will show, it too refracted its time like a mirror. And it poses some of the issues raised above: the connection between modernity and tradition, between specific actions and experiences of individuals and groups, between tourism, leisure, and the individual's encounter with the miraculous and its sustained attraction, all calls of its demise to the contrary. But before addressing Lourdes as a case for pilgrimage in the age of mass tourism, it is worth briefly summarizing some salient facts of premodern pilgrimage to elucidate the above mentioned points: pilgrimage, the paradigm of religious mass phenomena, began as a highly individual pursuit, with the exception of the Crusades.

Jerusalem—as the medieval maps of the world document with great persuasion—was in the eyes of most Jews and Christians the center of the world, the *umbilicus mundi*, because it was the place where the divine had most profoundly encountered the human. Here Jesus' salvific nature had first been recognized, in the temple "which is of his father's" (Luke 2:22), Jesus had first preached, Jerusalem witnessed his passion, and Jerusalem was also considered the place were the final judgment would take place and where the heavenly Jerusalem, at the end of time, would come down to earth (*UM,* 5). Thus, for Christians, Jerusalem represented—beginning with the second century and the recognition of the intrinsic link between Old and New Testaments after the challenges of Marcion—both the place where Jesus had lived and also the locus where the Christian history of salvation had taken its origin and would find its fulfillment.[11] And although from the beginning there were those who insisted that God could be worshipped everywhere and that no one place offered a more privileged access to the sacred truth than another (following, for example, John 4:19–21, 23), many ancient persons were deeply influenced by the contrary notion, namely that certain places offered particular access to the divine and hence needed to be seen and touched for curative and divinatory purposes.[12]

The earliest account of a Christian pilgrimage is therefore, not surprisingly, a road map to Jerusalem: a short, laconic itinerary describing the route from Bordeaux to the Holy Land and back, written by an anonymous pilgrim in AD 333.[13] The *Itinerarium Burdigalense,* as it is known, composed twenty-one years after Constantine had made Christianity legal, follows a form of travel writing that had a long-established tradition, a kind of topographical enumeration of place names and distances; after all, the traveler enjoyed the infrastructure of the Roman roads.[14] What makes the *IB* into a document of a sacred journey is its focus on the Holy Land and Jerusalem, a city that did at that time not really exist and had to be completely reinvented and rebuilt because the emperor Hadrian had sacked ancient Jerusalem and refounded it as a small Roman colony called Aelia Capitolina. It was in this enterprise that the laconic Bordeaux pilgrim participated. As soon as he entered Palestine, he or she traveled more leisurely and began to gloss place-names with a host of allusions to Old and New Testament persons and places. Indeed, the Bible itself now became the guidebook.[15] To cite a sample entry: "city of Isdradela (Jezreel): 10 miles. It was here that King Ahab held his throne and Elijah prophesied" (585.7–588.2). And the Bordeaux pilgrim described Jerusalem in depth, imagined it as a biblical city, while remaining mostly mute with regard to the great urban centers of the Roman empire that he had also passed—for example, Antioch.

The anonymous pilgrim traveled as an individual, but he or she consistently invited the reader along—"here you ascend; here you cross and you enter"—as if addressing a companion, thus rendering the journey vivid and present. Indeed, many soon followed the same path. The account of the pilgrim Egeria, who traveled with a small entourage from Spain or Southern Gaul in the 380s, is perhaps the most vivid late fourth-century travelogue, but she shared her experience with many who came to Jerusalem.[16] Not even the capture of Jerusalem by the Sassanids in 614 could stem the small but steady stream of individual pilgrims, the Muslim Arabs, the eighth-century Abbasids, or the Fatimid Caliph al-Hakim, who was the first to prohibit pilgrimage to Jerusalem and in 1009 even began to dismantle the Church of the Holy Sepulcher, which had been begun by Constantine—perhaps in response to an increase in pilgrimages around the year 1000, as suggested by the eleventh-century chronicler and Cluniac monk Rudolf Glaber.[17]

But over these centuries, how many actually went to Jerusalem? I have mentioned vague numbers indicating "not very many," and indeed, it is very hard to say. Our early sources evoke multitudes "from the entire world."[18] Thus Jerome, the famous church father from Dalmatia who settled in Bethlehem after 385, continuously complained of the "multitude" of visitors, but he also praised Bethlehem's "solitude."[19] Both Jerome and his friend Paula had themselves traveled with "many virgins," several monks, a presbyter, and Jerome's brother. Like Egeria and many other early pilgrims we know by name, they belonged to the upper echelons of society and traveled in style, which means with an entourage of slaves, grooms, and guards. The actual size of the entourage also depended on the type of voyage, by land or by sea, and in the latter case, it made a difference whether one threw in one's lot with all the rest as part of an ordinary cargo ship or whether one hired a special vessel. But we do not only know of the very wealthy. Some early pilgrims traveled alone with the barest of financial means, passing the voyage as deckhands or "blind passengers," and others wandered along on foot for the entire duration. Yet smallish groups that changed size throughout the journey were probably the norm, not least because imperial legislation limited the size of an entourage for private travelers who used the road system to persons necessary for the "protection of life and the performance of necessary labors for the traveler," a rule enforced under penalty.[20] However, in societies that knew only armies and the travels of the imperial court as examples of movements en masse, even parties of twenty or thirty would have attracted a great deal of attention, and the numbers that came to Jerusalem were significant enough to lead to the erection of special hostels to receive the stream of visitors. Common to all travel, however luxurious, were numerous dangers and discomforts, crowded lodgings, and long periods away from home. The very act of travel over a great distance was a considerable hardship under any circumstance.[21]

After the Islamic conquests of the Holy Land and the eastern and southeastern shores of the Mediterranean, pilgrims to Jerusalem faced additional hazards. Pilgrimages did not cease; indeed, Muslims thought of Christian pilgrims wishing to see Jerusalem as persons "obeying the dictates of their law." But what had always been performed by a small minority now shrank to a trickle, until the reversal of the trend after 1009.[22] According to Rudolf Glaber, writing in the 1040s, at that time "from all over the world innumerable crowds began to flock to the Sepulchre of the Saviour in Jerusalem—in greater numbers than anyone before had thought possible." Those who went to Jerusalem again were "some of the common people and of the middling sort, but there were also several great kings, counts and noblemen . . . many noble ladies set out with the poor people" (*History*, 680)—propelled perhaps by apocalyptic fears of the millennium just passed as well as al-Hakim's attempts to destroy the Church of the Holy Sepulcher. As had been done before, most went by sea from southern Italy. But new land routes had also opened up, for example through Bohemia, Poland, and Hungary; even seaworthy Viking chieftans, newly Christianized, took to visiting the Holy Land, fearlessly sailing round the Iberian Peninsula. This incremental increase, whatever its absolute numbers (still small), meant that many at least knew of someone who had gone to Jerusalem, and such familiarity no doubt prepared the way for the new mass movement that began in 1095, the Crusades (*PPMW*, 17–20).

When on November 27, 1095, Pope Urban II called upon the French nobility to free Jerusalem from the hands of the Muslims, the response was extraordinary. Many who were assembled at Clermont on the occasion of a great church council shouted *deo lo vult* (God wills it), and many "of any and all occupation" begged to join. What they joined was, in everyone's understanding, a pilgrimage. Whoever went to Jerusalem "for devotion alone, not to gain honor or money," would liberate not only the city, but him- or herself from all sins, a reward of immense spiritual significance that previously would have required joining a monastery. About fifty to sixty thousand persons made use of the opportunity—the first mass pilgrimage ever. And even though the endeavor required armed force and was thus antithetical to all other Christian concepts of pilgrimage—peaceful; a remedy for individual sin and promise of salvation; in essence an individual pursuit—it was the liberation of Jerusalem and the desire to see the *loca sancta* that truly motivated most: the approximately 10 percent who were knights, and the rest, other pilgrims, servants, the poor, old, sick, women, and children. Furthermore, these "masses" did not travel in one cohesive group, but in many smaller, regional units, intending to assemble in Constantinople in 1097. Of those who got there, many fewer actually arrived in Jerusalem in 1099, not least because a significant group remained in Antioch, which was taken in 1098 after a prolonged siege.[23]

Actual numbers, much less the precise composition of the masses, are impossible to establish, as is usually the case in premodern history: there are no police reports like those accessible to George Rudé when he sought to establish the social composition of the "crowd in history" during the French Revolution.[24] Perhaps fifty to sixty thousand in all heeded the call, those who engaged in battles were many fewer, and only a small percentage of those ever reached Jerusalem (for the battle of Hattin in 1164, the estimates are thirteen hundred knights and about fifteen thousand foot soldiers; the numbers for Jerusalem 1099 were far fewer; Fulcher of Chartres recorded that in 1101, three hundred knights had remained there) (*C*, 81).

Yet all chroniclers of the events, particularly when describing the sack of Jerusalem in June 1099, speak of astounding numbers, both of those who had arrived, and even more so with regard to the enemies slaughtered. Several chroniclers who had themselves participated in the sack of Jerusalem later spoke of knights wading ankle-deep through the blood of slain Muslims and of corpses everywhere. Fulcher of Chartres counted the number of the dead as a hundred thousand, a figure soon doubled and quadru-

pled, or rendered so vast that it was only for God to know its magnitude.[25] Conversely, the Byzantine writer Niketas Choniates gave the number of the second crusading army as 9,876,543. However, the most probable count is the one mentioned above, approximately 16,300 in all.[26] Given the scarcity of urban centers and their small size—Paris, for example, is estimated as having a population of fewer than twenty thousand at the end of the eleventh century—even the most conservative numbers of those who participated made this armed pilgrimage, for contemporaries as well as for modern scholars, into a mass movement. Still, the enormity of the figures provided by the medieval authors is significant, especially given the tendency of ancient authors use numbers to indicate orders of magnitude.

The vast numbers of the chroniclers are neither accident nor simple exaggeration. Just like modern estimates of the numbers participating in any given protest or rally, all computer-generated, grid-based data to the contrary, are never clear but always vary in size depending on their source (rally organizers versus the police force, for example), those of the crusader chroniclers, too, are part of a carefully crafted argument. In fact, they are actors in an ancient dramaturgy: the battle between good and evil. The hundreds of thousands slaughtered were not simply enemies. They represented the demonic forces of Satan, evil incarnate; the others represented the triumph of God and his followers. The greater the evil surrendered, the greater the glory of God. All subsequent calls for Crusades and all the media available at the time—sermons, songs, chronicles, liturgical texts, vernacular poetry, even Church windows—emphasize this point: God himself wished the destruction of his enemies, the triumph of good over evil, as he had done countless times beforehand. Hence, the armed pilgrims followed in the footsteps of Moses, David and Goliath, the Maccabees who had cleansed the Temple, and the Roman emperors Titus and Vespasian, whose destruction of the Temple in AD 70 had long been interpreted as divine revenge for the crucifixion of Christ.[27] Therefore, before the final assault on Jerusalem in 1099, the cross-bearing pilgrims, not yet known as crusaders, fasted and walked barefoot around the city behind priests carrying holy relics and preaching sermons on the Mount of Olives. Those who died during the following siege died in a particular manner, as Bohemond of Taranto, the great Norman warrior, wrote in a letter he sent back to the West: "in peace . . . and without a doubt they will be glorified in the eternal life." His recipients would have understood what he meant. Fulcher of Chartres said it even more clearly. Whoever died en route to Jerusalem or in Jerusalem itself, died "enshrouded in faith and hope. . . . As soon as he had been laid to rest on earth, he was already crowned in heaven. Blissful, whom the Lord grants such glory, to be crowned by the laurel of martyrdom and counted among the martyrs" (*UM*, 28–33).

Imitatio Christi, through the pain and sufferings of pilgrimage, the thirst, hunger, illness, uncertainty, poverty, and nakedness of the journey, was the principal aim of many crusaders, as expressed by the anonymous author of the *Deeds of the Francs*, the *Gesta Francorum*. Such *imitatio* was the reason for the great remedy of sin granted to "cross-bearing" pilgrims by Urban II and his successors, which proved to be such a draw. But the ultimate victory, the crowning achievement was to die en route to Jerusalem for the glory of God, as manifestation of his power, which means to die as a martyr—and the notion of martyrdom runs through the accounts of the Crusades like a leitmotiv (*PPMW,* 19–23; *FC,* 4–10; *C,* 63–66; 9–18). In the end, therefore, many pilgrims sought their individual salvation, but in this quest they were joined with many kindred souls, both present on the road with them, and even more so in the collective imagination. Each crusader who returned and brought back mementoes or relics (pieces of the Holy Cross, amulets) was living proof of God's power and of that of his followers. Each crusader was the ultimate representative of the entire community by having united in his person two supreme ideals: pilgrimage and chivalry. Those who died, however, acted as the ultimate multipliers of the collective imagination because of the enormous power of martyrdom.

Martyrs—The Ultimate Mass Crystals

Jerusalem was and remains until today the *umbilicus mundi* for many; and Jerusalem pilgrimage flourished even after the recapture of Jerusalem by Saladin in 1187 and the end of the Crusades in 1197. However, from its very beginning in the fourth century AD, Jerusalem had not been the only magnet for pilgrims. At the same time, a separate yet connected phenomenon emerged. For every visitor who completed the long and hazardous journey to the Holy Land, the were numerous others who also traveled out of religious motivation, not to Jerusalem, but to many other places, some, Rome among them, closer to home. This localized form of pilgrimage emerged out of three roots: first, the cultivation within early Christian communities of their honored dead, the martyrs; second, travel to their epigones, the living martyrs, or the holy men and women, soon known as saints, who lived in the deserts of Syria and Egypt (and thus en route to the Holy Land), as well as in numerous other remote localities or *deserta;* and, third, the ancient custom, known all over the Greco-Roman world and beyond, of taking refuge to particularly hallowed places for curative and divinatory purposes—or to use the words of Thucydides, "to go, to sacrifice, to consult the oracle, to be spectators, at the common sanctuaries."[28]

Martyrdom, the ostentatious death as self-sacrifice in a public setting for the glory of God, is one of the central aspects of Christianity, as the short overview of the Crusades has already made evident. Indeed, the image of Christians, both male and female, devoured by the lions of the persecuting Romans until their eventual triumph, which immediately caused the fall of Rome itself, is perhaps the most widely known synopsis of Roman history, put perhaps most succinctly by the second century North African author Tertullian: "*semen est sanguis Christianorum*—we multiply whenever we are mown down by you; the blood of the Christians is a seed."[29]

But why should martyrdom, almost always the act of a single person, figure prominently in a volume on *Crowds*? The answer lies in the fact that martyrs were and still are today a fitting example of what Canetti has termed *Massenkristalle*, or crowd catalysts. Each individual death that claims to be an act of martyrdom is always a mise-en-scène for a large collective. It therefore always has to make use of the best available means of mass communication. The death must be staged in manner that communicates to the widest possible audience the "author's" intention: his death is no mere suicide, but martyrdom through its direct link to a transcendental, religious, legitimizing authority. It occurs in opposition to and as protest against present, surrounding (mass) forces, which are clearly marked as opposing the transcendental authority and hence are a threat to the collective of its followers, on whose behalf and for whose salvation the self-sacrifice occurred. The manner of the death must therefore always be public, and—as in the case of the crusaders—the size of the "opposing crowd" underscores the power of the martyr and his or her transcendental power, or God. Such a death equals a victory over the opposition, which represents evil, and is thus a manifestation of divine will and power already on earth, rewarding the martyr with eternal glory.

Martyrdom is thus yet another version of a dance between an individual and a vision of collective-vision, because the masses, the collective, need not be present in its entirety. In fact, what should and must be present at the site is a crowd of opponents, preferably of sufficient size. But the true addressee and recipient of the author's message may be physically far removed. They are the crowd that is constituted, reconstituted, and reaffirmed not so much by the actual deed, but by its continuing and repeated representation through the appropriate media, narrative or visual or both. Thus the essential elements: an individual's spectacular death in front of a crowd (seen as opposition and often implicated in the death) becomes the catalyst for a collective of addressees, the martyr's crowd, which gains cohesiveness as well as expansion through the multiplier effect of the continuous narrative reenactment of the spectacular death, which attracts epigones, and so repeats the cycle.

Historically speaking, the acts of martyrdom so central to early Christianity, which spawned imitators in the form of ascetics and saints, men and women who sought to lead a life of extreme pain and suffering they termed a "daily martyrdom," and who became the focal point for numerous pilgrims, were only possible because of the existence of a particular form of "religious crowd": the games, both gladiatorial and other, *ludi* and *munera gladiatoria*, celebrated by enormous masses in the ancient world in honor of the gods, the cities, and the honored dead. Although perhaps uncomfortable for some today, early Christian writers were perfectly aware of the crucial link between Christianity's rising popularity and the ancient world's most important religious mass entertainment: "although we are beheaded and crucified, and exposed to wild beasts and chains and flames, and every other means of torture, it is evident that we will not retract our profession of faith; the more we are persecuted, the more do others in ever increasing number embrace the faith."[30]

Gladiatorial games and other types of games play a crucial role for the historian of the crowd for the simple reason that they are one of the very few types of mass gathering of the premodern world that permits any kind of numerical accuracy. We can measure with a fair degree of certainty the number of persons who could be seated in the theaters,

6A 'Hamon': Hebrew

Na'ama Rokem

In contemporary Hebrew, the word *hamon* unambiguously refers to a large group of people. Another meaning of the word, "noise," continues to be cited in contemporary dictionaries, but it is actually an archaism that contemporary users of the language are barely aware of.

I suggest that since the Bible, there have been two shifts in the use of *hamon* in relation to this latter meaning. The first coincides with the transition to Talmudic and medieval Bible commentary: after the advent of the Diaspora, the tradition of biblical commentary begins to understand *hamon* primarily as a sound. Thus, Jewish commentators of the Bible follow the dictum to suppress visual images by embodying the notion of a Jewish nation or congregation exclusively by means of sound. The second shift occurs with the transition from this essentially religious tradition to the building of a nationalist movement. In this context, even when *hamon* is used to describe a crowd, it is the sound of this crowd that is most salient.

Although some of the eighty-one instances of *hamon* in the Bible refer to sound, the word is also used in relation to agglomerations of people. God's promise to Abraham is, "Thou shalt be a father of many nations [*hamon goyim*] . . . for a father of many nations have I made thee" (Genesis 17:4–5).

For centuries after late antiquity, biblical commentary throughout the Diaspora seems to emphasize the "sound" aspect of *hamon*. A Talmudic source quoted by Ben-Yehuda says, "Three

amphitheaters, and arena—all considered *templa,* sacred places belonging to the gods—excavated throughout the towns and cities of the Roman empire (at Verona, Arles, Nîmes, El Djem) as well as in the great sites in Rome itself, the Colosseum (fifty thousand), the theater of Marcellus, the Circus Maximus (about two hundred thousand) or the Campus Martius. Further, we know the number of days devoted to games, both gladiatorial and other: in Rome, about 176 in an ordinary year in the fourth century AD, slightly less in the major cities. And we possess numerous laws, inscriptions, tax reports, and literary writings in a great variety of genres to impress on us the enormous expenses incurred and the vital importance attributed to the practice throughout the history of the Roman Empire, even after its Christianization.[31]

Gladiatorial games, the one-on-one combat between man and man, man and beast, and occasionally woman and woman, which led eventually to the death of Christians as martyrs, originated as part of the obligatory offerings owed to important men after their death, whether as a form of sacrifice, as sign of death and renewal, as a celebration of the importance and the warriorlike qualities of the honored, or as a combination of the above. Over time, although still linked to the honor due to death, they became part and parcel of all public spectacles, especially during the empire, when, at least in the city of Rome, only the (eventually divine) emperor was allowed to honor his family and himself in like manner. However, unlike other forms of public spectacles, gladiatorial games were relatively rare, only about ten per year in Rome, all celebrated—again perhaps in connection with death and renewal—around the end of the year. Other types of games, held much more frequently, involved staged hunts and wild beast fights (*venationes*), during which many exotic animals, brought to the venue at enormous cost and difficulty, were proudly displayed. Common to all types of games was their lavishness and their popularity, which extended not only to the person or persons who had offered these games, but also to the gladiators themselves, who frequently achieved real celebrity, despite their social status as slaves.

But gladiators were not the only ones fighting in the arena. *Venationes* and gladiatorial games also served a different function: they were the means by which criminals were publicly executed. As is by now well known thanks to the movie *Gladiator,* neither gladiatorial combats nor wild beast fights were left to progress arbitrarily. Rather, they were usually staged to evoke quasi-historical events, or mythological or religious themes. In the case of condemned criminals, their deaths as part of the mythological games in the arena were staged so that the punishment fitted the crime. Thus an arsonist would be condemned to death by burning, but the event might be staged to reenact Icarus's fatal ascent to the sun. In the process, the condemned were humiliated and mocked, but the very public manner of their death also signified that the wrongs they had inflicted on individuals and the community were now rectified.[32]

It is here that the Christian martyr enters the scene, as it were. Some (historically speaking, very few) Christian inhabitants of the Roman Empire were condemned to death, not because they were Christian, but because of their refusal (which was based, however, on their Christian belief) to sacrifice to the gods. Such a refusal was, according to Roman law (*ius in sacris*) and religious understanding, the equivalent of recklessly endangering the public welfare, a grave sacrilege.[33] Therefore, such persons, if they insisted in their refusal, were then publicly executed like any criminal as part of the games, as best illustrated once more by Tertullian in his *Apology* for his religion (15.4–5): "But you are still more religious in the amphitheater, where over human blood, over the polluting stain of capital punishment, your gods dance, supplying plots and themes for criminals—unless it is that criminals often adopt the roles of your deities. We have seen at one time or another Attis, that god from Pessinus, being castrated, and a man who was being burnt alive had taken on the role of Hercules."

Some of these criminals thus burnt alive as Hercules (the penalty of *crematio*), gored and devoured by animals, as a Europa raped by a bull or an Orpheus killed by a bear (the penalty *ad bestias*), are now known as saints and martyrs: Perpetua, Polycarp, Felix, Agnes, Donatus, and so on.[34] This is so because their deaths were recounted in detail, shaped and interpreted by other Christians for the Christian communities in narrative forms that used the most popular literary models, in particular the so-called romance novels. These literary reenactments were circulated widely and continuously for centuries to come. In these narrative reenactments of the mythological death scenes in the context of gladiatorial games, the painful public torture and the gruesome death of the Christian imitated the equally public and painful death of Christ, which had preceded his resurrection. Each martyr's death manifested Christ's continuing divine power, because the pain narrative of the martyr stories always represents the hero or heroine as visibly enduring the extreme tortures unfazed. Because public killings are traditional means to establish dominance, the victim's endurance represents a reversal of the power dynamic. Christ's martyrs, visibly empowered to endure extreme pain through his divine might, become his soldiers, the *militia Christi*, who overthrow Rome's might as represented by the opposing crowds in the theaters and the extraordinary splendor of the games. These opposing crowds are, of course, evil: the martyr Perpetua

voices reach from the end of the world to its end. And they are: the sound of the wheel of the sun, and the sound of the noise of the city [*hamona shel ha'ir*], and the sound of the soul as it leaves the body" (translation mine). A commentary on the Book of Lamentation composed in Palestine in late antiquity explains, "Oh the sound/multitude of many peoples [*hamon 'amim rabim*] they sound like the murmur of the seas [*ke'hamot yamim yehamiun*] and the noise [*sha'on*] of many nations is like the noise of great waters" (translation mine). Radak (ca. 1160–1235) finds interest in the conjunction of masses of a foreign nation with the sounds that they make in a commentary on Isaiah 13:4.

The revival of the Hebrew language precipitated by the awakening of a Jewish national movement in the nineteenth century had two prominent features: the mining of earlier sources for vocabulary that could be used in a modern language, and the production of a great number of neologisms. Considering the ideological context in which this project unfolded, one might expect that the masses would now become reembodied and understood through their corporeal presence rather than through their sound. What actually occurs is an apparent separation between the two meanings that had become increasingly associated in the commentaries on the Bible: namely, "sound" and "multitude." The use of *hamon* to refer to sounds, based on biblical usage, continues for some time. Accordingly, in Bialik (1874–1934), the voices of nature are described as "the voice of the sound of the woods [*kol hamon ha'ya'ar*]" or in Uri Zvi Greenberg (1894–1981) as "the voice of the sound of dark waters [*kol hamon mayim afelim*]." At the same time, *hamon* begins to be used to describe the crowd in the modern, urban sense of the word.

This tendency was strengthened by the creation of neologisms such as *himun*—a verb describing "vulgarization" used by such writers as Halkin and Shtaineman—and *hamonai*, used by Shlonsky (1900–1973) both as a noun describing "simple and vulgar people" and as an adjective describing mass production (which he associates with America). Neither of these neologisms was incorporated into contemporary Hebrew.[1]

says, "I understood that I was not fighting *ad bestias*, but against the devil" (*Pass. Perp.* 10.14).[35]

The collective of the martyrs and their followers, the *ecclesia martyrum*, thus represented the true opposing crowd. The martyr's victory over pain and death embodied their collective's triumph over the assembled masses of Rome and its leaders, the emperor chief among them. In the words of Minucius Felix, "nay, our boys and tender women are so inspired to sufferance of pain that they laughingly scorn crosses and tortures, wild beast and all the paraphernalia of punishment"— that is, all that represented the power of Rome (*Octavius* 37.5). Ironically, however, it was precisely through the very use of the Roman mass media, the fatal charades of the games, and the literary model of the romances that the central Christian notion of martyrdom took shape and gained its impact.[36]

Martyrs to Saints: Pilgrimage and the Ecclesia Martyrum

Martyrs, so nearly all early Christian writers maintained, had died as human beings who enjoyed, through the manner of their death, close intimacy with God. Therefore, a martyr was a friend of God who had once been human and so had a particular quality: she could intercede for and protect fellow mortals. Because of that particular relationship with God, in the martyr and all that she had touched on earth, the place of her tomb, fragments of the body, wells in which she had washed, other physical remains, resided a particular power: the power to make present the divine. Such presence had many consequences. The physical remains of the honored dead, such as fragments of bone, were no longer seen as corpses, and the site of the remains (graves, tombs), were seen as memorials, places where the continuous presence of the martyr would be particularly and powerfully felt. Hence, these were places of intense spirituality that inspired deep devotion, a devotion made manifest through miracles, most often miraculous cures for the sick, the blind, the crippled. But they also helped those who visited them wash away their sins, especially if the narratives of the martyr's death were read aloud during a visit.[37]

In short, at the very latest from the fourth century onward, the cult of martyrs began to be transformed into the cult of saints, and the many places where such martyrs had lived or where they had been buried themselves became shrines for pilgrimage. At the same time, living martyrs, especially those en route to the Holy

Land, also became focal points of attraction for similar reasons. These living martyrs were men and women like Anthony, Theodora, or Paul the First Hermit who had gone to remote, deserted areas, traditionally equated with the arena of the devil, in order to fight the very same devil and his demons through a strictly disciplined life of fasting, vigils, prayers, abstinence, and mortifications, through which they sought to imitate Christ in a "daily *martyrium.*" Their miraculous deeds—expressed through their superhuman way of life, through prophecies and miraculous feedings but also through manifold cures—were the manifestation of divine presence, and they were recounted in numerous accounts, hagiographies, which circulated as widely as the pain narratives of the earlier martyrs. Thus, almost all known early pilgrims to Jerusalem, from Egeria to Jerome and his companions, also visited Syria and Egypt, and "the companies of monks . . . paid a round of visits to the heavenly family on earth."[38]

Wherever Christianity existed in the Roman world, there were martyrs and hence their *memoriae* or tombs, and deserted places that offered potential sites for living martyrs and future saints. Soon special churches were erected, custom-built shrines with attached facilities for lodging and feeding permanent guardians as well as the increasing number of visitors—pilgrims—and hospitals for those among the pilgrims who were sick and infirm. Their numbers increased even further when relics, the physical remains of martyrs and saints, were exported and translated, which created new shrines in areas well beyond the former boundaries of the Roman Empire, Ireland, Saxony, Norway, and so on, so that eventually a dense network of local sanctuaries arose that attracted numerous pilgrims. New martyrs continued to join the crowd through the expansion of Christianity into hostile territories, as the result of the Crusades, and—importantly—in the context of colonization and the discovery of the New World.[39] Pilgrimage thus motivated many people to travel shorter and longer distances for many centuries—but we have little idea how many went at any given period. We do know that most of them went in small groups or alone, despite the occasional mass movement like the Crusades, or the not improbable number of 200,000 attracted to Rome in 1300, or the 147,000 supposedly counted in Aachen during a fifteen-day indulgence period in 1496. That plague and then the Reformation caused a shift toward more local pilgrimage is also possible, but it was not until the seventeenth and eighteenth centuries, when leisure travel, the Grand Tour, and travel for exploration became fashionable, that pilgrimage, at least long-distance pilgrimage, declined—declined as an elite activity, one should say, and indeed not for long: in the second half of the nineteenth century, the practice reemerged with a force and in numbers it truly had never seen before.[40]

6B Beyond the Blindfold

Luiz Costa-Lima

My interest in politics developed late when, at age twenty-seven, having completed my undergraduate work, I went to study in Spain. Until then, my family's social class and the fact of being a single child with a precocious commitment to the life of the mind had led to mostly sporadic contacts with the multitudes. These assumed the form of attending festivities such as soccer games and *carnaval.* As an aspiring intellectual, my formative experiences were shaped by atomized individuals and by books. It was Franco's Spain that, in 1960 and 1961, taught me to abhor right-wing regimes and to tilt toward a left that sought to address the needs of the masses. Admittedly, certain right-wing movements also claim to represent the masses' interests (Franquist fascism was well aware of this). But although I was still ignorant enough to be unaware of the difference between Le Bon's and Tarde's concepts of the masses, I had already developed my own intuitive understanding. Either the masses could be envisaged as a *crowd,* which is to say, as an anonymous assemblage in which "the feelings and ideas of every individual are oriented towards a single end" (Le Bon), arising thanks to *contagion* and to the presence of a charismatic leader. Or the masses could be conceived of as a *public* that arises thanks to *suggestion,* understood as "the expression of certain *beliefs* or *desires*" (Tarde). A further insight, formulated by Tocqueville, would later impose itself: "Equality gives rise to two tendencies: one spurs the individual towards new thoughts; the other spurs him to abandon thought altogether." In the end, Franquism led me to opt for Tarde's equation of mass and public.

Although still ignorant in the domain of political theory, I returned to Brazil at the beginning of 1962 and began a phase of involvement in leftist movements. My interactions with the masses were either anonymous, the result of participation in political rallies, or they were the result of my work in the literacy campaign imagined and put into action by the educator Paolo Freire. From the latter I learned that rhetoric, contrary to the negative valences the word has retained to this day, could serve as an instrument in the service of the logic of desire (precisely as Tarde would have it).

The experience didn't last long. In April 1964, a coup d'état took place and brought about a dictatorship that, as would later be the case in Pinochet's Chile, carried out a modernization of traditional structures in the name of combating the Red Peril and firming up Brazil's ties to the West. I was arrested several months later, fired from a university position that I had barely begun to occupy, and forced to start a new life in another state. Until that point I had resided in Recife, the capital of Pernambuco; now I moved to Rio de Janeiro.

The *mass* = *public* equation became obligatory under the dictatorship, for one's writings had to rely on code words, and secret small group assemblies were the rule. My face-to-face contact with the multitudes was limited to street demonstrations that ended in head-bashing on the part of the police and in clouds of tear gas, although there was also the occasional public protest tolerated by the regime because it was under international pressure. My passport had been revoked,

Lourdes and the Modern Masses

Between 1830 and 1933 the Virgin Mary appeared in least at nine places in Europe in a manner that defied by now well-established secular explanations. In her appearances, she proclaimed urgent millenarian messages, often addressed to women, chosen in a fashion that responded well to the concerns of the post-Enlightenment world. This world responded with all the modern means at its disposal: newspapers, best-selling novels,—after initial periods of intense skepticism—trains, scientific "corroboration," and the construction of sites ready to receive millions of visitors. Pilgrimage now involved the enormous religiously motivated crowds that so preoccupied Le Bon, Zola, Freud, Canetti, and others. Among the various sites of Marian apparitions in Europe, especially Fatima in Portugal (1917), Beauraing (1933), Banneux (1933), Medjurgoje in Croatia (1981), or the earlier Czestochowa in Poland, Lourdes holds a special place, not least because it emerged during the period of the third republic and the rise of crowd psychology.[41]

Situated on the old pilgrimage road from Arles to Compostela, Lourdes belonged to a region in which supernatural apparitions and the presence of God, the Virgin, and other saints had never lost their power. When the fourteen-year-old Bernadette Soubirous, born into a poor family and suffering from the onset of tuberculosis, reported eighteen visions of the Virgin speaking to her in dialect and revealing the presence of a healing spring in a decidedly unwholesome grotto, she communicated beliefs that were shared in her community by the genteel, the clergy, and the poor alike. However, although linked to local traditions, Bernadette's epiphany was not a remnant of a bygone age. It also resonated with "urban, educated Catholics around the world, influenced subsequent apparitions, and transformed the veneration of the virgin in contemporary Catholicism."[42] Lourdes gained its importance like most other international sanctuaries because of a fortuitous conflux of a variety of variables in its initial and subsequent stages. Briefly put, Bernadette's visitation stood out from other contemporaneous ones (for example, at nearby La Salette) because the Virgin appeared not as a mother but as a girl; she called herself the "Immaculate Conception," confirming only recently promulgated dogma; she had appeared in France, home of revolutionary traditions, but also of a burgeoning cult of Mary, of protagonists of science and secularization but also of stubborn royalists and pro-Catholics (ultramontanists); and her apparition was free of any anticlericalism. Lourdes flourished, further, despite initial resistance, in a France torn by the collapse of Louis Napoleon's empire, indeed because of the chaos after Franco-Prussian war and the Commune.

Because the visitation had been taciturn, and because Bernadette stoically refused to elaborate her message, the site offered many options for emotional and spiritual attachment. Those who wanted to restore the monarchy in the early 1870s chose Lourdes for national penitence and repentance. Other supporters, especially women, often aristocrats, together with members of the clergy, found new networks of devotion and charity, in which personal contact was paramount: through the cure for the very sick and dying, and the establishments of hospitals and the so-called white trains. Others again used the wide reach of the mass media, authors like Lasserre or Zola, whose competing accounts were read by millions and translated into various languages, and the miraculous cures, examined since 1883 at the site by a specially established Medical Bureau, and shaped and reshaped in curing narratives, became focal points for debates among the leading Parisian physicians regarding hypnotism, the unconscious, and mediumistic power and hygiene—the paramount pressing medical issues of the fin de siècle.[43]

Of course, the site itself was physically transformed. The establishment of a railway connection in 1866 dramatically increased the number of visitors, and from 1858 onward, the originally rather inaccessible grotto became transformed. The river was diverted, broad avenues opened up, and new churches constructed. An entire infrastructure, including the healing baths, was built to receive hundreds of thousands of visitors.[44] Today they come in charter planes and as members of a packaged tour. What endures, so it seems, is the need for consolation for those afflicted with pain and illness. Bernadette's illness and physical weakness echoed the physical pain of Christ and the sufferings of his mother. At Lourdes, from the very beginning, the sick, ill, and infirm take center stage, surrounded by the healthy, who clamor to take care of total strangers who gain spiritual significance precisely because they are suffering, deformed, ill, and in ordinary life relegated to the sidelines. Lourdes assembles in a defined space at the same time persons who are mostly unknown to each other, without clear internal structure except for what guides them toward their common goal: the spiritual experience of finding solace in a crowd of the like-minded, attended to by a crowd of the otherwise indifferent, in the presence of a "mass crystal" who had experiences of divine presence at that place, even though she was poor, young, and sickly. Although this mass experience may lead to cures, today's literature at the shrine instead stresses this spiritual dimension, and the fact that bathing washes away sins.

This very brief overview of Lourdes has perhaps shown that religion—and that includes religious mass phenomena—are neither static nor easily compressed into the dialectic between progress, modernity, science, and elites, on the one hand,

so I couldn't even dream of going abroad. And although my political activities had been modest, I found myself arrested once again in 1972, only weeks before I was to defend my doctoral thesis.

Progress had been made in the domain of repressive measures. In 1964, my torturers were mere hobbyists. In 1972, they were professionals. I was placed in a white isolation chamber. The room was soundproofed, although sometimes one could hear the cries of torture victims, perhaps real, perhaps recorded. Temperature and light varied continuously, to the point that I lost all track of day and night. To go to the bathroom, I had to pound on the door and be led out blindfolded. There was also a large and empty interrogation room where, because I was always blindfolded, my interrogators retained their anonymity. The only furniture was a table, bathed in shade and therefore congenial to sleep. On one occasion, I dared to try to read the inscriptions atop a series of wall sockets written in English. Some were clear, such as the word *shock*. Others were either illegible, or I no longer remember them.

The day came when, blindfolded as always, I was thrust in a car by my captors, who forced me to keep my head down. The vehicle advanced for several minutes, after which the blindfold was ripped off and I found myself tossed out into the street. Dressed in a T-shirt and underpants, I viewed the urban masses anew. And what I saw was neither a *public* nor a *crowd:* just a busy agglomeration of individuals.

Translated from the Brazilian
by Jeffrey T. Schnapp

and, on the other, superstition, nostalgia, reaction, popular culture, or "the masses" in the negative sense of Le Bon. Lourdes, with its packaged tourism, rampant consumerism, and use of all the latest techniques of mass communication and mass mobilization, appears as a vibrant example of modernity. Its content too shows, from the beginning, a great sensitivity to the intellectual currents of the time. Yet at its center there remains the ancient draw of the supernatural and the miraculous, the desire "to go, to sacrifice, to consult the oracle, to be spectators, at the common sanctuaries," to touch and experience, as part of a collective, the presence of the divine in the places touched by the physical remains of particular persons who had enjoyed a particular intimacy with God as humans. What made that intimacy possible, in almost all cases, was the experience and endurance of these human beings, in their lifetime, of pain and suffering, in imitation of the suffering of Christ.

Travel for such purpose, although it may look and smell and feel like mass tourism, is nonetheless different, because it differs in intention. It seems to permit the reaffirmation of a particular aspect of individual identity that other leisure travel does not offer: a finding of oneself, a biographic construct of before and after, a new authenticity through the common experience of ancient sentiments. Hence, especially the globalization of experiences, including religious experiences, furthers such mass movements to particular sites, because these sites remain fixed points of an enduring antiquity, or, to cite Simon Coleman, an "arena of action and meaning, within the shifting, liminal, chaotic space of the global world."[45] The sensory experience of this arena at the pilgrim's destination and the community of others at the site appear to be irreplaceable. As anyone who has ever experienced a crowd knows, although it may offer better visuals, live television is not yet life.

7 Movies and Masses

Anton Kaes

I

On July 15, 1927, an angry mob of workers stormed the Palace of Justice in Vienna and set it on fire—an unprecedented event that sent shock waves through Europe for years to come. It began as a spontaneous demonstration against an offensively unjust acquittal of three members of a right-wing organization accused of murdering a striking worker, but turned into a rapidly growing mass rally in front of Austria's highest court. The Social Democratic leadership, completely unprepared, feared unrest and decided against an organized protest march, trying instead to calm the incensed masses with speeches. But it was too late. Elias Canetti, then a student in Vienna, recalls,

> From all districts of the city, the workers marched in tight formation to the Palace of Justice, whose sheer name embodied the unjust verdict for them. It was a totally spontaneous reaction: I could tell how spontaneous it was just by my own conduct. I quickly biked into the center of town and joined one of the processions.
>
> The workers, usually well disciplined, trusting their Social Democratic leaders, and satisfied that Vienna was administered by these leaders in an exemplary manner, were acting *without* their leaders on this day. When they set fire to the Palace of Justice, Mayor Seitz mounted a fire engine and raised his right hand high, trying to block their way. His gesture had no effect: the Palace of Justice was *burning*.[1]

Once the large and amorphous mass of demonstrators had become an uncontrollable mob, Vienna's police chief gave the order to shoot into the crowd—an action that brought a quick and bloody end to the protest. Eighty-nine people were killed and hundreds critically injured. As Heimito von Doderer writes at the end of his novel *The Demons*, one could hear "constant shooting coming closer from a nearby street, a volley of shots actually." Moving in closed ranks, the police became "armed troops, advancing in step, firing and driving everything before them."[2] The crowd quickly disbanded, realizing that the battle against the heavily armed police was hopeless. The brutal shooting brought back memories of the war, but now civilians were the enemies. It was an unequal match; they had no chance against the police's heavy weaponry. The uprising yielded little except the realization of the masses' absolute powerlessness when faced with armed opposition. The aftershocks of this event were momentous: there were no more spontaneous rebellions by the urban masses against injustice and misuse of power. Their fear and resignation benefited the subsequent fascist governments across Europe for the next two decades.

In 1932, five years after this debacle, Ernst Jünger claimed in *Der Arbeiter* (The Worker) that the old masses—those storming the Bastille, those involved in street uprisings and political gatherings, and those still cheering the outbreak of the war in August 1914—were a thing of the past. "The actions of the masses," he declared as if referring to the events in Vienna, "have lost their magic wherever they meet resolute resistance, just as two or three old warriors behind an intact machine gun have no reason to be worried even when told that a whole battalion was approaching. Today, the masses are no longer able to attack, they can no longer even defend themselves."[3]

In Vienna, it was, ironically, the leaders of the Social Democratic Workers Party who immediately denounced the behavior of the revolutionary masses as reckless, imprudent, and irrational, using a terminology that dates back to Gustave Le Bon's well-known treatise of 1895, *Psychologie des foules*.[4] When the Social Democrats convened for a party congress in October 1927, three months after the event, they reiterated their critique of the undisciplined and lawless masses and emphasized the importance of transcending class differences for the sake of social harmony. Henry Ford, the car manufacturer, had indeed replaced Karl Marx; consumer capitalism had superseded communism; and "practical solutions" had triumphed over ideology.[5]

II

The July 1927 uprising in the streets of Vienna strangely follows the script of the staged worker uprising in Fritz Lang's film *Metropolis,* which debuted only a few months before. Both crowds (in the streets and in the movie) seemed deaf toward attempts at appeasement; instead, they pursued the path of blind rage and an orgiastic desire to destroy. After the violent rebellion has run its course, both are presented with the chimera of a harmonious society beyond class struggle and political enmity. Both come to realize the senselessness of their revolt.

Metropolis spared no expense to stage the proletarian revolution and class reconciliation in unabashed opulence. The stylized presentation of revolutionary masses that cost 5.3 million Reichmarks—three times its budget—bankrupted Germany's foremost film production company UFA. The film, which (except for the ending) critiqued ruthless and cold American capitalism from the perspective of excitable German idealism, needed the financial support of two American production companies, Paramount and Metro Goldwyn, in order to make it to the big screen. After almost two years of production, *Metropolis*, the most expensive and ambitious film to date in Europe, would finally open on January 10, 1927, in a festive premiere.

Two thousand five hundred invited guests, including the German Reichskanzler, members of the diplomatic corps, and the leaders of industry and banking, filed into the Berlin Zoopalast, the city's largest and most lavish movie palace, to watch the spectacle of a self-destructing proletariat. In his film, Fritz Lang sent the anonymous working masses into battle against the heroic entrepreneur modeled after Henry Ford. With robot-Maria as the classical rabble rouser, the staged revolt in *Metropolis* recalled Rosa Luxemburg and the failed 1918–1919 revolution while also serving as a blueprint for the disastrous revolt in Vienna. The vertical structure of the film's architecture enforces the tension between the classes: every movement upward (Maria into the ruler's domain) or downward (Freder in the machine rooms) results in major destabilization of the fixed social order. Stylistically, the film oscillates between Bible and Bauhaus, catacombs and futuristic skyscrapers, occultism and the cult of technology. After the revolutionary masses suffered defeat and possible self-annihilation, they are reintegrated into a unified body, marching in formation, in the film's final reconciliation scene at the steps of a Gothic church—a phantasmagoric vision for the utopian political union of all classes. After the political body's destruction through war and revolution, Lang's *Metropolis* pursued a project of regeneration. In its fusion of theater, architecture, and music, the film itself embodied a kind of unified *Gesamtkunstwerk* for the masses, with the synthesis of different arts in cinema enacting the wish for a new unity of the national body.

III

Metropolis, a film of transitions and transformations in the social realm, begins with a montage of visual superimpositions. Gleaming pistons and wheels are projected onto brightly lit skyscrapers, suggesting a union of urban architecture and technology in the modern metropolis. Interspliced with images of cityscapes and stomping machines, two battalions of workers meet as they change shifts. With one battalion marching toward the camera, the other marching in the opposite direction, they slowly fill the screen. With their black uniforms and their conformity in size and shuffling gait, they resemble the faceless soldiers of World War I. Lang depicts them as automatons controlled by some invisible power.

Michel Foucault argued in *Discipline and Punish* that in the eighteenth century the factory had joined the army in becoming one of the institutions in which "teachable bodies" are produced:

Historians of ideas usually attribute the dream of a perfect society to the philosophers and jurists of the eighteenth century: but there was also a military dream of society; its fundamental reference was not to the state of nature, but to the meticulously subordinated cogs of a machine, not to the primal social contract, but to permanent coercion, not to fundamental rights, but to indefinitely progressive forms of training, not to the general will but to automatic docility.[6]

7A 'Samuuha': Sanskrit

Peter Samuels

The word *samuuha* in Sanskrit signifies a crowd, multitude, or assemblage (fig. 7A.1, below). Although *samuuha* has survived into our own time through *prakrit* (vernacular) languages such as Hindi, which grew out of Sanskrit, its modern usage markedly differs from that found in the spiritual and epic writings of the Vedic and classical periods.

Figure 7A.1

Many of the major sacred texts and epics written in Sanskrit were composed during the Vedic period, before the "common era" of the western calendar. As nonvernacular texts written in an esteemed language of purity and perfection, these texts either issue moral injunctions or didactic messages through narratives involving the interplay of relationships between gods, kings, and mortal humans. It is within this thematic structure that the figure of the crowd is often invoked in order to reflect the singular might of the higher being to which crowds are juxtaposed.

In the hymns of *Rigveda*, reputed as being the earliest and most significant of the *Vedas*, and composed between 1500 and 1200 bce, the figure of the crowd plays just such a role:

Agni, the God resplendent, giver of great joy, has on his lovely vehicle encompassed the lands with might.

Let us with pure laudations in his house approach the high laws of this nourisher of multitudes. (3, hymn 3, line 9)

In the legendary historical-spiritual epic Vyasa's *Mahabharath* (ca. 1400 bce)—a mythological tale of a feud between two families in which thousands are killed—crowds feature even more significantly and are often spectators at battles and bear public witness to expressions of triumph and defeat: "The citizens consisting of thousands . . . came out and gathered to behold the fight. The crowd became so great that it was one solid mass of humanity with no space between body and body" (book 23). Another key Vedic text, the *Laws of Manu* (ca. 1280 bce), contains spiritual injunctions for everyday life. Here crowds are invoked as markers of the public domain of social life and can be seen to represent the divide between the public and the private, the sacred and the profane. For example, the *Laws of Manu* state that the *Vedas* must not be recited under certain conditions, one of which is a gathering of a "crowd of men" (book 4, line 108).

Although Vedic Sanskrit had ceded considerable ground to its classical form by 250 bce, *samuuha* continued to be used in reference to crowds and can be found in some of the later writings of the classical period. For example, it features in the writings of the poets Somadeva and Jayadeva in the twelfth and thirteenth centuries, after which Sanskrit had been largely supplanted by a number of *prakrit* languages such as Hindi and Pali, the spiritual language of Buddhism. Nevertheless, Sanskrit continues to be extremely highly regarded as a spiritual and scholarly language, and many attempts have been made to "sanskritize" certain *prakrits* in order to refine them.

The word *samuuha*, however, remains in use

In *Metropolis*, the military dream of "automatic docility" rests on Taylorism as the theory and praxis of industrial production. In Freder's hallucination, a machine metamorphoses into the heathen god Moloch, to whom, in a visually stunning scene, entire battalions of working slaves are sacrificed. When the exploited workers finally destroy their machines in a blind rage, echoing Ernst Toller's 1924 play *Machine Wreckers,* they realize the degree to which industrial technology controlled their lives.

According to Ernst Jünger, it was technology that had transformed the latently dangerous masses of the nineteenth century into the homogeneous masses of modernity's worker-soldiers. Masses were not solely formed through the work process but rather, as Jünger had long recognized, through institutions of modernity: "The traffic system, the supply of basic necessities, such as fire, water and light, a developed system of credit and many other things . . . are similar to the strands, the free-flowing veins, through which the amorphous body of the masses is connected to death and life."[7] In his pivotal 1932 study *The Worker*, Jünger claims that enormous integrated systems like technology and bureaucracy, in addition to disciplinary institutions such as school, church, military, and, I would like to add, cinema, have addressed the growing threat of the masses and devised ways to monitor and control them. Film had become an instrument of subliminal and unforced discipline—perhaps because it was the place where the masses gathered without coercion.

The visually striking Tower of Babel scene in *Metropolis* shows how closely entertainment and instruction are interwoven in this process. We first see the exploited workers stream toward a cavernous secret meeting place deep under the city. The workers become a movie audience when Maria presents the parable of the Tower of Babel as a film within a film. They watch and listen respectfully, visibly moved, as Maria, the prophet standing before an altar covered with crosses and candles, conjures up the vision of an ancient society that destroys itself because of disunity. The planning, erection, and destruction of the Tower of Babel has mythical as well as futuristic dimensions. It reveals to the workers of Metropolis the consequences of proletarian rebellion and turns them into spectators who can view their own fate in biblical-mythical terms. Maria's short instructional film exposes "false" behaviors of the proletarian masses and their consequences. Her film's message—that once unleashed, class struggle will inevitably lead to devastation and self-destruction—is very clear. Ironically, however, the working masses learn nothing from the film. Soon afterward, they attack the machines.

Metropolis's overwhelmingly bourgeois audience in 1927 could feel superior to the unenlightened, politically activist, and slightly outdated proletarian masses in the film—an attitude that undoubtedly boosted the entertainment value of the film. What in the Bible was human hubris, which caused the destruction of a unified language, is here retold as a parable about class and power—the confusion of languages appears as a mere consequence of labor division. The workers do not understand the lofty designs of the rulers, and the rulers show no awareness of the workers' suffering. Ultimately, the mediation between hand and head, not class divisions themselves, are called into question. In order to anchor Maria's message—rebellion against the authorities destroys not only social peace but is also self-destructive—as deeply as possible in the cultural memory and to present it as "natural," the film borrows from classical painting: the Tower of Babel derives from the famous 1563 painting by Pieter Bruegel, while the chief architect's pose is from Auguste Rodin's well-known sculpture, *The Thinker*, of 1882. The vertical steps (a graphic image of the power relations and hierarchies in *Metropolis*'s class society) are products of Max Reinhardt and Leopold Jessner's stage artistry.[8] The last scene is the reversal of the first: the Tower of Babel is in ruins, just as much of Metropolis is destroyed at the end of Lang's film. However, another ending follows the destruction of the machines.

In the irritating, although completely intelligible, closing scene of *Metropolis*, the worker-soldiers march again in clear formations after the failed uprising, re-emphasizing the parallels, in both form and function, of factory and army. The "disciplined crowd" at the end of the film becomes witness to the denouement of private as well as public story. The love story between the idealist, industrial tycoon's son and the charismatic worker's daughter culminates in a positive, class-transcending end, complete with hug and kiss, while the struggle between management and working class is set aside peacefully (after some hesitation) with a handshake—a solution in the spirit of Henry Ford, whose plan for the production of social peace was well known in 1920s Germany.[9] Later, in American exile, Fritz Lang denounced this quick and simple reconciliation between the classes as a fairy-tale ending and pushed the responsibility for it onto Thea von Harbou, his former wife and screenplay coauthor. Lang said that he had only been interested in machines.[10] Still, the fairy-tale ending certainly has a logic of its own: it suggests, only a few years after the double trauma of military defeat and failed revolution, the common dream of a modern nation born again and reunited through work and discipline.

today, albeit in a slightly different way from its deployment in the Sanskrit texts cited above. In modern Hindi and Nepali, among the closest *prakrits* to Sanskrit, *samuuha* refers to a collectivity produced in the spirit of community and service, banded together, for example, by a common humanitarian goal and often with a basis in shared experiences. Thus, *samuuha* in modern India and Nepal can be found in the titles of various community organizations and social movements.

Conversely, quite another word for *crowd* exists in modern Hindi: *bheedh*. Rather than invoking an image of throngs gathering to bear witness to the epic feats of gods and kings, this word refers more accurately to a crowded market or bus stop—in short, to congestion more than a gathering of spectators or a reverent mass. This ostensible splitting of *samuuha* and the crowd from Sanskrit to the present time is, perhaps, a product of the phenomenon of the modern crowd itself, an example of the ways in which language changes to express new social and cultural realities in new contexts.

The word *samudra*, meaning "the ocean" in Sanskrit and Hindi, and remarkably close in its phonemic structure and associative meaning to *samuuha*, is still used to refer to the ocean.[1]

7B Dolores Park, Dyke March, June 2002

Tirza True Latimer

Dolores. Imagine naming a baby for pain. Imagine spending your life responding to that name. A woman's name. Dolores Park. Today, there are only women here. Or if you think that the word *women* only makes sense within a patriarchal, heterosexual syntax, there are no women here.

Dolores Park is the staging ground for San Francisco's annual Dyke March. Speakers and performers, vying for the attention of those assembled, tax an over-amped sound system to its limits from a black stage erected where the grass ends and the concrete begins. But the dykes, sitting on the lawn in clusters, dressed to the nines, undressed, underdressed, standing with their arms around each other in the thick of the action, standing with their hands in their pockets at the margins of the gathering, shifting from foot to foot, are not easily distracted from their own pursuits; they scope out the comings and goings, the rows of kick-standed motorcycles framing the green; they converse, they embrace, they comb the steadily growing crowd of lesbians, greeting passers-by, known and unknown, avoiding or soliciting the gaze of ex-lovers, future lovers. We are all lovers today or we wouldn't be here.

By the time the gathering swells into a crowd and takes to its feet to become a demonstration, a march, the park, can no longer contain its dyke population. Ten thousand? Fifteen thousand? Twenty? Who's counting?

In 1927, the same year in which proletarian revolts were quelled both in *Metropolis* and in front of the Viennese Palace of Justice, Alfred Döblin began work on *Berlin Alexanderplatz*, a novel about the existential status of the working class in the big modern city. His protagonist Franz Biberkopf's desperate and futile search for community marks the transition from the traditional (exploited and rebelling) worker to the new (pacified and subjugated) *typus* of worker-soldier described by Ernst Jünger in *The Worker* five years later. The novel begins with Franz Biberkopf's release from Tegel prison, where he has been serving a four-year sentence for murder (a duration that alludes to the four years of World War I). Once outside of the prison (or rather, after the war), he is brutally exposed to the overpowering metropolitan world swirling around him. The roaring street traffic and the proliferation of signs produce an information overload that makes him dizzy. As Biberkopf meanders through the city, a movie theater magically attracts him. He enters and watches a melodrama with the telling title *Parentless, Fate of an Orphan in 6 Acts*. However, what he sees is not as important to him as what he physically experiences in the dark theater among similarly "parentless" moviegoers: "It moved Franz greatly when the giggles around him began. So many were there, free people, were amusing themselves; no one could tell them what to do, magnificent, and I am right in the middle of it all."[11] An oceanic feeling of community and solidarity overcomes him in the dark, womblike space of the densely occupied movie theater. It seems as if the masses of the postrevolutionary era have claimed the illusionary world of the movies—an imaginary dream world projected in a dark space walled off from the surging life outside—as a refuge from their alienated existences; the movies promised life in its plenitude, even if simulated and limited to two hours. For the uprooted masses of the cities, movies promised a short, intensive, communal experience, a temporary relief from the daily discriminations due to class status, ethnic origin, sex, age, religion, or political orientation. It was a community that raised no claim to identity and consequently did not depend on exclusion.[12] At least in principle, all were equal before the flickering images in the darkness of the movie theater. In the mid-1920s, the movie theater was seen as warm shelter from the "coldness" of the modern metropolis; it became not only a home to all who yearned for a feeling of community, but also a counterworld to the technologized city, notwithstanding the paradox that the movies themselves were a product of technology and urban life.

V

"The many millions," wrote film critic Eugen Tannenbaum in 1923, "who sit in the cinemas every night, under the spell of life that twitches across the screen from countless kilometers of lit celluloid strips—traders, workers, craftsmen, academics, clerks, snobs and ladies of the real world, but after a few scenes they become a *homogeneous mass* that has gathered for a theme, a problem, a thought, a film star, formed under the suggestion of passion—they all want to see the world newly arisen."[13] Statistics show the drawing power of movies for the masses: in 1927, Berlin alone boasted more than three hundred movie theaters with 165,000 total seats; around thirty of these "distraction palaces" (Kracauer) seated between a thousand and three thousand people. The German Reich had no fewer than two million moviegoers a day.

After the end of inflation in 1924 and at the beginning of an economic upturn, Germany's working class developed new attitudes, spurred on by countless images from American cinema that defined "modern life" in terms of consumption. The working masses in offices and factories perceived themselves increasingly as consumers and less as exploited victims or revolutionary subjects. The film industry satisfied their wishes: in the mid-1920s, lavish movie palaces were built, production costs of films rose drastically, and the films themselves, most of them Hollywood imports, embodied style, glamour, and urban coolness. German films, in contrast, tried to define themselves as high art (for example, F. W. Murnau's 1926 version of *Faust* or Lang's *Metropolis*), which married avant-garde aesthetics to an ambitious social message.

"The more people perceive themselves as a mass," writes Kracauer in his 1926 essay "Cult of Distraction: On Berlin's Picture Palaces," "the sooner the masses will also develop productive powers in the spiritual and cultural domain that are worth financing."[14] For Kracauer, a "homogeneous cosmopolitan audience" emerged "in which everyone has the same responses, from the bank director to the sales clerk, from the diva to the stenographer."[15] The menacing masses of the nineteenth century evolved into paying film audiences in the 1920s, and movies became a second home for these new consuming masses.

Standing on the steps of the Mission Dolores Basilica, my lover and I watch the marchers go by—ten or twenty abreast—for an hour. We are struck, uplifted, by the variety of marchers reclaiming these streets with their bodies in the name of dykes—all colors, sizes, shapes, ages, and styles jostling each other, cuddling, sparring, signaling in a range of languages and body languages that frustrate any impulse to generalize.

How long have I been grinning? The muscles around my mouth ache. I am surrounded by people whom I do not know but whom I do not perceive as potentially hostile. A novel experience. Thrilling.

My lover and I join in at the tail end of the parade. Leaning out the windows of the Victorian houses that line the parade route, Castro-dwellers whistle and cheer. Our brothers. They give their streets over to us gladly. In a few hours, this ad hoc legion of dykes will disperse, melting into the population at large. Tomorrow, the world, these streets, will bear little trace of this moment.

What will these few hours of taking to (and taking over) the streets—of loving each other in public—mean to us in a week? A month? How long will the power of these sympathetic bodies bolster us?

VI

The universalism of silent film language—gestures need no linguistic proficiency—lent the film a global dimension. Audiences around the world intuitively understood Charlie Chaplin's slapstick films. Benjamin noted that Chaplin's worldwide appeal came from laughter as the "simultaneously most international and revolutionary affect of the masses."[16] Because Chaplin's movies transcended national boundaries as well as class barriers, movie-going crowds recognized themselves as part of a global community united in laughter.

Even though cinema has in the last few decades rapidly expanded from a refuge for "homeless" metropolitan masses to a worldwide entertainment industry, the original practice of "going to the movies" has remained unchanged: a mass of people assembles in a public space and constitutes a momentary and radically contingent community. Even though the gathering may be more arbitrary and coincidental than in the theater or in church, a sense of communality is nonetheless produced through sheer physical proximity and collective reactions such as laughing, crying, or (in horror films) screaming. These are spontaneous bodily reactions that may be capable of transforming a heterogeneous mass into a relatively homogeneous group—a group that transcends, at least for the film's duration, barriers of class, gender, age, race, ethnicity, and national identity. In contrast to a sports arena, the movie theater is dark; the spectators are alone with themselves (they often lose themselves under the hypnotic effect of the projected images), but they are also part of the surrounding audience, undeniably present with its noises, smells, and physical bodies. Whereas the theater presupposes an "aesthetic community" (Ernst Jünger), popular movies address the general public, which is hybrid, undefined, and unstable. The transitory and restless nature of the movie audience makes it into a temporary community that has no other identity than that of a consuming audience.

VII

Lang's depiction of the long-suffering but then irrationally rebelling masses in *Metropolis* must have seemed behind the times to a modern movie audience of 1927. Workers who in their fanaticism destroy the system that sustains them could not expect great sympathy from the metropolitan masses that had learned to pursue realistic goals. *Metropolis*, on the other hand, displays masses easily misled to use violence, act irresponsibly, and blame their behavior on a scapegoat ("the witch"). Lang's film exaggerated all the classical stereotypes and threats associated with the masses since Le Bon's fearful account of them at the end of the nineteenth century. The rebellion of the oppressed working class is shown to be doubly ineffective, even comical in its Luddite approach, within the ultramodern setting of a science fiction film. *Metropolis* clearly catered to a new classless, even blasé mass audience that considered social turmoil an obstacle to consumption.[17]

From this perspective, a new look at the controversial and unanimously criticized closing scene in *Metropolis* is warranted because it illustrates the historical change in the representation of the masses. An orderly crowd of pacified workers (Jünger's "worker-soldiers"), filmed from above, moves slowly from the bottom part of the screen into view. When the mass stops, it forms a triangle in front of the cathedral, a geometric form that precludes individuality. The workers, who had suffered under and rebelled against their exploitation at the beginning of the film, now become silent witnesses to a public reconciliation between their representative (who had betrayed their trust before) and management. The workers have come to terms with their ultimate role as spectators, as has the movie audience, which sits in front of the screen as the workers' mirror image. Disillusioned and relieved of all revolutionary determination, the masses, both in the film's narrative and in the film theater, have become consumers who silently watch a spectacle, in which their own cause is negotiated. The camera, shooting them from a bird's-eye view, transforms the previously rebellious workers into a "mass ornament" (Kracauer) of thousands, enjoyed by thousands in the Zoopalast in 1927. Only in the mass medium of film do the masses become visible to themselves—as spectators.

8 Mass, Pack, and Mob: Art in the Age of the Crowd

Christine Poggi

AMONG THOSE WHO TOOK NOTICE of the powerful presence of the masses on the political and cultural stage of his time, Charles Baudelaire was nearly alone in extolling the experience of the urban crowd. His prose poem "Crowds" describes the phenomenon as a dialectic of "multitude, solitude," in which these terms are interchangeable, even identical. For Baudelaire, enjoying the crowd is an art that depends on "the love of masks and masquerading, the hate of home, and the passion for roaming." Like the fully self-possessed dandy, who spends his days strolling the urban street and attending to its spectacular effects and chance encounters, the poet can easily abandon his identity to assume another. Such a man does not automatically surrender his reason and conscious will on immersion in the crowd, as most crowd theorists assumed, but intentionally selects whose personality to inhabit: "The poet enjoys the incomparable privilege of being able to be himself or some one else, as he chooses. Like those wandering souls who go looking for a body, he enters as he likes into each man's personality. For him alone everything is vacant; and if certain places seem closed to him, it is only because in his eyes they are not worth visiting." Baudelaire describes the rare ability to transcend the confines of the ego as the precondition for experiencing "feverish delights," moments of "a singular intoxication in this universal communion." Paradoxically, however, such communion is given only to the few, for whom the multitude presents an open site for colonization. Indeed, Baudelaire imagines that the "founders of colonies, shepherds of peoples, missionary priests exiled to the ends of the earth, doubtlessly know something of this mysterious drunkenness."[1]

The Parisian crowd, newly on display in the era of Haussmannization, provides Baudelaire with an opportunity for an exhilarating encounter with an unknown, but still particularized "other." The thrill of imaginatively entering the "stranger as he passes" recalls Baudelaire's peculiarly modern definition of beauty (exemplified by the dandy), which must offer the frisson of the unexpected and strange, the fleeting and the eternal.[2] The threatening homogenization that characterized crowds was palliated in part through a pose of aristocratic distinction, which allowed the dandy to remain master of the gaze while remaining unseen.[3] Yet elsewhere in the prose poem Baudelaire writes of being submerged in the multitude, of "relish[ing] a debauch of vitality at the expense of the human species."[4] If the poet/dandy is only at home on the boulevards of the modern city, it is because he is also its quintessential product, the counterimage of the bustling crowd. His exaggerated individuality, elegant fashions, and cool demeanor constitute a protective mask, a defense against urban shocks and the threat of a leveling anonymity so acutely analyzed by Georg Simmel.[5] As Baudelaire put it in his essay "The Painter of Modern Life," the artist/dandy is like a self-conscious mirror reflecting the kaleidoscopic patterns of life, "an ego athirst for the non-ego, and reflecting it at every moment in energies more vivid than life itself, always inconstant and fleeting."[6] Cosmopolitan in his tastes, rootless but at home in a world of electrifying spectacles, the artist/dandy seeks to amplify his identity by becoming a reflective surface shimmering with the transient and alluring effects of modern, commodity culture.

The chiasmic interchange between multitude/solitude and ego/non-ego that drives Baudelaire's reflections on his experience of the crowd also announces a dialectic that would be central to crowd theory as it developed in the late nineteenth century. Social psychologists including Gabriel Tarde, Scipio Sighele, and Gustave Le Bon all sought to understand the apparent loss of individuality that occurs whenever a crowd forms to create a new, mentally unified organism. For Le Bon, whose popular book *La Psychologie des foules* of 1895 synthesized many of the theories that

were circulating at the time, "the sentiments and ideas of all the persons in the gathering take one and the same direction, and their conscious personality vanishes."[7] Similarly, the Italian criminal anthropologist Sighele argued that "the most marvelous phenomenon is precisely this obliteration of the singular personality in a single, immense personality, different from each of those who compose it. One would say that each individual loses the ability to feel and to think and becomes a blind instrument of an unknown brain and spirit."[8] Although both theorists admitted that the crowd could occasionally be heroic as an instrument of historical change, for the most part, they viewed the loss of individuality with horror, seeing in the crowd a reversion to a primitive, unconscious state, similar to that of a hypnotized subject. And like the hypnotized subject, those immersed in a crowd became highly suggestible and tended to follow what Tarde called "the laws of imitation"[9]—hence their "feminine" volatility and their proclivity for excessive sentiment, violence, and crime. Members of crowds were transformed from heterogeneous individuals into homogeneous ciphers, easily seduced by a charismatic, prestigious, and often authoritarian leader. The crowd constituted an *informe* mass, mere raw matter, which the leader would infuse with spirit and thereby shape according to his wishes. Le Bon had written his book precisely to apprise potential leaders of their task, that of shaping and dominating the crowd.

Crowd psychology emerged as a field of inquiry in the second half of the nineteenth century as a response to the rapid progress of urbanization and industrialization, as well as the decline of traditional forms of belief and custom. Indeed, for Le Bon, the "modern age represents a period of transition and anarchy" (*C,* 14). Newly dislocated and discontented popular classes demanded political power, inspiring in many a fear of riots or even revolution. As Le Bon observed, "the divine right of the masses is about to replace the divine right of kings" (*C,* 16). And because in the estimation of Tarde and Le Bon, invention and civilization are always the achievements of a small aristocracy, never of the masses, the decline of traditional hierarchies threatened to destroy civilization itself (*C*, 18, 182; *LI*, 2). But such destruction could occur only because profound instability and decay already existed within a given social structure. For many observers, French society of the second half of the nineteenth century—in its uncertain class relations, in the proliferation of commodities and commercial culture, in the rise of mass media, and in its pervasive materialism—presented such symptoms of decline.[10]

The artists who sought to represent the varied phenomena of the modern crowd, whether gathered provisionally on a boulevard or assembled for entertainment, a riot, political demonstration, or a public event, also meditated on the forms of its psychological cohesion, and on the relation of the individual to the larger social mass. How they viewed the crowd, how they positioned themselves in relation to it, and how they chose to appeal to it through their work reveal a great deal about historical transformations in the public sphere, commodity culture, and media since Baudelaire's time. If the nineteenth-century crowd still primarily depended on the physical proximity of individuals, usually on the street, in a theater, or public square, the contemporary crowd is often a virtual collectivity, achieved through the exchange of information, advertising, and opinion. Yet the roots of the dispersed crowd were already well established by the late nineteenth century and first analyzed by Le Bon, who reflected on the role of national events in generating such crowds, especially when the prior circulation of ideas and sentiments predisposed individuals to a particular response:

For individuals to succumb to contagion their simultaneous presence on the same spot is not indispensable. The action of contagion may be felt from a distance under the influence of events which give all minds an individual trend and the characteristics peculiar to crowds. This is especially the case when men's minds have been prepared to undergo the influence in question. (*C*, 126)

The threatening example he cited was the "revolutionary movement of 1848, which, after breaking out in Paris spread rapidly over a great part of Europe and shook a number of thrones" (*C*, 126). Like Le Bon, Tarde called particular attention to the role of newspapers in the creation of opinion, and eventually of publics (which he came to distinguish from crowds).[11] Today's virtual crowds, which communicate through electronic media with a speed Tarde could scarcely have imagined, must be seen as linked to the rise of new industrial forms of culture and mass subjectivity in the nineteenth century.

One of the earliest avatars of the emerging commercial mass culture of the late eighteenth and early nineteenth centuries can be found in the panorama, which was invented in 1787 by the Irishman Robert Barker. The panorama enjoyed successive waves of popularity throughout Europe and America until the end of the nineteenth century, when the birth of cinema led to its gradual demise. The panorama's success lay in its mobilization of a circular format and meticulous hyperrealism to create a seamless illusion that could transport viewers to the scene of a war, to near or faraway cities, or to the site of historical events. Spectators would enter a rotunda and ascend to an elevated central viewing platform through a dark stairway, designed to conceal the panorama's physical structure. Once on the platform, and still in relative darkness, viewers would behold a painting illuminated from above by natural light, whose source was filtered (to reduce shadows) and concealed by a suspended false ceiling that made the upper edge of the canvas impossible to see. The lower edge was similarly masked by a fence or by *faux terrain* (imitation terrain) that created an imperceptible transition from the viewing gallery to the image. No dissonant reminder of reality was allowed to interrupt the spectator's field of vision. The suppression of the frame, darkened viewing platform, and circular horizon gave observers the exhilarating experience of unfettered, total vision of the world displayed before them, but from which they were also safely distanced. Not surprisingly, the propaganda uses of such a visual machine were not missed by those who sought to promote nationalist sentiment, justify colonial ventures, or advertise particular sectors of industry.

Although Barker's first panorama in Edinburgh was designed for an elite clientele, the high investment cost of this self-financing operation quickly determined that access be given to all classes.[12] Some panoramas provided two viewing platforms with different entrance fees: a lower, crowded platform with poor visibility for the working and middle classes, and an upper, aristocratic platform where places were limited and viewing could occur at greater leisure. It was a commonplace that different strata of society were attracted to the panorama for different reasons; the educated classes were thought to appreciate the interpretive originality of the images, whereas the masses were said to be attracted by the illusory effects and thrilling sensations the new format made possible (*P*, 115). Yet ironically, the lower viewing platform offered a vantage that was out of true, whereas the upper platform provided a convincing perspective and better illumination, suggesting that visitors to the upper platform may have been more easily taken in by the illusion before them. For the most part, however, a heterogeneous crowd flocked to the panorama seeking entertainment and spectacular effects.

Scenes of war, which allowed crowds of spectators to view their heroic counterimage, or even to project themselves into the fray of battle, were among the more popular subjects. One of the most successful was Jean-Charles Langlois's *Naval Battle of Navarino* of 1831 (which survives only in a drawing providing a cross section, elevation, and plan). Langlois was an officer of the Legion of Honor and a veteran of Napoleon's campaigns who had studied military painting with Horace Vernet. His *Naval Battle of Navarino* depicted a battle off the Greek coast at Navarino (now Pylos) of 1827, in which French, English, and Russian ships, arrayed on one side, fought against the Turks on the other. The painting was unveiled at the inauguration of Langlois's new rotunda, the largest in Paris at fifteen meters high and thirty-eight meters in diameter, in the Rue des Marais-du-Temple. This panorama sought to surpass all previous examples in scale and illusory effects in order to bring an episode of recent history to life. Langlois's innovations included replacing the usual viewing gallery with a section of the deck of the frigate *Scipion* (which had taken part in the depicted battle), having viewers pass through a reconstruction of an officer's cabin and then up a stairway to the captain's dining room on their way to the platform, perfecting the use of imitation terrain, using gas burners to enhance the effect of the burning ship, and using ventilation to simulate sea breezes.[13] For panorama architect and historian Jacques Ignace Hittorf, the result was an unparalleled "manifestation of reality": "The site was transformed into a fully armed and rigged vessel, the end of which gradually merged with the canvas at the back with the help of the authenticity of the relief, the shapes of the bas-reliefs and the painting. This *tour de force* of art and ingenious industry in the pursuit of *maximum* illusion was crowned by an epoch-making success."[14] Germain Bapst commented that whereas other panoramas preserved a sense of distance from the painting, Langlois situated the viewer in "the very center of the action."[15] Such theatricality gave rise to equally theatrical responses, with one young woman reporting that she had had a genuine hysterical attack when viewing Langlois's panorama (*P*, 103). Some sense of Langlois's realism and use of special effects can be gleaned through his subsequent work, *The Battle of Moscow* of 1838 (fig. 8.1). Here makeshift fences, rocks, and overturned canon in the foreground open onto the field of battle, in which massed troops confront each other amidst the wreckage of fallen men, weapons, and horses. The smoke of fired cannons envelops the scene in the atmosphere of war while allowing the artist to obscure certain areas and highlight others, and to balance

Figure 8.1 Jean-Charles Langlois, Detail, *Study for The Battle of Moscow.* Oil on canvas, 1838. Musée de l'Armée, Paris.

distant views of the vast plain of battle with detailed close-ups of heroic individuals. Thus Langlois achieved both anecdotal legibility and epic scale without sacrificing dramatic effects or a sense of historical accuracy.

Langlois's *Naval Battle of Navarino* and *The Battle of Moscow* brought the panoramic form to an apex of illusion, in which the image replaced the reality it represented, thereby affirming its version of truth. With the advent of photography just a few years later, the academic realism these and other panoramas relied on would have to be modernized. When Langlois set out to create a new panorama representing the siege at Sebastopol in the Crimean War in 1855, he traveled to the site to document the topography of the zone, the fortifications, positions of the troops, and war action. This time he used photographs as the basis for his preparatory drawings, a practice that became increasingly frequent as artists sought to guarantee the authenticity of their images.[16] As in the earlier practice of juxtaposing drawings made from a single rotated axis, here, a series of partly overlapping photographs would be joined to create the basis for a continuous 360-degree image, with the inevitable perspectival distortions smoothed out in the painting. The panorama experienced a last wave of popularity at the end of the nineteenth century before ceding to other, related forms of hyperrealist display. In the twentieth century, the film, the circular or environmentally scaled photomural, and even the foldouts in popular magazines, can be seen as panoramic in their effort to create an uninterrupted field of vision in which the image displaces reality. These media were frequently put to use whenever it was a matter of interpellating the masses, of providing an exhilarating sense of total vision, or of compelling belief in political causes. As we will see, panoramic media were especially prominent in the depiction of crowds—whether revolutionary masses, political rallies, marches, or scenes of battle—during the interwar period. Their use corresponded to the requirements of propaganda, as articulated by crowd theorists and consciously adopted by the fascists, communists, and even democratic nations, although some important differences in technique and ideology may also be observed.

If Langlois set out to represent events of the recent past—or, in the case of *Siege of Sebastopol*, a current conflict in which some viewers would recognize the topography and remember the action—other artists similarly sought to represent a contemporary scene in which viewers might find their idealized mirror reflection. Edouard Manet's *Music in the Tuileries* of 1862 (fig. 8.2) is frequently heralded as one of the first depictions of the heroism and beauty of modern life celebrated by Baudelaire's famous essay, "The Painter of Modern Life" of the following year. The painting pictures a fashionable gathering for a concert in the Tuileries garden, with all the markers and protocols of class on display. As T. J. Clark has observed, this painting should be regarded as transitional in that the public realm it portrays is still composed of particular individuals who are legible in terms of profession and rank, and who are recognized by friends and relations. Listeners exchange glances, converse, and enjoy an easy conviviality.[17] No obvious heterogeneity intrudes on this gathering, and no mixing of classes destabilizes it.

The picture is tightly cropped, with figures pressed close to each other and to the edges of the frame, so much so that the abandoned chair in the near right foreground seems to invite our entry into the scene. A few individuals look directly out, as if to acknowledge our proximity. The artist himself stands, partly cut off, at the extreme left of the canvas, accompanied by his friend Albert de Balleroy, and between them is the critic Champfleury; other identifiable figures include Baudelaire, Théophile Gautier, and Aurélien Schol. If Manet depicts a familiar world of which he is an integral part, he nevertheless chooses to view it from a marginal position, as a dandy who observes but remains nearly unseen.

Despite the legibility and apparent social cohesion of the crowd depicted in *Music in the Tuileries*, signs of fragmenta-

Figure 8.2 Edouard Manet, *Music in the Tuileries.* Oil on canvas, 1862. National Gallery, London. Photo © The National Gallery, London.

tion and dispersal can also be found there. With the source of the entertainment out of view and the figures looking in different directions, no focal point generates a larger sense of unity or hierarchical organization; rather, individuals coalesce into small, random, scattered groups that seem to extend indefinitely beyond the picture's frame. Anomalies in the rendering of space and scale cause foreground and background to become elided in places, with some figures looming too large and others strangely diminished. Passages of realist description alternate with crudely scumbled areas, as if the artist had wiped out certain sections but neglected to repaint them. Yet the thickly smeared white, black, and gray brushstrokes at the lower right and center can also be read as evidence of fresh vision, or a willful naïveté, also marks of modernity. If we cannot make out the relations of the figures in the right foreground, or if the forms at the center of the composition—including the seated, veiled woman, who offers a music program to the standing man in the top hat—dissolve into a vaguely construed mass, this may be a symptom of the growing indeterminacy of certain social signs.

Many of the figures in *Music in the Tuileries* can be identified, yet there is also a tendency for the repetition of fashionable top hats, frock coats, and canes to counter these portraits with a sense of overall sameness, of "uniformity." Baudelaire had already ironically observed the paradox of men's fashions: the "much abused frock coat" exemplified contemporary beauty and native charm while simultaneously introducing "the inevitable uniform of our suffering age, carrying on its very shoulders, black and narrow, the mark of perpetual mourning." The frock coat, an object of fashion, also boasted of "political beauty, which is the expression of universal equality" ("1846," 105). Those who wished to distinguish themselves would have to be content with subtle differences of cut and design, avoiding color and ornament ("1846," 105–6). The field within which social distinctions could be expressed was thereby reduced,

in itself a cause of mourning for Baudelaire. He compared the result to "an immense procession of undertakers' mutes, political mutes, bourgeois mutes. All of us are attending some funeral or other" ("1846," 105).

A more distinct sense of unease, perhaps due to a recognition of social uniformity and isolation within apparent diversity and collectivity, emerges from an examination of the neoimpressionist Georges Seurat's many works that portray crowds. Paintings such as *Sunday Afternoon on the Island of the Grand Jatte* of 1884–1886, *Parade de Cirque* (Circus Parade) of 1887–1888, and *Cirque* (Circus) of 1890–1891 (fig. 8.3) focus on popular entertainments and the ambiguous relations of social classes within the urban world of commodified spectacle. Each of these paintings depicts an occasion for shared enjoyment, which is contradicted by the rigid postures, frozen smiles, and insularity of the figures. If a social aggregate is implied by the gathering of individuals in leisure activity or in attending to the same proffered diversions, the paintings fail to offer a convincing picture of spontaneous cohesion across class lines. Like the dots and dashes from which Seurat composed his paintings, the figures in his works point toward an ideal of unity through homogeneity, but that unity emerges only provisionally, as an elusive optical effect that dissolves on close scrutiny.

Although Seurat never made a clear statement of his political point of view, he was closely associated with anarchist circles during his brief life. His works have therefore generally been read by his friends and contemporary critics, as well as by later interpreters, as expressing an anarchist-inspired critique of capitalist forms of sociality and spectacle. *Cirque,* for example, depicts a scene drawn from studies of the Cirque Fernando, situated near the artist's atelier, as well as from the pictorial formulas and clichéd types to be seen in popular posters by Jules Chéret and possibly in the films for praxinoscope by Emile Reynaud.[18] Such prototypes suggest an interest in using the language of commercial visual culture to reveal its internal contradictions—in

Figure 8.3 Georges Seurat, *Cirque* [Circus]. Oil on canvas, 1890-1891. Musée d'Orsay, Paris, legs John Quinn, 1924.

Chéret, the application of a standardized faux-naïf style to all subjects, in which sexually alluring, evanescent images of young girls and their male patrons simulate gaiety while advertising products or entertainment.

The Cirque Fernando, not one of the more luxuriously appointed circuses of its time, drew most of its working-class and petit bourgeois clientele from Pigalle and Montmartre and was especially known for its equestrian attractions.[19] In *Cirque*, Seurat preserved and distilled the class distinctions to be seen in the actual seating arrangement at the Cirque Fernando, where social rank is legible from the types who occupy the various tiers. The first five rows, with 420 seats, were the most expensive, with red velvet backrests; separated by a white barrier, the second class comprised three rows with 630 seats, followed by a third class with 1,000 seats (which Seurat combined with the second-class section); behind a further barrier, there was room for standing viewers. The critic Georges Lecomte, writing in 1891, noted the static quality of the audience in *Cirque* in contrast to the "powerful sense of movement" conveyed by the performers, as well as the clichéd types Seurat portrayed: "the spectators watching the show remain completely impassive. They have stereotyped faces and poses, denoting particular types and classes of people; those sitting in the upper rows are slumped carelessly and wearily over the parapet."[20] If the working-class audience in the far row leans casually (or wearily) over the balustrade, the bourgeois men and women in the front rows sit more stiffly, hands resting in their laps or politely clapping. Little communication among the members of the audience occurs, and even those who sit in small groups of two or three seem isolated from each other. Most of the schematic visages bear a V-shaped sign denoting a smile, but the subdued bodily poses and gestures of the spectators cancel any impression of gaiety. As Lecomte observed, Seurat establishes a clear contrast between the dynamism and upward movements of the performers, and the impassive audience, relegated to a tiered setting dominated by strong horizontals.

Drawing on the theories of Charles Henry, Ogden Rood, Humbert de Superville, and others, Seurat believed that emotional qualities could be conveyed scientifically, and therefore universally, through the use of particular colors and lines.[21] In a letter of 1890 to Maurice Beaubourg, he explained:

> Art is Harmony. Harmony is the analogy of contrary and similar qualities in *tone, color and line*, considered with reference to a dominant and under the influence of a scheme of lighting in happy, calm or sad combination . . .
> Gaiety of *tone* results from a luminous dominant; of *color*, from a warm dominant; of *line*, from angles above the horizontal. . . .
> Calmness of *tone* results from a balance of dark and light; of *color*, from a balance of warm and cold; of *line*, from a horizontal.
> Sadness of *tone* results from a dark dominant; of *color*, from a cold dominant; of *line*, from angles below the horizontal.[22]

The depiction of the performers in terms of the striking use of rising lines, gestures, and even coiffures, as well as luminous reds and yellows, is intended to express gaiety and the unfettered expansion of energies; the viewers, rendered in more muted tones and visibly rooted to their seats, are portrayed as closed in on themselves, calm, reserved, and in some instances, distracted. Yet a certain unity, established through the flattening and decorative treatment of the composition, the repetition of the primary colors, and the ubiquitous dots, joins the two realms. The schematization that converts the smiles of the spectators into frozen grimaces is also present in the poses and exaggerated smiles of the performers, for whom the enactment of laughter and gaiety is a professional skill. It is difficult to discern whether any genuine gaiety is present, or whether we witness merely the commercial simulation of its "universal" signs.

The repetition of diagrammatic smiles and rising diagonals in the visages (moustaches, eyebrows) and in the clothing of the spectators seems to mirror those of the performers, thereby exemplifying Tarde's "law of imitation." For Tarde, whose social theories were published in the late

1880s and 1890s, "a society is a group of people who display many resemblances produced either by imitation or by counter-imitation" (*LI*, xvii). Such imitation could occur as a result of sheer proximity, but it could spread through other modes of communication as well, in a process he likened to contagion or the effect of electromagnetic vibrations; in either case, it depended on the natural suggestibility of individuals, who remain unaware that most of their seemingly conscious choices are socially dictated and automatic. Such mimicry suggested that behavior and thought were largely under the command of the unconscious, even in the absence of the explicit formation of crowds. In Tarde's pithy summary, "society is imitation and imitation is a kind of somnambulism" (*LI*, 87). Somnambulism, a term Tarde later replaced with hypnotism, implies a dreamlike state of heightened suggestibility, which could be reciprocal but was usually one-sided (*LI*, 77). A *magnétiseur* would occasionally appear, even in modern secular times, with the power to fascinate, to generate mimicry and command obedience through the effective use of images and illusions: "The magnetizer does not need to lie or terrorize to secure the blind belief and the passive obedience of his magnetized subject. He has prestige—that tells the story" (*LI*, 78). As Jonathan Crary has argued, by constructing his painting out of "dynamogenic" elements (the rising lines, V-shaped mouths and hair), Seurat used a pictorial language he believed would have similarly contagious emotional and psychomotor effects on its viewers.[23]

Seurat seems to have distilled certain of his caricatures from known personalities. His friend, the artist Charles Angrand, sits alone in a top hat in the front row. His prominent viewing position indicates that he may be a surrogate for the artist as social observer and participant. The clown in the foreground, who unveils the scene for us, is probably based on the well-known Spanish clown "Boum Boum" Medrano, who had been associated with the Cirque Fernando until 1889, and who later bought the establishment,

changing its name to Cirque Medrano.[24] Here he may also represent the figure of the hypnotic leader, who holds sway over his audience, seeking to absorb them in the spectacle as if in a dream world.[25] Do the strangely lethargic spectators with their mimetic smiles indicate that he has succeeded in making them into mass subjects, stupefied before the phantasmagoric illusions that unfold before them? Or does their impassive demeanor and dispersal suggest that genuine social unity—Seurat's dream of harmony—cannot be achieved through the amusements of modern capitalism? Finally, we note the presence of a mirror over the entrance to the arena, impossibly reflecting a distant white balustrade and implying the extension of spatial depth before the picture. Are we not invited to imagine ourselves sitting in the rows on the other side of the ring, stratified by class and type, with a schematic smile on our faces, perhaps responding automatically to the language of tones, lines, and colors? Yet it remains difficult to imagine oneself into this scene, or to establish empathic relations with its stereotyped spectators. As Meyer Schapiro observed, "The figures in the late paintings are more and more impersonal and towards the end assume a caricatural simplicity or grotesqueness in expressing an emotion. They have no inner life, they are mannequins capable only of the three expressions—sadness, gaiety and neutral calm—which his theory of art also projects on the canvas as a whole."[26]

In such a mechanical reduction of the range of human feeling, Seurat diagnosed his own and his contemporaries' response to the spectacles offered them, which they are meant to consume passively, the stimulus engineered to achieve a statistical (rather than individual) effect.[27] Yet his disenchantment allows for certain moments of humor and disruption, as in the inclusion of a little girl in the fourth row who holds an orange, no doubt intended for the performers, or the young man in second-class seating holding flowers, perhaps intended for the dancer on horseback. Such figures, also caricatures in their way, nonetheless demonstrate the interpenetration of observation and schematization that is central to Seurat's paintings, as well as the difficulty of drawing a precise line between images of gaiety and of anomie, a difficulty that is itself symptomatic of social confusion and decline. In mourning Seurat's death in 1891, his follower and friend Paul Signac referred to "the synthetic representation of the pleasures of decadence: dancehalls, *chahuts*, circuses, as the painter Seurat did them, he who had such an intense feeling for the ongoing vileness of our epoch of transition."[28]

Seurat exerted a powerful influence on several generations of artists, who saw in his art both a commitment to depicting transformations in the urban world of his time, as well as a technique that seemed resolutely modern and objective in its reliance on science. Yet relatively few artists chose to focus with similar intensity on the phenomena of crowds and collective spectatorship of commodified spectacles. One who did was the Italian Futurist Umberto Boccioni, who had learned a version of Seurat's neoimpressionist method through his teacher, Giacomo Balla. Like Seurat, as a young man Boccioni was associated with anarchist and socialist circles, and his early work pictured the outskirts of Milan with its factories and workers. But inspired by the rhetoric of F. T. Marinetti, who founded the Italian Futurist movement in 1909, Boccioni turned his attention to the city itself, and in particular, to the crowds, urban construction, and popular entertainments that were integral to its modernity.

Boccioni's *Riot in the Galleria,* of 1910, seems to respond directly to Marinetti's "The Founding and Manifesto of Futurism," which proclaims, "We will sing of great crowds excited by work, by pleasure, and by riot."[29] It is one of the first paintings Boccioni created after joining the Futurist movement, and it pictures a riot in the Galleria Vittorio Emanuele in the heart of Milan (fig. 8.4). But rather than a political demonstration (the Galleria opens onto the piazza before the Milan Cathedral, where many demonstra-tions occurred), Boccioni represents a brawl between two fashionably dressed women, probably prostitutes, at night under the glare of several electric orbs.[30] Before the women, two men attack each other while a third seeks to hold them apart, indicating that the violence may have erupted as a result of a sexual dispute, insult, or jealousy. Boccioni, however, seems more interested in revealing the effects of the brawl than its causes. Waves of individuals flow toward the women, as if compelled by a magnetic force that extends to the far reaches of the arcade. With bodies flung forward and arms outstretched in a posture that is repeated throughout the composition, these individuals exemplify the propagation of sentiment, as if by contagion or electrical current. Drawing on the ideas of Tarde, Sighele had also written of the crowd's susceptibility to suggestion and imitation: "the cry, the gesture of one person can stir it to a delirium of enthusiasm or of fury, can make it vile or heroic."[31] The effects of this mimicry seem destined to expand until they encircle and "magnetize" even the painting's viewers; indeed, the man with arms flung upward in the center foreground is cropped so that he appears to pitch forward, beyond the fictive space of the picture. He gestures in an effort to block our inward rush into the depicted field, as if the painting exerted its own force of contagion. In its theme and formal organization, *Riot in the Galleria* draws on Boccioni's understanding of the psychology of the crowd, in order to achieve the Futurist aim of putting "the spectator in the center of the picture."[32] Yet the elevated perch he assumed also suggests that Boccioni preferred to survey the crowd from above, distanced, like the dandy, from its hypnotic effects and violent action. A similarly elevated point of view would characterize many images of crowds in the twentieth century, whether paintings, photographs, or films, thereby instantiating a quasi-panoramic optic that grants the observer a thrilling sense of omniscience and power.

With two violent women at its center, Boccioni's *Riot in*

Figure 8.4 Umberto Boccioni, *Riot in the Galleria.* Oil on canvas, 1910. Pinacoteca di Brera, Milan. Gift of Emilio and Maria Jesi.

the Galleria also conforms to the prevalent idea that crowds were essentially "feminine" in their excitability, irrationality, and proclivity for crime. For Le Bon, "crowds are everywhere distinguished by feminine characteristics" (*C*, 39). Sighele similarly argued that "the crowd—like woman—has an extreme psychology, capable of all excesses, possibly capable only of excesses."[33] Like Manet's Tuileries and Seurat's circus, the Galleria is a space of modern spectacle, where the signs of class and of commodity consumption circulate. Insofar as we witness a riot in an environment associated with decadent pleasures and consumerism, the crowd that gathers there is further feminized.

The brilliant artificial light that illuminates the scene activates the metaphor, so common in discussions of the crowd, of an electric current coursing through it, linking each individual to the others. Flecks and daubs of complementary color dissolve the figures into a single vibrating field, so that a particular face or set of limbs is often indistinguishable from those nearby, or from the pictorial ground. Many of the figures also lack clearly defined feet and hands; they seem to float in a turbulent sea, impelled by forces they cannot control. Where in Seurat the pointillist application of paint is a means of democratizing technical expertise by negating the individual flourish of the artist's hand, in Boccioni, it serves primarily to create a shimmering, luminous surface in which the corporeal and psychic unity of the crowd finds its formal equivalent.

Like Boccioni, Sonia Delaunay was also drawn to the optical and psychological experience of electric light within the nocturnal urban environment. Born Sarah Stern in 1885 in Ukraine, Delaunay studied art for two years at the Karlsruhe Academy before moving to Paris in 1905. There she soon established relations with a group of young artists and poets drawn to the emblematic phenomena of modern life and inspired by the vivid color of Cézanne, Van Gogh, Gauguin, and the pointillist technique of Seurat. In 1910 she married Robert Delaunay, and together they embarked on a pictorial exploration of the city of Paris and its spectacles, including the Eiffel Tower, the Bal Bullier, Blériot's flight over the English Channel, and views of Paris seen through the refracting prism of a window. By 1912, Robert Delaunay's Windows on the City series would lead him to the creation of quasi-abstract paintings based on the sense of movement and depth achieved through the juxtaposition of contrasting areas of color. Sonia Delaunay's contribution to the style that came to be known as Simultanism or Orphic Cubism (as it was called by Guillaume Apollinaire) is less well documented but equally interesting. Her little-known series of twelve crowd studies of spring and summer 1913, executed in sketchbooks with gridded paper as well as on various other scraps, reveals a lyrical response to the kaleidoscopic phenomenon of the Parisian crowd, seen under the recently installed electric lights on the Boulevard St. Michel (fig. 8.5).

These new arc lights can be viewed as one of the modernizing effects of Haussmannization, in which expansive new boulevards, among them the Boulevard St. Michel, cut through the narrow streets of old Paris, opening them to greater circulation and the production of new forms of visuality and spectacle. As Wolfgang Schivelbusch observes, arc lights were like small suns with a spectrum similar to that of daylight. In contrast to the gas lamps they replaced, they were extraordinarily bright and could not be looked at directly. As a result, they had to be fixed much higher on posts, where they were out of view. For those entering one of the places illuminated by arc lights from a dim, gas-lit side street, the transition could be dramatic.[34] Delaunay's memoirs evoke her experience of the modernity of the site, the brilliant color and disorienting spatial effects created by the arc lights inducing a sense of "madness":

I liked electricity. Public lighting was a novelty. At night, during our walks, we entered the era of light, arm-in-arm.

Rendez-vous at the St. Michel fountain. The municipality had substituted electric lamps for the old gas lights. The "Boul Mich,"

Figure 8.5 Sonia Delaunay, *Crowd Study, Boulevard Saint-Michel*. Colored crayons on graph paper, 1913. Musée National d'Art Moderne, Centre Georges Pompidou, Paris. © L & M Services B. V. Amsterdam 20051204.

highway to a new world, fascinated me. We would go and admire the neighborhood show. The halos made the colors and shadows swirl and vibrate around us as if unidentified objects were falling from the sky, beckoning our madness.[35]

Blaise Cendrars, a poet with whom Sonia Delaunay collaborated at this time, evokes a similar experience of "raining globes of electric light" in his poem *Contrasts*.[36] Inspired by the use of simultaneous contrasts of color in the paintings of both Delaunays, he writes of a Paris apprehended in its momentary configurations as dazzling color, sound, and movement. This is also a world of commerce and entertainment, of bistros, advertising, newspapers, fashion, and traffic; and it is one that is already in the process of being transformed into poetry and art through Linotype printing and colored stencil techniques such as those used by Cendrars and Delaunay in their jointly created *La Prose du Transsibérien et de la Petite Jehanne de France*, also of 1913.

Les fenêtres de ma poésie sont grand'ouvertes sur
les Boulevards et dans ses vitrines
Brillent
Les pierreries de la lumière
Écoute les violons des limousines et les xylophones des linotypes
Le pocheur se lave dans l'essuie-main du ciel
Tout est taches de couleur
Et les chapeaux des femmes qui passent sont des comètes dans l'incendie du soir . . .
Il pleut les globes électriques
Montrouge Gare de l'Est Métro Nord-Sud bateaux-mouches monde
Tout est halo
Profondeur[37]

The windows of my poetry are open wide on
the boulevards and in its store windows
Shine
The jewels of light
Listen to the violins of the limousines and the xylophones of the
     linotypes

The stencil printer washes himself in the towel of the sky
Everything is spots of color
And the hats of the women who pass by are comets in
the night fire . . .
It is raining electric globes
Montrouge Gare de l'Est Métro Nord-Sud ferries on the Seine
world
Everything is halo
Depth

Delaunay's sketches of nocturnal crowds gathering at the fountain of the Boulevard St. Michel share this vision of Paris as a multicolored, cacophonous metropolis whose forms and rhythm have been altered in the "era of light." In the sketches, which were rapidly executed in rough sheaves of strokes, individual masses are distinguished primarily as areas of pure color. But the strokes also contribute to a sense of movement, and in their vertical or diagonal alignment, they even hint at posture and gesture. The color patches, which partly overlap and lack clear edges or boundaries, suggest merely provisional social groupings in the processes of formation and dispersion. In some of the drawings, the cropping of figures at the edge of the sheet also points toward a modern, Baudelairean sense of the beauty inherent in the fleeting impression, or in the stranger as he or she passes out of view.[38] Occasionally a top hat, black tie, boot, or extended arm allows one to identify human forms and provides a summary indication of gender and social class as displayed through fashion. Other planes of color, adjacent to or above the figures, seem to connote elements in the environment, perhaps posters or advertisements on nearby buildings, or streams of light from the arc lamps overhead. These patches of color also serve to integrate figure and ground, fusing the crowd with its environment to create an overall, nearly abstract field of fluctuating color relations.

As in Boccioni's *Riot in the Galleria*, individuals are linked to each other and to the pictorial ground in an effort to convey a sense of the (contingent) unity of the crowd.

But for Delaunay, the primacy of pure color relations also signifies the immediacy of visual sensations that have not yet congealed into fully distinct and separate subjects and objects. The openness, fluidity, and lack of precise ego boundaries evoked by such an optical experience seem to correspond to the qualities that Delaunay found exhilarating in the crowd. These are qualities also captured in the unanimist poems of Jules Romains, written just a few years earlier and known to Delaunay, who made a collage cover for her copy of his book:

La ville aurait envie de jaillir comme un feu
D'artifice, un grand peuple insurgé d'étincelles.
Elle voudrait lâcher des milliers de ballons
Qui porteraient tous ces hommes dans leurs nacelles.
Elle voudrait se dilater sans se dissoudre,
Mêler à ses maisons de l'espace et du vent,
Faire couler le ciel dans ses rues élargies,
Rester une et devenir illimitée.[39]

The city would have wished to burst forth like
Fireworks, a great people sparkling with insurgency.
It wished to release thousands of balloons
That would transport all its men in their small airships.
It would like to expand without dissipating,
To mingle space and wind with its houses,
Make the sky flow into its enlarged streets,
Remain one and become limitless.

Such a euphoric view of the city—as a powerful, animate being able to embrace all its diverse inhabitants while retaining its unity—depended on an aesthetic perception of its dazzling colors, lights, and rhythm. Similarly, for Delaunay, all objects, regardless of their unique material qualities and uses, could be perceived as areas of pure, contrasting color dispersed through a nonhierarchical pictorial field. Significantly, Delaunay experienced this "modern" mode of vision near the fountain on the Boulevard St. Michel, a crossroads or "highway" as she called it, where the commercial spectacle of the city and the circulation of its inhabitants and visitors were especially heightened. As she recalls, she would go "to admire the neighborhood show," but the swirling electric lights made it seem as if "unidentified objects were falling from the sky." According to Simmel, the money economy of the metropolis can be correlated with a sense of the qualitative equivalence of all objects, whose differences can be registered only as quantity:

To the extent that money, with its colorlessness and its indifferent quality, can become a common denominator of all values, it becomes the frightful leveler—it hollows out the core of things, their peculiarities, their specific values and their uniqueness and incomparability in a way which is beyond repair. They all float with the same specific gravity in the constantly moving stream of money.[40]

Delaunay's sketches of crowds under the destabilizing effects of electric light may be understood as a response to this leveling, which affects both people and things. These works acknowledge the reduction of difference within a money economy while seeking to restore "color" to the world. But it is now an artificially produced color, and it supplants traditional forms of representation that sought to convey a sense of the material specificity of things, their weight, spatial position, and uses: "The fragmentation of objects and of forms by light and the birth of colored planes led to a new pictorial structure . . . color is liberated, it becomes in itself the subject."[41]

After World War I, this quasi-abstract approach to depicting the city, and of the masses that inhabit it, would come to seem outdated, even decadent. If prewar artists attended to urban crowds in environments associated with modern spectacle and entertainment, after the war, many artists focused instead on the politically organized crowd, whether in labor, protest, or revolution. Given the specific ideological function of many postwar images of the masses, it is not surprising that reproducible media, including cartoons, photography, photomontage, photomurals, and film, play a more prominent role than painting. The crowds figured in such works tend to emphasize anonymity and homogenization as correlatives of the new forms of social engineering that emerged in the postwar era: socialism in Russia, and fascism in Italy, Germany and Spain. Individuals, when they appear, are often heroic types who represent a particular class of worker or a social (or racial) ideal. The hierarchical relationship of the anonymous masses to the leader, who gives them an identity and a purpose, provides a recurrent theme. The masses, frequently photographed or depicted from above, seem to multiply endlessly, their sheer quantity signifying the erasure of particular subjectivities in favor of a increase in raw group power. The leader, on the other hand, is a singular, charismatic personality—in Tarde's term, a *magnétiseur*. His ideological function is to galvanize and embody the will of the people, now reduced to identical, interchangeable elements, leveled less by a capitalist money economy than by the political requirements of totalitarianism. Images of the masses under fascism and socialism are fascinating for what they reveal about state propaganda, and in particular about the constitution of a new mass subjectivity and its relation to a cult of the leader. Such pictures not only represent the masses, but seek to interpellate them in a manner consonant with the prevailing understanding of mass psychology.

Early in 1915, before Italy's entry into World War I, the Futurist Giacomo Balla painted several semiabstract works representing patriotic crowds in the form of swelling waves. These crowds gathered before a symbol of the Italian flag, or of the House of Savoy, to demand intervention in the war.[42] After the war, like many of the Futurists, Balla embraced fascism, producing images that sought to construct a heroic vision of the regime in its role of rebuilding a war-torn Italy. From 1923 to 1927, during the period of the consolidation of power, his propaganda drawings appeared regularly in the Futurist-fascist journal *L'Impero*. Given Balla's earlier social-humanitarian representations of individual

workers, these largely unknown drawings are shocking for their unadulterated enthusiasm for the Duce, as well as for their depiction of the people as anonymous cogs in the machine of the state.[43]

Tutte le forze nazionali verso il Duce per L'Italia (All the National Forces Toward the Duce for Italy), reproduced in *L'Impero* in August 1923, exemplifies Balla's dynamic but highly legible figurative style (fig. 8.6). Mussolini, crowned by the star of Italy and with flamelike forms on his brow, looms large in the foreground, his raised hands and lower legs cropped at the edges of the image, as if his dominating presence were too large to contain. Along the lower right foreground lies the fasces, its ax raised so that it appears, at least in my reading, to menace the workers who are pressed together just above it. Their small scale, schematically rendered bodies, and repeated gestures figure forth the ideal of perfect psychic and corporeal homogeneity. As if they were members of a single organism, they strive toward the Duce with an arm raised in salutation. Behind them, the repeated word *lavoro* (work) emanates like smoke from factory chimneys in a linguistic doubling of the indexical sign of productivity. The rising "smoke" of collective labor generates a cloud in the sky above: the profile of Italy. The nation will be constructed, the image tells us, through the disciplined, industrial work of its people, in turn guided by the all-powerful leader.

The repetition of the word *lavoro* also marks it as a rhetorical "affirmation," relentlessly hammered home, as Le Bon had advised. In order to "imbue the mind of a crowd with ideas and beliefs," Le Bon recommended "affirmation, repetition, and contagion." Affirmations should be as concise as possible, free of proof, and "constantly repeated, and so far as possible in the same terms." Eventually the affirmed idea would become embedded in the unconscious and accepted as a demonstrated truth, thereby forming a current of belief that would be propagated through contagion (*C*, 124–26). The repeated slogan *lavoro* functions

Figure 8.6 Giacomo Balla, *Tutte le forze nazionali verso il Duce per L'Italia* [All the National Forces Towards the Duce for Italy]. Ink on paper, 1923. Lost. Reproduced in *L'Impero* 1, no. 133 (14 August 1923), Rome, p. 1. © 2005 Artists Rights Society (ARS), New York /SIAE, Rome.

similarly as an affirmation and ultimately a command; it is directed to the viewers of the image who are meant to receive its message and mimic the response of the depicted workers.

A related drawing, published in *L'Impero* in October 1923, adopts another technique favored by Le Bon: the condensation of an idea into a simple, compelling image.[44] Balla inscribes the single word *Obbedire* (obey) over the stern forehead of a gigantic Mussolini, while crowds flock to him and the towering fasces on which he rests his hands. Such drawings address the masses through repetition and easily grasped, highly charged images and symbols. As Le Bon explained, "Whatever be the ideas suggested to crowds they can only exercise effective influence on condition that they assume a very absolute, uncompromising, and simple shape. They present themselves then in the guise of images, and are only accessible to the masses under this form" (*C*, 61–62). Mussolini, who had read Le Bon, acknowledged that he used many of these principles in his propaganda campaigns.[45]

Artists working in the Soviet Union after the revolution also sought effective visual techniques for creating images of collective labor. As in Balla's drawings, captions and slogans frequently lend greater clarity and precision to an image by linking its visual and verbal registers. A poster designed by Valentina Kulagina in 1930 to celebrate International Working Women's Day adopts many of the strategies of political montage under discussion at the time (fig. 8.7). Although photomontage had existed as an avant-garde practice in Germany and Russia since the war, its use was often criticized either as too formal or as lacking in unity and legibility. In 1928 a group of photographers, media designers, filmmakers, and critics formed the October Association to promote a productivist approach to the integration of art and life. Gustav Klucis, Kulagina's husband, published the article "Photomontage as a New Kind of Agitational Art" under its auspices in 1931, arguing for the suc-

cess of photomontage in conveying political and economic messages.[46] Unlike those who advocated a return to realist painting or to conventional documentary photography, Klutsis, Kulagina, and their colleagues embraced fragmentation, diversity of scale, unusual points of view, and the combination of drawing, typography, photography, and other media within a single image. The photography section of the October Association articulated its program in an essay also published in 1931:

We are for a revolutionary photography, materialist, socially grounded, and technically well equipped, one that sets itself the aim of promulgating and agitating for a socialist way of life and a Communist culture. . . . We are against . . . flag-waving patriotism in the form of spewing smokestacks and identical workers with hammers and sickles. . . . We are against picturesque photography and pathos of an old, bourgeois type.[47]

Kulagina's poster, *International Working Women's Day*, exemplifies this effort to put avant-garde techniques to work for the revolution. Her image does not purport to reflect reality, as demanded by some, but is obviously constructed, comprising lithography, photomontage, and typography. Kulagina, who sought to avoid "spewing smokestacks and identical workers" (as in Balla's cartoon), composed her mass of women workers out of individual photographs of heads, some covered with superimposed red scarves. Each visage remains visible in its particularity, even as Kulagina assembled a virtual parade of workers who march along a dynamic diagonal toward the viewer. The faces in the foreground are the largest and seem to seek our reciprocal gaze. Receding into depth along an orthogonal perpendicular to the parade are the hand-drawn forms of a monumental textile machine. We see only a fragment of it in close-up, so that its streamlined, repetitive machine parts create a nearly abstract, geometrical pattern. The machine is operated by two heroic women, who lack all specificity; as proletarian types, they symbolize the strength, skill, and commitment

Figure 8.7 Valentina Kulagina, *International Working Women's Day.* Lithograph, 1930. Private collection.

of the textile workers. Significantly, Kulagina chose to represent these figures and their machine in the medium of lithography, which allows for the requisite generalization in the creation of a type. The drawing and application of color is sober and proficient but not seductive or overtly personal, as was common in "bourgeois" practice. Thus Kulagina identifies her own artistic skills with those of the heroic woman worker/engineer, who integrates the artisanal craft of the hand with advanced technology. In contrast, she represents the marching women through the medium of photography, thereby retaining a strong sense of their particularity. Yet Kulagina's parade is clearly also a fabricated rather than documentary image; close examination reveals it to be constructed of cropped photographs of both individuals and groups of women, repeated (in differing scales) and redistributed throughout the montage. The randomly placed red scarves serve to link the marchers to their larger idealized type, but also to disguise the photographic repetition of their faces.

Rather than hammers and sickles, Kulagina's marchers are accompanied by two small red banners and a larger orange one in the foreground, which clarify the poster's message to them. The red banners (repeating the text in the red strips to right and left) proclaim "International Working Women's Day," while the orange banner refers to the "Day of Viewing Socialist Competition." In related posters, Kulagina uses the term *shock* or *strike worker* (as in lightning strike), common parlance at the time, to emphasize the virile ideals of discipline and commitment to the patriotic cause of increased production.[48] Yet the assimilation of the marching women to a regimented formation is partly undone by their heterogeneity, disorderly ranks, and profusion of smiles. These qualities may have served to demonstrate that the female worker "preserves her womankind despite severe schooling."[49] One wonders how such posters, intended for broad distribution, were received by their female audience. Kulagina's poster seems positioned between an earlier productivist model, in which the artist as engineer/inventor constructed a utopian proposal for the future, and the emerging role of the artist as mere publicist for the totalitarian state. In the latter role, artists were expected to provide easily consumed images and slogans for the purposes of social engineering.[50] As in fascist imagery, the subordination of the masses to the leader as the very embodiment of the state was increasingly emphasized. Beginning in 1932, Kulagina frequently found her work rejected by the Central Committee of the Communist Party.[51]

Photomontage and related graphic techniques also played a significant role in posters, murals, print media, and exhibition design in National Socialist Germany, despite their left-wing, modernist origins and "degenerate" associations. In 1933, the importance of photography as a mass medium was highlighted in the first successful Nazi propaganda exhibition, *Die Kamera* (The Camera). Both amateur and commercial associations of photographers participated, under the aegis of Joseph Goebbels's motto: "The experience of the individual has become the experience of the people, thanks solely to the camera."[52] The entrance hall to the exhibition featured sixteen enormous photomurals, each an enlarged press photograph of a mass march or meeting of the Nationalsozialistische Deutsche Arbeiterpartei (NSDAP) by Hitler's personal photographer, Heinrich Hoffmann (fig. 8.8). Such photomurals had become possible just that year as a result of the invention of new enlarging techniques. Hoffmann had taken the source photographs from an elevated perch that emphasized depth of field and raised the horizon line. This allowed the teeming crowds and serried ranks of marchers to be fully displayed within their framing, architectural context—or in some cases, to overflow the boundaries of the photograph. Tilting the horizon upward also brought the foreground closer to the actual ground, as if it were opening up before the spectators.

Figure 8.8 Anonymous. Entrance hall to the exhibition *Die Kamera* [The Camera], Berlin. Photomurals and text, 1933.

Architect Winfried Wendland, the exhibition designer capitalized on these effects by setting the photomurals high on the upper walls of the entrance hall; by aligning the visitors' upward gazes with the ascending orthogonals of the images, the photomurals seemed to invite their entrance into the scene. Visitors were thus encouraged to assume two seemingly contradictory points of view: that of their actual situation in the entrance hall (from below), and that provided by Hoffmann's panoramic optic, which doubled as that of the Führer (from above). The central panel on the far wall made this double perspective, and its ideological implications, explicit; the only vertical panel in the series, it dropped below the other photographs to nearly meet the floor. Visitors were invited to imagine themselves entering the scene that unfolded before them in order to follow the party officials marching up the center of a grand parade ground flanked by patriotic masses while simultaneously retaining an elevated vantage point. If here the visitor was addressed as a solitary, heroic, omniscient individual,

the neighboring photomurals of crowds and mass marches encouraged identification with the party's workers and participation in its group rituals. The prevalence of flags with swastikas in the photomurals, and the captions that ran around the lower perimeter of the frieze (identifying the date and location of each party event), provided symbolic framing devices that reinforced the ideological message. Although the photomurals appear as distinct images, set side by side rather than seamlessly joined, the exhibition designer nonetheless sought to approximate the all-encompassing experience of the panorama. By placing the photomurals on the upper register of the walls, Wendland avoided the interruption of doors and entrances to other exhibition rooms. The result was a continuous flow of related images, unified by the raised viewpoint, the repetition of crowd scenes, the recurrence of flags and banners, and the captions.

Herbert Bayer, a successful painter, commercial artist, and photographer, designed the brochure for *Die Kamera*, as well as for the catalog of the 1936 *Deutschland Ausstellung*, organized on the occasion of the Olympic Games in Berlin. Although he had once been a student as well as a teacher of typography and advertising at the Bauhaus, which the Nazis closed in 1933, he apparently saw no contradiction in putting his skills in the service of National Socialism.[53] Whereas the photomurals of *Die Kamera* adopted a severe factographic format, which emphasized the single, unified, documentary image, Bayer's brochures combined this technique with elements of photomontage. The brochure for the Deutschland exhibition catalog comprised twenty-eight montages that used photographs from a number of prominent artists as well as from photographic agencies, engravings, and graphic art. Seemingly innocent, it celebrated German cultural and economic success through images that portrayed idyllic farmland, a happy and prosperous rural population, peaceful views of small-town life, typical examples of various German architectural styles, and the portraits of prominent cultural figures such as Bach, Beethoven, Goethe, Kant, and Gutenberg. Yet a double-page spread of a huge crowd at a rally of National Socialists gave the brochure a more manifest ideological content (fig. 8.9). Onto a dense image of the masses that extends beyond the limits of the pictorial field, Bayer superimposed the motif of an eagle bearing the swastika, the enlarged heads of a farmer, a worker, and a soldier, and an open book bearing a text. The three figures embody heroic types of National Socialist manhood, each representing the people and their allegiance to Hitler. In their particularity, the people appear virile and forward looking, attentive to the words of their leader, even as in the teeming crowd below, they coalesce to form the merely ornamental, feminized vehicles of his will. The text in the open book proclaimed (in German, English, French, and Spanish), "The Führer speaks! Millions hear him. The working population, the farming community, the military in their regained freedom, are the pillars of National Socialist Germany."[54] In or-

der to manufacture the image of "millions" required by the motto, Bayer reproduced the same crowd image on both pages (cropping the right hand-page a little higher, as is especially visible along the lower edge where individuals carry flags), and he probably also eliminated gaps.

Hitler, although absent from this photomontage, is strongly implied. His monumental figure appeared instead in the foreground of an enormous photomontage before the Hall of Honor at the entrance to the Deutschland Ausstellung (fig. 8.10). Hitler, flanked on his right by the smaller figures of a party member and two workers with muscular, bared chests and distinctly Aryan features, and on his left by uniformed members of the military, raises his right hand in salute before the exhibition's visitors. The scene of a mass rally behind him filled every crevice of space to the point of seeming to surge beyond the borders of the photo-

Figure 8.9 Herbert Bayer. Double-page spread from the brochure for the *Deutschland Exhibition* catalogue, Berlin. Photomontage, 1936. © 2005 Artists Rights Society (ARS), New York/VG Bild-Kunst, Bonn.

montage. This crowd figured forth the motto "Volk ohne Raume" ("People without space"), and thereby sought to justify Hitler's ruthless expansionist policies. Similar representations of the cult figure of the leader and his hierarchical relation to the masses could be found in Italy, as we have seen in Balla's cartoon of Mussolini, in posters by Xanti Schawinsky, or in the foldouts of popular fascist magazines[55]; and in Russia, in the many heroizing posters and paintings of both Lenin and Stalin, or in the famous concluding scene of part one of Sergei Eisenstein's film *Ivan the Terrible* (commissioned by Stalin), where a close-up of the czar's head looms over a winding procession of the people who have come to beg him to rule over them.

Similar formal techniques were also appropriated for propaganda purposes in the United States, where Bayer em-

igrated in 1938. Despite his work for the National Socialists, Bayer's talents in photography, advertising, and exhibition design were held in high regard. His famous installation design for Edward Steichen's 1942 exhibition, *The Road to Victory: A Procession of Photographs of the Nation at War*, was commissioned by the U.S. government and mounted at the Museum of Modern Art.[56] The installation, which occupied the entire second floor of the museum, with a single entrance and exit, enacted a "procession" of 150 photographs arranged in eleven stations. Bayer sought to activate the viewer's experience through the use of variously angled, large photomurals placed on walls, or positioned as freestanding elements on the floor. As conceived by Steichen, the exhibition told a simple, mythical story of American manifest destiny, primarily through photographs and a few wall texts by Carl Sandberg: the narrative began with pictures of the "virgin land" and the "Red Men" who occupied it; it continued with the arrival of an "endless tide of white men in endless numbers with a land hunger," then moved to the pioneers who spread out across the continent until they reached the "long sunsets of the west coast." Various achievements in industry and farming were represented, along with heroic images of "tough strugglers of oaken men—women of rich torsos." After celebrating these "fathers and mothers," the exhibition wall text proclaimed, "tomorrow belongs to the children." No mention was made of the fascists in Germany or Italy, or of the war in Europe; the bombing of Pearl Harbor appeared as the sole cause of America's declaration of war—an unexplained catastrophe that must be met by the implacable will of the people. This was followed by images of the armament, "the boys at war,"

Figure 8.10 Anonymous. Entrance hall to the Hall of Honor at the *Deutschland Exhibition*, Berlin. Photomontage, 1936.

Figure 8.11 Herbert Bayer, Exhibition design for *The Road to Victory: A Procession of Photographs of the Nation at War*, Museum of Modern Art, New York. Photomontage and wall text, 1942. Photo: Bauhaus-Archiv. © 2005 Artists Rights Society (ARS), New York/VG Bild-Kunst, Bonn.

including the army, navy, and air force, and the first war photographs of the Pacific and Bataan.

The sequence of sober black-and-white photographs culminated in a huge curved mural, extending from the floor to the ceiling, composed of a seamlessly repeated picture of marching columns of soldiers by Samuel H. Gottscho (fig. 8.11). The blank, stupefying uniformity of these men, whose individuality is masked by their helmets and weapons, was no doubt intended to signify the relentless

power of the American military. This tidal wave of marching soldiers was relieved by the interpolation of six smaller photomurals, placed against the large background panel or before it as a series of freestanding elements. Depicting the soldiers' fathers and mothers as ordinary, if archetypal, white Americans, Gottscho's pictures pose them before clapboard houses, on front porches, in interiors with fireplaces, or against the open sky (in apparent imitation of images by Walker Evans and Andrew Wyeth). The fathers

8A 'Mob': English

Maria Su Wang

Tracing the semantic history of a word as rich and varied in its linguistic genealogy as the term *mob* obliges one to start somewhat in the middle, go backward, and then again go forward in time. Mob is a shortened version of *mobile*, belonging to the epithet *mobile vulgus*, which literally translates as "excitable, fickle crowd." By using *mobile vulgus* as a starting point to uncover the Latin roots of the term *mob*, we will chart its ensuing evolution into the term's modern form.

Mobile vulgus derives from Latin philological ancestors such as *moveo, mobilis*, and *vulgo*. *Mobilis* has the following connotations: (1) quick in movement, nimble, active; (2) capable of being moved; (3) varying, changeable, shifting; capable of being modified, mutable; and (4) inconstant, fickle, easily swayed.

Vulgo, the main root of *vulgus*, means (1) to make available to the mass of the population, to make common to all; to make of general application; to prostitute one's body; (2) to scatter abroad, to spread out; and (3) to make widely known, to spread a report, to make public, to expose. *Vulgus*, which draws on the ideas of mass dissemination and general application, comes to signify the common people or the general public, the multitude of undifferentiated or ordinary people, a flock (of animals), and the members as a whole of a particular class or category.

Moveo and *mobilis* both find their trace in the English word *move*, used in the fourteenth and fif-

and mothers—exemplifying every available patriotic cliché—appear as hale, hardworking, and virtuous, associated with the land and its natural fertility. Whereas the photomontages of Kulagina, Klucis, and El Lisstizky had sought to preserve a sense of the individual within the mass and had revealed the material structure of their images, Bayer for the most part used the single perspective, seamless image, and large scale of the factographic "document." Working with Gottscho's already stereotyped photographs, he masked the joins and distortions occasioned by the process of making enlarged photomurals from strips of photographic paper forty inches wide; seams were lightly airbrushed, imperfections were retouched by hand, and finally the whole mural was covered with a dull varnish to eliminate any reflections caused by the surface of the photograph paper.[57] Rather than allow disparate montage elements to compete for the viewers' attention or encourage a dialectical process of interpretation, the photographic insets and freestanding panels create a superficial sense of variety and movement while invoking well-known clichés. By rendering familiar themes in heroic and monumental terms, the exhibition sought to instill in its viewers a sense of identification with the land, its people, and their mutual promise, culminating in support for the "nation at war." As Benjamin Buchloh and Ulrich Pohlmann have observed, Bayer converted the formal strategies of photomontage and dynamic exhibition design, first invented by the German dadaists and Russian constructivists, with a critical or emancipatory function, to the ideological demands of fascism, and eventually to those of capitalist culture and propaganda.[58]

During the postwar period, such heroic propaganda images of the masses in support of revolution, war, or a particular state ideology would increasingly be met with skepticism, even when such images were produced (as they continued to be in the Soviet Union with the cult of Stalin). Compromised by the devastating effects of the war and the Holocaust, as well as by association with totalitarian regimes, representations of the masses as a surging force devoted to a leader or a cause receded in favor of celebrations of the individual. Cold war rhetoric further pitted western individualism against the conformity of the Soviet bloc, an opposition partly belied by the emphasis on patriotism, political conformity, and consumerism in the United States.

Images of the people, in the form of crowds at concerts, on the beach, or at rallies, political demonstrations, or mass marches returned in the 1960s, but in ways that avoided both constructivist and fascist prototypes. Rather than assert a specific political stance, American Pop artist Andy Warhol simply re-presented the stultifying effects of the postwar mass subjectivity and media culture. In the wake of 1950s McCarthyism and the prevailing opposition between the free and communist worlds, Warhol ironically called attention to the convergence of Soviet and American ideologies, remarking blandly, "I want everybody to think alike. Russia is doing it under government. It's happening here all by itself."[59] Warhol associated the peculiarly American brand of equality not with a democratization of the means of production, but with uniform access to everyday consumer products and to the mass media. As he explained, "What's great about this country is that America started the tradition where the richest consumers buy essentially the same things as the poorest. You can be watching TV and see Coca-Cola, and you can know that the President drinks Coke, Liz Taylor drinks Coke, and just think, you can drink Coke too." Moreover, the same advertisements, newspapers, films, radio, and television shows are available to everyone: "Rich people can't see a sillier version of *Truth or Consequences*, or a scarier version of *The Exorcist*. You can get just as revolted as they can—you can have the same nightmares. All of this is really American."[60] In this proliferation of mass experience, we all share the same desires, consume the same products, think the same thoughts, and "have the same nightmares." Standardized consumption leads to repetition (you can have Coca-Cola every day), to predictable and automatic responses, and to an apparent absence of feeling. Rather than try to reassert his individuality, Warhol mirrors the affect of the vacant, superficial, homogeneous mass subject, but to such an exaggerated degree that his work and person refuse to occupy a fixed, neutral position. For if Warhol claims to want to be a machine, and to like eating Campbell soup every day, he also performs the role of the Baudelairean dandy who retains an aristocratic distance as he voyeuristically observes the crowd. He operates on both sides of the media world: as a cult figure and as a fan, as a producer and as a consumer.[61] And like the dandy, he cultivates a cool and detached pose, which masks intense feelings of desire and pain, as well as a sharp, analytic awareness of the failures in the American dream of social equality and freedom.

Warhol's pictures tend toward two compositional types: the overall, homogeneous pattern of mechanically repeated motifs, and the isolated, centered motif, raised to the status of a single, glamorized object. These aesthetic strategies, designed to avoid giving evidence of subjective preferences, also function as correlatives of the relation of the individual to the crowd. Similarly, on the level of subject matter, Warhol's single *Campbell Soup Can* assumes an individual consumer, whereas his *200 Campbell Soup Cans* corresponds to the masses. But as in Baudelaire, there is a reciprocal relation between the terms *individual* and *multitude*. The artist once remarked, "Somehow, the way life works, people usually wind up either

teenth centuries as meaning "to change or shift position, to lodge and displace someone or something." In the sixteenth century, *move* could also signify the application or administration of a remedy and the promotion or advancement for an office. All of these significations contain the same thread of movement and motion. *Movable*, the adjectival form of *move*, is the primary predecessor of *mobile*. *Movable* signifies a readiness or aptitude for motion but also comes to mean "fickle," "inconstant," and "changeable," recalling the connotations of *mobilis*.

With the appearance of *mobile* as an English word, we first approach the modern sense of *mob*. *Mobile* originally derives its sense from phrases like *Primum Mobile* ("first moving thing") in the sixteenth and seventeenth centuries. *Primum Mobile* refers to the outermost sphere added in the Middle Ages to the Ptolemaic system of astronomy. This sphere was supposed to revolve round the earth from east to west in twenty-four hours, carrying with it the (eight or nine) contained spheres. *Mobile* grows to signify the capacity for movement or for being free and unattached. Christopher Marlowe, in his play *Doctor Faustus* (1604), deploys *mobile* and *Primum Mobile* with reference to the nature of Faustus after he makes a pact with Lucifer. Faustus's servant, in describing his master, says, "For is he not Corpus naturale, and is not that *mobile*?" (1.2), implying that Faust's ability to move around freely is an attribute of the human condition. Faustus becomes so mobile that he can even reach the *Primum Mobile*, which the second Chorus testifies to:

Learned Faustus, to find the secrets of Astronomy,
Graven in the book of *Jove's* high firmament,
Did mount him up to scale *Olympus'* top.

Where, sitting in a Chariot burning bright
Drawn by the strength of yoked Dragons' necks,
He views the clouds, the Planets, and the Stars,
The Tropics, Zones and quarters of the sky,
From the bright circle of the horned Moon
Even to the height of *Primum Mobile*. (4.1)

In the seventeenth century, *Primum Mobile* was also a figurative term for the source or mainspring of an activity or motion, an erudite synonym of cause. Early in the seventeenth century, *mobile* is first used as a term denoting the common people or populace.

Alongside the development of *mobile* in the seventeenth century, *mob*, stemming from *mab* (meaning "a woman of loose character" in the sixteenth century), begins to signify a promiscuous woman or a piece of negligée attire. In Jane Austen's *Mansfield Park* (1814), Tom Bertram urges Fanny Price to play the role of the cottager's wife in their play by saying, "You must get a brown gown, and a white apron, and a *mob cap*, and we must make you a few wrinkles, and a little of the crowsfoot at the corner of your eyes, and you will be a very proper, little old woman." A *mobcap* is a woman's indoor cap in the eighteenth and nineteenth centuries, preserving the connotation of an article of clothing worn in private.

These senses of *mob* are demonstrated in its subsequent usage as a verb, meaning "to dress untidily," "to go in disguise so as to escape recognition," or "to frequent low company." This connotation of *mob*, the association with loose or disorderly character and conduct, combines with *vulgus* in the late seventeenth century to forge the meaning of an excitable common people. In *On Liberty* (1859), John Stuart Mill refers to an "excited mob assembled before the house of a corn-

in crowded subways and elevators, or in big rooms all by themselves. Everybody should have a big room they can go to and everybody should also ride the crowded subways."[62] Whether alone or in a crowd, Warhol tells us, we should all do what everyone else is doing. Conspicuously missing is the possibility of meaningful collectivities or a genuine public sphere.

If many of Warhol's images refer to the techniques, products, and effects of a commodified, spectacular culture, a few explicit pictures of crowds also occur. They include the optically colored versions of the *Race Riots* of 1963, as well as a work (in two versions) simply titled *The Crowd* of the same year (fig. 8.12). As Jeffrey Schnapp has observed, both silk screens derive from a single United Press International source photo dated November 4, 1955, bearing the caption, "Rome, Saint Peter and the Crowd: The huge statue of Saint Peter seems to look down benignly upon the crowd in Saint Peter's Square that gathered to hear the Pope's blessing on Easter Sunday. It was impossible to estimate the tremendous throng accurately, but guesses range from 300,000 to 500,000."[63] The final works, however, retain no reference to the pope or Saint Peter, although the presence of a few nuns and priests can be detected. As cropped and silk-screened, the purpose of this gathered multitude is obscured, although it is clearly a well-dressed and orderly crowd. As such, it differs from the contemporary crowds that marched or rioted to demand civil rights, perhaps presenting their neutral or complacent counterpart. Yet the image still resonates with its time, drawing its emblematic status from the wealth of more clamorous crowd images in the newspapers and magazines of the period.

In one version, *The Crowd* comprises four identical, rectangular silk screens arranged in superimposed pairs, thereby exemplifying the tendency toward mimicry and multiplication said to be inherent in its subject. Yet Warhol subtly misaligned the repeated quadrants, so that they fail to meet at the center, or to establish an even perimeter. The other version makes the (mis)constructed character of the crowd even more evident: here, the repeated images vary in size as well as scale. The join is moved off center, and more visible gaps occur between the silk screens, which Warhol patched with crude pencil marks.[64] The grainy quality of the image in both versions evokes a poor newspaper source, whose reproduction has caused further random degradations in clarity. Or the blur may suggest the erasure of the lingering remnants of individual subjectivity. Unlike Bayer's photomural of endlessly marching soldiers, here, everything has been done to interrupt the unity and to reduce the detail and legibility of the whole. Although the *Race Riots* are historically specific and violent, this crowd is white, middle class, passive, and seem-

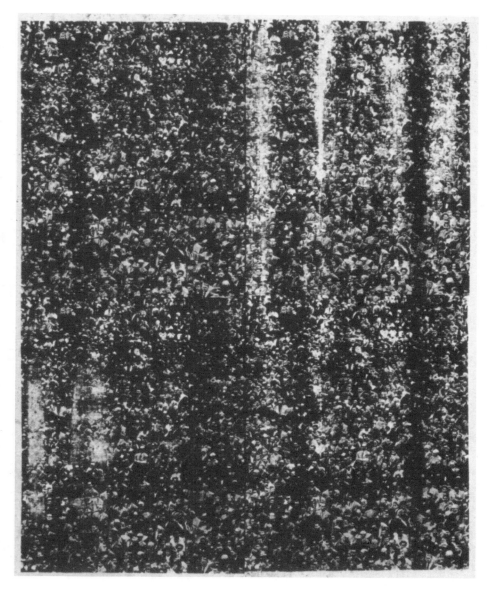

Figure 8.12 Andy Warhol, *The Crowd*. Silkscreen ink on canvas, 1963. © 2005 Andy Warhol Foundation for the Visual Arts/ARS, New York.

dealer," utilizing the term in its Latin origins.

Mobile vulgus is first shortened to mob in Burnet's *History* in the early eighteenth century, leading to censure and reproach from Swift in Addison's *Spectator* No. 135 in 1711. *Mob* now signifies the common mass of people, particularly the uncultured or illiterate class. Thomas Paine uses mob in this context in *The Rights of Man* (1791), writing, "How then is it that such vast classes of mankind as are distinguished by the appellation of the vulgar, or the ignorant, *mob*, are so numerous in all old countries?" As the eighteenth century progresses, *mob* acquires a variety of meanings, including an assemblage of the rabble or a tumultuous crowd, an aggregation of persons regarded as not individually important, or a heterogeneous collection. Austen probably has the latter connotation in mind in *Mansfield Park*, where Edmund Bertram declares, "A clergyman cannot be high in state or fashion. He must not head *mobs*, or set the ton in dress."

Since Swift's criticism, Samuel Johnson sealed the modern meaning of mob in his *A Dictionary of the English Language* (1755), defining it as "the crowd; a tumultuous rout." Concurrent with Johnson's definition, *mob* circulates as a verb in eighteenth-century English. It now comes to denote attacks carried out by disorderly crowds; crowding around and molesting or annoying; pressing unduly upon; thronging; and congregating in a *mob* or disorderly crowd. Edmund Burke uses mob in this sense in his *Reflections on the Revolution in France* (1790), writing, "The Assembly, their organ, acts before them the farce of deliberation with as little decency as liberty. They act like the comedians of a fair before a riotous audience; they act amidst the tumultuous cries of a mixed *mob* of ferocious men." Paine, in another portion of *The Rights of Man,* deploys *mob* with the same connotation: "There is in all European countries, a large class of people of that description which in England is called the 'mob.' Of this class were those who committed the burnings and devastations in London in 1780, and of this class were those who carried the heads upon spikes in Paris."

In the nineteenth century, *mob* becomes slang for a company or gang of thieves or pickpockets working in collusion. This connotation eventually finds its way to the twentieth-century meaning of *mob,* signifying a more of less permanent association of violent criminals, also known as the mafia.[1]

ingly unorganized. And whereas the *Race Riots* glow with red, blue, and mustard (mustard gas?) tints, *The Crowd* appears in muted monochrome. Warhol's crowds, pictured from above, like so many crowd scenes from the 1920s on, nonetheless differ from established norms by representing the mass in antiheroic form, as a constructed surface pattern without inner coherence or meaning. Repetitions occur and figures partly fuse, not to create a sense of oceanic totality, but to become mere abstracted ornament: the crowd as wallpaper, as background noise.

Among the artists of the post–World War II era, only German artist and political activist Joseph Beuys equaled Warhol in his ability to create a mythic persona that unified his art and life while also fostering the rise of a cult with numerous followers and "believers." And like Warhol, Beuys was drawn to the open wounds in his society, generated both by the traumas of the war and by the alienating effects of modern technology and mass consumption. In his staged "actions" and other oratorical events, he proved to be a master of the crowd, projecting a strong charismatic presence and aura of mystery. Despite his rejection of radio, television, and other modern forms of communication (in favor of writing on blackboards, making animal sounds, speaking directly to an audience, and remaining silent for long periods), few artists have so successfully orchestrated their reception by the media.

Central to his work was the project of reintegrating the masses into the political process and forming more organic communities. In some cases, animal aggregates (such as bees) and even the primitive herd provided models of cooperative democracy, or simply a hope for group survival in a time of catastrophe. One of the most compelling of these works is an installation of 1969 titled *The Pack* (*Das Rudel*) (fig. 8.13). It comprises an extremely weather-beaten, rusty Volkswagen bus from the back of which spill forth twenty-four identical sleds arranged in three rows. Each sled is equipped with those elements Beuys deemed essential for survival: a roll of felt for warmth, a lump of fat for nourishment, and a flashlight. This idiosyncratic use of materials, as well as the topos of emergency and escape, derive from Beuys's years as a Nazi combat pilot. The artist, who was shot down by the Russians in neutral Crimea in 1943, recalled being saved by Tartars who wrapped his body in felt and fat, and accepted him as a fellow nomad. His crash and near death take on a mythic status in the artist's (partly fictional) autobiography, allowing him to be transformed through rebirth.[65] (The artist would continue to assume multiple and overlapping identities throughout his career, including that of shaman, shepherd, proletarian, educator, political activist, and martyr.)

The Pack figures a crisis and its provocation of fear flight, recasting a personal

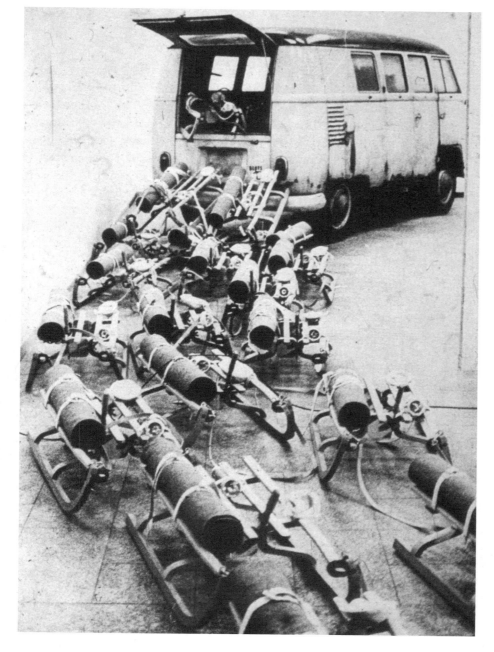

Figure 8.13 Joseph Beuys, *The Pack.* Volkswagen bus, 24 sleds equipped with a roll of felt, fat, and flashlight, 1969. Neue Galerie, Kassel. © 2005 Artists Rights Society (ARS), New York/VG Bild-Kunst, Bonn.

8B Crowd Writings

Armando Petrucci

In September 1966, the Italian historian Delio Cantimori pointed out a particular task of historical research, that of investigating "sets of deeds and of conscious and unusual actions or phenomena of long duration" that were nonetheless concrete and possible to document.

The phenomenon that I intend to study here, evoking a series of diverse situations in which it has manifested itself in the past and continues to manifest itself today, is the use of written texts that are publicly exhibited by human masses, or crowds, present and active within urban realities.

In societies that are more or less partially literate, there exist, and have always existed, situations in which organized masses, more or less numerous, of men and women, participate in or attend a public event, bringing with them, individually or in groups, objects (panels, signs, pieces of fabric, banners, and so forth) covered with written texts that are legible from a distance and that are used in various ways.

Thus far, scholars' attention has been concentrated on the immobile, so-called exhibited writings, affixed or inscribed in a stable way in some public place, on walls or monuments; thus it has been until now and thus it will continue to be for all those writings of a communicative, political, or advertising nature that have populated and populate the spaces of cities, from Pompeii to New York. But it seems to me that, so far, a completely different phenomenon has not been examined: the phenomenon of autonomous displayed writings, produced spontaneously and exhibited ostentatiously by human masses in movement, crossing an inhabited place or standing in an open place like a square or a stadium, or even in closed places, such as sufficiently large rooms.

I will state, right away, in order to clarify for my readers the scenarios that I intend to dwell on, that I am thinking about public events such as processions, parades, and demonstrations on the one hand, and sports events or ceremonial and political meetings on the other. The protagonists of these events are, to turn to the interpretative categories delineated in his time by Elias Canetti, "still masses," such as those concentrated in closed squares, in stadiums, and in rooms, and "masses in motion," slow or rapid. In the first case, the "still masses," although remaining such, can move the exhibited writings more or less rhythmically, and in the second case, the mobile masses can transform their motion, their march charged with aggression, actually using the supports for the exhibited writings themselves (sticks, poles, bars, clubs) as blunt arms against opposing formations (political or sporting opposition, the police) that seek to impede them or to stop them.

If we primarily consider the contemporary period, from the nineteenth century to today, it seems to me that we can proceed to another distinction, and that is to a distinction between "celebrating crowds" and "demonstrating crowds," in that the attitude of the protagonists, very different in the two cases, radically modifies the use and the nature of the writings exhibited. A celebrating crowd, present at a religious procession or at an official procession (for example, in the past, the "entrance" of a king, a pope, or an ambassa-

war trauma in collective terms. Beuys provided this scenario: "This is an emergency object: an invasion by The Pack. In a state of emergency the Volkswagen bus is of limited usefulness, and more direct and primitive means must be taken to ensure *survival*. The most direct kind of movement over the earth is the sliding of the iron runners of the sleds."[66] The Volkswagen bus, of course, is highly symbolic in Germany. As the people's (*volk*) vehicle, it is a proxy for the masses, but it also functions as an emblem of German technology and its limits. The severely corroded surfaces, dirt-covered windows, and frayed front seat of this abandoned bus signify its decay and ruin. As one of his critics of the time pointed out, Beuys regarded modern technology as a source of moral corrosion: "Fear seems to be his mainspring; it is deep and ubiquitous within him. Technology is evil, today is evil, automobiles are dreadful, computers inhuman, televisions likewise, rockets are horrible, splitting atoms destroys the world."[67] The name "Beuys," accompanied by a cross and inscribed in *braunkreuz* on the panel of the driver's side and back of the bus, marks its homeopathic appropriation by the artist. *Braunkreuz*, an opaque reddish-brown paint made of an iron solution combined with commercial rust-proofing, has associations with blood and healing, as does the cross, with resonances that evoke both the Christian cross and the Red Cross.[68] Beuys thus converts his Volkswagen bus into a kind of ambulance, a vehicle he would choose to transport him to the site of his exhibition at the Block Gallery in New York five years later. Significantly, only the driver's seat remains in this bus, the others having been taken out to make room for the sleds. One individual, it seems, must still play the role of shaman/leader even under conditions of collective flight and defense.

Beyond its personal resonances, Beuys's *The Pack* may be interpreted through the typologies that appear in Elias Canetti's famous *Masse und Macht* (*Crowds and Power*) of 1960. Many of the chapters in this book could have attracted Beuys's attention, especially those that address "the survivor," "the command," the "crowd crystal," "flight crowds," and "the pack." Although Canetti uses the term *die Meute* (pack of hounds, gang, rabble), and Beuys uses the more peaceable term *das Rudel* (flock, herd, or pack), both allude to an originary group with affinities to animal packs. For Canetti, the crowds of today ultimately derive from this oldest of all social units, the pack, which he defines as a small horde of roaming men in a state of communal excitement.[69] Because of its limited size and vulnerability, the pack always desires greater density and growth. But within the pack, there is a strong sense of equality and a shared concrete goal, such as lamentation or hunting, which leads to movement and action. Similar to the hunting pack is the war pack, which presupposes a second pack of men or at least the fear of one. Although the enemies do not differ very much from each other, the cleavage is absolute and endures as long as a perceived or real threat exists (*CP*, 27–31).

The Pack combines elements of the flight crowd and the war pack, in which the goals of escape and survival subsume that of counterattack. The absence of weapons or even hunting equipment seems to signal its nonviolent, purely defensive status, although the lack of individuating elements in the sleds, each equipped with the same standardized provisions, also intimates a military form of homogenization and discipline. Driven by fear, always in rapid movement over deterritorialized, open space, the members of this closed and uniform(ed) group fall back into a primitive, communal social order (although a leader is still implied). Their very survival depends on their banding together and on each individual being known to the others. Unlike the modern crowd, which may be an effect of the media and therefore dispersed in time and space, the pack derives its purpose and strength from physical proximity, immediate joint action, a common direction, and speed. It is self-contained and autonomous, requiring no assistance from other groups, who by definition remain beyond its closed borders. Through *The Pack* Beuys evokes a world of strife and aggression that can be survived only by reversion to the most archaic social formation and to basic sources of protection, energy, and movement. As such, he also reveals a nostalgia for a simpler, face-to-face communal life, in harmony with animals and nature, and possible only through isolation and a rejection of modern technology and warfare.

Although Beuys's interest in Canetti's *Crowds and Power* remains conjecture, California conceptual artist John Baldessari acknowledges reading this book in 1984, and remembers that it sparked his series of representations of crowds begun that year. He also read Freud on the crowd, and possibly other theorists as well. Indeed, Baldessari continues to be intrigued by the fact that crowds are an unusual subject in modern art, and he speculates that this may be due to the emphasis on individualism in our culture.[70] The series *Crowds with Shape of Reason Missing*, of 1984–1985, draws on photographs of historical events as well as movie stills. The artist alters these photographs through cropping and by superimposing a white geometric shape onto the central figures and the space they command, thereby rendering invisible the crowd's raison d'être. This masking of the focal point does not so much subtract meaning as repress its specificity while directing attention to formal configurations of space, and hence of power. The type of crowd pictured in each image remains evident—whether (to use Canetti's terms) the crowd is open or closed, slow or quick, stagnating or caught in a moment of discharge.

dor into a city), displays writings composed and prepared, even materially, by others. These writings are provided to them or imposed on them by the true "rulers" of the ritual situation: imagine, for instance, public processions under dictatorial regimes, entirely ritualized and militarized, in which not only the development of the action is organized and controlled from the beginning to the end with a precise choreography, but also, or perhaps above all, the symbols that are exhibited, figural or written, are rigidly designed according to an unchangeable plan.

From this point of view, the nature of writings exhibited by demonstrating crowds is completely different, if not entirely opposite, to that of the writings exhibited by a celebrating crowd. The demonstrating crowd displays its own written products, usually put together by the participants themselves for the occasion, in an explicitly aggressive and strongly individualized fashion, corresponding to the participating groups as distinct from each other in different segments of the procession. In the first case, therefore, we can say that we encounter the exhibition of writings put together *for* the crowd, and in the second, quite the opposite: writings put together *by* the crowd.

One final aspect that I would like to examine is that of the impact of these writings, the texts of which are usually obsessively repeated out loud by the participants, on the public space (streets or squares of a city) that they cross. In general, these are the most aristocratic, important, and ancient areas of a single inhabited center, those in which one finds the "buildings of power," the most important historical and religious monuments, traditionally reserved for the public rites of institutions and the dominating class, from afternoon strolls to attendance at shows to shopping. Doubtless the impact is of a hostile nature, psychologically intent on frightening the hypothetical adversary and on communicating a terrorizing impression of overwhelming force by means of a physical action of "armed" crossing, that symbolically configures itself like an act of explicit violence: thus not so much a crossing as much as a "penetration," in which the exhibited, brandished writings constitute the symbolic and declarative meaning.

Another, very contemporary phenomenon must, from this point of view, be considered apart from the previous discussion: the writings exhibited by crowds made up of organized sports fans, generally located within places designated for such events (stadiums, gyms, fields). This phenomenon must be considered separately because of the formal contiguity of these writings with the spontaneous written productions of a political nature and because the protagonists are almost all young.

In these highly ritualized situations, the writings, exhibited on rigid cards or on large or even enormous banners of cloth, constitute real and authentic works of art by anonymous artists, or, better, by groups, the language of which is strongly expressive and aggressive, tinged with jargony self-representation, sex, and violence. Because the protagonist public is constrained in the place where the sports event takes place, that event at which the public is spectator and participant, the writings are the entities that move, that, accompanied by slogans sung or screamed in chorus, are lifted up, are lowered, are rolled up and unrolled, configuring a show within the show in the form of a actual warrior dance, which is often followed by, in the moment of the final paroxysm, a serious physical clash that concludes the presentation.

In *Two Crowds (With Shape of Reason Missing)* of 1984, Baldessari selected images with clear, powerfully visualized gestalts that reveal a great deal about the crowd's character and its performative function (fig. 8.14). The source materials, published alongside the final work, allow one to gauge the effects of the artist's cropping and deletions.[71] The first image, probably a film still, is of a ceremony in a cathedral, perhaps a coronation or royal marriage (and hence an image of the alliance of church and state). Two rows of knights in armor flank the sides of a long center aisle; behind them stands the congregation, also in ceremonial dress. This crowd is marked by its closed, hierarchical formation, all eyes directed down the aisle toward the figures enacting a ritual at the altar. In the final version, Baldessari crops the altar and covers the aisle with a white, diagonal shape.

The second image records the proclamation of war in Berlin on August 1, 1914.[72] Again the mass of witnesses is controlled by military figures, who surround the central speaker and lend a ritual significance to the event. As representatives of the army, they embody Germany's national crowd symbol, the mythic force in which Canetti believed Germans feel themselves united, invincible (*CP*, 173–74). Although the actual army is a closed and highly regimented crowd, the army as symbol (often associated with the forest) is open, embraced by heterogeneous groups of citizens. Identification with this symbol played a vital role in the nation's enthusiasm for war. Indeed, Canetti described the very event pictured in Baldessari's photograph:

On the outbreak of the first world war the whole German people became one open crowd. The enthusiasm of those days has often been described. Many people in other countries had been counting on the internationalism of the Social Democrats and were astounded at their failure to act. They forgot that the Social Democrats, too, bore within them this forest-army symbol of their nation. . . .

But those first August days of 1914 were also the days in which National Socialism was begotten. Hitler himself is our authority for this. He later described how, at the outbreak of war, he fell on his knees and thanked God. It was his decisive experience, the one moment at which he himself honestly became part of a crowd. (*CP*, 180)

In the photograph, the ringed observers see themselves reflected and multiplied in the faces before them, thereby constituting a self-mirroring world from which all outsiders are excluded. (A few members of this crowd do look away, to others behind them or toward the photographer, suggesting they are not fully caught up in the sense of group identification promoted by this event.) This is a dense, open crowd that wishes to grow and exults in its unity and power. The direction and discharge that it seeks has now been promised. Baldessari crops this photograph so that the crowd becomes more symmetrical and the space around the speaker more centered within the image. He then superimposes a white oval shape over the speaker and the space that distances him from the crowd.

Baldessari's photoworks ironically suppress the "reason" for the crowd's appearance, the ritual event or command that galvanized it, while nevertheless preserving the abstract "shapes" of power, characterized by clear geometry, reflexive symmetry, and a hierarchical relation to the leader or ritual. Most theorists agree that crowds are formations united through shared unconscious desires and identification with a "magnetizer" or mythic ideal, not through reasoned discourse. Theorists as diverse as Le Bon, Freud (who was much indebted to Le Bon), and Canetti have emphasized that a crowd demands a leader, a goal, and a direction.[73] It requires the imposition of a shape, but one that conforms to its latent sentiments and myths. In suppressing this "shape of reason," Baldessari exposes its irrational, phantasmagorical basis. The crowd in each image stands solemnly at attention before a precisely defined void. Yet this void, this mark of repression, nonetheless has the force to shape the crowd, to address it, to rouse its passions and illusions of power. The white shapes trace both the calling forth of the crowd, and provide a blank screen for the crowd's projective fantasies.

Baldessari's *Two Crowds (With Shape of Reason Missing)* also raises the question of the relation of the crowd to the public, which may take on some of the characteristics of the crowd but is not identical with it. As early as 1895, Le Bon had recognized the importance of the newspapers in the propagation of public opinion (*C*, 149–54). Tarde further developed this notion, arguing that "the invention of printing has caused a very different type of public to appear, one which never ceases to grow and whose indefinite extension is one of the most clearly marked traits of our period." He defined this public as "a purely spiritual collectivity, a dispersion of individuals who are physically separated and whose cohesion is entirely mental."[74] For Tarde, the seemingly instantaneous transmission of ideas over great distances through printing, the railroad, and the telegraph proved a more powerful force than the transport of armies. The bond created between readers of the same newspapers lay in their shared convictions and passions, and in their awareness of forming a united mass.[75] Before the diffusion of the press, opinions were developed and propagated in distinct and separate communities through conversation. Now, Tarde argued, "The press unifies and invigorates conversations, makes them uniform in space and diversified in time. Every morning the papers give their publics the conversations for the day." The result was the rise of mass subjectivity: "This increasing similarity of simultaneous conversations in an ever more

I affirm that it is exactly this most recent kind of situation, in its explicit mixture of sport and of violence, through the rhythmic movement of millions of bodies and hundreds of writings, that constitutes a new and original use of the exhibition of the writings of urban crowds.[1]

Translated from the Italian
by Heather Webb

Figure 8.14 John Baldessari, *Two Crowds (With Shape of Reason Missing).* Gelatin silver print, 1984. Private collection. Photo: Courtesy of John Baldessari.

vast geographic domain is one of the most important characteristics of our time."[76] Even those who do not read the newspaper, but who speak with those who do, "are forced to follow the groove of their borrowed thoughts" ("OC," 304). Rather than small and diversified crowds, based on class, local tradition, profession, or religion, Tarde saw that "the newspaper will create an immense, abstract, and sovereign crowd, which it will name opinion" ("OC," 318).[77] And opinions, as Le Bon recognized, are more often counted than analyzed. As older beliefs and traditions lose their influence, the power of transient public opinion grows until it supplants that of governments, which now have become the observers and servants of opinion (*C*, 149–54).[78]

Tarde's recognition of the important role played by the means of communication in determining the structure and character of publics, and the ways in which it generates mass subjectivity, is increasingly relevant today. The speed with which information and opinions can now be transmitted through new electronic media including television, radio, fax, and the Internet exceeds anything Tarde might have imagined. These media have produced dispersed publics that transcend local and national boundaries, allowing simultaneous knowledge of, and response to, events and issues deemed newsworthy.

German photographer Andreas Gursky's *Stock Exchange, Tokyo*, of 1990, addresses this phenomenon and its effect on the market economy of the late 1980s and 1990s (fig. 8.15).[79] As a barometer of opinion, the stock exchange exemplifies the constantly fluctuating reactions of the investors to the day's news and recent and projected economic trends. In Gursky's photograph, a bird's-eye view allows us to grasp the combination of distraction and group frenzy that characterizes the brokers' activities. Small clusters form, passions rise and fall (as observed in the dense group with raised arms in the right foreground), deals are made or fall through. The omnipresence of computers throughout the hall points to the role of electronic media in the production of symbol-

Figure 8.15 Andreas Gursky, "Stock Exchange, Tokyo," 1990. Courtesy: Matthew Marks Gallery, New York and Monika Sprüth / Philomene Magers, Cologne/Munich © 2005 Andreas Gursky / Artists Rights Society (ARS), New York / VG Bild-Kunst, Bonn.

ic (rather than industrial or finance) capitalism. Although concentrated in this image, its effects are dispersed globally and produce a new kind of mass cyborg. In another set of photographs, titled *Hong Kong Stock Exchange, Diptych*, of 1994, male and female brokers no longer form groups but sit in rows before their computer screens wearing identical red vests. Its counterpart is *Chicago Board of Trade II, 1999*; here the number of brokers is vastly increased and the floor is littered with paper (a sign of the rapid obsolescence of data), but the pervasive presence of telephones and computer screens, many showing the same image, alerts us to the uniform and instantaneous dissemination of information and its effects on subjectivity. The individual, now indistinguishable from the mass, must adjust his or her speed to the flows of the market and the media. Direct conversation gives way to deals brokered through electronic means among dispersed people unknown to each other.

Gursky's stock exchange pictures, like his other contemporary photographs, are digitally scanned, montaged, and then conventionally printed from enlarged negatives in order to enhance the wealth and density of vivid detail as well as the proliferation of like elements within a mural-scale format. Thus manipulated, these pictures mimic the deadpan, frontal photographs of archetypal industrial buildings taken by Gursky's teachers in Düsseldorf, Bernd and Hilla Becher, while rejecting their serial composition. Or we might say that Gursky has made seriality and the structure of the grid internal to the image. As has often been noted, his photographs seem both factual and fantastic, mundane and sublime, in their attention to minute particles as well as to large, overall patterns, both exceeding the capacity of human vision. As one critic remarks, it is "as if we were peering simultaneously through binoculars and a microscope."[80] The hyperreality he thereby constructs, intensified by fully saturated color and monumental scale, seeks less to document the world of global exchange, communication networks, advertising, and commodified spectacle than to find its visual equivalent. His images of stock exchanges, like those of overabundantly stocked store shelves, sprawling parking lots, mobbed automobile shows, and traffic jams, present us with a mirror in which we can view our increasingly deindividualized selves within the environments we have created, rendered simultaneously strange and uncannily familiar.

We might also consider the *Truisms* of Jenny Holzer as a reflection on the collective, if contradictory, opinions and dogmas of our time. Holzer's *Truisms* (written between 1977 and 1979) recirculate popular clichés in the form of stickers, T-shirts, posters, and LED signs, often situated in public venues (fig. 8.16).[81] We read: "Abuse of Power Should Come as No Surprise," "An Elite Is Inevitable," "Anger or Hate Is a Useful Motivating Force," "Money Makes Taste," "Any Surplus Is Immoral," "Morals Are for Little People," "Most People Are Not Fit to Rule Themselves," and so forth. Not surprisingly, many of these *Truisms* are reminiscent of the clichés advanced by turn-of-the-century crowd theorists, which, ironically, were also presented in concise, declarative form. Holzer's *Truisms*, which imitate the rhetoric of the mesmerizing leader or the ideas of the anonymous crowd, take the form of pure affirmations, without explanation or apparent origin. They are simple, lively, and direct, and hence easily repeated and remembered. As such, they pass for truth in a culture of automatic thinking, with little concern for testing ideas and prejudices. In the posters of the late 1970s, Holzer would include forty or more mutually contradictory *Truisms* listed in a neutral alphabetical order, thereby confronting her viewers with their own inconsistent and irrational doxa. The LED signs that followed put the *Truisms* into motion, mimicking the speed, evanescence, and flashiness of advertising or the news announcement (and their confusion). No sooner is one *Truism* read than it is followed by another, and another. Displayed on LED signs at the Philadelphia Bourse, on the baggage carrousels at the McCarran International Airport in Las Vegas, on the Spectacolor Board in Times Square, and on the spiral ramp of the Guggenheim Museum, her signs address a distracted mass public, one that is usually heterogeneous and already in motion. The transient public thus constituted will soon be dispersed in space and nonsynchronous in time. Yet by bringing into view the ways in which our opinions and passions are produced and propagated through mass media, Holzer's *Truisms* undermine their own absolutism. They seek to produce critical thinking, even perhaps a genuine public sphere.

The animated films of South African artist William Kentridge provide a more politically charged view of the masses "on the move," in which images of the crowd seem alternately abject and powerful, oppressed and on the cusp of emancipation. As a South African of Lithuanian Jewish descent, Kentridge sees himself as occupying a marginal, although hardly neutral, position within his society.[82] He is conscious of "the tyranny of our history" and the "moral imperative arising from that"[83] while also seeking to avoid indulging in nostalgia for prior moments when a utopian art was still possible (as exemplified by the Russian revolution and its constructivist art). As the artist explained, "I am interested in a political art, that is to say an art of ambiguity, contradiction, uncompleted gestures and uncertain endings. An art (and a politics) in which optimism is kept in check and nihilism at bay."[84]

Images of crowds occur with great frequency in Kentridge's drawings and films, sometimes associated with the

Figure 8.16 Jenny Holzer, Selections from *Truisms*. Spectacolor Board, Times Square, New York, 1982. Sponsored by the Public Art Fund, Inc., New York. © 2005 Jenny Holzer / Artists Rights Society (ARS), New York.

irresistible force of rising tides and floods, as in *Tide Table* of 2003, with the dehumanizing labor of the mines, as in *Mine* of 1991, and in the many *Arc Processions* that picture an incongruous assemblage of the dispossessed, some carrying their belongings on their backs, arranged in an arc-like frieze. Kentridge's film *Monument* of 1990 crystallizes many of his concerns, weaving personal memories into a three-minute narrative that links a sense of political crisis with feelings of ambivalence toward his own role as an artist (fig. 8.17). The protagonist, the capitalist Soho Eckstein (modeled both on the artist's grandfather and to some extent on himself), seeks to absolve his guilt by creating a monument to the masses who work in his mines. Eckstein, appearing in the guise of civic benefactor, mumbles unintelligibly into the many microphones that surround him while the crowds gather in a decimated landscape before his shrouded gift. When the monument (contained in a cage-like scaffolding) is unveiled, it proves to be the stony figure of an anonymous laborer, seen earlier in the film carrying an enormous weight on his back as he passed through the outskirts of the city and then vanished into the landscape. This laborer, who is associated with the scarred land, as Dan Cameron observes, represents the moral dilemma at the center of Eckstein's mining empire. For although Eckstein may wish to acknowledge the workers by erecting a monument in their honor, he cannot fully recognize their humanity and retain his power and wealth.[85] Instead, the monument serves to further hypostatize Eckstein's oppression of the workers, who have been assembled so that they may contemplate their reified image. Indeed, the laborer, still carrying his burden, is chained to the base; yet in the final moments of the film, he raises his head and opens his pained eyes, suggesting the survival of some measure of dignity and resistance.

Like Kentridge's other animated films, *Monument* is based on a series of charcoal drawings, which the artist transforms through a process of erasure and new figura-

tion, captured one frame at a time by a camera. The result synthesizes a traditional, low-tech, static medium, with the movement made possible by film. As Rosalind Krauss emphasizes, the technique itself demands a constant back and forth, shuttling between the drawing and the camera, introducing a strong sense of temporal mediation and reflective distance into the very process of image-making.[86] In *Monument*, this palimpsestic structure allows thought to follow unexpected metaphorical paths, from the opening image of the weary laborer, to the exploited landscape strewn with billboards, lampposts, loudspeakers, microphones, and other signs of political speech, to the crowd gathering in this blighted zone, to Eckstein, the monument, and back. A sense of instability and imminent change infuses these layered and recurring motifs, lending them a quotient of historical possibility that might seem more remote in a fixed image. Kentridge's open-ended films of crowds respond to the epochal transformations occurring in South Africa during the late 1980s and early 1990s; in 1989 the state of emergency was extended for its fourth year as defiant masses marched to slogans and chants accompanied by red flags. The following year Nelson Mandela was released, and De Klerk announced his intention to negotiate with the black opposition to draft a new constitution, finally lifting the state of emergency. Referring to the crowds in his first four films, Kentridge remarked, "they are more directly political crowds. It may be of interest to note (and here I do not know how to apportion responsibility) that these images of crowds emerged in my work in 1989, the year that the political thaw in South Africa began, when for the first time in my memory huge political processions surged through the streets."[87]

Kentridge's animated films project the crowd as a highly mediated phenomenon, called into being by bullhorns, megaphones, billboards, and radios, interpellated by these and other techniques, and finally represented through newspapers, photography, posters, television, drawings,

Figure 8.17 William Kentridge, *Crowd and Covered Monument 1*. Drawing for the film *Monument*. Charcoal on paper, 1990. Johannesburg Art Gallery, Johannesburg.

and film. The ever-present megaphones, bullhorns, and billboards that address his protagonists in deliberately outmoded, relatively low-tech forms, refer to earlier twentieth-century emblems of political speech. Kentridge remembers having seen similar devices in the photomontages of the Russian constructivists and in Max Beckmann's paintings.[88] Yet he can no longer believe in the utopian optimism of those times. Like other contemporary artists, his crowds are neither heroic nor oceanic, although they sometimes fill streets or march through desolate landscapes. They figure forth the reality of their oppression and instantiate a demand for change, but Kentridge refrains from providing an image of naive optimism in the future.

Kentridge's work, although grounded in the particular historical moment in which it was made, during the violent final years of apartheid in South Africa, nonetheless speaks to the larger question of the role of crowds in contemporary social and political processes. Today's crowds are increasingly the result of overt mobilization, whether through the press, television, or, as in the recent phenomenon of the flash mob, through Internet communication. Frequently the crowd's physical presence in a single time and place is staged for media coverage, to demonstrate support for a particular cause, and it therefore implies an address to a larger, virtual crowd or public. The recent stunning success of the Ukrainian masses in demanding new elections was not due to their collective presence and courageous action alone; it was supported by Ukrainian television as well as by the presence of an international media, and by strong protests abroad.

The action of the contemporary crowd seems to converge, increasingly, with that of the public, a collectivity dispersed in time and space but connected through shared media channels. Such publics, however, do not always conform to Tarde's thesis that the media serve only to foster mental unity through a mysterious process of contagion; at times the media can also promote debate and the contestation of ideas, even the emergence of a public sphere. Whether the fact of gathering as a mass retains any political agency seems to depend on specific historical circumstances and on the relation of the crowd to the media that interpellate its potential members, circulate ideas and images, and represent its virtual or physical staging and actions. Contemporary images of the crowd engage this process of representation while allowing us to glimpse the modes of social cohesion and dispersal characteristic of our time.

9 The Return of the Blob, or How Sociology Decided to Stop Worrying and Love the Crowd

John Plotz

ON THE LOOKOUT FOR MELODRAMA in the most arid reaches of social science? You couldn't do better than peruse sociological writing about crowds. The pathos of large numbers is already there in Gustave Le Bon's dire warning that the crowd is the sphinx of our century, dying to consume us; it waxes in Sigmund Freud's worry that "groups" exist in no other form than ego-abating worship of their ego-ideal leader; and it still burns strong in Serge Moscovici's pseudoscientific pronouncement that political riots only prove "the veneer of civilization is very thin." Even in the twenty-first century, you can still hear echoes of the oracular tone of Thomas Carlyle or Joseph de Maistre, post–French Revolution reactionaries who feared that any mass action from below would set the social order ablaze.

In the United States, a country that was arguably born out of crowd-fueled, democratically arrayed civil unrest, the fear of crowds was a lot quieter in the nineteenth century. It did, however, still reach a predictable apex in the McCarthy era. This generation can be rescued from crowd thinking, writes one 1950s hyperbolizer, only when citizens "discover that their own thoughts and their own lives are quite as interesting as other people's, that, indeed, they no more assuage their loneliness in a crowd of peers than one can assuage one's thirst by drinking sea water."[1]

Perhaps largely derived from a distrust of totalitarianism most ably articulated in Hannah Arendt's *The Origins of Totalitarianism*, the "mass critique" of the social scientists of the midcentury extrapolated from the worst of Nazism and Stalinist communism a generally coercive force called "the social," which seemed now to be terrorizing not Germany and Russia but, in a different guise, America itself. Small wonder that Hannah Pitkin called her account of Hannah Arendt, preeminent theorist of the threat that "society" poses to an orderly political realm, *The Attack of the Blob.* For Arendt, social life—with its tendency to annihilate privacy and collapse public arenas into overseen and government-managed cages—had stopped being one aspect of human culture and become a dangerous underlying assault upon human freedom.[2] To writers like Arendt—those in her train included C. Wright Mills, Theodor Adorno, Elias Canetti, Richard Hofstadter, and arguably even the young Jürgen Habermas,[3] the enemy was all the more terrifying for being uncanny, an aspect of our own familiar selves suddenly recognized as part of an external assailant.

We may not be quick to recognize the central worry of such mass-critique writers as panic about what crowds can do, because what they mostly described themselves as denouncing was instead "society" or "the social." The legacy of Mill trains us to see in their words mostly introspective unease about one's lack of control over one's own actions, rather than crowd-control protocols. But to these writers, worry about the unrestrained, licentious, and determinedly egalitarian danger of crowds was, in the final analysis, the way that "the social" became visible (and hence vulnerable).

Richard Pells describes what made the dominant intellectual liberalism of the 1950s distinct from preceding decades: "What the writers of 1930s called 'community' the postwar intelligentsia labeled 'conformity.' Cooperation now became 'other-direction'; social consciousness had turned into 'groupism'; solidarity with others implied an invasion of privacy; 'collectivism' ushered in a 'mass society'; ideology translated into imagery; economic exploitation yielded to bureaucratic manipulation; the radical activist was just another organization man."[4] In William H. Whyte's 1956 *The Organization Man*, aggregation itself gets hypostatized into a collective noun with its own ideational motivations ("Is the Organization to be the arbiter? The Organization will look to its own interests, but it will look to the individual's *only as The Organization interprets them*").[5] And in *The Lonely Crowd* (1950), by Riesman et al., the underlying emphasis is on rescuing democracy by protecting individual difference from the homogenizing barbarism of the crowd: "the idea that men are created free and equal is both true and misleading; men are created different; they lose their social freedom and their individual autonomy in seeking to become like each other" (*LC,* 307).

Consider for a moment how greatly the suspicious 1950s divagated from the collectivist or at least crowd-cheering ethos of the 1930s. In King Vidor's 1928 *The Crowd,* for instance, much of the film's visual delight comes from conglomeration shots: lines of chatting women leaving an office building at quitting time, spinning through the revolving door, or climbing together onto rides at Coney Island. In among these teeming masses, the occasional deviation is generally for disaster—the one man struck down in the street is distinct from the crowd that gathers around him. When a happy couple is picked out, they are applauded in their moment of most perfect conformity with their surroundings. That was a 1930s dream, of the average hero, but by the 1950s it reappears in Whyte and Riesman as a nightmare of stagnation and immersion.

This brief history of popular sociology's dependence on a paradigm that feared the social, particularly the social as manifested in crowd actions, may seem to omit key components of midcentury social theory—notably, sociology's flirtation with "hard" science. After all, beginning as early as his 1937 publication of *The Structure of Social Action,* wasn't the functionalism or "structural functionalism" of Talcott Parsons immensely influential within the circles of professional sociology? True, and yet the stunning popularity of such voluntarist and morally/politically prescriptive work as Arendt's and Riesman's suggests that the appeal of functionalist models beyond academia was limited.[6]

If Todd Stillman is right to propose the dominance of a resolutely unselfconscious scientific sociology in midcentury America was "an exception to the rule" that "reflexivity is natural feature of intellectual communities," then perhaps the work of writers like Arendt can be seen as restoring to the discipline a striking measure of reflexivity, an assessment of how much the discipline's own vocabularies are shaped by its time and place.[7] If so, then the popularity of these exceptions to the scientific sociology norm (with their abhorrence of data sets and their open rejection of what Harold Garfinckel dismissively called "Parson's plenum"—that is, the hypothesis of complete macrolevel mappability of society) may be consistent with a public desire, even in the 1950s, not for "objective" accounts of society, but compelling, inspiring ones.

That Whyte and Riesman were ultimately as inspiring to their generation as Hannah Arendt was terrifying is evident. Witness the manifest appeal of both Whyte and Riesman's books, which were both middle- and high-brow conversation books from decade to decade: Michael Schudson describes them as the twin bibles of his sociologically savvy childhood, the two classics whose status was unquestioned.[8] Both are formative books for the 1960s generation—along with Betty Friedan's 1960 *The Feminine Mystique*, a book that manifestly shares the same anxiety about depraved social forces that underpin a misogynist suburban way of life.

What remains fascinating about this generation's antisocial manifestos is not how clear their enemy is, but how opaque, how confused and confusing. Both Riesman and Whyte posit as an enemy the aggregated hypostatized entity that comes into being when individuals assemble into a system larger than their individual volitions. In Whyte, this is called "Organization," and in Riesman, it is referred to as becoming an "other-directed man." This is their central figure for the crowd—the unavoidable social phenomenon that presses in on the individual with an unavoidable and exit-blocking social force, compelling a uniform response form each person so constrained.

But neither Whyte nor Riesman is looking for a way to

diagram escapes from this overcrowded situation. In both writers, it is a reflexive feature of such crowd situations that participants are unable to see the crowd as something that necessitates escape. The overcrowding is thus "realized" only by the reader (and perhaps not even then). Those who are imprisoned by crowds by definition lose sight of that fact. It is not simply that they are trapped by Big Brother, or even simply that they grow to prefer Big Brother. In fact, they themselves change so that they comprise the core of the very Organization that is busy curtailing or compromising their own freedom. They do not flee Big Brother, they become Him.

One purpose of this essay, therefore, is to explore why this rather unlikely, almost masochistic account of crowd triumph succeeded so well in the 1950s. Why for so long did people choose a paradigm to explain their own actions that seemed implicitly both on the one hand to blame them for their acquiescence to social forces, and on the other to assume that their acquiescence or resistance was largely beyond their own control?

I also want to explore the swing of the sociological pendulum back toward an unexpected, rather troubling kind of affection for certain sociable crowds. How has sociology in the last decade come to embrace sociability in what once seemed its most "crowdlike" aspects? What makes Riesman's work revisiting in this context is how perfectly it seems to invert a certain troubling trend in present-day popular sociology.

If we are living in what looks more and more like a return to McCarthyite America in many respects—as regards the curtailing of civil liberties, the distrust of social protest, the valorization of certain kinds of religious cohesion—one glaring difference remains. It is clear that popular sociology nowadays has no interest in preaching a fear of either "the crowd" or of "the social" more generally. "Social capital" is the order of the day, and sociologists from Christopher Lasch to Alan Wolfe to Robert Putnam—alongside both left and right communitarians such as Michael Sandel and Amitai Etzioni—can't hurry us back to church and PTA meetings fast enough. Nowadays, it's de rigueur if not to love the homogeneous society, then at least to hate those who tell us to hate it, to fear those who favor withdrawing from it in fear. It is no longer normal to fear a crowd because it is a crowd, and it no longer makes sense to criticize suburbia for its mindless conformity.

Now social scientists speak of suburbia's emptiness, it lack of "binding social capital" or its "dispersal" and "avoidance." The enemy is what Zygmunt Baumann calls "glocalization," in which the dual punishments of our privileged and our deprived are to be trapped, either in empty (lonely) motion of the deracinated and hence bereft rich, or in the privation of having to live, as a poor person, a great distance from the world's real centers.[9] Even our suburbs now are problems, sociology informs us, not because they brainwash us (as Riesman worried), but because they fail to make any demands on us at all.

It was not always thus. In the late 1950s and 1960s, suburban chroniclers like Edmund Wilson and John Cheever worried about the strange synchronization of private lives that Lewis Mumford condemned as "the collective effort to live a private life." Like "the lonely crowd," that phrase oxymoronically stresses the ways in which our new exposure to one another in a collectivity is linked, inextricably and depressingly, with our alienation from one another. The closer to one another we grow (physically, socially), the farther away from one another (morally, politically, ethically) we become. It had been a common lament ever since Wordsworth's *The Prelude* (ca. 1805), but the suburbia panics of the 1950s took it to new heights.

By the late 1990s, though, D. J. Waldie's *Holy Land* sees only empty squares, burned-out consciences, a city hall that is no more than a way station for sparsely attended zoning hearings—the bowling alleys deserted, the softball teams disbanded.[10] Baumgartner tells us now (1988) that the *Moral Order of a Suburb* is characterized not by excessively other-directed cohabitation, as Riesman feared, but by the same kind of "avoidance" that Eskimos and the plain nomads of West Africa use—no violence, no adjudication, no confrontation; mere anomie is loosed upon the world.[11]

Science fiction's tale is the same. The days of *Invasion of the Body Snatchers* and *The Stepford Wives* (that 1970s phobic fantasy of the 1950s) are gone.[12] In their place, Ang Lee's brilliant fin de siècle logic in *The Ice Storm* entails his arguing that suburban Connecticut is a nightmare because the suburbs are empty—all human contact is prevented from occurring by a thin and deadly sheet of ice. In Ray Bradbury's Martian idylls (*The Martian Chronicles*, 1950), small-town Ohio is imagined as a durable enough community to reestablish itself creepily on Mars. Fifty years on, though, the worrying enemy is not overly cohesive community and a smothering social life but sociality's absence. In *The Matrix* (1999), Sunday picnics have been replaced by the big empty skies and by empty minds; all that computer brainwashing only covers up the fact that each human is lying alone in a vat somewhere. The nightmare is not our collective insertion into the world of dreams but the fact that beneath that dreamscape, we "really" vegetate in solitude. To dream alone is the worst delusion of all.

We have entered an era in which sociology's most popular book, Robert Putnam's *Bowling Alone*, the only current contender for Riesman's sociological best-seller title, is an encomium to just the sort of all-encompassing group activity that Riesman warned us about.[13] Exhortatory social science texts now are cautioning us to tune in, turn on, and drop in—to a church social, a party meeting, a bowling league. Gaining a rejuvenated social life appears to entail accepting the compulsory and arbitrary nature of propinquity and cherish it. The crowd that haunted us fifty years ago beckons us today.

The Lonely Crowd's Crowd

Between 1950 and 1965, the same impetus that spurred the "mass society" critique spurred an unprecedented battery of phobic writing about crowds, from Arendt's influential 1951 *Origins of Totalitarianism* to Elias Canetti's memorable 1960 *Crowds and Power*. Alongside placid Eisenhower Republicanism and rabid McCarthyism sprang up social critiques whose suspicion of the actions of ordinary social forces bordered on the paranoid.

There did exist, certainly, a kind of moderate social critique. Pells emphasizes the way in which most critics of conformist "false consciousness" still strove to have their cake and eat it too: "Most intellectuals who tried to maintain their critical perspective . . . could not ignore the psychological and cultural costs of middle-class affluence, or the moral compromises involved in the individual's readiness to embrace the attitudes and expectations of his peers. So while they accepted the basic structure of society, they believed that the private citizen must somehow resist the enticements of material comfort and the pressures to conform."[14] However, Riesman and Whyte were more blistering than the mainstream Pells describes—and it seems clear that it is on account of their extremity that they were more successful in their day—and widely read even today. Indeed, Pells himself concedes that the dominant mode of critique in the age was laid out by Whyte's "barely concealed antagonism to the collectivist sentiments of the 1930s" and by Riesman's (extreme but not anomalous) contention that "much-praised voluntary associations were 'not voluntary enough'; they intensified 'the pressure on any individual to *join*, to submerge himself in the group—any group'" (*LC*, 233–34, 244).

The point worth stressing here is not simply the widespread fear that certain kinds of social aggregation would submerge individual identity. It is, rather, the all-inclusiveness of the dread of social life that strikes us in retrospect as extreme. In Riesman's account, dronification is simply what groups do. Riesman, like Whyte, brushes aside ostensible distinctions between organizations, or types of organizations. That phrase "any group" gets Riesman's tone perfectly. The putative voluntary nature of the groups, in Riesman's account, disguises the fact that the pressure is overpowering to sign up somewhere, and so lose the traction of withdrawal, the apathy that is the only present form of meaningful dissent.

Even joining, say, a civil liberties group is in Riesman's account only another form of conformity to groupthink, rather than a substantive protest against the deliberalization of the age.[15] It turns out that *The Manchurian Candidate* was even righter than its makers knew. It is not just costume parties concealing communist agents (Angela Lansbury dressed up as the Queen of Hearts) that are dangerous. In fact, *all* costume parties are part of the rot. Anybody dressed as a card is part of the corruption. At times, the barest hint of freely transacted social interaction is enough to send Riesman off in a fury. We should recall his denunciation of medals for the best children's books, as well as his hatred of *The Joy of Cooking*, a book he thought was guilty of encouraging a freely social attitude towards mealtimes and of promulgating the notion that meals must be "pleasant" (*LC*, 142).[16]

The hyperbole connected with the imagined loss of individual agency is a notorious feature of both 1950s and 1960s social science: looking out at World War II's horrible detritus, what writers from Heidegger to Clinton Rossiter saw was not so much lost life as lost meaning.[17] "What we fear," Riesman wrote, "is more than total destruction, it is total meaninglessness."[18] The crucial development here appears to be a sense that the aggrandizement of a crowd form of life has deprived us—that perhaps even democracy itself has deprived us—of individual agency, of opportunities for meaningful consideration and attainment. What looks like the open skies of liberalism are in fact fixed flight paths: the palpable fulfillment of our wishes in fact bespeak our very implication in a machine that seems to serve us but truly rules us.[19]

This leads both Whyte and Riesman to embrace a fruitful set of paradoxes like Riesman's title: solitude is actually crowdedness, consumption actually means being consumed, moving actually means being anchored to one place (in the corporate chain). These paradoxes are frequently inconsistent and in tension with one another; their palpable strangeness helps to clarify how seriously Riesman, White, and others took their diagnosis of complete social immersion. At one point, for example, William Whyte points to the ceaseless movement of junior executives in "the organization" from one town to another as proof not of their atomization but of their ultimate attunement to the desires of the machine (*OM*, 268–73). Such movement, because nationwide and predictably replicated by other execs, makes them all better in tune with one another and better, not less, able to function in a group. Atomization breeds not individual isolation but inescapable conformity—out of loneliness comes the crowd.

Jason Kaufman has recently argued that in America's golden age for voluntary associations (1890–1920), the social groups that Riesman sees as nothing but homogenizers were in fact created for just the opposite reason: precisely to serve the cause of heterogeneity.[20] That is, such groups were either markers or actual producers of ethnic or vocational division, convenient ways to disaggregate society—distinctly not party to "massification" or the rise of social homogeneity. Riesman would be able to make nothing of this argument; in fact, the existence of meaningful ethnic or national homogeneity *within* our social fabric as a whole never emerges as a possibility in *The Lonely Crowd*. In Riesman's thinking, the social always comes back to another incarnation of the omnipresent crowd.

"Enforced and empty gregariousness" (*The Lonely Crowd's* preface labels this our worst current enemy) is the smile we muster in response to other smiles; and it is the acquiescence that a fourth grader gives to a friend who wants him to agree that a particular comic book hero is stupid, or that a plot twist was "neat."[21] In a gradually more impassioned crescendo of simple social compulsions cataloged—although each on its own means little more than common courtesy—Riesman argues that the modern world is unable to stop other people's thoughts, voices, and values from spilling into our own heads. Like the John Cheever story "The Enormous Radio" (in which a woman goes mad eavesdropping on her neighbors) Riesman's "other-directed" psychic eavesdroppers tune in to others so well that their own navigation systems seize up.

The metaphor that readers tend to remember from *The Lonely Crowd* is that of the "radar" that "other-directed" persons are said to be equipped with—the diametrical opposite of the "gyroscope" that an earlier generation's "inner-directed" people had. The catch is that in a world of radars, you'd risk crashing into everyone else if you flew by gyroscope.[22]

The enemy in Riesman is finally this kind of adjustment. Randall Jarrell's wry version of the same notion is Riesmanian in spirit: "President Robbins [a character in Jarrell's novel *Pictures from an Institution*] was so well adjusted to his environment that sometimes you could not tell which was the environment and which was President Robbins."[23] Todd Gitlin oddly describes David Riesman as wanting to "counsel society, not lecture it" (foreword to *LC*, xiv). But counseling and society are the two things that Riesman feared most—counseling connoted the therapeutic culture of an "other-directed" age, in which aspired to perfect adjustment. And *society* as a word for the whole of the country's culture—well, it was just that inclusive model of sociability he wanted to avoid.

As only *Dissent* magazine was churlish enough to note in

its obituary, David Riesman began his professional life in the law, writing "briefs for the anticommunist Rupp-Coudert Committee, hunting down reds in the city's schools."[24] There were a great many reasons for young liberals to feel and act anticommunist in the early 1940s, but Riesman's commitment to unearthing communists at work in the schools has a macabre resonance with his later invective against schools' susceptibility to the creeping conformity of materialist capitalism. In each case, what he feared was that we'd be corroded into conformity, into crowdishness, without knowing it.

Fictional Knowledge: The Double Life of Conforming Novels

The striking thing about Riesman's prognostications, in retrospect, is how much such gloom and dooming seemed to fit rather than bravely defy the culture of the 1950s. If Riesman depicts a world in which everybody but a few lonely social scientists is busy forfeiting individuality for a shot at complete social integration, the texts of a wider cultural realm suggest that his concerns were shared and his diagnoses implicitly echoed—even in the very realms where Riesman believes he is seeing the worst kind of conformity. What makes Riesman and his sociological ilk far more interesting than their notions alone would warrant are the ways in which texts in the broader popular culture realm at times echo the very Riesmanesque diagnoses that would seem to apply most perfectly to that pop cultural realm itself.

It is immediately noticeable that even the very texts that William Whyte and David Riesman single out as typical of the small-minded conformism of the period are themselves busy preaching against small-minded conformism. And it is the texts that now seem to us the most dated, the most perfectly typical of the depressing era of McCarthy,

jitterbugs, and brainwashing phobias, that present the most seemingly heartfelt indictments of just the phenomena that sociologists like Riesman most feared. Take, for example, Sloane Wilson's novel, *The Man in the Gray Flannel Suit* (1955), which was made famous by the 1956 film starring Gregory Peck.

If this book lingers in our memories at all, it is as an indictment of the era's lockstep conformity in business matters, in praise of its hero's ability to buck the system and win. And yet, why? Indeed, William Whyte calls the novel one of the acmes of "sanctimonious materialism," an indictment that makes perfect sense given that the hero leaves a job with a philanthropy to go to work for a go-getter corporate type, straighten out his foundation work, and get his boss the national recognition he craves. Where's the critique in that?

It lies, seemingly, in the attitude with which the author and the protagonist gaze down at the Byzantine coilings of the machine. The book is admittedly autobiographical in parts—in fact, its successor, the deservedly forgotten *Man in the Gray Flannel Suit 2*, is an out-and-out memoir, and openly laudatory of its hero's success in both climbing and gently shaking the corporate ladder. In any event, the love-hate relationship established between the novel's protagonist and the ordinary world of striving nine-to-fivers seems to be shared by the author of the book. However, a closer look at the novel itself reveals why it was such a confusion and delight to Wilson's once-legion readers. The novel is two things at once: very quick to criticize the conformist ethos of contemporary business, and its "Organization" underbelly—but also quick to diagram how inadvertently easy success in that material and vocational world can be, once one has attuned oneself properly to the social surroundings.

In a pair of linked scenes that probably best synopsizes the whole novel's concerns, Wilson issues an indictment of his society—and then reveals his own dependence on the very phenomena that he criticizes. It begins when young business executive and protagonist Tom Rath has a chance to meet with his boss to tell him what he really thinks of him and his ideas. Rath explains carefully to his wife that this meeting is a transparent exercise in what Erving Goffman (in a 1957 article) was about to label "face work." But if for Goffman (as we shall see below), face work is simply what we do all the time in order to avert embarrassment, then in Wilson's account, the careful social acquiescence involved in such face work is particularly suited to the servile truckling that the corporate hierarchy demands of its low dogs. Rath explains to his wife what will happen when he goes in to meet his boss:

There's a standard operating procedure for this sort of thing. . . . It's a little like reading fortunes. You make a lot of highly qualified contradictory statements and keep your eyes on the man's face to see which ones please him. That way you can feel your way along, and if you're clever, you can always end up by telling him exactly what he wants to hear. . . . For instance, I'll begin by saying, "I think there are some wonderful things about this speech. . . . " If Hopkins seems pleased, I'll finish the sentence by saying "and I have only the most minor improvements to suggest." But if he seems a little surprised at the word wonderful, I'll end the sentence with "but as a whole, don't think it comes off at all, and I think major revisions are necessary. . . . " As I say, it's standard operating procedure, the first thing the young executive must learn.[25]

This cynical passage seems to align Wilson as well as his character with the "mass society" critics because it suggests that the Organization has a comprehensive logic all its own, to which one must religiously conform in order to gain advancement—at the cost of one's own ego and personal honor. Tom's wife Betsy, who knows that for Tom's salary to increase he must go into the corporation wholeheartedly (and hence willingly), reprimands Tom's cynicism. The face-off seems clear: Tom stands for a Riesmanesque skewering of social conformity, while his wife buckles down and does what society demands.

Given Tom's anatomy of what's required of him, you'd expect his showdown with the boss to end in disaster or in passive acquiescence, either in the open revolt his critique seems to require, or in the yes-sirring his wife urges on him as the best way to a pat paycheck. What's striking about the novel, however, is that neither occurs.

Rather, the carefully guided sycophancy that Tom was describing to his wife gets reenacted, but with this difference—that Tom doesn't feel he is a lickspittle. In the "face work" interaction, he finds a way to kowtow while feeling that he's being his own man. At the moment that Tom is about to speak, the novel enters into a free indirect discourse that renders us greater immediacy of his thought processes and his actions than we've yet had—an entrance marked by Tom's own sudden awareness of the gap that opens up between what he *thinks* and what he actually *does* in the world. Tom finds that he is so acutely tuned in to his surroundings, so engrossed in the present moment as both human and organizational encounter, that what he says has everything to do with his boss's magnetic effect on him, and nothing with what he had planned to say before the actual meeting: "The hell with it, Tom thought suddenly, so clearly that he half thought he had said it. Here goes nothing. It will be interesting to see what happens. In defiance of his intentions he heard himself saying aloud in a remarkably casual voice, 'To tell you the truth, Mr. Hopkins, I read the latest draft of your speech, and I'm afraid I question it pretty seriously.'"[26] And of course *that* (Tom's minor criticism, offered brashly but with an implicit solution built in) is exactly what the boss wants to hear. The free indirect discourse at this moment allows Wilson to convey that Tom's body clearly knows what to do, without his conscious mind knowing that he knows it. Tom's social being has taken over completely for the exchange; he's become a cog in the machine—but a cog so willing that his behavior doesn't even feel mechanical. Nor is this a horrifying moment (my body is acting without me!). It is instead a fulfillment of the promises that the corporate world holds for Tom. Through the corporation, he can not only be part of something larger than himself, he can even find a self that is guided by social directions he need not consciously understand for them to work upon him.

The Man in the Gray Flannel Suit suggests that the novels of the period were capable of bemoaning the ways in which social conformity was enacted—and yet simultaneously capable of exhibiting as valid or attractive the very forms of behavior that most perfectly exemplify such conformity. But the point about Sloane Wilson goes deeper. Why is it that this generation was so attached both to the sort of behavior that Riesman criticizes and to critiquing that behavior? Why wish to guide one's social actions by the strong force of other's opinions and bodily coercions surrounding one, and at the same time to bemoan one's society's tendency to do just that?

What's the pleasure in anatomizing the very same things that one upholds, in eroding the values that are, apparently, one's own and one's society's? Especially if one is committed to an account, as Riesman and his ilk obviously are, that collapses the will, agency, viewpoints, and ideology of each member of the society into a larger social viewpoint. In other words, if we are all operating under the shared assumptions of an inadvertently homogenized society, what possible pleasure can be derived from flagellating one's own flesh, from gravely describing as errors the very same behaviors that one doesn't only endorse, but actually practices? Can this have been a generation that enjoyed being told its pathologies almost as much as it enjoyed having them?

Face to Face with Erving Goffman

When individuals are in one another's immediate presence, a multitude of words, gestures, acts, and minor events become available, whether desired or not, through which one who is present can intentionally or unintentionally symbolize his character and his attitudes.

—ERVING GOFFMAN, *Interaction Ritual*

If so, then it must have been a generation utterly flummoxed by Erving Goffman. Pleasure there may be in watching others' autonomy slipping away, or in thinking of ways to win back from the suburbs, or the communists, the precious free agency that our ancestors had. But what pleasure can lie in being told that the very notion of individual agency subsequent to social forces is itself an illusion? What satisfaction can the conformity fighters have derived from the argument that there is no way to behave or even to be in public which is not by definition conforming? In such an account, individualist ethics and politics abruptly vanish, along with the fear of the crowd. What's to be feared if the crowd is no different from any other kind of social interaction—and if there is no prior selfhood against which the counts as an assault?

Goffman, whom Blackwell's recent *Companion to Major Social Theorists* called "arguably the most influential American sociologist of the twentieth century" even though he "does not fit easily fit within a specific school of sociological thought," offers the most innovative way, between Riesman's pessimism and Putnam's Panglossian optimism, of rethinking the appeal and alarm of the social realm.[27] But he does so by repudiating entirely the notion that there might be a moral stigma or a moral value attached to the social realm as completely as he does the notion that the social and the political realms might be dissevered from one another. Yes, there is an ideal state of what might be called "socializing," but it makes no sense to orient oneself for or against that state. It simply is where human beings dwell.

Goffman's lasting contribution to American sociology was his account of the well-nigh irresistible social role played by "face work"—a phrase that fuses in Goffman's account a universal concern for "saving face" with a similarly universal notion that all meaningful human interactions are those that take place "face to face." This makes the notion of the "social" in Goffman a happy fusion of the considerations of immediacy and of intimacy. As Adam Kendon points out, Goffman's perennial concern is the question of "co-presence" or mutuality. According to Goffman, persons sharing the same physical space (however broadly defined) are always either in a "focused" or "unfocused gathering" in relationship to one another—even pedestrians passing by in the street have an unfocused interaction in which each one both "gives" signs (by a wave or a deferring bow, say) and "gives off" unintended information about action (by a purposeful acceleration).[28]

There is little or no room for deep agency in Goffman. Rather, sophisticated social structures cast a shadow that resolves as a kind of shallow agent within what Bourdieu would call the habitus. Persons matter for the parts they are willing to play in an extant order; parts that are foreordained not because they have been programmed or have had their freedom removed, but because there is not much to human agency apart from its enactment of these roles. In Goffman's account, the "interaction order" provides so rigorous and well developed a basic structure that very little is required from individual actors to play their parts in it: "interaction sequences establish slots, and slots can be effectively filled with whatever is available: if you haven't got a sentence, a grunt will serve nicely; and if you can't grunt, a twitch will do."[29]

Goffman's approach is manifestly radically divergent from Riesman's. Rather than being immersed in an interaction order which in its turn constituted selves from its interstices, in Riesman, selves precede the interaction order and are perpetually at risk of being lost within it. Although Frederic Jameson is wrong to assert that Goffman can only imagine selves emerging from formal recombination of social parts because he is responding to the freewheeling and overly existential 1960s (Goffman's face work pieces were first published in the 1950s), he is still right to discern in Goffman a deep skepticism about any plan—political, social, or ethical—that presumed a way to develop or maintain a self without reference to the constitutive force of society.[30]

The space that opens up between Riesman and Goffman may seem primarily defined by this disagreement about where agency resides. Riesman holds a contradictory notion of subsumable free agency (we were free, then the crowd/society took it away from us). Goffman (in a move that Giddens criticizes for its avoidance of the complications of real arguments about agency) says that the external social world is where decisions reside and occur, and the persons who feel themselves behind the social realm matter far less than they think: "not, then, men and their moments. Rather, moments and their men."[31]

One upshot of this radical (for an American sociologist) account of agency is that both "the political realm" and "privacy" disappear into what might be called the social matrix—or, more aptly, the omnipresent crowd. Simply put, nothing is not a crowd to Goffman. Although Goffman works hard to distinguish between pedestrian interaction (unfocused) and conversational face work (focused), he also makes it clear that there's no bright line in social action. Shared physical presence is enough to make a social scene (and hence in effect a crowd) for Goffman; no amount of vicarious contact can substitute for it, and no amount of avoidance can erase its facticity. Solitude is a quiescent interlude only.

I vividly remember first reading Goffman's acute observations about how people share or fail to share seats on a bus. It is not that Goffman erases consciousness from that account—indeed, he even includes an apt account of what people feel when yielding or being yielded a choice seat. It is just that even such feelings are for Goffman—as they were for Marcel Mauss in his account of gifts—epiphenomena of the social process, rather than personal, particular, and precipitating factors that somehow precede or originate the social practice. You might think of Tom Rath suddenly finding himself telling his boss "the truth" about his speech: that kind of action before thought, or against one's prior judgment, is just what Goffman predicts that face work will produce: moments making their men, not the other way around.

Ultimately Goffman's is a god of small things, easily wounded by pettiness, easily charmed by the completion of what might strike many as a totally minor social transaction—what might strike Riesman as mere acquiescence to a coercive society. Here, for example, is how Goffman imagines the sad fate of a character we might usefully compare to Virginia Woolf's Mrs. Dalloway:

At a small social gathering the hostess may be expected to join in with her guests and become spontaneously involved in the conversation they are maintaining, and yet at the same time if the occasion does not go well she, more than others, will be held responsible for the failure. In consequence, she sometimes becomes so much concerned with the social machinery of the occasion, and with how the evening is going as a whole that she finds it impossible to give herself up to her own party.[32]

For Goffman, the moment of "giving herself up" to a social interaction is the acme, the light of the world, precisely because he has scant time for any kind of mental activity that takes place otherwise than in face-to-face interaction. So it is for Mrs. Dalloway too—but in Woolf's novel, the creepiness of her involvement in her social life is expressed by the fact that the suicide of a young man, Septimus, is what it takes to make her "feel the fun of it all." Woolf is anatomizing and undercutting Mrs. Dalloway, showing how limited her life is because everything in her life is experienced with reference to the "fun" of social goals. In Goffman, such goals really are all there can be to life. In fact, it is worth noting that Goffman even has considerable difficulties dealing with what might be presumed to be an easier case for a student of interaction studies—namely, the meeting of different cultures.[33] For Goffman there must always be normative and then deviant social behaviors.

What light does Goffman have to shed on the waning of a Riesmanian account of social lives, and of the threats that crowds were or were not felt to pose to our American autonomy? It may seem that the most salient point here is the comparative failure of Goffman's views to sway his contemporaries. It is admittedly dangerous to theorize too broadly about a field that has changed so much in fifty years, and undergone several conceptual revolutions around just this question of agency and social determination. But it is fair to say that Goffman made it possible to see the incursion of an omnipresent crowd mentality in all social interactions not as an abomination or a loss of freedom, but as an everyday irrefutable fact of life.

Although Goffman himself never reached any kind of mass audience, however, he has had a sort of trickle-down or flow-through effect in some thoroughly unexpected ways. So too did the roughly contemporaneous "ethnomethodology" of Harold Garfinckel, which—with less wit but a broader claim to theoretical generality than Goffman—also proposed studying ordinary behavior in public with a view to understanding the laws that govern interpersonal behavior that we may be mistakenly tempted to see as autonomous. Salient to both Goffman and Garfinckel is the notion that sociability is so purely omnipresent that embracing it, or indeed failing to embrace it, has no ethical valence at all: that Goffman's work on people who failed to be properly social was largely contained in his most famous book, on *Asylums*, tells us enough about Goffman's account of what it would mean to deny the necessity of playing by generally agreed-on rules.[34]

One thing that seems to follow from Goffman's rejection of the ethically overloaded, the practically paranoid accounts of agency in writers like Arendt or Riesman, is that the ground is cleared for a fascinating kind of ethical inversion. From being simply what we do, in our everyday social lives, face work becomes, in an increasing number of social scientists of the very late twentieth century, an actual telos of human culture, something to aspire to rather than simply to enact.

You might simplify the movement from the 1950s to nowadays like this: Riesman told us that we were being lumped together into one blob when we'd be better off trying to establish ourselves as autonomous islands; Goffman came along to proclaim that no man was an island; Putnam righteously opines that we'll be better human beings if we cut out being islands. Goffman's position is really no closer to Putnam's than to Riesman's because both Riesman and Putnam are prescribing about a phenomenon of social life that Goffman endeavors only to describe. Yet it is easy to see how Goffman's studied value neutrality on that hot-button topic of sociability's role serves to clear the ground for thought like Putnam's. The remarkable evolution of William Whyte's thinking from the 1950s to the 1980s is perhaps the best test case for how the gradual transformation from sociophobia to sociophilia could occur.

Endearing Sociable Elements: The Changing Work of William Whyte

The downfall of the mass society critique is certainly striking, and it would be putting the cart before horse to as-

cribe it, as many do, to the radical experimentation with antiauthoritarian anarchy in the 1960s. The change in disciplinary logic that I have argued is strikingly evident in Goffman can be seen to precede the most explosive years of the 1960s—and to unfold more slowly and thoroughly throughout the 1970s and 1980s. One way to chart the gap between the "mass society" worries of the 1950s and the turn back toward the virtues of homogeneous sociability is to chart the evolution of the work of William Whyte.

As an early adapter of Riesman's ideas, Whyte can hardly be bettered in the world of popular sociology. True, his *Organization Man*, published only six years after *The Lonely Crowd*, quotes Riesman by name only twice, only one of those involving the phrase "other-directed." But the pervading influence is evident. Whyte fears both a hypostatized Organization that is the acme of the group-minded suburbanite and the "moral imperative" that makes individuals treasure the group living "that defines our era" (*OM*, 394, 393). In Whyte's formulation, the "generation of technicians" runs the risk of becoming instead a generation of machines: "they are becoming the interchangeables of our society and they accept the role with understanding" (*OM*, 594–95). Whyte's 1956 logic in many ways perfectly mirrors that of Riesman—save that he is even more willing than Riesman to hypostatize the invisible enemy of the social realm and call it "Organization."

So it is all the more striking, thirty-plus years later, to come across Whyte's valetudinary 1988 *City: Rediscovering the Center* and the accompanying film, *The Social Life of Small Urban Spaces*. *City*—which sparked major crowd-friendly changes in New York's urban planning—speaks of "sociable elements" as the extreme desideratum of street life, and praises the kind of park benches that allow (or, more usefully, actually force) people to clump together in groups of two or three.

Whyte also has a compelling and detailed study of the movement of street traffic around corners and other places of high traffic, showing that people seek out high-traffic areas for their interactions rather than moving out of the flow of pedestrians. That is, although people questioned about their beliefs will report disliking crowds, they will still be observed unconsciously moving into the flow of pedestrian traffic on "100 percent location corners" so as to be bathed in it. Gazing down at the timed interactions on the plazas, discovering how easy it is to predict when one person will leave a lunch, when another will move into the center of the street for a conversation, Whyte does not, as he did in *The Organization Man*, bemoan regularity. Rather, he now delights in predictability, knowledge about pedestrians that is deeper than their own self-knowledge. Whyte's suggestions are all geared toward increasing the kind of clumping and temporary confinement that city dwellers want (without knowing) out of their streets. Despite what we think about ourselves, Whyte explains at one point "we come to its green spaces not to escape from the city but to partake of it."[35]

Whyte's book is unmistakably marked by Jane Jacobs's magisterial 1961 *The Death and Life of Great American Cities*, with its compelling paean to the vital necessity of "useful great city diversity." In Jacobs's account, the existence of multiple voluntary associations, and the "hop-skip" weak ties that link such organizations, are the ligaments of a urban skeleton, and perennial pedestrian interaction is the city's lifeblood: of the four "generators of diversity" that Jacobs deems indispensable to a city neighborhood's life, the one that still leaps out at us is "3. Most blocks must be short; that is, streets and opportunities to turn corners must be frequent."[36] In some sense Whyte's entire book is an effort to extrapolate from the brilliance of that categorical topological insight.

And yet Jacobs's work alone is not enough to explain Whyte's emphasis on the underlying predictability of a flourishing organic urban street life. Jacobs's mantra was urban diversity, her keynote was complexity, and her descriptions and prescriptions all rely on a separation between sociologically homogeneous associations and inherently polymorphous urban interactions.

Jacobs's work was so revolutionary and so beneficial to urban redesign because it predicted urban success on the basis of a city's openness to multiple uses—simultaneous, overlapping, and even over time, so that people could change jobs or lives completely but remain living in the same neighborhood. It made the fact that people lived among others with whom they had nothing but geography in common, that they found multiple ways of living with others with whom they felt no positive alliance into a virtue of city life, not a negative. The very fact of our changing jobs and life interests over time, so that we might not even like or care to talk with our own younger selves, is exactly why, Jacobs argues, a city is a great place to live: we can make those changes, snub a whole different set of neighbors, without leaving the same block.

But Jacobs's work as it filters down to us through the lens of Whyte's *City* erases that account of diversity and complexity in favor of Jacobs-inflected descriptions of how statistically predictable pedestrian flow can be massaged and ameliorated. This selective reading of Jacobs is certainly preferable to Robert Putnam's mistaken assertion, in *Bowling Alone*, that Jacobs endorsed the concept of ultimately homogenizable communities. But Whyte is still "following" Jacobs where she never intended to go. Whyte misreads Jacobs in this way, I believe, because *City* was published in an age when "sociable elements" already seemed a laudable and integral part of public life, when politicians of the left and right alike were both groping for rhetoric of togetherness. Adjustment had come back in—perhaps because Goffman said that there was no action that was not either successful adjustment or a failed attempt at it, perhaps for some other reason altogether, related to the irritations of "the Me Decade" or to the success of successful business forces in portraying their corporations as leaders of an all-inclusive community.

9A 'Foule,' 'Folla': French/Italian

John B. Hill

At the heart of *foule* and *folla* is the idea of pressure. Their parent, the Latin *fullo, fullonis,* was a person who tread upon or beat cloth in order to clean or thicken it. In France it was first cloth that was *fulled* underfoot, and later, by analogy, grapes and wheat. For a period of time the Old French *foule* signified both the place where one beat cloth and the season in which one pressed autumn's harvest. *Foule*, however, developed a range of metaphorical uses much sooner than its English counterpart *full*. As early as Chrétien de Troyes's *Perceval,* the verb *fouler* could mean to oppress mentally: "Le rouge chevalier qui ne se *fouloit* point/Faisoit tant d'armes" (The Red Knight, who felt no pressure, fought energetically) (ca. 1190). The Red Knight is unpressured, confident—to a fault, for Perceval defeats him several lines later. By the Renaissance, the action of kicking open a door was regularly expressed by *fouler,* but so was sullying someone's reputation. So the diplomat and memoirist Phillippe de Commynes writes that song may be used both "a la louenge des vainqueurs et a la foulle du vaincu" (to praise the victors and to trample the vanquished) (1490). To dishonor or discredit someone was imagined as trampling their reputation. Another form of pressure that *fouler* could express was economic and political. In his royalist propaganda, Pasquier's writes that "Nos roys sont arrivez a cette grandeur . . . sans foule et oppression de leurs subjects" (Our kings have reached their present greatness . . . without

Whatever the chain of causation, Whyte's book in retrospect does not look like the continuation by other means of Jane Jacobs's prescriptions for a city of social complexity and sidewalk accessibility. As attractive as those nuts-and-bolts prescriptions are, as engaging as Whyte's short film about behavior on sunny and shady streets is, *City* still strikes me an early and unheralded member of a wave of books that, without being communitarian per se, managed to make respectable the idea that simply being involved in social activities with other bodies, no matter what the activity or what the nature of the interaction, was a positive good in and of itself. And that is a line of thought that may have found fertile soil in Goffman's apparent endorsement of face work—but one that was not to find its most outspoken, and wildly popular, exponent until Robert Putnam published first an article and then a book on the phenomenon of "bowling alone."

Putnam's Passion for Crowds

Robert Putnam's *Bowling Alone* may not yet have entered into the same retail league as *The Lonely Crowd,* whose sales of 1.4 million tower over all sociological competitors.[37] But the more than fifty thousand copies sold in its first three years are not the only way to gauge the impact of both the book and the 1995 article on "Bowling Alone" with which Putnam began the "social capital" furor. "Bowling alone" shows up in mainstream newspaper articles a staggering 650 times since Putnam's article came out in 1995. By the same token, "social capital" (a phrase Putnam did not invent, but did popularize)[38] appears 244 times just in the last year in major newspapers, and more than 1,000 times over the past ten years, 411 times in major journals.[39] As Benjamin Barber's memoir *The Truth of Power* demonstrates, Putnam had a clear impact on Bill Clinton's presidency; a series of celebrated appearances in England, Ireland, and points farther east in Europe shows that Putnam was a knight errant of "social capital" overseas as well.[40]

It is crucial to note how completely Putnam's thinking and his phrase-making have shaped even concerted opposition to what his ideas are understood to be. When rebutters assail Putnam (a professor of public policy at Harvard University), they are still liable to talk in manifestly Putnamesque terms like "kicking together." Even the Web site Meetup.com, a progressive rallying point for local activists that is explicitly opposed to communitarian tendencies, invokes *Bowling Alone* as philosophical inspiration.[41]

Both for those who love him and those who hate him, both for the left and for the right, Putnam has articulated not only the problem—absence of bowling leagues and similar associations—but also the range of debatable solutions. Some of these solutions are explicit in his work—Turn your TV off! Copy North Dakota! Don't come from the South!—whereas others are only implicit. Might women not do better as homemakers with plenty of volunteer time than as overtasked professionals? Couldn't the young imitate the Depression generation?

It is true that Putnam's brief is for "social capital" specifically—meaning the value derived in part from the sharing of norms and the assumption of predictable homogeneity in other's ethical stances—rather than "sociability" in general. But the response to his work certainly leans toward the sociable side. Critics and fans alike, with a few vocal exceptions in the heart of academe,[42] agree that social capital's version of sociability is good, and whatever we can do to increase congregation must in itself be a good thing. It is also worth noting that even popular writers whose inspiration clearly comes from the rational choice theorists of the Chicago School find reasons, sometimes arcane ones, to throw in their lot with an ideology that values what one such free marketeer, James Surowiecki, calls "the wisdom of crowds." Although Surowiecki is at pains to emphasize that a market-based individualism is manifestly the best way to govern a country or to operate an economy, he makes ingenious arguments about the collective powers of individuals operating en masse (for their own interest) as a way of wedding the best of free markets with the desirability of some sort of crowd-based social cohesion.[43]

The key to Putnam's argument is that he finds it nearly impossible to conceive of any kind of social assembly that is not in and of itself a blameless good. So for example, critics of his 1995 article pointed out that by Putnam's logic, even violent street gangs would be a good thing. In *Bowling Alone*, Putnam responds by agreeing—violent drug gangs *are* good things! Such gangs have great social benefits (increasing camaraderie, looking out for one another, developing a strong sense of community). He then goes on to admit that such palpable benefits do, alas, get outweighed by a gang's violence, interruption of educational and economic opportunities, and so on.

At the heart of Putnam's diagnosis is his vision of the erosion of social values that held our society together in the 1950s, a high-water mark of voluntary associationism.[44] "Bowling Alone," the 1995 article that laid the groundwork for the book that followed, began simply by claiming that the decline of league bowling was a leading symptom in a general decline in America's civic life. As we failed to associate with one another for play—play being the very realm where Riesman saw the

oppressing their subjects) (ca. 1555). François de la Noue is of a different sentiment when he writes in 1587 that "il semblera peut estre que ceste foule soit petite; mais je pense qu'elle se monte . . . par an" (It may seem that this oppression is small, but I think it is rising . . . each year). He's referring, of course, to new taxes.

It is around this same time that *fouler* regularly begins to refer to the action of a mass of people as well as of things. Montaigne writes in his *Essais* of the common occurrence of people struggling to be first: "les ames [que] seroient a se fouler a qui prendroit place la premiere" (the souls who would press to take the first place). A century later, at the opening of Racine's play *Athalie*, Abner describes a crowd of worshippers thus: "le peuple saint en foule inondait les portiques" (the devout people in large numbers inundated the church porticos). One notes here two opposing images of the multitude: stagnation, as in the example from Montaigne, or power, as in the example from Racine. Although *fouler* could mean to stamp one's feet—the same action used to stamp fresh wool or grapes—it never developed the sense of forward motion, that is, of gushing or streaming. Another set of images quite apart from those of textiles or the harvest (and often clichés) had to be added.

Italian has the words *follare* and *folla* from the same Latin root, and it takes a similar course from the textile mill and the winepress into the streets; however, the noun forms in French and Italian have divergent histories. In French, *foule* was used to refer to a multitude of people in one place as early as the thirteenth century, although more frequently it was used to mean the place where the action of "pressing," literally or figuratively, occurred. Italian, however, doesn't produce an equivalent in *folla* until the seventeenth century. Modern dictionaries always cite the example of the Jesuit orator, Paolo Segneri, who in a work from 1673 writes, "Non vedi tu ciò che accade in un'altra folla? Quanto entra in chiesa chi allor fa forza ad entrarvi, tanto pur v'entra chi lascia in essa portarsi dall'impeto della calca, che gli vien dietro" (Don't you see what happens in another crowd? However much one might struggle to enter a church, so much easier it is to relinquish one's movement to the force of the crowd which comes behind). Here *folla* begins to describe not just a mass of things under pressure, but specifically a mass of people. Before Segneri, and indeed for some time after, the transitional locution was "folla di gente" or "folla del popolo" (mass of people).

In both French and Italian the idea of pressure inherited from the Latin *Fullo* finds specific application in the crowd. But in France, at the end of the eighteenth century, there is yet another wrinkle: the idea of pressure becomes internalized in the pair *refoulement* and *defoulement*, which express the notions of repression and release, respectively. When, at the beginning of the twentieth century, Freud's works were translated into French, these words became official psychoanalytic vocabulary.

complete cooptation of formerly autonomous individuals—so too would we fail to participate in any of the meaningful markers of our shared political and social lives: fail to vote, to help one another out in need, to assist the needs in our neighborhoods. And it is to the desertion of the broadly defined public realm, a realm that is social and political together, that all our other present woes can be traced.

Putnam hails the very features of the 1950s that Riesman dreaded. As he sees it, the social world in an ideal era of associationism actually *becomes* the political realm, and a good thing too. It is not just that small social groups taught America political skills; it is that they actually constitute a kind of Jeffersonian freehold realm, politically vibrant in bowling alleys and Kiwanis bars. It was an era when those Putnam calls "moderates of all stripes" actually went to local political meetings so that "extremists" didn't get control of local organizations (*BA,* 339–41).

The first key to understanding Putnam's direct connection to the crowd alarmism of the 1950s is to note that like Riesman and company (and like Goffman), Putnam effectively erodes the distinctions between any sort of social organizations and the larger "crowd." The social simply is a form of crowd life—one is out in the larger world, forced to rub together with everyone else and to come to share their judgments in due course. Putnam offers many reasons for liking local organizations, but each time, these return to one of two things. On the one hand, he praises the generalizable features of such associations, the way that they fit seamlessly into a national fabric. On the other, he embraces local manifestations of national collectivity as the only medium whereby properly compulsory physical meetings can ever happen. In other words, the local is admirable in other words because only locally can one become part of a properly compulsory crowd.[45] This may be Putnam's most curious wrinkle: he likes getting local because there is no getting away from these (unchosen) others around one: we must all perforce get along, since none of us is going anywhere.[46]

This leads Putnam to some very odd claims. He dislikes computer socializing, but only because there is too much freedom associated with it. One can post and run away, one can choose to speak only with other BMW owners, one can avoid neighbors while seeking out distant mental kin. Earlier ages had a useful kind of group balkanization he maintains, which allowed for comforting sameness within the group. Today, however, we are cursed with a universally accessible medium (the Internet) that has the effect of allowing places where identities can vanish and pure volition can reign: as the *New Yorker* cartoon puts it, "on the internet, nobody knows you're a dog."[47] For Putnam, the obligation to huddle together with others is precisely what made the groups of the 1950s (from bowlers to readers) desirable, and the failure of today's social networks is precisely that they have succeeded in becoming too inner-directed, leaving individuals free to turn on the television.

Television is Putnam's emblematic bad individual choice—not because, as earlier critics like Adorno had it, such media consumption will synchronize one with other members of the lonely crowd, but because television is the one social activity that doesn't synchronize us in any way: it requires no investment of self in the difficult but necessary social face work that Putnam so valorizes. You might compare Richard Hoggart's moving description, in *The Uses of Literacy* (1957), of a thousand lonely viewers each getting programmed by exactly the same show.[48] The great good thing in Putnam is the great bad thing in Hoggart—socialization, into the vast involuntary grouping that is a nation taken all together.

The recent history of television as a social activity seems to suggest an underlying national agreement with Putnam's critique of TV's anomic force, as we witness a remarkable upsurge in forms of collective television watching. This shift is not necessarily visible in the field of television studies, which has always (even in the 1960s, long before it was delineated as a field) tended toward the sociological, not the aesthetic, and hence has always tended to overstudy and overestimate the significance of generalizable "group reaction" to television as medium. It is therefore not surprising that most academic work on the topic of television has—despite what Robert Allen has identified as a 1970s turn toward valuing "popular" cultural forms and hence toward developing reading and analytical strategies for television shows as texts—generally stressed the experience of viewership and of television's "influence" far more than its "content."[49]

Despite that orientation, scholars, with a few laudable exceptions such as Anna McCarthy, do not seem to have dwelt on the recent explosion of what might be called "watching together."[50] The sort of group TV watching that used to be reserved for neighborhoods with few televisions, or for spectacularly publicized events like the Super Bowl and the last episode of *M*A*S*H* has now become a weekly part of many people's lives. Parties for something mildly unusual, such as, say, the final episode of *Survivor*, have given way to simple weekly group consumption of *Buffy the Vampire Slayer* or *The Sopranos*. Television is bad alone; well, then, let's screen together. Again, as with *The Man in the Gray Flannel Suit*, we can witness the culture in a striking kind of lockstep with the dictates that emanate from popular sociology. It is almost as if people were reading Putnam, as if groups from California to Maine mobilized to fight the diagnosis of "watching alone" as soon as Putnam told us how troubling a trend it was.

However, this synchronicity represents not Putnam's ability to set trends but to

9B My Summer of Solitude

David Humphrey

New York in 1976 was much darker than it is now, especially downtown. Black clothes seemed blacker then. The municipal government was broke, and nights in my neighborhood were lit by the regular torching of abandoned buildings and stripped cars. I moved to the city that aggressively cold winter, dazzled by the activities of people making new art in big, cheap industrial spaces. I was twenty and attracted by what I imagined was solitude en masse; it was my existential/romantic notion of the urban artist/loner. I remember entering the determined tides of work-bound people each day to realize, months later, that I had never recognized a single person I had passed previously.

Independence Day that year was the Bicentennial. New York hosted a proud and very fancy Disney/Macy's celebration with fireworks at the bottom of the island. Purposeless curiosity and loneliness propelled me that day from my home in the East Village down Broadway into the enveloping dusk. A slow trickle of people thickened with each southward block to become a crawling density at the recently completed World Trade Center. I don't think the streetlights were working—I remember the space becoming less and less discernible, slightly disorienting, even threatening. Thousands of us eventually impacted to a complete halt in the dim canyons just below the towers. A collective sense of frustration nearly boiled over as the first booms of the fireworks rolled over us. A slow surge forward squeezed away personal space we thought had already been surrendered. There was no way to get out and no way to see the show except in flickering reflections on the upper windows of the after-hours skyscrapers. The anticipated ecstatic fusion with the national television audience and cheering crowds who limned the harbor never happened. We missed the biggest pyrotechnical entertainment spasm in history. Ten thousand pleasure boats had joined the massive fleet of tall ships watching from the water along with hundreds of thousands of people on shore. Marines, Coast Guard, and the Army Corps of Engineers took orders from a command center in the Trade Center's south tower. We, the blocked ones, could only hear the countless shells and mortar fusillades launched from barges and islands. The next day's newspaper informed us that we also missed patriotic music, celebrity readings, and a helicopter pulling a giant flag across the sky. That same paper also contained news of an almost simultaneous raid by Israeli commandos to free hostages held at Entebbe airport in Uganda.

Thousands of us had been cut off. We were failed witnesses, clotted and stagnant, blinded by the buildings meant as a backdrop for the television audience relaxed safely at home. It was an indignity for us to be smeared against the very cause of our frustration. We were an inconvenience to each other and to the crowd-control authorities. I naively hated those people. They were the others, the ones art was happy to offend or confuse. They were the undifferentiated ones we artists needed to frame our absurd singularity. My conception of this art-world "we," however, was

articulate them, to unburden the American conscience of what has been troubling far more people than simply Putnam himself. Why assume that sixty minutes of gangland badinage unites any worse than thundering pins, if we simply agree to participate together? You might ask Putnam that question; or you might ask the growing numbers who, although they haven't yet joined bowling leagues or the PTA, are willing to sign on for this piece of social capitalization.

Long Live Face Work!

Putnam's praise of compulsoriness as the way out of our current social anomie—television viewing parties would be good, one imagines Putnam saying, if an entire apartment block were required to attend—makes clear what exactly Putnam conceives his debt to Goffman to be. For Putnam, the upshot of Goffman's interaction studies is simple: meeting face to face is a good kind of sociability, whereas technological mediation allowing communication beyond the immediate vicinity is bad. One of Putnam's Goffman footnotes is appended to the following claim: "experiments that compare face-to-face and computer-mediated communication confirm that the richer the medium of communication the more sociable personal, trusting and friendly the encounter is" (*BA*, 176). Putnam doesn't despise computers. Instead, he detests "cyber-balkanization"[51] because he hates the idea that a thoroughly interest-driven conversation can be sustained online. (Unsurprisingly, Riesman fantasizes about just such a medium being available for a lonely schoolchild to connect up with others who truly think like him.) Putnam fears people being brought together via our most pressing interests: "A comment about Thunderbirds in a BMW chat group risks being flamed as 'off topic.' Imagine by contrast the guffaws if a member of a bowling team or a Sunday school class tried to rule out a casual conversation gambit as off-topic" (*BA*, 178).

Putnam's claim is more than merely wrong; it is revealingly off base. After all, if I brought up Thunderbirds in a Sunday School class, I would risk, if not eternal damnation, then at least strong disapprobation. Why can't Putnam see that? Because his ideal model for social interaction is an all-in form of social universality, where each group, no matter what named or doing, will feature just the same sort of face-to-face interaction and the same kinds of conversations. He wants to believe that the voluntary associations of his own youth were, in exact counterpoint to what Riesman argued, a laudable model of compulsory universal community. Philip Larkin begins a 1974 poem with an unappealing invitation:

My wife and I have asked a crowd of craps
To come and waste their time and ours.[52]

In Putnam's world, there can be no finer sort of invitation, no better promise of future happiness than this: mutual waste.

Refusing the Blob

Of course, this Toquevillian take on modern America malaise is not just Putnam's. There has been a notable resurgence of people who endorse community self-policing—often, as in Amitai Etzioni's work, without much sense that individual rights ought to stand in the way of an overall social decorum. And in fact there is a mainstream of sociological thought now that left and right look to "civil community" or (most famously in Eastern Europe) "civil society" to save us from the depredations of state and economic pressures alike.[53] Moreover, in a wide range of left-wing sociology, the dominant emphasis has been of documenting the decline of the old networks and "weak ties" that formerly ensured economic survival or social inclusion.

Thus, for example, Eric Klineberg's *Heat Wave* achieved national prominence (and a review in the *New Yorker*) because it documented the same loss of civic nodes that Putnam bemoans—here, it was the decay of a neighborhood's social fabric that allowed many old people to die when Chicago boiled in the summer of 1995. And *Sidewalk*, by the prominent young sociologist Mitch Dunier, circles back in its conclusion to the same insight: that the key difference between success and failure on the streets of New York is how much a neighborhood chooses to define its street people as "part of us"—how much latent social capital is in place, in other words, to enable trusting activities like letting the homeless use a bathroom proceed.[54]

In short, Putnam's call for a return to the glory years of "social capital" resonates with those on the right and the left who are looking for a way to climb out of the hole that many believe was dug by the 1960s insistence on autonomy and on the individual's separability from society. It is not only sociologists who are telling us to forego the claim to un-crowd ourselves and accept that even in our most existential moments of putative separation from the world, the cheery crowd was grinning over our shoulder all along—or should have been.

Hannah Pitkin wrote *The Attack of the Blob* to point out the error involved in supposing that rather than simply an adjective like "political," "public," or "pri-

a fantasy, as I had yet to obtain even the tiniest milieu. I was as cut off as that Independence Day crowd. My goal was to build a studio in my head and treat the world as a hallucination. I was proud to imagine myself as socially unintegrated.

The crowd and I were an unhappily fused horde of grumbling consumers—hungry sheep unconsciously obeying nebulous orders. We wanted a big show, but our frustration had made us stale and viscous, not volatile like the blackout rioters of the next summer, the antiwar demonstrators of 2002, or the rock audiences I had joyously merged with as a teenager. We eventually dispersed into an ebb tide of aversion and disappointment. On the long walk home, however, the throng atomized into fellow New Yorkers: attractive, eccentric, and driven people, neighbors, protofriends, colleagues, and lovers.

vate," "the social" is a blobbish enemy, a crowd endowed with superhuman agency and capable of subsuming individual lives and agency uninvited. Pitkin's critique of Arendt's attempt to divide "political" and "social" too strictly from one another applies equally well to Whyte (ca. 1956) and to Riesman. We are lucky no longer to see the world through such blinkers.

Still, there is no need to embrace the opposite extreme. Robert Putnam's mellifluous praise of a general American social life that is compartmentalized into smaller (compulsory) locales without forfeiting its potentially nationwide (or global) hold as a social force deserves as comprehensive a critique as Pitkin's of Arendt. The challenge now is to achieve the same kind of clarity about Putnam and the partisans of the Blob that Pitkin achieved about foes of "the social."

Some questions arise. Are we justified in mounting such a contemporaneous attack? Pitkin, after all, waited until thirty years after Arendt's death before pinpointing her faults. And you might reasonably object (communitarians and followers of Michael Sandel certainly will object), to attacking social capital with full-gale force in any event. After all, wasn't such extremism in the putative defense of liberty the vice that got Riesman and his antisocialists into such trouble in the first place?

The worry is a false one: Putnam's errors are made no smaller by the fact that fifty years ago Riesman and Whyte fell into an opposite mistake. Nor should the genealogy I've sketched exonerate Putnam. Putnam's wholehearted attempt to make full social participation into the only ethical path forward may indirectly derive from Goffman's notion that to be social is inescapable. However, it grievously misreads him. At worst, Goffman is fatalistically suggesting that everything we do is oriented not toward our own perceived intentions, but toward social conformity or "embarrassment avoidance." Goffman's determinism cannot translate into a positive endorsement of becoming more

caught up in the daily whirl of social activities. Wherever we go, in front of the TV or bowling (alone or together), we bring social energy with us. And to begin proclaiming such a wholesale embrace of the more directly coercive and compulsory of such actions a good thing is as misguided as proclaiming it, like Riesman, a bad thing.

Putnam's is a worldview that calls for us all to do our best to form social units with those around us, regardless of what the political or ethical implications of such a grouping may be. Putnam never calls the social capital that he wants to endorse "the realm of the crowd." But he might, because what he idolizes is an undifferentiated space of social agglomeration that prevents any individual from exercising judgment about how one form of association differs from another (he even produces statistics purporting to find that membership in one group, any group, can double the years of life remaining to you—and that joining a second will add half as much again).

Putnam assumes—like Riesman—that one form of social life is exactly equivalent to another. Therefore he forgets, or deliberately passes over, the crucial political category that Hannah Arendt called "solidarity." To Arendt, there are two ways to decide to aid our fellows, one requiring face-to-face contact and the other equally effective with and without such contact. The former, "compassion," results from the chance to share another person's feelings, or to be swayed by their social needs, or even to be moved in their immediate presence, by the desire to avert embarrassment. By contrast, the best forms of political "solidarity," Arendt believed, could be achieved as well sitting alone in a room as they could be out on the barricades.

"I am least alone when by myself," Arendt wrote (quoting Cato), because contemplation allowed one to draw away from one's immediate surroundings, and the result was that one could best connect with those whose thoughts most closely and interestingly aligned with one's own. Solidarity need not occur in solitude—it can occur in a properly political public realm, where we meet others as particular, nonfungible members of a species which we are indebted to as a whole.[55] But alone or together, we will be moved by solidarity to do well by others. And for that, we need neither bowl with them, nor share an ethnic grouping with them, nor (to refute Riesman) protect ourselves from their tangible presence in our rooms or in our hearts. Given the proper frame for encounters, we can exercise individual judgment to override both the thrill of solitude and the social excitement of being among the crowd.

Florence Nightingale's *Cassandra* mentions the gruesome feeling that a young Victorian lady feels when she has finally begin to pursue (in private or in correspondence) something that genuinely interests her: she has to appear among her family and friends, to lose the possibility of "imagination" and "power" to mealtimes: "If she has a knife and a fork in her hands during three hours of the day, she cannot have a pencil or a brush. Dinner is the great sacred ceremony of this day, the great sacrament."[56] The bedroom (like the street) is a place of refuge, a site of abstraction where we can potentially perform any kind of intersubjective or private action, and dinner is the kind of "convivial" and compulsory social space (laudable *because* compulsory, remember) that Putnam would like to prescribe for all of us.

Communitarianism and its near relatives need not go as far as mandating "community standards of morality" to begin trespassing on meaningful aspects of our intellectual emancipation. Putnam makes repeated effort to convince us that our imaginative forays—pursued alone or via abstracted affiliations on Internet or paper—are worth less than the shared commitment to waste time together. Each time he does so, we should feel behind his imposing statistics on membership and longevity the dead hand of an earlier age's conformity pressing our arms. Are our interest groups, our advocacy and our strikes, really best viewed through their resemblance to bowling leagues? Is what we say and do in them of less concern than the fact that they,

like a Victorian dinner party, exist to give shape to our week and order our intersubjective action?

Putnam is probably right to be contemptuous of using the Internet to do nothing more than find other BMW enthusiasts, with whom one can discuss BMWs and only BMWs for as long as one wants. But mental dislocation, attained through a novel, a TV show, or an Internet search, can also have that otherworldly quality that Proust describes in the opening pages of *Swann's Way:* "I had been thinking, all the time, while I was asleep, of what I had just been reading, but my thoughts had run into a channel of their own, until I myself seemed actually to have become the subject of my book: a church, a quartet, the rivalry between Francois I and Charles V."[57]

Riesman's near-paranoia can certainly stand a reminder that social practices are at the heart of imaginative, rational, and physical lives, and that we ignore our sociable existence at our peril. But by the same token, Putnam could stand to be reminded of something that Goffman never quite admitted: that there is more to our lives, more that goes on in our thoughts, than simple association with those who surround us can explain.

As I write this, I am locked in a not-quite interaction with all the other patrons of my library's reading room, a companionable agreement to allow one another to visit whatever peculiar haven our own computers, documents, or paperbacks allow. I avoid catching their eyes as I woolgather; they agree not to bump into me as they search for reference books. Are we in the kind of nonbinding social interaction that Goffman proposes? I suppose so. And yet we are also, like Proust's reader, potentially anyone and anywhere. Why should Putnam fault us for foregoing the occasional Recycling Committee meeting for that? Some of us will connect to the world most perfectly in that committee. Others will do better, feel freer, know their neighborhood better, by roaming unaccompanied down dark streets.

10 From Crowd Psychology to Racial Hygiene: The Medicalization of Reaction and the New Spain

Joan Ramon Resina

Matter Revolts Against the Mold

In his entry on "mass society" in the *International Encyclopedia of the Social and Behavioral Sciences*, Salvador Giner calls José Ortega y Gasset's *The Revolt of the Masses* (1929) "the first fully-fledged interpretation of such phenomenon."[1] Although Ortega's priority in the definition of mass society is open to debate,[2] his importance as a theorist of the phenomenon "masses" is undeniable. Little in the book is original, yet by combining strands of nineteenth-century crowd psychology with his aristocratic view of history, he left an influential if ambiguous legacy to Spanish and Latin American politics.

The ambiguity begins with Ortega's description of the phenomenon, which he sees, at first, under its quantitative aspect. His notion of the "mass" appears at the intersection between the prepolitical concept of the multitude (or the crowd) and the spatial one of agglomeration. But he moves immediately toward a qualitative definition, drawing a sharp distinction between the multitude and the civilization it uses without feeling responsible for it. Suddenly and unexpectedly, the multitude has sprung up, fed by the dislocation of people and groups who used to occupy their own places. Topsy-turvy and turbulent, the crowd has become visible by taking up social space—and not just any space, but the best places, those formerly reserved for the privileged few. It is this being-out-of-place that Ortega calls "the revolt of the masses," whereby he stresses not the quantitative and visual aspect of the mass but its social and moral side.[3] If the masses now occupy the best places, then it follows that they have acceded to social power, that they are, in effect, the new paradigm setters. Although he admits as much (*RM*, 11), Ortega disputes the masses' legitimacy, nay, their ability to create a new principle of coexistence.

Ortega probably found the idea of mass as amorphous quantitative accumulation and as an inert throng in Werner Sombart. In 1924 Sombart had written, "people call 'mass' the unrelated, amorphous agglomeration of population in the modern metropolises, which lacking all internal articulation and abandoned by the spirit, that is, by God, form an inert throng of pure units."[4] Then again, the early mass psychologists had advanced Ortega's idea of the masses as an explosion of primitivism. Scipio Sighele, for instance, had written in 1891 that in the masses, "atavistic inclinations triumph over the accumulated results of centuries of education."[5] Ortega drew conspicuously from these early mass critics, but especially from Gustave Le Bon. In *La psychologie des foules* (1895), Le Bon stressed both the civilizing role of select minorities and the destructive behavior of crowds.[6] Like Sighele, he referred to the crowd's regressive nature and described its rule as a barbarian phase in the history of civilization, a phase during which the instincts prevail. "Moreover, by the mere fact that he forms part of an organized crowd, a man descends several rungs in the ladder of civilization. Isolated, he may be a cultivated individual; in a crowd, he is a barbarian—that is, a creature acting by instinct" (*C*, 32). Moreover, by demanding immediate gratification, crowds preclude the work of social mediations. "Like the savage, [the crowd] does not permit any obstacle between its desires and their realization."[7] Ortega would later link the impatience of crowds to the anarchist principle of direct action, adapting Le Bon's "civilized" barbarian in his own notion of the vertical invasion of the barbarians. Oswald Spengler had also formulated this idea toward the end of *The Decline of the West*, where he speaks of the "age of the masses," during which civilization is undermined by the "barbarians from below."

But if, according to Le Bon, the individual became a barbarian as soon as he joined the crowd, Ortega reversed the order. For him, the sociological problem of the masses was real insofar as it could be traced to individuals—indeed, to whole classes of people, who in themselves, and independently of whether they ever joined a crowd, revealed the traits of "mass" psychology. A qualitative perspective that revealed Ortega's enduring individualism blunted the quantitative edge of the "mass." His notion of the mass-person found support in Le Bon's remark that, under certain circumstances, crowds could precede their own formation.

The disappearance of conscious personality and the turning of feelings and thoughts in a different direction, which are the primary characteristics of a crowd about to become organized, do not always involve the simultaneous presence of a number of individuals on one spot. Thousands of isolated individuals may acquire at certain moments, and under the influence of certain violent emotions—such, for example, as a great national event—the characteristics of a psychological crowd. It will be sufficient in that case that a mere chance should bring them together for their acts to at once assume the characteristics peculiar to the acts of a crowd. (*C*, 24)

With the qualifiers "may," "at certain moments," and "under the influence of certain emotions," Le Bon cautiously suggested that special conditions could on occasion predispose otherwise fully rational individuals to form a crowd. With much less circumspection, Ortega posited an abiding disposition where Le Bon had spoken of unusual moments: "Strictly speaking, the mass, as a psychological fact, can be defined without waiting for individuals to appear in mass formation. In the presence of an individual we can decide whether he is 'mass' or not" (*RM*, 14). Such faith in the possibilities of the categorical judgment founds an ontological rather than a social blueprint. Ortega's social universe, furthermore, is drawn less by painstaking sociological or psychological research than by rule of thumb. Just by standing before a person, we can, Ortega thinks, assign him or her to a social niche, either to the Olympus of the heroes or to the Hades of the vulgar. In the last analysis, the mass ceases to be a matter of great numbers and becomes one of self-elevation:

For me, then, nobility is synonymous with a life of effort, ever set on excelling oneself, in passing beyond what one is to what one sets up as a duty and an obligation. In this way the noble life stands opposed to the common or inert life, which reclines statistically upon itself, condemned to perpetual immobility, unless an external force compels it to come out of itself. Hence we apply the term mass to this kind of man—not so much because of his multitude as because of his inertia. (*RM*, 65)

Heteronomy defines Ortega's mass-person, one that will not budge unless he is acted upon. The mass is history's dead weight. But this means that it is the rare individual who is capable of autonomous motion through "un esfuerzo espontáneo y lujoso" that drives history forward. The masses, on the contrary, are material awaiting the form-giving action of the few: "for anyone who has a sense of the real mission of aristocracies, the spectacle of the mass incites and enflames him, as the sight of virgin marble does the sculptor" (*RM*, 20). Ortega's condescending hylomorphism blends with class divisions to form a bizarre sociological category defined by the idea of a predetermined mission.

Yet from his attribution of subjectivity to the mass, Ortega might have inferred that the era of the masses implied the absolute triumph of the very values he associated with the ruling few. In this period, as Peter Sloterdijk notes, "the metaphysical privileges of the lord—will, knowledge, and the soul—penetrate that which formerly appeared to be mere matter and endorse the claims of the subjugated and unrecognized part to the honors of the other side."[8] In the spectacle of the masses saturating the places in which they "did not belong," Ortega ought to have recognized the undisputed victory of the form-giving spirit as it passes from the select few to ever larger groups of people hitherto reduced to the status of *res extensae*.

It was, in all certainty, their will to subjectivity that drove the masses to the places where it had last been seen: to the theaters, the forums, the public places where the masses could become aware of themselves as a moving, living thing. Through its self-presence, the mass could experience the vertigo of self-fascination. And out of its becoming-spectacle to itself, it could objectify its fascination with itself in obeisance to whomever or whatever would embody that fascination. Le Bon asserted that crowds desire nothing so much as to submit to a strong authority. "Abandoned to themselves, they soon weary of disorder, and instinctively turn to servitude" (*C*, 55). And Ortega, following up, forecast: "Before long there will be heard throughout the planet a formidable cry, rising like the howling of innumerable dogs to the stars, asking for someone or something to take command, to impose an occupation, a duty" (*RM*, 136). Ortega's prophecy was surely fulfilled, but it was hardly one. Authoritarian regimes were already in place—in the Soviet Union, in Italy, in Spain—and Ortega saw them rightly as expressions of the rule of the masses. Ortega's liberalism, however, had little to do with egalitarian democracy. In American society he saw the paradigm of the civilization crisis he denounced: "America is, in a fashion, the paradise of the masses" (*RM*, 116).

For Ortega, the key political question was not how to structure society but how to induce the many to accept the authority of the few. Le Bon thought that because the masses are irrational, they could be influenced by hypnotic means such as the repetition of simple messages, the use of vividly iconic language, and deception if necessary. He was the first to draw propaganda uses from the contemporary speculation on hypnotic states. Especially interesting for its potential political applications was the recently discovered phenomenon of *fascination*, as the Belgian crowd magnetizer Alfred d'Hont, alias Donato, called his hypnotic technique. Magnetism and hypnosis had been around for some time when Donato appeared on the stage of a Turin's theater. What was so unique about his performances?

Unlike many of his predecessors, Donato did not claim to have fluid or divinatory powers, or to influence his subjects through somnambular states, but rather to possess a sharp gaze whose sudden contact could shock the nervous system of impressionable individuals. Because his gaze acted merely as a catalyst, it became clear that hypnotic states were not triggered by any secret gift of the hypnotist, but by a particular weakness of the hypnotized subjects themselves.

Not all subjects responded to suggestion, however, and this psychic peculiarity soon led to what Enrico Morselli, a contemporary student of hypnotism, described as the pathologizing of suggestible individuals. These people were now seen as deficient in free will.[9] The political consequences of this new distinction between the inherently willful and the innately will-less were easy to perceive, and Morselli linked Donato's hypnotic spectacles to what he saw as a political crisis at the heart of Europe.[10] The crisis of liberal democracy had, of course, broader causes, but Morselli was not alone in tracing the social upheavals to the crisis of the rational subject, now crushed by a strong determinism that invalidated the free will. Performances like Donato's showed how flimsy individual autonomy could be and how vulnerable the personality was to control by a stronger agency. What struck the witnesses of Donato's performances most was the ease with which many of his subjects lost control of their actions even in a wakeful state and impersonated roles dictated to them by Donato. Psychology had become a source of political power. Henceforth, domination would be cast as a form of suggestion.

Ortega, writing thirty-three years after Morselli, began his book with the assertion that Europe was undergoing the severest crisis that any nation or culture could experience (*RM,* 11). Ortega warned that the term "revolt of the masses," which designated the crisis, did not mean exclusively or even primarily something political but referred more generally to a social phenomenon (*RM,* 11). Later in the book, he insisted that "the theme I am pursuing in these pages is politically neutral, because it breathes an air much ampler than that of politics and its dissensions" (*RM,* 96). However, as the book progresses, Ortega's reflections reveal an unmistakably political horizon, to the point of making a surprising ontological claim for politics: "Politics is much more of a reality than science, because it is made up of unique situations in which a man suddenly finds himself submerged whether he will or no. Hence it is a test which allows us better to distinguish who are the clear heads and who are the routineers" (*RM,* 158). Politics, then, is not only inescapable but also becomes the ultimate touchstone for Ortega's anthropological approach to the social hierarchy.

Ortega denies any overlap between his social categories and the dichotomies of class: "The division of society into masses and select minorities is, then, not a division into social classes, but into classes of men, and cannot coincide with the hierarchic separation of 'upper' and 'lower' classes" (*RM,* 15). Nonetheless, it remains true, in his own terms, that each category is concretely realized at the heart of the political. And in the next lines, Ortega acknowledges that excellent minorities tend to crystallize into dominant groups. He regards the aristocratic principle as foundational, an opinion he shares with Le Bon, according to whom, "As soon as a certain number of living beings are gathered together, whether they be animals or men, they place themselves instinctively under the authority of a chief" (*C,* 117). For Ortega, "human society *is* always, whether it will it or no, aristocratic by its very essence, to the extreme that it is a society in the measure that it is aristocratic, and ceases to be such when it ceases to be aristocratic" (*RM,* 20). Society automatically establishes the rule of the best. There is no society without vertical distinction. And this remains true in the era of the masses, when society is threatened at its foundations by the refusal of the masses to acknowledge the structuring will of the few. Invertebration, as Ortega dubbed the political consequences of the breakdown of this fundamental law, was the political term for the becoming mass of the social body.

Ortega's aristocrat is not merely the creative individual, but the individual who shapes and directs the masses. He is Donato's equivalent in the social scene: "There is not and there has never been an aristocracy that is not based on the power of psychic attraction, a sort of law of spiritual gravitation that draws submissive individuals in the wake of a model," he asserted in *Invertebrate Spain* (1921).[11] Devoid of autonomy, the mass is there to be "directed, influenced, represented, organised" by the select few (*RM,* 115). Because this is its destiny, no wonder that it secretly desires nothing better than its own subjugation by an external will. Le Bon's insight into the masses' longing for subordination was not lost on Ortega, whose formula for social integration was based on a form of collective hypnosis. His "suggestive project for a life in common" (a more literal but also more accurate rendering of "proyecto sugestivo de vida en común" [*ES,* 56] than Adams's correct but imperceptive translation, "an inspiring plan" [*IS,* 25]) is never a goal in itself but the means to secure and preserve society's "natural" hierarchy. This means, in effect, that in itself, the project is indifferent. What counts is that it succeed in enticing the masses, just as the roles Donato imposed on his subjects were incidental to the purpose of controlling them on stage. Once more, Ortega found the idea crisply formulated by Le Bon:

The crowd has become a people, and this people is able to emerge from its barbarous state. However, it will only entirely emerge therefrom when, after long efforts, struggles necessarily repeated, and innumerable recommencements, it shall have acquired an ideal. The nature of this ideal is of slight importance; whether it be the cult of Rome, the might of Athens, or the triumph of Allah, it will suffice to endow all the individuals of the race that is forming with perfect unity of sentiment and thought. (*C,* 205)

A "perfect unity of sentiment and thought" closely corresponds to Ortega's idea of the state. Race, blood, geography, and social class do not determine citizenship for him; adherence to the state's project does (*RM,* 171). Now it becomes clear why Ortega conceived the state in terms of mission and conditioned citizenship, the rights of the political subject, on willing collaboration with the state's enterprise. Because the unanimous participation of the masses in the state's enterprise presupposes forms of collective suggestion, Ortega's important qualification that the state's project must be "suggestive" implies some form of *panem et circensis.* The unifying project must resound with the masses, but on no account should it be determined by the masses themselves. The masses, constitutionally incapable of self-direction, always await the historical genius that will seduce them with the substance of his imagination.

Ortega borrows from Le Bon the idea that Caesar— "the greatest imagination of antiquity," as Ortega calls him (*RM,* 155–56)—is the paradigm of the leader of the masses. For Le Bon, "The type of hero dear to crowds will always have the semblance of a Caesar. His insignia attracts them, his authority overawes them, and his sword instills them with fear" (*C,* 54–5). That is why Ortega's "suggestive project" turns out to be an imperial one: "there is no empire without a programme of life; more precisely, without a programme of imperial life" (*RM,* 144). States live or die according to their capacity for expansion. Even in periods of apparent stagnation, the state is always "conquering other peoples, founding colonies, federating with other States; that is, at every hour it is going beyond what seemed to be the material principle of its unity" (*RM,* 163). When the process is reversed, the state enters a period of disintegration and fatally declines. Ortega's notion of "invertebration" echoed Le Bon's description of the phase in which a people, having exhausted its formative ideal, falls into the typical anomie of the crowd. "What constituted a people, a unity, a whole, becomes in the end an agglomeration of individualities lacking cohesion, and artificially held together for a time by its traditions and institutions" (*C,* 206).

On history's large canvas, the social distinction between masses and select minorities translates for Ortega into the imperial distinction between mass-peoples and the great nations who act on history's inert matter (*RM,* 134). And because empires are of necessity the result of a great mass set in motion by a historical genius, Ortega's advocacy of this motion inevitably passes into the idea of a mass movement based on contempt for the masses. Soon this idea was to crystallize in fascism. Ortega's paradox lies in the fact that, while reproving fascism as an embodiment of mass society, he underwrote the essence of its ideological edifice. The same ambivalence marked his conception of the state. On the one hand, he deemed it the greatest danger for the autonomy of the great individual; on the other hand, he regarded it as the clearest embodiment of the great man's will.

It will always be possible for readers to bracket out the Caesarean overtones of *The Revolt of the Masses.* And yet an icier view of the "suggestive project" informs *España invertebrada,* where Spain's lack of cohesion is openly attributed to the dissipation of its expansive ideal. That Ortega repeatedly refers to this earlier work in *The Revolt of the Masses* indicates that he looked on it as a valid preamble to the questions of authority, state formation, and mass control, which continued to occupy him. Notwithstanding his assertion that "we must make up our minds to search for the secret of the national State in its specific inspiration as a State, in the policy peculiar to itself, and not in extraneous principles, biological or geographical in character" (*RM,* 169), the Nietzschean overtones of *Invertebrate Spain* continued to inform his approach to the nation by way of the masses. Both books aligned themselves with a number of other works devoted to the regulation of the crowd since the end of the nineteenth century, when the European right began to feel the presence of the masses as a danger.

Ortega distilled his view of the masses in an historical anecdote that his American translator considered dispensable. In 1759, the people of the Andalusian town of Níjar, celebrating the proclamation of Charles III, were seized by monarchical frenzy and destroyed the town's grain reserves, the food stores, and finally all private possessions. Ortega does not analyze the causes of this gigantic potlatch or the power structures in the town, although, as his source indicates, the priestly clan urged the women to sacrifice every object in their homes. He merely remarks, sarcastically, "Admirable Níjar! The future is yours!"[12] But although Ortega does not probe into the background of this eccentric collective act, he is aware that in the Andalusian countryside, starvation wages and high food prices produced bursts of popular anger well into the twentieth century. The anecdote is appended to a passage in which Ortega ironically notes that a hungry populace will often revolt by destroying the bakeries.

Because he is only interested in the exemplary value of a crowd running amok and smashing the property that keeps it physically alive, Ortega does not relate the next logical episode, when the troops march into the town to reestablish distances, thinning the crowd through brutal repression. The two forms of destruction are, for Ortega, incommensurate, and for good reason. As Paul Connerton points out, "the destructiveness of the crowd is unlike that of the army, which aims at the instrumental defeat of the enemy."[13] Although Connerton's observation is meant to question Freud's use of the army as a paradigm of mass formation, it has the virtue of throwing into relief the fact that the army is a crowd whose violence has been harnessed and redirected against a mediated object. Seen in this light, Ortega's comparison of the masses to a mutinous population reveals the implications of the "suggestive project" for common action as a strategy to force the masses into ranks. At this point, his organic metaphors take on new meaning, for the body representations associated with the mass depend on maximal closeness. In that proximity, all places are interchangeable, because no one stands above or below any other and no one is untouchable. An army, on the contrary, is "vertebrated" along an axis of authority that keeps the vertebrae at a distance from each other. Sitting at the top, the head represents the visionary and hypnotic powers of the leader. In a topographic translation of the body metaphor, the head had a precise ethnic meaning. "Only Castilian heads," says Ortega, "contain the special organs required to comprehend the great problem of an integral Spain" (*EI*, 61).

Ortega translated Hegel's notion of the struggle between lord and bondsman into the tension between the mass and the select few. But this dialectic is not all that he adapted from German romantic thought. Following Fichte's conception of Romania as a territory of hybridized and debilitated Germanism, (*IS*, 70–71) Ortega pictured the Visigothic hordes that overran the Iberian Peninsula in the sixth century as Germans in decline (*IS*, 75–76), but still as the forgers of Spain's "vertical" unification. The raw division between conquerors and conquered appeared to Ortega as the permanent structure of modern European nations, as "the typical feature of their historic biology" (*IS*, 75). And according to biological laws, it was the privilege of conquerors to shape the mass of the defeated. Hence, Ortega traced Spain's defective fulfillment of the western norm to the insufficient will of its conquerors. Their softness, due to their intensive romanization, was to blame for the faulty foundations of a national edifice crisscrossed by the stress lines of centrifugal particularisms. Spain could not be said to be decadent because it had never been racially healthy, and the symptom of its chronic disease was its insufficient hierarchization, both vertically, as a caste society,[14] and horizontally, as a radial territory governed by the supreme organs located in the Castilian center. Ultimately, for Ortega, authority was the key political problem and the final test of a society's character. "Who must rule? The Germanic answer is quite simple: he who can." And he clarifies: "I do not mean to replace right with might, but to discern in the fact of being able to impose one's will on others the indisputable sign that one is worthier than others and, therefore,

deserves to rule" (*EI*, 115; passage deleted from the American translation). Might is right, then, not by one's willful decision but by the incontestable force of things.

Ortega's "Prussianism" was almost certainly influenced by Sombart's "Patriotic Reflections" on *Merchants and Heroes* (1915) and especially by *The Bourgeois* (1913), where Sombart describes the history of capitalism as a gradual loss of the heroic and an increasing predominance of the masses. Sombart's conception of heroism as a minority virtue is similar to Ortega's notion of the elite. Also pointing the way to Ortega's definition of the masses is Sombart's idea that the generalization of a previously restricted institution (such as capitalism) necessarily hands it over to mass instincts and capacities.[15] For Sombart, military organization saves a society from the scary picture of the anthill by shaping the masses into immense marching columns,[16] an idea that we have already encountered in Ortega's "suggestive project" for the national masses. Sombart pathologizes commerce, heaping abuse on the British as the embodiment of the commercial spirit, whereas the Germans, although temporarily infected with the "English disease,"[17] remain true to the precapitalist military ideal.[18] And Ortega, asserting that "the industrial ethic . . . is morally and vitally inferior to the warrior's ethic," measures "the historical quality" of a people by its army's performance in war (*EI*, 57, 58; both deleted from the American translation).

Furthermore, Ortega translated Sombart's nationalistic projection of the capitalist and precapitalist dichotomy into Iberian terms, attributing Spanish unity to Castile's superior historical quality. Hawkish Castile was the guarantor of Spanish health, and industrial Catalonia was the focus of the particularistic disorder that threatened to spread to the entire national body. Ortega, following in Sombart's footsteps, translated a cultural and socioeconomic gap into a difference of degree in racial vigor among the various peninsular peoples. "Castile made Spain and Castile has unmade it" (*IS*, 38); yet it remained

Castile's task to awake the national energies and reclaim Spain's mission. Diagnosing the cause of decadence in the feebleness of the German input in Spain's "historical biology" (*IS*, 80), Ortega prepared the terrain for the identification of Habsburg imperialism with racial virtues. And through the use of medical metaphors, as when he notoriously called force "la gran cirujía histórica" (the great historical surgery) (*EI*, 57), he justified in advance the nationalistic violence that would soon erupt against the peripheral nationalities. Force steps in to do the work of suggestion when the masses fail to enthusiastically follow their hypnotist. It would be vain, says Ortega, to try to remove those resistances through persuasive reasons (*EI*, 57). And we know why. The mass lives permanently in a somnambulistic state, subject to superficial representations. Likewise, the peoples who refuse the yoke imposed on them by a foreign nation are ruled by "collective prejudices on the surface of the popular soul" (*IS*, 26).

Ortega's Spanish readership would not have entertained any doubts that he had the so-called Catalan problem in mind. Particularism was the reason for Spain's decomposition, which was reaching the point where a surgical intervention would be required to prevent the entire country from becoming an invertebrate mass. Le Bon had explained why national units decline and fall apart: "with the progressive perishing of its ideal the race loses more and more the qualities that lent it its cohesion, its unity, and its strength" (*C*, 206). Ortega's diagnostic for Spain's malady was cut out for him. The rise of the periphery (always understood as a necessarily subordinate member of an organic whole) was an unmistakable sign of disintegration and of the weakening of the unifying will. The old imperial ideal, however, could not be resuscitated and a new one had to be found. But since Ortega prescribed the kind of project that only Castilian heads could hatch, his suggestive project for a life in common risked going up in the smoke of nostalgia.

Even so, should this project fail to arrive or to seduce everyone, then Castile's imperative virtues could always be relied upon: "The genius that is capable of inventing a suggestive program for a life in common always knows how to forge an exemplary army, which is the effective symbol and the best promotion of that program" (*EI*, 59; deleted from the American translation). The ability to forge an army capable of imposing a "project" was the ultimate proof of an elite's superior vitality. In keeping with his biological tropes, Ortega defined "vitality" as "the power which a healthy cell has of begetting another cell, and vitality is likewise the secret force which creates a great historic empire" (*IS*, 76; translation slightly modified). The health of the race depended on the metastatic power of the Germanic cells in the national body, but it also depended on the mystical force that ordered the cellular plasma into an exemplary army.

Ortega's plea for an ambiguous aristocracy that passes effortlessly into the classless concept of meritocracy helped him retain substantial political and philosophical capital among Spanish liberals. But this ambiguity did not prevent his critique of the masses and his philosophic-historical endorsement of imperialism from feeding the most reactionary strains of Spanish thought. Antiliberal intellectuals intensified Ortega's spite against modern society, understood as the revolt of the masses, and his superlative nationalism based on the permanent overcoming of the state's borders. With the admixture of prebourgeois ideologies, these ideas combined into a regressive rehash, which the new intellectuals of the right bedecked with the mantel of the leader cult and with a deep hatred of bourgeois society. Le Bon had written off the bourgeoisie as incapable of leadership, calling for Caesarean men to take that role. Likewise, Ortega collapsed bourgeois rule with the empire of the masses (*EI*, 126–27; passage deleted from the American translation).

Spanish fascism owed much to Ortega's national philosophy of history. Franco himself seemed to echo Ortega in the script of the film *Raza* (1941), which portrays the fictionalized story of the Caudillo's selection as a member of the elite. In the film, Franco cast himself as the heroic (and fanatic) Captain José Churruca. Like Spain, the Churruca family is polarized in a conflict of values between José's military ideals and his older brother's bourgeois values. The conflict takes on territorial dimensions because the older brother serves the Republic in Catalonia, which is shown time and again as the bastion of the unruly masses. Although Paul Preston believes that the title of the film reflected Franco's infatuation with Nazism,[19] obsession with *la raza* had long pervaded Spanish conservative thinking. Ortega's elevation of the military over the industrial ethic could only flatter a career officer like Franco, on whom the racial source of the will to power would hardly have been lost. Ortega had declared the bourgeoisie's efforts to reform the traditional state ineffectual, because, in his opinion, the periods when wealth seems to drive a society are transitional, and their egalitarian ideal is soon superseded by a new hierarchical impulse.[20] These words, which were written in 1927, during the dictatorship of Miguel Primo de Rivera, betrayed Ortega's relief at the termination of a period marked by the rising influence of the Catalan bourgeoisie and by the concomitant rise of organized labor. This was the period, to put it in his terms, in which the rebellious masses climbed to the political stage.

Spanish fascism conflated industrialism with the lower values of the masses and was ready to provide the hierarchical backbone that Ortega missed in the country. As in central Europe, where many of Ortega's ideas about mass society originated, Spanish reactionary thought deployed medical and biological terminology to pathologize the masses and medicalize society in an effort to justify the most aggressive interventions in political life.

To the biological metaphors, which flourished especially in the imperialist climate between the 1870s and World War I, crowd psychology contributed the ideas of psychic contagion, emotional infection, and suggestion as metaphors for the "weak subjectivity" of certain groups and categories. Le Bon was not alone in claiming that "the opinions and beliefs of crowds are specially propagated by contagion, but never by reasoning" (*C*, 128). In Spain, this doctrine led to the belief that political forms of "the revolt of the masses," such as communism or syndicalism, were cases of mass contagion afflicting individuals with a constitutional psychic weakness.

If the concept of "mass" had always been pejorative, now the pathology attributed to certain masses implied the existence of "healthy," docile masses. Years before his famous diatribe against the rebellious masses, Ortega had bluntly defined their existential assignment as the acceptance of leadership: "The mission of the masses is no other than to follow their betters" (*EI*, 126; passage deleted from the American translation). With the discovery of the invincible compliance of the masses, fascism had found its raison d'être. From the amorphous, untamed mass it had to produce a self-restrained, abnegated national body. Matter awaited form, and the doctrine of eugenics rose to meet the challenge.

Racial Eugenics

From the moment the term *eugenics* was coined in the 1880s by Francis Galton, an English aristocrat and a nephew of Charles Darwin, it was associated with the biology-inspired view of society that came to be known as social Darwinism. The new "science" quickly penetrated those societies where economic modernization underwrote a competitive view of life. From the turn of the century to the 1930s, eugenics spread through North America, Europe, and other parts of the world. States developed eugenic policies to increase the birthrate of selected classes and to discourage or altogether prevent the reproduction of negatively targeted groups. Shortly before World War I, Bruno Laquer expressed the aim of this doctrine in his article, "Eugenik und Dysgenik," published in the popular journal *Grenzfragen des Nerven—und Seelenlebens—Einzeldarstellungen für Gebildete aller Stände*. Laquer, speaking on behalf of the public interest, concluded his article by affirming that for the upper classes, the new science consists "*for the time being* only in the enlightenment over the duties of individual partner selection according to the principles of eugenics." For the lower strata, however, it will mean "in the not-so-distant future the construction of a restrictive, many generations-long eugenics." According to the author, this policy entails "the weeding out of the asocial lines, insofar as they develop through inheritance on the basis of bad, inappropriate seed."[21]

Early on, eugenics became synonymous with the idea of *racial hygiene*, a term coined by Alfred Ploetz in his book *Die Tüchtigkeit unserer Rasse und der Schutz der Schwachen* (1895). Ploetz, a physician and economist, took the ideas of social Darwinism into the terrain of racial thinking, proposing a racial hygiene as the precondition for Germany's racial purity and higher "national fitness."[22] The term *racial hygiene* reappeared in the title of a text published by the Munich physician Wilhelm Schallmayer in 1916: "Brauchen wir eine Rassenhygiene?" Schallmayer stated that "Crucial for the prosperity of the race is not only the quantity of the offspring but also its quality, the racial fitness," and he concluded that "inferior germ-cells should have no part in the reproduction of the nation."[23] Out of the turn-of-the-century concern with degeneration emerged a biological mobilization of society for the purpose of succeeding in the competition among nations. Doctors anointed themselves as planners of the strategy for this heartless evolutionary war. Gynecologists in particular were seen as the enforcers of the principles set down by geneticists. As early as 1894, Alfred Helgar, in his book *Der Geschlechtstrieb*, had proposed the interdiction of marriages among "the inferior," a class that included the mentally ill, the deaf-mute, and the blind, but also those considered to be "instinctive criminals." And in 1913, Max Hirsch, in a study on the applications of racial hygiene to gynecology, advocated the permanent sterilization of women with alleged hereditary maladies. Hereditary were, in his view, the various psychoses, but also alcoholism, advanced tuberculosis, syphilis, and anemia. He concluded by hoping that medicine might be able to guide the instincts, so that people would "reject the physically and mentally inferior for the propagation of a healthier progeny, just as they today . . . spurn the members of lower races."[24] Partaking in the growing medicalization of racism did not prevent Hirsch from being persecuted and driven into exile as a non-Aryan after 1933.

Around World War I, medicine subordinated itself to a worldview shaped by extramedical values, claiming an unofficial advisory role to the state. In the crisis-ridden Weimar Republic, physicians elevated the tone of the eugenics debate, demanding obligatory sterilization and confinement of the "congenitally inferior." The thought that some individuals carried dangerous genes that caused the "social illness of the German nation"[25] led to a differentiation between the worthy and the unworthy of biological participation in the life of the people. After the consolidation of the Nazi regime, "social conspicuousness" was diagnosed as hereditary, and in Hamburg, the ordinance on "Heredity Care" (*Erbpflegeverordnung*) of August 31, 1939, made orphans, "education-resisting" children, people liable to prosecution, prostitutes, and some prisoners subject to sterilization. Also coming under the sterilization ordinances were dysfunctional individuals who worked as unskilled or semi-skilled laborers, the chronically ill, the mentally retarded, the handicapped, whoever was deemed incapable of full productivity, and anyone who was perceived as a liability to the state. Those affected were mostly members of the lower classes.[26]

Considering the increasingly authoritarian and racially oriented character of German medicine since the early twentieth century, it does not come as a surprise that from the beginning, physicians were overly represented among Hitler's followers.[27] Easing the transition from caring for the (infirm) human body to acting as self-appointed custodians of the national body or *Volkskörper* was the rampant organicism of the predominant social metaphors. But the fervor with which physicians embraced eugenics derived less from scientific evidence than from a messianic faith in the idea of national mission, which found fertile ground in the political and economic depression of the 1920s. Providentialism, which always accompanied the rise of imperialism, now grew into a national destiny. And it was a physician, Dr. Gustav Sondermann, who infused national socialistic ideas with messianic Christianity in a pamphlet that he published in 1924 with the title *Der Sinn der völkischen Sendung.*[28]

As we have seen, Ortega had already enunciated the idea that the masses had a preordained mission, consisting in the enthusiastic acceptance of a "suggestive project" for national life as established by a select minority. In itself, the "suggestive project" need not entail racial representations. The idea of molding the national mass by means of a common goal lies at the heart of the cultural nationalism developed by Fichte in his *Addresses to the German Nation*. In the first address, Fichte proposed a common cultural goal as the basis for ethnicity: "By means of the new education we want to mold the Germans into a corporate body, which shall be stimulated and animated in all its individual members by a common interest."[29] Fichte's recourse to culture and, above all, language as the reservoir of ethnic superiority[30] was meant to fend off the Germans' spiritual absorption by their French conquerors. But by the time this idea reached Ortega, German nationalist thought had appropriated Nietzsche's contempt for the masses and combined his Darwinian legitimization of the strong with the doctrine of racial superiority.

Thus the concept of "race," the biological equivalent for the sociological notion of "mass," also featured in the discourse of Spanish fascism. Nevertheless, in Spain, the word *race* retained a prebiological sense, betraying the country's impenetrability by the scientific worldview. Still, a curious mixture of pseudoscience and traditionalism emerged in the 1930s when some Spanish doctors adopted eugenics as the Nazis were turning it into a program of racial purification. Dr. Antonio Vallejo Nágera, a psychiatrist and a devotee of the Spanish national movement who dedicated one of his books "To the glorious Spanish Army" and another "To the undefeated Imperial *Caudillo*," borrowed extensively from German eugenics with a view to regenerating the Spanish "race." The influence of Ortega on Vallejo's racial thought transpires in the latter's absorption with the biological conditions of the select few while remaining indifferent to the genetic "mass" of the population. Such profound conservatism explains the failure of Spanish fascism to carry out a "national revolution." Nazi ideology decked out Spanish fascism with the rhetoric of modernization, but Spain was still far from that phase of capitalist development in which Ortega's alarm at the brimming proximity of the masses could find a factual correlative.

In an attempt to reconcile "science" with the ethnic sense of the word *race*, Vallejo attributed to the Nazis a distinction between eugenics and racial hygiene. Eugenics supposedly tried to preserve the genetic health of an entire people by intervening in its reproductive practices. Racial hygiene aimed to strengthen the superior individuals, a postnatal goal that required the assistance of social agents rather than the geneticist's. Yet Vallejo seemed unwilling to part from either concept, promoting "a positive eugenics based on stimulating the fertility of select individuals, since we do not believe that in biology quantity rules out quality."[31] Although he and other Spanish apostles of the Übermensch flirted with biology, they adapted social Darwinism to traditional authoritarianism, stressing the moral, cultural, and metaphysical traits of Spanish history as the locus of racial struggle. Their avoidance of the more secular racism of the Nazis has often been attributed to the persistence of a humanistic layer in Spanish culture. More convincingly, the reason lies in the fact that modern Spanish racism was born of impotence and nostalgia, and these conditions played themselves out in an exalted idealism.

Comparison between Nazi Germany and fascist Spain shows the extent to which similar ideologies have different outcomes in different cultures. Both movements sought legitimization in historical archaism, but they did so in opposite directions. If the Nazis strove to preserve the "continuity" of the present with the Holy Roman Empire and the pre-1918 German empire by creating the third empire that Moeller van der Bruck announced in *Das dritte Reich* (1923), the Falangists, although lacking in utopian imagination, also filled their doctrine with reveries of imperial overhaul. Their fascist costume had no purchase on the urban masses, and their social base remained the backward petit bourgeoisie of Castile's rural towns. Theirs was an anachronistic empire stitched together with dissipated glories. It was made up of nostalgia for world domination, the grotesque hallucination with which a handful of provincial intellectuals tried to patch their resentment against modernity. And nothing symbolized modernity better than the urban masses and the industry that had called them into being. Nazism also drew upon chiliastic faith, but unlike its Spanish imitation, it did not translate technological backwardness into spiritual superiority.

In Germany, racism "had to" concern itself with bodies, because the nation, recently unified and still expansive, looked forward to the incorporation of lands populated by masses of ethnic Germans. The embodiment of its *Volksgeist* in a *Volkskörper* could be measured concretely by the physical extension of the Reich. In Germany the notion of *Deutschtum* was inextricably linked to the expansion of the habitat of a people that Hans Grimm called a *Volk ohne Raum* in 1926.[32] In Spain, on the contrary, racism could not rely on an expansive national body. Ortega had decried the encroaching masses, but he had also denounced a national decline that had left Spain with a maladjusted skeleton. Lack of adequate embodiment idealized Spanish racism, which found its imperial conduit historically foreclosed. "Hispanidad," like "Deutschtum," entailed the racial control of the biosphere. But the impossibility of reclaiming the physical basis of the empire forced Spanish racism to stake its claims not so much on the body as on the soul.

Without hope of politically reuniting the Hispanic body, Spanish fascism strove for an animistic equivalent. Because the imperial body was now beyond reach, the Hispanic race took refuge in the spirit. "The race is spirit, Spain is spirit, the Hispanic world is spirit," asserted Vallejo Nágera in the heady days leading to the civil war.[33] Cut off from matter, Ortega's masses were redeemed from their "mass" quality by their appointed historical mission. By virtue of the Hispanic ideal, they existed in the realm of the universal. Henceforth the crowd, emerging from its barbarous natural state, would become a people. Vallejo's language was a great deal more vehement than Ortega's, but the retention of certain motifs is unmistakable. The "suggestive project" that Ortega prescribed for the masses was none other than the ghostly empire haunting the Spanish soul since 1898.

Spanish fascism extended Ortega's distinction between masses and spiritual few, dividing the world into countries dominated by material concerns, the so-called bourgeois democracies, and the Axis powers, whose spirituality transpired in the spectacle offered by masses shaped by the will of a new Caesar. Such feats of the spirit could only be achieved by a healthy race, and Vallejo, calling for a policy of racial hygiene in 1934, prescribed precisely Ortega's "suggestive project" as the ideal that could turn Spaniards from invertebrate masses into a people.

We Spaniards have reached a stage in our historical development that is extremely delicate and dangerous for the future of the race. Either we allow the positivistic and materialistic currents dominating the greatest part of the world to carry us away or, joining the German and Italian peoples, we go back to the arena to demand the restitution of the racial and spiritual values that made it possible for us to civilize immense territories, which after one century of material independence are still attached to Mother Spain by racial and cultural bonds. (*HR,* 1)

The invectives against materialism were part of the eccentric claim that Spain's empire had been an altruistic venture, just as, in Ortega's words, Caesar's had been a display of prodigious fantasy. To be pure spirit acting upon the raw matter of uncivilized lands—could there be better proof of Spain's membership in the most exclusive club of world-historical nations? Since the days of the American conquest, the idea of a Christian mission had been Spain's version of the white man's burden. Fascism took over this ideology, but its emphasis on spirit was overdetermined by the loss of Spain's political hegemony. The empire must be retrieved at all costs—if not materially, then ideally. Spain could still exert spiritual leadership over the masses of an entire continent, shaping them into one race.

Our patriotism, the patriotism that propelled the National Movement, feeds on the desire of revitalizing the universal values of the Hispanic idea on the world scale. Our patriotism is that Hispanic idea. We are now at war for the sake of the Hispanic idea, and when we achieve peace, we will build a New Spain steeped in the Hispanic spirit and with the zeal of expanding that spirit, for this is the nature of our Imperialism.[34]

The world must be forced to acknowledge the premodern values to which Spain clung. Like Unamuno before him, Vallejo transvaluated the superior material culture of the bourgeois democracies into a sign of decadence. In *Eugenesia de la Hispanidad* (1937), he attacked modern society explicitly: "From the time of their infancy, men must be freed from the dogmas of industrial civilization and the mate-

rialist principles on which modern society is based" (*EH,* 97). The reason was clear: industrialization required a mass market, which in turn presupposed egalitarian principles and, in the long run, a democratic state. Surely Germany's industrial might was the condition of its military power, and Hitler with his *Autobahnen* and his Volkswagen would never have endorsed Vallejo's rabid antimodernism. But Hitler could be seen as the knight who bridled Germany's industrial bourgeoisie and curbed the financial oligarchy. For Vallejo, it was not Germany or Italy that exemplified materialism but the Anglo-Saxon "race," especially the Yankee upstart. Ortega had called the United States "the paradise of the masses," and Vallejo, playing on Ortega's definition of the mass-man as a latter-day barbarian, affirmed that the "semi-civilized Yankee society" was driven by ancestral tribal instincts (*HR,* 8).

Because of its psychological makeup, this most unspiritual people had been the first to introduce artificial selection by means of sterilization laws and in this way had initiated its own decadence (*HR,* 121). Vallejo, a staunch Catholic, considered birth control a mistake. He did not oppose racial selection, but his imperialism required demographic growth. So he was loath to intervene in the reproductive organs, although not in the reproductive patterns, of the population, which he tried to modify through his doctrine of "total segregation."

In tune with a cohort of Hispanic thinkers—including Miguel de Unamuno, the Mexican José Vasconcelos, and Ortega himself—Vallejo predicted the vindication of the Spanish worldview in modernity's exhaustion. In *Eugenesia de la Hispanidad,* he augured the proximate decline of Spain's rival for influence in the Spanish American countries: "The failure of materialism can be seen to advantage in the immense North American nation, the richest of all, the most democratic, the militarily most powerful, about to sink in the quagmire issuing from its worldview and idea of happiness: the spirit of money" (*EH,* 97). Le Bon had considered popular democracy and a material veneer sure symptoms of the downfall of nations: "The populace is sovereign, and the tide of barbarism mounts. The civilization may still seem brilliant because it possesses an outward front, the work of a long past, but it is in reality an edifice crumbling to ruin, which nothing supports, and destined to fall in at the first storm" (*C*, 207). Accordingly, the Spanish right pinned its hopes on the historical demise of democracy and, at its most delirious, saw in fascism a new cosmic paradigm. The following excerpt from *Biopolítica* (1942), by Dr. Antonio de la Granda and Dr. Eduardo Isla, is concocted from a number of ideas given course by Ortega in the previous decades and now placed at the service of the reaction:

Once again we see Hellenism and Romanism face to face, the rising German-Roman world with its will to power and its vital-dialectic synthesis, and the Russian-Anglo-Saxon world with its materialistic rationalism. The triumph of the former is assured by the fact that they represent the dialectic realization of history. The transition from the rationalistic antithesis to the vital-dialectic synthesis agrees with the ongoing spiritual transformation of men and nations. Rationalism, exalted individualism, freedom and democracy, the omnipotence of natural science... all these things seem old, imperfect, and barren. More or less intensely, a new common sentiment stirs Western European men. This sentiment places once more philosophy and science at the service of life and of faith in a better destiny. It promotes the heartfelt union between Church and State; enhances the significance of blood, race, and family; it gathers together and organizes different peoples into empires with a single mission. Pure reason yields to the will and nations prepare themselves to conquer the world. The empire, the Caesar, an efficient Realpolitik is something everyone can feel and everyone longs for with impatient hope.[35]

De la Granda and Isla echoed Vallejo's theory of racial degeneration: "When a nation receives customs alien to its nature, to its biological make-up, it fatally degenerates" (*B*, 354) and declared democracy—the dictatorship of the majority—"biologically unacceptable" (*B*, 277). Likewise, for Vallejo, the only reliable form of racial selection was the "natural" result of oligarchic or aristocratic government (*HR*, 118). From Le Bon and Ortega he had learned that the masses could be upgraded to a race through the creative work of the select minority. Ortega himself had appealed to an "imperative of selection" to bring about "the refinement of the race" (*EI*, 128; deleted from the American translation). Such an imperative was for him the only reliable method of "racial purification and improvement" (*IS*, 87). Following Ortega's hint, Vallejo preferred a tutorial "care of the race" to biological eugenics: "True racial hygiene consists in encouraging the creation of select individuals." Because the world was naturally divided into masses and minorities, racial hygiene must be oriented exclusively to preserving the correlation between the two. Vallejo abhorred democracy because it posed the danger that inferior members of the species would find their way to the top (*EH*, 127). He did not entertain the possibility that democracy enhances selection by stimulating competition, nor that hierarchical societies stagnate.

Spain was an obvious case of a stagnant society, and Vallejo saw its lack of influence as an unambiguous sign of racial deterioration. He considered "imbecility" to be on the rise and the Spanish race near extinction (*EH*, 7). The race had been sliding since the end of the Habsburg dynasty and was fast approaching its demise under the young democratic republic. Never mind that for most of this period Spain had absolute rulers. The structure of government might have been right, but the national body was infected by a wave of foreign courtiers that had invaded the country with the Bourbon dynasty at its head. Like viruses, these alien bodies had corrupted not so much Spanish blood as Spanish thought, the fountainhead of the racial virtues (*EH*, 109). A closer look revealed that the spread of democratic ideas was responsible for the Spaniards' betrayal of their ontological mission: "Over the last two hundred years we have been losing our soul by trying to become what we are not, instead of trying to be ourselves but with all the power we can muster. These two hundred years are the era of Revolution" (*EH,* 112). Spaniards, in other words, had fallen into the existential attitude that Américo Castro later called "to live undoing one's life."[36]

A few decades earlier, on the eve of the Spanish-American War, Angel Ganivet had set forth the view that Spain had swerved from its predestined course. In *Idearium español,* Ganivet called for a remedy to this historical deviation through the concentration of national life. He also called for a dictator and expressed the need to "throw one million Spaniards to the wolves" in order to save Spain from spiritual bankruptcy.[37] Following in Ganivet's and especially in Ramiro de Maeztu's footsteps, Vallejo gave their views a semblance of medical erudition and provided a scientific alibi for the reaction: "For biological reasons," he wrote during the Civil War, "we are partial to dictatorship and unified command."[38]

Vallejo's prescription against racial degeneracy followed from his diagnosis: Spain must retrieve the matrix of religious faith and imperial will. Anti-republican and autocratic, in line with such conservatives as Joseph De Maistre, Donoso Cortés, and Carl Schmitt, Vallejo staked everything on the question of authority:

We must start an intense hygienic war against the noxious germs that vitiate the Hispanic race, leading it to the most abject degeneration. The point is not to simply go back to the humanistic values of the XVth or the XVIth centuries. We must reintroduce them into the thought, the habits, and the actions of the people for the purpose of cleansing the moral environment and psychologically reinforcing the phenotype in order to keep the genotype from degenerating. Racial politics includes everything that biology and hygiene teach, but its highest goal is to attain the civilization that has its source in philosophy, translating the latter into a healthy morality for the people. (*EH,* 109–10)

Vallejo's discourse is peculiar for a physician. He tropes medical terms into aggressive ideologemes amounting to

the proposal of shock treatment for the masses. Le Bon, mindful of the endurance of tradition, had stressed heredity as the only trustworthy means of social modification (*C,* 82). This meant that for an ideal to enliven the masses, it must resonate with the nationally accumulated past. Revolutionary changes could only damage the social organism; therefore, the people were best served by a conservative institutionalization of the past (*C,* 83). Ortega made exactly the same point when he praised England for preserving the monarchy and opposing the principle of continuity to the revolution.[39] Accordingly, Spanish Falange attempted to reconnect Spaniards with the imperial institutions, overlooking the fact that continuity, as Ortega maintained, implied the retention of a people's *entire* past.

Vallejo was so confident of the hygienic benefit of traditional Castilian values that he wished to make them universally compelling. Indeed, he offered them as the only means to avert the threat of communism—a position, incidentally, that Franco would later take to curry favor with the United States: "If the clash between East and West is to be avoided, we must urgently revive and spread over the entire planet that Spanish spirit that looked upon all men as brothers, although it distinguished between those having seniority and those not yet grown up" (*EH,* 112). *Fraternité,* yes, but there was no question of *égalité.* The distinction between the masses and the select few was crucial to the health of the race. As for liberty, it was strictly a relation between the minority's guidance and the masses' willingness to follow. Democracy per se was a source of social morbidity: "Democracy has liberated the psychopathic tendencies in every country, with crime increasing in direct proportion to what we could call the national democratic index" (*EH,* 129).

Initially, Spanish fascism allotted its hostility equally between communism and democracy. Both represented the triumph of the masses; both dissolved society's traditional structures and declared patrimonial hierarchies obsolete.

10A 'Gente': Spanish

Jeronimo Ernesto Arellano

The word *gente* is defined as a "group or plurality of people" by the *Real Academia Española*. In contrast to *pueblo* or *masa*, *gente* appears as a politically neutral term when used on its own, as indicated by several contemporary colloquial expressions such as "quedar con la gente" (to set up a meeting with a group of people). When used as part of a composite phrase, however, as in "lowly crowd" (*gente baja*), *gente* suggests a marking of racial or socioeconomic difference, which in turn may provide us with a vantage point in relation to its semantic history.

Gente derives from the Latin *gens*, generally defined as "race," "nation," or "family." Archaic colloquial expressions in Spanish such as *gente fosca* ("brown-skinned folk") and *gente non sancta* suggest the distance of an observer that characterizes a group from the outside. It is perhaps then not surprising that Christopher Columbus uses *gente* repeatedly when describing the indigenous communities of the Caribbean in his travel journal; Columbus notes that it will be difficult to travel to scout for copper in the island of Carib, for example, "because [the] people [there] eat human flesh" (puesto que sera dificultoso en carib por q aqll *gente* diz que come Carne humana). In the texts of the first chroniclers, *gente* refers to the indigenous troops that served within the Spanish armies. This is in fact a term for *troop* commonly used in Spain from roughly the fifteenth to the seventeenth centuries, but as the process of conquest and colo-

Despite these "analogies," though, Vallejo's perception of the maximal racial danger shifted during the civil war, as the invigoration of the Spanish Communist Party through the sale of Soviet arms and the presence of the international brigades caused him to reevaluate his estimation of the racial pathogenesis. Before the war, popular democracy—the more immediate threat to Spanish conservatism—had carried the onus of social morbidity, but as the western democracies turned their backs on Spain and the republic became dependent on the Soviet Union, Vallejo readjusted his target. In his wartime book, *Psicopatología de la conducta antisocial* (1937), he claimed that the revolution was the supreme racial threat. As evidence, he pointed to the morbid psychosomatic constitutions of its leaders and inspirers:

The pathographic study of the instigators and leaders of the French and Russian revolutions proves the madness and degeneration of Rousseau, Robespierre, Marat, Hébert, etc. Nietzsche and Lenin suffered general paralysis. Alcoholic degeneration is very frequent among the Russian people. Men who are misanthropic, irritable, explosive, paranoid and psycho-asthenic, as well as liars and homosexuals have been able, at certain historical moments, to exert such influence over the masses, that taking hold of power, have submerged whole nations into a bloody chaos. The psychopathological features of the preachers of the Spanish Marxist revolution do not differ much from the actors in other revolutions. (*PCA*, 53)

Those were for Vallejo the consequences of the revolt of the masses. Far from being the masses' royal road to their own subjectivity, the revolution defined the aberrant moments of history when asocial individuals were able to seduce the masses. Wherever revolution struck, one found a shapeless, dysfunctional social body. Degeneracy, though, was as much a cause as a consequence of racial derangement. According to Vallejo, subversion seized nations that were afflicted with negative racial factors. Revolutionary ideals and racial debasement always coexisted, for both were each other's effects. Spain's decadence, then, spelled the triumph of the revolution. This prognosis, however, could be averted through a program of racial hygiene.

Eugenics claimed to eliminate the negative racial factors, but Vallejo's belief that race was grounded in tradition, not genes, discouraged the practice of select breeding. Still, for all his claims about the spirituality of the race, he indulged in physiognomic exegesis. He freely adapted Ernst Kretschmer's theory of the relation between body form and psychological constitution and correlated physical appearance and ideological proclivity. After all, racial degeneracy must show in the body, and it must be possible to tell the select genius apart from the mass-men.

Whereas Franco's body appeared to him as the model of racial virtues, Azaña's revealed an inclination to antisocial behavior (*SR*, 21). For the discerning eye of the physiognomist, each of these bodies exposed the nature of the competing racial forces. With a stretch of the imagination, Vallejo managed to see an epic ideal of classic harmony in the short and chubby Caudillo, whereas the president of the republic's ill-favored, bespectacled figure revealed the lowest passions of a rebellious populace.

For all that, Vallejo was not interested in aesthetics but rather in cosmetics, not in physical beauty but in the social order. Given genetic indeterminacy, the eugenicist's task was not to weed out the inferior genes but to increase the birthrate while keeping the class proportion steady. When he wrote against the practice of sterilization in 1932, he claimed that the greatest racial danger lurked in the insufficient reproduction of the elite: "The threat to the race does not lie in the reproduction of degenerate individuals but in the lack of reproduction of the healthy, gifted persons. A population does not degenerate when all its classes reproduce proportionally."[40] According to his theory of proportional social reproduction, the Hispanic body would grow stronger only if it did not place hierarchy at risk, and this could only be guaranteed if internal homeostasis balanced external expansion (*EH*, 117). The masses were vital to the race, but racial health required that they obey the imperative of selection by serving the racial values. To that end, indoctrination, not genetic tinkering, held out the promise of success. Crowd psychology had taught Vallejo that the masses were prone to emotional manipulation. Consequently, he recommended an intensive propaganda, which in fact became pervasive for many decades after the war (*SR*, 9).

Ortega's dichotomy of rebellious masses and select minorities is an undialectical adaptation of Hegel's fable of the lord and the bondsman. Whereas Hegel's slave develops a superior consciousness through bondage, Ortega's masses do not attain rational subjectivity and remain beholden to the select minority for any action that is mediated by reflexive consciousness—exactly like an army. The elite, in turn, needs the masses—and distance from the masses—for its self-recognition. "The social value of the men who lead depends on the capacity for enthusiasm which the mass possesses" (*IS*, 61–62). It is ultimately the masses that declare the elite through their recognition. Enthusiasm, an irrational state akin to fascination, measures the quality of the masses. But their essence remains their numerical strength, which is vital to the racial fitness of the few. The empire's dependence on numbers, exacerbated by Spain's low demography, explains the repugnance Vallejo feels toward sterilization and his insistence that the "true" racial politics is

nization of the New World advances, *gente* is replaced by the term *hueste* in America, possibly during the first decades of the sixteenth century. As opposed to the more loosely organized troops known as *gente*, *hueste* entails a hierarchical military structure.

Similar changes take place on the religious front. The naked folk, or *gente desnuda*, that Columbus had considered as ideal targets of conversion—interpreting lack of clothing as a sign of a childish innocence or "blankness" of soul—are narrativized as a Christian pueblo (from the Latin *populus*) in accounts by missionaries in the sixteenth century. Here, in a manner comparable to the organization of the *huestes*, the emergence of the term *pueblo* seems to reflect the refashioning of a social collective into an institutionally regulated and stratified structure.

During the early decades of the seventeenth century, the Dutch jurist Grotius and the Spanish jurist Francisco Suárez develop a doctrine of law known as *iure gentium* or *jus gentium*, translated in Spanish as *derecho de gentes* ("law of nations"). This doctrine assimilates and actualizes the rules of engagement between armies that belong to different *gens*—often Christian versus barbarians—as described in military manuals of the past centuries, recalling the ancient meaning of "family," "race," or "nation." Yet when the discipline of international law begins to emerge from the doctrine of *jus gentium*, the term *gens* is dropped altogether, as it becomes perhaps an archaism in relation with a crowd with a political organization that requires the formulation of new concepts. And thus whereas Simón Bolívar, in his "Letter from Jamaica," praises Grotius for proposing that equal principles of law should apply to all, even to infidels and barbarians, the term *gente* is entirely absent from his discourse. Rather, Bolívar makes use of a concept of *pueblo* clearly influenced by Rousseau's political philosophy but also by the notion of popular mass developed by the early Christian missions to America.

A point of comparison between these two very different projects—evangelization and national sovereignty—remains perhaps the desire to crystallize the energy of a crowd into manageable units, both in terms of actual organization and symbolic power, that may then be realigned to suit a specific agenda. The identification of differences between communities, at the heart of the word *gente*, seems then to be mobilized and shaped to facilitate—at least discursively—diversified processes of social engineering. It thus seems possible to suggest that the current status of *gente*, as an informal and, to a certain extent, neutral term for a plurality of people in contemporary Spanish might be the result of a series of transformations of the notion of the collective that signal the gradual rise of the word *pueblo* in the vocabulary of modern states.[1]

antigeneticist. Social, rather than biological selection, and specifically the implantation of the old imperial values, would guarantee that quality "biotypes" would again flourish.[41]

Vallejo wavered between the moral and the biological. Nazi prestige ran high among Spanish fascists, and he indulged in the use of debased medical concepts to identify the "racial pollutants." If the Nazis had turned their advanced cancer research into a source of lethal metaphors for unwanted social groups, and Goebbels had repeatedly attacked the "cancerous tumor" of communism,[42] Vallejo would also perform a "blood test" on the Hispanic body to determine its health. In a raving article published in 1938, he traced all the modern evils, from rationalism and materialism to the class struggle, Marxism, and the Spanish republic to the *conversos*, the Christianized Jews who avoided expulsion and continued to work secretly against Christian civilization and western culture.[43] Fortunately, he claimed in a different text of the same year, Jewish endogamy had prevented the infusion of but a few drops of Semitic blood into the racial mainstream. Somewhat higher was the affluence of Moorish "blood cells," but not enough to alter the Roman-Hispanic-Gothic, or, in contemporary terms, Italian-Spanish-German, admixture that made the Spanish race (*PR*, 16). All was not well, though, because even if inferior racial groups had not harmed the Spanish stock, they had still damaged the Spaniard's "bio-psychical" traits. "The complexes of rancor, resentment, and inferiority that weigh on the race were sown first by the Jews, then by the Moors, and later by the influence of the *philosophes* and of rationalists enamoured of foreign ideas" (*PR*, 18). Jews, Moors, and the French—they were all to blame for Spain's misfortunes, from the loss of the empire to the modern class struggle.

During the war, Vallejo was assigned the direction of the Military Psychiatric Services. On August 23, 1938, he received Franco's authorization to create the Cabinet for Psychological Research, "whose primary purpose will be to research the psycho-physical roots of Marxism." Vallejo intended to investigate the relations between the "bio-psychological" makeup of war prisoners and "Marxist political fanaticism."[44] The high number of prisoners at his disposal gave Colonel Vallejo a unique opportunity to test his old idea about the existence of a link between psychopathology and Marxism. With the help of anthropometrics, he set out to prove experimentally that Marxism's "simplicity" lured chiefly the mentally retarded by teasing their lowly passions with the promise of material satisfactions—a strategy that communism shared with democracy. The crowd's irrationality (and communism was, according to Ortega, a quintessential mass doctrine) could only attract the feeble-minded. And because the mass was by definition inert—or worse, cancerous matter—it propagated through the hope of an enhanced material existence.

Proving this hypothesis would facilitate early detection of individuals predisposed to contract the Marxist disorder and would make it possible to segregate them at an early age.[45] This grim proposal did not fall on deaf ears. After the war, the new state exercised mandatory custody of children of republican prisoners, subjecting them to a stern reeducation in racial values. Repatriated children were often snatched en route to their families and their names changed to prevent reclamation by relatives. The regime even went to the length of abducting refugee children from foster homes in foreign countries, a difficult mission that was greatly simplified after the German army occupied asylum countries.[46]

Reeducating children to learn their place in life would redress the racial degeneration evinced in their parents' revolutionary proclivities. Learning one's place was the mission Ortega had assigned to the masses, whose revolt began precisely with their encroachment on the places reserved for the few. Vallejo tried to revive Dr. Juan Huarte de San Juan's sixteenth-century doctrine of the "temperaments" as a criterion for regulating the choice of profession. Pushing this pseudoscientific form of career counseling, he proposed barring access to higher education to working-class children, and also to the children of their employers: "Es peligroso para el Estado y para la Sociedad que el hijo del comerciante o del industrial ejerza profesiones liberales, porque suele mercantilizarlas" (It is dangerous for the state and for society if the son of a merchant or an industrialist exercises the liberal professions, for he will only mercantilize them) (*PR*, 28–30). Following Ortega's assertion that the industrial ethic is morally and biologically inferior to the warrior's, Vallejo considered wealth creation and material improvement unworthy of the racial elite. Because Ortega had indulged in the use of biological and medical metaphors, it was fitting that a physician inspired by his philosophy of national salvation would place the entire range of his specialized terminology at the service of Spain's historical mission.

In the name of racial values and state security, Vallejo was calling for a policy of not only class but also ethnic discrimination. Since the eighteenth century, Spaniards had associated commerce and industrial enterprise with Catalonia, a region completely shut out from political power. By the end of the nineteenth century, industrial growth and modernization had given Catalonia a political self-confidence that translated into demands for a fairer treatment by the central government (Memorial de Greuges [1885; Memorial of Grievances]) and for a degree of self-administration (Bases de Manresa [1892; Manresa Basic Guidelines]). This process culminated in 1932 with the establishment of Catalonia's Statute of Autonomy, which

10B   Take It

Ann Weinstone

At thirteen, Roger and I married under a tree in the front yard of his parents' three-bedroom bungalow. "Quakers can marry people," Roger had told me. He was a Quaker, so naturally we decided to do it.

One of us must have boasted about the blessed event. My parents, Roger's parents, and some school functionary ordered the newlyweds to attend an emergency meeting. "What exactly does this marriage entail?" my father asked Roger. Roger was an innocent. I understood exactly what my father wanted to know. The whole procedure disgusted me. My parents' relationship hadn't indoctrinated me into the concept of legal matrimony as serious business. Weren't we allowed to play, too?

Later that year, Roger and I attended a rock concert. Marriage first. Rock concert later. We had committed ourselves to reversing the natural order of things.

I wore a white Mexican wedding dress sans bra or underwear. Patches of teen-pink flesh showed through the lacy cotton. And I had shortened the dress. A lot.

We moved along with the throng of long-haired and peasant-topped ticket holders toward one of the concert arena's arched entryways. I squinched my eyes so that the streaming panorama before me tipped and I saw it as a two-dimensional canvas—an enormous Brueghel painting come alive. Then I stepped into the scene. This was my way of intensifying the immediacy of experience: put everything on a single plane and have it all at once.

This crowd intensification technology, however, played only a supporting role. The real drama emerged from my own interior narration of the Story of Ann and the Crowd.

The Story of Ann and the Crowd

Ann glides through an ocean of bodies, sound, and color. She is sensitive, able to detect and precisely narrate the shifting patterns of human expression. At a glance, she can discern secret alliances, undeveloped potentials, and future calamities. Employing sophisticated bioperceptual terrorist weapons, Ann can metamorphose you into a hallucinatory, Jackson Pollock blob; a visiting alien secretly trolling the planet for genetic material; or, perversely, the boring nine-to-five adult you are actually destined to become.

My bohemian parents hadn't taught me much about the sanctity of marriage, but they had taught me how to inhabit the position of the flaneur.

I remember the moment I stepped into the concert hall's steeply banked and darkened interior. The people who, outside, had presented the young flaneur with opportunities for enacting individualized extreme makeovers now formed a single, undulating mass: a shape-shifting labyrinth of human form from which single faces appeared and then winked out as they passed through columns of light issuing from spots hanging high overhead.

Roger and I plunged in. We had seat assignments on one of the higher levels. The Real Mission, of course, was to reach the starred and jeweled stage pulsing at one end of the oval concert floor far below.

The warm-up band pounded out a massively loud rockabilly beat. Like mute, programmed

immediately became the bête noire of Spanish conservatism and one of its principal reasons for launching the civil war. Vallejo, writing in the middle of the war but already certain of victory, knew what lay in store for Catalonia. Because this region was tainted with the inferior ethics that had led to racial deterioration, it must not have any part in the political or even the professional leadership of the New Spain. Vallejo recommended closing the universities to children born outside Spain's traditional sources of privilege: the landed aristocracy and smaller landowners, the military establishment, the state's bureaucracy, and the liberal professions, each group intermingling with the others in a tight castelike social bubble. He warned that undertaking unsuitable university studies often led to physical harm in the form of tuberculosis and drug addiction. If such dire prospects did not deter the unfit, eugenics should have the last word, because professional failure and the onset of disease were not individual but racial matters (*PR*, 32).

Vallejo furnished the dictatorship with a pseudoscientific rationale. About democracy, he said that by catering to the base instincts, it granted social equality to the insane, the imbecile, and the degenerate. "Social imbecile" was one of the categories into which Vallejo classified the war prisoners that he studied; another was "mystical-political schizoid." He defined *social imbecile* as "that multitude of uneducated, awkward, suggestible beings, who lack spontaneity and initiative and contribute to the largest part of the gregarious mass of anonymous people."[47] Clearly recognizable in this group are those suggestible people whom Donato had manipulated on stage. Converted by the social psychologists into the leading trait of all temporary aggregations of individuals, heteronomy was later transformed by Ortega into the inherent condition of human beings who no longer moved in and out of a crowd but constituted the permanent category of the masses.

According to Vallejo, democracy, the political order that permits the self-regulation of the faceless, anonymous masses, upsets the natural social order and endangers the race. Hence, the right to vote must be derogated or at least restricted to the elite: "Universal suffrage has demoralized the masses, and since the latter are shot through with mental deficiency and psychopathy, the equivalence between the votes of select and undesirable individuals will cause the latter to predominate in the leading positions, with great damage to the future of the race" (*EH*, 129). The masses were not just rebellious, as Ortega contended, but pathological as well, and universal suffrage demoralized them by encouraging political equality. In a representative democracy, the mental feebleness of the masses transcended to the entire society and hurt the race. Vallejo obviously had in mind Ortega's naturalizing definition of "mass" rather than Le Bon's dissection of crowd psychology. For even though Ortega defined the "mass-person" qualitatively, as the condition of this or that individual, he clearly broke society down into two incommensurable groups: a vast majority of mass-people and a small minority of select individuals. Le Bon, on the contrary, dissociated the mental quality of individuals from that of the crowd, so that "From the moment that they form part of a crowd the learned man and the ignoramus are equally incapable of observation" (*C*, 42). Ortega was partial to liberal democracy, as it was understood in the nineteenth century; Vallejo considered democracy a mass phenomenon and the vote as its catalyst. By matching the "select" with the "undesirable," the vote produced the mental leveling that Le Bon had detected in the formation of crowds.

Vallejo identified democracy with "social crime," providing psychological endorsement for the death penalties of numerous persons whose vindication of democratic standards had violated racial law. In fact, he became the only military officer in charge of producing the scientific reports on the juridical responsibility of people sentenced to death by court-martial: "Social crime has its votaries, the same who have expelled the death penalty from the code of law. The select races have been able nonetheless to counter the antisocial democratic invasion in some fashion. Feebler races, like ours, are in grave danger of being swamped by the predominance of psychopathic social tendencies" (*EH*, 129–30). Vallejo was determined to expunge the influence of liberal medicine on legislation and jurisprudence. In 1890, Dr. Josep de Letamendi, a professor of medicine at the University of Barcelona, had criticized Cesare Lombroso's fashionable school of penal anthropology for naturalizing the species of the criminal and relying on the death penalty as a means of social selection.[48] Letamendi, who opposed the death penalty, invoked neuropathology to reduce the scope of imputation on the assumption that certain defendants suffered from a severe limitation of the will. Vallejo, on the contrary, went to great lengths to impute social marginality and physical degeneracy to a moral error. For the time after the war, he advocated an intense retaliatory climate, in which even those whom the courts declared innocent would permanently bear a social stigma.[49] His prognosis proved all too accurate, in part because of Vallejo's prestige in the new regime. His medical approach to political disaffection greatly influenced the corps of medical doctors who received posts in the penal institutions after the war and attended Vallejo's special workshop or his courses at the Escuela de Estudios Penitenciarios. His influence is apparent in Dr. Francisco Marco Merenciano, one of Vallejo's students, who took his teacher's identification of Marxism as a disease to its logical conclusion. Doctors, said Marco to an audience of high-ranking Falangist officials in 1942, could infer the existence of a Marxist complex from a

corpuscles, we pressed on through the concert body's ever-constricting arteries. The band acted as a pumping system, sending rushes of vibratory sound to speed us toward our One True Goal.

A guard stopped our progress at a waist-high corrugated wall that divided the risers from the concert floor. He asked to see our tickets. A discussion ensued.

During this exchange, the rockabilly band exited. The lights came up as the stage crew prepared for the next performer. Now we could hear the conversational hum of the crowd and see the littered concrete floor. It all seemed so ordinary. I registered my own disappointment as an arena-wide drop in energy. Roger and I slunk off, following the divider toward what we hoped would be some less well-guarded spot.

The lights dimmed again. The music kicked in. Roger and I held our position. I want to be able to tell you something about that set. I want to remember the songs or special moments. We loved Joe Cocker, but now, all I can recall is a single, frozen-in-time long shot of Cocker's spastic body jerking in the spotlight.

We were only thirteen. Perhaps that explains it. We thought the concert was finished when Cocker played his encore and left the stage. But shortly, after we'd noticed that no one else was leaving, another rockabilly, bluesy beat hit the house in its midsection. This time, I barely looked up. My only concern was to get to the stage. Just to get there. This was, after all, The Story of Ann Gets to the Stage.

I tugged Roger's arm and straddled the wall. A guard stuck his hand up my dress and caught a fistful of flesh. This didn't slow me down. Not at all. I landed on the concert floor and kept going, pushing through the dark, vibrating labyrinth.

A woman had been singing.

Nah na na na na na na.

My head stayed down in battle formation. As we got closer to the stage, thousands of bodies pressed forward. My robust adolescent self-absorption was short-circuited by the psychokinetic frenzy beginning to build up around me. Only two or three people separated us from the front stage bulwark. I could no longer move.

Now nuh now nuh now nuh now.

I lost all awareness of Roger. Instead of looking up at the stage, I turned to face the crowd. Shoulders strained against shoulders, faces against faces—a wall of faces angling for position in all directions. I flashed on one of my favorite photos from a book in my parents' library: Weegee's edge-to-edge image of a crush of girls at a Sinatra concert in New York in the 1940s. Most of the faces here were male, and they were saturated with desire.

I'd seen male desire and registered it as a fascinating-frightening state of inebriation. This was different. This was desire-amazement. Or desire-innocence. Or desire-trauma.

I couldn't describe it. I was overcome by surprise. The flaneur disarmed, all interpretive weapons deactivated.

I looked up at the screaming woman on stage.

Hear me when I cruh-ai-ai-ai!

She was sweating hard. As she belted out the song, her face crumbled like my childhood friend Katie O'Brien's face crumbled when her dad got drunk and yelled.

Her hair hung wild and long over her face. She doubled over the mike, her fist buried in the crease of her thigh. She was ugly, or so I thought. And

person's bearing, even if that person did not realize his or her Marxist condition: "it does not matter that many resentful individuals are unaware that they are authentic Marxists; it is enough that we know it in order for us to remedy that malady."[50]

The mere lack of enthusiasm for the new regime could be perceived and treated as a disorder. Vallejo had already shown that social failure and marginality were culpable forms of existence. Although, according to him, more than 50 percent of prostitutes were mentally retarded, they were so as a result of a wrong moral choice. Poverty, alcohol addiction, parental mistreatment, rape—none was a significant coadjutant in a woman's recourse to prostitution (*EH*, 133). Furthermore, woman's psychological makeup made her the mass subject par excellence. Women were more liable than men to lose self-control and engage in violent revolutionary action:

In order to understand the extremely active participation of the feminine sex in the Marxist revolution, it is enough to remember woman's characteristic psychic frailty, weak mental balance, inferior resistance to external influences, low control over the personality. . . . When the deterrents that restrain woman socially disappear and the inhibitions that impede her impulses are lifted, then the instinct for cruelty is aroused in the feminine sex and surpasses all the imaginable possibilities, because it lacks the intelligent and logical inhibitions.[51]

Despite his pretense of culling empirical evidence from his study of republican women prisoners, Vallejo was rehearsing inveterate prejudices of the reactionary mind. Since the turn of the century, mass psychologists had asserted that women were especially active in social upheavals. Gabriel Tarde alleged that crowds consisting of women were more depraved than crowds of men. Fortunately for women, their relative isolation in the privacy of the home kept their crime rate below that of the other sex. But their irrationality and psychological instability made them more dangerous; in fact, the crowd itself was like a woman, even if it consisted exclusively of men.[52] Down the road, the sexualization of the mass led to the appearance of mass-leaders who displayed an exaggerated manhood, overwriting the psychological force of "suggestion" with the vigor of erotic seduction. Thus, democracy, the regime of the masses, was tainted by feminine irrationality and its institutions afflicted with woman's most elusive and dangerous ailment. For Sighele, "considered from a psychological viewpoint," parliament was "a woman, often a hysterical woman."[53] Democracy, a sexualized regime, was crying out for a manly leader who would still its symptoms. And so, from the turn of the century to the 1920s and 1930s, the reaction clamored continuously for a man who would reduce the hysterical masses to passivity.

Vallejo's misogyny combined with his antimodernism to make women who left the privacy of the home responsible for the demographic decline, which he related to Spain's decadence: "We must blame modern woman's treason for part of the evils of depopulation. This modern woman given to sports, to drinking, to smoking, to literary or artistic fantasies, to card playing, to domestic film criticism, or to any kind of pleasure except rocking her children in the cradle" (*EH*, 72). He was not alone in the conservative medical establishment to relate racial well-being to fecundity. In 1932, Dr. Fernando Enríquez de Salamanca laid out the rationale for a high birthrate policy, which would be implemented after the war. Social, rather than genetic, selectivity would permit the controlled amelioration of the race, making it possible to jettison the unworthy and undesirable: "It is not desirable for the race to care solicitously for a few puny beings, but to have abundant offspring from which to choose, and improve what is defective through education, without insisting on preserving what does not deserve to be preserved."[54] Physicians like Enríquez de Salamanca and psychiatrists like Vallejo and Juan José López Ibor offered the "scientific" rationale for the Catholic-inspired ban on contraception, which produced an erotically puerile and sexually high-strung society for many decades. The goal of a state-regulated sexuality looms large in the following convoluted passage, where Vallejo uses the term *biological laws* as a code word for the state's intervention against any form of sexuality and gender relations that does not further reproduction: "From a racial point of view, sexual relations with individuals of the opposite sex must be regulated according to biological laws after the adult has reached sexual maturity" (*EH*, 131). The requirement of sexual normativity became more explicit in his later definition of citizenship in the new state: "The exemplary citizen of the New Spain will be married and prolific" (*PR*, 55).

Vallejo anticipated a totalitarian intervention in every nook and cranny of social and private life: "Aware of the influence of the environment on the genotype, the racial hygienist must act on the physical, psychic, economic, professional, pedagogical, cultural, political, moral, and religious environments: on the totality of the peristasic factors" (*EH*, 137–38). Clearly, such a program was too ambitious for the medical (or any other) profession. Carrying out this project required an authority able to assert its will down an extensive and pervasive chain of command. The racial hygienist could only act on each of those spheres if he were at the helm of a paternalistic state with a clear monopoly on agency. When every environmental factor was taken into account, only an empowered *caudillo* could be a racial hygienist in the full sense of the word. The obverse of this unique privilege was the

she was screaming. Real screaming. Real pain.

Each time I tell myself that I can't stand the pain, you hold me in your arms, and I'm singing once again!

I asked a guy next to me who the singer was. He told me a name I didn't recognize.

So won't you just come on . . . come on. . . .

I looked at her. I looked at the crowd. I didn't get it. A wild woman screaming. The faces of desire. But I felt it. It's what I remember most about that concert. The true pain and joy of that sound and the crazy, open intensity on the faces of boys.

Come on!

Come on!

Now, take it!

leader's duty to pursue a racial politics. Such a duty, Vallejo explained, was also a form of self-preservation, because the new totalitarian and imperialistic state (his words) would otherwise soon be ruined through racial degeneration (*PR*, 21).

From Le Bon, for whom "a civilization involves fixed rules, discipline" (*C*, 18) and Ortega, whose "imperative of selection" was marked by an incessant training (*RM*, 183), Vallejo drew the idea that only an exceptionally stern education guaranteed Ortega's "program of imperial life." In the fascist context of the 1930s, the soft civilian concept of the masses began to firm up into a regimented corps. In Spartan fashion, the new imperialistic state would abolish the distinction between military and civilian education. Teachers would be storm troopers of the race: "We must take military discipline to the schools. Students respect professors in military uniform more than they do those with top hats" (*RM*, 25). This program, reminiscent of the Nazi Napola (National Politische Lehranstalt), was all but realized through the replacement of career teachers with Falangists and fascist veterans in the public schools and with the austere conditions prevailing in orphanages and asylums. Racial politics demanded the persistence of the spirit of the war well into the peace, the prevalence and the precedence of the winners in the new society that they would forge with their racial qualities: "For many years the spirit of the front must vibrate in the social environment, a spirit of lofty sentiments, fraternity, and sacrifice. In peace time the war heroes, those select men forged in combat, must impregnate the social environment with the virtues that have shone in the vanguard during the war" (*PR*, 100). Those virtues were folded into a rigid hierarchy maintained with the iron discipline of a marching army.

The distinction between the select few and the masses found expression in the highly stratified state that issued from the organization of the war machine. Henceforth, and for a long time, the masses would be the collective of losers and the elite the avant-garde of imperial revivalism understood as an expression of a higher and dominant will. In the New Spain that issued from the civil war, the nostalgia for world domination found in crowd psychology a renewed justification. The undying dream of a Hispanic commonwealth that would regenerate Spain's world historical mission merged at this time with fear of the masses embodied in the World War II Allies and their disparate political systems. In turning away once more from the currents of thought that would reshape the world for the next fifty years, Spanish absolutism was haunted by memories of the turn of the century experiments in hypnosis and suggestion. Psychiatry, led by Dr. Vallejo Nágera, identified Spain's slow and hesitant modernization with its sinking into the condition of a mass country led away by a heteronomous will. He and his colleagues not only certified the origin of the disorder, but felt called upon to provide psychic defenses against environmental threats to the race: "Come the peace, the adequate psychic disposition to oppose to the encompassing Marxism, liberalism, and democracy will be the reconquest of the Hispanic empire" (*SR*, 7).

To Ortega's bleak vision of an empire of the masses, fascism opposed a Hispanic empire, the very project that Ortega thought most likely to capture the imagination of the Spanish masses and turn them into docile followers of their natural betters. The Hispanic doctrine thus became an alternative to the abhorred philosophical snares born of the Industrial Revolution, each, in its own way, proclaiming the triumph of the masses.

Gloomy grammarians in golden gowns. . . .
—WALLACE STEVENS, "OF THE MANNER OF
ADDRESSING CLOUDS"

11 Crowds, Number, and Mass in China

Haun Saussy

THE INTELLECTUAL PROBLEM OF THE crowd falls under the heading of mereology—the subdivision of ontology that deals with parts, wholes, and their relations.[1] Do crowds exist, or does the expression "crowd" merely transmit a value judgment (as in "two's company, but three's a crowd")? What is the mode of existence of a crowd? Is a crowd adequately accounted for as (and thus, *merely*) the sum of the individuals composing it? Or is it a collective subject acting in ways that transcend the intentions of any of its participants? Is it a collection of defective subjects, individuals whose power of choice has been hypnotized away, and thus the vast plaything of the one presumably whole individual who manipulates it? Is it a collection of individuals, each doing and seeing what the individual might do in any case, but whose total power is somehow more than the sum of its parts, a case of "emergent behavior"?[2] Determining what a crowd is has some of the complexity of another battlefield of reductionism, the definitional dispute surrounding reports of thought and reports of brain activity.[3]

Much of the high ground in these disputes is pretheoretical. Language allows us to take sides without being aware of so doing. A great deal can hang on an article, a capital letter, a comma. The difficulty can be captured in a sentence from Geoffrey Hartman's first book, *André Malraux*. In it he describes Malraux's last novel, *Les Noyers de l'Altenburg* (*The Walnut Trees of Altenburg*), as the surviving part of "a larger work destroyed by Nazis."[4] Not "destroyed by *the* Nazis," as a more conventional wording would have it—the *the* serving to singularize the twelve-year experience of National Socialist terror and war, to give Nazism the qualities of a proper noun (definiteness, public notoriety, collective personality). Rather, whether intentionally or by an inspired typographical error, Hartman's dropping the *the* reduced those Nazis to the condition of an anonymous swarm, a periodic chance event like locusts, dry rot, or flood, as if to say, "Destroyed by Nazis—one of those things that happens." Sheltered from explicit discussion, an article, a bit of punctuation, a pairing of verb and subject mark a collectivity (such as a crowd) as having this or that type of duration, consistency, agency, purpose.

These classic problems of crowd theory—ochlology?—fall in line with some of the classic positions in the study of Asia, for if Asia is home to a majority of the human race, the populousness of Asia has long been described as a mere plurality without individuality, a passive reservoir of labor power awaiting orders from an imperial throne—in short, a crowd of the "defective" kind, observed by individuals who see themselves as members of a purposive historical movement (Christianity, progress, the dialectics of freedom, and so on).[5] Montesquieu's, Herder's, and Hegel's understandings of Asia as the preindividual soup from which (and in contradistinction to which) European individuality arose resolve into a psychological application of mereology and an anticipation of later crowd studies.

The Chinese *Geist* . . . emerges from the same general principle, namely the immediate unity of substantial and individual spirit; and that is the spirit of Family, which extends over this most populous land. The moment of subjectivity, that is to say, the self-reflection of the individual will against substance (seen as the power oppressing it), or the positing of this power as the individual's own essence, in which it can recognize itself as free, is *not present*. The General Will acts immediately through the individual: the latter has *no* knowledge of itself as distinct from the substance. . . . Here in China, the General Will says directly what the individual must do, and the individual follows and obeys utterly *without* reflection or selfhood.[6]

When nineteenth-century sociologists announced the coming of an age of crowds, descriptions such as Hegel's are part of what made the prophecy so threatening. But these are merely outsiders' accounts of distant empires; the fact that those observers were unable to detect internal differentiation in the Asian crowd may only indicate the observers' lack of insight. What do crowds do, and how do crowds attain linguistic expression, in texts written by and for Asian observers? Where to begin the survey? What periods and what countries to consider? How to compensate for the situatedness of those reporters most likely to have left records that were passed down within Asian civilizations (officials, historians, moralists)? No comprehensive examination is going to be possible, only a roster of samples each as thin, but doubtless not as translucent, as a laboratory slide.

The Crowd as Medium

For almost as long as there has been writing in China, there have been statements about "the people" (*min*), or various types or groups of people (warring tribes, the loyal tillers, the king's army, prisoners of war), but there is little point in looking for a theory of crowd action there. These texts are preformed by attitudes about governance that fit the mass into the role of the recipient of royal attention, praise, hectoring, displeasure. With the rise of states based on intensive agricultural exploitation of limited territory, laborers become the focus of concern, for discontented populations could and did after all pick up and leave; so political advisors elaborated paternalistic, benevolent theories of the relation between the rulers and the ruled.[7] But the chronicles and polemics of the period of the Warring States (403–221 BCE) continue as well to show "the people" as standing army, as farming labor force, as numbered chattels to be transferred with their territory by inheritance or conquest. The first ruler formally to be called emperor (*huangdi*), the First Emperor of Qin (r. 221–209 BCE), conscripted vast numbers of convicts and corvée laborers to build his palaces and defensive walls, an exploitation without corresponding benefit that led to a series of rebellions during the reign of his ineffectual son, the Second Emperor. One hundred-odd years later, the court scribes and astrologers Sima Tan (d. 110 BCE) and Sima Qian (ca. 145–ca. 86 BCE), in their *Shiji* (*Records of the Grand Historians*), recounted the events leading to the fall of the Qin, laying blame on domineering rulers and power-hungry ministers for alienating the population: "The Second Emperor plotted with [his chief palace administrator] Zhao Gao, saying: 'I, the sovereign, am still young and have just ascended the throne, and the black-headed people [*qinshou*, the commoners] are not yet won over to me.'" Zhao Gao advises exterminating the hereditary nobles and chief ministers, so as to show the Second Emperor's uncontested mastery. Singled out for more detailed narration is the fate of one of the Second Emperor's sons, Prince Jianglü:

Jianglü looked up to the sky and called thrice on heaven, saying: "O Heaven! I am without guilt!" His three brothers, weeping, drew their swords and killed themselves.

The members of the imperial family were terror-struck. Those officials who had remonstrated with the emperor were considered to be slandering him. The great ministers, maintaining their salaries, adjusted their deportment. The black-headed people were terror-struck.[8]

Here the "black-headed people"—the commoners—are either a substance whose possession is a general condition of successful kingship or a member of a set of functional groups (royal house, officials, ministers, people) whose reactions monitor the effects of Zhao Gao's policy. They are acted upon rather than actors. When the actual rebellion occurs, responsibility devolves to named actors: "In the seventh month, Chen Sheng and others on their way to become garrison soldiers rebelled. . . . Chen Sheng enthroned himself as the king of Chu. . . . The youths in the local seats of government east of the mountains, having suffered under Qin's officials, all killed their governors, commandants, prefects and assistants, rising in revolt in response to Chen."[9] Thus in the *Shiji* the mass is defined—narratologically—not as an agent but as a medium or material on which agents act. Should some part of the mass take on the role of agent, it is necessary for it to be individuated, given a personality and a motive (as when Chen Sheng, rising, incites others to rise).

Some one hundred fifty years later, another court historian, Ban Gu (32–92 CE), writing the history of the Former Han dynasty—the dynasty under which Sima Tan and Sima Qian lived—tells the story of a rise to power in which active, vocal popular support is indispensable. Wang Mang, prime minister for a series of incapable or underage kings, was perhaps the first Chinese politician to muster up letter-writing campaigns in his own behalf. "The many common people, the Confucian masters, the Gentlemen, the lower officials, and those holding higher positions, who thereupon came to wait at the palace Portals to present letters to the grand Empress Dowager, numbered more than a thousand daily; some of the ministers and grandees went to the middle of the principal court and some prostrated themselves outside the doors of the Inner Apartments," all of them supporting Wang's daughter as the best choice for an imperial consort—a manipulation of public opinion that does not gain Wang Mang any points in the eyes of his later chronicler.[10] "In the fourth year [of Emperor Xiaowen], Mang's daughter was raised to the rank of empress. Throughout the empire, general amnesty [*tianxia da she*]."[11]

The verb (if it is a verb, because it could just as well be a noun) in the second sentence is impersonal and intransitive, even though masses of people (criminals and suspects) are receiving amnesty—a remoteness from detail befitting the lofty origin of the command. An analogous passage later in the same chapter reads, "In the spring of the third year, earthquake. Great amnesty throughout the empire."[12] To put it anachronistically, it is as if the imperial situation room contained a button marked "amnesty." Populations feel its effect as a condition—a state of general pardon suited to national rejoicing or mourning.

Somewhat later, for his services to the dynasty, Wang Mang is summoned to receive the bestowal of an estate, which he humbly declines.

At this time, because Wang Mang had not accepted the cultivated fields of Xinye, the officials and common people who sent letters to the Emperor, including previous and later times, numbered 487,572 persons. Moreover, the vassal kings, the highest ministers, the full marquises, and the members of the imperial house, when they had audiences, all kowtowed, saying that it would be proper immediately to give rewards to [Wang Mang].

At length, the Grand Empress Dowager's investiture, addressed to Wang Mang, includes the observation:

Verily, Duke, your achievements and virtuous conduct are the most brilliant in the empire. For this reason the vassal kings, the highest ministers, the full marquises, the members of the imperial house, the various masters, the lower officials and the common people were of one accord and said the same things. They continually waited at the gate towers and the great court, hence their writings were referred to the throne by the proper officials.[13]

This all sounds rather democratic, or at least responsive, in a way that we do not usually associate with the Chinese emperors. Wang Mang clearly was riding high in a popularity contest that presupposed two-way communications networks and literacy skills widely distributed across the immense Chinese empire. Half a million petitions is an impressive number, whatever the population and literacy figures for the time may have been. Although it manifests its will by sending in written memorials rather than by demonstrating in the streets, there is a crowd here, and an active one. But this by no means indicates that Ban Gu, the later-born historian, endorses Wang Mang or sees his popular mandate as a good thing. Nor will Wang Mang's amnesties, his exceptionally punctilious observance of the rituals and moral codes of the ancients, or his attempt to legislate into existence a Confucian utopia, benefit him in the eyes of history; quite the contrary. Ban, a legitimist to the core,

condemns Wang Mang for putting the reigning Liu family of the Han dynasty in the shade and manipulating public opinion through his various good deeds. From a legitimist point of view, to gratify the crowd is necessarily to corrupt it, unless you are the person entitled to act as "father and mother of the people." And it is made to seem inevitable when, in 9 CE, Wang Mang eventually puts aside his title of regent and takes the throne for himself. An activist crowd is a sign of something gone badly wrong.

These examples and the analysis given them, it may be said, tell us nothing about crowds but only about perspectives, about techniques for writing about crowds; the crowds themselves, what they do and what they want, barely emerge from the shadows. Fair enough: the question of crowds is inseparable from questions of representability.[14] Media such as written language cannot express the crowd directly, but only fashion devices for showing it. Those devices in turn are constrained by factors that stand at a remove from the crowd itself (they might include grammatical features, ideological options, and considerations of audience). Crowds *as represented* in early Chinese historical texts can be as passive, inert, and thoughtless as you like, but this should be taken as a fact about the aims, audience, limitations, and capabilities of the representers (in this case, dynastically sponsored historians) rather than as necessarily expressing properties of the early Chinese crowd itself. These ochlologies, or crowd theories, express a mixture of wishfulness and blindness proper to a point of view that it is the design of official history to make any possible reader adopt.

"Governing the Crowd" Through Fiction

Although two-way pagers, instant messaging, and cell phones may create a twenty-first-century category of "smart mobs," no mob worthy of the name has ever been entirely "dumb"—if by "dumb" we mean lacking direction, self-awareness, and collective purpose.[15] (The volatility of those purposes, not their absence, is what worries crowd theorists from Gustave Le Bon forward.) A crowd knows itself as a crowd: every member receives feedback from shouts, jostling, gestures, smells, and every other ingredient of the *bain de multitude*. Even an imaginary crowd that "meets" only in the delivery of basketsful of correspondence, like the supporters of Wang Mang, has to have some means of mutual awareness. New media mean new channels for such awareness. With the spread of literacy and cheap printing, "the crowd," says Walter Benjamin, "became a customer; it wished to find itself portrayed in the contemporary novel, as the patrons did in the paintings of the Middle Ages."[16] It is an open question whether the crowd motif belongs to the history of culture or to the history of communications technology.

Nor is the relation between technology (here, distribution mechanism) and content an empty or random one. At the latter end of the long career of the Chinese empire (221 BCE–1911 CE), a genre that had grown out of the cracks in the edifice of official historical writing, *xiaoshuo* (fiction) took on special importance because it was thought to be *faster* than other, more hallowed or profound kinds of writing. "There is nothing equal to fiction for moving people's hearts and minds and causing them to change their ways," wrote the missionary and publisher John Fryer in an advertisement soliciting new novels that would dramatize the need for social change. "With its *wide and rapid* circulation, fiction can, *within a short period of time, become known to one and all*, making it possible without difficulty to reform current practices."[17] Unlike the elite genres of poetry, discursive essays, and history, the fiction supplements in the newspapers could be followed by people whose repertoire of characters was small, or even enjoyed when read aloud. "To renew the people of a nation," Liang Qichao said in

allusion to the opening passage of the Confucian classical work *The Great Learning*, "one must necessarily begin by renewing that nation's fiction." Fiction took people to a different world; made them adopt the point of view of people different from themselves; directed them to observe the consequences of right and wrong choices. People took their emotions, desires, and beliefs from the fiction they read, as Liang put it in his 1902 essay "On the Relation of Fiction and the Governance of the Masses." They became the very people they read about.[18]

How did the Chinese develop the idea of holding scholars successful in the official examinations and prime ministers in such high esteem? It stems from fiction. What is the origin of the Chinese obsession with beautiful ladies and talented scholars? It lies in fiction. Where does the Chinese sympathy for robbers and brigands hidden away in the river and lake areas spring from? It springs from fiction. . . . . Alas! Fiction has entrapped and drowned the masses to such a deplorable extent! The thousands of words of the great sages and philosophers fail to instruct the masses. But one or two books by frivolous scholars and marketplace merchants are more than enough to destroy our entire society. . . . As the nature and position of fiction are comparable to the air and food indispensable to life, frivolous scholars and marketplace merchants in fact possess the power to control the entire nation.[19]

Hence a strong link existed between fiction and mass action. It was time, said Liang, for scholars and social reformers to embrace this heretofore unprized genre and begin addressing people unlike themselves—to write for the crowd. By putting good models before the people, novelists could incite imitation and "renewal." Fryer's remarks suggest the technological preconditions of this transformed genre: the steam-driven press made it possible to put thousands of copies of a new work, within hours, in the hands of a newly urbanized and often newly literate public. Unlike previous narrative genres, which had circulated in recitation, manuscript, and woodblock-printed books, the new Chinese fiction of the late nineteenth century sought its audience through serialization in daily newspapers. The line between journalism and fiction was narrow. Wu Jianren's bildungs-roman, *Ershinian mudu zhi guai xianzhuang* (Strange things eyewitnessed during the past twenty years), serialized in 1903–1910, gave the central role to a naive young man finding his way in the world and thus familiarized the reader step by step with the new era of steamships, compradors, and treaty ports.

I said: "So the secret passwords they use, what are they like? Could you. . . . " I hadn't finished my sentence when suddenly we heard an enormous boom as if the sky had fallen, followed by a roar that made the windowpanes rattle in their frames and the teacups and chopsticks dance on the table. We all jumped. . . . That noise was soon forgotten, for just then a stampede of people in the street gave me a big shock. Shunong stood up and said: "Let's go have a look!" As he spoke, he dragged me out the door, and walking up the street said: "Today they're having torpedo practice. I hear they're going to shoot off three of them. Hurry up, we may be in time to see them go." Then I understood. You see, the war between China and France was still going on. A few days before, we'd had news of the loss of Taiwan. The French had landed at Keelung. In the Jiangnan Arsenal, they were especially tense, so the commander was making a show of zeal and had ordered them to do torpedo practice, and it was set for tonight. When Shunong and I got to the riverbank, night had fallen and the rain was just clearing. A bright moon had risen in the east, and the beams rippled in the waves in the river like ten thousand golden snakes. If you'd had a few drinks, and came upon this view, it would give you a feeling of delight. But unfortunately a lot of people had turned out to watch the torpedo practice. Although the place wasn't exactly packed, we were definitely standing in a crowd. Suddenly we heard a loud boom, followed by four echoes, and the water went up like a wall for about eight hundred feet. The hiss of the billows gave way to a crash like a wind-flattened pine. And as the echoes among the mountains and valleys hadn't died out, the two kinds of sound met and collided. The people standing there let out a gasp of surprise. Never in my whole life had my ears heard a sound like that! And then they

shot off another. Although it wasn't exactly "divine rapture and soul's bliss," it was sure enough a novelty for the eyes and ears. When it was over, Shunong and I went back, rinsed the cups and had another drink.[20]

Wu Jianren's narrator, a curious urban spectator like the rest of the crowd standing on the riverbank, is drawn by the marvels of new technology: explosions that stir them to a shared gasp of astonishment. The description of this event in serial form communicates it yet more widely, makes it an experience that thousands of readers will henceforth have in common—no small part of the attraction of this genre of eyewitness fiction. A "news culture" coalescing around the themes of urbanism, technology, and spectatorship, and often involving crowd activities, is one of the durable inventions of the generation of 1900, continuing to dominate popular writing (although not its "serious," more politicized counterpart) throughout the Chinese twentieth century.[21]

Crowds also fill the frame of another novel often read in eyewitness mode, Li Boyuan's *Wenming xiaoshi* (A brief history of modern times; 1903–1905).

The military cadets who were camped in the village waiting to be examined on their martial skills were a bunch of idle lads easily led astray, the kind of young people who like to get into scrapes, and moreover the Miao tribesmen and the Han among them were constantly accusing each other of one thing and another. If they encountered an intelligent local official who knew how to calm them down, everything was all right, but if he did anything, major or minor, to annoy them, they would forever after be picking at the faults of the officer in question and treat him with no regard at all. The man in this town, Prefect Liu, was known to advocate the New Learning and made much of diplomacy; he was a valuable, solid official. But because he tried too hard to be conciliatory toward the foreigners, and now he had arbitrarily put off the military exercises, so that the cadets were unable to go home, they naturally felt they had been treated unfairly. And the cadets, now that they were all staying in one place, began to collect in groups of three or five and visit teahouses and wine shops, spreading rumors and causing trouble. Nothing serious, just a bit of trouble for the hell of it and to see what would happen.

That day, ten or so of them were in a teahouse drinking tea, and suddenly one of their fellow cadets came in shouting, "This is too much!" He looked so beside himself that they all stood up and asked him what was the matter. He told them: "I was just hanging around the courthouse, and I saw them come out and start sticking bills on the wall, and a lot of people gathering to watch. One old fellow who knew how to read told everybody, this Mr. Liu who's been posted here is going to sell all the mountains in the prefecture to some foreigners for a mine. Now think about it. Which of us doesn't live up in the mountains? And if he's going to sell them to the foreigners, so that we don't have a place to put our head, isn't it just too much?" He hadn't finished speaking when another cadet came running in and told the same story. In a moment three or four others arrived, each bearing the same tale. By now there were two hundred or more people shouting in that place, some of them saying, "My house is in the mountains, and they're going to pull my house down!" Another said, "I have a field in the mountains, they're going to take it away from me!" Another said, "My ancestors have been buried up in the mountains for hundreds of years, am I going to have to dig them all up, break into the coffins, collect the bones and move them somewhere else?" And another said: "I don't live in the mountains, but I'm in the valley at the mountain's foot, and my front gate looks right out at the mountains. If they start digging and moving earth, and leave it all lopsided, won't that ruin my good fengshui? We've got to find a way to stop them!" And there were some who said, "Let's go tear down the courthouse and beat those pestilent officials to death. Then we'll see if they still want to sell our land to some foreigners! Since we're not going to get to take our examination, let's just go all out and make an end of it this way!" So what with people yelling back and forth and arguing with each other, the place was boiling over. More and more people were stopping on the street to see what was going on. At first it was mostly examination candidates, but then people who had nothing to do with the examination got drawn in. Just as the noise was at its height, in came the very worst, the most deplorable de-

gree-holder in the town. Breaking through the crowd he came running into the teahouse, asking what it was all about. Everyone instantly began to explain: it was like this, no, it was like this, this way, that way, until the story was told. This degree-holder had done nothing his whole life long but peddle gossip and present accusations, trying to influence this or that official; he would stoop to anything, and his reputation was foul. When he had heard the story, he saw an opportunity for himself to shine, and said, "Incredible! This pestilent official doesn't give a damn about anybody. He thinks he can get away with selling off the mountain lands of our dear Yongshun Township and exterminating the good townspeople of Yongshun. So grave a matter deserves to be discussed in a more suitable forum than this teahouse. Let's all adjourn to the Temple of Harmonious Relations and work out a plan there. So why are we standing around here?" As soon as he had put the idea in the people's heads, off they went with a shout, at least a thousand strong by now. The teahouse owners were left holding the unpaid bills for the tea, not to mention a great number of tea bowls that had been broken. Vexed but with no one to blame, they could only glare at the people as they marched away; lucky enough that they hadn't burst the building, was there any point in complaining?[22]

Li Boyuan's description traces the mob's emergence from a set of prior conditions: restless young men forced to stop in a strange place; resentment at the official who has delayed them there; hatred and mistrust of the foreigners who are "snatching away" China; a rumor that crystallizes all these grievances; and a would-be leader who seizes the moment. The anonymous faces in the crowd all have their own motives for joining the march, and the very expression of their motives recruits new members who see themselves as similarly situated. The vortex continues beyond the page, for the crowd's worries about their mountain territory would have easily mapped onto the likely anxieties of Li's readership, who read the international news in the same paper that printed his novel. Even though the next chapter shows the foreigners to be less threatening than suspected (in the event, they are just a party of geologists invited by the provincial government to prospect for resources), Li's staging of the crowd presents as if in a mirror-lined case the argument for fiction as a miniature version of Chinese society, a magic doll on which operations could be performed that would transfer to the body it represented. Depictions of the crowd supplied a conducting medium for that transferential energy.

Chinese history from 1900 onward has been, if any era deserved the name, an Age of Crowds, punctuated by explosions of crowd energy: the Boxer Rebellion (about which Li Boyuan wrote a narrative ballad, *Gengzi guobian tanci*), the May Fourth demonstrations, the Shanghai strikes of 1927, the flow of refugees this way and that during the war with Japan (1937–1945), the civil war of 1945–1949, the Hundred Flowers movement (1957), the Tian'anmen demonstrations of 1976 and 1989—not forgetting the Cultural Revolution (1966–1976), the only one of these defining events to be channeled, not merely recorded, by mass media productions.

The Calligraphic Crowd

Sima Qian, Ban Gu, Wu Jianren, Li Boyuan—each has his techniques for constructing images of the crowd in action, and each technique expresses a theory of what a crowd is and can do. Technique is a momentary application of a tacit grammar. *Grammar* may seem an overspecific term. Certainly it is tautological to say that in narration, an actor can act only as the grammar of the sentences describing him permits him to act because narratives are made up of sentences, and these must necessarily render events through such values as active or passive, singular or plural, nominative or accusative (or whatever semantic alternatives are available in the language at issue). Techniques are specific: they have histories, they develop, they are constrained by properties of a medium (in this case, the resources of the Chinese literary language over a two-hundred-year period).

Figure 11.1 "Use The 'Yan'an Talks' as a Weapon to Thoroughly Destroy the Black Line of Counterrevolutionary Literary Revisionism." All images in this chapter are used by courtesy of the Hoover Institution, Stanford University.

Figure 11.2 "Raising the Great Red Flag of Mao Zedong Thought, Complete the Proletarian Cultural Revolution."

Figure 11.3 "The Sunlight of Mao Zedong Thought Lights the Road of Proletarian Cultural Revolution."

Figure 11.4 "Long Life to the Victory of the Great January Revolution!"

So to approach the problem of technique and content in a more general way, perhaps it will be appropriate to examine the ways in which crowds come into being in a nonverbal medium: visual art.

Like advertising, propaganda art occupies a place between two points of view, two technical projections of the crowd or mass: the point of view of the mass that is purportedly expressing itself through propaganda, and that of the mass that is the audience for propaganda. A perfect circuit is established if only the receiver will recognize his or her desires as having been expressed, or anticipated, in the artwork: the proper response is "Yes!" Since Freud's *Group Psychology and the Analysis of the Ego* (1921), we have learned to recognize in the heroes and leaders of the mass age figures of the "ego-Ideal," vastly enlarged representations of the (for Freud) fathers who speak in us with the voice of authority. If the audience, viewing a perfect piece of political art, gives its assent, then the two implicit points of view

Figure 11.5 "May the Closeness of the People and the Army Lead to New Accomplishments in the Midst of Great Revolutionary Critiques!"

各国反动派也就是这样的一批蠢人。他们对于革命人民所作的种种迫害，归根结底，只能促进人民的更广泛更剧烈的革命。

毛泽东

毛主席语录
下定决心，
不怕牺牲，
排除万难，
去争取胜利。

港九爱国同胞动员起来，坚决反击英帝国主义的挑衅！

Figure 11.6 "Loyal Compatriots of Hongkong and Kowloon, Resolutely Fight Back the Challenge of British Imperialism!"

collapse into one, confirming the unity of the ego and its ego-ideal. This mirroring function (achieved at the expense of whatever does not match in the confrontation of the two self-projections) might account for the art-historical course of agitprop in the twentieth century, studded with departures from mimetic canons of representation (as in constructivism or epic theater), but always returning to them as the social order for which the art claim to speak consolidates itself. Jean-Jacques Rousseau imagined that theater would be superseded in a perfect polity as the people lost interest in fantasies and unreal projections and instead took its joy in sitting down together in a common space and looking at itself.[23] How does the crowd recognize itself in representations of the crowd proposed to the crowd?

Chinese propaganda posters solve this problem in various ways. There are pictures of archetypal crowds—recognizable as such because none of the faces is the face of anyone in particular—performing the actions the audience-crowd is exhorted to emulate (figs. 11.1 and 11.2). There are the images in which the people as a whole is represented to itself through anonymous, but recognizable, "functional constituencies": the groups of distinctively attired ethnic figures (fig. 11.3), or the professional groups each in the costume appropriate to its work (for example, soldiers, sailors, airmen, farmers, scientists) (fig. 11.4). As variants of personification allegory, these images also designate (from within) the limits of their genre, as when the anonymous figures show up to welcome Chairman Mao—the individ-

Crowds, Number, and Mass in China   **261**

11A 'Zhong': Chinese

Ka-Fai Yau

Whether as a part of many other compounds (*heti zi*) designating "crowd" or as a monosyllabic simple word (*duti zi*), the Chinese word *zhong* illuminates an abyss of meaning in the Chinese language. From its ancient form to its modern, simplified form used in mainland China, *zhong* (fig. 11A.1) is basically formed by combining three *ren* words (fig. 11A.2); each of these is a pictograph visualizing apparently a person, and symbolically a human being in general.

Figure 11A.1 Simplified form of *zhong*.

Figure 11A.2 Various scripts of *ren*.

Xu Shen (AD 30–124) categorizes the word *zhong* as *huiyi*—that is, a combination of different meaning elements to make a new meaning. One could argue that seeing three persons together symbolically is in effect a pictographic representation of a crowd. It is the gaps and clashes among, as well as combinations of, these three persons

我们伟大的导师、伟大的领袖、伟大的统帅、伟大的舵手毛主席检阅文化革命大军

Figure 11.7 "Our Great Commander, Great Leader, Great Ruler, Great Helmsman Mao Zedong Reviewing the Cultural Revolution Great Army."

ual, not as representative of the "Han nationality" or the "Hunanese." A group of such nameless universal representatives frequently battles—in the name of all good Chinese—the contorted, insectlike individuals who have fallen from grace and must be expunged (figs. 11.5 and 11.6). Thus, for human images, three possibilities are designated: exalted individuality (the status of the leaders), exalted generality (the personifications), and debased individuality (the criminals). The crowd audience must see itself in the middle position, as participating in the images of exalted generality.

Another subject position and solution to the problem of recognition is provided by perspective. The Chairman (in foreground) waves from the reviewing stand to a million or so fellow Chinese (the background) massed in Tiananmen Square; unless the viewer happens to be the Chairman, he will recognize himself as a particle in the cheering throng (fig. 11.7). (The recognition is helped along by the title of the picture, which hails the leader in the crowd's own immense voice.)

你们要关心国家大事·要把无产阶级文化大革命进行到底！

毛泽东

Figure 11.8 "We Will Take Affairs of State Into Our Own Hands and Carry the Great Proletarian Cultural Revolution to its Conclusion," detail.

When the crowd's image is generated not by photography but by human hands, the stakes of representation change somewhat. How is a painter to designate the vast multiplicity of a crowd of people? The degree of detail achievable by silver nitrate film and optical lenses is beyond a painter's capacity; some choices have to be made. And so the people in the crowd will be reduced to abbreviated calligraphic strokes (a circle for the head and a flourish for the body, repeated as required) or a colorful blur, their holiday mood expressed through a few high-riding balloons or flags (figs. 11.8 and 11.9). Or some faces will be hastily sketched on a loosely delineated ground of marching bodies (fig. 11.10). The devices indicate a hierarchy of relevance, for the large personages in the foreground benefit from much more artistic work. The public's attention is directed thereby to focus on the giant figures who matter, and to skim over the dabbled walk-ons in the background—interchangeable as individuals, indispensable as a mass. The degree of "impressionism" the painters bring to the rendering of the crowd indicates varying effects of solidarity and anonymity, as the citizens melt, or are imagined as melting, into one substance (fig. 11.11). From this substance can be molded the ultimate "mass ornament," a new Great Wall to resist foreign invasion (fig. 11.12).

that form *zhong*'s pictographic and semantic dimensions.

But why three? The *Discourses of the States* (*Guoyu*) explains that "three persons make a crowd" (*A Concordance of the Guoyu*, 2). But why not two or four, or even more? In some Buddhist classics, *zhong* is defined as more than four, up to hundreds, thousands, and infinity (*Tiantai guan jing shu*), more than four up to twelve thousand (*Fa hua yi shu*), as well as simply more than three (*Fa hua xuan zan*). But the number three does have special implications in Chinese culture, as in many other cultures. In *Lao zi*, three is the path to everything. *Shuowen jiezi* explains that three is "the way of the sky, the ground, and the human" (Xu, 15). At the same time, other classical characters composed of *ren* parts have meanings unrelated to crowd formations: *yu* 猋, "to predict" or "to prepare," and *dao* 猋, "to steal" or "to rob."

In pre-Qin (pre-221 BC) historical, literary, ritual, and philosophical works, such as *The Book of Songs*, *The Analects*, and *The Book of Rites*, *zhong*, meaning "plenty" and "many," appears in connection with people already.

Apart from its connection with people, *zhong* can also be used in relation to animals and things. In "The Sorting Which Evens Things Out" (*Qi wu lun*) in *Zhuangzi*, *zhong* can also be an adjective for monkeys (if they are not simply regarded as ancestors of human beings) (54). Regarding things, *zhong* designates just "many things," as in *The Book of Rites*'s "*Zhongni yanju*," in which social order and disorder are connected to "the motions of all things [*zhong*]" (*A Concordance of the Li ji*, 137, translation mine).

Later, in Chinese Buddhist terms, *zhong* refers to both Buddhist believers and human beings in general. In *Chapters of the Mahayana Doctrines* (*Dacheng yi zhang*), the *zhong*, meaning "many" or "everyone," becomes a constituent in *he he zhong,* a term designating a Buddhist monk. *Ci yuan* considers that the term *dazhong* derives from this use (2215). *Zhong* lingers between ordinary people in general and certain (kinds of) people in particular.

In his critiques of the Chinese national character, the modern writer Lu Xun (AD 1881–1936) twists *zhong*'s reference to people in general in a national context when China was encountering western challenges, modernity and modernization. In his short story title "*Shizhong*" (Lu Xun, 291–96), the word *zhong* corresponds to the English word *crowd*, meaning "a mass of spectators," "an audience," and "a collection of actors playing the part of a crowd" (*Oxford English Dictionary*). The story, alluding to a Chinese crowd apathetically standing around a man accused by the Japanese of spying for the Russians during the Russo-Japanese War, focuses on the spectators and sketches out the way passersby rudely and curiously look for better positions to view the spectacle, of which they know little. The title of the story, "*Shizhong*," has a twofold meaning: it denotes both "showing things to the crowd" (like in the saying *"zhan shou 'shi' 'zhong'"* [cutting the head off and showing it to the public/crowd]) and "revealing the crowd as spectacle" (*zhan "shi" qun "zhong"* [showing the crowd]).

Such an affinity between revelation and the crowd in the compound *shizhong* is telling. Like the crowd seeing things revealed and the crowd being revealed, the mentioned abysses of meaning also reveal, and get revealed.[1]

Figure 11.9 "Closely Follow Mao Zedong's Great Strategic Directions; With Unity and Bravery Advance!" Detail.

Techniques, then, and yet they have nontechnical implications: to say that a representation is generated by such-and-such a technique, and say no more, leaves out of consideration the impact or effects of that technique on an audience. Propaganda painting is a genre that leaves little to chance: styles, content, motifs are determined by ideological necessity, vetted by committees, discarded after policy shifts. Over hundreds of examples, a grammar of possibilities and mutual implications emerges, parallel to the grammar that relegated crowd movements and individual actions to different types of function in the early court historians. It is chiefly a grammar of desires about the crowd, an attempt to present the masses with an image of their capacities for historical action that will answer a political, narrative need. From the outside, and compared with the contemporary upheavals in Europe and North America, the Cultural Revolution seems a weirdly obedient youth movement: those vast crowds of teenagers turning out to declare their

(text continues on p. 268)

毛泽东选集

要特别警惕象赫鲁晓夫那样的个人野心家和阴谋家，防止这样的坏人篡夺党和国家的各级领导。

毛泽东

向党内头号走资本主义道路当权派猛烈开火！

Figure 11.10 "Violently Open Fire on the Top Party Faction That is Taking the Capitalist Road!" Detail.

11B   Crowd Control

David Theo Goldberg

Crowds promote a sense of identification and belonging, prompting possibilities of action individual inhibition might prohibit. But they might equally give rise to fear and loathing, avoidance and flight. The surge of a crowd can exhilarate, but it can also threaten. The crowd at a large sporting event or political rally suggests support for a team or cause, energizing action; but it can also spiral out of hand, fueling violence, calling forth surveillance and indeed crowd control. A group in fusion, to use the Sartrean formulation, can grow quickly into a crowd, an internally coherent collective with at least a finite and more or less well-defined purpose; but it can also be established from without, its boundaries imposed for the purposes of oversight and order. The former logic is well known by anyone who has witnessed fanfare at a sporting event or concert, or suffered through a convention; a recent experience while traveling will serve to exemplify the latter more clearly.

Israel seems to have perfected the security apparatus of almost absolute surveillance predicated on what we might usefully call controlling the chaos of, or in, a crowd. The point is to promote panic among a population or crowd of people, at once observing—gaining insight into—the reactions of members of the multitude. Random attacks in public places, invasions, unannounced searches, bombs apparently missing targets, purposeful collateral damage in public places: all this always visited on those assumed to be ethnoracially distinct,

伟大的一月革命胜利万岁！

革命的"三结合"是

Figure 11.11
Enlargement of
Figure 11.4.

as already possibly suspect, exhibiting habits, behavioral dispositions, and cultural expressions deemed peculiar. The point of creating controlled chaos in crowded places is to force those present to resort to "natural instinct," to flush out those trying for what is considered terrorizing purposes to blend in by making manifest their cultural habits, their hidden difference, uncovering their hidden agenda. Crowd control becomes a matter of checking out reactions to the randomization of reaction in the face of dramatically unpredictable possibilities.

On a recent visit to Israel we had an impossibly early morning flight that required a 3:00 am airport check-in. If driving across darkened highways, the twinkling lights of Tel Aviv off to the side, conjured the alienation of Godard's *Alphaville,* arriving at the airport was more like *City of Lost Children.* We expected relative sleepiness at the airport, but instead, we were shocked to find ourselves in a terminal busier than any airport worldwide at the height of rush hour. Pressed between seven or eight layers of formal security passage from the entrance to the airport until one boarded the flight were irregular lines of people pushing and pulling, stress-making uncertainties about what line one was in or what the line was for, where one was headed, or how long it would take. Sleepiness and solitude quickly gave way to a sense of sleep deprivation and acute anxiety. Panic displaced the confidence of seasoned travelers. The ticking of time passing grew louder as the looming possibility of missed flights approached.

Watching over all of this seemingly random chaos were further layers of all-seeing eyes, some mingling easily in the crowd, others overhead, picking out panic, distinguishing difference amidst sleep-deprived activity: a too-quick movement, furtive looks, sweat on the brow, foam at the corners of the mouth, too obvious attempts to blend in, a mixed couple traveling under different names and on different national passports signaling different places of origin—the civic equivalent, one might say, of carpet-bombing Baghdad. Insecurity manifest through unnerving norms. Security predicated on acute insecurity, the heat of a familiar crowd edging to the margins the heat of one made unfamiliar, *unheimlich,* uncanny. Belonging, longing to be—in this case part of something—is always predicated on a distinguishing absence, on the constitutive outside(r).

Street savviness takes over, the product of intuitions minted on the anvil of years of air travel but also of antiapartheid street protests wending their way between "Casspirs Full of Love," as William Kentridge so aptly characterizes apartheid's armored vehicles, and Central Park summer pop concerts featuring the likes of Diana Ross. Surging crowds constituted through exploding tear gas canisters and flying dum dums, snatched jewelry, and jockeying for prime position across the span of decades. The political surge of 1970s crowds, the pop of 1980s public culture, the privatizing docility of 1990s libertarianism give way to born-again paranoias of strangers at the gate, of conjured crowds breaking down the boundaries of Babylon, their members careening into buildings, exploding dreams along with bodies. That fraternal crowd, the one of supposed support across otherwise anonymous and fragmented folks—the Harley rally, the hundred or so scooters on an Amsterdam Sunday street outside my window, their collective fumes and furious motorized humdrum invading my thoughts as I write this, the parade

Figure 11.12 "A Truly Great Wall."

(continued from p. 264)

loyalty to the septuagenarian leader and his latest "revolutionary line," searching out, humiliating, and sometimes killing suspected "class enemies," unquestioningly attentive to direction from the top—a revolution that appears to confirm its painted image. But personal narrations from those years tell more familiar stories of opportunism, idealism, suspicion, betrayal, and the rest. Perhaps the crowd was only pretending to be a crowd?

These examples—merely a few of the shapes that crowds have taken in the cultural vocabulary of China—bear on the nominalist question of whether crowds exist apart from their being perceived as crowds (or from the simultaneous self-awareness of every member of a crowd). Herbert Spencer once called language the sensorium of the species, reworking Newton's suggestion that space was the sensorium of God. Here we see language discovering new objects, making old objects newly speakable. The means of describing crowds keep pace with communicative techniques that address readers as observers of crowds, address individuals as members of crowds, even address crowds as such.

Devices like those discussed here are found in every nation. What is specific and historical about these examples is the interaction, each time, of semantic categories and a social order through technologies of representation. Could Sima Qian have recognized a crowd in our sense of the word—that is, recognized it as a body able to do the things we think of crowds as doing? Did Cultural Revolution propaganda posters persuade their viewers of the glory and grandeur of becoming granules in the stream of revolutionary action, or was their hyperbole always obvious? The nominalism that would make *crowd* a mere designation in the mind links with the verbal magic that "does things with words," for to describe a crowd is, in a more than phantasmatic way, to summon it.

of this or that group for this or that cause, or for sheer entertainment or whiling away an otherwise lonesome weekend—harboring, even occasionally cultivating, the seeds of something more insidious, more threatening because less thoughtful, unself-conscious, uncritical.

A sense of safety gives way to the defensive society, to states of security. The surge of the protesting crowd is considered now an internal threat, an unpatriotic act akin to, if not in cahoots with, the foreign terrorist. Crowd control secures not just behavior but beliefs too.

> The crowd is usually wrong.
> —HUMPHREY NEILL,
> *Tape Reading and Market Tactics*

> The bigger the crowd, the better the performance.
> —INSTINET.COM,
> AN ONLINE BROKERAGE

12 Market Crowds

Urs Stäheli

IN 1967, THE POPULAR FINANCIAL journalist and former portfolio manager George Goodman (alias "Adam Smith") asked, "Is the market really a crowd?" And without hesitation, he suggested a crowd psychology of financial markets: "*The market is a crowd,* and if you've read Gustave Le Bon's *The Crowd* (1895) you know a crowd is a composite personality."[1] In his best-seller *The Money Game,* Goodman refers to crowd psychology as the primary tool for grasping the market—moreover, he does not simply aim at a polemical description of the market, but he also suggests a practical guide for succeeding in the market. "Adam Smith" is no exception, with his suggestion that financial markets may best be described and analyzed with the tools of crowd psychology. Excerpts from Le Bon on crowd psychology are often reprinted in anthologies of investment theory;[2] and in 2002, Robert Menschel, senior director of Goldman & Sachs, published a whole reader on the crowd and the market with the title *Markets, Mobs, and Mayhem,* also including reprints of Le Bon and other crowd theorists.[3] Additionally, a whole subdiscipline within economics has emerged that calls itself "behavioral economics"[4] and that also refers to Le Bon as one of its founding fathers. While Le Bon has been expelled from other social sciences, such as sociology or political science, we can observe a resurrection of crowd psychology within investment theory and finance guidebooks.[5]

This is even more amazing because financial markets are often also seen as one of the most rational and efficient features of modern society. In 1931, Richard Whitney, the former director of the New York Stock Exchange, who was later imprisoned for financial fraud, praised the stock exchange as an "efficient institution."[6] It is the stock exchange where the great economic fiction of the *homo oeconomicus* finds its ideal stage: the stock market promises nearly complete price information and a minimum of transaction costs. Thus, the preconditions for establishing an autonomous and rational economic individuality seem to be met perfectly. How, then, does this paradigmatic realm of economic individuality turn into the nightmare of the crowd market? What makes the semantics of the crowd so attractive for describing financial markets?

At first sight, discourses on the crowd and those on financial markets seem to be quite distinctive, bearing few parallels or points of connection. At the turn of the century, crowd psychology tried to come to grips with the dark underside of modernity, exemplified by lynch mobs, mass crimes, and masses deluded by demagogic political leaders and the irrationality of crowd behavior. It was in this context that crowd psychology tried to account for that which was related to, but not in accordance with, the optimistic ideals of modern western societies: rational individuals turn into blind and passionate elements of a crowd, democracy is not ruled by enlightened citizens, but dominated by the cruel "demon of the demos."[7] In short, the diagnosis seems to be clear: rationality is superseded by irrationality, endangering the project of modernity.

Crowd semantics was introduced as a discursive means for diagnosing and dealing with this crisis of modernity. Le Bon exclaimed that with the advent of the twentieth century, the "era of the crowd" has begun.[8] The crowd becomes a typically modern phenomenon, and not only because it emerges at places and institutions that are representative for modernity, such as the city. It also suggests a critique of modernity by showing what happens when the ideals of modern society—universality and equality—are radicalized and, from the perspective of the crowd psychologist, unduly overstretched. Now modern universalism, best exemplified with common suffrage, turns into a tyranny of the crowd, and the ideal of equality starts to resemble a viral contagion. However, crowd semantics not only formulates a conservative critique of modernity, but it also prepares the discursive terrain for thinking about social groupings that are no longer based on stratified identities such as class and gender. This modernity of crowd semantics is often overlooked, but it is crucial to understanding its success. In what follows, I first discuss Charles Mackay's *Extraordinary Popular Delusions and the Madness of Crowds* (first published in 1852), which also deals with speculative "market crowds" before the advent of crowd psychology.[9] My reading of Mackay tries to show why the semantics of the crowd proves to be so attractive for describing financial speculation. Although Mackay establishes crucial elements for understanding the crowd as a modern phenomenon, he does not address the question of how to deal with the crowd. In the second part of the paper, I want to show how the investment philosophy of the *Contrarians* benefited from crowd psychology. It is here that crowd psychology becomes a tool for constructing the ideal speculator.

Speculative Frenzies: Charles Mackay's Description of Financial Delusions

In 1841 the Scottish poet and journalist Charles Mackay published the first volume of his monumental study on *Extraordinary Popular Delusions and the Madness of Crowds,* which was completed in 1852.[10] This book has no theoretical ambitions. Rather, it uses the semantics of the crowd as the common denominator for a heterogeneous collection of phenomena ranging from witchcraft, alchemists, and beard fashions to speculative frenzies. The first three chapters—three historical cases of speculative mania—focus on exemplary cases of "speculative delusions": tulipomania in the Netherlands, John Law's Mississippi Scheme in France, and the South Sea Bubble in England. Let me only briefly point to how Mackay uses the semantics of the crowd when describing financial crazes (without going into historical details). Mackay introduces money and financial speculation as one central cause for "popular delusions": "Money, again, has often been a cause of the delusion of multitudes. Sober nations have all at once become desperate gamblers, and risked almost their existence upon the turn of a piece of paper. . . . Men, it has been well said, think in herds; it will be seen that they go mad in herds, while they only recover their senses slowly, and one by one" (*EPD,* xviii). Mackay argues not from the perspective of an economist who is interested in market dynamics and failures, but rather from the perspective of a political observer who notes that "whole nations" turn into gamblers. But how does he relate the English or French people to the financial mobs and crowds? It is the process of *delusion* that describes the strange transformation into an irrational collective—a transformation that cannot be explained by the internal logic of the people. A nation becomes mad not because it is already pathological,[11] but rather it requires an external catalyst—money—that makes it deluded.

Although Mackay describes the emergence of crowds as a maddening process, the meaning of the crowd is not exhausted by its irrationality. Rather, his description of the crowd starts to oscillate between its irrationality and, at the same time, an unheard-of modernity. My contention is that Mackay uses crowd semantics to describe a paradigmatically modern form of collectivity that stands in stark contrast to older ideas of communal belonging. Thus, crowd semantics is neither simply the remnant of a rebellious folk culture, nor an elitist denunciation of the "popular," as British cultural studies would have it.[12] It tries to envisage what consequences the modern ideals of equality and inclusion have. This becomes clearest when we try to identify how crowd semantics organizes meaning. We can do so by distinguishing three different dimensions of meaning which undergo crucial transformations: the social, the temporal, and the fact dimension of meaning.[13]

The *social dimension* deals with the problem of how to conceive of the relation between ego and alter ego. The notion of the crowd is an attempt at dealing with the anonymization of the alter ego. This semantics is a big challenge to older ideas of society that focused on its hierarchical organization into different classes and sociocultural identities. Crowd semantics describes the breakdown of stratified forms of differentiation, such as feudalism, and replaces it with a picture of a classless assemblage of anonymous people. One of the great discursive advantages of crowd semantics lies precisely in being able to speak about collective transformations that are not restricted to a particular stratum or group of society. The wish to be a part of the speculative crowd is universal: "Every fool aspired to be a knave" (*EPD,* 55). The crowd seized by a speculative frenzy is not simply a lower stratum of society; everyone may become victim of this maddening process (see *EPD,* 21, 55, 59, 97). The crowd, then, indicates the leveling of social, cultural, and sexual identities, because everybody can become its member. Mackay often describes speculative crowds as a chaotic assemblage of people coming from a wide variety of social and cultural origins. Speculative crowds consist of "all ranks of society," or simply "every body" (*EPD,* 55). It is precisely this all-inclusive and equalizing force of the crowd that fascinates Mackay (and his contemporaries). Descriptions of speculative crowds, then, often point at this social heterogeneity of crowds and at this most improbable mixture of classes, professions, and gender: Speculative crowds include "Cookmaids and footmen" (*EPD,* 20), but also "persons of distinction, of both sexes" (*EPD,* 59). The crowd affected by Dutch tulipomania, for example, is described by a list of heterogeneous identities: "Nobles, citizens, farmers, mechanics, seamen, maid-servants, even chimney-sweeps and old clotheswomen, dabbled in tulips" (*EPD,* 97). It is no accident that Mackay describes these crowds by using lists and enumerations: there is no pregiven identity that could provide a common foundation.

The crowd is an enumeration within which the singular

element loses its distinctive identity—and it is this equalizing and deindividualizing logic that is also diagnosed as excessive and pathological. The equality produced by the crowd does not know any limits: everybody who approaches a speculative crowd soon becomes a deluded speculator him- or herself. Even before crowd psychology invoked the vocabulary of contagion and suggestion, Mackay describes the social logic of the crowd as a contagious psychopathology ("frenzy," "mania," "panic," and "delusion") that ignores already existing social differences. The behavior of the crowd cannot be regulated because all established strategies of control are dependent on the social strata of society. The description of speculative crowds starts to resemble depictions of carnival. During the peak of the Mississippi scheme in France, a huge crowd of speculators and would-be speculators gather in front of John Law's mansion: "Their various colours, the gay ribands and banners which floated from them, the busy crowds which passed continually in and out—the incessant hum of voices, the noise, the music, and the strange mixture of business and pleasure on the countenances of the throng, all combined to give the place an air of enchantment that quite enraptured the Parisians" (*EPD,* 17). The variety of the crowd is best exemplified by its noisy character—a noise that is not only a nuisance, but also the celebration of the chaotic and equalizing logic of the crowd.[14]

But how is this strange equality within the speculative crowd generated? It is here that the "fact dimension" (*Sachdimension*) of meaning becomes crucial. The crowd is not held together by the identification with a leader, but with an impersonal object.[15] The speculating crowd is unified by "a vision of boundless wealth" (*EPD,* 15). It is important to note that the common "thing" of the crowd is a highly individualized fiction. The idea of "boundless wealth," then, is not the wealth of a community of speculators (that is, a common good), but the wealth aspired to by individual members of the crowd. It is this common thing that becomes the cause of a paradoxically individualizing collective delusion. What is interesting is that the effect of this delusion is primarily based on the fictionality of its common thing: the wealth is not yet realized, but may be realized in the future, often at an imaginary exotic place geographically far away in some colonies.[16] The breakdown of a speculative frenzy, then, is consequently described as defictionalization—as getting back to reality: the South Sea Bubble "fixed the eyes and expectations of all Europe, but whose foundation, being fraud, illusion, credulity, and infatuation, fell to the ground as soon as the artful management of its directors were discovered" (*EPD,* 73). What Mackay links is the semantics of the crowd with that of fictionality: Fiction becomes the source of delusion, and delusion is the mechanism which transforms a sober nation—or even Europe—into a speculative crowd. The crowd phenomenon, then, shares with the fictionality of its "thing," its instability: As soon as the illusion of boundless wealth breaks down, the crowd starts to dissolve.

The fictional "thing" of the speculative crowd is not only unstable, but it also becomes addictive. Speculation "would hold out a dangerous lure to decoy the unwary of their ruin, by making them part . . . for a prospect of imaginary wealth" (*EPD,* 53). The articulation between speculation and the crowd is based on the role of the imaginary. Speculation is an economic communication working with imaginary values—and it is, in other words, contrasted with the "real" economy, defined by work and production. The crowd, in turn, is usually characterized by a loss of reality: be it the loss of sound reasoning and rationality, or be it of a mere sense of reality, because the crowd believes even most improbable suggestions if they are presented appealingly. Thus, the highly fictionalized economic practice of speculation finds its correlate in the crowd, which is held together by just as fictional a common concept.

Let me now turn to the temporal dimension of meaning. Speculative crowds are characterized by a time structure also common to other crowd phenomena. They are marked by a temporal discontinuity, because a speculative crowd does not develop slowly, but emerges suddenly: "We find that whole communities suddenly fix their minds upon one object, and go mad in its pursuit; that millions of people become simultaneously impressed by one delusion" (*EPD,* xvii). A crowd, then, does not have a long history, providing it with a foundation—such as the history of a nation. Thus, crowd semantics attempts to grasp a collectivity without history—a collectivity where sudden emergence replaces cultural and historical traditions.

It is precisely because there is no common past of the crowd that its presence and future become crucial for its definition. Here again, crowd and speculation ideally complement each other. As we have already seen, the fictional good "boundless wealth" is a highly temporalized good: it is wealth of the future (that is, the prospect of wealth) that creates the present effects of delusion. The future tense of speculation is based on the celebration of contingency: there are possibilities in the future that have not yet been discovered. Thus, speculation is based on future possibilities hidden in the "not yet"—and it is this aspect that, in turn, further qualifies its fictional status. It is a fiction that flirts with reality: its raison d'être is precisely being a realistic fiction; a fiction whose realism will be tested by the way things go. That is why the end of a speculative frenzy is often described as the breakdown of an illusion, and as getting back to reality. This emphasis on the fictional nature of financial speculation is also a crucial argument for discourses on speculation in the twentieth century. Every successful broker will have to develop some sort of "speculative fantasy," without, however, succumbing to the lure of its delusions. Success in financial markets, then, will be measured by one's capacity for handling the distinction between reality and fiction.

Let me briefly summarize my argument so far. Mackay understands the crowd as a frightening and modern pheno-menon. Speculative crowds are, first, *egalitarian* crowds— and this egalitarianism is so successful that it ignores all established boundaries: everybody hopes to make easy money by speculation and joins the heterogeneous crowd of hopeful speculators. Thus, speculative crowds do not respect older social, ethnic, and gender distinctions. Second, the speculative crowd is integrated by an indeterminate *fictional object:* the hope for future wealth. Thus, it is a celebration of thinking in terms of future possibilities and options, contrasting the force of traditions. The contingency of the future becomes an economic opportunity in the present. That is also why, third, speculative crowds define themselves not in terms of a shared past (which they do not have), but in terms of a *future* prosperity. It is crucial to understand that the speculative crowd does not believe in a *common* future good, but in individual success. To put it differently, the fictional object is highly individualized, and it is this individualization that is shared by all members of the speculative crowd.

Crowd Psychology as Market Psychology

Although Mackay provides a dense description of these early speculative crowds, they are still treated as an exception to the normal working of society. Speculative crowds are like an illness that suddenly emerges and that will disappear after some time. This also shows itself in the structure of the book, which resembles a collection of curiosities— that is, odd phenomena that are a bit frightening but that are, above all, entertaining. What makes speculative crowds so appealing is their carnival-like structure. They point to the frightening possibility that society could be structured differently: a society governed not by hierarchies, but by a strange form of equality. As we have seen, Mackay does not paint a positive picture of this new form of equality and self-organization; rather, he underlines the irrationality, amorality, and threat of these crowds. Still, we should not forget that even Mackay's critical description hints at the modernity of crowd phenomena. It is in this sense that the semantics of the crowd becomes a "crisis semantics" of modernity: a semantics that, on a most general level, tries to deal with the transformation of stratified societies into functionally differentiated societies.[17]

That is also how the affinity between the market and crowd semantics is generated. Both, at least in their self-descriptions, suggest a radical form of equality. The logic of the market is no longer governed by stratified rules of inclusion and exclusion, because, at least in principle, everybody who has the necessary financial means (or credit) is welcome to participate in markets. And crowd semantics, similarly, stresses that everybody can become an element of a crowd because its dynamics erases the particularity of the individual. Against the modern optimism of an increasing universalism permeating all spheres of society, crowd semantics polemically exhibits the limits of this universalism. With the advent of crowd psychology in the beginning of the twentieth century, this skepticism initiates a discussion that juxtaposes the possibility of universal access with the competency of those who are going to be included. From this perspective, key ideas of modern universalism, such as the postulate of universal suffrage in the political system or free access to markets, are seen as intrinsically deficient. Often, this problematization is only understood as a conservative reaction to the emergence of new societal structures.[18] This is certainly a legitimate reading, although it tends to neglect the fact that this critique also attempts to address this tension within universalism. To put it differently, whereas the rhetoric of equality and universalism presents these concepts as if they had no limits, crowd semantics points precisely at the other side of modernism. In what follows, I want to argue that despite its initial conservative articulation, the notion of the crowd is used by func-

tional systems for observing and organizing their modes of inclusion. Such a rearticulation goes beyond Mackay because it no longer understands the crowd as accidental to the spheres of modern societies, but as constitutively linked to the specifics of these spheres.

What does this mean in the context of financial speculation? First of all, speculative crowds are no longer seen as contingent epidemics, but as a pathology generated by economic processes. It is no longer the fate of the nation that is at stake, but the future of the economic system. Now, the notion of the crowd refers to an often repeated lament over the increasing number of incompetent speculators. In his 1908 memoirs, the former broker Henry Clews criticizes the belief "that any man who has money can speculate." The reason for this is that "people forget that the business of speculation requires special training, and every fool who has got a few hundred dollars cannot begin to deal in stocks and make a fortune."[19] Although Clews does not resort to the rhetoric of the crowd, he plainly formulates the problem that the notion of the crowd tries to describe: the widening access to financial markets has led to a popularity of speculation that is no longer in line with even the most basic forms of economic competency. To put it differently, financial markets are even open to those who, from the perspective of economic rationality, do not know anything about how these markets work. In a similar way, the trader M. C. Brush also notes, "I wish you would leave this off the records. Well to be perfectly frank with you, it is a pathetic basis on which the average man buys stocks."[20]

This diagnosis of an overstretched universalism, which leads to the inclusion of highly incompetent speculators, is not always seen as necessarily problematic. Charles Emery, who was one of the eminent early theorists of stock speculation, also observes positive effects of mass inclusion. Although speculation may be tragic for the unfortunate small speculator and may even be morally illegitimate, the widening of the market is seen as stabilizing.[21] Or to put it like a recent slogan of the online broker Instinet.com: "The bigger the crowd, the better the performance."[22] Whether the inclusion of an incompetent crowd is seen as problematic or not on the macroeconomic level, it still poses a problem for the individual speculator. Even if the overall effect of the crowd may increase liquidity, the individual speculator wants to succeed as an individual. It is here that the usage of crowd psychology (and not only of the more general crowd semantics that was exemplified with Charles Mackay) becomes important because it promises a tool for survival on the market. Thus, the crowd is now being formulated as a problem that confronts every speculator—and crowd psychology offers tools for success on the market by understanding the psychology of market crowds.

It is the formulation of the crowd as a problem that opens up the discursive horizon for the development of different strategies for regulating and controlling the crowd. This change of interest also indicates itself in the prefaces to more recent editions of Mackay's compendium, which read it as if it were already a market psychology. Now Mackay is turned into a *guidebook* for succeeding on the market. The finance manager Ron Baron, for example, distributes Mackay's book free to all his employees.[23] Furthermore, the legendary financier and speculator Bernard Baruch opens his preface to a reprint of Mackay with a generalization of crowd semantics: "All economic movements, by their very nature, are motivated by crowd psychology. . . . Without due recognition of crowd-thinking (which often seems crowd-madness) our theories of economics leave much to be desired."[24] It is with this generalization that a problem emerges that Mackay only casually addressed: there is not only an intrinsic connection between the economy and crowd psychology in times of crisis, but this connection is the normal state of financial economy.

This normalization of crowd semantics requires a different way of dealing with the crowd. The crowd is no longer seen as a transient phenomenon, and that is why it has to be accepted as a normal feature of financial markets. Thus, those who participate in the market have to know crowd psychology in order to understand the market. In contrast to Mackay's account of the crowd, an analysis of the crowd is now automatically an analysis of how the market works. Taking seriously this "crowd" definition of the market makes Gustave Le Bon's crowd psychology highly attractive. The reason for this is that it presents not only psychological laws of crowd behavior, but, more importantly, it also introduces the leader as an element confronting the crowd. What Le Bon envisaged as the power technologies of political leaders gets translated into a managerial discourse on how to beat the crowd.

In the beginning of the 1920s and 1930s, crowd psychology became the intellectual foundation of the investment philosophy of the "contrarians." Humphrey Neill, who is often seen as one of the founding figures of the contrarians, draws heavily on Mackay and Le Bon.[25] Although I will focus on Neill's position in what follows, it is worth mentioning that elements of crowd psychological thinking are not unique to the somewhat obscure contrarians in Vermont. There is a whole academic branch specializing in behavioral management that also refers to Le Bon to understand market dynamics.[26] But perhaps nobody has better described the role of the crowd for investment theory than John Maynard Keynes: "The actual, private object of the most skilled investment today is to 'beat the gun,' as the Americans so well express it, to outwit the crowd, and to pass the bad, the depreciating, half-crown to the other fellow."[27] For Keynes, crowd thinking in the economy is scandalous because it accepts the irrationality of the economy instead of defeating "the dark forces of time and ignorance." The skilled speculator, then, has to study, and possibly even partially to adapt to the judgment of the crowd instead of finding a sound judgment about the "true" economic value of investments. Thus, the full scandal of the market crowd is that economic rationality requires one to relate to the irrational-

12A 'Ochlos': Ancient Greek

Sebastian De Vivo

Greek language possesses a rich and varied terminology for the concept of crowds. This is hardly surprising, in light of the relentless preoccupation with the political realm that swept the city-states of Greece at the end of the so-called Dark Ages (up to the eighth century BCE). The turmoil of the Greek Renaissance saw the advent of the *polis,* innovations in interregional trade and commerce, and the shifting of political power from chieftains and tyrants to the citizen body. The Greeks developed a complex vocabulary to conceptualize "the people," as the totality of a city-state's citizen body, and as the integral participants in highly visible political and military groups, in contrast to a tyrannical leader and an elitist oligarchy.

The standard definition of the Greek term *ochlos* (ξλοω) is "a crowd, throng." In this it closely parallels the term *homilos,* "assembled crowd, throng of people," and *ochlagogeo,* "crowd, mob," literally "a led crowd," as opposed to similar terms with broader political implications, such as *laos,* "people, folk," and *demos,* "country, land, citizenry." In its standard sense, *ochlos* is often used in relation to armies and soldiers and their camp followers. It is also a fairly unmarked way to refer to a group or crowd.

The term *ochlos* also carries a political connotation, as "populace, mob." For Plato, *ochlos* can refer to a popular assembly, and for the oligarchic philosopher, the term certainly carried a nega-

ity of the crowd: "It may profit the wisest to anticipate the mob psychology rather than the real trend of events, and to ape unreason proleptically."[28]

It is precisely this relationship to what Keynes calls the "mob psychology" of the market that is the basis for the rearticulation of the distinction between the crowd and the leader in the contrarian investment philosophy. The central question is how to behave in markets, which are governed by the logic of the crowd—and for the contrarians, all financial markets are eventually based on this logic. The aim is to beat the market, or to outsmart the crowd by observing it. The foundation and legitimation of this investment philosophy is an a priori knowledge about the quality of crowd judgment: "The crowd always loses because the crowd is always wrong. It is wrong, because it behaves normally."[29] Or briefly: "The crowd is usually wrong."[30] It is this "normal falsity" that generates speculative opportunities. It is the "stupidity of the many" (*WYWL*, 21) that enables a few investors to act intelligently: "The crowd is always 75% wrong marketwise. Were it otherwise, the market would be unprofitable for the Insiders."[31] Speculation, then, is seen as zero-sum game: "Speculation can be worth while only when a few are taking advantage of the stupidity of the many" (*WYWL*, 174–5). Thus, the basic idea of contrarian speculation is to position oneself against the crowd in order to arrive at good investment decisions: "The art of contrary thinking consists in training your mind to ruminate in directions opposite to general public opinions; but weigh your conclusions in the light of current manifestations of human behavior."[32] What this quote already indicates is that it does not suffice to oppose the crowd; the investor must take into account the specific situation. Contrarianism is not simply a pure "counter-mimicry"; it also requires a "subjective synthesis" (*ACT,* 143), which reintroduces the ability to think against the logic of affect which governs the crowd.

Thus, the contrarians fully accept that markets are crowd or mob markets—and that there is only one consequence to be taken from this diagnosis. It is not to make markets more rational (as Keynes, in theory, may have wished), but rather to construct a speculator who can withstand and make use of the crowd. Whereas Le Bon was still interested in controlling the market, the contrarian speculator has given up this hope. And there is a good reason for this: he profits from the madness and mistakes of the crowd. The contrarian investor is not interested in how a certain company whose shares he possesses develops or what the economic prospects of a particular branch are. Rather, he uses crowd psychology as a tool for second-order observations: he is only interested in the judgments and observations of other investors. It is for this reason that contrarianism shifts the meaning of economic reality. While Keynes was disappointed about disregarding "real" economic trends, the contrarian is happy to stress the reality of observations: "Is not human action also fundamental?" (*ACT,* 58). A contrarian, then, has to become a true second-order observer: he does not observe how the economy develops, but how the economy is observed by other speculators—and he takes his observations of others as the basis for investment decisions.

But this redefinition of economic reality in terms of mutually observing market participants is not the whole story.[33] For the contrarians, it only prepares the terrain for the construction of the ideal speculator. What contrarian investment philosophy inaugurates is a whole program of disciplining and individualizing a speculator firmly posited against the crowd. In order to sustain his identity and to secure his chances for profit, he always has to be in the position of the minority: "Contrarians are a permanent minority, comfortable only in articulate opposition to the placidly received wisdom or panicked self-delusion of the majority."[34] But how is it possible to maintain this difficult position? How does the speculator protect himself against the delusions of the crowd? It is here that Le Bon's distinction between the leader and the crowd becomes crucial. However, the contrarians do not simply copy Le Bon's idea of the leader, but rather rearticulate it in an important way. Although Le Bon was skeptical about the possibility of governing a crowd, he still expected that at least a precarious mode of control could be established that would help to maintain the very distinction between the statesman as leader and the crowd. Thus, Le Bon suggested a couple of techniques that help to seduce and control the crowd. In the contrarian idea of market crowds, the figure of the leader is neither simply copied nor abolished. The speculator is supposed to take the role of the leader, but without aiming at governing and controlling the crowd. It is this difference that makes it necessary to split the figure of the leader into two very different functions that can no longer be occupied by one single person. The function of seduction and control becomes impersonalized to a large extent. Financial crowds do not require a figure of identification external to the market,[35] but it is the market itself that becomes seductive.

How does it accomplish this task? Neill points to this problem when he explains that it is the movement of *prices* that attracts and seduces investors (*TR,* 35). In a similar vein, Bond argues that the popular speculator buys because of tips and "prices going up before his eyes."[36] The idea that prices replace the leader has become very successful and has also been repeated more recently. Neil A. Costa, a professional trader and director of Market Masters, explicitly refers to this transformation of the leader: "In the case of trading, the crowd leader becomes 'price.'"[37] Certainly, the old personalized form of the leader also survives—there

tive implication. In the dialogue *Gorgias,* Socrates states that "the rhetorician's business is not to instruct a law court or a public meeting [*ochlos*] in matters of right and wrong, but only to make them believe; since, I take it, he could not in a short while instruct such a mass of people [*ochlos*] in matters so important" (455a).

For Plato's pupil Aristotle, the term is likewise politicized. In *The Politics,* he refers to oligarchs playing the role of demagogues and currying to the mob in their bid for power (1305b). In this, he is directly indebted to the great Athenian lawmaker Solon, who in his elegiac poetry harangues the citizens of Athens for their mindless support of the tyrant Pisistratus, crystallizing the oft-repeated notion of the crowd as a mindless entity swept away by charismatic oratory and unable to see or realize its best interests.

The term appears 641 times in the Greek main corpus, from the tragic and comic poets, through the great philosophers Plato and Aristotle, and on to the New Testament. The term survived into the Middle French *ochlocratie,* "a government by the populace," and modern Italian *oclocrazia,* "mob rule, rule of the plebs," from the Hellenistic coinage *ochlokratia,* "mob rule." It was soon to enter the English language as *ochlocracy,* "rule of the populace, mob," a term used in 1991 by the *Observer,* in quoting the Russian newspaper *Pravda* as claiming that Boris Yeltsin's run for the presidency was backed by an ochlocracy.

12B Barneys New York: The Warehouse

Jessica Burstein

All that glitters is gold.
—Smash Mouth, "All Star"

Three truisms:
Shop alone; friends are for bars.
You don't make art out of good intentions.
No amount of irony can redeem teal.

—Flaubert

You arrive early and walk into a room after having surrendered your backpack, and possibly a kidney. Walk is a euphemism; you stand in line, hopping from one foot to the other impatiently, and then once you are past the metal detector, you break into a low-key sprint; you do not want to get winded early. Travel light, because this is serious. If you are smart, you have worn shoes that slip on and off easily, no bra in case you find a sleeveless or backless number, and nothing that buttons: zippers are optimum. The smart and the brave wear swimsuits, thus avoiding wasting time by periodically redressing. Although not necessary, it is recommended that you spend the prior week dieting, because this will make you feel worthy and cruel. The latter characteristic will be especially helpful.

There are four versions of Barneys New York, and they all come crowd-equipped: (1) the stores; (2) the outlets, the best of which is in California (Camarillo, about thirty minutes outside of LA, which is about as close to LA as it's worth getting); (3) the Barneys Warehouse Sales Event, held semi-

are investment stars and analysts who may figure as leaders, thus governing the market crowd by their predictions.[38] However, only focusing on star traders tends to neglect the fact that the function of the leader has undergone a deep transformation by becoming largely impersonal. What survives is the idea that the crowd only reacts to clear and easily understandable signals: It is not a slight change in prices that attracts the crowd, but "very obvious changes"[39]—it is not least the sensual phenomenon of fast movement that may catch the attention of the crowd.

These movements reduce the complexity of market volatility to a clear signal that does not require the investor to understand the mechanisms producing the changes. The rapid movement starts to resemble a clear-cut signal that catches the attention even of the small speculator. Moreover, it makes the function of the leader democratic: the small investor who observes such a movement knows that it is created by other members of the crowd. Instead of imitating the slogans of a leader, who may have been once part of the crowd but is now removed from it as figure identification, the market crowd starts to imitate itself.[40] The investor knows that he could not only have been caught up within the price movement, but also that he could have profited from it. And it is precisely this observation of a possibly missed opportunity that makes him want to join the crowd before it is too late. To put it in terms of a more formal argument: Markets observe themselves by producing prices[41]—and it is this self-observation that takes on the role of the leader.

However, I have mentioned that the classical function of the leader is not fully absorbed by this impersonal mechanism of prices. The second function of the classical figure of the leader was to control the crowd. Quickly changing prices may seduce the crowd, but they do not control the crowd. Thus, the control function of crowd psychology becomes significantly altered because it changes its reference: it is no longer the crowd that has to be controlled; the contrarian investor has to learn how to control *himself*. To put it very simply, the contrarian investor has to position himself *against* the market crowd. In order to do this, he has to know how to maintain his individuality and autonomy—especially because he cannot seek approval of his position by the majority. It is this positioning that is central to the success of investing: like the leader, the investor has to maintain the distinction between himself and the crowd. But in contrast to the leader, the contrarian investor is, in most cases, not visible to the crowd. He prefers that his investment decisions not be observed as exemplary because this would threaten his minority strategy. For in taking advantage of the "stupidity of the many," he must not become himself part of the many. There is no easy solution to this agonistic position, which is best described by a popular investment slogan: The investor has to *beat the market*—and, one might add, without becoming a popular hero.

The leader is thus transformed into a second-order observer whose decisions are based on these observations. This position, however, creates considerable problems for the contrarian investor because he has to accomplish two very different things: on the one hand, he has to produce mass observations; on the other hand, he should not simply observe the market, but also make independent investment decisions. The semantics of the leader, then, tries to solve this problem: The leader is, by definition, different from the crowd: the crowd is his adversary. Thus, crowd semantics not only structures his observation of the market, but it also supports him in upholding the distance separating him from the crowd. To put it differently, the semantics of the crowd tries to formulate a solution to the epistemological problem of the contrarian market observer: How to observe the market without becoming a member of the crowd.

It is only now that the whole rearticulation of crowd semantics becomes clear: it is not simply a metaphorical substitution of the classical leader, either by prices or by the contrarian investor. The contrarian investor does not use crowd semantics for controlling the crowd; he has given up the idea. Moreover, it is precisely the irrationality of the crowd that produces investment opportunities. Instead of controlling the masses, crowd semantics helps the investor to individualize and control him- or herself. What is being individualized is not the crowd but the contrarian investor who has to develop a strong identity in order to withstand the temptations of the market crowd. The test for every speculator is "how you behave when the crowd is roaring the other way . . . the crowd, the elusive Australopithecus, is still largely an unknown, an exercise in mass psychology still not accomplished" (*MG,* 41).[42] The relation between the contrarian and the market crowd is not only a contest, but it is also the scenery of a possible seduction[43]—the seduction by the mass, against which the contrarian has to posit himself, withstanding the comfortable pleasure of joining the majority. That is why "Adam Smith" stresses that a stable individual identity is a prerequisite for successful speculation: "If you don't know who you are, this is an expensive place to find out" (*MG,* 26, 80). However, the solution to this problem is not that easy, as many contrarian guidebooks prove. They aim to provide not only a tool of observation, but also guidelines for how to keep on knowing who one is. The threat of the market crowd is precisely that it transforms individuals into deindividualized streams of affect. The struggle against the crowd becomes internalized; it is hidden within even the most stable and self-reflexive identity.

annually; and (4) lunching with Simon Doonan. Here I shall focus on the Warehouse Sale.

There is nothing like entering a large room filled only with racks of designer clothing, between which are hordes of women ripping off their clothes, standing naked or nearly so in the aisles (if you sleep with women, the effect of this can be dizzying, but the race goes to the dedicated: keep your mind on your work), squirming into or out of a Viktor and Rolfe. How does this snap? Is this Velcro? Is this meant to wrap around the waist or is it a little floaty thing? What was Rei Kawabuko thinking? You don't have time to snap, button, or even toggle, and forget about hemlines: you get into it, and if it fits, you grab it and move on. This is Malthus, baby. Get outta my way. You may or may not choose to note the swizzle stick with the screaming infant locked into the $800 Bugaboo like a tiny little Hannibal Lector from the Upper East Side. If you are there for tourism, you can waste time wondering whether she or her cell phone has more body fat, but if you're there for real reasons, you step over the caterwauling kid and grab the Helmut Lang, ignoring the fact that the swizzle stick is now yelling at you that she was going to try that on. The Botox makes her face strangely expressionless as she screams, a fact which you will later find amusing over a martini; at the moment, though, this is simply noisy wallpaper. She's slow; she's soft; she's been doing *Pilates,* for Christ's sake. Well, a hundred double-leg kicks aren't going to get mommy any closer to this little felt number, sister, so just play past it. Not having wasted time with children, you are accordingly empathy-free.

The anger that Simmel identified as lurking beneath the blasé surface of metropolitan encounters is laid bare at the Warehouse Sale. Other people's bodies seem constructed solely as impediments to one's own negotiation of space. There are hundreds of would-be models, which on the street makes for nice scenery but right now means that one's sight is frequently obstructed. You see racks, and skin wandering around between them. Don't look at prices right now; you can hunker down and do triage later. Right now, you live a life without latent content.

If someone has grabbed something away from you, there are questions to be asked before actually assaulting them.

1. Was it in your hands? If so, you can and should grab it back.

2. If it was not actually in your hands but on the rack next to the really interesting corset-like evening jacket that turned out to have some unfortunate rouching in the back, and you realize you've ended up with the aftermath of a Shirley Temple suicide bombing, etiquette dictates that you wait your turn. "Waiting your turn" consists of brief intervals of staring at the woman who somehow got the current object of desire before you did. Rummage onward, but with an eye toward the moment in which she discovers that she is not now and has never been a size 0.

3. Is it by Olivier Theyskens? If so, all bets are off: go for the throat. Say that it is not her color. Claim you have already paid for it. Ask her what her child's name is, tell her that you recruit for Brearley and are struck by such obvious infant beauty and intelligence; when she reaches for her BlackBerry so that you may give her your office phone number, grab the Theyskens and run away.

You will often encounter men assisting their girlfriends, wives, friends, or clients. These men

Disciplining the Speculator

Crowd semantics, then, opens the terrain for the development and usage of individualizing technologies. There are at least four different technologies that are closely intertwined: techniques of observation, time management, affect control, and techniques of isolation.

Techniques of Observation

The individualization of the contrarian speculator is foremost a particular mode of self-observation. The speculator has to reassert his individuality by taking an "impersonal view point" (*TR,* 64), which helps him to observe himself "objectively." This mode of observation is closely linked with a highly flexible attitude toward himself: Past decisions are not necessarily right decisions, and the permanent screening of one's own decision should enable the contrarian to adapt his decisions to the market situation. What is required is "pliability" in the sense of an "ability to change an opinion, the power of revision."[44] This pliability, however, does not mean adjusting one's opinions to those of the crowd. On the contrary, the parameters of this process are generated by a scrupulous process of self-observation—and it is only these observations that may guide a reorientation of the decision-making process. What becomes clear is that the ideal speculator is a figure of the present and the future. He uses his past decisions only for critically evaluating his shortcomings, not for relaxing the doxa of the past. The speculator has to keep in mind that even his successful decisions may just be "luck and no skill"—that is why the imperative of the speculator is, "Analyze all of your transactions!"[45] The particular mode of self-observation, then, is to analyze oneself by focusing on one's investment decisions. Because the contrarian is aware that the context for his decisions changes all the time, self-analysis always also means avoiding overidentification with one's successes: "Pride of opinion and impatience will be your worst enemies" (*SSM,* 125). Thus, the aim of these self-observations is to generate and maintain the decision-making capacity of the speculator as a capacity directed toward the *future.* It is not the past that defines one as a successful speculator, but how one deals with the challenges of the future. At the same time, it is this present and future orientation that makes the contrarian speculator vulnerable, because his identity lacks a firm foundation. As a man of the future, he always has to prove himself anew—and he always has to reestablish the distance that separates him from the crowd. Although the artist may identify himself with his works of art, which distinguish him from the crowd, the speculator always has to reestablish this distance that is so crucial to his survival.

Still, at the same time, he must not concentrate only on himself. In order to position himself against the crowd, he has to know the crowd. Thus, self-observation is aided by "mass-observation," but as I have tried to show, the contrarian is not interested in controlling or steering the crowd. This is quite cynical because the mistakes of the crowd are his investment opportunities. Observing the market crowd, then, means identifying the opinions he is not going to share—to which he will be opposed. The aim of these market observations is precisely to beat the gun.[46] Although classical crowd psychology conceived of the relationship between the crowd and the leader as public spectacle (at least in Le Bon's work), now the battle between the lonely contrarian and the crowd becomes privatized. The battlefield is switched to the identity of the contrarian speculator who struggles between opposition to the crowd and attraction to its dynamics. The self-positioning against the crowd becomes difficult because it requires one to permanently distinguish between oneself and the crowd. That is why the contrarian has to make sure that he draws the correct line between self- and other-observation: "Is this truly a generalized viewpoint, or is it perhaps a composite of my own views which the 'mirror' misleads me to think are those of the crowd?" (*TR*, 157). What the contrarian is confronted with is a difficult epistemological problem: How is it possible to recognize the crowd? The problem is not only how to know the market; it also affects the subjectivity of the speculator: In order to know the market, he has to be absolutely himself. This is also why the contrarians emphasize the importance of these observational techniques: The permanent monitoring of oneself is a prerequisite for observing the market. However, at the same time, the contrarian is not at all independent; rather, he has to define himself in relation to the market crowd. And it is precisely this relation that is seen as dangerous—the distinction between the contrarian and the market crowd is far from stable.

Time Management

One reason for this instability is that one cannot always posit oneself against the crowd. This is not only because of the difficulty of correctly identifying mass opinion, but also because sometimes even the crowd is right. That is also why Neill has to relativize his leitmotiv: "'The crowd is usually wrong'—at least, in its *timing* of events" (*ACT*, 2). Thus, one has to participate partially in the mass trends of the markets without getting lost in them. It does not pay to oppose the crowd

are the equivalent of shrubbery. Do not be shy about undressing in front of them. They are holograms, albeit holograms who seem to be enjoying themselves. Under no conditions make eye contact, unless you see that they are guarding that amazing Rochas double-breasted oyster-gray silk coat with the high waist and super-skinny three-quarter-length sleeves made to overlay the watery pink silk dress that looks like a cross between the lifestyles of F. Scott Fitzgerald and Jan Svenkmajer. In that case, deep and meaningful eye contact is called for. Otherwise, not. However, if they offer an opinion as to your own vestmental choices, you are free to do with them what you will, but remember: every moment spent executing a cutting comment is a moment not spent in the presence of a Dries van Noten.

Although it is in your interest to be ruthless, it is not unusual to encounter strange acts of reciprocal humanity or even politeness: an appreciative murmur once you have verified it isn't your style, but will probably look good on the person who is holding it; a shared eye roll at the third party who is waving what looks like an Oscar de la Renta suit jacket at a guard and asking if this comes in her size; or the unholy joy of that amazing black chick coming up to as you peel out of the Gucci, and when you sadly hand the thing over to her—impossibly long—she says, Cool thong. Yeah, you say, La Perla. Simple pleasures for simple people.

As incredible as it is, shoplifting still exists. This is a stupid pastime, even for kleptomaniacs. Despite your terrible upbringing, do not partake. Everything you do is watched, recorded, wired; your pulse rate is a known factor, and there is less intimacy in an intravaginal probe. Nonetheless, you will occasionally stumble onto a Winona

Ryder wannabe who is busy trying to stuff a cocktail gown into her socks. Feminism means you keep on walking.

The crowd ebbs and flows. There will be what seem like hours spent wriggling into a plastic Prada dress with black sight lines à la Etienne-Jules Marey, an achievement executed between twenty-three other women who are so tightly wedged together that for several seconds running you can't figure out whose left arm it is that you have inadvertently inserted into the dress sleeve, because it does not seem to be yours. Any smaller, said Robert Benchley about the office he shared with Dorothy Parker, and it would have been adultery. Crowd etiquette entails taking nothing personally: not looking up, removing the stray limb, and using your hips to make a small lacuna in the flesh so you can shimmy out. By now the racks are in disarray, skidded off center, with clothing, iPods, wallets, cell phones—and is that a diaphragm?—on the floor, lost children wailing, beautiful women on their hands and knees, crawling around in an orgy of Helmut Newton outtakes. The Chanel dress with the faux-prim plaid pleats now has a large footprint on it. Many have fallen, but the strongest survive. Pain is just weakness leaving your body. You will suddenly find yourself in small bubbles of empty space. Take this time to store up oxygen, but do not waste time wondering is this is a reflection of the quality of the clothing at hand. The crowd has no reason; it just is.

Yoox.com has done much to dissipate the frenzy attendant upon Barneys Warehouse Sale, so this may be something of a historical exercise. Shopping online, however, deprives you of the reason Barneys was invented: the negotiation of crowds, punctuated by instant gratification, or in the par-

dogmatically because this would also mean that one cannot profit from ongoing trends. The difficulty is to follow the crowd partially, and, at the same time, to keep a firm distance. The solution of the problem suggested by Neill is the distinction between a stimulus-driven crowd and a thinking individual. Following Le Bon's emphasis on suggestion, Neill notes that the crowd cannot think, but can only receive affective stimuli.[47] One of the most important stimuli is the rapid price movement mentioned above. Because of its dependency on such stimuli, which do not require any reflection, the crowd does not develop the time consciousness that would be necessary for knowing when to act against the crowd. Thus, the primary mistake of the crowd is not simply that it is wrong, but that its decisions are always too early or too late. This time consciousness is closely linked to one's abilities as an observer: it is only "thinking" that makes it possible not only to receive impulses, but also to *read* them and to understand them as an element of larger economic trends. Of course, there is a price to be paid for dealing reflexively with the temporality of speculation: the speculator is slowed down because he cannot immediately react to impulses, but has to invest time in reading and reflecting on them. Still, it is precisely in the different way of relating to the temporality of speculation that the crowd and the individual speculator can be distinguished.

Affect Control

However, maintaining one's identity as contrarian speculator is not only based on cognitive techniques; it also has to do with controlling and structuring affect. Drawing from classical crowd psychology, the contrarians describe the market crowd as highly affective and contagious. Although this affectivity of the market may clash with the ideal of the economic man, it is seen as an affectivity generated by the market itself: "It may seem that the statement that stock prices are merely the resultant of market actions based on hopes and fears of gain and loss, is so plain as to be hardly worth such emphasis."[48] It is not only the force of its opinions that makes the crowd attractive, but also its affective structure. Crowd psychology was fascinated and frightened by how easily affect moves from one member of a crowd to another. Crowd semantics, then, describes the market as a battlefield between hope and fear, resulting in enthusiasm and depression. The struggle of the contrarian investor is even harder than that of the average speculator: Because he deliberately positions himself against the crowd, he does not find supporting comfort in the company of others. In addition to the contagious feelings he is confronted with, he is exposed to the challenge of being one of the few who does not follow the crowd. That is why it is emphasized that being a contrarian requires not only an independent intellectual stature, but also a hard psychic determination. The contrarian needs "a complete mastery over one's impulses, emotions, ambitions under the most heroic tests of human endurance."[49] Contrarian literature combines a psychological stance with a highly antipsychological one: On the one hand, it explains market dynamics by the "human" factor, basically understood as crowd psychology. On the other hand, the ideal speculator seeks to get rid of his psychology—or at least of those dimensions of it that he cannot control. Most mistakes of speculators are seen as psychological mistakes—as a failure to master oneself totally.

Techniques of Isolation

Affect control is based not only on self-discipline, but also on techniques of isolation. Foucault has shown that the individuality of the prisoner is generated by his or her architectural isolation from other prisoners.[50] The technique of isolation is a primary tool for producing individuals and overcoming the threat of a chaotic crowd. Although the contrarian is not put into a cubicle, he still has to rely on physical techniques of isolation. The contrarian is not only a man of independent opinions and self-discipline; he also has to separate himself from other speculators: "Trade alone! . . . Close your mind to the opinion of others; pay no attention to outside influences. Disregard reports, rumors, and idle board-room chatter. . . . Be a calm, unpleasant cynic" (TR, 44). However, it was also Neill who recommended establishing a contrarian position precisely by observing the opinion of other speculators. Total isolation is impossible, but nevertheless, isolation is a powerful technique for producing and maintaining one's identity.

That is why the lonely speculator in the countryside has become a popular figure for exemplifying the contrarian speculator. Charles Dow—the originator of the Dow Jones Index—points to the advantages of the "out-of-town trader": "The outsider who will wisely study values and market conditions and exercize patience enough for six men will be likely to make money in stocks."[51] S. A. Nelson, the author of one of the first stock market psychologies, also recommends retreating to small places like Newport or Saratoga, especially during heavy market dynamics.[52] Spatial isolation, then, is supposed to cool down the speculator during hot market times, to help him to keep his autonomy. Still, this technique is also paradoxical because it presupposes what it is supposed to produce: a highly self-disciplined speculator. Bluntly put, "staying away from the market place means

lance of the industry, "retail therapy." Then, too, there is the pleasure of knowing you got it right. Do you know what it feels like to figure out later that that Yohji Yamamoto sleeveless blouse with that strange zipper at the bottom hemline actually transforms into a little purse, so you got two things for the price of one? Dar-ling, you have no idea.

self-discipline" (*SSM,* 122). Only those speculators who are not addicted to the stock market are able to withdraw from it for a while. The "suckers"—as the naive small speculators have been called—do not have this discipline and become easy victims of market affect and rumors.

However, spatial isolation was not the only suggestion. For many reasons, its efficiency was seen only as limited. First of all, its paradoxical nature—requiring self-discipline in order to practice self-discipline—restricted its uses. Additionally, it was not that easy to escape the market. Even in remote parts of the United States, there were broker offices with a ticker reporting the most recent quotes.[53] With the advent of new media technologies, the market started to be everywhere—and small crowds gathered at broker's offices and restaurants equipped with a ticker. Thus, the idea of spatial isolation was supplemented with the more abstract idea of communicative isolation. These techniques allow the speculator to be at the marketplace, but to separate himself from the surrounding crowd. In order to do this, he has to become indifferent toward rumors, which are the communicative equivalent of contagious affect. What is recommended here is that the speculator not only refrain from participating in or listening to "idle talk," but also that he actively withdraw from the oral culture of the marketplace. Thus, Neill recommends never attending the marketplace without a notepad and a pencil: "Use pad-and-pencil since it will occupy your mind and concentrate your attention. Try it; you will not be able to chatter and keep track of trades at the same time" (*TR,* 44). Necessary isolation is now produced in a more refined way: the dangerous and contagious oral culture of the marketplace is replaced by writing. Although orality and visuality are seen as the medium of the crowd, writing is that of the individual. In this sense, the contrarian speculator separates himself from the crowd not necessarily by retreating to a lonely place, but by using the media technique of writing. Writing, then, articulates two very different purposes: it combines the permanent observation of the market with the individualization of the speculator. Writing is presented as a technique to keep from losing oneself within the noise of the marketplace and the never-ending circulation of rumors and tips.

These four techniques of inclusion are survival techniques for the lonely speculator who has to prove himself on the battlefield of the market. From the perspective of crowd and market psychology, being a speculator becomes a never-ending test and a self-assessment that is intimately linked with the subjectivity of the contrarian. The lure of the crowd and the comfort of the majority may appeal to the contrarian in those moments of "human endurance," when he has to struggle not only with his emotions, but also with his role as a cynic observer set apart from the speculating majority.

Let me return to my initial question: Why has the semantics of the crowd been so successful for describing markets? A first answer might suggest that it tries to rationalize the irrational: market panics and euphorias, deluded speculators, and imitative trading. Such an answer, however, does not really address the function of crowd semantics for the finance economy—it treats crowd semantics merely as an ideology that rationalizes the intrinsic irrationality of global finance capitalism. My argument has tried to escape such a reading of crowd semantics by addressing two different questions. First, I tried to take Le Bon seriously when he wrote that we are entering into an "era of the crowd." Of course, my intention was not to argue for a renewal of crowd psychology, but rather to ask how such a link between modernity and crowd psychology is established. In order to do this, I returned to Charles Mackay's *The Madness of Crowds,* which is one of the crucial source books for crowd psychology. My reading of Mackay tried to show that, despite the denunciation of the crowd, the crowd also represents a highly innovative semantics. The reason for this is that it tries to develop a descriptive vocabulary for a form of a social "collectivity" radically different from well-established forms of social groupings. Speculative (and other) crowds are presented as social forms open to everybody. Thus, crowds prove to be indifferent to the prevalent identities of stratified societies, such as class, gender, and ethnicity. Certainly, masses are often characterized as proletarian, feminine,[54] and southern European, if not African. However, this characterization does not alter the astonishing dynamics of the crowd, which includes persons from all strata and professions, from every gender and ethnicity. Thus, crowd semantics is the attempt to develop a semantics that addresses inclusion into social spheres, such as politics or the economy, in universal terms. Of course, it presents this universal inclusion as a crisis, but it also prepares the discursive terrain for thinking about inclusion in a new way. My argument is that it is precisely this semantic innovation that is complementary to the semantics of the free market, which also presupposes, at least in principle, the inclusion of everybody who has the necessary financial means or credibility. Thus, the notion of the crowd is able to describe this new mode of universal inclusion and to criticize it at the same time.

Mackay's phenomenology of speculative crowds remains, however, basically descriptive. It was only with the advent of crowd psychology and its economic rearticulation that it could become fully integrated into the working of financial markets. Now the crowd is not only seen as an adequate description of the working of the finance economy, but also transformed into a tool for constructing the ideal speculator. Although Mackay presented the crowd as an odd (albeit innovative) pathology of modern society, crowd psychology "normalizes" crowds in two ways. First, market crowds are not only an excrescence of an otherwise rational economy, but the normal logic of markets. Second, this is linked to the usage of crowd psychology for processes of normalization. Thus, crowd semantics ceases to work exclusively as a crisis semantics and becomes a tool for organizing the process of inclusion. Whereas in Europe (notably in France and Germany) crowd semantics was primarily used for excluding small speculators from the market, the American investment philosophy of the contrarians accepts universal inclusion into financial markets and becomes a tool for constructing a contrarian speculator—a speculator who is able to withstand the temptations of the market crowd. In order to do this, it became necessary to rearticulate Le Bon's crowd psychology in at least one crucial aspect. Although market crowds are based on imitation, suggestion, and affect, the position of the figure of the leader has radically changed. Now the leader becomes a truly lonely figure because he ceases to serve as the point of identification for the market crowd. Otherwise, he could not benefit from the mistaken judgments of the market crowd. In line with this goes a crucial rearticulation of the idea of control. Although classical crowd psychology tried to control the crowd (although with skepticism regarding the odds of success), now it is the contrarian who has to control himself! Thus, the object of control has shifted from the crowd to the former leader. The ingenuity of this "market crowd psychology" is that it simultaneously provides a technique for observing the market crowd and one for controlling the contrarian speculator. The need to draw a permanent distinction between the observed crowd and one's self-observation becomes a generative principle. The contrarian speculator finds himself in a never-ending test—a test not only of the economic rightness of his investment decisions, but also a test of whether he is still himself or has already joined the crowd. Crowd psychology has thus become a technique for individualizing the ideal speculator. Paradoxically, the semantics of the crowd, which is also always a lament for the end of individualism, serves here as technique for constructing the speculator as *homo oeconomicus*.

13 WUNC

Charles Tilly

AT HOMER, ALASKA, COOK INLET meets the Gulf of Alaska. According to its Chamber of Commerce, the town of four thousand people occupies a spectacular site on Kachemak Bay in sight of the Kenai Mountains. Once a coal-mining town, Homer now relies for its livelihood mainly on commercial fisheries—salmon and halibut in abundance—and tourists. With moose, bear, puffins, eagles, porpoises, and killer whales close at hand, it seems like the antithesis of my own New York City, and well worth the visit.

Residents of Homer might be surprised to learn that their weekly routines owe something to the violent victories of a dissolute demagogue in London during the 1760s. But they do. The online *Homer News* posted an intriguing story in April 2003:

Monday has become the day for war supporters and peace activists to stage simultaneous demonstrations on the corner of Pioneer Avenue and Lake Street, prompting a barrage of honks and hollers—and the occasional profanity—from passing motorists. Saturday, meanwhile, has become the day that Anchor Point stakes its claim as the hub of patriotic rallying.

Deanna Chesser said there were no peace activists present as roughly 90 people gathered to show their support for military action in Iraq and the efforts of the men and women in the U.S. military. "And we don't have any Women in Black," said Chesser, referring to Homer's contingent of the global network that advocates peace and justice. The organizers of the Anchor Point rally are planning a repeat performance for noon on Saturday, with the addition of music and speakers. Chesser, whose son Davin recently was deployed to Kuwait, said she expects an even bigger turnout.

While those showing their support for the U.S.-led war in Iraq have Anchor Point all to themselves on Saturdays, they have only begun joining the peace activists on the corner at Pioneer and Lake for the past several weeks. For weeks prior to that, passersby out around noon on a Monday would see a subdued silent vigil taking place on the corner, which is also the site of Homer's Veteran's Memorial. The presence of protestors in front of the memorial stirred up resentment among some residents, prompting a call to begin a counter rally at the same time. "We want to take the corner back," said one flag-waving demonstrator. "Why don't you pray for our troops instead of for the Iraqis?" yelled a passing motorist, responding to the Women in Black assertion that their vigil is in observance of those lost in war.

But Sharon Whytal said she believed the choice to stand near the Veteran's Memorial symbolizes a concern for all those who are lost in military conflict. "It's true that many of us are there because we're grieving for the loss of veterans," Whytal said, adding that having both groups share the site also provides a powerful symbol—freedom in action.

Although there had been reports of some unpleasant exchanges between the two groups, there was little sign of it on Monday as close to 100 people stood on the corner, split evenly. The group waving flags stood out front on the sidewalk, lined up at the curb waving flags and cheering as passing motorists honked and waved. Standing 15 yards behind them, a line of Women in Black joined by a number of men, also dressed in black, remained silent for the duration of their vigil. "I don't feel offended that there are two groups there expressing their minds," Whytal said, referring to a sign bearing a slogan popular at many protests around the country: "This is what democracy looks like."[1]

Anchor Point, site of the solo prowar celebrations, lies sixteen miles west of Homer on the Sterling Highway, which leads up Kachemak Bay to Anchorage. With only an elementary school at home, Anchor Point's adolescents bus down the Sterling Highway to Homer for their high school educations. Thus the two towns often interact.

The same day that the *Homer News* reported Homer's dual displays of antiwar and prowar sentiment, it also ran a dispatch from Anchor Point describing the yellow ribbons tied to trees throughout the smaller town, and inviting people out for a new rally along Sterling Highway. Participants, it said, should bring American flags and pictures of family members serving in the Iraq War.[2] Inside Homer, the corner of Pioneer and Lake, where the two bands of around fifty people each stood fifteen yards apart, features not only the town's war memorial but also its police and fire departments. These activists stage their peaceful confrontations at one of Homer's central locations.

No one who stayed alert to national and international news during the spring of 2003 should have any difficulty decoding April's events in Homer and Anchor Point. Not just Americans, but people across the world, can easily recognize them as street demonstrations, a standard means of broadcasting support or opposition with regard to political issues. In this case, demonstration and counterdemonstration represented opposition to, and support for, American military intervention in Iraq. On the same days when citizens of Anchor Point and Homer took to the street, hundreds of street demonstrations were occurring elsewhere in the world. Some of them concerned the Iraq War, but most of them took up other locally urgent questions. In the early twenty-first century, the street demonstration looks like an all-purpose political tool—perhaps less effective in the short run than buying a legislator or mounting a military coup, but within democratic and semidemocratic regimes, a significant alternative to elections, opinion polls, and letter writing as a way of voicing public positions.

Although the news from Homer and Anchor Point does not tell us so, the twenty-first-century demonstration actually has two major variants. In the first variant, Homer style, participants gather in a symbolically potent public location where, through speech and action, they display their collective attachment to a well-defined cause. In the second, they proceed through public thoroughfares offering similar displays of attachment.[3] Often, of course, the two combine, as activists march to a favored rallying place, or as multiple columns converge from different places on a single symbolically powerful destination.

Occasionally, as in Homer, counterdemonstrators show up to advocate a contrary view and to challenge the demonstrators' claim over the spaces in question. Frequently, police or troops station themselves along the line of the march or around the place of assembly. Sometimes police or troops bar demonstrators' access to important spaces, buildings, monuments, or persons. At times, they deliberately separate demonstrators from counterdemonstrators. As in Homer, passersby or spectators often signal their approval or disapproval of the cause that the demonstrators are supporting. The symbolism and choreography of the street demonstration rival those of baseball and debutante balls.

Street demonstrations also have some identifiable kin: municipal parades, party conventions, mass meetings, inaugurals, commencements, religious revivals, and electoral rallies. Most citizens of democracies know the difference. But participants in such events sometimes bend them toward the forms and programs of demonstrations—for example, by wearing ostentatious symbols or shouting slogans in support of a cause. And many of the same principles apply: the separation of participants from spectators, the presence of guards to contain the crowd, and so on. Considered as a whole, this array of gatherings exhibits at once remarkable coherence, systematic internal variation, and type by type impressive uniformity across places, programs, and participants.

Another glance at the gatherings of Homer and Anchor Point reveals something more: an implicit scorecard against which participants, observers, and opponents measure demonstrations. The scorecard measures WUNC: worthiness, unity, numbers, and commitment. The term may be unfamiliar, but the idea is not. WUNC displays can take the form of statements, slogans, or labels that imply worthiness, unity, numbers, and commitment: Citizens United for Justice, Signers of the Pledge, Supporters of the Constitution, and so on. But collective self-representations often act them out in idioms that local audiences will recognize, for example:

Worthiness: somber dress; presence of clergy, dignitaries, and mothers with children.

Unity: wearing badges or headbands, marching in ranks, chanting.

Numbers: filling streets, signing petitions.

Commitment: braving bad weather; visible participation by the old and disabled.

Particular idioms vary enormously from one setting to another, but the general communication of WUNC connects those idioms. With no suggestion that people assign actual numerical ratings to demonstrations and their participants, we might schematize the rating system as:

$$W \times U \times N \times C = \text{IMPACT}$$

If any of the four values falls to zero, then the action as a whole loses impact; entirely unworthy or completely uncommitted participants, regardless of how numerous and/or unified, quite undermine the impact of any demonstration: imagine five thousand drunken dancers in a public plaza. More interestingly, a high value on one component compensates for a relatively low value on another; a very small number of highly worthy, unified, and committed persons can produce a large impact. The Women in Black, with their silent vigils, exemplify the potential impact of small numbers in the presence of worthiness, unity, and commitment.

Disputes over demonstrations often center on one component or another of the scorecard. Advocates, for example, usually provide higher estimates of the number participating in a demonstration than their critics do. But public disagreements also spring up over the other three components: Did the organizers bring in disreputable people in order to swell their numbers or intimidate their enemies? Did everyone there actually support the same cause? Did almost everyone run when the cops advanced? The frequent fierceness of such disputes indicates that the scorecard represents serious stakes.

Why? More than the pride of organizers is at risk. To see the stakes, step back and place the demonstration in its political context. Both the demonstration and the WUNC scorecard belong to a wider set of political interactions: those we call social movements. As it developed in the West after 1750, the social movement emerged from an innovative, consequential synthesis of three elements:

1. A sustained, organized public effort making collective claims on target authorities; let us call it a *campaign*.

2. Use of combinations from among the following forms of political action: creation of special-purpose associations and coalitions; public meetings; processions; rallies; demonstrations; petition drives; statements to and in public media; pamphleteering; call the ensemble of variable performances the *social movement repertoire*.

3. Participants' concerted public representations of WUNC on the part of themselves and/or their constituencies; call them *WUNC displays*.

Unlike a demonstration, a petition, a declaration, or a mass meeting, a *campaign* extends beyond any single event—although social movements often include petitions, declarations, and mass meetings. A campaign always links at least three parties: a group of self-designated claimants, some object or objects of claims, and a public of some kind. Even if a few zealots commit themselves to the movement night and day, the bulk of participants move back and forth between public claim making and other activities, including the day-to-day organizing that sustains a campaign. Homer and Anchor Point show us two small-scale local campaigns in progress. As the Women in Black suggest, however, both local campaigns connect with larger, longer campaigns occurring at national and international scales.

The social movement *repertoire* overlaps with the repertoires of other political phenomena, such as trade union activity and electoral campaigns. During the twentieth century, special-purpose associations and coalitions in particular began to do an enormous variety of political work across the world. But the integration of most or all of these performances into sustained campaigns marks off social movements from other varieties of politics.

That brings us back to WUNC. Worthiness, unity, numbers, and commitment characterize effective demonstrations. But they also characterize other activities of an effective social movement: participants' petitions, press interviews, pamphlets, ribbon tying, badge wearing, flag displaying, and just plain attendance at meeting after meeting after meeting.[4] WUNC matters politically because it conveys crucial political messages.

Let us roughly distinguish among three sorts of political claims that people make by means of WUNC displays: program claims, identity claims, and standing claims. *Program* claims involve stated support for or opposition to actual or proposed actions by the objects of movement claims. *Identity* claims consist of assertions that "we"—the claimants—constitute a unified force to be reckoned with. *Standing* claims assert ties and similarities to other political actors, for example as excluded minorities, properly constituted citizens' groups, or loyal supporters of the regime. Put together and backed by WUNC displays, program, identity, and standing claims convey the message that a distinct political actor has marched onto the scene. That actor may simply represent a public conscience to which officials ought to pay attention. But under the right circumstances, it could also form a voting bloc, create a new political party, organize a boycott, provide forces for an uprising, or otherwise interfere with politics as usual. WUNC says: pay attention to us; we matter.

What of the dissolute eighteenth-century English demagogue I promised you at the start? He represents a moment at the beginning of WUNC history, as social movements and WUNC displays were just starting to acquire a place in public politics. Before the 1760s, ordinary people had sometimes made spectacular displays of WUNC in moments of popular rebellion. But the regularization of social movements and WUNC displays as visible, available ways of making political claims first occurred in Great Britain and North America during the half century of incomplete democratization that included the American Revolution, but also saw unprecedented mobilization against slavery, for workers' rights, and on behalf of civil liberties across the Atlantic.

London's culprit—or hero—was John Wilkes. Wilkes was an agitator, but certainly no plebeian. Using his own money and his position as a member of the lesser gentry, he had entered Parliament in 1757. While in Parliament (1762), he started to edit an opposition newspaper, the *North Briton,* in response to Tobias Smollett's proadministration paper, named the *Briton.* Wilkes's title referred slightingly to Scots in the royal administration, especially the king's favorite, Lord Bute.

The *North Briton's* issue number 45 (1763) criticized a royal speech, written by his minister, in which the King praised the Treaty of Paris that had just ended the Seven Years' War:

The *Minister's speech* of last Tuesday is not to be paralleled in the annals of this country. I am in doubt whether the imposition is greater on the Sovereign, or on the nation. Every friend of this country must lament that a prince of so many great and admirable qualities, whom England truly reveres, can be brought to give the sanction of his sacred name to the most odious measures and the most unjustifiable public declarations from a throne ever renowned for truth, honour, and unsullied virtue.[5]

For this statement, the crown's attorneys charged Wilkes with seditious libel. In the legal environment of the time, not even a member of Parliament could publicly imply that the king had lied. For that offense, Wilkes spent time in the Tower of London. In his subsequent court appearances, Wilkes challenged the general warrant on which the king's officers had arrested him and seized his papers. He also explicitly identified his personal wrong with a general cause. In the Court of Common Pleas (May 1763), Wilkes declared that "The LIBERTY of all peers and gentlemen, and, what touches me more sensibly, of all the middling and inferior class of the people, which stands most in need of protection, is in my case this day to be finally decided upon: a question of such importance as to determine at once, whether ENGLISH LIBERTY be a reality or a shadow."[6] He eventually won his case and received compensation from the government for his illegal arrest and for seizure of his papers. He also appealed to freedom of speech, which won him cheers in the courtroom and the streets. His courtroom speeches launched the cry "Wilkes and Liberty!" as a fateful slogan for resistance to arbitrary power.

Later in 1763, Wilkes not only reprinted no. 45, but also produced a pornographic pamphlet called *Essay on Woman.* When government agents seized the proofs, began new proceedings against Wilkes, and assigned the London sheriff and the hangman to burn no. 45 publicly in Cheapside, an assembled crowd assaulted the sheriff and hangman, rescuing the sacred text from their hands. Wilkes himself soon fled across the Channel into France to escape prosecution. Parliament expelled him, and the courts declared him an outlaw. In 1768, however, he secretly returned to England, stood again for Parliament, won the poll, entered jail to be tried for his earlier offenses, and saw Parliament refuse to seat him.

During Wilkes's turbulent election campaign of March–April 1768, great crowds of his supporters marched to the polls with him and stopped carriages on the street to demand that their occupants cry "Wilkes and Liberty!" After Wilkes went to jail, his supporters thronged the surroundings of his prison, vying for a glimpse of their hero and still calling for Wilkes and Liberty. On April 28, 1768, the day after Wilkes went to jail, a massive gathering of

Wilkites near the King's Bench Prison called for Londoners to light up their windows; that was a standard sign of celebration for royal birthdays, military victories, and similar events. But they also held their own ceremony in which they burned a boot and Scots bonnet. The ritual punned on the name and Scottish origins of the king's minister, Lord Bute.

In the course of 1769, Parliament formally expelled Wilkes again. It then rejected three more parliamentary elections that he won from his prison cell. While Wilkes served his term as a popular hero, he received ample press attention, distinguished visitors, and gifts from all over the country; supporters in the town of Stockton, for example, sent him forty-five hams, forty-five tongues, and forty-five dozen bottles of ale.[7] The number forty-five was becoming a patriotic icon.

Wilkes went on to a distinguished career as public official and dissenting voice. In 1769, he managed election as a London alderman while still serving his prison term. He only went free (to great popular acclaim, fireworks, illuminations, and salvos of forty-five artillery shells) in 1770. He became London's sheriff in 1771 and soon began campaigning for the supreme municipal post of Lord Mayor. He actually won the City of London poll for the office in 1772, but the aldermen chose his less tainted competitor James Townsend. At that point, three thousand people entered the yard of Guildhall (the Lord Mayor's residence), shouting, "Damn my Lord Mayor for a scoundrel, he has got Wilkes' right, and we will have him out."[8]

After one more failed attempt, Wilkes gained election as Lord Mayor in 1774 and finally reentered the House of Commons that same year. He became a major speaker for the American cause during the bitter years of the Revolutionary War. Despite his time in prison, his court cases definitively established the legal rights of British periodicals to report and criticize governmental actions, including those of the crown. He not only commanded widespread popular support (including bands of activists from among the Spitalfields silk weavers), but also found allies among London merchants and officials who sought a counterweight to arbitrary royal power. An elite association that began as Friends of Mr. Wilkes and the Constitution soon became the Society of Supporters of the Bill of Rights, an important force for parliamentary reform. Although no one then used the term *social movement,* the association laid some of the foundations for the social movement as a new form of public politics in Great Britain.

In the very process of supporting Wilkes for Parliament, Wilkes's plebeian backers innovated. Almost no workers could vote in parliamentary elections of the 1760s, but workers came out in droves to accompany Wilkes to the polls. After Wilkes won the first round at Brentford on March 28, 1768, his followers began the attacks on opponents and the demands for cheers that continued through the election:

The mob behaved in a very outrageous manner at Hyde-park-corner, where they pelted Mr. Cooke, son of the city marshal, and knocked him from his horse, took off the wheels of one of the carriages, cut the harness, and broke the glasses to pieces; several other carriages were greatly damaged. The reason assigned for their proceedings is, that a flag was carried before the procession of Mr. Wilkes' antagonists, on which was painted, "No Blasphemer."[9]

Over the long run, Wilkites pushed out the boundaries of previously permissible public assemblies. They not only expanded electoral processions and public meetings into mass declarations of support for their hero, but also converted delegations and petition marches into opportunities to fill the streets instead of simply sending a few dignified representatives to speak humbly on behalf of their constituents. They pioneered the synthesis of crowd action with formal appeals to supporters and authorities. Although Wilkites remained stronger on unity, numbers, and commitment than on public displays of worthiness, they helped fashion the connection between the social movement repertoire and displays of WUNC.

Long before the 1760s, ordinary English and American people had made public claims of one kind or another. Authorized public assemblies such as holidays, funerals, and parish assemblies had, for example, long provided opportunities for people to voice complaints and to express support for popular leaders. Within limits, organized artisans and militia companies exercised the right to parade on their own holidays, and sometimes they used that right to state their opposition to powerful figures or oppressive programs. With proper shows of respect, they could also send humble delegations to petition for redress of collective wrongs. Within their own communities, workers, consumers, and householders repeatedly mounted resistance or vengeance against offenders of local rights or morality.[10] The implicit British theory of popular public politics ran something like this:

British subjects group into legally recognized bodies, such as guilds, communities, and religious sects, which exercise some specifiable collective rights—for example, the right to meet regularly in designated places of assembly.

The law protects such collective rights.

Local authorities have an obligation to enforce and respect the law.

Chosen representatives of such recognized bodies have the right—indeed, the obligation—to make public presentations of collective demands and grievances.

Authorities have an obligation to consider those demands and grievances, and to act on them when they are just.

Outside this framework, no one who has not been convoked by established authorities has a clear right to assemble, to state demands or grievances, or to act collectively.

Anyone who presumes to speak for the people at large out-side these limits infringes illegally on the prerogatives of Parliament; in fact, even electors have no right to instruct their parliamentary representatives once they have gained election.

Local and national authorities often looked the other way when local people violated these principles by activating customary routines of vengeance, approbation, and control. But authorities commonly invoked the principles—as represented, for example, in the Riot Act—when popular action threatened ruling class property, targeted influential members of the ruling classes, or banded together across local boundaries. During major episodes of rebellion and civil war like those that beset the British Isles between 1640 and 1692, to be sure, ordinary people frequently voiced radical claims in the names of religion and political tradition. But before the later eighteenth century, postrebellion repression always shut down those dangerous forms of popular expression.

On both sides of the Atlantic, however, members of the ruling classes had less risky ways of making claims. Authorities tolerated their clubs, dinners, pamphlets, and sometimes boisterous legislative assemblies. Elections to assemblies, especially to Parliament, provided splendid opportunities for license, as candidates treated electors, paid them off, and made extravagant public shows of their patronage. (Wilkes's 1757 election to Parliament cost him seven thousand pounds, when a farm laborer in London's hinterland was lucky to earn thirty pounds in a year.[11]) Social movements innovated not by inventing any one of these elements, but by converting and expanding them into disciplined vehicles for the expression of popular demands. Equally important, social movement efforts created a contested but genuine legal space within which their combination of campaigns, claim-making performances, and WUNC displays acquired political standing.

The Seven Years' War (1756–1763) gave this sort of political innovation a major impetus. For half a century before the 1750s, France and Great Britain had fought each other intermittently in Europe, on the high seas, in Asia, and across the Americas. France, which had earlier conquered Louisiana and what eventually became eastern Canada, found itself under attack in North America from both British colonists and British armies. Because colonists and armies alike were pushing back American Indian settlements, the French recruited ready allies within the major Indian federations. For residents of North American colonies, the Seven Years' War therefore became the French and Indian War.

Although the British side won dramatically—seizing Canada from the French, for example—momentous military efforts in Europe, India, and the Americas left the British treasury depleted and the government heavily in debt. In the North American colonies, British authorities tried to recoup some of their financial losses and to spread the cost of their greatly expanded military establishment. They tightened customs surveillance and imposed expensive duty stamps on a wide range of commercial and legal transactions. Resistance against customs and the Stamp Act united colonists as never before. It stimulated boycotts of British imports and the formation of extensive communication among cities of the thirteen colonies, as well as some of their Canadian counterparts. Chapters of the Sons of Liberty organized and enforced boycotts throughout the colonies. The Stamp Act's repeal (1766) only came after merchants, artisans, and other city dwellers had created an elaborate resistance network.

Boston and Massachusetts led the early effort, but other colonies soon joined them. Boston merchants had formed a Society for the Encouragement of Trade during the early 1760s; that society became a nucleus of dignified opposition to excessive taxation and regulation. It coordinated elite resistance to the Stamp Act, for example, in 1765 and 1766. At the same time, a group of smaller businessmen with substantial ties to workers began speaking out as Boston's Sons of Liberty, thus linking the mercantile community with the street activists who burned effigies, sacked houses, and assailed tax collectors.

Late in 1767, a meeting of Boston inhabitants organized by the expanding web of patriotic associations resolved to encourage American manufacturing and reduce reliance on British imports. "These resolutions," reported the *Annual Register,*

were adopted, or similar ones entered into, by all the old Colonies on the continent. In some time after, a circular letter was sent by the Assembly of Massachuset's Bay, signed by the Speaker, to all the other Assemblies in North America. The design of this letter was to shew the evil tendency of the late Acts of Parliament, to represent them as unconstitutional, and to propose a common union between the Colonies, in the pursuit of all legal measures to prevent their effect, and a harmony in their applications to Government for a repeal of them. It also expatiated largely on their natural rights as men, and their constitutional ones as English subjects; all of which, it was pretended, were infringed by these laws.[12]

Although leading merchants pursued their program by means of deliberate legal action, Boston sailors and artisans frequently took the law into their own hands. They forcefully resisted press gangs, blocked the quartering of soldiers, attacked customs agents, and hung effigies of British officials or their collaborators on the so-called Liberty Tree near the common that had been a flashpoint of action during the Stamp Act crisis of 1765–1766. They often doubled mercantile and official resistance with direct action.

When negotiations with the governor (as the representative of the crown in Massachusetts) and the British government grew rancorous, for example, the populace of Boston joined in. In May 1768, British customs officers seized Boston merchant John Hancock's ship *Liberty* for its failure to pay duties, whereupon Bostonians manned another ship, cut loose the sequestered vessel, and took it away: "The populace having assembled in great crowds upon this occasion, they pelted the Commissioners of the Customs with stones, broke one of their swords, and treated them in every respect with the greatest outrage; after which, they attacked their houses, broke the windows, and hauled the Collector's boat to the common, where they burnt it to ashes."[13] The customs officers fled first to a royal warship and then to Castle William in Boston Harbor. Town meetings of protest convened without official authorization throughout the Boston area. When word reached Boston (September 12) that two regiments were coming from Ireland and another body of military assembling in Halifax, Nova Scotia, to restore order in Boston, members of the Massachusetts Bay assembly began organizing resistance committees throughout the colony.

Massachusetts patriots quickly gathered allies throughout the other colonies. Mostly the allies began by using the established forms of elite public politics: resolutions, petitions, and solemn meetings. Innovative forms of contentious gatherings elsewhere in America, furthermore, regularly adapted the forms of previously tolerated assemblies. Consider this account of the King's birthday celebration of Charles Town (Charleston), South Carolina, in June 1768:

the same was celebrated here, with every demonstration of joy, affection and gratitude, that the most loyal subjects could give. The morning was ushered in with ringing of bells: At sun-rise, the forts and shipping displayed all their colours. Before noon, the detachment of his Majesty's troops posted here, under the command of Capt. Lewis Valentine Fyser; the Artillery company in a new and very genteel uniform, commanded by Capt. Owen Roberts; the Light-Infantry company, in their uniform; and the other companies of the Charles Town regiment of Militia, commanded by the honourable Colonel Bexie, were drawn up in different places, and marched to the Parade, where they made a handsome appearance, and were reviewed by his honour the Lieutenant-Governor, attended by his Council, the public Officers, &c. At noon, the cannon, &c. were fired as usual, and his Honour gave a most elegant entertainment at Mr. Dillon's, to a very numerous company, consisting of the Members of his Majesty's Council,

and of the Assembly, the public officers, civil and military, the Clergy, &c., &c. The afternoon was spent in drinking the usual, with many other loyal and patriotic toasts, and the evening concluded with illuminations, &c.[14]

Note the parallels with the fall's elections to the colonial assembly, when "mechanicks and other inhabitants of Charles Town" met at Liberty Point to choose candidates:

This matter being settled, without the least animosity or irregularity, the company partook of a plain and hearty entertainment, that had been provided by some on which this assembly will reflect lasting honour. About 5 o'clock, they all removed to a most noble LIVE-OAK tree, in Mr. Mazyck's pasture, which they formally dedicated to LIBERTY, where many loyal, patriotic, and constitutional toasts were drank, beginning with the glorious NINETY-TWO *Anti-Rescinders of Massachusetts Bay,* and ending with, *Unanimity among the Members of our ensuing Assembly not to rescind from the said resolutions,* each succeeded by three huzzas. In the evening, the tree was decorated with 45 lights, and 45 skyrockets were fired. About 8 o'clock, the whole company, preceded by 45 of their number, carrying as many lights, marched in regular procession to town, down King Street and Broad Street, to Mr. Robert Dillon's tavern; where the 45 lights being placed upon the table, with 45 bowls of punch, 45 bottles of wine, and 92 glasses, they spent a few hours in a new round of toasts, among which, scarce a celebrated Patriot of Britain or America was omitted; and preserving the same good order and regularity as had been observed throughout the day, at 10 they retired.[15]

In addition to its impressive capacity for alcohol, the Charleston electoral assembly's blend of political elements boggles the mind. In general form, it resembles the king's birthday, except for the notable absence of military and royal officials. But Charleston's Liberty Tree directly emulated its Boston model. The toast to ninety-two antirescinders (those members of the Massachusetts assembly who voted against withdrawing a strong circular letter of February 1768 that had condemned new taxes and called for united resistance to Britain across the colonies) identified the

South Carolinians with Massachusetts patriots. The number forty-five, obviously, marked the legacy of John Wilkes. Lighting up (in this case the procession rather than the city's windows) likewise enacted a public declaration of allegiance and solidarity.

As of 1768, opponents of arbitrary rule had not yet invented WUNC displays and social movements in London, Boston, or Charleston. Nevertheless, their innovations moved popular public politics toward social movement forms. They enlisted ordinary citizens such as artisans and sailors in campaigns of sustained opposition to royal policies. (In contrast to Boston's small merchants, Charleston's Sons of Liberty expanded from a volunteer fire company composed largely of artisans.[16]) They combined special-purpose associations, public meetings, marches, petitions, pamphleteering, and statements widely reported in the public media. To some extent, they even adopted displays of WUNC. The *South Carolina Gazette* remarked on "the same good order and regularity as had been observed throughout the day."

Although the "mechanicks and other inhabitants" of Charleston remained quite capable of attacking royal officials, resisting customs agents, and sacking the houses of their designated enemies, at least on ceremonial occasions, they abandoned direct action in favor of program, identity, and standing claims: we are upright people, we deserve a voice, and we oppose arbitrary rule with determination. In fact, Charleston's artisans "spearheaded" the city's anti-importation agreements in alliance with merchant-patriot Christopher Gadsden.[17] Integration of popular forces into elite opposition campaigns split the ruling classes but made an important step toward the creation of the social movement as a distinct form of public politics.

The social movement emerged in England and America against the background of profound political and economic changes. Four catchwords tag the essential changes: war, parliamentarization, capitalization, and proletarianization.

As the influence of the Seven Years' War has already suggested, war did not simply mobilize national populations; it expanded state structures, inflated governmental expenditures, increased extraction of resources from the government's subject population, created new debt, and at least temporarily fortified the state's repressive apparatus. On the British side, the wars of American independence dwarfed the Seven Years' War in all these regards, only to seem puny themselves by comparison with the gigantic wars of the French Revolution and Napoleon.[18]

In North America, the aftermath of the Seven Years' War weighed heavily: the British stationed a peacetime army of ten thousand men, tightened control over customs, and imposed a series of revenue measures such as the Stamp Act of 1765. The Revolutionary War (as it came to be known in the thirteen rebellious colonies) cost the Americans incomparably more in personal services, money, and debt than had British impositions after the Seven Years' War. The war effort created the relatively exiguous national state structure that prevailed for decades.

During the European wars of the French Revolution and Napoleon, the new United States first evaded, then abrogated, its treaty obligations to France, which had provided crucial aid to the American cause during the American Revolution. With minor exceptions, the United States kept its distance from the European war until 1812, warring mainly with Indians on its western and southern frontiers. But in 1812 the Americans ended five years of uneasy negotiation by declaring war on Great Britain, invading Canada, battling Indians deemed to be allied with Britain, and conducting a series of maritime battles in the Great Lakes, the Atlantic, and the Gulf of Mexico. They also suffered the torching of Washington and the invasion of Maine before the European war ground to a halt in 1814.

Parliamentarization occurred more subtly than making war, but with no less effect on public politics. It had two related components: a general expansion of Parliament's power, and a shift of national political struggles from king to Parliament.[19] War-driven taxation and debt increased parliamentary power; each governmental request for new funds initiated a struggle in which Parliament extracted new concessions. (Parliamentary consent to taxes also reduced open rebellion against taxation, in contrast to eighteenth-century France and the American colonies.)[20] As parliamentary power increased, royal patronage became less crucial to political success, Parliament intervened more broadly in public affairs, and the stakes of parliamentary actions for national constituencies (whether enfranchised or not) greatly increased. The Americans replaced the king with relatively weak executives, investing heavily in parliamentary power at the national and, especially, state levels.

Capitalization occurred on both sides of the Atlantic as agrarian, commercial, and industrial capital all greatly increased in scope. Great Britain was becoming the world's greatest center of manufacturing and trade while its agricultural production increased dramatically in scale. The American colonies and their successor United States served chiefly as tributaries to the British economy, but they too experienced momentous agrarian, commercial, and industrial expansions after 1750. Although landlords certainly did well and manufacturers were beginning to make their marks, merchant capitalists in particular gained heft within the British and American economies.

By proletarianization, let us understand not just the growth of routinized factory labor (although that did occur to an unprecedented extent), but more generally an increase in the proportion of the population depending on wage labor for survival. In British agriculture, concentration of landholding and leaseholding greatly increased the share of wage-laborers among all cultivators. Proletarianization occurred even more rapidly in manufacturing, where self-employed artisans lost ground to wage-dependent workers in shops, factories, and their own households. The picture differed significantly in North America, where slaves performed an increasing proportion of all labor in southern agriculture, proletarianization resembling its British counterpart occurred in the coastal zones of commerce and manufacturing, but the expanding frontier provided abundant opportunities for smallholders and petty traders.

What connects war, parliamentarization, capitalization, and proletarianization, on one side, with the growth of WUNC and social movements, on the other? To put complex matters schematically:

Mobilization and payment for war simultaneously increased the influence of governmental activity on ordinary people's welfare and engaged government in negotiation over the terms under which landlords, merchants, workers, soldiers, sailors, and others would contribute to the collective effort.

Despite the exiguous franchise, the shift of power toward Parliament meant that the impact of legislative actions on everyone's welfare greatly increased, and that because of representation's geographic organization, everyone in Great Britain and the colonies acquired a more direct connection to the men—the elected legislators—who were taking consequential political actions.

Although great landlords continued to dominate national politics, capitalization expanded the independent influence of merchants in London and elsewhere, and these men increasingly became the government's creditors and managers of capital.

As many a social commentator feared, proletarianization reduced the dependence of workers on particular landlords, masters, and other patrons, and thereby freed workers to enter political life on their own.

In combination, these changes promoted contingent alliances between dissident aristocrats and bourgeois (who lacked the numbers for independent action against the bulk of ruling classes) and dissatisfied workers (who lacked the legal and social protection supplied by patrons).

13A 'Csőd,' 'Tömeg,' 'Csődtömeg': Hungarian

Dániel Margócsy

The Emergence of New Words

During the early nineteenth century, tens of thousands of Hungarian words were coined in order to reform and modernize the Hungarian language. In contrast to the relatively large semantic fields of the old Hungarian equivalents of crowd (*sokaság*, "multitude, manyness," and *nép*, "people, folk"), the two new crowds-related words that were coined in the nineteenth century, *tömeg* and *csőd*, had more specific meanings. *Tömeg* was derived from the verb *töm*, "to fill." *Csőd* is a truncated version of the verb *csődül*, "to run together." *Csőd* very quickly lost its connections to the crowd and only retained the more popular meaning "bankruptcy" or simply "failure."

According to *A Magyar Nyelv Történeti-Etimológiai Szótára (TESz)*, *tömeg* was first used in 1828, coined probably by the Hungarian poet Vörösmarty, and it referred to the "multitude of gathered people." Although it could also refer to a "heap" and "vastness," these uses went out of fashion by the early 1840s, and *tömeg* most often referred to "crowd." The expression *néptömeg*, "people-mass," was used by the translator of Tocqueville's *Democracy in America*.

Although other meanings took over rather quickly, the *TESz* informs us that *csőd* originally had the meaning of crowd. The less frequent *csődület* has retained its connotations to crowd, however; in 1844, Ignác Nagy wrote of *csődületi*

Such alliances, in their turn, facilitated appropriation and expansion of special-purpose associations, public meetings, petition campaigns, disciplined marches, and related forms of claim making by working-class and petit bourgeois activists while making it more difficult for authorities to maintain legal prohibitions of those activities.

Such alliances turned the same working-class and petit bourgeois activists away from direct, destructive action as a means of making claims.

Joint actions of dissident aristocrats, radical bourgeois, indignant petit bourgeois, and workers thus created precedents and legal spaces for social movement actions, even when current campaigns and alliances ended.

Of course, these changes did not occur in an instant. Between the turbulent events of 1768 and the clear availability of social movement politics to a wide variety of actors on either side of the Atlantic, another half-century of struggle and evolution elapsed.

On the British side, London provided the first major setting for social movement innovation. The city of London, which grew from about 675,000 to 865,000 inhabitants between 1750 and 1800, competed with Istanbul for the rank of largest European city, and thus (after Beijing) of earth's second-biggest metropolis. By that time, London had become Europe's greatest port, a vastly influential center of trade, and the world center of banking. London's financiers had their fingers on the pulse (or their hands on the throat) of the entire British Empire.

Within London, however, financiers did not become radicals. On the contrary: the bourgeois who supported Wilkes and his radical successors concentrated disproportionately among middling tradesmen.[21] They aligned themselves against both the court and great capitalists. Their popular backers, in turn, came especially from workers in London's better organized trades: sailors, coal heavers, silk weavers, and a host of other artisans and clerks.

Not that all London workers supported radical causes; the thousands mobilized by Lord George Gordon's anti-Catholic Protestant Association in 1780, for example, also seem to have come chiefly from the London working classes. Members of the Protestant Association first marched with Lord Gordon to Parliament for presentation of a petition for repeal of a 1778 act that had made minor concessions to Catholic rights, then (on parliamentary refusal to negotiate under pressure) broke into groups, some of which went on to sack Catholic chapels, houses of prominent Catholics, and houses of officials reputed to be protecting Catholics. Of those apprehended and prosecuted for participating in attacks on Catholic properties, "two in every three of those tried were wage-earners, journeymen, apprentices, waiters, domestic servants and labourers; a smaller number were petty employers, craftsmen and tradesmen."[22] Broadly speaking, nevertheless, London's major mobilizations of the later eighteenth century pitted worker-bourgeois alliances against coalitions of finance and Court, with some segment of Parliament typically aligned against the Court.

As the Protestant Association's temporary prominence suggests, mass-membership associations figured ever more centrally in British popular mobilizations. The eighteenth century's greatest surge of associational activity occurred during the early years of the French Revolution. During those years, elite demands for parliamentary reform that had been active for two decades coupled with popular demands for democratization in the French style, based in clubs, societies, and popular associations as well as in religious congregations. Revolution societies, constitutional societies, and corresponding societies took the French Revolution, the American Revolution, and Britain's own Glorious Revolution of 1689 as their points of reference. Defenders of church and king likewise mobilized against secular democrats by means of specialized associations. From 1794 to the end of the Napoleonic Wars, governmental repression damped down associational activity, especially on the part of workers. Associations returned in a great burst after war's end. By that time, with the prominent exception of still-illegal workers' "combinations," associations and their public meetings had become standard means of popular expression.

At what point, then, can we reasonably say that the social movement had become a distinctive, connected, recognized, and widely available form of public politics? We are looking for times and places in which people making collective claims on authorities frequently form special-purpose associations or named coalitions; hold public meetings; communicate their programs to available media; stage processions, rallies, or demonstrations; and through all these activities, offer concerted displays of worthiness, unity, numbers, and commitment. If the complex occurs together regularly outside of electoral campaigns and management-labor struggles, we will be more confident that the social movement has arrived on its own terms. We recognize all the individual elements in British public politics of the later eighteenth century. But by these standards, British politics did not institutionalize social movements until after the Napoleonic Wars.

In Britain, the immediate postwar years proved crucial. Soon after 1815, nationwide campaigns arose for parliamentary reform: broadened franchise, more equal representation of electors, annual meetings of Parliament, and often further refine-

betegség, "urban disease," describing the maleficent effects of the putrid scent of the dirt and water in the city of Pest.

Sándor Petőfi, the most successful poet of the 1840s (and, possibly, of all Hungarian literature) is another example of the popularity of *csőd* both as a word and as an urban practice in the period:

Így múlik éjünk s napunk,
Nincs híja semminek,
Mig végre csődöt nem kapunk,
Mi boldog pestiek.

That's how our days and nights pass by,
We are not in want of anything,
Until we go bankrupt,
We, happy citizens of Pest.
—A Boldog Pestiek, 1844

By 1846, *csőd* seems to have ceased to have the connotations of "mass," "amassing," "running together," because the term *csődtömeg* was coined in order to describe the goods in possession of an insolvent company. István Pajor used this new word in 1846 in his work on the Hungarian laws of bills of exchange.

Beyond the Midcentury

There is some evidence that suggests that by the end of the nineteenth century, of the two new coinages, *csőd* ceased to denote crowd, and *tömeg* denoted a very clear concept of crowd, although it also retained the scientific meaning of "ponderable mass."

Ballagi's dictionary from 1873 does not mention *csőd* as having anything to do with crowds. In 1902, the second volume of the linguistic journal *Magyar Nyelv* indicates that it "used to mean tender, and even gathered people."

In contrast, by the beginning of the 1900s, *tömeg* seems to have only predominantly one meaning outside scientific contexts: "crowd." The Hungarian poet Endre Ady uses the word only in this sense in his poetry. For him, *tömeg* is not a positive concept, as the following lines suggest:

Parfümöt még Nietzsche sem izzadt
S a tömeg ma sem illatos.

Not even Nietzsche sweated perfume,
And the masses are not fragrant nowadays either.
—Henrik úr lovagol

Révai Nagylexikona gave a definition of *tömeg* in 1925 that still seems to hold. It is "the multitude [*sokaság*] of men who have common feelings and intentions. We often call a multitude of people *tömeg* if they are together in space, but it is necessary that they show similar spiritual characteristics. In modern democracies, the concept of *tömeg* becomes more and more important, because its political importance grows, cf. *tömeglélektan*." This clear-cut definition is then further elaborated under the heading *tömeglélektan* (mass psychology, *Massenpsychologie;* in contrast to *néplélektan*, *Völkerpsychologie*), where the reader is referred to the works of Le Bon and Tönnies's *Kritik der Öffentlichen Meinung.*

It seems probable that by the 1940s, *tömeg* acquired a meaning that was more influenced by contemporary psychological theories than by its etymological origins. It has taken up such connotations more easily than *nép*, which remains polysemous until today. *Csőd* no longer has the meaning "crowd," and *sokaság* is less and less frequently used.[1]

ments such as secret ballots and stipends for members of Parliament that would make holding office possible for poorer men. At the same time, and in overlapping efforts, unprecedented efforts went into organizing workers to demand parliamentary action on their behalf. Because officials often refused authorization for popular reformers to meet in public buildings, assemblies repeatedly took place on the streets or in open fields. They thus became half meeting and half demonstration. What is more, delegations frequently marched to the place of assembly, thus linking the twinned forms of the demonstration: the street march, and the disciplined assembly in a public space. Although London continued to play a significant role, greater innovations occurred in England's northern industrial districts, where workers organized and acted energetically during the postwar years.

In the cotton manufacturing center of Stockport, the formation of the Stockport Union for the Promotion of Human Happiness in October 1818 helped mobilize people of the industrial North on behalf of relief for political prisoners, but also on behalf of parliamentary reform. The Stockport Union sponsored repeated reform meetings, organized petitions for political prisoners, issued remonstrances, and staged demonstrations. The union sent a delegation of some fourteen hundred men and forty women marching in ranks with banners to the famous reform meeting of August 16, 1819, at St. Peter's Fields, Manchester, attacked by the Manchester and Salford Yeomanry, and thenceforth infamous as Peterloo. Of the delegation's march, Manchester merchant Francis Philips reported,

On the 16th August I went on the Stockport Road about eleven or a little after, and I met a great number of persons advancing towards Manchester with all the regularity of a regiment, only they had no uniform. They were all marching in file, principally three abreast. They had two banners with them. There were persons by the side, acting as officers and regulating the files. The order was beautiful indeed.[23]

Particular organizations such as the Stockport Union rose and fell with the times, and they continued to face governmental surveillance or outright repression. But by the 1820s, all the essential elements of social movements—campaigns, repertoires, and WUNC displays—had cohered and become widely available to organized interests in Great Britain. The vast, effective mobilizations of the 1820s and 1830s for workers' rights, Catholic emancipation, and parliamentary reform locked those elements in place.[24] By the 1830s, furthermore, social movement strategies had become available not only to reformers and radicals, but also to conservative activists such as the widely effective English opponents of Catholic emancipation.[25]

In 1925, J. Franklin Jameson devoted an influential lecture series to "The American Revolution Considered as a Social Movement." As celebrations of the Revolution's one hundred fiftieth anniversary were beginning, Jameson called for students of the American Revolution to emulate specialists in the French Revolution by expanding from political and military to social history. "The stream of revolution," he argued,

could not be confined within narrow banks, but spread abroad upon the land. Many economic desires, many social aspirations were set free by the political struggle, many aspects of colonial society profoundly altered by the forces thus let loose. The relations of social classes to each other, the institution of slavery, the system of land-holding, the course of business, the forms and spirit of the intellectual and religious life, all felt the transforming hand of revolution, all emerged from under it in shapes advanced many degrees nearer to those we know.[26]

He closed his lectures with his major claim "that all the varied activities of men in the same country and period have intimate relations with each other, and that one cannot obtain a satisfactory view of any one of them by considering it apart from the others."[27] For Jameson, it turns out, "social movement" equaled large-scale social transformation rather than a specific form of politics. As our earlier looks at Boston and Charleston might lead us to expect, Jameson drew attention away from the heroic leaders and dramatic moments of revolutionary action to the broad participation of colonists in the struggles of 1765–1783.

Might we nevertheless claim the American Revolution as a social movement, or a series of social movements? Considering the same period we have examined in London and Boston, Sidney Tarrow points to innovations in political actions: amid the burning of effigies and sacking of houses, the organization of boycotts and nonimportation agreements signaled the creation of "modular" forms of politics that could easily migrate from place to place, group to group, issue to issue:

Thenceforth, nonimportation and boycotting became the modular weapons of the American rebellion, employed most clamorously in the controversy over tea in Boston harbor. The effectiveness of the tactic was not lost on Britain: in 1791, the English antislavery association used a boycott on the importation of sugar from the West Indies to put pressure on Parliament to abolish the slave trade. From a parochial response to new taxes from the periphery of the British Empire, the boycott had migrated to its core.[28]

Tarrow rightly identifies the invention of quick-moving modular tactics as a hallmark of social-movement activity, and a significant contrast with the more parochial attachments to local settings involved in effigy burning and house sacking.

13B   Protest Crowds

Tom Seligman

Then in a youthful "purple haze." Now trying to sort out memories from subsequent reflections, shared stories with friends, and media accounts. The period from 1964 to 1969 was turbulent for me as a young San Franciscan opposed to the war in Vietnam and the draft and as an activist for civil rights and social equity. The psychedelic and drug scene was pervasive, as were organizing antiwar and civil rights demonstrations, some of which turned violent, happenings and "love-ins" in Golden Gate Park, concerts at the Fillmore and Avalon, and lots of Haight-Ashbury street action. How to find and reconstruct memories? The strongest are of an abundance of desire to alter the world, stop wars, live in love and peace, radically change the way the American "establishment" controlled social and economic activities at home and abroad. Individuals and crowds are significant in these memories.

The single most powerful and probably most significant mass action I was involved with was the occupation of the Mall in Washington D.C. in the spring of 1968. My ex-wife and I were living in New York and with friends were planning to build one of the "resurrection schools," a geodesic dome, on the Mall to provide classroom space to teach inner-city, mostly African American children during the summer. We drove in our VW to Washington, arriving at dusk to a remarkable absence of any traffic, with fire engines and smoke all over the skyline. We had no radio in our car, no knowl-

edge that Martin Luther King had been assassinated, that D.C. was in a state of emergency, or
that a curfew had been imposed. On the outskirts
we stopped at a traffic light, and a pickup pulled
alongside. A man in plain clothes pointed a shot-
gun at us. He asked what we were doing driving about. After hearing our story, he told us to go
directly to our friend's in southeast D.C. without
stopping. We arrived safely and found our friends
and others locked in their apartment. Throughout the night, tanks and National Guard troops
rolled down the street to the Capitol area. After
a sleepless night of intense discussion, we ventured forth to the Mall to try to see what was going
on—to figure out what to do—what was possible. After a day or two, we were on the Mall along
with thousands of others, camping, making music, building resurrection schools, and conducting antiwar demonstrations. We protested the
presence of troops and tanks by placing flowers in the barrel of rifles held by men my age or
younger. For several days after the rioting qui-
eted, we built the school and returned to New
York—drained—upset—confused—frightened.

Why were crowds essential? The sense of solidarity and belonging in such a clear and visceral
way was the most important reason and the most
enduring sensation. We were together—optimistic—and we gained strength through our numbers—strength for a shared cause. The rain, the
muddy Mall, the troops, the tanks—the hardships
brought us even closer together. We worked hard,
believed passionately, cared to extremes, and as a
result, we were comrades.

Another memory is fear. Fear of losing control—
of the crowd out of control, of armed, equally frightened young soldiers shooting us (as later happened

Those tactics generalized WUNC displays. But does the emergence of modular
tactics qualify the American Revolution as a social movement?

We are still looking for times and places in which people making collective
claims on authorities frequently form special-purpose associations or named coalitions; hold public meetings; communicate their programs to available media; stage
processions, rallies, or demonstrations; and through all these activities offer concerted displays of worthiness, unity, numbers, and commitment. As in Great Britain during the same period, the answer is clear: all the individual elements existed
in the new United States of 1783, but they had not yet congealed into a distinctive,
widely available form of popular politics. As in Great Britain, the proliferation of
interconnected associations from 1765 onward transformed popular politics and
laid the basis for emergence of full-fledged social movements.

Might antislavery mobilization, as Tarrow hints, constitute a crucial exception? During the 1770s and 1780s, jurists in both Great Britain and North America began to deliver rulings that challenged the legality of slavery. The Vermont
constitution of 1777 banned slavery, and between 1780 and 1784, Pennsylvania,
Massachusetts, Rhode Island, and Connecticut took legal steps toward general
emancipation. (New York did not join the move toward general emancipation
until 1799.) In both Great Britain and the American colonies, organized Quakers
were creating antislavery associations during the 1770s. In fact, Friends congregations on both sides of Atlantic were then expelling members who refused to free
their own slaves.

In 1783, English Quakers sent Parliament its first (but by no means its last) petition for abolition of the slave trade. Britain's nationwide campaigns against the
slave trade began, however, in 1787, with mass petitioning and formation of the
Society for the Abolition of the Slave Trade. The initiative did not come from London, but from the industrial North, especially Manchester. The eleven thousand
signatures on the Manchester petition of December 1787 represented something
like two-thirds of all the city's men who were eligible to sign.[29] As Tarrow says, furthermore, antislavery activists introduced another weighty innovation: a general
boycott of sugar grown with the labor of slaves, with perhaps three hundred thousand families participating in 1791 and 1792.[30]

New petition drives surged from 1806 to 1808, in the midst of which both Great
Britain (or, rather, the United Kingdom, which had formally joined Ireland with
England, Wales, and Scotland in 1801) and the United States outlawed the slave
trade. After multiple mobilizations, Parliament finally passed an Emancipation
Act applicable throughout its colonies in 1833. The United States remained fierce-

ly divided on the issue and eventually fought a civil war over it. Yet by the 1830s, abolition had become the crux of a vast American social movement. Where in this sequence might we reasonably say that full-fledged social movements were flying?

We face a classic half full–half empty question. Somewhere between the Manchester petition of 1787 and the 1833 parliamentary banning of slavery in the British Empire, the full panoply of campaign, repertoire, and WUNC displays came together. When did it happen? Let us split the question into two parts: When did antislavery meet all the tests for a genuine social movement? When did the political form represented by antislavery become widely available for other sorts of claims? To the first part, we may reply that some time between 1791 (the sugar boycott) and 1806 (the second great petition drive), British abolitionists assembled campaign, repertoire, and WUNC displays into a single political package; they thus have some claim to constitute the world's first social movement.

For the second part, however, we must allow another decade to elapse: on models drawn quite directly from antislavery, we then find workers, reformers, Catholics, and others regularly forming special-purpose associations, holding public meetings indoors and outdoors, adopting slogans and badges, staging marches, producing pamphlets, and projecting claims with regards to programs, identities, and political relations. For such a complex and momentous change, the quarter century from 1791 to 1816 looks like a very rapid transition indeed.

Might Francophiles then make a case for French priority? As the Revolution of 1789 proceeded, French activists certainly formed politically oriented associations at a feverish pace, made concerted claims by means of those associations, held public meetings, marched through the streets, adopted slogans and badges, produced pamphlets, and implemented local revolutions through most of the country.[31] If such mobilizations had continued past 1795 *and* if they had become available for a wide variety of claims thereafter, we would probably hail the French as inventors of the social movement—or at least coinventors with their British counterparts. As it happened, however, the full array of social movement claim making did not acquire durable political standing in France for another half century, around the Revolution of 1848.[32] Even then, repression under Louis Napoleon's Second Empire delayed the full implementation of social movement politics through much of the country for another two decades.

More unexpectedly, Dutch eighteenth-century activists might also have some claim to have institutionalized social movements, at least temporarily. In what Dutch historians call the Fourth English War (1780–1784), Dutch forces joined indirectly in the wars of the American Revolution, taking a severe beating from

at Kent State)—of riot—of serious injury—to my friends—to me.

With memory dim, what is the legacy for me filtered through subsequent years? I guess I learned that for social action to be successful, it often requires mass action. While mass action is powerful, crowds and social actions can be subverted from their goals. Governments, tradition, and inertia are powerful forces resisting change—thus when change comes, it comes slowly. I also realize that what I perceive as social gains that have been "won" (or legislated) can be later lost if those who care are not constantly vigilant—remaining activists. (I think of *Roe v. Wade* in this context.)

Having had three male children, I have also seen that because I am an activist does not mean they will be. Those of us from the pre–baby boom civil rights and anti-Vietnam days often turn our children and their friends off by frequently recounting the glorified experiences of the late 1960s. They see us as stuck in nostalgia. Because they have had no similar major issues directly affecting their own lives until 9/11/01, my children and their generation nonetheless require their own space and time to effect change—with or without mass action.

superior British naval power. As the disastrous naval engagements continued, a sort of pamphlet war broke out within the Netherlands. Supporters of the Prince of Orange attacked the leaders of Amsterdam and Holland as the opposing Patriots (based especially in Holland) replied in kind; each blamed the other for the country's parlous condition. Drawing explicitly on the American example, Patriots called for a (preferably peaceful) revolution. Earlier claim making in the Low Countries conformed to local variants of the older repertoire we have already seen operating in England and America.[33] But during the 1780s, petition campaigns began in earnest: first they demanded recognition of John Adams as a legal representative of that contested entity, the United States of America, and then they proposed remedies to a whole series of domestic political problems.

Citizens' committees (possibly modeled on American committees of correspondence) soon began to form along with citizens' militias across Holland's towns. In a highly segmented political system, their incessant pressure on local and regional authorities actually worked. Between 1784 and 1787, Patriot factions managed to install new, less aristocratic constitutions in a number of Dutch cities, and even in a whole province, Overijssel. The Prince of Orange and his followers, however, still disposed of two crucial advantages: British financial support and military backing from the Prince's brother-in-law, King Frederick William of Prussia. Late in 1787, a Prussian invasion broke the Netherlands' Patriot Revolution.[34]

The next invading army arrived in 1795, when French revolutionary forces established a Batavian Republic with active support from revived Patriots. Despite governmental alterations on a French model, the new republic soon deadlocked between advocates of centralizing reforms in the French style and the customary federalism of the Netherlands. From 1798 to 1805, a quartet of top-down coups—unaccompanied by widespread popular mobilization—produced the major political changes. The republic gave way to a French satellite Kingdom of Holland (1806), then to direct incorporation into France (1810–1813). The post-Napoleonic settlement created a bifurcated kingdom that until 1839 nominally included both the Netherlands and what became Belgium.

From the French takeover onward, the Dutch state assumed a much more centralized administrative structure than had prevailed in the heyday of autonomous provinces. With the Batavian Republic of 1795, committees, militias, and Patriots returned temporarily to power, only to be integrated rapidly into the new sort of regime, with French overseers never far away. Recognizable social movements did not start occurring widely in the Netherlands until after Napoleon's fall. Thus counterrevolution, reaction, and conquest wiped out another possible candidate for the social movement's inventor. Great Britain retains priority, in close interaction with its American colonies. Since the Anglo-American invention of social movements and their WUNC displays, both of them have spread throughout the world with democratization, and with glimmers of democracy. Both of them still occur chiefly in democratic or democratizing countries rather than authoritarian regimes.

Although it could have gone otherwise, then, the good citizens of Homer, Alaska, are participating in a worldwide form of political broadcasting that originated especially in Anglo-American struggles of the eighteenth century. Over the last two hundred fifty years, WUNC displays and social movements have changed with their times. Still, they exhibit impressive continuities. Long may they thrive.

14 Far Above the Madding Crowd: The Spatial Rhetoric of Mass Representation

Andrew V. Uroskie

Introduction: Counting Crowds

On February 21, 2003, the *San Francisco Chronicle*, Northern California's largest paper, led with a headline "Photos Show 65,000 at Peak of S.F. Rally." The occasion was an unprecedented collective protest—potentially "the largest synchronized global dissent in history"—across the major capitals of the world.[1] It marked a decisive end to the sympathy which had greeted the United States in the aftermath of 9/11, and revealed the depth of incomprehension, fear, and anger to which the policies and rhetoric of the Bush administration has so quickly given rise (figs. 14.1 and 14.2). The specific number presented by the *Chronicle* was taken not as an indication as to the size and strength of the protest, but rather of its paucity and weakness. In fact, the specific number—and the story that would unfold beneath it—did not concern themselves with the situation to which this mass of people had gathered to respond, but only with the situation of the mass gathering itself.[2]

The original number of demonstrators, reported at two hundred thousand by both organizers and police alike, had been disseminated to news agencies throughout the world. So although this story was about the relative paucity of the crowd (at least compared to the initial estimates), it was essentially about the more general problem of visually representing the crowd—that is, of representing a phenomenon that was itself in a particular act of representation. In so doing, the *Chronicle* unconsciously placed itself in a long line of questioning, within the arts and philosophy of the modern era, of this problem of "mass representation." This tradition concerns both the crowd as a specific problem of visual representation, and the way in which this particular question of representing the

307

Figure 14.1 Anti-War Protests in Madrid, Spain,

Figure 14.2 and Rome, Italy, February 15, 2003.

masses comes to stand in for a more general question of mass representation as such within twentieth-century visual culture. This number reproduced in the headline—sixty-five thousand—was shocking at the time because both organizers and police had estimated a much higher number. Throughout the 1990s, as various groups became adept at organizing large-scale demonstrations in Washington, Americans were treated to the Million Man March, the Million Mom March, the Promise Keepers rally, and so forth. In a quintessentially American supersizing of the demonstration, these increasingly regularized spectacles were greeted with progressively less and less media attention. According to Todd Gitlin, the practice of splitting the difference between often widely divergent estimates of the protesters and the police agencies was finally abandoned in the 1990s in favor of simply reporting both numbers, thereby admitting a certain representational instability. The size of the crowd is by necessity what Alex Jones of the Harvard Center on the Press, Politics and Public Policy calls "an emotional issue, not a factual issue" precisely in that, by seemingly adjudicating the significance of the demonstration, it stands to confirm or deny the very existence of the situation to which the demonstration was ostensibly responding.[3] For tens of thousands, the desire to be "seen,

heard, and counted" was much more than an articulation of disagreement with state policy; it was a primary instance of subjectification—a rare moment of collective disidentification from the world-as-presented through the often totalizing lens of the mass media.

Yet the *Chronicle*, which commissioned this particular survey, organized a very different kind of truth-claim based around a very different account of representation. Its representation of the demonstration was presented as the truth of the detached, objective view—a truth ostensibly beyond emotion and politics, gained through the resources of aerial photography and "scientific" procedure. "The world from above looks different than it does from street level" here signifies, "above the clamor of the street, above the intense emotions of the interested parties, above all that would *distort* one's perception, there is a clear, objective view to be found—a 'detached' and therefore 'truthful' perspective" (fig. 14.3). In the upper-level corner of the page, under the heading "The Camera," we encounter a torrent of seemingly superfluous technical minutiae. We find, for instance, that the camera's aperture had been set to f4, its shutter speed was 1/300 of a second, and that the film used had been AFGA Pan 80. Rhetorically, this detail is essential to the overall message being conveyed, namely, "This sur-

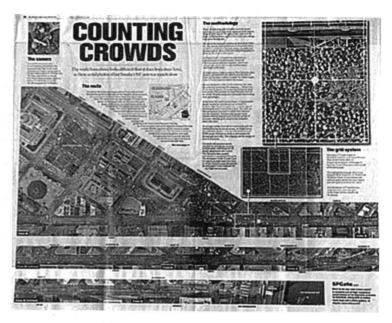

Figure 14.3 "Counting Crowds: The world from above looks different than it does from street level, as these aerial photographs of last Sunday's S.F. Anti-War march show."

vey has been well-done. It was scientific. Advanced equipment has been used by trained professionals. As such, the data, however controversial, is objectively accurate and the message it conveys can be trusted."[4] Far from the madding crowd—and specifically far *above* that crowd—such a perspective yearns to offer much more than an accurate count. It would offer a truthful accounting of the event outside the normal give-and-take of the various involved parties—outside the concrete, lived perspectives of the demonstrators, the police, and the bystanders. The "neutrality" and "objectivity" of its method would proclaim not simply a particular perspective on the event, but what we colloquially term "the long view"—the descendent of the god's-eye view of the Middle Ages. Not just any perspective, it is the privileged perspective that, in transforming the subjective image into an objective data set, would secure the social and political normalcy that the very existence of the crowd was taken to challenge.[5]

The *Chronicle*'s "scientific" technique certainly seems to provide a more precise means of ascertaining the number at a mass gathering, especially compared with the necessary vagaries of personal eye-witness testimony. Doubtless such a technique will become, in time, the established practice for the measurement of large demonstrations. Yet because it has not yet hardened into routine, this particular image and imagination of the crowd—mass representation figured as a detached, objective measurement—can still strike us as uncanny. Yet it is precisely because of this that we should pause to consider what such a practice of representation, and the desire for such a practice, signifies—above all when it is applied to such a peculiar kind of phenomenon as the mass demonstration. For the mass demonstration is, of course, already itself an instance of representation in both the visual and political sense of the term. In accepting the technical question as to the validity of the data, as the question to be answered, we unwittingly accept not simply a particular representation of the crowd, but a particularly narrow conception of the very practice and goals of representation as such. For these "objective" numbers, upon which such rhetorical importance is placed, can only acquire significance within a particular social, cultural, and political context, and against other numbers, from other times and other places. Even if such measurements were to become standardized, so many variables remain that such precision would likely have only a negligible effect on the necessary interpretation of the historic significance of any individual event. Far more important than the scientific precision of this technique, then, is the desire for such precision, and the idea—which usually goes unquestioned—that this specific kind of measurement, objectification, and distanced perspective is the most appropriate modality of representation.

The Long View: From the Picture Window to the Data Set

We might begin to approach these questions of distance and representation by considering the imbricated history of aerial photography and the instrumentality of vision. The desire to employ photography for the distanced gathering of information is, in fact, as old as the apparatus itself. In 1858, Albrecht Meydenbauer wrote that experience has proven that one can see, not everything, but many things better in scale measurement than on the spot. Meydenbauer had been charged with measuring the facade of a cathedral in Wetzlar, Germany. To save the time and expense of erecting scaffolding, he traversed the length by means of a hanging basket. One evening, so the story goes, as he tried to climb directly into one of the upper windows from the suspended platform, he suddenly lost his balance—just managing to catch the window and save himself from falling by kicking away his platform. "As I came

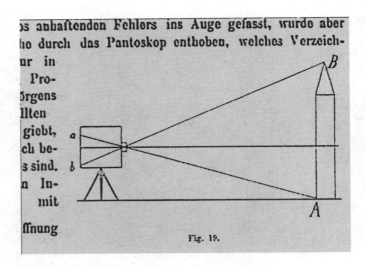

Figure 14.4 Meydenbauer's illustration, as reproduced in Farocki, *Images of the World and the Inscription of War* (1988).

down, the thought occurred to me: is it not possible to replace measurement by hand by the reversal of that perspectival seeing which is captured in a photographic image? This thought, which eliminated the personal difficulty and danger involved in measuring buildings, was father to the technique of scale measurement."[6] Meydenbauer's experience was a traumatic one—born literally from a suspension between life and death. Thus photography—already a technology of memorialization—is given an additional apotropic role, charged not simply with preserving the memory of the body, but protecting the body itself against the threat of death, giving the eyewitness an ever greater physical and temporal distance from that which he surveys.[7] In Meydenbauer's text, we find the physical experience of danger eviscerated by the elegance of a geometric theorem (fig. 14.4). The same year that Meydenbauer was attempting to transform the photograph into a data set, the great early portraitist Nadar (né Felix Tournachon) was reorienting the very ground of the perspectival frame. With the simple act of successfully exposing a photographic plate 262 feet over Bièvre, France, Nadar caused photography to break with the Quattrocento rules that had gov-

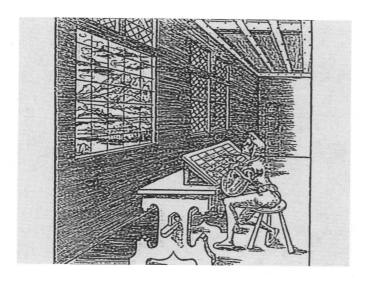

Figure 14.5 The reorientation of perspective, from picture window to data-set. Alberti (left) and Auschwitz (right), film stills from Farocki, *Images of the World and the Inscription of War* (1988).

erned visual representation since the Renaissance. It is the same break with which Leo Steinberg, a hundred years later, would famously characterize the radicality of Rauschenberg's work of the late 1950s and 1960s—the so-called Flatbed Picture Plane.

Despite "the most drastic changes in style" artists had developed over the centuries, Steinberg argued that a single axiom could hold together all western artistic representation from that of the old masters through American abstract expressionism, and this was "the conception of a picture as representing a world . . . which reads on the picture plane in correspondence with the erect human posture . . . [even] where the Renaissance world space concept almost breaks down, there is still a harking back to implied acts of vision, to something that was once actually seen." Yet for Steinberg, Rauschenberg's radicality consisted in upending this representational doxa, operating through "a radically new orientation, in which the painted surface is no longer the analogue of a visual experience of nature but of operational processes . . . I tend to regard the tilt of the picture plane from vertical to horizontal as expressive of the

most radical shift in the subject matter of art, the shift from nature to culture," a surface "on which data is entered, on which information may be received, printed, impressed" (fig. 14.5).[8]

Steinberg's discussion contains a number of important themes for our inquiry into the history of the aerial perspective. "As a criterion of classification, [the flatbed picture plane] cuts across the terms 'abstract' and 'representational,'" he concludes, and we can locate a similar representational ambiguity within the aerial photograph a hundred years before. It is an image which represents visual data—but no longer as it had been experienced in nature by the human eye. "Abstract," as Siegfried Kracauer would say with regards to the ornamental formations of the Tiller Girls, and yet still referential, analogical.[9] It is a new category of image that is part of the human world, and operationally useful to human affairs, but which no longer represents that world from an embodied, human perspective. Rather, it *models* that world—as information to be recorded, data to be analyzed and processed.[10] Yet this newly oriented image as a site of the informational, as a site of

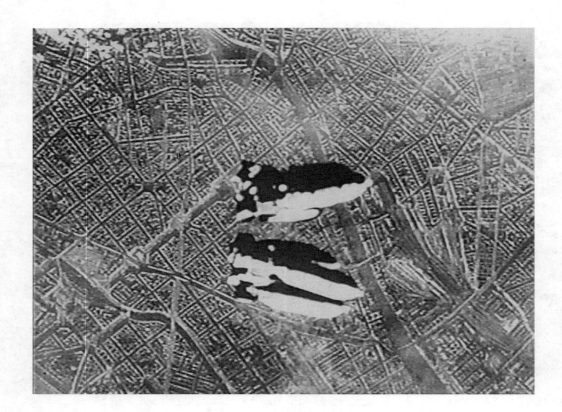

data processing rather than naturalistic vision, had already issued forth—a hundred years before Rauschenberg and others would "rediscover" it for contemporary art—in the historical conjunction between Meydenbauer and Nadar. Their simultaneous inventions would become increasingly bound together by the turn of the century and would augur a radically new relation between the human body and the image within twentieth-century visual culture. What we might call the abstract and the informational were together conjoined the moment Nadar was asked to undertake photo reconnaissance for the French army. He refused, but by 1882, unmanned photo balloons—joined soon after by photo rockets, kites, and even carrier pigeons—had already taken aerial photography out of human hands.[11] When Wilbur Wright produced the first photograph from an airplane in 1909, the potential value of aerial reconnais-

sance is judged to be of such importance that in the space of just a few years, as many as ten thousand photographs were being developed and delivered to field commanders in World War I each day.

Harun Farocki relates Meydenbauer's story in his *Images of the World and the Inscription of War,* in which his narrator adds the text, "Arduous and dangerous, to hold out physically on the spot. Safer to take a picture, and evaluate it later, protected from the elements, at one's desk."[12] Like the work of Paul Virilio and Michael de Landa, Farocki's film seeks to trace the imbricated history of visual technologies of distanciation with the modern instruments and policies of surveillance and war.[13] Because many, if not most, of the technologies of aerial photography were developed for military use, aggression and surveillance have come to be indissociable from the perspective it provides. And the technologies of distanced imaging—from the radar technology that enabled Britain's Royal Air Force to defeat the much larger German Luftwaffe in World War II's Battle of Britain to the satellite imaging, the global positioning system, and airpower that enabled the U.S. victories in Serbia, Afghanistan, and the Persian Gulf—have played an ever-greater role in military supremacy and, by extension, the character of globalization within the last half-century (see fig. 14.6).[14] These authors help us to understand that this association of visual and militaristic technologies was not simply a historical accident, but a profound imbrication of new technologies of representation, technologies that would occasion a transformation in the epistemology of representation within the modern era.

Whereas Virilio has developed the important historical and cultural association between militarism and technologies of representation, between "War and Cinema," as it were, there is a more fundamental, and potentially more disturbing, genealogy that Farocki's film, in its dialogue with the work of Martin Heidegger, is interested in tracing. It is a story of the world becoming picture, becoming representation, and our human capacities for perception—capacities crucially linked to the ambiguities, blind spots, and above all the reciprocity and mutual imbrication of seer and seen, viewer and world, being renounced in favor of what Heidegger calls the securing and mastering of practices of a modality of representation—that sets the world before us as picture, something to be evaluated from a safe distance, or as Farocki's narrator puts it, "protected from the elements, at one's desk." It is a transformation that leads away from an experience of the world grounded in the phenomenology of embodied vision, toward an experience and epistemology of the visual field that we might describe as "informational," increasingly mediated through the instrumentality of calculation and regulation.

The Rationalization of Sight

The recent work of Lev Manovich can help us place the inventions of Meydenbauer and Nadar within a longer historical perspective that both clarifies their relation to the Quattrocento system of perspective and links them to the future developments of radar and satellite imaging. Manovich has taken up the larger cultural trajectory of what William Ivans, in his influential 1939 book, called "the rationalization of sight," to propose that a particular modality of representation, for which he coins the term "visual nominalism," has accounted for an influential, although under-acknowledged, tradition arising out the Renaissance invention of perspective. He defines visual nominalism as "the use of vision to capture the identity of individual objects and spaces by recording *distances and shapes*," and he goes on to trace how "the rationalization of perspectival sight" proceeded simultaneously along two directions throughout the nineteenth century: "On the one hand, perspective became the foundation for the development of the *techniques* of descriptive and perspective geometry that became a standard visual language for modern engineers and architects. On the other hand, photographic *technologies* automated the creation of perspectival images."[15]

The system of perspectival imaging that had begun, for theorists like Alberti and painters like da Vinci, as a mere aid for what was acknowledged as an infinitely more complex practice of painterly representation by and for man, became instrumentalized in the nineteenth century for the acquisition and analysis of all matter of objective data. And with modern technologies of the automation of vision, the difference between human perception and the mere acquisition of this visual data becomes increasingly pronounced. Aerial photography begins the break with embodied vision, even in the increasingly rare instances when it is carried out by human photographers, because the images it produces no longer correspond to a shared experience of the visual world. Manovich describes radar technology as the culmination of this tradition, for there the essential data of identity and location becomes completely divorced from all other "extraneous" aspects of human perception:

All it sees and all it shows are the positions of objects, 3–d coordinates of points in space, points which correspond to submarines, aircrafts, birds, or missiles. Color, texture, even shape are disregarded. Instead of Alberti's window, opening onto the full richness of the visible world, a radar operator sees a screen, a dark field with a few bright spots . . . but it performs [its delimited function] more efficiently than any previous perspectival technique or technology.[16]

Manovich cites Lacan's contention that, "what is at issue in geometric perspective is simply the mapping of space, not sight," and that "the whole trick . . . of the classic dialectic around perception, derives from the fact that it deals with geometric vision, that is to say, with *vision in so far as it is situated in a space that is not in its essence the visual*."[17] If what Manovich calls the "automation of visual nominalism" has reached such an apogee within the contemporary era that the traditional foundation of representation in the human act of seeing is henceforth both unnecessary and inconvenient for its operation, we may well be in a better position to ask after those aspects of "seeing" that this tradition so actively/aggressively forecloses.

Farocki's film does so in an extended dialogue with the work of Heidegger, effecting precisely the kind of "Questioning Concerning Technology" that Heidegger considered an ethical necessity within an age in which the world has, as he put it, "become Picture."[18] In Heidegger's work, we must situate the specific ideology of militarism only within a much broader domain of instrumentality—the fantasy of managing the complexity of human affairs with a detached scientific objectivity that lent itself, throughout the twentieth century, to the most destructive of human acts being justified through nebulous conceptions of "progress." Heidegger's critique of a particularly modern conception of representation as *Vorstellung*, or "setting-before," is that it is not really a matter of perception as such, so much as an ordering and securing of the visual field in advance of its exercise. It is a modality of representation necessarily involved in the domination of that which it would figure—even when it is not directly used, as it so often comes to be, in the exercise of destructive force.[19]

Thus when the trope of the "view from above"—our modern equivalent of the god's-eye view—replaces the Quattrocento perspectival system, it brings with it an inescapable ambivalence. On the one hand, it seeks to present a single, comprehensive view of the totality, a mastering view that would survey and take in everything that lies below it. But unlike the traditional Quattrocento system, the "view from above" is no longer, in its essence, a view *for man*. It is first propelled by daring individuals in balloons or airplanes, but almost immediately it is replaced by all manner of unmanned vehicles, from the first kites and unmanned balloons of the nineteenth century to the orbiting geosynchronous satellites of the twenty-first, to convey photographic information which no human eye could ever independently grasp. Thus even as Manovich is correct to find the roots of this system in the Renaissance techniques, their elaboration within contemporary technologies of vision effects a dramatic change in the basic trajectory: man is no longer the measure of that which he surveys. Instead, the world has become so much data—increasingly only 1s and 0s—which can only confirm, or fail to confirm, to the preexistent frames laid down to contain it. Unable to occupy, even theoretically, the locus of vision, man has increasingly allowed technologies of perception to see, even to interpret, in his place—hence the increasing "automation of perception" within computerization.

The tradition of visual nominalism that Manovich describes is one that, as Lacan says, loses the very essence of the visible, in that it rejects the reciprocity between viewer and viewed that lies at the heart of the experience of human perception. And while he is often regarded as the origin of the modern tradition of scientific perspectival construction, Alberti had been careful to note that he had no intention of settling what he termed the "truly difficult question" that had occasioned considerable dispute among the ancients, namely, "whether these rays emerge from the surface or from the eye."[20] This phenomenon has been addressed and described in many ways since ancient times, but in the contemporary era it has been put forth most forcefully by Merleau-Ponty as a bidirectionality of perception, the bivalency or chiasmatic intertwining of viewer and viewed, and the immersion of both the seer and the seen within a single, overlapping visual field. Farocki writes, "the photographic image is built up of points and decomposes into points. The human eye synthesizes the points into an image. A machine can capture the same image, without any consciousness or experience of the form, by situating the image points in a coordinate system. . . . To conceive of a photographic image as a measuring device is to insist on the mathematicality, calculability, and finally the 'computability' of the image-world."[21] The photograph is made up of points, of data, and thus can certainly be again so decomposed through instrumental calculation. Yet in so doing, the image is no longer an image, but a data set. "Secured-in-advance," as Heidegger would say, it can no longer provoke a true encounter, because its field of intelligibility has already been posited in advance of its visibility. The information required of it functions to delimit its possible operation—just as the photographic evidence of the concentration camp at Auschwitz accidentally captured by U.S. surveillance would not be recognized until decades later, because those examining the images had not been instructed to look for it.

When Farocki uses the terms *image* and *form* in the passage above, they stand opposed to that kind of "image-world" that can be rationalized and automated because they function in an affective, and not simply a cognitive, register. In the *Chronicle's* story with which I began, the reporter approvingly cited Jones's assertion that the size of a crowd is an "emotional" not a "factual issue." This strikes at something true, but not simply, as the *Chronicle* seems to imply, because people are too caught up in their own emotions to see what "really is." Rather, it is fundamentally because human perception, as such, is always and irreducibly bound to affect and affective identification, and this "truth" is something that numerical data can neither change nor even adequately address. And yet human perception is not the inevitable result of our looking. The possibility for affective encounter is bound up with the possibility of visual reciprocity, the extent to which the object is capable of returning our gaze. Without this dimension of reciprocity, the world—and even the people within that world—become reduced to what Heidegger termed *standing-reserve*, mere data to be analyzed and manipulated according to its potential use value. What Heidegger considered the "greatest danger" within contemporary visual technologies may lie in the fact that the very difficulty in seeing, the complexity and ambivalence involved in human perception, becomes obscured within a field of instrumental rationalization that increasingly serves as its own justification.

This "rationalization of sight" that Farocki, Manovich, and Heidegger all describe as a dominant feature of our current representational era is crucially related to the distanced perspective of aerial photography through this dimension of what I am calling visual reciprocity. It is not simply the sense that the other sees back, but rather that the other seen is recognized as a seer in the first place, as one capable of returning the gaze.[22] If the crowd can only be seen as crowd from a spatially divergent position—specifically from an elevated, distanced, detached perspective—it might seem that identification and disidentification would be predictable, perhaps ineradicable psychological correlates of its visual representation.

This association between the detached perspective, in-

Figure 14.7 "Would you really feel any pity if one of those . . . *dots* stopped moving forever?" Aerial view from *The Third Man* (1949), text spoken by Orson Welles.

strumentalization, and violence has a long history within numerous forms of twentieth-century visual culture. A poignant cinematic example occurs in the pivotal scene of Carol Reed's *The Third Man* (1949), in which the two central characters ride a Ferris wheel high above the amusement park they survey (fig. 14.7). Harry's highly profitable practice of smuggling diluted penicillin is revealed to have caused the death and insanity of dozens of people in destitute postwar Vienna. When Holly, his childhood friend, demands whether Harry had ever seen his victims, Harry insists the question is melodramatic. Opening the door to the car and looking out, he instructs Holly to look down on the tiny figures below. "Would you really feel any pity if one of those . . . *dots* stopped moving forever?" Harry asks.

"If I offered you [a quarter million dollars] for every *dot* that stopped, would you really, old man, tell me to keep my money? Or would you calculate how many dots you could afford to spare?"[23] Later, making an explicit connection to the kind of instrumental vision that characterizes the bureaucracy of modern states, capitalist and communist both, Harry (Welles) declares, "Nobody thinks in terms of human beings . . . governments don't, why should we? They talk about 'The People' and 'The Proletariat,' I talk about the suckers and the mugs—it's the same thing. They have their 'Five Year Plans,' so have I."

The identification and disidentification that almost always appears correlative to the distanced perspective could be said to be the primary reason that the figuration of the crowd became such an acute dilemma for progressive politics in the first part of the twentieth century, as well as why—despite the great desire and relative ease of photographically representing large collectivities—artists, filmmakers, and theorists of artistic modernism devoted so much time and energy to the problem of how to represent the multitude as phenomenon, as event, and as subject. The crowd was perhaps the quintessential object for the social scientist and the policy maker to "get into hand" through representation, such that the regularity and calculability of such an admittedly volatile object could be ensured. As Jeffrey T. Schnapp and others have argued, the crowd represents both the power and the legitimacy of the modern state, after the traditional markers of authority were dispersed through the progress of the Enlightenment. And yet we might consider how, within the visual rhetoric and theoretical reflection of artistic modernism, the crowd continued to defy this particular logic of representation, to inhabit a space "outside the picture" I have so far been describing. In whatever guise it appears, the collective subject tends to emerge as a site of representational breakdown; it is that which cannot be representationally secured. This is why, within the tradition of artistic modernism, the crowd

tends to be figured either through a kind of essential ambivalence, or else as a particularly liminal kind of object—fleeting, insubstantial, transitory. And precisely because it seems to defy representation, the figure of the crowd often comes to stand in for the perceived limitations of both the practice, and the epistemology, of the particular modality of representation I have been describing.

The New Vision of the Modern Metropolis

In his discussion of the radical reorientation of perspectival relations within postwar art, Steinberg concludes by claiming that this transformation of the "picture window" into the "flatbed picture plane" was what "let the world back in again. Not the world of the Renaissance man who looked for his weather clues out of the window; but the world of men who turn knobs to hear a taped message, 'precipitation probability ten percent tonight,' electronically transmitted from some windowless booth. Rauschenberg's picture plane is for *the consciousness immersed in the brain of the city.*"[24] Here Steinberg locates what we have been calling the "informational" structure not only with a new modality of vertically oriented perception, but specifically with the urban—with a change in contemporary consciousness structured by the experience of urban modernity.

In "The Metropolis and Mental Life," Georg Simmel argues that "the metropolis presents the peculiar conditions which are revealed to us as the opportunities and the stimuli for the development of psychic existence," and historically, the rise of the crowd—as objective fact and as psychological condition—was certainly tied to the growth of the industrial city. Only with the rise of the new industrial economies of the nineteenth century did the extreme density of the urban population make the crowd such a potent site of cultural and political struggle. It is thus no coinci-

Figure 14.8 The verticality of the city as *unheimlich*—a new strangeness at the heart of the domestic. Photo collage by Aleksandr Rodchenko, 1925.

dence that during this decade in which visual and theoretical reflection on the crowd was to take on such visibility and importance, we find a concomitant discourse on the spatial topography of the modern metropolis. Both are organized, to some extent, around this topos of verticality and elevation as it was understood to engender both a new somatic economy of vision and a new level of visibility for the crowd.

Aleksandr Rodchenko, the Soviet constructivist, would be one of the most vocal proponents of the necessity of a "new photographic vision" tied to the specific spatial, perceptual, and somatic experience of the new urban environment. Nor was he alone: throughout Europe, one of the unifying threads of the otherwise widely divergent styles of the photographic New Vision, as it came to be known, was an attention to the heretofore unexamined representational possibilities and characteristics of the metropolis.[25] A 1925 photomontage by Rodchenko would give his visual economy programmatic illustration (fig. 14.8). Within its frame, two radically different perspectives are forced into collision. In Rodchenko's constructivist project, the word *perspective* can be seen to take on both a visual and ideological valence. The country house is placed, rather mockingly, in center stage; framed in a Renaissance tondo, it is presented as a kind of quaint little picture, a memory trace. The modern apartment building rises up all around, enveloping it with armlike walls. Unframed, it continues to the edge of the page. Although the small house presents us with a total image, whole and detached—seen as if through a telescope, from a distance—the apartment building is necessarily incomplete. We immediately feel the structure continuing beyond the frame, just as we inescapably feel that particular embodied perspective—on the street, craning our neck—from which this image was captured.

The ideological message is unmistakable: the space of the city, of modernity, has radically shifted from that of the country, of tradition. It demands a new kind of representation and a new kind of spectator. Within the image, the isolation of the individual family gives way to the congregated masses of the apartment building. The fantasy of a total vision, the view from a distance, has given way to a fractured and partial perspective. Rodchenko insisted on this ideological program through a privileging of the snapshot over the "artistic photograph," of the multiple and temporal over the singular and eternal. But he also did so by reinserting the specificity of the corporeal experience of vision into a traditionally detached, generic practice of representation.

This corporeal experience of vision was one on which the vertical topography of the city simply insisted. The city is not simply an object but, as Simmel would have it, a total perceptual and psychic environment. And its most obvious and striking new feature, for Rodchenko as for many of the New Vision photographers, was precisely the conspicuous verticality of its topography. Despite the complexity of the metropolis, the impossibility that sociologists like Simmel found in attempting to describe the multiplicity of its conditions and transformations, there was a single architectural form that symbolized the ambivalent hopes and fears about modernity, one that traversed both capitalist and communist countries, both avant-garde and popular representation, that emerged as a synecdoche for the modern metropolis as a whole. That form was the American skyscraper.

Rodchenko's specific fascination with the high-rise emerged on account of the basic disjunction between our lived experience of the new urban environment and the decidedly disorienting effect of simply reproducing this experience photographically. Because we spend only the smallest fraction of our lives looking above a thirty-degree incline, representations of such "natural" perceptions become coded as deviant. Rodchenko increasingly found himself accused of "formalist distortion" for shooting from these angles. Tall buildings, ironically enough, only seem natural when photographed from miles away. Yet within the me-

Figure 14.9 Aerial view of the New Vision—the world as "ornament," as "data." Zeitbilder's "St. Paul's Cathedral, London."

tropolis, between its unprecedented congestion and verticality of its architecture, such distanced views no longer correspond to perceptual experience.[26]

The Dada artist Raoul Haussman had been arguing since 1921 that technology and the metropolis had together given rise to an epochal shift in visual culture and sense experience, and Moholy-Nagy's unrealized film script *Dynamic of the Metropolis* (1921–1922) had called for a plethora of radical perspectives on the city.[27] Yet perhaps more influential than either of these would be a rather prosaic book of pho-

tographs of new American skyscrapers taken by the German architect Erich Mendelsohn on his trip to New York in 1924. Because neither Europe nor the Soviet Union had any real skyscrapers at this time, Mendelsohn's images were influential in bringing the new spatial dynamics of the New York skyscraper into the European aesthetic debates and practices of the mid- to late 1920s, as well as helping nourish a growing collective European fantasy of America's power, efficiency, progress, and triumph over nature. In his review of the book, the constructivist El Lissitzky was so taken by surprising angles and perspectival disjuncture to which these massive structures gave rise that he exclaimed the only proper way to look at these images was to "hold the book above your head and rotate it"—specifically acknowledging the corporeal dimension that the representation of this new spatial topography seemed to imply.[28] By contrast, this famous image of Zeitbilder illustrates what we might call, after Siegfried Kracauer, the "ornamental" dimension of the aerial view—its tendency to de-realize what it portrays (fig. 14.9).[29] In this image, it is difficult to feel any sense of identification with either the photographer or the world depicted. Despite the extreme heights and possible danger the photographer endured, one feels nothing of the vertigo or precariousness that inhabits the camerawork of Rodchenko or Vertov. At such an extreme distance, there is no longer anything human with which to identify; the human world has been photographically decomposed into pure form and rendered as an abstract series of shapes and tonalities.

Rodchenko's aerial perspectives do not abstract from corporeal experience, but become inescapably vertiginous only through their appeal to embodied perception. In this way, they call to mind the Stenberg Brothers' contemporaneous poster for *Man with the Movie Camera,* in which we are placed on the street, craning our necks to stare up at the lofty peaks of the skyscrapers (fig. 14.10). Out of the sky, a woman appears to be falling directly onto us—but something about those receding buildings is so vertiginous, they

Figure 14.10 The (dis)embodied experience of the metropolis—loss of center, loss of gravity. Sternberg Brothers, Poster for *Man with a Movie Camera*, 1929.

seem to extend downward, as if we were the one falling through the air, tumbling from the edge of one of the skyscrapers. The spiraling text redoubles this vertiginous descent, marking an inversion of both the physical and ideological valence of the skyscraper's verticality. The traditional

subject cannot remain whole against the dynamic energy of cinematic technology and the new metropolis, the Stenbergs' poster seems to declare, but comes flying apart. And indeed, Vertov's masterpiece will be about the deconstruction and reconstruction, both visual and ideological, of the new Soviet city and the new Soviet citizen.

The View from Above, the View from the Street

Aerial photography did not become a truly widespread aspect of visual culture until its use in World War I, and it is thus no surprise that the New Vision of the 1920s, just a few years after, would take up this "view from above" within the city from the perspective of the newly towering structures to which it was giving rise. And what kinds of objects did this newly elevated perspective suddenly make visible to the photographer? Precisely that curious and seemingly unrepresentable phenomenon of urban modernity: the crowd as such. Seen from above, the crowd gathers a solidity, an objectivity, that it could never possess from the street. And because it can be represented photographically—captured, as we say—it achieves an objective existence of a particular kind (fig. 14.11). One might consider the ways in which the securing aspects of the view from above might serve to inoculate the viewer against that which is inherently unstable and ambiguous in visual representations of the crowd. Matthew Tiews has traced out the importance of a rhetoric of contagion in nineteenth-century cultural history of the crowd that remains crucial to a consideration of how this desire for a distanced representation begins to operate within the twentieth-century visual rhetoric of film and photography. The desire to see from a distance is not only the desire for mastery over, but that of inoculation from. The crowd is something to be feared, from the perspective of the bourgeois individualist subject, because it threatens desubjectification on a primary level. This desubjectivification occurs, as we know from Tarde, Le Bon, and others, through some irrational vector of transmission—not the Enlightenment model of rational discussion and individual choice, but the murky and nebulous realm of identification, affect, and seduction. "The opinions and beliefs of crowds are specially propagated by contagion," Le Bon succinctly declared. Thus in distinction to the "distanced mastery" of the aerial perspective, "the street" emerges as a rhetorical locus of traffic and transmission—an especially difficult place to represent, administer, and control.

Within the visual and discursive rhetoric of early twentieth-century modernity, "the view from above" and "the view from the street" become much more than mere spatial relation. Scott Bukatman suggests that what is at stake is nothing less than competing versions of the modernist project—a fundamental opposition between the modernism of "the rational, planned city of efficient circulation, perhaps epitomized by the designs of Le Corbusier" and "another modernism entirely . . . the experience of the city described by Simmel, Benjamin and Kracauer—disorganized, heterogeneous, street-level."[30] Michel de Certeau describes the unique pleasure of looking from atop a skyscraper in New York in terms of both a ritual of transubstantiation and an "erotics of knowledge." The spectator is lifted, "out of the city's grasp. One's body is no longer clasped by the streets that turn and return it according to an anonymous law; nor is it possessed, whether as player or played, by the rumble of so many differences and by the nervousness of New York traffic . . . up there, he leaves behind the mass that carries off and mixes up in itself any identity of authors and spectators . . . his elevation transfigures him into a voyeur."[31] No longer necessarily "possessed" of a body, he places himself

at a distance. It transforms the bewitching world by which one was "possessed" into a text that lies before one's eyes. It allows one to read it, to become a solar eye, looking down like a god . . .

Medieval or Renaissance painters represented the city as seen in a perspective that no eye had yet enjoyed. This fiction already made the medieval spectator into a celestial eye . . . the 1370 ft high tower that serves as a prow for Manhattan continues to construct the fiction that creates readers, makes the complexity of the city readable, and immobilizes its opaque mobility in a transparent text.[32]

For de Certeau, the aerial perspective of the skyscraper turns the embodied viewer into the disembodied reader of what seems a transparent text of social relations. Although the city dweller of Simmel, Benjamin, and Kracauer is similarly a kind of reader, the spatial text—seen from the vantage of the street—is seen as decidedly more ambiguous and polyvalent in its message.

Aspects of the 1920s New Vision might be productively understood as interrogating this particular dialectic of the skyscraper and the street, as analyzing how the spatial topography of the modern metropolis was transforming not only the formal characteristics of perception but also the dynamics of intersubjectivity and identification within which visual reciprocity plays a crucial role.

The Crowd (1928)

King Vidor gave a particularly vivid expression to conjoined dynamics of visibility and identification within the new metropolis in his silent-era masterpiece *The Crowd* (1928). Despite its matter-of-fact title, Vidor's film is a complex and compelling portrait within which the crowd is considered not an objective fact to be recorded so much as a psychological disposition to be analyzed. The film begins with the birth and childhood of a certain John Sims, an American Everyman, who, despite his failure to evidence any particular distinction, is repeatedly told—practically enjoined—that he will grow up to "*be* somebody."[33] After his father's abrupt death and his own coming of age, John travels to New York to make a life for himself. In so doing,

Vidor presents him as exchanging the horizontal openness of the country, and the past, to vertical congestion of the city of the future.

Within the metropolis, Vidor depicts John's desire to prove himself equal to his father's mandate through an explicit visual rhetoric of verticality. Throughout the film, this verticality—the constant struggle to move up, to distance himself from that below—conditions John's struggle for subjectification as one that can only take place against the street and against the crowd.

Upon first seeing New York, Vidor's camera remains curiously divorced from both the narrative and any possible point of view within the film's diagesiss. When we emerge from this detached view from above, we are given the film's only real crowd scenes: images of the congested New York streets, taken from above, filled with all manner of vehicular and pedestrian traffic. As befits the expressionist style he often appropriated, Vidor presents these images not as objective evidence of material reality, but as subjective evidence of a psychological reality. These crowd images, although associated with the view from above, would seem to mock that perspective through their obvious framing and overt manipulation. In the first, two separate images of a crowded street are superimposed upon one another, creating an unrecognizable visual cacophony. We cut to another superimposition, this time of a busy intersection, where ghosted cars and pedestrians seem to pass through one another unscathed. Yet as Vidor's camera pans right, we see that this cacophony was simply the result of an intervening windowpane, casting reflections from another street. The street ahead is relatively clear and orderly, its perceived chaos merely the result of an intervening screen.

When Vidor shows us the next image of a high-rise, the one that begins the story, it is from the perspective of the street. As if illustrating the very enacting of "embodied perception" with which Lissitzky characterized Mendelsohn's New York, Vidor's camera abandons the still,

fixed distance of his earlier aerial shots for the movement and perspective of the man on the street, turning his body to face the structure. The camera, no longer distanced or abstract, suddenly seems to stand in for a distinctly human gaze, perhaps marveling at the imposing structure before it. But then, suddenly, we are flying up the side of the building, higher and higher, seemingly about to surmount the structure completely.[34] Slowing near the top, and turning in toward the building's surface, the monumental unity of the form begins to dissolve into a serial arrangement of identical windows that themselves dissolve into a serial arrangement of desks, each with its own identical employee. While John dreams of climbing above the crowded street, the reality of this elevated position allows no escape from the dehumanization of the Taylorized workplace. The project of representational mastery with which I have characterized the distanced perspective is encoded into Vidor's dramatic use of perspective as soon as we enter John's workplace, high above the street. The desks completely cover the visual field in a perfect grid-like formation, organized and ordered for optimal surveillance. At the center and limit of that field, Sims lies trapped, himself reduced to a number. His occupation—endlessly calculating sums—likewise concerns only numbers. By locating the protagonist precisely at the vanishing point of a deep perspectival field, Vidor explicitly associates the Quattrocento's organization of the visual field with the Cartesian rationalization of sight and the alienated production of data.

In *The Production of Space*, Lefebvre writes that "the arrogant verticality of skyscrapers . . . is to convey an impression of authority to each spectator." Yet the equation Vidor's visual rhetoric makes between the monumentality of the skyscraper and the seriality of the windows and desks illustrates how this authority can develop not only through confrontation with, but also through, incorporation of the spectator. By allowing individuals to recognize themselves in relation to its own repetitive structure, the monumental can build itself out of the serial—can allow the individual to sign on to something greater, and so magnify his individual importance.[35] This logic of amalgamation is one of the basic principles of mass psychology, according to Le Bon, and is found in successful corporations of all kinds.[36] Yet Sims's tragedy lies in that he is either unwilling or unable to recognize himself within this metonymic logic, and so is destined perpetually to strive for differentiation.

In his work, John might be considered one of the white-collar office workers whom Siegfried Kracauer was writing about at this time.[37] In *Die Angestellten*, Kracauer argued that although this burgeoning species of relatively untrained office worker was essentially proletarian in his working conditions, he based his ostensibly middle-class status on a fantasy of upward mobility and a concomitant disidentification with those below. John is similarly disgusted by the crowd; from the moment he gets out of work, he attempts to distinguish himself through disassociation. We see John walking with the crowd for the first and only time in the film when he is finally talked into going on a double date.[38] Yet just moments later, this organic relation is once again given over to differentiation as the two couples climb on top of a double-decker bus. The bus is something of an interstitial space from which the perception of the crowd remains decidedly ambivalent. While it is *above* and away from the crowd—enabling the crowd to be seen as such—it remains *on* the street, continuing to afford the potential for interaction. Because it is neither wholly detached, like the aerial perspective, nor involved, like the view from the street, this liminal space is perhaps more open to identificatory transformation in that it does not preclude visual reciprocity. Within Vidor's film, it thus becomes the site of a decisive identificatory transformation.

After climbing into their seats in the front, John basks for a moment in the reflection he finds in the monumental towers around him, and his date, Mary, seems taken by his grand aspirations. But John's first and decisive vision is that of the crowd he has left below. "Look at that crowd!" he exclaims of those they have just left behind on the street—"the poor boobs, all in the same rut." Rather than agreeing, Mary simply looks at him in incomprehension as his expression—never taking his eyes from the crowd—changes from contempt to melancholy recognition.

Admonished to "cut out the high-hat" by his buddy, John focuses his attention on Mary, insisting that although "most people" give him a pain in the neck, "she's different." Although she initially denies such distinction, she visibly begins to relish the thought. While the bus is momentarily stopped, a clown on the street catches their eye, and John is clearly disquieted by this visual reciprocity. He relegates the clown back to the facelessness of the mass by telling his companions, "the poor sap, I bet his father thought he'd be president someday."[39] This time Mary joins him in the mocking laughter as their companions look on with disgust and disbelief. To win John's heart, Mary surprises everyone by spitting off the side of the bus, onto the crowd. Obviously made for each other, they are soon married.

It is significant that "*the* crowd," as an objective visual phenomenon, is almost entirely absent from Vidor's film. Instead, we are shown a world that, in being ironized or blatantly contradicted, emerges as John's solipsistic fantasy. Throughout the rest of the film, Vidor will depict John's struggle with the crowd as a struggle with himself, with his own need to master and overcome, as well as with the isolation and social anomie generated by an individuation that can only ever set itself against the other. In a particularly amusing moment, John and Mary have gone to the beach on vacation, and we see John, playing his ukulele, singing about being "gloriously alone." The camera pans to reveal both a fully crowded beach, as Mary—enjoying somewhat less of a vacation—juggles preparing lunch, keeping the fire lit, and corralling their screaming child.

Rather than conquering against all odds, as we might

expect within the ideology of Hollywood, Vidor depicts Sims's resolute individualism as obstinate, even pathological: although he tries to wall himself off from the crowd, he is ultimately swallowed up by it. Because John's identity comes to consist solely through his *dis*identification with the crowd, his destiny is forever tied to it, whatever his fortune brings. Vidor presents his starkly individualistic ethos, his desire for strict separation and autonomy, as a pathological form of self-imposed alienation. It is the noisy, uncontrollable street, Vidor seems to suggest, that contains John's only real chance for happiness and even freedom, but paradoxically, it is a freedom with the crowd and not, as he dreams, apart from it.

In the final scene, we find John reduced to juggling for pennies on the streets—a mirror image of the clown he had begun his married life by mocking. His wife and child have finally given up and left him in disgust. Nevertheless, John hopes to win back their hearts, if only for a night, by taking them to the theater. A kind of social reciprocity there ensues that has been unknown for John—he slaps a stranger on the back to aid his coughing, and moments later, the stranger congratulates him upon seeing John's winning advertisement in the show's program. Yet immediately after, the camera begins to slowly crane up and back, revealing row upon row of people, bobbing back and forth with what now seem identical, mechanical movements. What seemed an ordinary amusement becomes increasingly freakish and inhuman the further we crane away until, at its limit and before the screen goes completely black, we are left with an unrecognizable orchestration of flickering lights. For John, Mary, and their immediate company, the moment is one of shared amusement and joy. Yet from our vantage point, above and apart, we cannot even make out individuals—only an abstract, ornamental pattern. As the crowd dissolves into visual data, a binary code of light and darkness, we return to the distanced view from above that characterized our initial approach to the city, and our initial perception of John's plight.[40]

Constructivism and the Apparitional Ontology of the Crowd

Even in the golden age of the crowd in the 1920s and 1930s many of the great photographers and filmmakers seemed to confront the possibility that the representation of the mass as a concrete thing tended to produce an empathic distanciation regardless of the sociopolitical context within which it is inscribed. This might explain why even the most threatening depictions of mass consciousness or mass action need not necessarily stir the viewer to any concrete political consciousness of their own situation—or in the case of the historical dramas that Kracauer analyzed, precisely the opposite.[41]

This question of location, of the viewer's standpoint vis-à-vis the crowd, was considered crucial for many visual theorists of the time attempting to wrestle with the difficulty of "mass representation." For instance, while otherwise affirming the importance of the singular take over the principle of disjunctive montage, Siegfried Kracauer insisted that the crowd was a special kind of cinematic object, one which could only be adequately addressed through a fragmentation of space. Constantly intercutting between the closeup and the long shot, cinematic montage alone had the ability to "launch the spectator into a movement enabling him really to grasp the street demonstration."[42] Pudovkin similarly considered disjunctive space and a mobile point of view crucial to any attempt to portray the revolutionary crowd cinematically. He wrote, "The observer must . . . climb upon the roof of a house to get a view from above of the procession as a whole and measure its dimension; next he must come down and look out through the first-floor window at the inscriptions carried by the demonstrators; finally, he must mingle with the crowd to gain an idea of the outward appearance of the participants."[43]

Before the fascist mass spectacles of the 1930s, Soviet constructivism was probably the twentieth-century aesthetic movement most specifically concerned with the problem of mass representation. Yet unlike the fascist aesthetics with which it would be replaced, constructivist photographic practice and theory proposed both the representation of the collective, and the newly collective means of representation, as an ongoing aesthetic, social, and political problem—not simply to create an art practice for the masses, but to question and reevaluate accepted aspects of aesthetic doctrine around the questions and problems of this category of mass representation itself. Within the constructivist movement, Dziga Vertov and Aleksandr Rodchenko both assiduously avoided the objectification to which even Eisenstein's cinema often fell prey, yet their own efforts were, perhaps paradoxically, only accomplished through a certain refusal of representation as such. Rather than presenting the mass—whether positively or negatively—as a thing to be grasped, their work might be said to invoke the mass, to imbue it with a kind of aleatory or spectral ontology.

In this canonical image from Vertov's *Man with a Movie Camera*, the cameraman—despite his revolutionary ambitions to relate organically with the crowd, to be in and among them—seems to be necessarily, structurally divorced from it (fig. 14.11). This very position seems to figure him maliciously—looking down on the crowd. A second camera, absent an operator, might even be said to instantiate the purely detached, inhuman view from above. Yet the image is decidedly ambiguous on this score. For despite the structural distanciation it projects, it also depicts the cameraman and his instrument as but ghostly and transparent, even insubstantial, entities. Furthermore, they do not simply float above the crowd, detached, but rather seem to rise up out of it from within. The cameraman stands both with the crowd and above it, and in neither place is he solid, obdurate—a living agent capable of providing the single representation or "photo-picture" that Rodchenko would condemn. Rather, this spectral cameraman shows us our own viewing position, essentially reduplicating our own perspective on the crowd below within the cinematic frame, thus marking this image of the crowd as itself a construction, contingent, provisional.[44]

Yet Vertov's most important image of the crowd emerges earlier in the film, in a paradoxical moment of temporal arrest. The image itself is not a photograph—or rather, it is not witnessed in the time, manner, or material in which we are accustomed to thinking about photographs. The image, or rather series of images, is assigned a particular temporal duration that serves to reflect back upon the temporality of the photographic moment itself—both its capture and its review. Inscribing the act of filming, and hence the spectator perceiving, into this image of the crowd, Vertov—in perhaps the central scene of his *Man with a Movie Camera* (1928), shows us an image of the crowd that is simultaneously still and in motion, both within and outside of time. The images in this sequence are shown to "come to life" as their photogram is replaced by the full-frame image, now in motion (fig 14.12). This scene has often been mentioned within the literature on Vertov's film for its paradigmatic reflexivity, the labor of production "now visible again back on the street rather than behind the scenes."[45] Yet significantly, and unlike the other shots of the sequence, Vertov never presents the crowd image as a celluloid photogram. Whereas the previous shots have exposed the brute materiality of the support in their construction of the experience of "plentitude," the crowd image is shown twice in full frame—first stilled, then, intercut with the children's wonder at the magician, in motion. The most probable reason for this omission seems quite simple: the image would have been too small to recognize. Presented as a photogram, it would have seemed nothing but a decorative pattern, an ornament. But this simple practicality points to an important discontinuity within the series.

The image of the crowd—apparently important enough

Figure 14.11 Still from *Man with a Movie Camera.* Courtesy of Kino International.

to take pride of place as the first brought back to life by the magic of the cinematic magician—cannot be similarly distanced by the foregrounding of the cinematic apparatus. This is because the image of the crowd is always already experienced as distanced. Its aerial perspective takes in the whole of the street, but only at the cost of losing the specificity of its inhabitants. As both an image of the crowd and an image of the production of that image, Vertov's act of representation here insists on its own temporal disjuncture, its own artificial scission from the flow of life, and its own mortification of that which it would portray (a mortification that fig. 14.13 must still portray). The crowd it presents is indelible, but gone in an instant. A moment later, through the magic of the editing table, we see it again, and now every individual dot, every individual, will begin to flicker and move, the whole beginning to swell with life. Yet this new "life" continues to recall to the deathlike stillness

the image had just contained—a paradoxical stillness this new image, even though it has now been placed in motion, *still* contains.

This movement between photography and film—between stasis and motion, the finality of an essence versus a kind of apparitional ontology—is of course the very question of the crowd, and it is thus no surprise that we can find, at this canonical moment in artistic modernism, the problem of representing the crowd thus standing in for the problem of representation as such. Rodchenko's "Assembling for a Demonstration" is a single, still image, but like Vertov's sequence, it too inscribes a kind of duration (fig. 14.14). Rodchenko depicts a formation in process, a figure not quite realized. A mobilization *in potentia*, it is an event just now unfolding. We seem to bear witness to the twilight moments of emergence: this crowd of people, this "formation," in the moment of its emergence as form out

14A 'Tolpa': Russian

Dustin Condren

The Russian noun *tolpa* has the principal definition of a large, disorderly congregation of people (*Slovar' sovremennogo russkogo literaturnogo iazyka*). Its usage in modern Russian also shares with its equivalents in many other languages a sense of chaos, loss of individuality, and unpredictable movement.

The earliest known written usage of *tolpa* appears in an ecclesiastical manuscript of the late eleventh century, the *Service Menology for November 1097* (*Sluzhebnaia mineia za noiabr' 1097 g.*), a text written in Old Church Slavonic, the clerical tongue and early literary language for much of the Slavic world. *Tolpa* is used in this selection in reference to the twelve apostles, suggesting that at this moment in time the term signifies merely a grouping of people, without the elements of mass and chaos that it bears today.

However, by the time that the Laurentian *Chronicle of the Tale of Bygone Years* (*Povest' vremmenykh let*) appears in the twelfth century, *tolpa* seems to have already developed its denotation of the large crowd, the term being applied in one instance to a large group of people thronging at the gates (*PVL*, 6582). Another interesting early occurrence of *tolpa* comes in the hagiography *Pecherskii Paterikon* (*Paterik pecherskii*), in which Isakii is able to distinguish one face among the crowd whose countenance is brighter than all the rest. This moment provides an exact indicator of the boundaries of the word *tolpa*: the crowd exists

Figure 14.12 Stills from *Man with a Movie Camera.* Courtesy of Kino International.

of a group of individuals. Oddly enough, the stains on the ground—likely water, tossed out from cleaning the street, evaporating in the afternoon sun—compete with the mass for our attention as figures. Despite emerging from opposite ends of the tonal spectrum, both are flattened against the ground; both take on the qualities of a surface. They even intersect near the top in an odd blending in that one dark-clothed man—clearly not part of the gathering crowd—almost disappears completely, dissolving into the ground, evaporating like the water spots that, from our particular vantage point, he seems to resemble.[46]

All this is visible as figure, of course, because we are not there, on the ground. In that case, the crowd, the organization, would not be visible as such. From an enclosed terrace, a woman happens to be gazing down, mimicking our gaze. Her presence calls attention to the spatial dynamics of the scene, to our position as spectator, and to the crowd's position as ornament against the flatness of Rodchenko's visual field. This redoubling inscribes our act of spectatorship into the visual field. The two women—one looking down, the other looking away—in fact form a sequence that inscribes a kind of duration to this process of looking, and to the gradual appearance of the mass as ornament.

The complex temporality, reflexivity, and aleatory status of the crowd are even more dramatically highlighted when compared with Rodchenko's contemporary

Figure 14.13 Stills from *Man with a Movie Camera*. Courtesy of Kino International.

"Courtyard of Vkhutemas" (fig. 14.15). There, it is as if all movement and temporality were consciously drained from the image of the crowd below. Rodchenko is brutally insistent on what Kracauer calls the "mass as ornament," presenting it from a wholly detached, aerial perspective. Without the mediation of an external viewer, without the slight angle of "Assembling for a Demonstration" that allows the visual field to continue up to our position upon the balcony, "The Courtyard" presents itself as an imperious, detached view of the scene below. This perspective, deprived of the temporality inherent in the process of perception, makes a durational event into a static thing capable of being definitively captured on film—a temporal shift registered in the grammar of the titles, from a gerund to a noun. Despite what was likely a banal occasion, there is something decidedly sinister about the image of the crowd thus portrayed. The formal dimension present in the previous image receives no counterbalancing degree of recognition or identification. If, in the previous image, the water spots blended together with the people's shadows, they here seem more directly identified with the people themselves. Not only the regimentation of the line but also its formal extension off either side of the pictorial space invoke stasis, the endless duration of idle waiting.

In aerial photographs like "Assembling for a Demonstration," the view from as a collective body, with which one may come face to face, yet if any member of that collective differs strongly enough from the whole of the body, this individual may be independent of the crowd, although located simultaneously within.

Another term that begins to appear in places where one might expect to find *tolpa* is the noun *chern'*. *Chern'* might also be translated as "crowd," but it brings with it the distinction of the crowd of common people—more directly translated, the black masses. The etymology of *chern'* is tightly woven with the adjective *chernyi* (black), which historically had its application with the common people (*prostonarodie*)—for example, the lower levels of society in ancient Novgorod were referred to as the *chernyi narod* (black folk), *chernaia sotnia* (black hundred), or *chernye liudi* (black people).

A conception of the crowd, in which *tolpa* and *chern'* are used interchangeably, is eloquently established in Pushkin's 1828 poem, "The Poet and the Crowd" (*Poet i Tolpa*). The poet is confronted by a "cold and haughty group of unconsecrated people" (*a khladnyi i nadmenyi/Krugom narod neposviashchennyi*) who listen to him without understanding. The poem is constructed partially in dramatic format with the character "Poet" having a dialogue with the character "Chern'," which, it should be noted, speaks with one voice. The poet is merciless in his upbraiding of this *chern'* and its members' inability to transcend their mundane terrestrial lives. He calls them "mindless slaves" (*rabov bezumnykh*) and creates a pun from the word *chern'* referring to the crowd as *cherv' zemli* (worm of the earth). This crowd is interested in poetry (and by metonymy, anything representing high culture) only as it becomes practical for use in the

Figure 14.14 "Assembling for a Demonstration," Rodchenko (1928-30).

Figure 14.15 "The Courtyard of Vkhutemas," Rodchenko (1928-30).

humdrum of daily life—for Pushkin, this is the core of their philistinism, their ignorance of the spiritual value of poetry.

Although the use of *chern'* is almost exclusively negative, the connotation of *tolpa* is dependent on usage, but varies mainly between neutral and negative. The negative connotation seems mainly due to the association with mindlessness, imperviousness to higher thought and feeling. This specificity for the two terms is especially important as the Marxist rhetoric of masses and proletariat begins to hold sway in the twentieth century. The *tolpa* remains somewhat undesirable, lacking direction, whereas the historically motivated forward movement of the proletariat *massa* gives the concept of the crowd an entirely new reading that departs wholly from the concept's previous lexical incarnation in both *tolpa* and *chern'*.[1]

above does not become detached, but rather still contains within it both the somatic locus of perception and the lack of finality that characterizes his works from the street. Thus while Pudovkin and Kracauer rightly point out the problem of spatial position with regard to the representation of the mass, the perspective inscribed by the camera cannot be reduced to the mere location of the camera in physical space. Of much greater import was how this perspective could be experienced by the viewer—whether it could be translated into a practice of identification, or whether it was inevitably detached, abstract, and informational.

Beyond Representation—The Mass in/as Movement

There were certainly aspects of the New Vision that, rather than foregrounding this complex interplay between identification and spatiality, were simply content to capture the most radical and shocking images possible. Often these practices lead to a total detachment—aesthetic and identificatory—between the image and its referent. Combined with an uncritical praise of industrialization and machine culture, these images set the stage for an overt politicization of the New Vision in the Soviet and German fascist visual culture of the 1930s. Yet in opposing the

14B Crowd Experiences

Hayden White

Crowds. I tend to avoid them. The most memorable experiences? Political riots in Rome in 1954, when Italians were protesting the British occupation of Trieste. I blundered upon a crowd that was bent on finding and punishing British citizens (or subjects), property, and institutions. I heard the swell of the mob as I walked from Piazza Capranica toward Via del Corso. It was the noise that was most unnerving, for it was like a swarm of bees or locusts, utterly without specific direction or target. What did I do? Melted into a side street and proceeded toward home. I never feel curiosity for what the mob will do. One can be sure it will be up to no good.

Then in 1971, during the anti–Vietnam War resistance in Los Angeles, on the campus of UCLA, a police riot. Police were called in to suppress a crowd that had been demonstrating peaceably enough until someone (it turned out to be an agent provocateur of the Los Angeles Police Department) threw something—a rock, a trash can, who knows?—into a store window. This infuriated the police, who immediately dispersed over the entire UCLA campus, beating up people indiscriminately, invading the library where they seized people working at their tables in the reading room, put them in police come-along grips, and escorted them to the nearby vans for arraignment. Police helicopters overhead, tear gas everywhere, panic on the part of the faculty (who immediately thought that the rioters would come and destroy their pre-

authoritarian detachment of the view from above, those who struggled with this question of mass representation were left with an aporia: the view from the street did not in fact represent the mass directly, as a thing with qualities, but only indirectly, as a temporalized process or event. Often the movement between different vantage points worked to allegorize this dynamic ontology of the collective subject.

Rhetorically, the German *Masse* often tends to be used interchangeably with the English *crowd* or *mob*, but the terms are actually quite different with respect to this issue of movement. *Mob* (Latin *mobile vulgus*) implies a dynamism, as well as a loose sort of direction and intentionality. *Mass*, by contrast, is something relatively inert—a thing to be shaped, molded, "pressed" into service by exterior forces.[47] Crowd (Old English *crudan*, "to press or drive") occupies something of a middle space between these two terms, as it implies a degree of movement without granting intention.

Samuel Weber has called attention to the fact that whenever Benjamin uses the term *mass*, he specifically goes against the grain of tradition by associating it with a movement or dynamism.[48] Weber thus wonders what it implies for Benjamin that the masslike quality of technical reproducibility itself leads to its *Aufnahmen* (reception/production) in a state of *Zerstreuung*—not simply distraction, but also the spatially oriented sense of being scattered or dispersed.[49] Although I cannot here rehearse the complexities of Benjamin's thought, for our purposes, it should suffice to say that it was, in part, the spatiality of this *Zerstreuung* that was seen to necessitate an indirect mode of mass representation. For himself, Benjamin famously turned to the poetry of Baudelaire to illustrate how the crowd could be invoked, rather than represented, through the figure of the individual *passante*. Weber describes her "ostensible individuality" as

anything but individual: she comes to be only in passing by. And in so doing, she reveals herself to be the allegorical emblem of the mass, its coming-to-be in and as the other, in and as the singularity of an ephemeral apparition. The mass movement—the mass in/as movement—produces itself as this apparition, which provides an alternative to the formed and mobilized masses of the political movements of the Thirties.[50]

This alternative conception of the "mass in/as movement"—what we might call the apparitional ontology of the crowd—was not exclusive to Benjamin's writing but, as I have attempted to show, can be found throughout the visual culture of artistic modernism as it wrestled, more or less explicitly, with this crucial yet intractable question of mass representation.

If the films of Farocki, Reed, and Vidor show us both the attraction and the dangers of this distanced perspective on the crowd, the liminal kinds of representation invoked by Vertov and Rodchenko illustrate a somewhat different possibility, one that might be said to continue the kind of apparitional ontology of the crowd found in Poe and Baudelaire. Here, the crowd is represented in motion precisely because it "is" not—its "being" is not solid and substantial but impermanent, temporal, aleatory—multiple, mobile, in progress. This is why, for those who truly grapple with the problem of representation in general and the problem of mass representation in particular, "the crowd" is so often represented as something ephemeral, fleeting—something incapable of *being* represented.

Authors such as Heidegger, Virilio, and Manovich show us how, as the mechanical eye has replaced the human eye in technologies of mass visual culture, the eye of the machine has become our modern substitute for the medieval "eye of god"—an ultimately detached perspective that could separate fact from fiction, sort through the competing discursive claims, and establish a final metaphysical "truth." When this modality of representation is turned on something as complex, multivalent, and aleatory as a collectivity, it necessarily forsakes these qualities in order to reconstruct it as an object of knowledge. Delimited in time and space, solid and bounded, it becomes "a crowd"—something that can be dissected, studied, and above all, factored into social, economic, and political calculations. It finally "appears" only when splayed out on the dissection table like a once-living creature.

By contrast, there has been, within the visual and theoretical discourses of artistic modernism, another kind of representation that in some ways refuses representation altogether. This struggle over representation might be said to go back to Leonardo da Vinci, whose drawings—despite their scientific value—stand opposed to the manner of scientific objectification with which Heidegger diagnoses our current "Age of the World-Picture." For Leonardo, technical precision did not necessitate conforming to the detachment of the perspectival grid. He instructed his students that they should refrain from placing hard outlines around those things they would represent, but instead should keep them soft and malleable, as they exist for the perceiving eye.

Within the artistic modernism of the 1920s, such a practice figures the crowd not as a concrete object, for which one can have a distanced judgment (either positive or negative), but as a kind of liminal, identificatory event—a spectral presence that seems flickering, insubstantial, precisely because it cannot exist apart from the viewing subject or the event of perception. As a durational experience, transforming in energy, purpose, and character, the collectivity can be finally represented as

cious research notes), a sense of high drama and delight among the principal student activists engaged in the event. I witnessed a crime committed by a police officer (he had been undercover, enrolled as a student in one of my courses, and his cover blown a couple of days before when he gave testimony against the antiwar agitators: he had been assigned to gather dossiers on faculty and students suspected of participating in antiwar activities), and (foolishly) reported it to . . . the police! As a result, I found myself charged with having attacked this officer, having torn his uniform from his back (he was in civilian clothes), and so threatening him that he had had to flee for his life. All this on Los Angeles television within a couple of hours. I was then investigated by the L.A. Police's Internal Affairs, who had only to take a look at me to realize that the idea of my attacking two police officers was ludicrous. Nothing came of it.

Peace demonstrations and civil rights demonstrations in Washington in the fall of 1972: peaceful, pacific, flower-power mood, lots of good, decent people with their kids, expressing their belief in the constitution and civil rights.

My experience of crowds: I stay away from them unless I am compelled by some obligation to a friend or political ally to turn up for a demonstration.

neither subject nor object, its outlines are never hard, but soft. Like Leonardo's drawings, it emerges as both still and in motion.

Just as the geography of the city at the beginning of the last century made the transformation of the conditions of representation into an acute question of aesthetic, social, and political investigation, so the electronic geography of the new century is in the process of transforming representational practices once again.[51] The globalization effected through the ever-expanding networks of multinational capitalism and the new transactional spaces of the globalized internet portend similarly novel transformations of space and relationality. How and to what extent these transformations affect our representational practices, or allow novel formulations of aesthetic, social, and political problems, remains to be seen.

Yet because the representation of collectivities within the visual rhetoric and discourses of artistic modernism was never a secure practice, but rather a difficult and ever-changing terrain of investigation, we can similarly expect that the crowd, as figure and metaphor, will continue to circulate as a persistent, if elusive, site of representational breakdown, and aesthetic, social, and political contestation.

In Memoriam, Michael Rogin (1937–2001)

15 Far from the Crowd: Individuation, Solitude, and 'Society' in the Western Imagination

Jobst Welge

IN THE "PROLOGUE ON THE THEATER" in Goethe's *Faust I,* the figure of the poet remarks,

O sprich mir nicht von jener bunten Menge,
Bei deren Anblick uns der Geist entflieht.
Verhülle mir das wogende Gedränge,
Das wider Willen uns zum Strudel zieht. (59–62)

Don't speak to me of crowds at whose mere sight
The spirit flees us! That you could confine
The surging rabble that draws us with might
To compromise our every great design.[1]

The passage is representative of an entire conception and epoch of modern literature: the poet in his ivory tower, aloof from, disdainful of, yet tempted by the crowd. Moreover, it also addresses the paradoxical relation between poetry and theater: "Die Masse könnt ihr nur durch Masse zwingen/Ein jeder sucht sich endlich selbst was aus" (The mass is overwhelmed only by masses/Each likes some part of what has been presented) (95–96). We might apply to these lines, and by extension to the character Faust, an observation by Georg Lukács, who has argued that the tragic hero is by definition a lonely figure who strives to elevate himself above the merely human and the masses: "Die Einsamkeit ist aber etwas Paradox-Dramatisches: sie ist die eigentliche Essenz des Tragischen" (Solitude is something paradoxical-dramatic: it is the true essence of the tragic).[2]

In this essay, I am concerned with the evolution of such anticrowd sentiments, with the public, literary performance of solitude, as well as with the perception and representation of crowds from an "individualist" perspective. In fact, what is absent from most sociological accounts of the masses, as well as from Elias Canetti's anthropological approach in *Crowds and Power*, is an analysis of the relation between individual observers and formations of the crowd. I will try to show that there is a long tradition of western literature, both modern and early modern, which expresses this relationship between the individual and the crowd. In contrast to sociological investigation and philosophical reflection, literary works do not show the masses (and, in a wider sense, the "public" or "society") from an objective, "scientific" perspective, but give us representative, historically conditioned accounts of the interaction between individuals and their social surroundings, in relation to which they see themselves as apart, or as distant observers. However, I will occasionally also draw on the work of philosophical writers. The writing of Nietzsche in particular is pertinent both for its formal links with early modern writers and its strong influence on writers at the turn of the twentieth century.

More specifically, the following account, necessarily highly selective, will privilege texts by writers who reflect on their own literary authorship as conditioned by, and as symptomatic of, the interaction between the individual and the collective. This is to say that the literary author becomes necessarily a "solitary" individual who shares his thoughts with a mostly anonymous public. In this sense, we are concerned not only with the historical evolution of subject/crowd formations (obviously an integral part of every subjective formation), but also with a central aspect of the mechanism of literary communication.

I take for granted the causal link between historical modernity and the semantic connotations of the "masses." However, rather than cordoning off the phenomenon of the masses from the categories of "crowd," "collective," "society," and "public," I'm interested here precisely in the—sometimes unsuspected—continuities between these terms, as I shall use them with regard to both modern and early modern texts. If our primary interest is not modern mass society but rather the phenomenon of individuation through and against the collective, it will help us to adopt a long, rather than a short, historical perspective.

The first section of this essay will look at the early modern conception of humanist authorship (Petrarch, Montaigne) as bound up with the state of solitude, as well as the (Neo-)Stoic rhetoric of a separation from the public, however temporary. The second part will look, in the wake of Benjamin, at some nineteenth-century examples where the perception of a specifically urban modernity poses new problems of vision, representation, and subject constitution. I have also included two eighteenth-century authors. Although Rousseau is grouped with the early moderns because of his retrieval of a Neo-Stoic rhetoric, Goethe's description of the Roman carnival opens the "modern" section because it can be seen as one of the earliest literary representations of the crowd in explicitly visual terms. The third and final section is mostly concerned with a tradition of typically modernist intellectual disdain for the masses and their political passions.

Early Modern Solitudes

Among early modern writers, Petrarch and Montaigne are the ones that have most insistently and influentially written about solitude in terms of a humanist retreat from society and the affairs of the world. In their writings, the condition of solitude is directly connected to what we would refer to today as the emergence of Renaissance subjectivity, as well as of secular authorship.

During the years 1342–1343, Petrarch retreated to Vaucluse near Avignon, where he penned not only a dialogue of spiritual self-investigation, the *Secretum*, but also *De vita solitaria* (*On the Solitary Life*). The text is a self-apologetic treatise in which Petrarch polemically opposes the solitary, forest-dwelling life of the poet to the self-alienating, active city life of courtly or clerical service, emblematized by the symbolic places of Sylvan Vaucluse and "Babylonian" Avignon, respectively. The text is informed not only by medieval monasticism but also by the classical ideal of secular *otium*, which entails a legacy already much more complex than simply advocating a retreat from the active life.

In *De vita solitaria*, the retreat from the public life is said to lead to spiritual fulfillment, but it is also described as the ideal condition for literary production: "To be absent or free . . . from affairs is the source of literature and the arts."[3] Not only is Petrarch writing about solitude, but writing and solitude are identified with each other, so that solitude becomes a place of conversation in a Ciceronian sense: "There are those for whom solitude is more threatening than death, graver than death. This happens to those ignorants who, without interlocutors, are not capable of talking to themselves, or to books, and therefore remain mute. Solitude without culture [*solitudo sine literis*] is certainly an exile, a jail, and a torture" (*DVS*, 47).

On the one hand, Petrarch describes his writing as an "interventionist" type of literature that ultimately aims at the moral improvement of society, by claiming that he wants "a non-solitary solitude, an *otium* neither sterile nor useless, a solitude that can be helpful for many" (*DVS*, 270/72). On the other hand, Petrarch explicitly rejects Cicero and other writers of the Roman Republic by fully adopting the Augustinian perspective of the City of God. He defends a stance of spiritual inwardness against the ornamental, external dimension of rhetorical culture. Thus he criticizes Cicero because his desire to derive glory from oratory pushes him inevitably into the public realm: "It is peculiar and characteristic of orators that they take pleasure in large cities and in the midst of the crowd [*populus*], in proportion to the greatness of their own talents. They curse solitude, and hate and oppose the silence required for decisions" (*DVS*, 250). Although the life in the urban crowd is generally rejected, Petrarch at one point seems to endorse the Senecan notion that solitude might be achieved also metaphorically: "But if some circumstance should push me towards the city, I know how to create solitude in the midst of the crowd, a haven in the middle of a tempest, by using a system not known to all: to control the senses in such a way that they don't feel what they feel" (*DVS*, 52). With regard to Petrarch, Timothy Reiss has recently argued against the modernist imposition of a rhetoric of heightened individualism, the anachronistic framework of private versus public, arguing that every "private" literary activity has an inherently "public" dimension as well. Petrarchan personhood, Reiss maintains, is imaginable only within the bonds of a larger community, with regard to a social or literary model of authority. To be sure, the rhetoric of public/private has a Habermasian ring to it that is highly problematic if applied to the late medieval context of Petrarch.

However, despite the semantic inadequacy, I find it necessary—contrary to Reiss—to insist on the general presence of a dialectic in Petrarch's thought. In fact, Reiss himself argues for the essential intermingling in Petrarch of the "contemplative" and the "social," the "personal" and the "civic," as well as the "ethical" and the "political."[4] Solitude has to be understood not as the stable, essential term of an antithesis, but as part of a complex constellation. But even as we recognize such intermingling, it is not possible to wholly dispense with a dualistic framework. In fact, beginning with Petrarch, a whole series of humanists reflected endlessly on the question of *vita solitaria* versus *vita activa,* a dialectic that tries to reconcile or to play out the ancient claims for a virtuous, active life (Cicero) versus the values of Christian introspection and withdrawal (Augustine). Leonardo Bruni, a later Florentine humanist, sets Petrarch against Dante as the typical embodiment of the "leisurely life."[5]

Even *De vita solitaria,* the Petrarchan text most directly concerned with the question of solitude, sees itself as ultimately promoting civic welfare. Petrarch, drawing on monastic ideals of eremitic seclusion, represents these ideals as unattainable for himself. His portrayal of the solitary life appears no longer as the ideal of a religious community or institution, but as a viable practice for individual, secular readers. The text was dedicated to Philippe de Cabassoles in 1366, the proprietor of the Vaucluse territory, who had visited Petrarch twenty years earlier during his state of solitude.[6] The figure of Cabassoles, constantly invoked throughout the text, is appealed to as a friend, a double of the Petrarchan self. As Petrarch remarks at the end of the treatise, "I realize that I have exalted the kind of solitude that flees from the multitude [*turba*], not the one which also flees from a friend" (*DVS,* 304). Petrarch is thus a pioneer of practices of solitude that are no longer tied to transindividual communities, practices that are characteristically associated with the medium of the book and thus develop the potential to claim a distance from institutionalized authority and academic scholasticism. This gradual transvaluation of monastic values is generally characteristic of Petrarch's unique tendency to "occupy" traditionally religious forms with a laicized or "secular" meaning.[7]

In the *Essais* of Montaigne (1533–1592), full of the rhetoric of self-containment, we encounter some of the most complex representations of the interactive tension between solitude and public service. In fact, the entire logic of the *Essais,* the reason for their existence and their mode of expression, is motivated by this dynamic. Montaigne belonged to the recently ennobled bourgeoisie, having inherited a private estate and the chateau de Montaigne. This social position allowed him to produce a rhetoric of self-ownership and self-possession, even as he was engaged in practices of public service.[8] Self-possession for Montaigne signifies a state of inner liberty, a withdrawal "out of the crowd" to some inner sphere.[9] Yet this self-possession and inner freedom are not contrary, but rather complementary to a principal obedience to all manifestations of lawful authority—a paradoxical phenomenon that also character-

izes the Lutheran, Protestant understanding of politics (although Montaigne considered himself an adherent of the Catholic church; cf. *E,* 1:56) and that lies as well at the heart of the treatise of Montaigne's friend, Estienne de La Boétie (1530–1563), *Discours de la servitude volontaire* (ca. 1550).

Despite his professions of solitude and withdrawal, Montaigne frequently participated in public affairs. For instance, he was elected mayor of Bordeaux twice, and thus he conceives of himself as being split between different roles: "Le Maire et Montaigne ont toujours esté deux, d'une separation bien claire" (*E,* 3:10, 1012) (The mayor and Montaigne have always been two, with a clear separation). He fulfilled this "public office without departing one nail's breadth from myself; and [gave] myself to others without taking myself from myself" (des charges publiques sans me despartir de moy de la largeur d'une ongle) (*E,* 3:10). Not only can one exercise a "metaphorical" solitude, but solitude also necessitates metaphorical sociability, achieved through the duplication of the self, following the saying of Tibullus, *in solis sis turba locis,* "in solitude be to thyself a crowd" (*CE,* 241). If living in the crowd appears to be "contagious," the simple strategy of physical withdrawal and moving away offers no solution to these problems, because this will not have us automatically lose our acquired vices. Rather, Montaigne advises the ideal of self-sufficiency right in the midst of the social world. The ideal of solitude, then, takes on a kind of metaphorical, psychological signification that is not (only) dependent on actual, spatial separation, similar to Horace, or the Stoics who advocated a form of spiritual retreat. What is needed, above all, is a technique of control and self-mastery: "it is not enough to have gotten away from the crowd, it is not enough to move; we must get away from the gregarious instincts that are inside us, we must sequester ourselves and repossess ourselves."[10]

A similar point is made in Essay 3.3, "Three Kinds of Association" ("De trois commerces"), where he relates withdrawn inwardness and sociability in a paradoxical fashion that he differentiates from the literal *solitude local*:

La solitude que j'ayme et que je presche, ce n'est principallement que ramener à moy mes affections et mes pensées, restreindre et resserrer non mes pas, ains mes desirs et mon soucy, resignant la solicitude estrangere et fuyant mortellement la servitude et l'obligation, [C] et non tant la foule des hommes que la foule des affaires. [B] La solitude locale, à dire verité, m'estand plustost et m'eslargit au dehors: je me jette aux affairs d'estat et à l'univers plus volontiers quand je suis seul. Au Louvre et en la foule, je me resserre et contraincts en ma peau; la foule me repousse à moy, et ne m'entretiens jamais si folement, si licentieusement et particulierement qu'aux lieux de respect et de prudence ceremonieuse. (*E*, 78)

The solitude that I love and preach is primarily nothing but leading my feelings and thoughts back to myself, restraining and shortening not my steps, but my desires and my cares, abandoning solicitude for outside things, and mortally avoiding servitude and obligation, [C] and not so much the press [*foule*] of people as the press of business. [B] Solitude of place, to tell the truth, rather makes me stretch and expand outward; I throw myself into affairs of state and into the world more readily when I am alone. At the Louvre and in the crowd I withdraw and contract into my skin; the crowd drives me back to myself, and I never entertain myself so madly, licentiously, and privately as in places full of respect and ceremonious prudence. (*CE*, 625)

In effect, the *Essais* are on some level the continuation of a dialogical communication with Montaigne's deceased friend la Boétie, as literary introspection replaces the practice of interactive conversation, or as it indeed requires the doubling of the self in order to make self-perception possible in the first place. This technique of self-doubling has to be seen in the context of the Stoic tradition: Seneca's advice to create an imaginary witness (*testis imaginarius*) in his *Letters to Lucilius*, Marcus Aurelius's "good demon," or Petrarch's designation of Christ as a true "witness" in *De vita solitaria*—all versions of an interior voice, or personalized conscience. Montaigne's rhetoric of privacy and solitary retreat has to be situated in a context of civil war and sociopolitical unrest. His views on dissimulation and masking in the social sphere can be compared to his Italian contemporary, Francesco Guicciardini. Although he generally advocates a more optimistic anthropology than his friend Machiavelli, in the *Ricordi* (1528–1530), Guicciardini advises servants of political power, such as himself, to assume a stance of prudence and discerning, flexible intelligence that elevates such individuals high above the common folk: "To speak of the people is really to speak of a mad animal gorged with a thousand and one errors and confusions, devoid of taste, of pleasure, of stability."[11] Writing in his characteristic gnomic-aphoristic style, Guicciardini coolly observes the masses' inclination to be deceived and manipulated—and how the powerful individual can achieve a position of self-preservation and control in a society generally characterized by dissimulation and suspicion.

In the eighteenth century, Jean-Jacques Rousseau practiced a rhetoric of intimacy and psychological inwardness that anticipated the romantic critique of the conformism dictated by society. In the case of Rousseau's "agoraphobic inclination" the condition of solitude is the result of an involuntary necessity: "I am now alone on earth, no longer having any brother, neighbor, friend, or society other than myself. The most sociable and the most loving of humans has been proscribed from society by an unanimous agreement. In the refinements of their hatred, they have sought the torment which would be cruelest to my sensitive soul and have violently broken all the ties which attached me to them."[12] After the Parliament of Paris had condemned his *Emile* on June 9, 1762, Rousseau spent the next twelve years fleeing from place to place, experiencing a state of enforced solitude. Whereas his *Confessions* aim to communicate the portrait of the self, the *Reveries of a Solitary Walker* (*Les rêveries du promeneur solitaire*, 1772)—much like, say, Petrarch's *Secretum*—is a text expressly written solely for the self-gratification of its author. In fact, it was published only posthumously, in 1782. Radical literary solitude of this kind always has the effect of engendering an imaginary society where the writer becomes his own sole reader. It is precisely this self-directed nature of his writing that has Rousseau distinguish his project not only from the *Confessions*, but also from the most famous model of self-writing in the French tradition, Montaigne's *Essais*:

My enterprise is the same as Montaigne's, but my goal is the complete opposite of his: he wrote his *Essays* only for others, and I write my reveries only for myself. If in my later days as the moment of departure approaches, I continue—as I hope—to have the same disposition as I now have, reading them will recall the delight I enjoy in writing them and causing the past to be born again for me will, so to speak, double my existence. In spite of mankind, I will still be able to enjoy the charm of society; and decrepit, I will live with myself in another age as if I were living with a younger friend. (*RSW*, 8)

Exiled from society, he engenders a circular bond between the writer and the writer-as-reader-of-himself. For Rousseau, the pleasures of meditative inwardness and solitude are a welcome by-product of his persecution anxiety: "Those moments of rapture, those ecstasies, which I sometimes experienced in walking around alone that way, were enjoyments I owed to my persecutors. Without them I would never have found or become cognizant of the treasures I carried within myself" (*RSW*, 9). Rousseau often uses such strategies of rhetorical inversion to turn enforced solitude into a welcome state: "Throughout his autobiographical writings he assures his readers that he has no need of others, that he is happiest without them, that he is grateful for their hostility, for they have forced him in this way to discover unsuspected treasures in himself."[13] For instance, in the "First Walk," Rousseau stresses the discontinuity between this text and the earlier *Confessions*. If he still registers the modifications of his soul, such an account remains entirely self-referential: "Everything is finished for me on earth. People can no longer do good or evil to me here. I have nothing more to hope for or to fear in this world; and here I am, tranquil at the bottom of the abyss, a poor unfortunate mortal, but unperturbed, like God himself" (*RSW*, 6).

In the "Third Walk," Rousseau links the current situation of enforced leisure to his natural predisposition during his youth when he already felt an "intense desire for solitude" (*RSW*, 20) and when he had already set himself a limit of forty years for accomplishments in the world of ambition: "The rural solitude in which I passed the flower of my youth, the study of good books to which I completely gave myself up, reinforced . . . my natural disposition to affectionate feelings and rendered me devout almost in the manner of Fenelon. Secluded meditation, the study of nature, and contemplation of the universe force a solitary person to lift himself up incessantly to the author of things" (*RSW*, 19). Yet there seems to be too much protesting in these continuously repeated assertions of radical autonomy and self-sufficiency. For Rousseau, both society and its opposite, solitude, are part of the condition after the "fall" from original nature. Thus human beings can never go "back" to a presocial stage, and, if not prevented by necessity, the individual's relation to society is generally seen in benevolent terms.

Modernity

The nineteenth century, it is often said, was the century of the masses. Literature responds to this situation by imagining new relations between individual observers and collective formations. In contrast to our previous examples, where the "crowd" functioned as the signifier of sociality in a series of essentially Stoicist reflections on solitude versus the *vita activa,* the "crowd" comes now into view, for the first time, as a primarily visual phenomenon and increasingly as a metonymic emblem of urban modernity. In fact, the initial literary reactions to urban modernity are all attempts to cope with the sensual and perceptive overload experienced in the modern city. Before the emergence of genuinely modernist modes of representation, the early reactions typically express a crisis of representation, a crisis of classical aesthetic and poetic concepts. To be sure, this problem of representation marks a crucial difference between premodern and modern representations of the crowd. However, the modern examples also develop a tension between the individual and the larger collective. Now the solitary individual is not so much withdrawn from society, but he is a distanced observer, as well as a part of what David Riesman calls the "lonely crowd."

A very early example of this type of representational crisis might be seen in a text rarely invoked in this context: J. W. Goethe's description of the Roman carnival as it appears as the major set piece in the (second) Rome section of his *Italian Journey* (*Italienische Reise*, 1814–1816; 1829).[14] From the beginning of his journey, the observational stance of Goethe as traveler is described in terms of individual autonomy and sovereignty. His first comments on Venice emphasize the idea of solitude within the crowd: "I can now enjoy the solitude for which I have so often yearned; for nowhere does one feel more solitary than within the crowd [*Gewimmel*], where one pushes through, unknown to anyone. In Venice I'm known by maybe one person, but this person will not encounter me immediately."[15] Now, once arrived in the eternal city, Goethe's program of seeing—a program of visual *Bildung*—takes on the goal of becoming "solid" (*IR*, 179). During his Grand Tour, Goethe, who describes himself repeatedly as a "stubborn hermit" eager for solitude (*IR*, 126, 245, 512), seeks only reluctantly the company of other men, a select group of fellow artists and Northern European travelers. Many pages are devoted to reflections on nature and art. At times, however, Goethe attempts sketches of the Italian people (*Volk*), always seen from the outside, from an observational distance that conceives of the Italian, "picturesque" character as an extension of primitive nature in the manner of Rousseau (*Naturmen-*

schen; *IR*, 189; cf. 279): "the people, a big crowd [*Masse*], a necessary, immediate being" (*IR*, 91). In fact, Goethe sees the people as the fundamental characteristic of Italian civilization as a whole, "good and bad at the same time," passionate, loud, and living their life openly in the public, "a basis upon which everything rests" (*IR*, 104).[16]

With these presuppositions, the phenomenon of the Roman carnival, with its formless and ecstatic crowd scenes, presents a particular challenge, which "defies all description" (*IR*, 639), because it does not allow for any observational distance: "The long and small street, in which innumerable men move back and forth, cannot be surveyed. There is hardly anything one can distinguish within the compound of the swarming [*Getümmel*] seen by the eye" (*IR*, 639). In fact, during Goethe's first Roman sojourn (February 1787), the carnival is mentioned, but only to deprive it of any literary or aesthetic dignity: "One has to see the Carnival in Rome, but only to get completely rid of the desire to ever see it again" (*IR*, 228).

The second time around, however, Goethe recognizes in retrospect that the difference in perception was helped by his artist's way of looking at things, the predisposition of an aesthetic sensibility, the *Kunstanschauung* "coming to my help even among the crowding [*Gewühl*] of this carnival madness and folly" (*IR*, 685).[17] During this second period (1788), Goethe realizes that the seemingly chaotic event still follows a recognizable, repeatable structure: "Because of this I was now reconciled with the swarming [*Getümmel*], I could now see it as one more significant natural creation and national event" (*IR*, 685). Having settled on this plan to make form visible where first only formlessness appeared, Goethe has to temporarily compromise his cherished sovereignty: "For this purpose, more than would otherwise have been the case, one had to descend among the masked multitude, which left a repellant, uncanny impression, despite its artistic aspect" (*IR*, 686).

The Roman carnival, he remarks, is unlike other orchestrated civic events, bonfires, or processions; it is an anarchic self-manifestation of the people and, in the last analysis, of nature itself. Goethe's account, somewhat quixotically perhaps, thus strives to convey to the reader, in an orderly and systematized fashion—the narrative is broken down into small, thematically organized chapters—"a survey and the pleasure of this overcrowded and bypassing happiness" (*IR*, 640). Although the participants in the festivities might not remember much after everything ends like a dream, the reader's "imagination" and "sense" are able to experience "everything in its entirety" (*IR*, 676). Even as the observer Goethe is temporarily threatened by the disorder and physical danger of the event on the Roman Corso, which apparently reminds him of the orgiastic moment of the French Revolution ("freedom and brotherhood can be enjoyed only in the dizzying moment of madness" [*IR*, 677]), he is still able to turn chaos into sense.[18] His narrative provides an orderly frame in order to bring out the underlying rules and rites in what only appears to be a formless dissolution. Although the carnival is anything but a modern phenomenon, it is retroactively associated with this contemporary, political event—the emergence of modern mass politics— and is thus perceived as a potential threat to Goethe's classicist aesthetics. Ultimately, the carnival is seen as an allegory of life itself, which is equated with an inevitably partial and confused (*unübersichtlich*) perspective and the ways in which the crowd delimits individual autonomy:

Still more the narrow, long, thickly crowded street reminds us of the ways of life in this world, where every spectator and participator . . . on the balcony or balustrade can only survey a small space before and next to him; where he moves forward only step by step, be it in a carriage or on foot; where he is more pushed than walking, more hindered in his movement than willingly pausing; where he strives to get wherever it is better and merrier—and then again will be brought into narrow straits and finally pushed away. (*IR*, 677)

The representational problems that Goethe encounters in the Roman carnival and its temporary Saturnalian dissolution of order, are very similar to the ones encountered in later writers' attempts to describe the dizzying spectacle of urban modernity. Goethe's solution, to wrest an allegorical significance from the seemingly meaningless, will be similarly encountered in literary representations of the urban crowd. His morphological technique of observation, schooled in the perception of landscape and nature, distances the phenomenon of the crowd from the observer and leaves him protected in his singular autonomy.

It is not surprising, then, that some of the most influential representations of the crowd during this period must essentially be understood as new modes of seeing, of coping with scenes of visual-sensual overload. This is particularly evident in E. T. A. Hoffmann's late, short tale "My Cousin's Corner Window" ("Des Vetters Eckfenster," 1822). The tale takes the form of a dialogue between the narrator and his older cousin, who stands so as to survey the crowded scene of a marketplace, the Gendarmenmarkt in Berlin (out of which the visiting narrator has emerged on the way to the house of the older cousin). As in the case of Hitchcock's *Rear Window*, the cousin's power of observation is accompanied by a condition of physical immobility, for, sitting in a wheelchair, he "has entirely lost the use of his legs owing to an intractable illness."[19]

Hoffmann's text is not so much a tale as a narrative experiment that takes the existence of the protourban, preindustrial crowd as a challenge to modes of visual perception.[20] In the wake of Benjamin's discussion of this text in his book on Baudelaire, it has become a canonical reference point in recent years in studies concerned with the literary representation both of Berlin and of urban modernity more generally. The central passage of Hoffmann's piece concerns the view through the window onto the market scene:

The entire market seemed like a single mass of people squeezed tightly together, so that one would have thought that an apple thrown into it would never reach the ground. Tiny specks of the most varied colors were gleaming in the sunshine; this gave me the impression of a large bed of tulips being blown hither and thither by the wind, and I had to confess that the view, while certainly very attractive, soon became tiring, and might give oversensitive people a slight feeling of giddiness, like the not disagreeable delirium one feels at the onset of a dream. ("CCW," 379)

Following the instructions of his older cousin, the narrator will be progressively capable of making out single figures and situations in what first appears as a confusing, proto-impressionistic field of formless colors. The window of the older cousin's house is associated with a position of visual mastery and distance: "he can overlook the entire panorama of the splendid square at a single glance" ("CCW," 378). The window as a visual framing device of reality is known since L. B. Alberti's theory of painting in the fifteenth century; its application to urban scenery extends from Hoffmann to Musil.[21] Although the older cousin, a writer—related through various autobiographical references to the old, sickly Hoffmann himself—is said to impart the "art of seeing" (Kunst zu schauen) ("CCW," 380) to his younger cousin, his mode of seeing is decidedly static in nature, even as it constantly zooms in and focuses sharply on individual figures. The younger cousin experiences a situation of sensual overload that can be seen as prophetic of representations of urban modernity, precisely through its failure to make "sense" of his initial impressions, the "motley, bewildering throng of people animated by meaningless activity" (Anblick eines scheckichten, sinnverwirrenden Gewühls des in bedeutungsloser Tätigkeit bewegten Volkes) ("CCW," 380).

In contrast, the older cousin's visual strategies, sometimes aided by "field-glasses" ("CCW," 384) master this complexity by assimilating the various scenes to genre tableaux, which Benjamin has associated with the harmless domesticity of the *Biedermeier* aesthetic.[22] They are explicitly compared to older visual models: Hogarth, Callot, Chodowiecki. (Through this principle of reducing form-lessness to "art," the cousin's mode of seeing recalls the framing devices adopted by Goethe in his description of the Roman carnival.) Moreover, whereas the younger cousin is instructed to scan the scene outside visually, the older cousin's elaborations on these views blend into a more interior vision associated with the imagination, which in turn is associated with his withdrawn life. Notwithstanding the autobiographical identification or the designation of the older cousin as a teacher of his younger cousin, Hoffmann might be said to underscore the outdated connotations of these visual strategies.[23]

The lessons in viewing and interpreting the members of the crowd lead the two cousins to follow the movements of individual characters and their interaction with others, and to develop all kinds of hypotheses about their history, social class, motives, and so forth. At times the "reading" of the individual people is explicitly physiognomic: "her whole appearance and behaviour revealed her moral propriety and her shamefaced poverty" ("CCW," 382).[24] The final observations of the older cousin veer toward a sociopolitical dimension when he contrasts the "delightful picture of prosperity and peaceful manners" with an earlier, unruly time when the market was the "scene of quarrels, beatings-up, deceit, theft" ("CCW," 400). Yet in the final analysis, the cousin's picturesque approach of viewing is anchored in the principle of allegory. His last comments can thus be directly compared with the allegorical implications that Goethe derived from the Roman carnival: "This market . . . is still a true picture of ever-changing life. Bustling activity and momentary needs brought the mass of people together; within a few minutes all is deserted, the voices that mingled in a bewildering tumult have died away" ("CCW," 401).

Goethe's and Hoffmann's texts can be seen as early, prophetic depictions of the masses as embodiments of urban modernity and a central topos of nineteenth-century literature. At the same time, a new observer of these masses is born: the floating flaneur, who simultaneously is and is not part of the masses. This experience of existential solitude within the medium of the masses can be seen as a fundamental moment of modernism.

Unlike the solitary perambulations of Rousseau in the countryside, the radical solitude of the flaneur occurs in the middle of the crowd, in the middle of the city. This new constellation, the crowd "as a new subject in lyric poetry," has been famously analyzed by Walter Benjamin, who identified it, above all, with the poetry of Charles Baudelaire (*CB*, 60). As Benjamin points out, in Baudelaire's writing, the masses, although absolutely central, are never represented directly; they are never the explicit theme of poetic representation: "Diese Menge, deren Dasein Baudelaire nie vergißt, hat ihm zu keinem seiner Werke Modell gestanden. Sie ist aber seinem Schaffen als verborgene Figur eingeprägt" (This crowd, whose being Baudelaire never forgets, has never served as a direct model for any of his writing. Yet it is impregnated in his works like a hidden figure).[25] Thus in *Les Fleurs du Mal* (*The Flowers of Evil*, 1857) the urban crowd becomes internalized in the artistic consciousness of the poet:

La rue assourdissante autour de moi hurlait.
Longue, mince, en grand deuil, douleur majestueuse,
Une femme passa, d'une main fastueuse
Soulevant, balançant le feston et l'ourlet.

The darkening street was howling round me when a woman passed on her way, so tall and slender, all in black mourning, majestical in her grief, with her stately hand lifting and swaying the scallop and hem.[26]

The apparition of a woman in "A une passante" is described here as a completely instantaneous, self-contained encounter, as the appearance of a human form from an amorphous mass where human voices have become indistinguishable from the noise of the street ("la rue . . . hurlait"). The immersion in the crowd confronts the observing subject with sudden, passing impressions, what Benjamin calls the experience of shock.

The glance of the observer penetrates the chaos of the city, always picking out the objects of his peculiar, sudden interest. Take the case of the "Little Old Women" ("Les petites vieilles"), from the series *Tableaux parisiens*, who arouse in the poet a sublime mixture of enchantment and disgust: "Et lorsque j'entrevois un fantôme débile/Traversant de Paris le fourmillant tableau" (When I catch a glimpse of a sickly ghost passing through the swarming Parisian landscape) (*CV*, 181). The observer extends his sympathy, his tenderness, to these *êtres singuliers*, but his eye is distant nevertheless, refraining from any direct interaction with the person or persons observed—no matter whether it is a passing beauty or *débris d'humanité*.

In the writings of Baudelaire, one can observe a constant interplay between the individualist retreat of the poet and his willful immersion in the crowd: "Er macht sich zu ihrem Komplizen und sondert sich fast im gleichen Augenblick von ihr ab" (He makes himself into its accomplice, and almost in the same instant separates himself from the crowd) ("UMB," 204). The interdependence is stated most programmatically in the prose poem "Les Foules" ("Crowds") from the collection *The Spleen of Paris* (*Le Spleen de Paris*, 1864): "Multitude, solitude: termes égaux et convertibles pour le poète actif et fécond. Qui ne sait pas peupler sa solitude, ne sait pas non plus être seul dans une foule affairée. Le poète jouit de cet incomparable privilège, qu'il peut à sa guise être lui-même et autrui" (Multitude and solitude are equal and interchangeable terms for the active and productive poet. Anyone who doesn't know how to people his solitude does not know, either, how to be alone in the midst of a bustling crowd. The poet enjoys the unique privilege of being both himself and other people, at will).[27] The poet figure in Baudelaire is the quintessential flaneur whose radical individuality paradoxically allows him to keep himself open to the possibility of a quasi-erotic communion, indeed a "holy prostitution of the soul" ("cette sainte prostitution de l'âme") with appearances that emerge instantaneously and unforeseen: "Le promeneur solitaire et pensif tire une singulière ivresse de cette universelle communion. Celui-là qui épouse facilement la foule connaît des jouissances fiévreuses, dont seront éternellement privés l'egoïste, fermé comme un coffre, et le paresseux, interné comme un mollusque. Il adopte comme siennes toutes les professions, toutes les joies et toutes les misères que la circonstance lui présente" (The thoughtful perambulating loner derives a special kind of uplift from this communion with all and sundry. He who can readily identify with the crowd enjoys ecstatic delights which are forever denied to the egoist who is locked inside himself as in a coffer, or to the lazy-minded fellow trapped in his own shell like an oyster. He can make every profession his own, and make his all those joys and miseries that circumstance may bring his way) (*PP*, 58–59). The flaneur derives pleasure and desire precisely from and within the fleeting movement of the crowd: "die Erscheinung, die den Großstädter fasziniert—weit entfernt, an der Menge nur ihren Widerpart, nur ein ihr feindliches Element zu haben—, wird ihm durch die Menge erst zugetragen" (the appearance that fascinates the urban dweller—far from seeing in the crowd only its opposite or antagonistic element—is actually brought toward him through the crowd) ("UMB," 200). Similarly, in *The Painter of Modern Life* (*Le peintre de la vie moderne*, 1863) Baudelaire describes the painter Constantin Guys's erotic communion with the crowd:

La foule est son domaine, comme l'air est celui de l'oiseau, comme l'eau celui du poisson. Sa passion et sa profession, c'est d'épouser la foule. Pour le parfait flâneur, pour l'observateur passionné, c'est une immense jouissance que d'élire domicile dans le nombre, dans l'ondoyant, dans le mouvement, dans le fugitif et l'infini. Être hors de chez soi, et pourtant se sentir partout chez soi; voir le monde, être au centre du monde et rester caché au monde. . . .

The crowd is his element, as the air is that of birds and water of fishes. His passion and his profession are to become one flesh with the crowd. For the perfect flaneur, for the passionate spectator, it is an immense joy to set up house in the heart of the multitude, amid the ebb and flow of movement, in the midst of the fugitive and the infinite. To be away from home and yet to feel oneself everywhere at home; to see the world, to be at the center of the world, and yet to remain hidden from the world. . . . [28]

The "convalescent" artist Guys is both immersed in and distanced from the crowd, which is here described not so much as a synecdoche of society, but as a feminine (*la foule*), watery element of nature.[29] For Baudelaire, then, the phenomenon of the crowd is the manifestation of modernity itself, insofar as it embodies "le transitoire, le fugitif, le contingent, la moitié de l'art, dont l'autre moitié est l'éternel et l'immutable" (the ephemeral, the fugitive, the contingent, the half of art whose other half is the eternal and the immutable) (*PML*, 13).

Benjamin points out the parallels of this *flânerie* with the essential anonymity of the urban crowd, as an enabling factor for the emergence of the modern detective story, notably in the works of Edgar Allen Poe, translated into French by Baudelaire himself (*CB*, 43). Yet he also connects the phenomenon of *flânerie* with more specific, "material" conditions of the urban environment, such as the emergence of the arcades in Paris, the capital of the nineteenth century. As Benjamin points out, the type of the flaneur is not to be confused with the "man of the crowd," because he observes the life of the city as a passing spectacle from which he always retreats to his privacy. His heightened consciousness and his dandyish posing always save him from the threat of indifferentiation presented by the masses: "Baudelaire loved solitude, but he wanted it in a crowd" (*CB*, 50).

An interesting counterpart—and an influential model— for Baudelaire's individualism can indeed be seen in Poe's narrative *The Man of the Crowd* (1840–1845). In this text, the similarly "convalescent" narrator/observer looks through the window of a coffeehouse on the swirling masses outside in the streets of London, passing by as night begins to fall. The observer, who is just recovering from an illness, is also distinguished by a heightened state of sensibility:

the tumultuous sea of human heads filled me . . . with a delirious novelty of emotion. I gave up, at length, all care of things within the hotel, and became absorbed in contemplation of the scene without. At first my observations took an abstract and generalizing turn. I looked at the passengers in masses, and thought of them in their aggregate relations. Soon, however, I descended to details, and regarded with minute interest the innumerable varieties of figure, dress, air, gait, visage, and expression of contenance.[30]

As in Hoffmann's text, the observing gaze proceeds from the indistinct mass to more specific appearances within the crowd. Yet in contrast to the tableaulike genre scenes in Hoffmann's tale, Poe's observer submits the individuals to a diagnostic analysis, where "in my then peculiar mental state, I could frequently read, even in the brief interval of a glance, the history of long years" ("MC," 135). Poe's observer moves his discerning gaze in such a way that he passes from one social group or professional class to another, in strictly descending order, all recognizable by individual—yet characteristic—features and traits. One example will suffice to illustrate this point: "The division of the upper clerks of staunch firms, or of the 'steady old fellows' it was not possible to mistake. These were known by their coats and pantaloons of black or brown, made to sit comfortably with white cravats and waistcoat . . . They had all slightly bald heads, from which the right ears, long used to pen-holding, had an odd habit of standing off on end" ("MC," 133). It is surely not coincidental that Poe prefaces his tale with a quote from La Bruyère's *Caractères* ("Ce grand malheur, de ne pouvoir être seul" [The great misfortune not to be able to be alone]), because the narrator's gaze is eminently physiognomic.[31] As night begins to fall, the features of individual figures in the crowd, passing in front of the window in quick succession, become increasingly uncanny. Midway through the text, the narrator notices the face of an old man among the crowd, and he decides to abandon his secure, immobile position of observation and follow the man through the night.

The man, who appears to carry a diamond and a dagger under his jacket, obsessively tries to blend in with the anonymous crowd. In the narrator's culminating observation, this individual illustrates the merging of the flaneur with the criminal: "This old man . . . is the type and the genius of deep crime. He refuses to be alone. *He is the man of the crowd*" ("MC," 135). Benjamin's observation in this regard, that this is "a view which would be capable of inspiring a great etcher—an enormous crowd in which no one is either quite transparent or quite opaque to all others" (*CB*, 49), appears to have been taken up by Alfred Kubin (fig. 15.1). In contrast to Hoffmann's older cousin, then, Poe's narrator abandons his secure observer position and develops a detective-like gaze in pursuing the old man through London's nightly streets. The tale effectively illustrates how the immersion into the crowd is not the opposite, but the correlate to the distance and autonomy of the individually shielded observer. Compared to Hoffmannn, then, Poe's tale, as Benjamin writes, illustrates the "difference between Berlin and London" (*CB*, 49), that is to say, between market and a generic street, between an incipient and a more fully developed state of nineteenth-century urban modernity.

In contrast to Hoffmann's primarily aesthetic concerns, then, Poe's "Man of the Crowd" implicates the observer in the general conditions of modern mass society. A still more fully developed sense of the social conditions of the "masses," or, in fact, of the modern masses *as* a social phenomenon, can be found in the writings of Heinrich Heine.[32] A republican polemicist and a late romantic poet, Heine viewed the masses—and the crucial liberal revolution of 1848–1849—with a characteristic ambivalence between humanitarian empathy and aestheticist disdain. With his trademark irony and wit, he maintains in his "Fragments from England" (1828, part of the *Reisebilder*) that a philosopher might well profit from the "pressing stream of living human faces" that he would encounter in the center of London, near Downing Street. However, a poet such as him is ill at ease among these crowds, moving forward "machinelike" and with "colossal uniformity":

Aber schickt keinen Poeten nach London; bei Leibe keinen Poeten! Schickt einen Philosophen hin und stellt ihn an eine Ecke von Cheapside, er wird hier mehr lernen, als aus allen Büchern der letzten Leipziger Messe; und wie die Menschenwogen ihn umrauschen, so wird auch ein Meer von neuen Gedanken vor ihm aufsteigen, der ewige Geist, der darüber schwebt, wird ihn anwehen, die verborgensten Geheimnisse der gesellschaftlichen Ordnung werden sich ihm plötzlich offenbaren. . . . Und wolltet Ihr gar einen deutschen Poeten hinschicken, einen Träumer, der vor jeder einzelnen Erscheinung stehen bleibt, etwa vor einem zerlumpten Bettelweib oder einem blanken Goldschmiedladen—o! dann geht es ihm erst recht schlimm, und er wird von allen Seiten fortgeschoben oder gar mit einem milden God damn! niedergestoßen.

But don't send a poet to London! Not a poet! Send a philosopher instead and put him on a corner in Cheapside; here he will learn more than from all the books of the latest fair in Leipzig. And as the waves of people storm around him, so will also arise a sea of new thoughts, the eternal spirit that hovers above will move towards him, the most hidden secrets of the social will reveal themselves to him. . . . And if you would even venture to send a German poet, a dreamer who stops before every single sight, say, a ragged beggar woman or a polished jewelry shop—oh! then he will really suffer, and he will be pushed from all sides, or even boxed down with a mild "Goddamn."[33]

It is immediately evident that Heine, to the difference of Baudelaire, is unable to assume the stance of the distant observer within the crowd. If *Les Fleurs du Mal* represents the first—and perhaps the last—attempt to perceive urban

Figure 15.1 Alfred Kubin, illustration for E. A. Poe, "The Man of the Crowd."

modernity through formally traditional poetry, Heine's late, ironic romanticism posits the modern city as the very death of poetry—graphically illustrated here by the image of the downtrodden poet. The stark juxtaposition of poverty and wealth in this scene, as well as the subsequent description of the frantic business mentality of "John Bull," render this scene more allegorical than realistic: the frantic movements of the crowd are metonymic for the rhythms of capitalism. When Heine contrasts this scene of English confusion and chaos with the peacefulness of "our dear Germany," his judgment is characteristically suspended between disdain for the conformism of modernity (England), *as well as* for the philistinism of the provincial (Germany).

Yet for Heine, the phenomenon of the modern city also presents a challenge to traditional—that is, idealist—philosophy. The urban reality of London is devoid of aesthetic qualities, yet as the manifestation of a concrete, "prosaic" social reality, it becomes the object of a "sociologically" enlightened philosophy. Heine, it appears, sees philosophical reflection and aesthetic perception as mutually exclusive domains. However, the irony of this passage seems also to imply that "philosophical" grasping of urban reality must be blind to the apprehension of singular, concretely human details. The apparent inadequacy and anachronism of the aesthetic-poetic predisposition has thus its counterpart in the abstraction of the quasi-sociological gaze—that is, even if the philosopher followed Heine's plea to go to Cheapside.

The very form of the *Reisebilder* (*Images of Travel*; first volume 1826), Heine's first publication—a characteristic blend of poetry and journalism—is indicative (not unlike Baudelaire's *prose* poems) of the changed conditions of literature, notably the end of classicist aesthetics. The "end of the period of art" (Ende der Kunstperiode), as Heine, adapting Hegel, calls it, produces a conflicted tension between poetic consciousness and public address; a "strange relation between world reference and subjectivity."[34] Of course, when Heine contrasts the more pacific atmosphere in Germany (à la Hoffmann) with the teeming masses in London (à la Poe, or Engels), we cannot but notice the irony in his lament about the masses.

If for Baudelaire the apparitions within the crowd are essentially aesthetic phenomena, the republican Heine is alert to the social differences within the crowd. Thus, he writes about the "müßigen Lord, der, wie ein satter Gott, auf hohem Roß einherreitet und auf das Menschengewühl unter ihm dann und wann einen gleichgültig vornehmen Blick wirft, als wären es winzige Ameisen" (the idle lord who rides along like a satisfied god, sometimes giving a distinguished glance to the crowding of people under him, as if they wire tiny ants) (*IR*, 512). In fact, Heine's ambivalence toward the masses is often complemented by a quasi-Marxist awareness of the socioeconomic conditions of their misery, as becomes clear from a passage of his *Confessions*:

These court lackeys of the plebs constantly extol its virtues and excellent qualities, crying out fervently, "How beautiful the common people are! How good! How intelligent!" No, you lie, the poor common people are *not* beautiful. They are, on the contrary, quite ugly. But this ugliness comes from dirt and will disappear with it, as soon as we build public baths where Their Majesty the people can bathe for free . . . The people, whose goodness has been so highly praised, are not good at all, they are often as evil as other potentates. But their malice is due to hunger, and we must see to it that the sovereign people get enough to eat.[35]

Heine as an urban flaneur is no longer a detached observer of the spectacle of the masses, but a political commentator on the deplorable conditions of the urban poor. The hybrid "antipoetic" style of his essayistic prose marks the transitional nature of his writing and a larger crisis within the paradigms of nineteenth-century literature. As Russell Berman has written, "Nineteenth-century literature is largely embedded in an institution of private contemplation and reception in which the category of the individual provides the central organizing principle. . . . The ideology of democracy provides literature with the *demos*—the people, the masses, the class—as a new interlocutor around which new literary strategies can crystallize."[36]

The iconic texts of the early twentieth century reconfigure the relation between subjectivity and the masses through entirely new ways of aesthetic representation. For instance, in R. M. Rilke's *Notebooks of Malte Laurids Brigge* (1910)—a classic high modernist text that explicitly exhibits its dependency on Baudelaire (the prose poem *A une heure du matin* is quoted toward the end)—the interiority of the quasi-autobiographical protagonist is not a region shielded from the influx of the city. On the contrary, interiority here is an effect of the experience of urban modernity. As John Plotz has remarked with regard to De Quincey, the internalization of the outside world can lead to distinctively traumatic effects, a veritable crowding of the mind itself: "the self can be preoccupied by a welter of voices that came from without, but now live within."[37] Malte never relinquishes his stance as a distant observer. Retreating to his room, he seeks refuge from the crowd and the incessant movement of city life in Paris:

Alone, finally! You only hear the rolling of some late, hurried carriages. For some hours we will have silence, if not more. Finally! The tyranny of the human face (De Quincey!) is over, no one can torture me any more but myself. Finally! Now I am permitted to refresh myself in a bath of darkness! First, I close all the doors. It seems as if this multiple enclosure enlarged my solitude, as if it strengthened the barricade that separates me now from the world.[38]

Rilke's novel is a central instance of German modernism—indeed, it is the first German novel to represent modern urban experience; yet the experience of modernity is filtered here through an essentially negative perspective. Like Döblin's *Berlin Alexanderplatz* (1930), Rilke's novel derives its formal and thematic originality from its confrontation of the genre of the bildungsroman with the phenomenon of modern urban experience. The tradition of the bildungsroman is invoked but ultimately subverted, insofar as the individual appears no longer as the determined subject of a trajectory of self-fulfillment, but rather as the object upon which external pressures impinge. In fact, Rilke's text contains numerous scenes of bodily fragmentation, which suggest that the boundaries of inside and outside are dissolved through an interpenetration of the subject with its environment. With a Nietzschean contempt for the prevalent history of the masses, Rilke's narrator Malte writes, "Ist es möglich, daß die ganze Weltgeschichte mißverstanden worden ist? Ist es möglich, daß die Vergangenheit falsch ist, weil man immer von ihren Massen gesprochen hat. . . . gerade, als ob man von einem Zusammenlauf vieler Menschen erzaehlte, statt von dem Einen zu sagen, um den sie herumstanden, weil er fremd war und starb?" (Is it possible that all of world history has been misunderstood? Is it possible that the past is a deception, because people have al-

ways talked of its masses . . . just as if one would talk about a congregation of many men, instead of talking about the single one, who was surrounded by them, because he was alien and died?) (*MLB,* 469). Rilke's *Malte* is indebted to earlier writers such as Baudelaire and De Quincey in that he investigates the individual's relation to the urban crowd as a primarily mental, psychological effect, a crowding, as it were, of the interior mind, an interpenetration of interior and exterior. John Plotz speaks here of an "urban-crafted interiority that contains not the 'authentic' self but external phenomena forced inward that rule one willy-nilly" (*BLPP,* 217n6). As he points out with regard to De Quincey's *Confessions of an English Opium-Eater,* "De Quincey conceives of crowds as extant both out on the streets and inside his brain: it is that doubleness which makes their quasi-tangibility such a permanent irritation and opportunity" (*BLPP,* 95).

Malte's negative stance toward the masses can be seen as a literary expression of Rilke's negative experience of urban modernity, as associated with his first stay in Paris, from August 1902 to June 1903.[39] During an early scene in the *Bibliothèque Nationale,* Malte invokes the image of a solitary poet, a poet he would have liked to become himself, as he notes with melancholy regret:

You don't know what that is, a poet? Verlaine . . . Nothing? No memory? No. You have not distinguished him, among those you knew? You don't make distinctions, I know. But the one I am reading is a different kind of poet. Someone who doesn't live in Paris, someone wholly other. Someone who has a quiet house in the mountains. Who sounds like a bell in clear air. A happy poet, who talks about his window and the glass doors of his book case, which pensively reflect a dear, solitary world. This is just the kind of poet I would have liked to become. (*MLB,* 482)[40]

A not-so-distant relative of Malte can be encountered in Fernando Pessoa, the towering figure of Portuguese modernism. In *The Book of Disquiet,* compiled during many years of the early twentieth century, the office clerk Bernardo Soares, one of Fernando Pessoa's many literary heteronyms, offers a proliferating variety of diary entries that reflect on an existence of radical solitude and "inaction" in which exterior reality is discounted in favor of an interior life of the soul, a life of dreams. Pessoa's late romantic sensibility sometimes comes close to Nietzsche's antisocial individualism:

With ironic sadness I remember a workers' demonstration, carried out with I don't know how much sincerity (for I find it hard to admit sincerity in collective endeavors, given that the individual, all by himself, is the only entity capable of feeling). It was a teeming and rowdy group of animated idiots, who passed by my outsider's indifference shouting various things. I instantly felt disgusted. They weren't even sufficiently dirty. Those who truly suffer don't form a group or go around as a mob. Those who suffer, suffer alone.[41]

Pessoa's literary imagination, much like Baudelaire's or Rilke's, is unimaginable without the backdrop of the modern city and its crowds, sometimes observed from the distance of the window, sometimes experienced, in Baudelairean fashion, as a surrounding, oceanic element. But if Baudelaire looks for asylum in the crowd, turning away in disgust from the bourgeoisie, Pessoa retreats to the impossible search for the self. To be sure, the crowd exists, as it vibrates with its complex multitude of personalities, yet it exists primarily inside the subject.

Enemies of the People: Intellectual Disdain for the Masses

After Rousseau, philosophical discourse about self and society diverges into two different strands. On the one hand, Hegel and Marx theorize the progressions of history and society as concrete universals. Søren Kierkegaard, writing against this Hegelian tradition, is the first modern philosopher to redeem concrete human existence, the freedom of the individual against the leveling and equalizing effects brought about by modern mass society. For Kierkegaard, the rise of the masses is understood as a key feature of modernity. He was one of the first thinkers to link this phenomenon to a critical understanding of mass media (notably, the press) and the ideological function of the public. In his writings, the "crowd" is not identified with a specific group or social stratum, but as the negative, abstract possibility of all contemporary individuals.

The most explicit statement of this view occurs in the latter part of the text known as *A Literary Review,* entitled "The Present Age." Kierkegaard's text (1846) is a long discussion of a now-forgotten Danish novel by Thomasine Gyllembourg entitled *Two Ages* (1845). In accordance with the general structure of the novel, Kierkegaard distinguishes the "present age" from a former revolutionary, passionate, and "heroic" age. The present is characterized by a universal "leveling" in which abstract processes—embodied by the idea of the public and the press—win out over concrete individual actions: "A particular individual can take the lead in an insurrection, but no particular individual can take the lead in leveling, for then he would, after all, become the commander and escape the leveling."[42]

The modern, "Christian" system of equality and representation has replaced an older dialectic between the "great individual" and the crowd. The present age has reduced this dynamic process of individuation to a simple practice of computation: "In antiquity the individual in the crowd had no significance whatsoever; the man of excellence stood for them all. The trend today is in the direction of mathematical equality, so that in all classes about so and so many people make one individual, and in all consistency we compute numbers . . . in connection with the most trivial things" (*TA,* 85). For Kierkegaard the "idolized positive principle of sociality in our age" (*TA,* 86) estranges the individual both from his own inwardness and from the Christian God, since all existential problems are reductively understood as sociopolitical problems. In contrast to

Rousseau, for Kierkegaard, the state is not the expression of the general will, but rather a necessary evil for the maintenance of peace and order. The universal process of leveling and the judgment of "reflection"—in the sense of living in a spectatorial society—"can be halted only if the individual, in individual separateness, gains the intrepidity of religiousness" (*TA*, 86).

Beyond the diagnosis of the present there emerges the hope that the individual's inwardness might be rescued from the crowd for a coming Christian community. Hence Kierkegaard's critique of the crowd is often seen as anticipating Ferdinand Tönnies's sociological distinction between *Gemeinschaft* and *Gesellschaft*—an organic community versus the specter of atomized individuation, in which social relations exist in terms of economic mediation. After Kierkegaard, this radically anticommunal strain of philosophy, where the crowd is recognized as one of the most fundamental features of modernity, is further developed by Nietzsche, Heidegger, and Ortega y Gasset. For all of these thinkers, the authentic self-realization of the individual must necessarily evolve out of and against the givens of modern mass society.[43]

In his text *The Use and Abuse of History for Life*, Nietzsche criticizes the tendency of contemporary historiography (Hartmann) to privilege the "world process" as the embodiment of world history. Instead, a new form of historiography must find its way back to those uncontemporary, "singular men who form a kind of bridge over the wild stream of becoming," a "republic of geniuses."[44] These exceptional heroes represent creative being and life force instead of the anonymous, abstract process that turns human history almost into a kind of natural history (*HL*, 319). The latter is tied to the "disgusting, uniform" masses: "The masses seem to me worthy of notice in only three respects: first as blurred copies of great men, produced on bad paper with worn plates, further as resistance to the great, and finally as the tools of the great; beyond that, may the devil and statistics take them!" (*HL*, 320). In the writings of Nietzsche, we encounter some of the most vitriolic anticrowd sentiments of the nineteenth century. In the allegorical-mythic narrative *Thus Spake Zarathustra* (1885), these anticrowd sentiments are dialectically linked with the identification of philosophy with solitude. The protagonist of this work is portrayed as an eremitic prophet-philosopher, nearer to the divine than to man, living in absolute isolation from the "herd," or crowd. The "last men" are the beings of the plain, always averse to the creation of new values emanating from Zarathustra, who is called "the danger of the masses."[45] At the beginning of the text, Zarathustra descends from the mountains to the marketplace of the city in order to preach his doctrine of the superman (*Übermensch*). Yet as will be explained later ("Of the Flies of the Market-Place"), Zarathustra is not the kind of man who is received well by the masses: "Where solitude ceases, there the market-place begins; and where the market-place begins, there begins the uproar of the great actors and the buzzing of the poisonous flies. In the world even the best things are worthless apart from him who first presents them: people call these 'great men.' The people have little idea of greatness, that is to say: creativeness."[46] The people, writes Nietzsche, don't recognize the singular beings, which are loving and creating, in the "solitude of all givers" (*TSZ*, 130). Thus Nietzsche's disdain for the masses is only the flip side of a revolutionary humanism that claims to serve (a new) society: "Truly, the cunning, loveless Ego, that seeks its advantage in the advantage of many—that is not the origin of the herd, but the herd's destruction" (*TSZ*, 86).

As Nietzsche himself writes with near-pathological self-confidence in his late "autobiography," *Ecce Homo*, shortly before his psychophysiological collapse in Turin, the text is a work of total negation and superhuman perfection. It lives in a "blue solitude," a high altitude of prophetic inspiration, unreachable even for the likes of Dante, who in comparison is a "mere believer." Paradoxically, *Zarathustra*, thanks to its "biblical attitude," and despite the "mostly embarrassing" rhetoric (Thomas Mann), has become Nietzsche's most popular book.[47]

In his essay on Nietzsche (*Nietzsche's Philosophy in the Light of Our Experience*), Thomas Mann contrasts Sorel's influential treatise, *Sur la violence*, according to which the masses represent the mythic motor of history, with the Schopenhauerian individualism and "heroic aestheticism" of Nietzsche: "He wants and announces a new time, in which one abstains wisely, ahistorically and transhistorically, from all constructions of the world process, as well as the history of humankind; in which the masses are no longer considered, but the great men, timeless and contemporaneous, which conduct their ghostly conversation over the historical crowding."[48] Similarly, in his review of European nihilism in *The Will to Power*, Nietzsche presents himself as a "philosopher and solitary by instinct"[49] who explains the genesis of nihilism as an effect of the masses' leveling of genius and heroic types: "The lower species ('herd,' 'mass,' 'society') unlearns modesty and blows up its needs into cosmic and metaphysical values. In this way the whole of existence is vulgarized: in so far as the mass is dominant it bullies the exceptions, so they lose their faith in themselves and become nihilists" (*WP*, 19). This vast, fragmentary compendium of notes contains the most extensive comments on the modern "masses" in Nietzsche's entire oeuvre: the index of the Kaufmann edition lists no fewer than seventy-two entries for the term *herd* (*Horde*). Nietzsche's diagnosis of and confrontation with the predominance of the "herd" instinct has sociological, political, economic, ethical, and ultimately physiological or biopolitical implications. As he had written already in the *Genealogy of Morals*, there is no unified system of ethics because the moral instincts of the herd—Christian love of the neighbor—are directly opposed to those of the virtuous individuals: the will to power. The ressentiment of the crowd toward superior men is echoed by the latter's disdain for the masses.

It is characteristic of Nietzsche's nihilistic overturning of nihilism that he sees the figure of the solitary sage-philosopher both as a symptom of and as a potential remedy for mass-dominated society: "Formerly the sage almost sanctified himself in the mind of the crowd by going apart in this way—today the hermit sees himself surrounded as if by a cloud of gloomy doubts and suspicions. . . . From my childhood I have pondered the conditions for the existence of the sage, and I will not conceal my joyous conviction that he is again becoming *possible* in Europe—perhaps only for a short time" (*WP*, 514–16). The figure of the sage removed from the crowd can function both as a sign of aristocratic distinction, as well as form of disguise or protection. Although a Stoic remoteness, a stance of dissimulation and prudential disguise—clearly Nietzsche is influenced by early modern moralistic writers—is advised for the life in the crowd, generally, Nietzsche is in favor of a physical withdrawal, avoiding in this way the danger of contamination with base men. Thus Zarathustra warns of the "poisoned wells" of the herd and states that he was compelled to "fly to the height where the rabble no longer sit at the well" (*TSZ*, 2:6).

Ultimately, the state of radical solitude is conceived of as a transitional phase, giving way to an elitist community of higher men.[50] Of course, the relationship of quantity (few/many) is directly contrary to the relationship of power (strong/weak): "A declaration of war on the masses by *higher men* is needed!" (*WP*, 458). The current predominance of the masses is associated with ideas of Christianity, democracy, and socialism. The "people" are consistently coded as feminine, which for Nietzsche amounts to being "weak, typically sick, changeable, inconstant"—not to mention "liberal" or "Jewish" (*WP*, 460, 462).[51] If the current state of affairs is characterized by the mechanization and minimization of the human ("leveling, higher Chinadom"), then the new, projected arrival of the "superman" does not so much overturn this situation but rather completes it through a kind of codependency or healthy antagonism: "He needs the opposition of the masses, of the 'leveled,' a feeling of distance from them! He stands on them, he lives off them. This higher form of aristocracy is that of the future" (*WP*, 464).

Nietzsche's idea of the strong, beautiful superman is a construction against the "democratic" spirit as it manifests itself from the doctrine of Christianity to the French Revolution, to modern, "English" ideas. As is widely known, Nietzsche's doctrine of the superman, of the "dangerous life," was adapted by the fascist ideologues of the 1920s and 1930s, but, as Thomas Mann points rightly out, with regard to this later adaptation, Nietzsche's thought must be seen as seismographic and strategic, rather than directly political. In fact, his aversion to the masses can be seen as a corrective inversion of the masses' suspicion of the genius, the elevated individual: "Nietzsche's incalculable provocation consists in the fact that he turns the masses' disdain for everything that transcends their horizon into the material and the antagonistic object for a correcting, multiplying disdain."[52]

Thomas Mann's own work, heavily influenced by Nietzsche, provides an illuminating commentary on the status of the individual during a crucial period of modern history. Notwithstanding his spectacular transformation from conservative reactionary to spokesperson for democracy, there is a remarkable consistency in his work, the concern with the predicament of the bourgeois subject in the early twentieth century. In his monumental essay *Considerations of an Unpolitical Man* (1918), Thomas Mann, still in his pre- and antidemocratic phase, argues, in the wake of World War I, against the cosmopolitan, "French" tendencies, as embodied by his brother, Heinrich Mann—the latter named, however, only through the eponym "literate of civilization" (*Zivilisationsliterat*). In the section on politics, he argues that the overemphasis on the social neglects the metaphysical aspects of the transindividual: "for it is the personality, and not the masses, that is the true embodiment of the general."[53]

The specifically German understanding of nationhood is grounded in the basis of "culture," as opposed to the western rhetoric of "civilization." Although Mann grants that democracy will come also to his nation, as well as the concomitant mass politics, he argues for the higher value of a "metaphysical" understanding of the state, an idea that he sees consecrated by his three chosen thinkers, Schopenhauer, Nietzsche, and Wagner:

We have there the difference between masses and people (*Volk*)—which is equal to the difference between individual and personality, civilization and culture, social and metaphysical life. The individualistic masses are democratic, the people is aristocratic. The first is international, the latter a mythical personality of a very special kind. It is wrong to locate the transindividual in the sum of individuals, or the national *and* human in the social masses. The metaphysical *Volk* is the embodiment of the universal. Therefore, it is spiritually wrong to conduct politics in the spirit and sense of the masses.[54]

And, of course, it is the mythic body of the people, the *Volk*, which is embodied more than anywhere else in Germany—where it is threatened by its degeneration through "foreign" influences: "The *Volk* of Germany has remained such more than elsewhere, here it is least degenerated into classes and masses" (*BU*, 377).

However, aside from the "metaphysical" difference between *Volk* and masses, even the Volk, the *people*, are seen with a very skeptical eye. For what, asks Mann, is democracy, if not, precisely, the rule of the people? (*BU*, 376). The *Volk* is dissociated from progress and enlightenment; neither can it justly be called a working class. ("Labor," on the contrary, is associated with the sphere of the bourgeois, that is to say, Thomas Buddenbrook—and Mann himself.) Mann quotes Nietzsche approvingly: "The tendency of the herd . . . is towards permanence and preservation, there is nothing creative in it" (*BU*, 380).

15A 'Vulgus': Latin

Alexandra Katherina T. Sofroniew

Vulgus is one of the Latin words for "crowd." Derived from the Sanskrit word *varga*, meaning "group," "category," or "class," *vulgus* stood for the general public or common people. It referred to a crowd not necessarily in the sense of people physically gathered together in the same place, but in the sense of being part of the same social order and sharing the same ideas and opinions. In contrast with other Latin words for "crowd," such as *turba*, which implied a state of disorder within a crowd, and *multitudo*, which denoted a crowd purely in a numerical sense, *vulgus* made a judgment on the social status of the people making up the crowd. Because the Roman elite saw anything connected to the populace at large as beneath them, *vulgus* came to stand for the lower classes. It was implied that the members of the *vulgus* were of lower intelligence and had lower moral standards. Thus Cicero, an orator and politician writing at the end of the Republic, contrasts *vulgus* with *intellegentium* when he asks, "Semperne in oratore probando aut improbando vulgi iudicium cum intellegentium iudicio congruit?" (Is it always true that in the approval or disapproval of an orator the judgment of the crowd coincides with the judgment of experts?).[1]

Vulgus was also used to describe the crowds at circuses and public events, such as the Triumphs held in Rome for victorious returning generals. Holding these mass public festivities was a crucial way for the emperors to keep their people happy,

For Mann, intellectuals and writers are disenchanted with the political to the degree that the metaphysical character of the state is overtaken by the social. Spiritually emptied mass politics is seen as a territory of moral degradation: "The democratic addition of humankind amounts not to an addition of the good, but of the evil in men; and the greater the sum, the closer it gets to the bestial. The social is a morally questionable terrain" (*BU*, 266). The distrust in democracy is associated with what he sees as "utilitarian enlightenment and the philanthropy of happiness" (*BU*, 271). Looking back on the war, he makes democracy responsible for the fact that the war can be perceived as inhuman and barbaric. War has been deprived of "dignity" and "spiritual values," and thus the last enticement for the "masses" to serve higher, idealistic, nonpragmatic values is gone. What seems especially murky here is not so much the vague difference between masses and *Volk*, but Mann's tendency to equate the rule of the masses with the system of democracy.

As the following years will show, the masses come to power in a way which supports totalitarian, rather than democratic regimes. All those who had prophesied or feared a coming age of the masses, writes Hannah Arendt, underestimated the masses' self-destructive and irrational tendencies, "this entirely unexpected phenomenon of a radical loss of the self, this cynic or bored phlegm with which the masses marched toward their own death . . . and their surprising tendencies for the most abstract conceptions, this passionate desire to conduct their life after senseless ideas."[55] In retrospect, Mann recognizes the anachronistic, untenable position of his wartime essay, as a belated expression of the "German-romantic bourgeoisie."

Mann dedicated many years of his life to an analysis of the crisis of his own artistry. It is significant that in the—retrospective—preface to the book, he defines the life-mode of the writer as "a public solitude, or a solitary publicity" (*BU*, 38). Not much different than for the early modern writers we considered, for Mann too, the solitary activity of the writer is released and redeemed by social use value. According to Mann, there exists a difference, as well as a complementary relation, between literary and civic-bourgeois publicity. Thus he speaks of the "literary publicity, spiritual and social at the same time . . . where the pathos of solitude becomes acceptable for society, possible for the bourgeois, even honorable for the bourgeois" (*BU*, 38).[56]

The essay itself, then, becomes a demonstration of a work worthy of "spiritual publicity": "This text, with the indecency of private letter writing, provides indeed, according to my best knowledge and intentions, what I had to give as an artist, and what belongs to the public" (*BU*, 39).[57] As a critical admirer of Nietzsche,

Mann seeks to reconcile the antisocial tendencies of the artist with his reintegration into, and his service to, democratic society. It is well known that since at least 1922 Mann's work had become increasingly politicized, accompanied by a constant flow of essays and speeches that spoke out for the republic and against the National Socialists.

In an essay from April 1935, "Attention Europe!," Mann takes a stance against the overriding of the self by the collective, the "popularization of the irrational, an event of the 1920's and 1930's."[58] In the development of new mass phenomena, Mann recognizes a new primitivism that has dispensed with the cultured, "more severe humanism" ("AE," 135) of the nineteenth century: "The mass ecstasy that liberates from the self and its burden has no purpose but itself; ideologies connected to this phenomenon, such as 'state,' 'socialism,' and 'greatness of the fatherland' are more or less imposed notions, secondary and really quite superfluous. The relevant purpose is ecstasy, the liberation from the self and thinking, in fact from the ethical and rational altogether" ("AE," 130). Such tendencies, the "mass man philosophizing against reason," and the "turning of spirit against itself" ("AE," 133–35), increased during the Great War but had been in evidence even before then: "The air is full of cheaply excited mass thinking" ("AE," 136). The cultural decline and moral regression with regard to the nineteenth century are attributed to the ascension (*Machtergreifung*) of modern mass man, as Mann notes with reference to the "brilliant" work of Ortega y Gasset, *La rebelión de las masas* (*The Revolt of the Masses*, 1928) ("AE," 131), who had similarly referred to the new mass mentality, and its affinity with fascism, as the "reason of unreason," as a "return to the common life or barbarism," or as an "essential retrogression."[59]

Although Mann envisions a "militant humanism" as the only possible remedy against this situation, it cannot be overlooked that his aversion to the pseudoculture of the masses shares at least in part a common rhetoric with a number of social conservatives, such as Oswald Spengler, Carl Schmitt, or Ludwig Klages, whose anti-Americanism led them to believe that the degraded masses would be reborn in the form of an authoritatively shaped collective, a passing over from civilization into community via the abhorred medium stage of the "masses."[60]

If this and related essays put forward an indictment of vitalist irrationalism, Mann's novella *Mario and the Magician* (1930) presents a more differentiated picture of the relationship between the hypnotized crowd and the charismatic leader.[61] The text straddles a fine line between realism and allegorical tale, which makes it the perfect medium to obliquely comment on the contemporary political situation. Although at first this more or less direct engagement with contemporary

or to momentarily distract them from the state of the city or the government, and the Roman calendar contained many festivals and holidays. Public events such as the circus were looked down on by the intellectual elite, who felt that there were more worthy ways of relaxing and entertaining oneself, and who felt that gathering people together in large numbers encouraged the spread of vice because it provided many examples of bad behavior. In the case of gladiatorial shows, the *vulgus* had the power of life or death over the competitors, condemning them with a turn of the thumb. Seneca argues that this teaches cruelty to those with compassionate sensibilities, because they cannot help but be swayed if the majority desires death.

Vulgus also had an active meaning, describing the spread of information to the public as well as referring to the public itself. The adverb derived from it, *vulgo*, meant "publicly," and the verb *vulgare* meant "to make widely known" or "to make common to all." These notions of popular availability led to the words being used to refer to promiscuity and prostitution.

Rome was a densely populated city, comprising a million inhabitants at its zenith and unsurpassed in size until London during the Industrial Revolution. The city contained a large number of people—slaves, unemployed, homeless, menial laborers, craftsmen—who existed on a level far below that of the literary Romans whose writings survive today. They used the word *vulgus* to refer to this shadowy mass of people who filled the buildings and streets and kept Rome noisy and bustling, but were largely unknown to the upper classes. The elite understood the potential power of this underclass as a result of its huge size, but they thought it mentally and morally inferior and easily manipulated. The *vulgus* was seen as easily susceptible to persuasion by rhetorical skill or even by the rumors that spread quickly through the packed city. Thus Cicero says, "Sic est *vulgus*; ex veritate pauca, ex opinone multa aestimat" (This is the way of the crowd; its judgments are seldom founded on truth, mostly on opinion).[2]

The Roman attitude of condescension toward the *vulgus* has survived to us in our use of the word *vulgar* to describe uneducated or ignorant people, or something common or otherwise beneath us.[3]

mass politics might appear to be unusual with regard to Mann's other, apparently more individual-oriented work, it really provides a focalization of his principal theme, the crisis of bourgeois individuality. The novella responds in particular to a new age of mass politics and mass psychology, and to the role of the charismatic, protofascist leader in it.

As Russell Berman has observed in a brilliant framing of this question, "the sense of the immanent crisis of traditional individuality pushing toward collective solutions [is] inherent in various versions of de-individuation" (*RMGN,* 262). Insofar as the novella presents its narrator as succumbing to the lure of an irrational collectivity, "the specific political material of the novella, the etiology of fascism, is implicitly linked to the origin of modernism in the crisis of liberal individuality" (*RMGN,* 266). As is so often the case in Mann's work, the narrative is located in a scene of cultural and personal encounter, a situation characterized by vacation and sickness. The story is told by an unnamed middle-class narrator who recalls events that happened to his family while they vacationed in an Italian sea resort named Torre di Venere. The story culminates with the account of a magician's evening performance, during which he provokes and hypnotizes his audience. As several critics have observed, what is especially remarkable about this resolution of the story is the fact that the savior Mario, who manages to break his own hypnosis and the general spell of the audience, is a distinctively working-class character. On the other hand, through his typically ironical presentation, Mann conveys that the middle-class narrator, in trying to make retrospective sense of the events, demonstrates his inability to extricate himself from the general seduction of the masses, despite his distanced stance of critical observation.

Although the narrator is assailed by doubts throughout the performance, especially with regard to the question of whether his children's continued attendance is really appropriate, his autonomous will breaks down. Because the narrator and his family are German visitors in an Italian place during Mussolini's fascist regime, Mann uses scenes of cultural encounter to suggest ways of ideological infection.[62] The narrative's principal contribution to an understanding of contemporary mass politics lies in its analysis of the connection between leader and mass as a subliminally sexual, libidinal relation, an analysis that resonates strongly with Freud's writings on mass psychology.[63] Finally, Cipolla's mastery of the audience can be seen to illustrate Gustave Le Bon's point about the crowd's—and especially the "Latin" crowd's—willing submission to forceful authority: "Crowds exhibit a docile respect for force . . . Their sympathies have never been bestowed on easy-going masters, but on tyrants who vigorously oppressed them."[64]

It is clear that both Le Bon and Freud have hypostasized their assumptions about the crowd into profoundly ahistorical, psychological generalities. Where Freud saw the workings of the collective unconscious, both Le Bon and Mann articulated fears about the disappearance of the individual will, associating the crowd explicitly with the condition of women, "primitive" people, and children (*C*, 36). For Le Bon, the person immersed in the crowd "is no longer himself, but has become an automaton who has ceased to be guided by his will" (*C*, 32). Similarly, when Cipolla compels a group of young men to join a dance on stage against their will, "he advised the audience that no fatigue was involved in such activities, however long they went on, since it was not the automatons up there who danced, but himself" ("MM," 170–71).

Mann's late novel *Doctor Faustus* (1947) integrates its account of the genesis of modernist music with a picture of the dramatic societal changes during the interwar period in terms that shed further light on the sociopolitical situation in *Mario*. Specifically, the narrator comments on the intellectual atmosphere of German irrationalism, the demise of human individualism, which emerged from World War I and which fostered the formation of protofascist thinking in the interwar period. The narrator Zeitblom relates his observations of the "Kridwiß" circle in Munich, where one had registered "the immense devaluation that the individual as such had undergone during the time of war."[65] According to these conservative revolutionaries, the French Revolution has inaugurated a new age, an "intentional re-barbarization" (*DF*, 491) that is drifting toward "the despotic, autocratic regime ruling over homogenized, atomized, unconnected, and—similar to the individual—helpless masses" (*DF*, 486). In this context, the narrator describes the fascination that Georges Sorel's *Réflexions sur la violence* have had on the artistic avant-garde and the cultural critics of the interwar period:

His uncompromising prophecy of war and anarchy, his characterization of Europe as the terrain of warlike cataclysms, his teaching that the peoples of the earth can be united only in one idea: to wage war,—all of this justified to call it the book of an epoch. Even more responsible for this was his insight and proclamation that in the age of the masses parliamentary democracy would show itself as entirely inappropriate as a medium for the formation of political will; that in its place henceforth would step the supply of the masses with mythic fictions, which as primitive battle-cries are destined to release and activate the political energies. This was indeed the shocking and exciting prophecy of the book, that popular or rather mass-appropriate [*massengerechte*] myths will henceforth be the vehicle of political movement. (*DF*, 366)

Mann's writings, then, locate their scenarios of beleaguered individuality in the

15B   MLK Rally

Richard Rorty

In August 1963, several hundred thousand people converged on the Mall in Washington, at the behest of A. Phillip Randolph and Martin Luther King Jr., in a rally "for jobs and freedom." Friends in Princeton (where I was then living) who were involved in the civil rights movement suggested to me that I might wish to go down to attend the rally on a bus that their group had chartered. My parents had once worked for Randolph, so I was familiar with his strategy of using real or threatened marches on Washington to win concessions from the federal government. I liked the idea of taking part of such a march. I was part of a contingent, perhaps half black and half white, who sang songs (usually "We Shall Overcome") during our three-hour bus trip from Princeton.

When we arrived in Washington, it was apparent that what was taking place was a rather loose gathering. At the end of the Mall nearest the Lincoln Memorial, where the speakers were, stood a mass of people, too thick to penetrate. Loudspeakers attempted to get the voices of the speakers to the rest of the gathering, which gradually thinned out the nearer it got to the Washington Monument end of the reflecting pool. But the loudspeakers were not powerful enough to do the job. I caught occasional lines of what Dr. King was saying (it was his "I have a dream" speech), but they were too intermittent to hold my interest, so

I just wandered around. Eventually I happened on an ex-girlfriend with whom I spent the rest of the afternoon, catching up on what we had been doing in recent years. We both had given up on trying to figure out what the speakers were saying; we figured that we were doing our duty just by being present in the general vicinity, identifiably part of the rally. When evening came, I went back to the bus and dozed my way home.

That 1963 event was, as it turned out, historically important. But at the time, there was no particular crowd spirit in evidence, at least none that I can remember. Everybody was glad to be there, since we all liked the sense of having contributed to the sheer number of those who had answered Randolph's and King's call. But we were not caught up in a common enthusiasm. Perhaps some segments of the crowd were, but not the part that I was in.

turbulent political context of the 1920s and 1930s, where the "masses" were variously marshaled for both progressive and regressive causes.

As the history of the early twentieth century has amply shown, the progression toward our modern democracies has taken a rather sinister detour in the shape of the various totalitarian regimes. As Hannah Arendt famously wrote, "The totalitarian leader is nothing but an exponent of the masses represented by him." In a recent essay, Peter Sloterdijk has similarly argued that the totalitarian regimes have given expression to the power of the masses through the figure of the leader, who is not so much a higher norm but rather a perfect expression of the banality and mediocrity of the masses, as well as their own aspiration to become a subject: "To become a subject through the elevated other becomes an intermediate step for one's own self-realization."[66] In his polemical essay, Sloterdijk seeks to demystify what he sees as the current ideology, the automatic connection between masses and the potential for progress and liberation. In contrast to much current sociologically correct thinking, Sloterdijk credits Elias Canetti's classic, highly idiosyncratic *Crowds and Power* as one of the few works that does not posit the masses as the enlightened bearer of the Hegelian world spirit, although he also recognizes the continuity between Canetti and the classic theorists of mass psychology: Tarde, Le Bon, and Freud (*VM*, 12–13, 14). For Canetti, the masses are not the protagonists of enlightened progress, but spontaneous agglomerations, *black dots*, always prone to the danger of violent regression, seduction and hypnosis. As Sloterdijk writes, "The term crowd becomes in Canetti's reflections a term which articulates the blockage of individuation precisely at the moment of its realization—which is why the masses, understood as agglomeration [*Auflaufmasse*], can never be encountered except in a state of pseudo-emancipation and half-subjectivity" (*VM*, 13–14).[67] Of course, while he attempts to counter the allegedly "predominant" ideology of the masses as bearers of progress, he succumbs to the opposite myth. It thus remains unclear what Sloterdijk refers to with the title of his treatise, *Contempt for the Masses* (*Die Verachtung der Massen*).

As I have argued here, the idea of the masses as a negative counterforce to individuality has a much older and longer history. It is an idea that has informed crucial moments of western literature and philosophy: the humanist or romantic withdrawal from "active," public life (Petrarch, Montaigne, Rousseau); the classicist or romantic despair vis-à-vis scenes of visual confusion and sensual overload (Goethe); the "death" of traditional poetry and the emergence of hybrid forms of representation (Baudelaire, Heine); and the Nietzschean reaction against the *demos* as an aesthetic, political, and moral disaster.

16 Agoraphobia: An Alphabet

Jessica Burstein

Introduction

Agoraphobia is alternately defined as a fear of open spaces, fear of public places, and a fear of crowds. The fourth edition of the *Diagnostic and Statistical Manual of Mental Disorders* defines it as "Anxiety about being in places or situations from which escape might be difficult (or embarrassing) or in which help may not be available in the event of having an unexpected or situationally predisposed Panic Attack or panic-like symptoms. Agoraphobic fears typically involve characteristic clusters of situations that include being outside the home alone; being in a crowd or standing in a line; being on a bridge; and travelling in a bus, train, or automobile." Given the apparent conflict—how might a fear of open places be the same thing as a fear of places filled?—the concept is as dizzying as the vertigo that often accompanies the phenomenon, and indeed was its primary means of definition in its earliest codification. In the spirit of the vertiginous, what follows is an alphabet of agoraphobia, which has the benefit of order, but one stripped of resolution's banalities. Each letter of the alphabet has one or more entries, some purely textual, and many involving images, each resonant with some aspect of the fear of public places. With apologies to Gustave Flaubert, Ambrose Bierce, and Edward Gorey.

A is for

Agora. The public meeting space in ancient Greece, located in the center of the polis. An open-air gathering spot for assembly or markets. The etymological basis of agoraphobia.

Allegory. Etymologically, wandering outside of narrative. Experientially, talking without being understood by one's fellow citizens. See *Tenure.*

Altamont. The worst rock concert ever. A projected audience of a hundred thousand, with three hundred thousand showing up. In 1969, in a free concert outside of San Francisco, arranged with twenty-four-hour notice at the Altamont Motor Speedway, members of the Hell's Angels, hired to provide security, murdered an eighteen-year-old black man as the Rolling Stones performed onstage. Crowd control gone very bad—notable in that the crowd was not responsible, whereas those hired to control it were.

APsaA. American Psychoanalytic Association. Founded 1911. A group of people paid to sit inside and convince people to go outside. See http://www.apsa.org/.

Atget, Eugène. Failed actor/premier photographer of interiors and exteriors, ignoring all that falls between.

B is for

Ballard, J. G. English novelist, specializing in technophilia and suburbs.

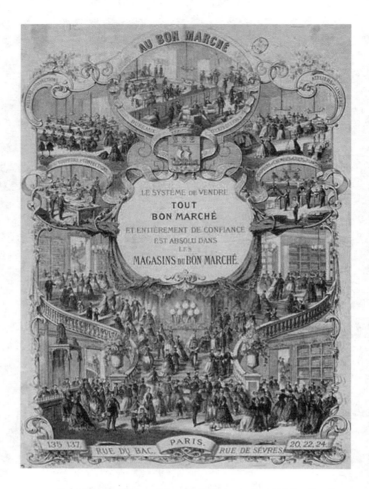

Figure 16.1 Image of Bon Marché interior, 1928. Bibliothèque nationale de France.

Benjamin, Walter. Perennial graduate student: he couldn't get done or, later, get out. "Nineteenth-century domestic interior. The space disguises itself—puts on, like an alluring creature, the costumes of moods. . . . To live in these interiors was to have woven a dense fabric about oneself, to have secluded oneself within a spider's web, in whose toils world events hang loosely suspended like so many insect bodies sucked dry. From this cavern one does not like to stir."[1]

Bon Marché. The first department store (see *Kleptomania*): Paris, Seattle. Commemorated in Zola's *Au Bonheur des dames* (*The Ladies' Paradise*, 1883). The Grand Magasins du Bon Marché was established by Aristide Boucicaut in 1852 and moved into 22, rue de Sevres, in the seventh arrondissement in 1869 (fig. 16.1).

Bosch, Hieronymus. Public distraction goes to hell.

C is for

Cabrini Green. Chicago's "ghetto in the sky," appearing in the films *Candyman*, *The Matrix*, and, having gone condo, *Matrix Reloaded*.

Claustrophobia. The fear of enclosed spaces. See *Tenure*.

Closet. Perennially a place for monsters, once a place for homosexuals, and recommended as a location for screaming.

Copycat. 1995 movie starring Sigourney Weaver as an agoraphobic profiler of serial killers. See *Weaver, Sigourney*.

Crowd. Three. See *Crowds*.

D is for

DNA. Deoxyribonucleic acid. A legal issue having to do with the right to privacy.

Dragnet. The agoraphobe's encroachment theme song: "Come out with your hands up!" Defined by Merriam-Webster as "A network of measures for apprehension (as of criminals)." The etymology is portmanteau-ishly simple: *drag* plus *net*. Also a television show airing 1951–1959, located in Los Angeles, the City of Angels. Starring Jack Webb as Sergeant Joe Friday, the series began with "The Human Bomb," with all but one of the following 274 episodes con-

16A   A Singular Month of May

Alain Schnapp

As far back as I go in my memory, the "events of May," which as far as the Latin Quarter is concerned I prefer to call, with Edgar Morin, "the student commune," are not identified with the crowd, in the sense of the enormous, powerful, at times formidable mass of people assembled at one protest; they remind me of something more discreet and more quotidian: the feeling of a period of liberty and engagement when the city was more fraternal, dreams more captivating, passersby and fellow travelers in the bus and the metro suddenly attentive to each other. Edgar Morin's formulation comprises a portion of the explanation: for several brief weeks "the student commune" incarnated students' desire to substitute for the current state of things a sort of ideal and deliberative city, where discussion, vote, and protest are a means of recovering the festal and poetic base of democratic invention. Certainly there have been other student movements in the world, but the Parisian events have a specificity which has to do with the architectural frame of the city, with its memory of revolutionary days, and with the place of intellectuals and students in the city. The Algerian War, not so distant, had revealed the violence of colonial warfare to draftees and had allowed students allied to intellectuals and to a party of "forces of the Left" to weigh in on the issue of combat and of the future of the Republic.

The spirit of May draws from the experience of the war in Algeria, the influence of Sartrean engagement, and the repertory of a social contestation combining anticolonial themes with a critique of the dominant classes. There are many meanings of the word "crowds" (*foules*), and one could first say that there were crowds of students in Paris (il y avait foule d'étudiants à Paris). Not in the sense of masses: students were not dominant in the population of Paris, but they were already much more numerous than ten years earlier, more determined and, especially, hardened in their critique of society. The "situationists" of Strasbourg and the students of Nanterre organized parodic actions, disruptions, and strikes. The occupation of the counsel hall of the University of Nanterre by 142 students unleashed a cycle of provocation and repression that led to the convocation of eight "leaders" before the counsel of the University of Paris, slated for May 6. When a fire broke out on May 2, 1968, on the premises of the Sorbonne student union, there was no doubt that it was due to a handful of students on the extreme right (the "Occident" movement) getting at the Sorbonne students, with whom they had constant skirmishes. The Sorbonne students and a small group already famous at Nanterre (the "movement of March 22") called for a manifestation in the courtyard of the Sorbonne on May 3 in response to this aggression.

We were hardly numerous that afternoon when everything began—maybe nine hundred at the most. Suddenly the rumor spread that commandos of the Occident were threatening to return. In the courtyard of the Sorbonne, some pieces of wood cropped up, a few people broke a chair or two with an eye to meeting up with the assailants: no big deal. But rumor of the presence of the Nanterre "fanatics" had spread. The rector and his secretary general became anxious. They asked

taining the adjective "big" in the title: prime among them were "The Big Parrot" (March 13, 1952), "The Big Doting Mother" (December 20, 1956), "The Big Smart Girl" (January 13, 1959), and "The Big Green Monkey" (February 9, 1958). Devoted to deadpan realism—"Just the facts, ma'am"—the show remains notable if only for the fact that the shoes Webb wore were a present from Richard M. Nixon.

DSM IV. The latest edition of the *Diagnostic and Statistical Manual of Mental Disorders.* Bedtime reading. Defines agoraphobia as "not a codable disorder. Code the specific disorder in which the Agoraphobia occurs (e.g., 300.21 Panic Disorder with Agoraphobia [p. 402] or 300.22 Agoraphobia Without History of Panic Disorder [p. 404])."

E is for

Enochophobia. The fear of crowds. Often confused with the fear of *Crowds,* which is more properly termed "Stanfophobia," the fear of Stanford, or "Stanfauxphobia," the fear of being mistaken for someone who went to Stanford.

F is for

Fascism. Italian political movement, founded in the early twentieth century, and a colloquial term for right-wing celebrations of groups headed by an often well-dressed demagogue. Used loosely by American academics as a means of referring to each other.

Fence. Makes good neighbors. Also a term for a person who links stolen goods to wider markets, and a form of male homosociality practiced in early French novels.

Fire. A word best heard in a crowded movie theater; relatedly, the study of free speech.

THE GASHLYCRUMB TINIES

Figure 16.2 Frontispiece from Edward Gorey, *The Gashlycrumb Tinies.* Reproduced by permission of The Edward Gorey Charitable Trust.

G is for

The Gashleycrumb Tinies, or After the Outing. 1963 alphabet book by Edward Gorey (1925–2000). The story of what happens to small people subjected to systematicity (fig. 16.2). In Gorey's allegory, a group of children is knocked off alphabetically, whether they are inside (fig. 16.3) or outside (fig. 16.4).

the police to intervene—an extremely rare act. The students were promised that they could go free if they left the property. But in several dozen minutes, the Sorbonne was sealed off. We were prisoners in the courtyard. A police brigade advanced and we negotiated, a bit stunned by what had happened. The police had never in students' memory (since the war!) entered into the Sorbonne to suppress a manifestation. The commissar who accompanied the policemen and the representatives of the rector was calm: he proposed letting the girls go and guaranteed that there would be no violence if we got into the police vehicles for an "identity check." We accepted and were made to enter the buses arranged in front of the Sorbonne. When my turn came, quite quickly, I heard the driver say to the policeman charged with watching over us in the rear compartment of the bus that the situation was tense and he should be careful: the quarter was in a state of joyful insurrection. Alerted by the girls who had been released and the *noria* of police buses, students throughout the Latin Quarter had spontaneously mobilized to the cry of "Liberate our comrades."

During the ride that led us to the commissariat from the Place de l'Opéra we heard cries, and through the bars we saw hundreds of protesters attacked, sometimes violently, by the overwhelmed policemen. One of my comrades suggested that I neutralize the policeman accompanying us in the rear of the bus, open the doors, and release the twenty or so students around us. Somewhat surprised, I replied that we would see what happened; in fact, we were received civilly at the commissariat and released around 10 o'clock at night, with the exception of Daniel Cohn Bendit, who, accompanied by Xavier Langlade, a famous militant at Nanterre, had to wait several hours longer. We talked late into the night and began to plan the action of the following days. We had the feeling that something was beginning, a spirit of insurrection that we had never encountered before. The symbolic intervention of the police into the Sorbonne had occurred on a Friday (May 3); the appearance of the accused Nanterre students before the disciplinary counsel was scheduled for Monday, May 6. The two weekend days were the occasion for feverish preparations. Without being entirely conscious of what was in the works, all the student groups were busy mobilizing their comrades and composing tracts. The day of May 6 witnessed an intense agitation: Nanterre and the Sorbonne were closed, and students were protesting in the Latin Quarter. Another protest was organized at Denfert-Rochereau on May 7. This time it brought together tens of thousands of people.

As soon as the action was launched, the revolt was no longer confined to the Latin Quarter: it reached the lycées and part of the populace. In the west of France, workers and peasants began to participate in the protests. The night of May 10 to 11, barricades were raised and then violently destroyed by the forces of order. It was as if the city had renewed its tradition of "revolutionary days," but with a notable difference: the students and the portion of the populace who supported them were protesting peaceably; the language was revolutionary, but the acts were in the tradition of classic student and popular manifestations. The night of May 10 to 11, the student service order tried with all its force to minimize the confrontation and to contain the physical violence. Despite the ineptness of power and the ministers' total incomprehension of the movement—and without underes-

G is for GEORGE smothered under a rug

Figure 16.3 "G is for George," from Gorey, *The Gashlycrumb Tinies.* Reproduced by permission of The Edward Gorey Charitable Trust.

Gogosian Gallery. Located in London, New York, and Beverly Hills. The New York branch, in Chelsea, reopened in September 2000 with a startling amount of space, much to the delight of agoraphilic New Yorkers. At the time, the gallery was teeming with works by the arty British equivalent of Eminem, Damien Hirst. The viewer was first confronted with "Hymn," "a 20–foot tall painted bronze anatomical model" of the human body.[2] The insides of a gargantuan anatomical learning device were exposed to the unhungry eye (fig. 16.5). Often confused with the fear of Damien Hirst. In *Love Lost*, and its twin vitrine *Lost Love*, large black carp swim in an enclosed environment of a gynecologist's office. A helpful critic glosses the allusion: "women smell like fucking kippers."[3]

Gursky, Andreas (b. 1955). German photographer, once a student of Bernd and Hilla Becher at Düsseldorf's Kunstakademie, and master of the late

H is for HECTOR done in by a thug

Figure 16.4 "H is for Hector," from Gorey, *The Gashlycrumb Tinies*. Reproduced by permission of The Edward Gorey Charitable Trust.

twentieth-century topophoto ("ToPoPho"). The hyperrealism born of digital manipulation ("FauxToPoPho"): libraries without floors, collapsed perspectives, and crowds made where none exist. In the case of *Untitled V* (1997), "a shimmering display of 204 Nike sports shoes," "there is no subject to visit—not just because Gursky constructed the display case and dismantled it after making the picture, but because he built only part of it, repositioned a new set of shoes for each of six exposures, then composed them in the computer to make a slender Minimalist image of something that never existed."[4] Gursky's digitally manipulated photograph of the Stockholm public library, "a perfect hemisphere of color-coded books, omits the actual floor, which, in reality, includes an escalator that would have marred the symmetrical beauty of the image."[5]

"Since it was impossible to take in the vast expanse of the building from a central vantage point," Gursky "[recorded] the left and right halves of the

timating the police violence—the sangfroid of the prefect of police and the interposition of intellectuals and some union representatives contributed to avoiding confrontations that could have been bloody. During the days of May, we never saw anything comparable to the awful repression of the Algerians on October 17, 1961, or even Charonne in 1962. On his return from Afghanistan on May 11, the prime minister, Georges Pompidou, decided to yield to the demands, to release the imprisoned students, and to reopen the universities, including the Sorbonne, which was immediately occupied. The most intense moment began May 16 and lasted until May 30, the date of the grand Gaullist and anticommunist manifestation that marked the resumption of power. It was the moment of the encounter between the students' revolutionary ideal and the reality of a country that relived in its depths the great working-class dreams of the popular front. While the students thought they were living episodes of the soviet of Petrograd, the unions rediscovered the paradigm of the "Matignon accords," which permitted a union-management agreement on May 27 in rue de Grenelle.

The revolt, begun by a modest student manifestation on May 3, was transformed into a giant social protest movement without the agents in the conflict—students, unions, parties, government—fully realizing what was happening. Since 1789, Paris has been a city where revolutionary days follow each other, each one calling forth the next, from July 14 to the Commune of Paris, passing through the fall of Charles X and of Louis-Philippe. Trained in this type of historical tradition, social actors always look backward to find in past crises a model for present crises. Students, often impregnated with a summary Marxism, thought

Figure 16.5 *Hymn* by Damien Hirst, 1996. Painted bronze, 240 x 108 x 48 inches. The New Saatchi Gallery at County Hall, London. Copyright David Levene 2004.

façade from separate viewpoints, then [merged] the two in the computer." "The two negatives also had the advantage of doubling the relative sharpness of what would become an enormous enlargement, in need of all the detail that could be mustered. Moreover, as Gursky has observed, the double viewpoint allows the viewer to see more deeply into the individual apartments—a gain in documentary information achieved thanks to a method that violates the conventions of perspectival realism."[6]

H is for

High Anxiety (1977), directed by Mel Brooks. A satire of multiple Hitchcock films, including *Vertigo* (1958), the movie recounts what happens when physicians attempt to cure themselves. See the title song: "High anxiety—you win!" See *Parents*.

Huysmans, Joris-Karl. Author of *À Rebours* (1884), alternately translated as *Against Nature* or *Against the Grain.* The ultimate agoraphobic reading—for us, about us (see also *Wolfe, Nero*). The character Des Esseintes, the last of a noble family line, retires to a French suburb and stays in for an extended weekend of several years in a world before DVDs. He creates the ultimate habitus, organizing his living arrangements to provide all that the world can offer, and much that it cannot, by creating rarified experiments in synesthesia (the mouth organ, an instrument played on the palate with arcane liqueurs) and sheltering (slippered and cowl-clad servants, all light blocked from intrusion). Organized with a chapter devoted to each aspect of the house and all but devoid of plot, the novel provides the perfect synthesis of agoraphobia and boredom. A home improvement manual for the enervated.

I is for

Isolation booth. Used in 1950s quiz shows as a means by which introspection is spatialized. Offshoots include tanning booths, sex booths, and the now extinct phenomenon of phone booths—the latter used, mostly by superheroes, in a world before the cell phone. Now we have Nextel and Nokia, and Clark Kent

they were the actors in a new October Revolution; unionists and men of the left, dazed by the extent of the strikes, imagined that they were seeing a new popular front that would rid them of a fifth republic and a man whom they identified with "personal power." The government and management lived in the confused fear of a plot bringing leftists, communists, and socialists together in one deadly front. This is why the history of the events of May is as much a historiographic adventure in which each camp, even each group poses in the position that seems most advantageous in the eyes of history, where everyone looks toward a past event to give his current attitude a certain style, incarnated as much in clothes as in postures. The rhetoric of discourse, the forms of action, the slogans draw from the historical repertory and from the traditions accompanying it.

I don't believe therefore that 1968 was one of the manifestations of the "age of crowds" in Serge Moscovici's sense. The student revolt was the fruit of a protest against archaism, authoritarianism, and the antiquated methods of a university caught up in the cult of elites and strangled by the poverty of its means. The workers' demand came from another gap that pointed to the contradiction between the modernization of institutions and the economy, proclaimed since 1958, and the workers' miserable condition. Preoccupied by the place of France in the world, de Gaulle had neglected the social and economic difficulties of a working class still powerfully influenced by the Communist Party, a class that had not forgotten the promises of a better world after liberation. May 1968 was born of the encounter of these repressions, and it made possible, beyond the political failure, a transformation of mores and an opening of the social space.

May 1968, in its exaggerations as in its successes, is one of the historical events where crowds are never unanimous, where from behind the collective and revolutionary phraseology peers out situationist humor: "be realistic: demand the impossible."

*Translated from the French
by Matthew Tiews*

has no place to change. The wired, operator-assisted telephone may make a comeback, and indeed is necessary as a portal for movement between states of reality in *The Matrix*.

J is for

Jawohl. German for "You betcha." Large numbers of people pronouncing this have been known to cause problems. See *Triumph of the Will*.

K is for

Kieslowski, Krzysztof. Polish genius. Directed, among others, *The Decalogue*, filmed for Polish television in 1988; tells the story of the Ten Commandments within the province of an apartment complex in Warsaw.

Kleptomania. The compulsion to steal. Invented in the nineteenth century, made possible by department stores. See *Ryder, Winona*.

Ku Klux Klan. Possible only in great numbers and with unlimited supplies of bedding.

L is for

Levi, Primo. Either a cockeyed optimist with vertigo or a hypocrite who came to terms with his past.

M is for

M (1931). Fritz Lang's tale of city life with Peter Lorre as a child murderer. One-half of a brightly colored candy seeking its exact other, i.e., sweet retort to *The Symposium*.

Malthus, Thomas (1766–1834). Political economist, early advocate of birth control.

Mimesis. Book by Eric Auerbach, scholar living in Pennsylvania at the time of writing. Therefore extremely lengthy, as well as providing its author with reflexive refuge. A term of praise for actors (example: "That was very mimetic." "Why thank you."); a term of suspicion for Mikkel Borch-Jacobsen.

Monogamy. At first blush, what seems to be the opposite of promiscuity, but is in fact its bedfellow. As the British essayist Adam Phillips says, "We are daunted by other people making us up, by the number of people we seem to be. We become frantic trying to keep the numbers down, trying to keep the true story of who we really are in circulation. This, perhaps more than anything else, drives us into the arms of one special partner. Monogamy is a way of getting the versions of ourselves down to a minimum."[7]

Movies. Civilization's highest achievement. Agoraphobic examples:

Alien (1979)
Bob and Carol and Ted and Alice (1969)
Copycat (1995)
Inside Out (1975)
Outbreak (1995) The crowd as contagion, riding on the "revenge of the rain forest" (Richard Preston, *The Hot Zone* [1994]), frisson of Ebola-phobia. An unlikely scenario, if only for the fact that Renee Russo would never marry Dustin Hoffman. Scariest line: "We've got to get that monkey!"
Panic Room (see *Panic Room*)
Rosemary's Baby (1968)
Safe (1995)
The Shining (1980)

N is for

Numbers. One may be the loneliest number, "much, much worse than two," but consider the alternatives. Two: company. Three: crowd. Four: a means by which many couples get through dinner with each other.

16B Crowds as Tear-jerking Opportunities

Luigi Ballerini

Crowds at political rallies make me weep. For this to occur, however, two conditions must be met. First, I myself have to be in the crowd. Second, the speaker cannot be an ordinary secessionist scumbag like Umberto Bossi, but must be a true political hero who is concerned with real ways and real means to turn our terrible world into a much better place to live. He must demand a fairer distribution of wealth and the public ownership of the means of production (when the products are of public interest). He does not have to go all out and ask for the abolition of the military or maintain, in fact, that the whole idea of defense is for the birds (for the cats, fat cats?). If he were to do that, he would not have much of an audience (yes, I know, a crowd) to address. So I put up with that omission on account of its structural relevance.

As a young man, I was very fond of Pietro Nenni, the secretary of the Italian Socialist Party, which, in my days, was a Marxist party. The difference from the Communist Party was that the socialists expected to implement socialism democratically, through persuasion and parliamentary action. The communists, on the other hand, kept talking about the need to bring about change in a revolutionary fashion, although they knew full well that they would not. In fact, in later years, under the leadership of Enrico Berlinguer, whom I also came to admire, the Italian Communist Party shifted gear and introduced the idea of entrepreneurship (in the public sphere). In the end, strange as it may seem, it became the first Communist Party to call itself Marxist and democratic—which, in my view, is better and by far more plausible, than "revolutionary and institutional," an oxymoron that did not do much for the welfare of Mexico, where it was conceived.

The official avowal of the democratic process did not result in a merger with the socialists, as it perhaps should have, simply because in the meantime the socialists had become downright capitalists and practiced with a vengeance what they had not preached: namely, the somewhat controversial doctrine of private profit and public losses. But to go back to Nenni: in terms of my weeping, he was better than any child lost in the crowd as shown today on TV, even when the child is Indian and his mother and father realize they lost him after days of bathing in the holy waters of the Ganges River. In fact, Nenni was impeccable. He never failed me. He was not a handsome man, and he spoke with a distinct vernacular accent. But he was "erotic" as Socrates was "erotic," according to Alcibiades. Or so I like to think of him in retrospect. He had guts. Life dealt with him shabbily; he lost a daughter in a Nazi concentration camp, spent years in exile, and saw his own party, which he loved dearly, become a boisterous gang of profiteers. His political passion never flickered, however, and he was no cheat. Quite the opposite: a superbly honest man who viewed politics as a noble art (like fistfighting, I suppose), or at least an honest craft: some know how to make boats, and some know how to make laws that are just.

He spoke of the necessity of nationalizing energy-related industries—and it was good to hear him

O is for

Outing. A sociopolitical practice used in the 1980s and 1990s in order to convince the general populace that homosexuality was not only not pathological but ubiquitous. Although the conclusions are correct, the methodology was as deviant as its victims were not. As the National Lesbian and Gay Journalists Association defines it, "outing" is "Publicly revealing the sexual orientation of an individual who has chosen to keep that orientation private (from out of the closet)."[8] See *Closet*.

Outside. A rumor. Alternatively, "Something I move between in order to get from the cab to my apartment" (Fran Liebowitz, *Social Studies*).

P is for

Panic Room (2002), directed by David Fincher, starring Jodi Foster. Panic rooms are trendy and expensive closets built for realists with too much time on their hands. The movie explores the frightening effects of being trapped for an extended period of time in an enclosed space with a precocious teenager who is denied candy bars.

The governmental equivalent to personal panic rooms is the "Continuity of Government Bunker," known as "Project Greek Island," "the code name for a mammoth bunker secretly constructed by the U. S. federal government during the Cold War. It was designed to shelter the members of Congress for up to sixty days in the event of nuclear war. This installation was placed underneath the posh Greenbrier Hotel in White Sulphur Springs, West Virginia. An entire wing was added to the hotel as a pretext for its construction."[9]

Paranoia. A psychological state brought on by an overly accurate grasp of reality. But why do you ask (fig. 16.6)?

Parents. "They fuck you up" (Phillip Larkin, "This be the Verse"). "It's not heights I'm afraid of—it's parents!" (Mel Brooks; see *High Anxiety*). A source of funding for APsaA.

Figure 16.6 Edvard Munch, *The Scream* (1893). Tempera and crayon on cardboard (91 x 73.5 cm). © 2005 The Munch Museum / The Munch-Ellingsen Group /Artists Rights Society (ARS), NY.

say so in front of thousands of people in Piazza del Duomo, the same spot where, in 1932, Mussolini had promised every Italian family a house made from good stone, only to deliver the entire city to the Nazis eleven years later. It was then that my grandmother blurted out, after days (weeks, in fact) of silence, that even among the Nazis, you could find fellows who were not as bad as we made them out to be, notwithstanding the number of her relatives and friends they had been beaten to a pulp or sent on to greener pastures—which goes to show how powerful denials can be.

In view of the mnemonic traces left in me by such complications, it felt good to hear Nenni, who must have been my grandmother's age, speak in one sweep of nationalization and ethics. And the good feeling remained with me and many other members of the crowd, even when it became clear that the transfer from private to public hands would cost Italy a pretty penny. Actually, I never understood why we could not just confiscate the whole damn thing. Why was it necessary to buy back what we had already paid for a thousand times over, every month, when the gas bill came, and the electricity bill came, and the god-knows-what bill came . . . and we paid. Well, we paid again. The only thing Nenni failed to tell us (or did he tell us and we forgot?) was that, after all this, nationalized electricity was going to cost more than before. But hey, what the heck, isn't a good weeping session worth more than any rate increase? Increase is actually a good thing, according to Shakespeare anyway. It is exactly what he says he desires to receive from the fairest of creatures. . . . Eugenicist that he was.

At any rate, the only way to avoid that increase could have come from the practice of honesty, which in turn is predicated on self-esteem—a very rare quality anywhere, and sorely lacking, I mean invisible, in people affected by a syndrome called public employment. It is much simpler to claim rights than to endorse duties. The claiming of rights, however, is a thing a crowd does very well also. Antileftist groups knew it and used to mock us with the following anecdote. Nenni (or any other leftist leader, for that matter) would ask his audience (yes, I know, his crowd): "Do you care for bread?" The crowd thunders back: "Yes!" *Leader*: "Do you care for wine?" *Crowd*: "Yes!" *Leader*: "Do you care for work?" *Crowd* (chanting the opening words of the Italian Communist Anthem): "Avanti o popolo, alla riscossa" (Go forward people, wake up, wake up)/"Bandiera rossa, bandiera rossa" (Red flag, red flag), and so on. All this in the early 1960s, when an experimental poet could bask in the idea of being a revolutionary of sorts.

Nenni died quietly on January 1, 1980. By then his party was securely in the hands of Bettino Craxi (Nenni's own *dauphin*, believe it or not) who would make the Socialist Party the necessary pivot of Italian politics, only to bury its glorious century-long history in a grave of scandals and corruption. Years earlier I had moved further to the left and lived in a state of velleity and confusion, a side effect of being frequently surrounded by crowds. My political passion peaked in the mid-1970s with a dastardly denunciation of literature as bourgeois art and the equation of poetry with silence (Nietzsche came to the rescue in the late 1970s and early 1980s). In the meantime, however, I had wept a few times listening to Enrico Berlinguer. Frail and unassuming as he was (communist mothers had a ball with him), he had a sensational sense of rhythm and could quote—although at times

Phobia. Fear. The first recorded phobia is hydrophobia, the fear of water. The second recorded phobia is the fear of cocktail parties at which people will tell you about their phobias.

Piazza. An Italian square. Identifiable by its proximity to basilisks and Cinzano. Freud liked the Piazza Colonna in Rome, writing to his family in on September 22, 1907, "When I turn to go I detect a certain tension in the attentive crowd [*der Menge aufmerksam*], which makes me look again, and sure enough a new performance has begun, and so I stay on. Until 9 PM I usually remain spellbound [*so der Zauber zu wirken*]; then I begin to feel too lonely in the crowd, so I return to my room to write you all."[10]

Polygamy. What Mormons do when everyone is looking. See *Monogamy*.

Q is for

Queue. British for "line." A group of people filed behind each other or in front of each other, depending on whether you are impatient or smug. In its American parlance, New Yorkers stand on them, other Americans stand in them, and rational people avoid them by staying at home, logging online, and ordering tickets in advance.

R is for

Rand, Ayn (1905–1982). The thinking girl's Danielle Steele, usually read by male MBAs. Russian-born novelist who appeared as an extra in Cecil B. DeMille's *King of Kings* (1927) and then went on to write large and eventful books such as *The Fountainhead* (1943) and *Atlas Shrugged* (1957); the use of recurrent initials for her main characters led many to believe that the author's thought was a systematic one, an illusion furthered by her founding of a school of philosophy. The central tenet of objectivism may be paraphrased as, "But enough about me—what do you think of me?" and flourishes at the University of Chicago. Her final wish was that she be commemorated under a large dollar sign.

Repulsion. 1965 movie directed by Roman Polanski starring Catherine Deneuve as a manicurist who carries a rabbit head in her purse. Her London flat has elastic walls, and the lack of central air conditioning sends her, during the sticky English summer of love, into a frenzy of interior redecoration.

Rosemary's Baby (1968), directed by Roman Polanski. Mia Farrow stars in this harrowing tale of the difficulties of finding decent housing in New York. See *Movies*.

Upside	Downside
Rent control.	Your landlord is the Antichrist.
Laundry room on site.	Yoko Ono lives in the same building.
Doctor makes house calls.	Vidal Sassoon doesn't.
Friendly neighbors.	They're in a coven.

Ryder, Winona. Ultimate method actress. See *Kleptomania*.

S is for

Sade, Marquis de. "Nobleman and pervert" (*Webster's Seventh New Collegiate Dictionary*, s.v. "Sade"). "Donatien Alphonse François" to his friends, who were few. The first to receive a full-time governmental grant stipulating no means of employment other than writing. Confused with European singer Sade by Brad Pitt's character in *Seven* (1995), the story of a man woefully misunderstood as a serial killer, when in fact he was working on a limited schedule: there are only a limited number of sins, and afterward he would have gone back to his lovingly decorated apartment.

Safe. Not bloody likely. Also a 1995 movie directed by Todd Haynes. See *Movies*.

Space (Ineffable). Le Corbusier's blueprint.

Stirner, Max. Author of *The Ego and Its Own: The Case of the Individual Against Authority* (1844; first English translation 1907). Opening chapter: "All Things Are Nothing to Me." Agoraphobia as self-expression.

he misquoted—big-shot literary types, including Dante, who remains to date a great crowd pleaser and the most profitable of all Italian industries. I remember in particular a speech Berlinguer delivered in 1975, at the newly built (a true engineering feat) Palazzo dello Sport (Sports Arena), the construction of which had been fiercely opposed by the Milanese section of the Communist Party (they changed their mind when they realized that Comrade Berlinguer was going to talk there). I believe that by then electricity had either been returned to private hands, or was going to be, shortly. Virtually all that had been nationalized reverted back to private hands. But the purchase this time was far less expensive. What was being bought, we were told, were money-losing concerns. The problem, this time, was a scandal named after the Lockheed Corporation—an ethical issue once again, but of a slightly different nature. Some prominent deputies from the Christian Democratic Party had pocketed vast sums of money, hiking the price of airplane engines delivered to the Italian government by the American company. Something like that. Some of the same people were also involved in petroleum-related scandals.

All in all, Berlinguer knew what he was talking about and successfully portrayed the Italian Communist Party as the only ethically reliable political organization left in the country. When he explained to the audience—a multitude of card-carrying, well-behaved, petit bourgeois communists and sympathizers—how Italy could be saved from the rapacious talons of those Christian Democratic vultures, whose thieving vocation was beyond dispute and made nineteenth-century robber barons look like archangels, the response was not just tears of happiness (on my part), but votes: the PCI got 35 percent of the national ballots, more than any other party—and it scared the hell of out of Uncle Sam. Upon exiting the arena, sobbing with delight, I was introduced to the secretary of a local communist cell who, having learned that I lived mostly in America, promptly produced a handkerchief, unfolded it, and waved it at me: clearly, he did not intend to dry my tears with it, but rather to dispel the symbolic stench emanating from my compromised persona.

Things became complicated after that. Negotiations between Christian Democrats and democratic communists were severely boycotted and came to a halt with the Moro affair. I stopped weeping, began to do some serious teaching, and went back to poetry.

Nowadays, to reach that emotional level, in which rage and feeling sorry for myself mix again and ward off any fear of death, I go to rallies against the war in Iraq, where crowds, however, are much thinner than those I seem to remember. You see, I can only love causes once I know they are lost. It's my way of behaving like a tragic hero. Italian style, naturally. As an Italian, I do not have to sport a stiff upper lip.

New York, December 2003

Streisand, Barbra. American singer, director, actress, diva. Singer of *Crowds* project theme song: "People, people who need people are the luckiest people in the world."[II]

Suburbs. Technically, "below urb," as in "sub rosa," or more precisely, "infra dig." A modern source of horror films and family life. See *Ballard, J. G.*

Symptom. The point at which killing time becomes mimetic. The first modern symptom was noting you had one.

T is for

Tenure. The point at which herding cats becomes literally metaphorical. And indeed preferable.

Three's Company. Topophobic nightmare: despite living in 1970s San Francisco, you are trapped in a small apartment with John Ritter, Suzanne Sommers [*sic*], and the woman from the L'egg's commercials. Your apartment is tended by Mr. and Mrs. Roper, a couple seemingly having fled from *Tales of the City*; they depart for their own sitcom and leave you in the care of Don Knotts.

Triumph of the Will. 1934 film by Leni Riefenstahl. Persuasive argument against governmental funding of the arts.

U is for

Urban. The ability to procure egg rolls at 1:30 AM without leaving one's home.

V is for

Versace, Viktor, and Rolfe, Dries Van Noten. Ostensibly to be worn when you're out on the town, but given the likelihood of having wine spilled on you, better to stay home and order more from Yoox.com.

Versailles. Marginal housing for the center of the universe. See *Atget, Eugène*.

Vertigo. Dizziness in the face of heights. See *Symptom, Movies*.

W is for

Wall. Great Wall of China, Berlin Wall, "Building Wall" (see *Fence*). Hit in the course of marathons and dissertations.

Weaver, Sigourney. Topohobic diva. She plays an agoraphobe in *Copycat* (see *Movies*), a murderous agoraphobe in *Death and the Maiden*, and, in the Alien sequence, a girl who hates Mother but insists on staying home anyway. Given the alternative, this is understandable. "In space, nobody can hear you scream."

Wolfe, Nero. The agoraphobe's detective. An eccentric, large-bodied genius who would repeatedly state to callers that he prefers not to leave his west Manhattan brownstone, which has been fitted for his every need: orchids on the roof, and a fine chef in the kitchen. "I repeat, Mr. Frost, it is useless," he declared, "I never leave my home on business. No man's pertinacity can coerce me."[12] "Wolfe started the conversation by explaining that he never left the office on business."[13] "I never leave my house on business."[14] Essential companion: Archie Goodwin: narrator, man about town, human tape recorder.

X is for

Xenia. The guest/host contract—the source of all wars, either through its misunderstanding or accurate grasp.

Y is for

Yodeling. Agoraphobic choral practice. The ultimate in isolation, but premised on the dream of the perfect audience: one kept at a great distance. "Repulsion and distance work to create a form of being together" (Georg Simmel, "The Stranger"). Conversely, Wagner, with hiccups, for one. See *Symptom*.

Z is for

Zeno's Paradox. A race between a turtle and Achilles, the sum of which amounts to the fact that you can never get to the other side of the room, and indeed that all motion is impossible if you really think about it. Comforting in its own way, and the nascent basis for many Thomas Bernhardt novels.

Zoos. The belief that we are different.

Afterword

N. Katherine Hayles

LIKE A LONE STRAGGLER LIMPING up the street after the crowd has come and gone, this afterword looks up and wonders what could possibly remain to say after all the fireworks are over. Nothing, perhaps, other than to offer a small comment on the shape of the multitude as it recedes into the distance. As the editors observe, by design and intention, this is a very crowded book. Although each essay has its singular voice, the effect of reading from essay to essay is much like lingering over faces in a crowd, each distinctive and yet in their cumulative effect composing a mass. Set against this mass are the alphabetized "crystals," sparkling gems of wit that give a pleasurable jolt of surprise, like the few individuals who are given red kerchiefs to make them stand out from the multitude. Embroidering the borders are the semantic histories and personal reminiscences, positioned on the outskirts, yet with clear affinities to the center of the mass.

Perhaps the most interesting feature of the project's form, to my mind, is its distributed existence as print artifact and electronic Web site. By spanning both media, the project optimizes the advantages of each and implicitly makes the case for recognizing the specificity of media. The print book, with its superior visual resolution, hacker-proof sturdiness, and easy portability, permits readers to continue long after eyestrain and repetitive stress syndrome would have taken a toll on even the most dedicated Web site visitor. The Web site, with its capacious storage space, multimedia capabilities, and sophisticated search functions, offers an ease of access and a diversity of material that enable research to be undertaken that often could not could be done at all from print material alone. Combined, the book and Web site offer unparalleled breadth and depth of research on crowds that will be likely to remain the gold standard on this topic for some time to come.

The advantages of combining both media in a single project invite reflection on the editors' suggestion that the functions served by the physical gathering of crowds may in part have been superseded by electronic media. I suspect that rather than displacing each other, physical congregations and electronic gatherings participate in a dynamic media ecology whereby the specificity of each defines itself in relation to the other. Whereas electronic media offer the advantages of easy access (no traveling required), multitasking (opening other windows and attending to various tasks while listening and/or watching crowded events), and large-storage accessible archiving, electronic gatherings lack the multimodal physical experiences of being immersed in a crowd, including odors, physical contacts, and the endorphin rush possible when in exhilarating contact with many other people. Electronic participation also tends either to be noninteractive or, in situations involving scrolling text, too linear to permit large-scale participation. On the other hand, the disappointing experiences recounted in the volume's first-person reminiscences of dangerous encounters, missing the event because the mass itself prevents access, being poked, pushed, and trampled, vividly illustrate why some prefer to remain safely and conveniently at home. Crowds are not apt to disappear, any more than electronic communication will fade from the scene. Rather, both will remain in active interplay with one another, just as they do in the Crowds project.

Finally, I want to comment briefly on the "Big Humanities" aspect of the project. It serves as an exemplary model of what collaborative research in the humanities can do and can be. With the spread of electronic communication has come the possibility for collaborative research on a scale never possible before; at the same time, the rapid circulation of information between and among disciplines and cultures has made collaborative research more necessary than ever before. The model of the Humanities Laboratory, a place where scholars gather to collaborate on large-scale research projects, is in my view one of the most promising and crucially important trends in contemporary humanities research. The resulting projects obviously differ in scale from single-author works; moreover, synergistic interactions and serendipitous convergences may make them different in kind as well. In its size, exuberant diversity, electronic research capabilities, and focus on a common topic, *Crowds* presents an exciting demonstration of what can be accomplished in collaborative humanities research. Left with the last word, I can only say that I am very glad I came along to be part of (the) *Crowds*.

Notes

INTRODUCTION

1. Lord Scarman, foreword to *The Crowd in Contemporary Britain*, ed. George Gaskell and Robert Benewick (London: Sage Publications, 1987), ix.

2. Gustave Le Bon, *The Crowd: A Study of the Popular Mind*, 2nd ed. (1895; Atlanta, Ga.: Cherokee Publishing, 1982), v; hereafter abbreviated as *C*.

3. Scarman, foreword, ix.

4. For a historical overview of the role of the crowd in western political theory, see J. S. McClelland, *The Crowd and the Mob: From Plato to Canetti* (London: Unwin Hyman, 1989).

5. See, for instance, Gabriel Tarde, *The Laws of Imitation*, trans. Elsie Clews Parsons (1890; New York: Holt, 1903); Hippolyte Taine, *Les Origines de la France contemporaine* (Paris: Hachette, 1875–1893), selections translated as *The Origins of Contemporary France: The Ancient Regime, the Revolution, the Modern Regime: Selected Chapters*, trans. Edward T. Gargan (Chicago: University of Chicago Press, 1974); Enrico Ferri, *Criminal Sociology* (1892; London: Fisher Unwin, 1895); Scipio Sighele, *La Folla delinquente: Studio di psicologia collettiva* (Turin: Fratelli Bocca, 1891; revised 2nd ed. 1895). For more on these and other "founders" of crowd psychology, see http://shl.stanford.edu/Crowds/theorists/theo.htm.

6. See Sigmund Freud, *Group Psychology and the Analysis of the Ego*, trans. James Strachey (1921; New York: Norton, 1959); Robert E. Park, *The Crowd and the Public and Other Essays*, ed. Henry Elsner Jr., trans. Charlotte Elsner (1904; Chicago: University of Chicago Press, 1972); José Ortega y Gasset, *The Revolt of the Masses*, trans Anthony Kerrigan (1929; Notre Dame, Ind.: University of Notre Dame Press, 1985); Elias Canetti, *Crowds and Power*, trans. Carol Stewart (1960; New York: Viking, 1962). For the proceedings of a recent conference devoted to Canetti's book, see *Die Massen und die Geschichte: Internationales Symposium Russe, Oktober 1995*, ed. Penka Angelova (St. Ingbert, Germany: Röhrig Universitätsverlag, 1998).

7. Gabriel Tarde, "The Public and the Crowd," in *On Communication and Social Influence*, ed. Terry N. Clark (Chicago and London: University of Chicago Press, 1969), 280–81.

8. Victor Hugo, *The Hunchback of Notre Dame*, trans. Catherine Liu (1831; New York: Random House, 2002), 6.

9. See, for instance, W. Trotter, *Instincts of the Herd in Peace and War* (New York: Mac-

millan, 1917); Sir William Martin Conway, *The Crowd in Peace and War* (New York: Longmans Green, 1915); Everett Dean Martin, *The Mob Mind vs. Civil Liberty* (New York: American Civil Liberties Union, 1920).

10. George Rudé, *The Crowd in the French Revolution* (New York: Oxford University Press, 1959).

11. Some of the major titles in this vein of scholarship are: Georges Lefevbre, "Revolutionary Crowds," in *New Perspectives on the French Revolution: Readings in Historical Sociology,* ed. Jeffrey Kaplow (1954; New York: John Wiley and Sons, 1965); George Rudé, *The Crowd in History: A Study of Popular Disturbances in France and England 1730–1848* (New York: John Wiley and Sons, 1964); E. P. Thompson, "The Moral Economy of the Crowd in the Eighteenth Century," *Past and Present* 50 (1971): 76–136; George Rudé, *The Face of the Crowd: Studies in Revolution, Ideology, and Popular Protest—Selected Essays of George Rudé,* ed. Harvey J. Kaye (New York: Harvester Wheatsheaf, 1988); Mark Harrison, *Crowds and History: Mass Phenomena in English Towns, 1790–1835* (New York: Cambridge University Press, 1988). A variant of this approach can be found in Pauline Maier's groundbreaking study of collective activity preceding the American Revolution, *From Resistance to Revolution: Colonial Radicals and the Development of American Opposition to Britain, 1765–1776* (New York: Knopf, 1972). Leftist economic and social histories addressing the formation of the notion of "mass" from a similar perspective include Asa Briggs, "The Language of 'Mass' and 'Masses' in Nineteenth-Century England" and "The Human Aggregate," in *The Collected Essays of Asa Briggs,* vol. 1, *Words, Numbers, Places, People* (1973, 1979; Urbana: University of Illinois Press, 1985), 34–54, 55–86; Eric Hobsbawm, "Mass-Producing Traditions: Europe, 1870–1914," in *The Invention of Tradition,* ed. Eric Hobsbawm and Terence Ranger (New York: Cambridge University Press, 1983).

12. Neil J. Smelser, *Theory of Collective Behavior* (London: Routledge and Kegan Paul, 1962).

13. Sam Wright, *Crowds and Riots: A Study in Social Organization* (Beverly Hills, Calif.: Sage Publications, 1978), 7–8. Other titles in this category include Hedy Brown, *People, Groups, and Society* (Philadelphia: Open University Press, 1985); Helen MacGill Hughes, ed., *Crowd and Mass Behavior* (Boston: Holbrook Press, 1972); Michael Brown and Amy Goldin, *Collective Behavior: A Review and Interpretation of the Literature* (Pacific Palisades, Calif.: Goodyear Publishing, 1973). An extensive attack from this perspective on the notion of a uniform "crowd mentality" can be found in Clark McPhail, *The Myth of the Madding Crowd* (New York: Aldine de Gruyter, 1991).

14. Robert A. Nye, *The Origins of Crowd Psychology: Gustave Le Bon and the Crisis of Mass Democracy in the Third Republic* (Beverly Hills, Calif.: Sage Publications, 1975); Serge Moscovici, *The Age of the Crowd: A Historical Treatise on Mass Psychology,* trans. J. C. Whitehouse (1981; New York: Cambridge University Press, 1985); Susanna Barrows, *Distorting Mirrors: Visions of the Crowd in Late Nineteenth-Century France* (New Haven: Yale University Press, 1981); Jaap van Ginneken, *Crowds Psychology, and Politics, 1871–1899* (New York: Cambridge University Press, 1992). For a straightforward reconstruction of crowd theory, see also Erika G. King, *Crowd Theory as a Psychology of the Leader and the Led* (Lewiston, N.Y.: Edwin Mellen Press, 1990).

15. See, for instance, Cynthia A. Bouton, *The Flour War: Gender, Class, and Community in Late Ancien Régime French Society* (University Park: Pennsylvania State University Press, 1993); Naomi Schor, *Zola's Crowds* (Baltimore, Md.: Johns Hopkins University Press, 1978); Nicolaus Mills, *The Crowd in American Literature* (Baton Rouge: Louisiana State University Press, 1986); John Plotz, *The Crowd: British Literature and Public Politics* (Berkeley: University of California Press, 2000); Thomas Reinert, *Regulating Confusion: Samuel Johnson and the Crowd* (Durham, N.C.: Duke University Press, 1996). A few studies have sought to do more than trace a single thematic thread; notable are Jeffrey Mehlman's *Revolution and Repetition: Marx/Hugo/Balzac* (Berkeley: University of California Press, 1977), which revisits nineteenth-century literary texts through a Marxian/deconstructionist reading of revolution; Mikkel Borch-Jacobsen, *The Freudian Subject,* trans. Catherine Porter (Stanford, Calif.: Stanford University Press, 1988), which takes seriously Freud's reliance on Le Bon to reinterpret Freud's theories of subjectivity; Mary Esteve, *The Aesthetics and Politics of the Crowd in American Literature* (New York: Cambridge University Press, 2003), which argues that "a heightened awareness of inhabiting a crowd culture could contribute, perhaps ironically, to more resolute distinctions between political and aesthetic categories of experience" (2); and Michael Tratner, *Modernism and Mass Politics: Joyce, Woolf, Eliot, Yeats* (Stanford, Calif.: Stanford University Press, 1995), which seeks to show the concordance between the description of the psychology of the crowd and the effects produced by modernist literature.

16. The one study that seeks to produce an interdisciplinary perspective on the topic is *Changing Conceptions of Crowd Mind and Behavior,* ed. Carl F. Graumann and Serge Moscovici (New York: Springer-Verlag, 1986). The interdisciplinarity in question is between social history, particularly of the Marxist variety, and "scientific" social psychology. See esp. chap. 13, Carl F. Graumann, "Crowd Mind and Behavior: Afterthoughts" for a description of the project. The approach in question bears little resemblance to that which characterizes the present volume.

17. Surowiecki's *The Wisdom of Crowds* (New York: Doubleday, 2004) is concerned with organizational behavior and markets. In *Smart Mobs: The Next Social Revolution* (Cambridge, Mass.: Perseus Books, 2002), Rheingold is concerned instead with the impact of technology on forms of distributed or virtual assembly. Negri and Hardt's *Multitude: War and Democracy in the Age of Empire* (New York: Penguin, 2004), develops a series of insights already present in their prior volume *Empire* (Cambridge, Mass.: Harvard University Press, 2001) within a framework of explicitly marxist derivation.

CHAPTER I

An earlier version of this chapter, titled "The Mass Panorama," was published in *Modernism/Modernity* 9, no. 2 (April 2002): 1–39. Used by permission of The Johns Hopkins University Press.

1. See Siegfried Kracauer, *The Mass Ornament (Weimar Essays)*, ed. Thomas Y. Levin (Cambridge, Mass.: Harvard University Press, 1995); Walter Benjamin, *The Arcades Project,* trans. Howard Eiland and Kevin McLaughlin (Cambridge, Mass.: Harvard University Press, 1999); *Illuminations,* ed. Hannah Arendt, trans. H. Zohn (New York: Schocken Books, 1976); and Wolfgang Kemp, "Das Bild der Menge (1780–1830)," *Städel-Jahrbuch* 4 (1973): 249–70, and the catalog *Der Einzelne und die Masse: Kunstwerke des 19 und 20, Jahrhunderts,* Ruhrfestspiele Recklinghausen (Recklinghausen: Städtische Kunsthalle, 1975). On the iconography of popular sovereignty, see also the catalog *Emblèmes de la Liberté: L'Image de la république dans l'art du XVIe au XXe siècle,* ed. Dario Gamboni and George Germann, Musée d'histoire de Berne (Bern: Staempfli, 1991). As indicated in the introduction to this volume, the publication of *Crowds* is coupled with the exhibition *Revolutionary Tides: The Art of the Political Poster 1914–1989,* held at the Iris & B. Gerald Cantor Center for the Arts,

September 14 through December 31, 2005, and at the Wolfsonian-Florida International University, February 24 through June 25, 2006; the exhibition catalog is published by the Iris & B. Gerald Cantor Center for the Arts and Skira in Milan (2005).

2. I have briefly sketched out the overall contours of this argument with a contemporary focus in "Ascensão e queda da multidão," *Veredas—A Revista do Centro Cultural Banco do Brasil* 6, no. 61 (January 2001): 26–31.

3. From the introduction to *The Crowd: A Study of the Popular Mind,* Project Gutenberg E-text 445 (http://www.gutenberg.org/). The original French edition of the work was published as *Psychologie des foules* (Paris: Felix Alcan, 1895). A powerful corrective to Le Bon's formulation was offered by Gabriel Tarde in "The Public and the Crowd" (1901), who concludes the opening section of his essay by stating "I . . . cannot agree with that vigorous writer, Dr. Le Bon, that our age is the 'era of crowds.' It is the era of the public or of publics, and that is a very different thing." Gabriel Tarde, *On Communication and Social Influence: Selected Papers,* ed. Terry N. Clark (Chicago: University of Chicago Press, 1969), 281. On various facets of the history of crowd sociology and psychology, see Robert A. Nye, *The Origins of Crowd Psychology: Gustave Le Bon and the Crisis of Mass Democracy in the Third Republic* (London: Sage, 1975); Jaap van Ginneken, *Crowds, Psychology, and Politics, 1871–1899* (New York: Cambridge University Press, 1992); and Damiano Palano, *Il potere della moltitudine: L'invenzione dell'inconscio collettivo nella teoria politica e nelle scienze sociali italiane tra Otto e Novecento* (Milan: V & P Università, 2002).

4. Introduction, *The Crowd,* Project Gutenberg E-text edition.

5. *The Crowd,* bk. 1, chap. 1. LeBon's ideas regarding atomic physics were developed in such publications as *L'Evolution de la matière* (Paris: Flammarion, 1905), *L'Evolution des forces* (Paris: Flammarion, 1907); and *La Naissance et l'evanouissement de la matière* (Paris: Mercure de France, 1908).

6. Letter to Scipio Sighele, printed in *La Foule criminelle: Essai de psychologie collective* (Paris: Alcan, 1901), 183–84 (my translation).

7. I am aware of two such instances, one direct and one oblique. In the preface to his work, Le Bon argues that "perceptible phenomena may be compared to waves, which are the expression on the surface of the ocean of deep-lying disturbances of which we know nothing," with specific reference to crowd behavior. In book 2, chapter 2, section 2, his example of collective

hallucination is the frigate *Belle Poule*, whose crew imagined that it saw "masses of men in motion, stretching out their hands, and heard the dull and confused noise of a great number of voices" when on a rescue mission at sea.

8. Sighele, *La Foule criminelle*, 22.

9. William Wordsworth, *The Prelude or the Growth of a Poet's Mind*, ed. Ernest de Selincourt and Helen Darbishire (Oxford: Clarendon Press, 1959), 7:701–4. Thomas De Quincey, *Confessions of an Opium Eater*, ed. Grevel Lindop (Oxford: Oxford University Press, 1985), 72. For a recent study of urban multitudes in the work of these two authors see John Plotz, *The Crowd: British Literature and Public Politics* (Berkeley: University of California Press, 2000), 15–42, 76–126.

10. Edgar Allan Poe, "The Man of the Crowd," in *The Works of Edgar Allan Poe* (New York: Funk and Wagnalls, 1904), 5:176. Charles Baudelaire, *Petits Poèmes en prose (Le Spleen de Paris)* (Paris: Flammarion, 1967).

11. Guy de Maupassant, *Sur l'Eau or On the Face of the Water*, in *Works* (Akron, Ohio: St. Dunstan, 1956–1959), 13:77; "Fondazione e manifesto del Futurismo," cited from *Marinetti e il futurismo*, ed. Luciano de Maria (Milan: A. Mondadori, 1973), 6 (my translation).

12. Cicero, *On the Commonwealth*, ed. and trans. George Holland Sabine and Stanley Barney Smith (Indianapolis, Ind.: Bobbs-Merrill, 1976), 148. The Latin original reads: "mare ullum aut flammam esse tantam, quam non facilius sit sedare quam effrenatam insolentia multitudinem." *De re publica*, ed. C. F. W. Müller (Leipzig: Teubner, 1878), 1:42.

13. Cicero's oceanophobia echoes that of Aristotle, who in *Politics* 7.6.5–6, had opined that it was good that cities "have ports and harbors which are conveniently placed in relation to the main city—distinct and separate, but not too remote" as a result of the threat that masses of naval oarsmen would represent to the rule of law. *The Politics of Aristotle*, ed. and trans. Ernest Baker (New York: Oxford University Press, 1962), 294–95. In Cicero's case, the polemic is not only antiproletarian, but also anti-Carthaginian and anti-Greek: "Why need I mention the Greek islands? They are surrounded by the sea and almost float—a description which applies no less to the customs and institutions of the states that existed on them." Cicero, *On the Commonwealth*, 158.

14. *The Aeneid of Virgil*, trans. Allen Mandelbaum (New York: Bantam, 1961), 6.

15. On this topic, see Horst Bredekamp's remarkable study, *Thomas Hobbes visuelle Strategien: Der Leviathan: Urbild des modernen Staates* (Berlin: Akademie Verlag, 1999).

16. Kracauer's argument in his essay "The Mass Ornament" is paradoxical on this score inasmuch as he considers modern choreographic geometries to be realistic and symbolic to the degree that "the mass ornament is the aesthetic reflex of a rationality to which the economic system aspires," while underscoring their ultimate abstractness. *The Mass Ornament*, 79, 81–83. He has nothing to say about their relation to prior forms of choreographic geometry.

17. Longinus, *On the Sublime* 9.13, in *Aristotle, "The Poetics"; Longinus, "On the Sublime"; Demetrius, "On Style,"* trans. W. Hamilton Fyfe (Cambridge, Mass.: Harvard University Press, 1973), 153.

18. Joseph Addison, *Spectator* 489 (September 20, 1712): 74–75.

19. Immanuel Kant, *Critique of Judgment*, trans. J. C. Meredith (Oxford: Oxford University Press, 1973), 122; hereafter abbreviated as *CJ*.

20. The links between sublimity and thrill in nineteenth-century culture are more fully elaborated in Jeffrey T. Schnapp, "Crash (Speed as Engine of Individuation)," *Modernism/Modernity* 6, no. 1 (January 1999): 1–49.

21. See in particular the opening chapter of *Civilization and Its Discontents*, trans. Joan Riviere (London: Hogarth Press, 1955), 8–21.

22. Dowie makes a cameo appearance in the Circe section of James Joyce's *Ulysses*, where he inveighs against Bloom: "Fellowchristians and antiBloomites, the man called Bloom is from the roots of hell, a disgrace to Christian men. A fiendish libertine from his earliest years this stinking goat of Mendes gave precocious signs of infantile debauchery recalling the cities of the plain, with a dissolute granddam. This vile hypocrite, bronzed with infamy, is the white bull mentioned in the Apocalypse. A worshipper of the Scarlet Woman, intrigue is the very breath of his nostrils. The stake faggots and the caldron of boiling oil are for him." *Ulysses* (Harmondsworth: Penguin, 1969), 463–64.

23. The city plan was, much like Mole's photographs, symbolic. It radiated outward from the site of the tabernacle, and its streets bore names like Aaron, Elijah, and Lydia. On the early history of Zion, see Philip L. Cook, *Zion City, Illinois: Twen-*

tieth Century Utopia (Syracuse, N.Y.: Syracuse University Press, 1996).

24. Seven panoramic photographs are preserved in the Library of Congress collection: "Welcome Home of the General Overseer, Rev. John Alex Dowie," "Industrial Parade," "Shiloh Tabernacle," "Fourth Anniversary of Consecration of Zion Temple," "Officers and Choir of Zion," "Zion Industries at Shiloh Tabernacle," and an aerial overview of the city. These may be consulted online through the American Memory project at http://memory.loc.gov/.

25. The bibliography on Mole is meager and largely focused on the novelty value of his photographs. Some valuable information may be gleaned from David L. Fisk, *Arthur Mole: The Photographer from Zion and the Composer of the World's First Living Photographs* (Tempe: School of Art, Arizona State University, 1983); and Doug Stewart, "How Many Sailors Does It Take to Make an American Flag?," *Smithsonian* 26, no. 10 (January 1996): 58–63.

26. A closely related image entitled "Figure of Zion," dated July 14, 1920, also appears to be by Mole, even though it is unsigned and wasn't published in *Leaves of Healing* until May 1937.

27. Barker cited in Scott X. Wilcox, "Unlimiting the Bounds of Painting," in Ralph Hyde, *Panoramania. The Art and Entertainment of the "All-Embracing" View* (London: Trefoil, 1988), 21.

28. Cited from the original patent in Wilcox, "Unlimiting the Bounds of Painting," 17.

29. For a complete catalogue and chronology of panorama art, see Silvia Bordini, *Storia del panorama: La visione totale nella pittura del XIX secolo* (Rome: Officina, 1984), 325–31.

30. The bibliography on the topic of panoramic photography is thin, but an excellent starting point on its early history is the Library of Congress's American Memory project, a section of which bears the title Taking the Long View: Panoramic Photographs 1851–1991 (http://memory.loc.gov/ammem/pnhtml/pnhome.html).

31. See Keith F. Davis, *George N. Barnard, Photographer of Sherman's Campaign* (Kansas City, Mo.: Hallmark, 1990).

32. On this topic, see David Harris with Eric Sandweiss, *Eadweard Muybridge and the Photographic Panorama of San Francisco, 1850–1880*, Canadian Center for Architecture (Cambridge, Mass.: MIT Press, 1993); and Robert Bartlett Haas, *Muybridge: Man in Motion* (Berkeley: University of California Press, 1976), 81–92,

although Haas's book contains inaccuracies such as the assertion that Muybridge was the first to use these techniques. Numerous photographers, such as George Fardon and Carleton Watkins, had preceded him in devising panoramas of San Francisco.

33. For a chronology of the development of panoramic cameras, see Bill McBride, "Panoramic Cameras 1843–1994," at http://www.panoramicphoto.com/timeline.htm.

34. For a survey of Soviet counterparts, covering the full spectrum of practices from documentarist photomontage to image enhancement to outright falsification, see David King, *The Commissar Vanishes: The Falsification of Photographs and Art in Stalin's Russia* (New York: Henry Holt, 1997).

35. Compare the doctored photograph of Lenin's speech in Dvortsovaya Square on July 19, 1920, published three years later with "blanks" in the crowd filled in through the substitution of one oceanic crowd with another (reproduced in King, *Commissar Vanishes*, 78–79).

36. Charles Baudelaire, "The Painter of Modern Life," in *The Painter of Modern Life and Other Essays*, ed. and trans. Jonathan Mayne (New York: Phaidon, 1984), 9.

37. *Rivista illustrata del Popolo d'Italia* 10, no. 10 (October 1932): 15–27. The lead article is by Manlio Morgagni, the magazine's director.

38. *Rivista illustrata del Popolo d'Italia* 19, no. 3 (March 1941).

39. See in particular Tupitsyn's essay "From the Politics of Montage to the Montage of Politics: Soviet Practice 1919 through 1937," in *Montage and Modern Life 1919–1942*, ed. Matthew Teitelbaum (Cambridge, Mass.: MIT Press; Boston: Institute of Conteporary Art, 1992), 82–127.

40. Sally Stein has some suggestive reflections on this topic in "Good Fences Make Good Neighbors: American Resistance to Photomontage Between the Wars," in Teitelbaum, ed., *Montage and Modern Life*, 128–89.

41. *In Focus—László Moholy-Nagy* (Malibu, Calif.: J. Paul Getty Museum, 1995), 78.

42. Warhol's photographic files, preserved at the Andy Warhol Museum archive in Pittsburgh, include a large number of photographs of Nazi mass rallies, as well as crowd scenes from political conventions and presidential campaigns (Kennedy, Stevenson, Johnson).

43. The photograph is found in the Andy Warhol Museum Archives, Archival Photo Collection, Source material (Crowd 1963), 6–2–14.

44. Compare the photomontage cover of *Udarniki* (1930) featuring the visage of Stalin against a backdrop made up of repeat prints of the same sea of faces (reproduced in King, *Commissar Vanishes*, 14–5).

45. *Gabriel Tarde: On Communication and Social Influence—Selected Papers*, ed. Terry N. Clark (Chicago: University of Chicago Press, 1969).

CHAPTER 1A

1. Theodor Mommsen, *The Digest of Justinian*, 47.8.4.3.

2. Richard M. Gummere, *Seneca, Moral Essays*, 7.1.

3. Sources: H. J. Edwards, *Caesar, The Gallic War* (Cambridge, Mass.: Harvard University Press, 1917); P. G. W. Glare, *Oxford Latin Dictionary* (Oxford: Clarendon Press, 1982); Richard M. Gummere, *Seneca, Moral Essays*, vol. 1 (Cambridge, Mass: Harvard University Press, 1917); Theodor Mommsen, *The Digest of Justinian* (Philadelphia: University of Pennsylvania Press, 1985).

CHAPTER 2

1. *Memoir of Thomas Hardy . . . Written by Himself* (1832), 16, cited in E. P. Thompson, *The Making of the English Working Class* (London: Victor Gollancz, 1963), 17.

2. Thompson, *Making of the English Working Class*, 21.

3. See Pierre Rosanvallon, *Le peuple introuvable: Histoire de la représentation démocratique en France* (Paris: Gallimard, 1998), 14–35.

4. For concise discussions of both reforms, see Mona Ozouf's articles "Département" and "Revolutionary Calendar," in *A Critical Dictionary of the French Revolution*, ed. Francois Furet and Mona Ozouf, trans. Arthur Goldhammer (Cambridge, Mass.: Harvard University Press, 1989), 494–503, 538–47.

5. Louis Chevalier, *Classes laborieuses et classes dangereuses à Paris pendant la première moitié du XIXe siècle* (Paris: Plon, 1958), 24.

6. Paul Rabinow, *French Modern: Norms and Forms of the Social Environment* (Cambridge, Mass.: MIT Press, 1989), 59.

7. Chevalier, *Classes laborieuses et classes dangereuses*, 22.

8. Keith Michael Baker, *Condorcet: From National Philosophy to Social Mathematics* (Chicago: University of Chicago Press, 1975).

9. Emmanuel Sieyès, *Qu'est-ce que le tiers état?* (Paris: Société de la révolution française; Editions Edme Champion, 1888), 37–40.

10. For a discussion of Quételet's *l'homme moyen*, see Georges Canguilhem, *The Normal and the Pathological*, trans. Carolyn R. Fawcett with Robert S. Cohen (New York: Zone Books, 1989), 151–62; and Rabinow, *French Modern*, 63–67.

11. There is a vast sociological literature—from Ferdinand Tönnies and Max Weber to Michel Foucault and Paul Rabinow—to support the thesis that the appearance of number in political and social thought is the symptom of a social and epistemological discontinuity.

12. Charles Baudelaire, *Intimate Journals*, trans. Christopher Isherwood (London: Blackamore Press, 1930), 29; "Journaux intimes: Fusées," *Oeuvres complètes* (Paris: Éditions de la Nouvelle Revue Française, 1937), 6:249.

13. Gustave Flaubert, letter to George Sand, September 8, 1871, in *Flaubert—Sand: The Correspondence*, trans. Francis Steegmuller and Barbara Bray (New York: Alfred A. Knopf, 1993), 240; *Correspondance*, ed. Jean Bruneau (Paris: Gallimard, Bibliothèque de la Pléiade, 1999), 4:376: "Un seul élément prévaut au détriment de tous les autres; le Nombre domine l'esprit, l'instruction, la race, et même l'argent, qui vaut mieux que le Nombre."

14. Edmund Burke, *Reflections on the Revolution in France* (Oxford: Oxford University Press, 1993), 33; hereafter abbreviated as *RRF*.

15. In general, the reception of Burke's work was critical, if not outright dismissive, and not only among radicals and liberals, but also within Burke's own conservative party. In particular, the book confounded and outraged its readers because of its gross inaccuracies in its description of French politics. See L. G. Mitchell's introduction to *RRF*, viii–xi.

16. Alexis de Tocqueville, *Democracy in America,* trans. Arthur Goldhammer (New York: Library of America/Penguin Putnam, 2004).

17. Ibid.

18. This is not the place to review the historical research on the social history of the French Revolution. For pioneering works of direct relevance to the discussion of "the masses," see Georges Lefebvre, "Les Foules révolutionnaires," in Paul Alphandéry, Georges Bohn, Georges Hardy, Georges Lefebvre, and Eugène Dupréel, *La Foule: Quatrième semaine internationale de synthèse* (Paris: Félix Alcan, 1934), 79–107; and George Rudé, *The Crowd*

in the French Revolution (Oxford: Oxford University Press, 1959).

19. Thomas Carlyle, *The French Revolution: A History* (1837; reprint, New York: Modern Library, 2002), 29.

20. Ibid., 178–79.

21. Interestingly, Carlyle's firebird prefigures Walter Benjamin's angel of destruction, that revolutionary power that frees men "by taking from them what they have, rather than making them happy by giving to them." Walter Benjamin, "Karl Kraus," in *One-Way Street and Other Writings,* trans. Edmund Jephcott and Kingsley Shorter (London: New Left Review, 1979), 289.

22. Antoine de Baecque, "Le Serment du Jeu de paume: le corps politique idéal," in *David contre David: Actes du colloque organisé au musée du Louvre,* ed. Régis Michel (Paris: La Documentation française, 1993), 2:776–80.

23. Rosanvallon, *Le peuple introuvable,* 35–55.

24. See Joan B. Landes, *Visualizing the Nation: Gender, Representation, and Revolution in Eighteenth-Century France* (Ithaca, N.Y.: Cornell University Press, 2001); and Susanne von Falkenhausen, "Vom 'Ballhausschwur' zum 'Duce': Visuelle Repräsentation von Volkssouveränität zwischen Demokratie und Autokratie," in *Das Volk: Abbild, Konstruktion, Phantasma,* ed. Annette Graczyk (Berlin: Akademie Verlag, 1996), 3–17.

25. Susanne von Falkenhausen argues that *The Tennis Court Oath* is above all a reflection of this opposition: David represents the sovereignty of the people as an ideal, but only at the cost of expelling the people outside the frame ("Vom 'Ballhausschwur' zum 'Duce'").

26. Jules Michelet, *The People,* trans. John P. McKay (Urbana: University of Illinois Press, 1973), 105; *Le Peuple,* ed. Lucien Refort (1846; reprint, Paris: Marcel Didier, 1946), 137: "Vous allez, la loupe à la main, vous cherchez dans les ruisseaux, vous trouvez là je ne sais quoi de sale et d'immonde, et vous nous le rapportez: 'Triomphe! Triomphe! Nous avons trouvé le peuple!'"

27. Flora Tristan, *Journal,* quoted in Chevalier, *Classes laborieuses et classes dangereuses,* 525.

28. Rosanvallon, *Le peuple introuvable,* 42–43.

29. Christopher Prendergast discusses this topos in *Paris in the Nineteenth Century* (Oxford: Blackwell, 1992).

30. Michelet, *The People,* 92; *Le Peuple,* 121–22: "En nationalité, c'est tout comme en géologie, la chaleur est en bas. Descendez, vous trouverez qu'elle augmente; aux couches inférieures, elle brûle."

31. Honoré de Balzac, *The Girl with the Golden Eyes,* in *History of the Thirteen,* trans. Herbert J. Hunt (Harmondsworth: Pen-

guin, 1974), 312; *Histoire des treize,* in *La Comédie humaine* (Paris: Gallimard, 1977), vol. 5.

32. Victor Hugo, *Les Misérables,* trans. Norman Denny (Harmondsworth: Penguin, 1982), 619–21; *Les Misérables,* ed. Maurice Allen (Paris: Gallimard, Bibliothèque de la Pléiade, 1951), 757–58; hereafter abbreviated as *M,* with page number to the French original last.

33. Chevalier, *Classes dangereuses et classes laborieuses,* 68–163, 451–68.

34. Honoré-Antoine Frégier, *Des classes dangereuses de la population des grandes villes* (Paris, 1840), quoted in Chevalier, *Classes dangereuses et classes laborieuses,* 159.

35. The political consequence of the distinction between passions and reason was made already by Hobbes. In his view, social order depends on the intrusion of a sovereign who forces everyone to restrain his self-centered passions. However, most theorists of absolutist monarchy, including Machiavelli, believed that it was the upper echelons of society that posed the greatest difficulty to the sovereign's attempts to uphold social peace. The aristocracy was perceived as comprising men of strong passions who did not easily submit to law. The common people, by contrast, subjected themselves to sovereign rule because their behavior was less emotional and hence more predictable. In the industrial age, the contents of the categories have shifted. The upper classes legitimize their power by investing themselves with the attributes of reason and social concord, and they justify the exclusion of the majority by portraying the lower classes as ruled by passions and hence incapable of acting in the interest of society.

36. See Helmut König, *Zivilisation und Leidenschaften: Die Masse im bürgerlichen Zeitalter* (Reinbek bei Hamburg: Rowohlt Taschenbuch Verlag, 1992), 56.

37. Daniel Stern, *Histoire de la révolution de 1848* (1850; reprint, Paris: Éditions Balland, 1985).

38. Eugène Sue, *Les Mystères de Paris* (Paris, 1851), 1.

39. Eugène Buret, *La Misère des classes laborieuses en Angleterre et en France* (Paris, 1840), 2:49: "Les ouvriers sont aussi libres de devoirs envers leurs maîtres que ceux-ci le sont envers eux; ils les considèrent comme des hommes d'une classe différente, opposée et même ennemie. Isolés de la nation, mis en dehors de la communauté sociale et politique, seuls avec leurs besoins et leurs misères, ils s'agitent pour sortir de cette effrayante solitude, et, comme les barbares auxquels on les a comparés, ils méditent peut-être une invasion."

40. Karl Marx, *Der achtzehnte Brumaire des Louis Bonaparte*.

41. Victor Hugo, *Choses vues: Souvenirs, journaux, cahiers 1830–1885*, ed. Hubert Juin (Paris: Gallimard, 2002), 567.

42. Gustave Flaubert, *Sentimental Education*, trans. Robert Baldick (Harmondsworth: Penguin, 1964), 151, hereafter abbreviated as *SE*; *L'Education sentimentale: Histoire d'un jeune homme*, ed. A. Thibaudet and R. Dumesnil (Paris: Gallimard, Bibliothèque de la Pléiade, 1952), 177, hereafter abbreviated as *ES*.

43. Flaubert was in this aspect preceded by Karl Marx, whose famous saying about history repeating itself as farce referred to the French history of 1848 (Marx, *Achtzehnte Brumaire*).

44. *SE*, 289–90; *ES*, 320:

> Et poussés malgré eux, ils entrèrent dans un appartement où s'étendait, au plafond, un dais de velours rouge. Sur le trône, en dessous, était assis un prolétaire à barbe noire, la chemise entr'ouverte, l'air hilaire et stupide comme un magot. D'autres gravissaient l'estrade pour s'assesoir à sa place.
> —Quel mythe! dit Hussonet. Voilà le peuple souverain!
> Le fauteil fut enlevé à bout de bras, et traversa toute la salle en se balançant.
> —Saprelotte! Comme il chaloupe! Le vaisseau de l'État est ballotté sur une mer orageuse! Cancane-t-il! Cancane-t-il!
> On l'avait approché d'une fenêtre, et, au milieu des sifflets, on le lança.
> —Pauvre vieux! dit Hussonet, en le voyant tomber dans le jardin, où il fut repris vivement pour être promené ensuite à la Bastille, et brulé.

45. *SE*, 290; *ES*, 321: "Dans l'antichambre, debout sur un tas de vêtements, se tenait une fille publique, en statue de la liberté,—immobile, les yeux grands ouverts, effrayante."

46. *SE*, 286; *ES*, 318: "Les tambours battaient la charge. Des cris aigus, des hourras de triomphe s'élevaient. Un remous continuel faisait osciller la multitude. Frédéric, pris entre deux masses profondes, ne bougeait pas, fasciné d'ailleurs et s'amusant extrêmement. Les blessés qui tombaient, les morts étendus n'avaient pas l'air de vrais blessés, de vrais morts. Il lui semblait assister à un spectacle."

47. *SE*, 287; *ES*, 318: "Cela faisait rire."

48. Gisèle Séginger, *Flaubert: Une poétique de l'histoire* (Strasbourg: Presses Universitaires de Strasbourg, 2000), 105.

49. Flaubert, letter to George Sand, September 8, 1871, in *Flaubert—Sand*, 240; *Correspondance*, 4:375–76: "Je crois que la foule, le nombre, le troupeau sera toujours haïssable."

50. *SE*, 282, translation modified; *ES*, 314–15: "Ils passèrent l'après-midi à regarder, de leur fenêtre, le peuple dans la rue."

51. *SE*, 276, 282–83, 288; *ES*, 308, 315, 319–20: "la foule tassée semblait, de loin, un champ d'épis noirs qui oscillaient"; "Un fourmillement confus s'agitait en dessous; au milieu de cette ombre, par endroits, brillaient des blancheurs de baïonnettes"; "flots vertigineux des têtes nues, des casques, des bonnets rouges, des baïonnettes et des épaules, si impétueusement que des gens disparaissaient dans cette masse grouillante qui montait toujours, comme un fleuve refoulé par une marée d'equinoxe, avec un long mugissement, sous une impulsion irrésistible."

52. *SE*, 292, translation modified; *ES*, 323: "Le magnétisme des foules enthousiastes l'avait pris."

53. *SE*, 283; *ES*, 315: "Car il y a des situations où l'homme le moins cruel est si détaché des autres, qu'il verrait périr le genre humain sans un battement de cœur."

54. Meissonier cited in T. J. Clark, *The Absolute Bourgeois: Artists and Politics in France 1848–1851* (1982; reprint, Berkeley: University of California Press, 1999), 27.

55. Adolphe Thiers, cited in Chevalier, *Classes laborieuses et classes dangereuses*, 459.

56. Clark, *Absolute Bourgeois*, 28.

57. Boissy cited in Jacques Rancière, *La Nuit des prolétaires* (Paris: Arthème Fayard, 1981), 195–96.

58. The letter was published February 17, 1863, in *L'Opinion nationale*, cited in Rosanvallon, *Le peuple introuvable*, 95–96.

59. See Susanna Barrows, *Distorting Mirrors: Visions of the Crowd in Late Nineteenth-Century France* (New Haven: Yale University Press, 1981).

60. Gustave LeBon, *La Vie: Physiologie humaine appliquée à l'hygiène et à la médecine* (Paris, 1872), quoted in Robert Nye, *The Origins of Crowd Psychology: Gustave LeBon and the Crisis of Mass Democracy in the Third Republic* (London: Sage, 1975), 28; hereafter abbreviated as *OCP*.

61. Letter to George Sand, April 30, 1871, in *Flaubert—Sand*, 228; *Correspondance*, 4:314: "Le peuple est un éternel mineur, et il sera toujours (dans la hiérarchie des éléments sociaux) au dernier rang, puisqu'il est le nombre, le masse, l'illimité."

62. Gustave Le Bon, *The Crowd: A Study of the Popular Mind*, reprint of 2nd ed. (Marietta, Ga.: Larlin, 1982), 123; *La Psychologie des foules* (Paris, 1895).

63. Le Bon, *Crowd*, 12.

64. This argument is developed at greater length in Stefan Jonsson, "Masses Mind Matter: Political Passions and Collective Violence in Post-Imperial Austria," in *Representing the Passions: Histories, Bodies, Visions*, ed. Richard Meyer (Los Angeles: Getty Research Institute, 2003).

65. Michel Foucault, *Histoire de la folie à l'âge classique* (Paris: Gallimard, 1972), 56–91.

66. Lucien Nass, *Le Siège de Paris et la commune* (Paris: Plon, 1914), 352–53.

67. Alexandre Calerre, "Les Psychoses dans l'histoire," *Archives internationales de neurologie* 34 (1912) 1:229–49, 299–311, 359–70; 2:23–36, 89–110, 162–77, 211–24.

68. Le Bon cited in *OCP*, 51.

CHAPTER 2A

1. Sources: *Dictionnaire de L'Académie française*, 1st (1694), 4th (1762), and 5th (1798) editions (hereafter DAF); Jean-Francois Féraud, *Dictionnaire critique de la langue française* (Marseille: Mossy, 1787–1788); Jean Nicot, *Thresor de la langue française* (1606); Jacob and Wilhelm Grimm, *Deutsches Wörterbuch*; *Oxford English Dictionary* (hereafter OED).

CHAPTER 3

1. Maria Wyke insightfully analyzes the "sword and sandal" film in *Projecting the Past* (New York: Routledge 1997); see also the general discussions in S. Joshel, M. Malamud, and D. McGuire Jr., eds., *Imperial Projections: Ancient Rome in Modern Popular Culture*, (Baltimore, Md.: Johns Hopkins University Press, 2001).

2. See Patrick Brantlinger, *Bread and Circuses: Theories of Mass Culture as Social Decay* (Ithaca, N.Y.: Cornell University Press, 1983).

3. This identification also serves the interests of popular satire, which operates within the same representational framework of cultural critique. An article in the *Onion* titled "Congress Approves 4 Billion for Bread, Circuses" uses filmic motifs to confuse Capitol Hill in Washington, D.C., with the Capitoline, one of the seven hills of Rome. Its parody of the Roman triumph links politics with entertainment, and the consumerist excess of the heartland with America's ignorant application of (virtually) imperial military force: "President Clinton announced news of the bill's passage to awaiting throngs from his purple-draped balcony at the White House. . . . [A] procession, attended by thousands of onlookers, featured a display of Exocet missiles; several Stealth bombers flying in formation; a phalanx of prominent military leaders, senators and bureaucrats; dancers, fire-eaters and contortionists . . . At the back of the procession were four dozen captured criminals and Serbian prisoners of war, who were repeatedly beaten by a prison guard as they slowly trudged under the weight of their chains and manacles. Following the massive parade, a state-sponsored feast was held on the Capitol Mall, and great quantities of such beloved American delicacies as hamburgers, hot dogs, bratwurst, potato salad, Lite beer, orange pop and sheet cake were served free of charge to vast and ecstatic crowds, who gorged themselves to excess" (August 19, 1999). The phrase "bread and circuses" is originally the first century CE satirist Juvenal's: "the people that once bestowed commands, consulships, legions and everything else, now contains itself and worriedly hopes for only two things: bread and circuses" (nam qui dabat olim imperium fasces legiones omnia, nunc se continet atque duas tantum res anxius optat, panem et circenses, *Sat.* 10.77–80).

4. The chariot scene provides a number of examples; also note the cycle of roar and hush in a massive crowd responding to barely visible gestures from Tiberius at a Roman triumph.

5. Hannah Arendt, *On Revolution* (New York: Penguin, 1963), 48; hereafter abbreviated as *OR*. See also Simon Schama, *Citizens* (New York: Vintage Books, 1989), 8.

6. I owe the insight into the emphasis on the performative in Arendt's text to Bonnie Honig, "Declarations of Independence: Arendt and Derrida on the Problem of Founding a Republic," *American Political Science Review* 85, no. 1 (1991): 206–10.

7. Arendt draws here on Machiavelli, *Discourses* 1.6, 2.2–3; cf. *On Revolution*, 202: "This notion of a coincidence of foundation and preservation by virtue of augmentation—that the 'revolutionary' act of beginning something entirely new, and conservative care, which will shield this new beginning through the centuries, are interconnected—was deeply rooted in the Roman spirit and could be read from almost every page of Roman history."

8. "Republican utopianism" is the phrase of Michael Hardt and Antonio Negri, *Multitude* (New York: Penguin, 2004), 354; see also their related discussion of "The American Revolution

and the Model of the Two Romes," in *Empire* (Cambridge, Mass.: Harvard University Press, 2001), 179–81. For the resurgence of republicanism in political thought, see J. G. A. Pocock, *The Machiavellian Moment* (Princeton, N.J.: Princeton University Press, 1975); Quentin Skinner, *Liberty Before Liberalism* (Cambridge: Cambridge University Press, 1998); Maurizio Viroli, *For Love of Country* (Oxford: Oxford University Press, 1995); Philip Pettit, *Republicanism* (Oxford: Oxford University Press, 1997); and John P. McCormick's critical survey of the development, "Machiavelli Against Republicanism," *Political Theory* 31 (2003): 615–43. I use the term *republic* in its Roman and neo-Roman sense as *res publica*.

9. The People: the capitalization is designed to fence the word from the dangerous threats of difference borne by its noncapitalized doppelgänger. Just as "People" is troubled by exclusivist nationalistic associations (*peuple, Volk*), the many local significances of "people" counterbalance the united front of the "People": race and kin ("my people"), religion ("chosen people"), class ("not our kind of people"), and so on.

10. Jeffrey T. Schnapp, "The Mass Panorama," *Modernism/Modernity* 9, no. 2 (2002): 243–81.

11. Edward Gibbon, *Decline and Fall of the Roman Empire*, 1.2, 3.

12. Elias Canetti, *Crowds and Power* (New York: Farrar, Straus, and Giroux, 1960), 313: "Anyone who has to give commands in an army must be able to keep himself free from all crowds, whether actual or remembered."

13. Montesquieu, *Considerations on the Causes of the Greatness of the Romans and Their Decline*, chap. 9.

14. On the reception of Athens in the west, see Jennifer Roberts's survey *Athens on Trial* (Princeton, N.J.: Princeton University Press, 1994). On Grote and Mill, see Nadia Urbinati, *Mill on Democracy: From the Athenian Polis to Representative Government* (Chicago: University of Chicago Press, 2002), 14–41.

15. I draw this line of thought from Ernesto Laclau, "Identity and Hegemony," 53–59.

16. Crowd "values," taking Hardt and Negri as influential examples: in *Multitude*, they praise performative transformation (199), crisis (348), and the collapse of boundaries (350); in *Empire*, conflict and immanence (180).

17. Judith Butler, "Poststructuralism and Postmarxism," *Diacritics* 23, no. 4 (1993): 3–11.

18. Louis Althusser, "Ideological State Apparatuses," 129–31; cf. Pierre Bourdieu, *The Logic of Practice* (Cambridge: Polity Press, 1980), 69.

19. Robert Morstein-Marx, *Mass Oratory and Political Power in the Late Roman Republic* (Cambridge: Cambridge University Press, 2004), 119–20, citing Josiah Ober, *Mass and Elite in Democratic Athens* (Princeton, N.J.: Princeton University Press, 1989), a useful and thoughtful discussion of the information in the following paragraphs.

20. Brunt, *Italian Manpower* (Oxford: Oxford University Press, 1971), 13–14, gives the latter figure for 28 BCE, on the basis of evidence from Augustus' *Res Gestae*; his work is usually interpreted as a conservative estimate.

21. Brunt, "The Roman Mob" in *Studies in Ancient Society* (London: Routledge, 1974), 90, cites Sallust and other contemporary sources for the migration of peasants into the city. He lists the ancient testimony for the events I describe here.

22. All elected magistrates, including the plebeian tribunes (whose original job it was to protect the interests of the people against the aristocratic senate, as we saw in Livy's account of the plebeian secession), had to meet high property qualifications in order to stand for office.

23. Vivid accounts of the *contio*'s doings appear in Pina Polo, "The Procedures and Functions of Civil and Military Contiones in Rome," *Klio* 77 (1995): 203–16; and Morstein-Marx, *Mass Oratory and Political Power*, 119–59.

24. For a discussion of the significance of this language of property, see Schofield, "Cicero's Definition of *Res Publica*," in *Cicero the Philosopher* (Oxford: Oxford University Press, 1995), 77–82.

25. A point emphasized by Andrew Lintott in *The Constitution of Rome* (Oxford: Oxford University Press, 1999), 3.

26. Livy, *Ab Urbe Condita*: *turba*, 1.7.2; *turba*, 1.8.6; *multitudo*, 1.9.9; *turba*, 1.12.3, *una civitas*, 1.13, *multitudo*, 1.59.6. For the record, Livy also uses *turba* in the preface to book 1, to describe his rival historians.

27. The Romans did not use the terminology or the practice of political representation in the modern sense. They elected executive magistrates, not representatives, and the magistrates were held accountable at the end of their year-long term for the legality of their actions, not their representation of the interests of any group, popular or otherwise.

28. Michel Serres, *Rome: The Foundations* (Stanford, Calif.: Stanford University Press, 1991), 112, 149–50.

29. Bill Buford, *Among the Thugs* (New York: Vintage, 1991), 166–67. Thanks to Osman Umurhan for the recommendation.

30. Roland Barthes, "Myth today," *Mythologies* (New York: Noonday Press, 1990), 124.

31. Ibid., 125.

32. Discussed in detail by Morstein-Marx, *Mass Oratory and Political Power*, 207–32.

33. "Politics was an activity reserved for a very small minority in Rome. We are therefore forced to distinguish between the political 'public' and the 'people.' Simply assuming that the populus and masses were the same merely perpetuates a particular ideological construction of the 'people,' first conceived by the Roman ruling class": so says Mouritsen, *Plebs and Politics in the Late Roman Republic* (Cambridge: Cambridge University Press, 2001), 145.

34. Cicero, *On Moral Duties* 1.124. See Schofield, "Cicero's Definition," 79–80.

35. Ferguson, *Essay*, 67–68.

36. Contrast Machiavelli's treatment of popular power in Rome, which he considers a genuine force in productive conflict with the nobles (*Discourses* 1.2–4).

37. Morstein-Marx, *Mass Oratory and Political Power*, 42–60.

38. Cicero, *Letter to his Brother Quintus*, 2.3.2.

39. Cicero, *On His House* 5.12: *nullo incitante*. Contrast his attacks on Clodius Pulcher (a popular rival) as a demagogic leader of crowd violence (e.g., *To the Priests* 11.22; *On His House* 21.54).

40. Cicero, *Letter to his Brother Quintus*, 2.1.5.

41. Brunt, "The Roman Mob," 96.

42. Asconius on Cicero, *Pro Milone* 32–33C.

43. Cited in *OR*, 241. She notes Robespierre's insistence in a 1794 speech before the convention that "laws should be promulgated in the name of the French people instead of the French Republic" (75).

44. Hardt and Negri, *Empire*, 344.

45. "The human flock that attends mass meetings amid the filth and dregs" (apud sordem urbis et faecem . . . contionalis hirudo, Letter to Atticus 1.16.11); "among those revolting, awful dregs of the people" (apud perditissimam illam atque infimam faecem populi); *Letter to his Brother Quintus*, 2.5.3; see also *For Flaccus*, 18, 24; additional references in Morstein-Marx, *Mass Oratory and Political Power*, 128n.49, 52.

46. Mouritsen, *Plebs and Politics*; Morstein-Marx, *Mass Oratory and Political Power*; and most provocatively, Egon Flaig, *Ritualisierte Politik* (Göttingen: Vandenhoek and Ruprecht, 2003).

47. North, "Democratic Politics in Republican Rome," 18; Morstein-Marx, *Mass Oratory and Political Power*, 284.

48. Serres, *Rome*, 15.

49. Toby Miller, *The Well-Tempered Self* (Baltimore, Md.: Johns Hopkins University Press, 1994), 228, explores a similar dynamic in the case of identity politics.

50. As Judith Butler critically notes in "Poststructuralism and Postmarxism."

CHAPTER 3B

1. Walter Benjamin, *Selected Writings*, vol. 3, *1935–1938*, ed. Howard Eiland and Michael Jennings, trans. Edmund Jephcott et al. (Cambridge, Mass.: Harvard University Press, 2002), 129.

2. Ibid., 129–30.

CHAPTER 4

Thanks are due to my assistants Andrew Franklin, Megan Pendergast, and Aimee Woznick, without whose tireless research this project would have been inconceivable.

1. Gustave Le Bon, *The Crowd: A Study of the Popular Mind* (Dunwoody, Ga.: N. S. Berg, 1968). See also Robert A. Nye, *The Origins of Crowd Psychology: Gustave Le Bon and the Crisis of Mass Democracy in the Third Republic* (London: Sage, 1973). As Walter Benjamin writes, "The crowd—no subject was more entitled to the attention of nineteenth century writers." Benjamin, "On Some Motifs in Baudelaire," in *Illuminations*, trans. Harry Zohn (New York: Schocken Books, 1968), 166.

2. Gabriel Tarde, *The Laws of Imitation*, trans. Elsie Clews Parson (New York: H. Holt, 1903).

3. The terminology and theses are those of José-Antonio Maravall. See in particular "From the Renaissance to the Baroque: The Diphasic Schema of a Social Crisis," trans. Terry Cochran, in *Literature Among Discourses*, ed. Wlad Godzich and Nicholas Spadaccini (Minneapolis: University of Minnesota Press, 1986), 3–41; and *The Culture of the Baroque: Analysis of a Historical Structure*, trans. Terry Cochran (Minneapolis: University of Minnesota Press, 1986).

4. See the analysis of Baltasar Gracián's work below.

5. I am grateful to Rebecca Haidt for this insight. Unpublished lecture, University at Buffalo, February 2003.

6. Gustave Cohen, *Histoire de la mise en scène dans le théâtre religieux français du moyen âge* (Paris: Librairie Honoré Champion, 1951), 48.

7. Le Bon, *Crowd*, 11, 6.

8. Elias Canetti, *Crowds and Power*, trans. Carol Stewart (New York: Viking Press, 1962), 15: "it is only in a crowd that man can become free of his fear of being touched," a statement that reflects both the modern thematic of abandon in the crowd, as well as the modern prejudice, prejudicial to our understanding of medieval group dynamics, which asserts a prior antagonism between the individual and the multitude. The arguments in this section derive from my *How the World Became a Stage: Presence, Theatricality, and the Question of Modernity* (Albany: SUNY Press, 2003). For a largely corroborating analysis of the English context, see Anthony B. Dawson and Paul Yachin, *The Culture of Playgoing in Shakespeare's England: A Collaborative Debate* (Cambridge: Cambridge University Press, 2001).

9. Engels, *The Condition of the Working Class in England*, quoted by Benjamin in "On Some Motifs in Baudelaire," 167.

10. Some of the best evidence for this generalization is collected and analyzed in Philippe Ariès and Georges Duby, eds., *A History of Private Life*, vol. 2, *Revelations of the Medieval World* (Cambridge, Mass: Belknap Press of Harvard University Press, 1988). See in particular Georges Duby, "Private Power, Public Power," 3–32. See also David Castillo and William Egginton, "The Perspectival Imaginary and the Symbolization of Power in Early Modern Europe," *Indiana Journal of Hispanic Literatures* 8 (1997): 75–94.

11. Hans Ulrich Gumbrecht, "The Body vs. the Printing Press: Media in the Early Modern Period, Mentalities in the Reign of Castille, and Another History of Literary Forms," *Poetics* 14 (1985): 190. Jelle Koopmans has made a similar point in the context of her discussion of the medieval theater of the excluded. Koopmans, *Le Théâtre des exclus au Moyen Age: Hérétiques, sorcières et marginaux* (Paris: Editions Imago, 1997), 31. Gumbrecht's notion of play, developed in part from Huizinga's famous thesis (*Homo Ludens: Vom Ursprung der Kultur im Spiel* [Ph.D. thesis, Hamburg, 1956]), argues that there was a practice of play peculiar to the Middle Ages that involved the generation of the very spaces that would normally distinguish the serious from the playful or fictional. See Gumbrecht, "Laughter and Arbitrariness, Subjectivity and Seriousness: The *Libro de Buen Amor*, the *Celestina*, and the Style of Sense Production in Early Modern Times," in *Making Sense in Life and Literature*, trans. Glen Burns (Minneapolis: University of Minnesota Press, 1992), 111–22.

12. See, for example, E. K. Chambers, *The Mediaeval Stage*, 2 vols. (New York: Clarendon Press, 1903), 1:187.

13. Elie Konigson, *L'Espace Théâtral Médiéval* (Paris: Éditions du Centre National de la Recherche Scientifique, 1975), 50.

14. Maravall, "From the Renaissance," 5.

15. See William Egginton, "An Epistemology of the Stage: Subjectivity and Theatricality in Early Modern Spain," *New Literary History* 27 (1996): 391–414.

16. "Súplica de la Ciudad de Sevilla al Consejo de Castilla, sobre licencia para representar comedias," quoted in Jean Sentaurens, "Sobre el público de los 'corrales' sevillanos en el Siglo de Oro," in *Creación y público en la literatura española*, ed. J.-F. Botrel and S. Salaün (Madrid: Editorial Castalia, 1974), 62–63. Unless otherwise indicated, all translations are mine.

17. Sentaurens, "Sobre el público," 63–64.

18. Ibid., 66.

19. Wallace Sterling Jr., "Carros, Corrales, and Court Theatres: The Spanish Stage in the Sixteenth and Seventeenth Centuries," *Quarterly Journal of Speech* 49 (1963): 20.

20. *Don Quijote de La Mancha* (Madrid: Cátedra, 1996), 1:557; quoted and commented in John J. Allen, "El papel del vulgo en la economía de los corrales de comedias madrileños," *Edad de oro* 12 (1993): 12.

21. Cervantes, *Don Quijote*, 1:557. The figure of the *vulgo* has a long and troubled history in Spanish letters, which we will only touch on here. Of note is the idea that one of the implicit butts of Cervantes's wit and resentment is his rival and far greater success in the world of the stage, Lope de Vega, who, as a writer who benefited extravagantly from the adoration of the *vulgo*, might be thought to treat them in a more generous light. See Kirschner's comparative study of the figure of the mob in Shakespeare and Lope, in which she argues that the Lopean mob is portrayed in somewhat better terms than its Shakespearean equivalent. Teresa J. Kirschner, "The Mob in Shakespeare and Lope de Vega," in *Parallel Lives: Spanish and English National Drama, 1580–1680*, ed. Louise and Peter Fothergill Payne (Lewisburg, Pa.: Bucknell

University Press, 1991), 140–51. Nevertheless, when speaking of the *vulgo* as the recipients of their own work, individual playwrights tended to be quite withering. See, for some examples, Hugo A. Rennert, *The Spanish Stage in the Time of Lope de Vega* (New York: Dover Publications, 1963), 117. The English context corroborates this disdain for the taste of the masses: for Jonson, for example, "the uninstructed reader is bound to be 'cozened' by plays . . . and the source of the cheat is to be found in 'the multitude, through their excellent [supreme] vice of judgment.'" Leo Salinger, *Dramatic Form in Shakespeare and the Jacobeans* (Cambridge: Cambridge University Press, 1986), 200. See also Nicoll Allardyce, *The Garrick Stage: Theatres and Audiences in the Eighteenth Century* (Athens: University of Georgia Press, 1980). As the case of the Drury Lane theater riots indicate, the threat of random or individual violence in the theater did not mean that theater audiences could not on occasion also act as more or less unified mobs. Henry William Pedicord, "The Changing Audience," in *The London Theatre World, 1660–1800*, ed. Robert D. Hume (Carbondale: Southern Illinois Press, 1980), 245. See also Leo Hughes, *The Drama's Patrons* (Austin: University of Texas Press, 1971), for descriptions of English audiences' behavior in the eighteenth century.

22. Egginton, "Epistemology of the Stage," 408. Cf., for the case of the English stage, Stephen Orgel, *Impersonations: The Performance of Gender in Shakespeare's England* (New York: Cambridge University Press, 1996).

23. Lemazurier's *Galérie historique*, quoted in W. L. Wiley, *The Early Public Theatre in France* (Cambridge, Mass.: Harvard University Press, 1960), 211–12.

24. For a historical examination of the "Cartesian theater," see Egginton, *How the World Became a Stage*, chap. 5.

25. I am grateful to Ciriaco Morón Arroyo for noting the semantic equivalence of this notion with the theme of Kant's third critique.

26. Baltasar Gracián, *El Criticón* (Madrid: Cátedra, 2000), 381; hereafter abbreviated as *C*.

27. Le Bon, *Crowd*, 8.

28. See William Egginton, "Gracián and the Emergence of the Modern Subject," *Hispanic Issues* 14 (1997): 151–69.

29. Maxim 94 of *Oráculo manual*; Gracián, *El héroe, el discreto, oráculo manual y arte de prudencia* (Barcelona: Planeta, 1984).

30. "Todo está ya en su punto y el ser persona en el mayor" (Everything is now at a crest, and being person is the utmost). *Oráculo,* maxim 1.

31. *Oráculo,* maxim 48.

32. For arguments concerning the history of publicity in this sense, see the articles collected in *A History of Private Life*, as well as Jürgen Habermas's influential *The Structural Transformation of the Public Sphere,* trans. Thomas Burger (Cambridge, Mass.: MIT Press, 1989). For more on this topic, see Jobst Welge's contribution to this volume.

33. Richard Sennett, *The Fall of Public Man* (New York: Knopf, 1976).

34. That the experience of anonymity is both ubiquitous within the historical epoch of modernity and pivotal in modern power relations is supported by a linguistic analysis of forms of address. More specifically, the burgeoning of publicity as the stage for the organization of power structures, which itself involves the bifurcation of experientiae along the axis of intimacy and anonymity, is registered in the language of address as the emergence of distinct forms for intimate and anonymous interaction, the latter being composed of formerly third-person and plural forms of address now appropriated as indicators of social distance as well as authority. See, for example, Ferdinand Brunot, *Précis de grammaire historique de la langue française* (Paris: Masson, 1937), 393. As regards the commonality of some third-person forms, "there is no sign of the Latin plural . . . being used with singular reference to indicate respect, a device widely adopted in Romance." Christopher J. Pountain, *A History of the Spanish Language Through Texts* (London: Routledge, 2001), 17. That there was a theoretical consciousness of the political nature of the relation between the singular and plural forms of address in France is evidenced by the attempt during the early years of the revolution to reduce all forms of address to the singular *tu:* "Les tentatives de niveler aussi la langue ne manquèrent pas. La plus notable a été sans doute le remplacement de *vous* par *tu*, décrété par la Convention, mais révoqué dès 1795." Walter von Wartburg, *Évolution et structure de la langue française* (Berne: A. Francke, 1946), 234. It is also noteworthy that this should have been revoked in the wake of some of the excesses of the Terror, suggesting perhaps the need for abstract embodiments of power in the modern state. The case of German is made in Paul Listen, *The Emergence of the German Polite* Sie: *Cognitive and Sociolin-*

guistic Parameters (New York: Peter Lang, 1999), 3. Ralph Penny argues that Spanish did in fact adopt a differentiated system from late Latin, expressed in the distinction between a more formal *vos* and a less formal *tú*. But, as he goes on to say, "during the fifteenth century the type *Vos sois/sos (<sodes)* became gradually less deferential, coming to be used among equals at various social levels and therefore often becoming indistinguishable in tone from *Tú eres*. Since society continued to require modes of deferential address, for occasions when one was speaking to someone of higher rank, speakers of fifteenth-century Spanish often remedied the situation by using two-word phrases consisting of an abstract noun preceded by the hitherto deferential possessive: *vuestra excelenceia, vuestra señoría, vuestra merced*, etc." *Variation and Change in Spanish* (Cambridge: Cambridge University Press, 2000), 152. Where I would intervene, of course, is to suggest that the emergence of these third-person forms in the fifteenth century was not inspired by the mere persistence of a need for modes of deferential address, but rather by a fundamental change in the kind of deferential address required—or, more specifically, by a change in the nature of deference itself, from the deference in the face of a personal, familiar source of power to the deference before abstract authority that characterizes the power structures of modernity.

35. I refer again to Castillo and Egginton, "Perspectival Imaginary." For a fascinating analysis of the emergence of what I am calling symbolic power in the writings of Gómez Manrique, who served as royal overseer of Toledo under the Catholic kings, see José María Rodríguez García, "Poetry, Politics, and Penal Practice in Fifteenth-Century Toledo: Re-Reading Gómez Manrique," unpublished manuscript.

36. See Michael Hardt and Antonio Negri, *Empire* (Cambridge, Mass.: Harvard University Press, 2002). Although the direction of my analysis is different, Anthony Gidden's claim that "the possibility of intimacy means the promise of democracy" can be seen to resonate here. *The Transformations of Intimacy: Sexuality, Love, and Eroticism in Modern Societies* (Cambridge: Polity Press, 1992), 188. The modern manifestation of democratic institutions is constructed on the idea of the public or anonymous negotiation of an intimate core of private desires. Hence, as he puts it, "political democracy implies that individuals have sufficient resources to participate in an autonomous way in the democratic process" (195), or to put it in Gracianesque terms, democracy is

the assertion of autonomy via the display and concealment of resources (*caudal*).

37. *Obras escogidas de Jovellanos* (Madrid: Imprenta La Rafa, 1930), 173; hereafter abbreviated as *OEJ*.

38. Dismay over disorder and desire for order was widespread in eighteenth-century European writings. See, for example, some of the descriptions quoted in John Kelley's *German Visitors to English Theaters in the Eighteenth Century* (Princeton, N.J.: Princeton University Press, 1936).

39. Although Jovellanos's reputation is deservedly that of a committed Enlightenment thinker, one cannot fail to notice what could be termed a "romantic" tug in these theater writings, an observation that is sustained by José María Rodríguez García's treatment in "The Avoidance of Romanticism in Jovellanos's 'Epístola del Paular,'" *Crítica Hispánica* 24, nos. 1 and 2 (2002): 93–110.

40. Explicitly political mass spectacle was, of course, an important recurrent practice of the French Revolution. David's *fête de Châteauvieux* as well as other spectacles at the time could be seen in some ways as a realization of the potential for the production of unity that Jovellanos so desires from the theater. See Mona Ozouf, *La fête révolutionnaire, 1789–1799* (Paris: Gallimard, 1982), 92.

41. Michel Foucault, *Discipline and Punish: The Birth of the Prison*, trans. Alan Sheridan (New York: Vintage, 1979).

42. Walter Benjamin, *Charles Baudelaire: Ein Lyriker im Zeitalter des Hochkapitalismus* (Frankfurt am Main: Suhrkamp, 1969), 52.

43. See again Jobst Welge's contribution to this volume.

44. Martin Heidegger, *Sein und Zeit* (Tübingen: Max Niemeyer Verlag, 1986), 126.

45. A psychoanalytic explanation for this phenomenon can emerge from a reading of the debate Freud stages in his *Group Psychology and the Analysis of the Ego* (trans. James Strachey [New York: Bantam Books, 1960]) with what he refers to as Le Bon's "deservedly famous work" on crowd psychology. If the libidinal bond constitutive of mass behavior requires explanation—in that love usually describes a relationality between individuals across a barrier distinguishing an object or another person, whereas the crowd phenomenon clearly seems at odds with this formulation—Freud solves this problem by arguing that individual members of the crowd "have put one and the same object in

the place of the ego ideal and have consequently identified themselves with one another in their ego" (61). Likewise, by attending in a nonparticipatory way to the performance taking place on the stage, audience members effectively shift toward the outside of the ego boundary normally demarcating the separation between self and other, the result being that the audience can react to affective input in a nondifferentiated way, thus producing the effect so characteristic of the crowd as described by Le Bon and others: that of "the collective mind."

46. For an analysis of a specific example of the political mobilization of theatrical crowds, see Jeffrey T. Schnapp, *Staging Fascism: "18 B L" and the Theater of Masses for Masses* (Stanford, Calif.: Stanford University Press, 1996).

47. *Obras de Don Ramón de Mesonero Romanos, Biblioteca de autores españoles*, vol. 200 (Madrid: Ediciones Atlas, 1967), 139; hereafter abbreviated as *RMR*.

48. Victor Hugo, *Notre-Dame de Paris* (Paris: Gallimard, 1975), 15.

49. Victor Hugo, *The Hunchback of Notre Dame*, trans. Walter J. Cobb (New York: New American Library, 1965), 21.

50. Ibid., 22.

51. Richard Miller, *Bohemia: The Protoculture Then and Now* (Chicago: Nelson-Hall, 1977), 26; hereafter abbreviated as *B*.

52. Critical Art Ensemble, *Electronic Civil Disobedience,* http://www.critical-art.net/books/index.html, 11.

53. See Lynn Jamieson, *Intimacy: Personal Relationships in Modern Societies* (Malden, Mass.: Blackwell, 1998), 19: "intimacy is again becoming attenuated not because people are being re-absorbed into a pre-modern type of communal life but because mass consumer culture promotes a self-obsessive, self-isolating individualism which is incapable of sustaining anything other than kaleidoscopic relationships."

54. " . . . that's RL [real life]. It's just one more window," as Sherry Turkle quotes from one of her wired informants. *Life on the Screen: Identity in the Age of the Internet* (New York: Simon and Schuster, 1995), 13.

55. Electronic Disturbance, http://www.critical-art.net/books/index.html, 3.

CHAPTER 5

1. Christian Bromberger, *Le Match de Football* (Paris: Édi-

tions de la Maison de l'Homme, 1995), 110.

2. Reproduced in Nicolaos Yalouris, ed., *The Eternal Olympics* (New Rochelle: Caratzas Brothers, 1979), 37.

3. Epictetus quoted in Moses I. Finley and H. W. Pleket, *The Olympic Games* (New York: Viking Press, 1976), 54.

4. Johann Heinrich Krause, *Olympia* (Hildesheim: Georg Olms, 1972), 192.

5. Roberto Patrucco, *Lo Sport nella Grecia Antica* (Florence: Olschiki, 1972), 21.

6. Finley and Pleket, *Olympic Games,* 57.

7. Dio quoted in H. A. Harris, *Greek Athletics and the Jews* (Cardiff: University of Wales Press, 1976), 89.

8. Ludwig Friedländer, *Roman Life and Manners Under the Early Empire,* trans. J. H. Freese and Leonard A. Magnus, 4 vols. (London: George Routledge and Sons, 1908–1913), 2:240–90; Georges Ville, *La Gladiature en Occident* (Rome: École française de Rome, 1981), 57–173.

9. Petronius, *Satyricon,* trans. William Arrowsmith (Ann Arbor: University of Michigan Press, 1959), 42.

10. Michael Grant, *The Gladiators* (London: Weidenfeld and Nicolson, 1967), 31.

11. Ville, *Gladiature,* 262.

12. Bollinger, *Theatralis Licentia* (Winterthur: Hans Schellenberg, 1969), 18.

13. Friedländer, *Roman Life and Manners,* 2:262.

14. Horace, *Satires and Epistles,* trans. S. P. Bovie (Chicago: University of Chicago Press, 1959), 148.

15. Augustine, *Confessions,* trans. E. B. Pusey (London: J. M. Dent, 1907), 106–7.

16. On the spectators' responses to the prospect of death, see Carlin A. Barton, *The Sorrows of the Ancient Romans* (Princeton, N.J.: Princeton University Press, 1993); Donald Kyle, *Spectacles of Death in Ancient Rome* (London: Routledge, 1998).

17. Friedländer, *Roman Life and Manners,* 2:243.

18. Louis Robert, *Les Gladiateurs dans l'Orient Grec,* 2nd ed. (Amsterdam: Hakkert, 1971), 301–2.

19. Juvenal, *Satires* [6.268–82], trans. Rolfe Humphries (Bloomington: Indiana University Press, 1958), 18.

20. Petronius, *Satyricon,* 43.

21. Seneca, *Ad Lucilium Epistulae Morales,* trans. R. M. Gummere, 3 vols. (London: Heineman, 1917–1925), 1:30–31.

22. Cicero quoted in A. Hönle and A. Heinze, *Römische*

Amphitheater und Stadien (Zurich: Atlantis, 1981), 20.

23. Ovid, *The Art of Love,* trans. Rolfe Humphries (Bloomington: Indiana University Press, 1957), 164–65.

24. Tertullian, *De Spectaculis,* trans. T. R. Glover (London: Heinemann, 1931), 271–73.

25. Novitian, *De Spectaculis* (Turnholt: Brepols, 1972), 171.

26. Barry Baldwin, "The Sports Fans of Rome and Byzantium," *Liverpool Classical Monthly* 9, no. 2 (1984): 29.

27. Rodolphe Guilland, "The Hippodrome at Byzantium," *Speculum* 22 (1948): 676–82.

28. Alan Cameron, *Porphyrius the Charioteer* (Oxford: Clarendon Press, 1973), 150.

29. Sotiris G. Giatsis, "The Massacre in the Riot of Nika . . . " *International Journal of the History of Sport* 12, no. 3 (December 1995): 141–52.

30. Eric Hobsbawm, *Nations and Nationalities Since 1780* (Cambridge: Cambridge University Press, 1990), 143.

31. Pliny, *Letters,* trans. Betty Radice (Harmondsworth: Penguin, 1963), 236.

32. Roger Sherman Loomis, "Arthurian Influence on Sport and Spectacle," in *Arthurian Literature of the Middle Ages,* ed. Roger Sherman Loomis (Oxford: Clarendon Press, 1959), 557.

33. Jean J. Jusserand, *Les Sports et jeux d'exercice dans l'ancienne France* (Paris: Plon, 1901), 12, 18. See also Richard Barber, *The Knight and Chivalry* (Ipswich: Boydell Press, 1974), 193; Charles Homer Haskins, "The Latin Literature of Sport," *Speculum* 2 (1927): 238.

34. Barber, *Knight and Chivalry,* 189.

35. Noel Denholm Young, "The Tournament in the Thirteenth Century," *Studies in Medieval History,* ed. R. W. Hunt (Oxford: Clarendon Press, 1948), 262.

36. Thomas Zotz, "Adel, Bürgertum und Turnier in deutschen Städten vom 13. bis 15. Jahrhundert," in *Das ritterliche Turnier im Mittelalter,* ed. Josef Fleckenstein (Göttingen: Vandenhoek und Ruprecht, 1985), 478.

37. Klemens C. Wildt, *Leibesübungen im deutschen Mittelalter* (Frankfurt: Wilhelm Limpert, 1957), 28; Walter Schaufelberger, *Der Wettkampf in der alten Eidgenossenschaft* (Bern: Paul Haupt, 1972), 46.

38. Norbert Elias, *Ueber den Prozeß der Zivilisation,* 2 vols. (Bern: Francke, 1969); Norbert Elias and Eric Dunning, *Sport im Zivilisationprozeß* (Münster: LIT Verlag, 1986); Norbert Elias and Eric Dunning, *Quest for Excitement* (Oxford: Basil Blackwell, 1986).

39. Sydney Anglo, *The Great Tournament Roll of Westminster,* 2 vols. (Oxford: Clarendon Press, 1968), 1:28.

40. Jean Verdon, *Les Loisirs au moyen âge* (Paris: Jules Tallandier, 1980), 179.

41. Anglo, *Great Tournament Roll,* 1:38.

42. Rosamund Mitchell, *John Tiptoft, 1427–1470* (London: Longmans, Green, 1938), 103–11.

43. Jusserand, *Les Sports et jeux d'exercice dans l'ancienne France,* 149–54; John McClelland, "Le Tournoi de Juin 1559," in *Le Mécénat et l'influence des Guises,* ed. Yvonne Bellenger (Paris: Honoré Champion, 1997), 177–85. Jusserand quotes Henri's moving epitaph: "Quem Mars non rapuit, Martis imago rapit" (He whom Mars was unable to take was taken by the image of Mars) (154).

44. Quoted in Anglo, *Great Tournament Roll,* 1:37.

45. Theo Reintges, *Ursprung und Wesen der spätmittelalterlichen Schützengilden* (Bonn: Ludwig Röhrscheid, 1963), 287; Arnold Wehrle, *500 Jahre Spiel und Sport in Zürich* (Zürich: Berichthaus, 1960), 7.

46. Kusudo Kazuhiko, *Doitsu Chûsekôki no Supôtsu* (Late-Medieval German Sports) (Tokyo: Fumaidô, 1998), 245–326.

47. Klaus Zieschang, *Vom Schützenfest zum Turnfest* (Ahrensburg: Czwalina, 1977), 80–81.

48. Herman Goja, *Die österreichischen Schützengilden und ihre Feste* (Vienna: Verlag Notring der wissenschaftlichen Verbände Oesterreichs, 1963), 45–84.

49. Wehrle, *500 Jahre,* 17.

50. Hans Germann, *Der Ehrenspiegel deutscher Schützen* (Leipzig: Thankmar Rudolf, 1928), 66.

51. Quoted in Eric Dunning and Kenneth Sheard, *Barbarians, Gentlemen and Players* (Oxford: Martin Robertson, 1979), 28.

52. Strutt quoted in Henry Alken, *The National Sports of Great Britain* (London: Methuen, 1903), n.p.

53. John Nichols, *The Progresses and Public Processions of Queen Elizabeth,* 3 vols. (London: John Nichols and Sons, 1823), 1:438n2; C. L. Kingsford, "Paris Garden and the Bear-Baiting," *Archaeologia* 70 (1920): 168. Kingsford indicated that Sundays were the day of closure.

54. Samuel Pepys, *Diary,* ed. Robert Latham and William

Matthews, 11 vols. (Berkeley: University of California Press, 1970–1983), 7:246.

55. John Evelyn, *Diary*, ed. E. S. de Beer, 6 vols. (London: Oxford University Press, 1955), 3:549.

56. *Gentleman's Magazine* quoted in Robert W. Malcolmson, *Popular Recreations in English Society, 1700–1850* (Cambridge: Cambridge University Press, 1973), 137.

57. Pierce Egan, *Boxiana*, 5 vols. (London: Sherwood, Neely and Jones, 1829), 1:58.

58. Ibid., 4:287.

59. Irving quoted in John Ford, *Prize-Fighting* (Newton Abbot: David and Charles, 1971), 163.

60. Egan, *Boxiana*, 4:374.

61. Zacharias Conrad von Uffenbach, *London in 1710*, trans. W. H. Quarrell and Margaret Mare (London: Faber and Faber, 1934), 90–91.

62. Mary Russell Mitford, *Our Village* (1824–1832; reprint, London: J. M. Dent, 1936), 63–64, 67–68.

63. Nyren quoted in Hans Indorf, *Fair Play und der "Englische Sportgeist"* (Hamburg: Friederschen, de Gruyter, 1938), 67.

64. Dennis Brailsford, "Sporting Days in Eighteenth Century England," *Journal of Sport History* 9, no. 3 (Winter 1982): 49; John Ford, *This Sporting Land* (London: New English Library, 1977), 87; Christopher Brookes, *English Cricket* (London: Weidenfeld and Nicholson, 1978), 71–72.

65. Keith A. P. Sandiford, "English Cricket Crowds During the Victorian Age," *Journal of Sport History* 9, no. 3 (Winter 1982): 19.

66. Wray Vamplew, "Sports Crowd Disorder in Britain, 1870–1914," *Journal of Sport History* 7, no. 1 (Spring 1980): 7.

67. Christina Hole, *English Sports and Pastimes* (London: B. T. Batsford, 1949), 62.

68. P. F. Warner, "The End of the Cricket Season," *Badminton Magazine* 35 (1912): 396.

69. Richard Cashman, *'Ave a Go, Yer Mug!* (Sydney: Collins, 1984), 11–14, 30–31, 48, 89.

70. J. Thomas Jable, "Latter-Day Cultural Imperialists: British Influence on the Establishment of Cricket in Philadelphia, 1842–1872," in *Pleasure, Profit, Proselytism*, ed. J. A. Mangan (London: Frank Cass, 1988), 175–92.

71. Joel Zoss and John Bowman, *Diamonds in the Rough* (Chicago: Contemporary Books, 1996), 52.

72. Melvin L. Adelman, "The First Baseball Game . . . ," *Journal of Sport History*, 7, no. 3 (Winter 1980): 132–35; Zoss and Bowman, *Diamonds in the Rough*, 52–59.

73. Albert G. Spalding, *America's National Game* (New York: American Sports Pub. Co., 1911), 55.

74. Harold Seymour, *Baseball* (New York: Oxford University Press, 1960), 15.

75. Ibid., 175; see also Marty Appel, *Slide, Kelly, Slide* (Lanham, Md.: Scarecrow Press, 1996).

76. H. Addington Bruce, "Baseball and the National Life," *Outlook* 104 (May 1913): 269.

77. C. L. R. James, *Beyond a Boundary* (New York: Pantheon Books, 1983), 51.

78. *Boston Globe* quoted in Stephen Hardy, *How Boston Played* (Boston: Northeastern University Press, 1982), 187.

79. Spalding quoted in Peter Levine, *A. G. Spalding and the Rise of Baseball* (New York: Oxford University Press, 1985), 42.

80. Seymour, *Baseball*, 90.

81. *New York Chronicle* quoted by Melvin Adelman, "The Development of Modern Athletics" (Ph.D. diss., University of Illinois, 1980), 406.

82. *Sporting News* quoted by David Q. Voigt, *American Baseball* (Norman: University of Oklahoma Press, 1966), 182.

83. Hardy, *How Boston Played*, 191.

84. Percy M. Young, *A History of British Football*, rev. ed. (London: Arrow Books, 1973), 113.

85. Adrian Harvey, "An Epoch in the Annals of National Sport," *International Journal of the History of Sport* 18, no. 4 (December 2001): 53–87; Adrian Harvey, "Football's Missing Link," *European Sports History Review* 1 (1999): 92–116.

86. Martyn Bowden, "Soccer," in *The Theater of Sport*, ed. Karl B. Raitz (Baltimore, Md.: Johns Hopkins University Press, 1995), 111–12.

87. Young, *History of British Football*, 132.

88. James Walvin, *The People's Game* (London: Allen Lane, 1975), 67.

89. Derek Birley, *Sport and the Making of Britain* (Manchester: Manchester University Press, 1993), 265.

90. Tony Mason, "The Blues and the Reds," in *Die Kanten des runden Leders*, ed. Roman Horak and Wolfgang Reiter (Vienna: Promedia, 1991), 174.

91. Walvin, *People's Game*, 31–68; Tony Mason, *Association*

Football and English Society, 1863–1915 (Atlantic Highlands, N.J.: Humanities Press, 1980), 21–68.

92. Neil Tranter, *Sport, Economy and Society in Britain, 1750–1914* (Cambridge: Cambridge University Press, 1998), 17.

93. Nicholas Fishwick, *English Football and Society, 1910–1950* (Manchester: Manchester University Press, 1989), 150.

94. Jeffrey Hill, "Cocks, Cats, Caps and Cups," *Culture, Sport, Society* 2, no. 2 (Summer 1999): 13.

95. Charles Edwardes, "The New Football Mania," *Nineteenth Century* 32 (October 1892): 627.

96. Mason, *Association Football and English Society*, 163–64.

97. For contributions to the debates over the nature and extent of sports-related spectator violence, see Eric Dunning et al., "The Social Roots of Football Hooliganism," *Leisure Studies* 1, no. 2 (1982): 139–56; Eric Dunning et al., "Football Hooliganism in Britain Before the First World War," *International Review of Sport Sociology* 19, nos. 3–4 (1984): 215–40; Gary Armstrong and Rosemary Harris, "Football Hooligans," *Sociological Review* 39, no. 3 (1991): 427–58; Eric Dunning, Patrick Murphy, and Ivan Waddington, "Anthropological Versus Sociological Approaches . . . ," *Sociological Review* 39, no. 3 (1991): 459–78; R. W. Lewis, "Football Hooliganism in England Before 1914," *International Journal of the History of Sport* 13, no. 3 (December 1996): 310–39.

98. Dunning et al., "Football Hooliganism in Britain," 229.

99. Steve Wulf, "Bad Mouthing," *Sports Illustrated* 68 (March 14, 1988): 17.

100. William Oscar Johnson, "The Agony of Victory," *Sports Illustrated* 79 (July 5, 1993): 31.

101. Cyril White, "An Analysis of Hostile Outbursts in Spectator Sports" (Ph.D. diss., University of Illinois, 1970), 100–107.

102. Ian L. Taylor, "Hooligans," *New Society* 14 (August 7, 1969): 206; see also Taylor's subsequent work, "Soccer Consciousness and Soccer Hooliganism," in *Images of Deviance*, ed. Stanley Cohen (Harmondsworth: Penguin, 1971), 131–64; "On the Sports Violence Question," in *Sport, Culture and Ideology*, ed. Jennifer Hargreaves (London: Routledge and Kegan Paul, 1982), 152–96. See also the following essays by Ian Taylor: "Class, Violence and Sport," in *Sport, Culture and the Modern State*, ed. Hart Cantelon and Richard Gruneau (Toronto: University of Toronto Press, 1982), 40–96; "Professional Sport and the Recession," *International Review of Sport Sociology* 19, no. 1 (1984): 67–82; "Putting

the Boot into a Working-Class Sport," *Sociology of Sport Journal* 14, no. 2 (June 1987): 170–91.

103. Brian Holland, Lorna Jackson, Grant Jarvie, and Mike Smith, "Sport and Racism in Yorkshire," in *Sport and Identity in the North of England*, ed. Jeff Hill and Jack Williams (Keele: Keele University Press, 1996), 165–86; Ian Taylor, "Professional Sport and the Recession," *International Review for the Sociology of Sport* 19, no. 1: 7–30.

104. Les Back, Tim Crabbe, and John Solomos, *The Changing Face of Football* (Oxford: Berg, 2001), 110.

105. John Williams, Eric Dunning, and Patrick Murphy, *Hooligans Abroad* (London: Routledge and Kegan Paul, 1984), 58.

106. Martin Polley, *Moving the Goalposts* (London: Routledge, 1998), 135.

107. Back et al., *Changing Face of Football*, 90.

108. Witter quoted in Les Back, Tim Crabbe, and John Solomos, "Lions and Black Skins," in *"Race," Sport and the British*, ed. Ben Carrington and Ian McDonald (London: Routledge, 2001), 90. See also Garry Robson, *Nobody Likes Us, We Don't Care* (Oxford: Berg, 2000).

109. Roman Horak, "Things Change," *Sociological Review* 39, no. 3 (1991): 531–48; Antonio Roversi, "Football Violence in Italy," *International Review of Sport Sociology* 26, no. 4 (1991): 311–30.

110. Kris van Limbergen, Carine Colaers, and Lode Walgrave, "The Societal and Psycho-Sociological Background of Football Hooligans," *Current Psychology* 8 (1989): 4–14.

111. Klaus-Jürgen Bruder et al., "Gutachten 'Fankultur und Fanverhalten,'" in *Fanverhalten, Massenmedien und Gewalt im Sport*, ed. Erwin Hahn et al. (Schorndorf: Karl Hofmann, 1988), 16.

112. Udo Merkel, "Football Identity and Youth Culture in Germany," in *Football Cultures and Identities*, ed. Gary Armstrong and Richard Giulianotti (Houndmills: Macmillan, 1999), 63.

113. Gunter A. Pilz, "Zur gesellschaftlichen Bedingheit von Sport und Gewalt," in *Gesellschaftliche Funktionen des Sports*, ed. Hannelore Käber and Bernhard Tripp (Bonn: Bundeszentrale für politische Bildung, 1984), 169.

114. Antonio Roversi, "Football Violence in Italy," *International Review of Sport Sociology* 26, no. 4 (1991): 311–30.

115. Dubravko Dolic, "Die Fußballnationalmannschaft als Trägerin nationaler Würde?" in *Fußballwelten*, ed. Peter Lösche,

Undine Ruge, and Klaus Stolz (Opladen: Leske und Budrich, 2001), 155–74.

116. Srdjan Vrcan and Drazen Lalic, "From Ends to Trenches and Back," in Armstrong and Giulianotti, *Football Cultures and Identities*, 177–78.

117. Eduardo P. Archetti, "Argentinian Football," *International Journal of the History of Sport* 9, no. 2 (August 1992): 227.

118. Vic Duke and Liz Crolley, "Fútbol, Politicians and the People," *International Journal of the History of Sport* 18, no. 3 (September 2001): 109–11; Marcelo Marió Suárez-Orozco, "A Study of Argentine Soccer," *Journal of Psychoanalytic Anthropology* 5, no. 1 (Winter 1982): 7–28.

119. Simon Inglis, *The Football Grounds of Great Britain*, 2nd ed. (London: Collins Willow, 1987), 29.

120. Phil Scraton, *Hillsborough* (Edinburgh: Mainstream, 1999).

121. White, "Analysis of Hostile Outbursts," 91–100.

122. *New York Times*, May 30, 1985. The first reports gave the number of dead as forty.

123. Peter Marsh, Elisabeth Rosser, and Rom Harré, *The Rules of Disorder* (London: Routledge and Kegan Paul, 1978); Armstrong and Harris, "Football Hooligans," 427–58.

124. Dunning et al., "Anthropological Versus Sociological Approaches," 459–78.

125. Bromberger, *Le Match de Football*, 213.

126. Ibid., 141.

127. In addition to *Le Match de Football*, see Christian Bromberger, Alain Havot, and Jean-Marc Mariottini, "Allez l'O.M.! Forza Juve!" *Terrain* 8 (April 1987): 8–41; Antonio Roversi and Roberto Moscati, "La violenza nel calcio in Italia," *Il Calcio e il suo Pubblico*, ed. Pierre Lanfranchi (Naples: Edizioni Scientifiche Italiane, 1992), 274–84; Christian Bromberger and Jean-Marc Mariottini, "Le Rouge et le Noir," *Actes de la Recherche en Sciences Sociales* 80 (November 1989): 79–89.

128. Richard Giulianotti, "Scotland's Tartan Army," *Sociological Review* 39, no. 3 (1991): 502–27; Henning Eichberg, "Crisis and Grace," *Scandinavian Journal of the Medical Science of Sports* 2 (1992): 119–28.

129. Matti Goksør and Hans Hognestad, "No Longer Worlds Apart?," in Armstrong and Giulianotti, *Football Cultures and Identities*, 206.

130. Chris Gratton and Peter Taylor, *Economics of Sport and Recreation* (London: SPON, 2000), 202.

131. Gunter A. Pilz and Andreas H. Trebels, *Aggression und Konflikt im Sport* (Ahrensburg: Czwalina, 1976); Peter Marsh, "Careers for Boys, Nutters, Hooligans, and Hardcases," *New Society* 36 (1976): 346–48; Marsh et al., *The Rules of Disorder;* Eugene Trivizas, "Offences and Offenders in Football Crowd Disorders," *British Journal of Criminology* 20 (1980): 276–88; Gunter A. Pilz, *Wandlungen der Gewalt im Sport* (Ahrensburg: Czwalina, 1982); Williams et al., *Hooligans Abroad;* Eric Dunning, Patrick Murphy, and John Williams, *The Roots of Football Hooliganism* (London: Routledge and Kegan Paul, 1988); Paul Murphy, John Williams, and Eric Dunning, *Football on Trial* (London: Routledge, 1990); Eric Dunning, "The Social Roots of Football Hooliganism," in *Football, Violence and Social Identity*, ed. Richard Giulianotti, Norman Bonney, and Mike Hepworth (London: Routledge, 1994), 128–57; Gordon W. Russell, "Personalities in the Crowd," *Aggressive Behavior* 21 (1995): 91–100; John Hughson, "Among the Thugs," *International Review of Sport Sociology* 33, no. 1 (1998): 43–57.

132. Jeffrey H. Goldstein and Robert L. Arms, "Effects of Observing Athletic Contests on Hostility," *Sociometry* 34 (1971): 83–90. For a classic statement of the frustration-aggression theory, see John Dollard et al., *Frustration and Aggression* (New Haven, Conn.: Yale University Press, 1939).

133. Robert L. Arms, Gordon W. Russell, and Mark L. Sandilands, "Effects of Viewing Aggressive Sports on the Hostility of Spectators," *Social Psychology Quarterly* 42 (1977): 279.

134. Edward Thomas Turner, "The Effects of Viewing College Football, Basketball, and Wrestling on the Elicited Aggressive Responses of Male Spectators" (Ph.D. diss., University of Maryland, 1968), 90; see also John Mark Kingsmore, "The Effect of Professional Wrestling and a Professional Basketball Contest upon the Aggressive Tendencies of Male Spectators" (Ph.D. diss., University of Maryland, 1968).

135. Leonard Berkowitz and Edna Rawlings, "Effects of Film Violence on Inhibitions Against Subsequent Aggressions," *Journal of Abnormal and Social Psychology* 66 (1963): 405–12; Leonard Berkowitz, "Aggressive Clues in Aggressive Behavior and Hostility Catharsis," *Psychological Review* 71, no. 2 (1964): 104–22; Leonard Berkowitz, "Some Aspects of Observed Aggression," *Journal of Personality and Social Psychology* 2, no. 3 (1965): 359–69; Russell G. Geen and Leonard Berkowitz, "Name-Mediated Aggres-

sive Cue Properties," *Journal of Personality* 34 (1966): 456–66; Leonard Berkowitz and Russell G. Geen, "Film Violence and the Cue Properties of Available Targets," *Journal of Personality and Social Psychology* 3 (1966): 525–30; Russell G. Geen and Leonard Berkowitz, "Some Conditions Facilitating the Occurrence of Aggression After the Observation of Violence," *Journal of Personality* 35 (1967): 666–76; Russell G. Geen and Edgar C. O'Neal, "Activation of Cue-Elicited Aggression by General Arousal," *Journal of Personality and Social Psychology* 11, no. 3 (1969): 289–92; Leonard Berkowitz and Joseph T. Alioto, "The Meaning of an Observed Event as a Determinant of Its Aggressive Consequences," *Journal of Personality and Social Psychology* 28 (1973): 206–17; Joseph X. Lennon and Frederick G. Hatfield, "The Effects of Crowding and Observation of Athletic Events on Spectator Tendency Toward Aggressive Behavior," *Journal of Sport Behavior* 3, no. 2 (May 1980): 61–80; Jeffrey H. Goldstein, "Violence in Sports," in *Sports, Games, and Play*, ed. Jeffrey H. Goldstein, 2nd ed. (Hillsdale, N.J.: Lawrence Erlbaum, 1989), 83–90; Dolf Zillmann and Paul B. Paulus, "Spectators," in *Handbook of Research on Sport Psychology*, ed. R. N. Singer et al. (New York: Macmillan, 1993), 600–619; Daniel L. Wann et al., "Beliefs in Symbolic Catharsis," *Social Behavior and Personality* 27, no. 2 (1999): 155–64.

136. For the argument that the sight of aggression induces aggression, see Albert Bandura, *Aggression* (Englewood Cliffs, N.J.: Prentice-Hall, 1973); Dolf Zillmann, *Hostility and Aggression* (Hillsdale, N.J.: Lawrence Erlbaum, 1979).

137. Hans Ulrich Herrmann, *Die Fußballfans* (Schorndorf: Karl Hofmann, 1977), 37.

138. Jennings Bryant and Dolf Zillmann, "Using Television to Alleviate Boredom and Stress," *Journal of Broadcasting* 28 (1984): 1–20; Jennings Bryant, Dolf Zillmann, and Arthur A. Raney, "Violence and the Enjoyment of Media Sports," in *MediaSport*, ed. Lawrence A. Wenner (London: Routledge, 1997).

139. Jennings Bryant, Paul Comisky, and Dolf Zillmann, "The Appeal of Rough-and-Tumble Play in Televised Professional Football," *Communication Quarterly* 29 (1981): 260.

140. Gordon W. Russell and Bruce R. Drewry, "Crowd Size and Competitive Aspects of Aggression in Ice Hockey," *Human Relations* 29 (1976): 723–35; Gordon W. Russell, "Does Sports Violence Increase Box Office Receipts?" *International Journal of Sport Psychology* 17 (1986): 173–83.

141. Norbert Elias and Eric Dunning, "The Quest for Excitement in Unexciting Societies," in *The Cross-Cultural Analysis of Sport and Games*, ed. Günther Lüschen (Champaign, Ill.: Stipes, 1970), 31.

142. Allen Guttmann, "The Modern Olympics," in *The Olympic Games in Transition*, ed. Jeffrey O. Segrave and Donald Chu (Champaign, Ill.: Human Kinetics, 1988), 433–43.

143. It is unfortunate that Wann has not synthesized the research in a monograph. See Daniel L. Wann and Nyla R. Branscombe, "Die-Hard and Fair-Weather Fans," *Journal of Sport and Social Issues* 14, no. 2 (Fall 1990): 103–17; Nyla R. Branscombe and Daniel L. Wann, "The Role of Identification . . . ," *Human Relations* 45, no. 10 (1992): 1013–33; Daniel L. Wann, "Aggression Among Highly Identified Spectators as a Function of Their Need to Maintain Positive Social Identity," *Journal of Sport and Social Issues* 17, no. 2 (1993): 134–43; Daniel L. Wann and Nyla R. Branscombe, "Sports Fans," *International Journal of Sports Psychology* 24, no. 1 (1993): 1–17; Daniel L. Wann, "The 'Noble' Sports Fan," *Perceptual and Motor Skills* 78 (1994): 864–66; Daniel L. Wann and Thomas J. Dolan, "Influence of Spectators' Identification on Evaluation of the Past, Present, and Future Performance of a Sports Team," *Perceptual and Motor Skills*, 78 (1994): 547–52; Daniel L. Wann, Thomas J. Dolan, Kimberly K. McGeorge, and Julie A. Allison, "Relationships Between Spectator Identification and Spectators' Perception of Influence, Spectators' Emotions, and Competition Outcome," *Journal of Sport and Exercise Psychology* 16 (1994): 347–64; Daniel L. Wann and Nyla R. Branscombe, "Influence of Identification with a Sports Team on Objective Knowledge and Subjective Beliefs," *International Journal of Sport Psychology* 26 (1995): 551–67; Daniel L. Wann, "Seasonal Changes in Spectators' Identification with and Evaluations of College Basketball and Football Teams," *Psychological Record* 46 (1996): 201–15; Daniel L. Wann, Jeffrey D. Carlson, and Michael P. Schrader, "The Impact of Team Identification on the Hostile and Instrumental Verbal Aggression of Sports Spectators," *Journal of Social Behavior and Personality* 14, no. 2 (1999): 279–86; Daniel L. Wann, "Further Exploration of Season Changes in Sport Fan Identification," *International Sports Journal* 4, no. 1 (Winter 2000): 119–23; Daniel L. Wann and Derek J. Somerville, "The Relationship Between University Sport Team Identification and Alumni Contributions," *International Sports Journal* 4, no. 1 (Winter 2000): 138–44; Daniel L. Wann and Anthony M. Wilson, "The Relationship Between the Sport Team Identifi-

cation of Basketball Spectators and the Number of Attributions They Generate . . . ," *International Sports Journal* 5, no. 1 (Winter 2001): 43–50.

144. Zillmann and Paulus, "Spectators," 604.

CHAPTER 5A

1. Sources: *The American Heritage Dictionary of the English Language,* 4th ed. (Boston: Houghton Mifflin, 2000); Middle English Dictionary, from Middle English Compendium, http://ets.umdl.umich.edu/m/mec; *Oxford English Dictionary,* 2nd ed. (New York: Oxford University Press, 1989).

CHAPTER 6

1. On average, twenty million adherents of various religions annually participate in some form of pilgrimage—which may occasionally also be simple tourism. For difficulties in estimating figures and the relationship between tourism and pilgrimage, see below, as well as Luigi Tomasi, introduction to William H. Swatos Jr. and Luigi Tomasi, eds., *From Medieval Pilgrimage to Religious Tourism: The Social and Cultural Economics of Piety* (London: Praeger, 2002), 1–24. The figures for the Kumbh-Mela ceremony are from the *Süddeutsche Zeitung,* January 15, 2001, and CNN, January 25, 2001; for Lourdes, from *Sanctuaires Notre-Dame de Lourdes, Services Comunication* (2001): 19. Irmengard Jehle, *Der Mensch unterwegs zu Gott: Die Walfahrt als religiöses Bedürfnis des Menschen—aufgezeigt an der Marienwallfahrt nach Lourdes* (Würzburg: Echter, 2002), 17–18.

2. A modern handbook of psychology defines a crowd as "a great number of persons who are mostly unknown to each other, gather at the same place at the same time, crowded together in a limited space, without clear internal structure, but guided towards a common goal, whereby they orient themselves at the same values, and hence can be empirically measured for a specific time. A crowd is thus not a cross section of society." Günter Laser, *Populo et Scaenae Serviendum Est: Die Bedeutung der städtischen Masse in der späten römischen Republik* (Trier: Wiss. Verlag Trier, 1997), 17.

3. Kaspar Elm, *Umbilicus Mundi: Beiträge zur Geschichte Jerusalems, der Kreuzzüge, des Kapitels vom Hlg. Grab in Jerusalem und der Ritterorden* (Brugge: Sint-Trudo Abdij, 1998), 25–28; hereafter abbreviated as UM.

4. Gustave Le Bon, *Psychologie des foules* (1895; reprint, Paris: Presses Universitaires de France/Quadrige, 1983), 3, 27, 93–95; hereafter abbreviated as *PF.*

5. *PF,* 113–24; Susanna Barrows, *Distorting Mirrors: Visions of the Crowd in Late Nineteenth-Century France* (New Haven, Conn.: Yale University Press, 1981), 162–76.

6. Sigmund Freud, *Massenpsychologie und Ich-Analyse* (Leipzig: Internationaler Psychoanalytischer Verlag, 1912), 46–56.

7. Elias Canetti, *Masse und Macht* (Hamburg: Claasen, 1960), 179, 80–81; hereafter abbreviated as *MM*. Translated as *Crowds and Power* by Carol Stewart (New York: Farrar Straus Giroux, 1962), 128, 24; hereafter abbreviated as *CP.*

8. Steven Lukes, *Emile Durkheim: His Life and Work* (London: Penguin, 1973), 462–63; Emile Durkheim, *Les formes élémentaires de la vie religieuse: Le système totémique en Australie* (Paris, 1912). Translated by Joseph W. Swain as *The Elementary Forms of Religious Life: A Study in Religious Sociology* (1915; reprint, New York: Collier, 1961), 13, 240–43.

9. Durkheim, *Elementary Forms,* 240–43, 247, 248; Stanley J. Tambiah, *Leveling Crowds: Ethnonationalist Conflicts and Collective Violence in South Asia* (Berkeley: University of California Press, 1996), 297–323.

10. Barrows, *Distorting Mirrors,* 2–6.

11. E. D. Hunt, *Holy Land Pilgrimage in the Later Roman Empire, AD 312–460* (Oxford: Clarendon, 1984), 2–5; hereafter abbreviated as *HLP;* Susanna Elm, "Perceptions of Jerusalem Pilgrimage as Reflected in Two Early Sources on Female Pilgrimage (3rd and 4th century AD)," *Studia Patristica* 20 (1989): 219–23.

12. Matthew Dillon, *Pilgrims and Pilgrimage in Ancient Greece* (London: Routledge, 1997); Simon Coleman, *The Globalisation of Charismatic Christianity: Spreading the Gospel of Prosperity* (Cambridge: Cambridge University Press, 2000), 10–29.

13. The second-century Christian author Melito of Sardis already claimed that he had gone to Palestine to see "the place where these deeds [told in the Bible] were accomplished and proclaimed." Eus. *Historia Ecclesiastica* 4.26.14; his account is not a travelogue, but he could be called the earliest Christian pilgrim. For the *IB,* see Jás Elsner, "The *Itinerarium Burdiagelense*: Politics and Salvation in the Geography of Constantine's Empire," *Journal of Roman Studies* 90 (2000): 181–95.

14. Elsner, "*Itinerarium Burdiagelense*," 184–86.

15. Simon Coleman and Jás Elsner, *Pilgrimage Past and Present: Sacred Travel and Sacred Space in World Religions* (London: British Museum Press, 1995), 83–88.

16. Susanna Elm, *Virgins of God: The Making of Asceticism in Late Antiquity* (Oxford: Clarendon Press, 1994), 272–73; *HLP,* 58–70, 155–85.

17. Diana Webb, *Pilgrims and Pilgrimage in the Medieval West* (New York: Taurus, 1999), 16–17; hereafter abbreviated as *PPMW; UM,* 10–12; John Wilkinson, *Jerusalem Pilgrims Before the Crusades* (Warminster: Aris and Phillips, 1977) 9–14.

18. Jer. *Ep.* 77.10; 66.11.

19. Jer. *Ep.* 46. 12.3; *Epp.* 66.14; e.g., 71.5.

20. *Codex Theodosianus* 8.5.4, and passim.

21. Dillon, *Pilgrims and Pilgrimage,* xviii; *HLP,* 63–70, 72–76, 141–60.

22. *PPMW,* 10–11, 16–18; Coleman and Elsner, *Pilgrimage Past and Present,* 94–95; Jonathan Riley-Smith, *The First Crusaders, 1095–1131* (Cambridge: Cambridge University Press, 1997), 1–2; hereafter abbreviated as *FC.*

23. *FC,* 3–34; *PPMW,* 19–21; Jonathan Philips, *The Crusades, 1095–1197* (London: Longman, 2002), 2–26; hereafter abbreviated as *C.*

24. George Rudé, *The Crowd in History: A Study of Popular Disturbances in France and England 1730–1848* (New York: Wiley, 1964), 3–15, 94–134.

25. Kaspar Elm, "'O beatas idus ac prae ceteris gloriosas!' Darstellung und Deutung der Eroberug Jerusalems 1099 in den Gesta Tancredi des Raoul von Caen," in *Es hat sich viel ereignet, Gutes wie Böses: Lateinische Geschichtsschreibung in der Spät- und Nachantike,* ed. Gabriele Thome and Jens Holzhausen (Munich: Saur, 2001), 155–59.

26. Nik. Chon. Annals of Constantinople; *C,* 81.

27. A. A. R. Bastiaensen, "*Ecclesia Martyrum:* Quelques observations sur le temoignage des anciens textes liturgiques," in *Martyrium in Multidisciplinary Perspective,* ed. M. Lamberigts and P. Van Deun (Leuven: Peeters, 1995), 333–49; Elm, "O beatas," 160–62.

28. Thucydides 5.18.2, i.e., the terminology of the Peace of Nikias between Sparta and Athens in 421 BC; Dillon, *Pilgrims and Pilgrimage,* xiii–xix, 60–123.

29. *Apologia* 50, an upper-class Christian from Carthage, who wrote at the end of the second and the beginning of the third century AD; the bibliography on martyrdom is enormous; for details, see Lamberigts and Van Deun, *Martyrium in Multidisciplinary Perspective;* and Wiebke Bähnk, *Von der Notwendigkeit des Leidens: Die Theologie des Martyriums bei Tertullian* (Göttingen: Vandenhoeck and Ruprecht, 2001), esp. 193–282.

30. As illustrated by statements like that of the philosopher Justin, himself later a martyr, *Dialogue with Trypho,* 110.

31. Hazel Dodge, "Amusing the Masses: Buildings for Entertainment and Leisure in the Roman World," in *Life, Death and Entertainment in the Roman Empire,* ed. David Potter and David Mattingly (Ann Arbor: University of Michigan Press, 1999), 205–55; Keith Hopkins, *Death and Renewal* (Cambridge: Cambridge University Press, 1983), 7–20; David Potter, "Entertainers in the Roman Empire," in Potter and Mattingly, *Life, Death and Entertainment,* 256–326; Thomas Wiedemann, *Emperors and Gladiators* (London: Routledge, 1992), 1–26.

32. Katherine Coleman, "Fatal Charades: Roman Executions Staged as Mythological Enactments," *Journal of Roman Studies* 80 (1990): 44–73.

33. Carlin Barton, *The Sorrows of the Ancient Romans: The Gladiator and the Monster* (Princeton, N.J.: Princeton University Press, 1993), 113–75.

34. Coleman, "Fatal Charades," 60–70.

35. Bähnk, *Von der Notwendigkeit des Leidens,* 28–76; Brent Shaw, "The Passion of Perpetua," *Past and Present* 139 (1993): 1–45.

36. Judith Perkins, *The Suffering Self: Pain and Narrative Representation in the Early Christian Era* (London: Routledge, 1995); Bähnk, *Von der Notwendigkeit des Leidens,* 282–315; Bastiaensen, "Ecclesia Martyrum," 333–49.

37. Peter R. L. Brown, *The Cult of Saints: Its Rise and Function in Latin Christianity* (Chicago: University of Chicago Press, 1981), 1–22; Patrick Geary, *Living with the Dead in the Middle Ages* (Ithaca, N.Y.: Cornell University Press, 1994), 77–92.

38. Jer. *Ep.* 3.1; Georgia Frank, *The Memory of the Eyes: Pilgrims to Living Saints in Christian Late Antiquity* (Berkeley: University of California Press, 2000), 1–101; Elm; *Virgins of God,* 1–22, 253–82 and passim.

39. *PPMW,* 1–16; Patrick Geary, *Furta Sacra: Thefts of Relics in the Central Middle Ages* (Princeton, N.J.: Princeton University Press, 1990), 5–45.

40. *PPMW,* 20–43; Coleman and Elsner, *Pilgrimage Past and*

Present, 104–35; Swatos and Tomasi, *From Medieval Pilgrimage,* 4–17.

41. Jehle, *Der Mensch,* 273–85; Liliane Voyé, "Popular Religion and Pilgrimages in Western Europe," in Swatos and Tomasi, *From Medieval Pilgrimage,* 115–35.

42. Ruth Harris, *Lourdes: Body and Spirit in the Secular Age* (London: Penguin, 1999), 13.

43. Ibid., 177–209, 226–49, 320–56.

44. Ibid., 250–88; Coleman and Elsner, *Pilgrimage Past and Present,* 128–29; Voyé, "Popular Religion," 124–32.

45. Coleman, *Globalisation,* 5 and passim; Voyé, "Popular Religion," 116–30; Swatos and Tomasi, *From Medieval Pilgrimage,* 181–92; Barry Gardner, "Technological Changes and Monetary Advantages: The Growth of Evangelical Funding, 1945 to the Present," in *More Money, More Ministry: Money and Evangelicals in Recent North American History,* ed. Larry Eskridge and Mark Noll (Grand Rapids, Mich.: Eerdmans, 2002), 298–310.

CHAPTER 6A

1. Sources: Shoshana Bahat and Mordechai Mishor, *Dictionary of Contemporary Hebrew* (Tel Aviv: Maariv Book Guild, 1995); Bar Ilan University, Responsa TIRS Project (CD-ROM Database of Biblical and Rabbinic Literature); Eliezer Ben-Yehuda, *A Complete Dictionary of Ancient and Modern Hebrew* (New York: Thomas Yoseloff, 1960); Avraham Even-Shoshan, *The New Dictionary* (Jerusalem: Kiryat-Sefer, 1993) and *A New Concordance of the Bible* (Jerusalem: Kiryat-Sefer, 1982); Yakov Kna'ani, *A Treasury of the Hebrew Language in its Different Periods* (Tel Aviv: Masada, 1962).

CHAPTER 7

1. Elias Canetti, *The Torch in My Ear,* trans. Joachim Neugroschel (New York: Farrar Straus Giroux, 1982), 245. The incident triggered Canetti's book-length meditation on the power of the masses. See Canetti, *Crowds and Power,* trans. Carol Stewart (New York: Farrar Straus Giroux, 1984).

2. Heimito von Doderer, *The Demons,* trans. Richard and Clara Winston (New York: Knopf 1961), 1261.

3. Ernst Jünger, *Der Arbeiter* (Hamburg: Hanseatische Verlagsanstalt, 1932), 115. Unless otherwise noted, all translations are mine.

4. Le Bon's book was translated into German as *Psychologie der Massen* (Leipzig: Kröner) in 1919. The first English translation, *The Psychology of Peoples* (New York: Macmillan) appeared in 1898. On Le Bon and his context, see Susanna Barrows, *Distorting Mirrors: Visions of the Crowd in Late Nineteenth-Century France* (New Haven, Conn.: Yale University Press, 1981). See also Serge Moscovici, *The Age of the Crowd: A Historical Treatise on Mass Psychology* (New York: Cambridge University Press, 1985); Helmut König, *Zivilisation und Leidenschaften: Die Masse im bürgerlichen Zeitalter* (Hamburg: Rowohlt, 1992). It may not be a coincidence that in the same year, 1895, in which Le Bon published his psychology of the masses, the first films were shown in Paris and Berlin.

5. See Jakob Walcher, *Freud oder Marx? Die praktische Lösung der sozialen Lage* (Berlin: Neuer deutscher Verlag, 1925).

6. Michel Foucault, *Discipline and Punish: The Birth of the Prison* (New York: Vintage Books, 1979), 169.

7. Jünger, *Der Arbeiter,* 116.

8. See André Combes, "A partir du 'Metroplis' de Fritz Lang: La Gestalt de Masse et ses espaces," in *Théâtre et cinéma années vingt: Une quête de la modernité* (Lausanne: L'Age d'homme, [1990]), 2:178–224; Heide Schönemann, *Fritz Lang: Filmbilder-Vorbilder* (Berlin: Edition Hentrich, 1992).

9. Henry Ford's German translation, *Mein Leben und Werk* (Leipzig: Paul List, 1923), of his autobiography of 1923, *My Life and Work,* was a best-seller in the Weimar Republic.

10. See Peter Bogdanovich, *Fritz Lang in America* (London: Studio Vista, 1967), 124.

11. Alfred Döblin, *Berlin Alexanderplatz* (Olten: Walter, 1961), 31.

12. Even though there were so-called blue-collar movie houses in Berlin, the separation by class was not absolute. Proletarian-revolutionary films such as Eisenstein's *Potemkin* (1926) or Brecht's *Kuhle Wampe* (1932; *To Whom Does the World Belong?*) premiered in Berlin's bourgeois movie houses, and Chaplin's films, for example, also ran in the blue-collar houses. Mühl-Benninghaus has proven that *Potemkin,* a classic among leftist intellectuals, enjoyed no success with the workers, even with free tickets. See Wolfgang Mühl-Benninghaus, "Deutsch-russische Filmbeziehungen in der Weimarer Republik" in *Positionen deutscher Filmgeschichte,* ed. Michael Schaudig (Munich: Schaudig and Ledig, 1996), 91–118. Even a classic revolution film such as *Potemkin* was

not acknowledged primarily as a movie and entertainment spectacle by spectators. Thus from a critical-historical perspective, the political differences diminish between the almost contemporary films *Metropolis* and *Potemkin*.

13. Eugen Tannenbaum, "Der Großfilm," in *Der Film von morgen*, ed. Hugo Zehder (Berlin: Rudolf Kämmerer, 1923), 62; emphasis mine.

14. Siegfried Kracauer, "Cult of Distraction: On Berlin's Picture Palaces, in *The Mass Ornament*, ed. and trans. Thomas Y. Levin (Cambridge, Mass.: Harvard University Press, 1995), 325. See also Miriam Hansen, "America, Paris, the Alps: Kracauer (and Benjamin) on Cinema and Modernity," in *Cinema and the Invention of Modern Life*, ed. Leo Charney and Vanessa Schwartz (Berkeley: University of California Press, 1995), 362–402.

15. Kracauer, "Cult of Distraction," 325.

16. Walter Benjamin, "Rückblick auf Chaplin," in *Kino-Debatte*, ed. Anton Kaes (Munich: dtv, 1978), 175.

17. Friedrich Zelnik's 1927 film *Die Weber*, based on Gerhart Hauptmann's play and released a few months after *Metropolis*, also depicted a hopelessly failed proletarian revolution.

CHAPTER 7A

1. Sources: Vidyadhar Vaman Apte, *The Student's Sanskrit-English Dictionary* (Delhi: Motilal Banarsidass, 1970); Vidyadhar Vaman Apte, *A Concise Sanskrit-English Dictionary: Containing an Appendix on Sanskrit Prosody and Another on the Names of Noted Mythological Persons and a Map of Ancient India* (Delhi: Gian Publishing House, 1986); Babulall Pradhan, *English-Nepali Dictionary* (Varanasi: Trimurti Prakashan, 1993); Theodore Benfey, *A Sanskrit-English Dictionary, with References to the Best Editions of Sanskrit Authors and Etymologies and Comparisons of Cognate Words Chiefly in Greek, Latin, Gothic, and Anglo-Saxon* (London: Longmans, Green, 1866); O. N. Bimali and Ishvar Chandra, eds., *Mahabharata: Translated into English with Original Sanskrit Text* (Delhi: Parimal Publications, 2000); S. D. Joshi and J. Roodbergen, eds., *Ashtadhyayi of Panini* (New Delhi: Sahitya Akademi, 2003); Monier Monier-Williams, *A Sanskrit-English Dictionary: Etymologically and Philologically Arranged with Special Reference to Cognate Indo-European Languages* (Oxford: Clarendon Press, 1899); Monier Monier-Williams, *A Dictionary of English and Sanskrit* (Delhi: Motilal Banarsidass, 1964); Jayadeva, *Gitagovinda,*

trans. Barbara Stoler Miller (New York: Columbia University Press, 1997); R. L. Kashyap and S. Sadagopan, eds., *Rigveda* (Bangalore: Sri Aurobindo Kapali Shastry Institute of Vedic Culture, 1998); *Complete Works of Kalidasa,* trans. Sudhanshu Chaturvedi (Thrissur: Geetha, 2000); Manu, *The Laws of Manu* (Oxford: Clarendon Press, 1886); R. S. McGregor, ed., *The Oxford Hindi-English Dictionary* (Oxford: Oxford University Press, 1993); Ravi Prakash Arya, ed., *Ramayana of Valmiki: Sanskrit Text and English Translation According to M. N. Dutt* (Delhi: Parimal Publications, 1998); T. Rhys Davids and William Stede, eds., *Pali-English Dictionary* (New Delhi: Munshiram Manoharlal, 2001); Somadeva, *Kathasaritsagara,* trans. C. H. Tawney (Delhi: Munshiram Manoharlal, 1968).

CHAPTER 8

1. Charles Baudelaire, "Crowds," in *Paris Spleen* (1869), trans. Louise Varèse (New York: New Directions Publishing, 1970), 20–21. My reading of this poem is indebted to that of Jeffrey T. Schnapp, in *Staging Fascism: 18 BL and the Theater of Masses for Masses* (Stanford, Calif.: Stanford University Press, 1996), 100–103.

2. In "The Universal Exhibition of 1855," Baudelaire offers this definition: "Beauty always has an element of strangeness." *Baudelaire: Selected Writings on Art and Artists*, trans. P. E. Charvet (Harmondsworth: Penguin Books, 1972), 119. In "The Salon of 1846," Baudelaire writes, "All forms of beauty, like all possible phenomena, have within them something eternal and something transitory—an absolute and a particular element." *Baudelaire: Selected Writings on Art and Artists*, 104; hereafter abbreviated as "1846."

3. For Baudelaire, the artist/dandy finds his natural habitat in the crowd where he can be at once at its center, and yet invisible: "The crowd is his domain, just as the air is the bird's, and water that of the fish. His passion and his profession is to merge with the crowd. . . . To be away from home and yet to feel at home anywhere; to see the world, to be at the very centre of the world, and yet to be unseen of the world, such are some of the minor pleasures of those independent, intense and impartial spirits. . . . The observer is a prince enjoying his incognito wherever he goes." Baudelaire, "The Painter of Modern Life," in *Baudelaire: Selected Writings on Art and Artists*, 399–400.

4. Baudelaire, "Crowds," 70.

5. For a discussion of the dandy as "a creature who is all masks and impenetrable surfaces because he needs to shock in order to shield himself from the shocks administered by the modern metropolis," see Schnapp, *Staging Fascism*, 103. For Simmel's analysis of the effects of urban shock and of the leveling of difference as a result of the money economy, see "The Metropolis and Mental Life," in *On Individuality and Social Forms* (Chicago: University of Chicago Press, 1971), 330; this passage is also discussed in Schnapp, *Staging Fascism*, 101.

6. Baudelaire, "The Painter of Modern Life," 400.

7. Gustave Le Bon, *La Psychologie des foules* (Paris: Alcan, 1895); trans. as *The Crowd: A Study of the Popular Mind* (1896; reprint, London: Ernest Benn, 1952), 23; hereafter abbreviated as *C*.

8. Scipio Sighele, *L'Intelligenza della folla* (Turin: Fratelli Bocca, Editori, 1903), 66. This book reprints essays Sighele published during the 1890s, and correspondence with other theorists, including, among others, Tarde and the socialist Enrico Ferri. Sighele's earliest writing on the crowd was *La folla delinquente* (The Criminal Crowd) of 1891. All translations, unless otherwise indicated, are my own.

9. Gabriel Tarde, *The Laws of Imitation*, trans. Elsie Clews Parsons from the 2nd ed. (1890; reprint, New York: Henry Holt, 1903); hereafter abbreviated as *LI*.

10. For a discussion of critical responses to the rise of consumerism, see Rosalind H. Williams, *Dream Worlds: Mass Consumption in Late Nineteenth-Century France* (Berkeley: University of California Press, 1982).

11. *C*, 149; *LI*, xiv, and Tarde, "The Public and the Crowd," from *L'Opinion et la foule* (1901), in *Gabriel Tarde: On Communication and Social Influence, Selected Papers*, ed. Terry N. Clark (Chicago: University of Chicago Press, 1969), 277–94.

12. Bernard Comment observes that Robert Barker's first panorama in Edinburgh was addressed to connoisseurs, with an entrance fee of three shillings. But the fee was soon dropped to two shillings, and then to one not long after Barker installed his panorama in London. See Bernard Comment, *The Panorama*, trans. Anne-Marie Glasheen (London: Reaktion Books, 1999), 115; hereafter abbreviated as *P*.

13. Stephen Oettermann, *The Panorama: History of a Mass Medium*, trans. Deborah Lucas Schneider (New York: Zone Books, 1997), 158–60, and *P*, 47–49.

14. Jacques Ignace Hittorf, "Description de la rotonde des panoramas élevée dans les Champs-Elysées: Précédé d'un aperçu historique sur l'origine des panoramas et les principales constructions auxquelles ils ont donné lieu," *Revue générale de l'architecture et des travaux publics*, 2 (1841); cited in *P*, 49.

15. Germain Bapst, *Essai sur l'histoire des panoramas et des dioramas: Extrait des rapports du jury international de l'Exposition universelle de 1889* (Paris, 1891); cited in *P*, 47.

16. See Silvia Bordini, *Storia del Panorama: La visione totale nella pittura del XIX secolo* (Rome: Officina Edizioni, 1984), 58–60.

17. T. J. Clark, *The Painting of Modern Life: Paris in the Art of Manet and His Followers* (Princeton, N.J.: Princeton University Press, 1984), 64.

18. Robert L. Herbert established the importance of Jules Chéret's posters for Seurat, and many direct borrowings of figures, in "Seurat and Jules Chéret," *Art Bulletin* 40 (1958): 156–58. Jonathan Crary has identified Emile Reynaud's phantasmagorical system of projecting film strips in an optical device called a praxinoscope as another possible model. One of the filmstrips for praxinoscope theater captures the acrobatic movements of a clown and the dispersed audience in images that are strikingly similar to their disposition in *Cirque*. Crary points out that Chéret and Reynaud were linked as exemplars of contemporary popular culture, and that Chéret made posters for Reynaud's *Pantomimes Lumineuses*. See Crary, *Suspensions of Perception: Attention, Spectacle, and Modern Culture* (Cambridge, Mass.: MIT Press, 2001), 259–78.

19. For an historical discussion of the Cirque Fernando, later called the Cirque Medrano, see Catherine Strasser, *Seurat: Cirque pour un monde nouveau* (Paris: Éditions Adam Biro, 1991), 10–12; and Michael F. Zimmermann, *Seurat and the Art Theory of his Time* (Antwerp: Fonds Mercator, 1991), 380–82.

20. Georges Lecomte, "Le Salon des Indépendants," *L'art dans les deux mondes* (March 28, 1891); cited in Zimmermann, *Seurat*, 380.

21. For analyses of Seurat's knowledge and use of the work of these and other theorists, see Herbert, "Seurat and Jules Chéret"; Zimmermann, *Seurat*; and Crary, *Suspensions of Perception*.

22. Georges Seurat, letter to Maurice Beaubourg, August 28, 1890; reprinted in translation in Richard Thomson, *Seurat* (Oxford: Phaidon Press, 1985), 225.

23. See Jonathan Crary's fascinating discussion of Seurat's *Parade de Cirque* and *Cirque* from the point of view of theories of social psychology and perception, including Tarde and Le Bon, as well as the "dynamogeny" of William James and Charles-Edouard Brown-Séquard, in *Suspensions of Perception*, 164–88, 230–47.

24. Strasser, *Seurat*, 10–11, 22.

25. For a discussion of the "controlling figures" in *Parade de Cirque* and *Cirque* as examples of "grands magnétiseurs," see Crary, *Suspensions of Perception*, 244.

26. Meyer Schapiro, "Seurat" (1958), in *Modern Art: 19th and 20th Centuries, Selected Papers* (New York: George Braziller, 1978), 108.

27. Ibid., 109.

28. Anonymous (attributed to Paul Signac), "Variétés: Impressionnistes & Révolutionnaires," *La Révolte*, June 13–19, 1891, 3–4; cited in T. J. Clark, *Farewell to an Idea: Episodes from a History of Modernism* (New Haven, Conn.: Yale University Press, 1999), 108.

29. F. T. Marinetti, "The Founding and Manifesto of Futurism" (published in *Le Figaro* [Paris], February 20, 1909); reprinted in F. T. Marinetti, *Let's Murder the Moonshine: Selected Writings*, ed. R. W. Flint, trans. R. W. Flint and Arthur A. Coppotelli (Los Angeles: Sun and Moon Classics, 1991), 50.

30. This painting, as Ester Coen has shown, was originally exhibited under the title *Una Baruffa* (A Brawl), in late 1910 and early 1911. See Umberto Boccioni, ex. cat. (New York: Metropolitan Museum of Art, September 15, 1988–January 8, 1989), 93. The work is related to another painting, now titled *The Raid*, depicting the arrest of a prostitute. This latter work was exhibited in 1911 with the title *Care puttane* (Dear Prostitutes). For further discussion of these works in the context of the Futurist appropriation of crowd theory, see Christine Poggi, "*Folla/Follia*: Futurism and the Crowd," *Critical Inquiry* 28, no. 3 (Spring 2002): 709–48.

31. Sighele, *L'Intelligenza della folla*, 7. Sighele was well known in Futurist circles because of his affiliations with the Nationalist movement. In 1911, he traveled to the Libyan War with Marinetti.

32. Umberto Boccioni, Carlo Carrà, Luigi Russolo, Giacomo Balla, and Gino Severini, "Futurist Painting: Technical Manifesto" (1910), in *Futurist Manifestos*, ed. Umbro Apollonio (Boston: ArtWorks, MFA Publications, 2001), 28. The text was largely written by Boccioni.

33. Sighele, *Intelligenza della folla*, 4. According to Sighele, the passage cited here refers to ideas already published in *La Coppia criminale*, 2nd ed. (Turin: Fratelli Bocca Editori, 1897).

34. For a cultural and scientific history of arc lighting, see Wolfgang Schivelbusch, *Disenchanted Night: The Industrialization of Light in the Nineteenth Century*, trans. Angela Davies (Berkeley: University of California Press, 1988), 52–57, 114–20.

35. Sonia Delaunay, *Nous irons jusqu'au soleil* (Paris: Editions Robert Laffont, 1978), 43; cited in Sherry A. Buckberrough, *Sonia Delaunay: A Retrospective*, ex. cat. (Buffalo, N.Y.: Albright Knox Art Gallery, 1980), 29.

36. In 1913 Sonia Delaunay and Blaise Cendrars created the first "simultanist poem," *La Prose du Transsibérien et de la Petite Jehanne de France*. The poem consisted of a text by Cendrars and stenciled colored forms intended to be read simultaneously. For a documentary history of this work, see Antoine Sidoti, ed., *La Prose du Transsibérien et de la Petite Jehanne de France: Genèse et dossier d'une polémique* (Paris: Lettres Modernes, 1987). See also Marjorie Perloff, *The Futurist Moment: Avant-Garde, Avant-Guerre, and the Language of Rupture* (Chicago: University of Chicago Press, 1986), chap. 1.

37. Blaise Cendrars, *Poésies complètes* (Paris: Éditions Denoël, 2001), 1:70–71.

38. See, e.g., *Light Study, Boulevard Saint-Michel*, Paris, 1912–1913, no. 205, and *Light Study, Boulevard Saint-Michel*, Paris, 1912, no. 208, in Jacques Damase, *Sonia Delaunay: Rhythms and Colours* (Greenwich, Conn.: New York Graphic Society, 1972), 70–71. The numbers refer to those in Sonia Delaunay's personal inventory.

39. Jules Romains, *La vie unanime: Poème 1904–1907* (Paris: Gallimard, 1983), 98.

40. Simmel, "Metropolis and Mental Life," 330.

41. Sonia Delaunay, cited in Dominique Desanti, *Sonia Delaunay, magique magicienne* (Paris: Éditions Ramsay, 1988), 147.

42. See Poggi, "*Folla/Follia*," 736–42.

43. See, e.g., Balla's series of 1898, *Macchiette romane* (Roman Characters) which portrays various street vendors, or *The Worker's Day* of 1904–1905, which shows workers at leisure.

44. For a reproduction of this drawing, see Giovanni Lista, *Giacomo Balla, Futuriste* (Lausanne: L'Age d'Homme, 1984), 224, no. 1219.

45. See Chanlaine, *Mussolini parle* (Paris: Tallandier, 1932),

61; cited in Serge Moscovici, *The Age of the Crowd: A Historical Treatise on Mass Psychology*, trans. J. C. Whitehouse (Cambridge: Press Syndicate of the University of Cambridge, 1985), 63.

46. Gustav Klutsis, "Fotomontazh kak novyi vid agitatsionnogo iskusstva," in *Izofront: Klassovaia bor'ba na fronte prostranstvennykh iskusstv: Sbornik statei ob'edineniia Oktiabr'* (Leningrad: Izofront, 1931), 124; discussed in Margarita Tupitsyn, *The Soviet Photograph, 1924–1937* (New Haven, Conn.: Yale University Press, 1996), 114–19.

47. [Aleksandr Rodchenko?], in *Izofront*, 150; cited in Tupitsyn, *Soviet Photograph*, 100–101.

48. My thanks to Ilya Vinitsky and Masha Kowell for their translations of the Russian text and explanation of its social context.

49. From Kulagina's diaries, August 24, 1934. Kulagina cites this response by Klutsis to a criticism that he had put sugary, smiling women in the foreground of one of his posters, and the courageous men in the background. See Tupitsyn, *Soviet Photograph*, 164–65. Kulagina's diaries further complain that Klutsis was paid five times more for government commissions than she was.

50. For an analysis of this transition within Soviet artistic practice, see Benjamin Buchloh, "From Faktura to Factography," *October* 30 (Fall 1984): 82–119.

51. In a diary entry from 1934, Kulagina noted these changes on the production of her posters, partly as a result of a new policy of sending poster designs to the Central Committee rather than IZOGIZ for approval: "As of the 21 [of August], none of the posters have yet been put into production; [they] have been sent to Tsk [Central Committee of Communist Party]. And of course, two of mine have been rejected. Try to work here! There are so many difficulties, whereas [posters] pass through IZOGIZ [a publishing house in Moscow, established in 1930 and initially charged with commissioning photomontage posters, books, and magazines on art]." Cited in Tupitsyn, *Soviet Photograph*, 161.

52. Goebbels cited in Ulrich Pohlmann, "El Lissitzky's Exhibition Designs: The Influence of His Work in Germany, Italy, and the United States, 1923–1943," in *El Lissitzky: Beyond the Abstract Cabinet: Photography, Design, Collaboration*, ed. Margarita Tupitsyn, ex. cat. (New Haven, Conn.: Yale University Press, 1999), 61. For a further discussion of Goebbels's speech and of the role of *Die Kamera* as Nazi propaganda, see Rolf Sachsse, "Propaganda für Industrie und Weltanschauung," in *Inszenierung der Macht: Aesthetische Faszination im Faschismus*, ed. Klaus Behnken and Frank Wagner (Berlin: NGBK, Nishen, 1987), 274–81.

53. As an adolescent, Bayer participated in the Austrian Youth Movement. In 1928 he left the Bauhaus, where he taught typography and advertising, to become director of art and design at the Dorland Advertising Agency in Berlin. Most books on Bayer make no mention of his work for the National Socialists, instead picturing him as bravely resisting the Nazis. See, e.g., Alexander Dorner, *The Way Beyond "Art": The Work of Herbert Bayer* (New York: Wittenborn, Schultz, 1947).

54. Cited in Pohlmann, "El Lissitzky's Exhibition Designs," 62–63. For a reproduction of several pages of the brochure, see "Inszenierung der Macht: Herbert Bayer, Kataloggestaltung," in *Inszenierung der Macht*, 285–96.

55. For a discussion of the mass panorama generally, and in particular for an analysis of the large-scale foldouts representing crowds in the Italian fascist daily *Rivista Illustrata del Popolo*, see Jeffrey T. Schnapp, "The Mass Panorama," *Modernism/Modernity* 9, no. 2 (2002): 243–81.

56. For a description of the exhibition, including the installation plan, wall texts, and installation shots, see "Road to Victory: A Procession of Photographs of the Nation at War," *Bulletin of the Museum of Modern Art* 9, nos. 5–6 (June 1942): 1–21. This exhibition was planned in October 1941, but it took on a new significance when the United States entered the war. Most of the photographs were supplied by departments and agencies of the government.

57. For a detailed description of the process of mounting the mural, see "Road to Victory," 19.

58. See Pohlmann, "El Lissitzky's Exhibition Designs," 59–64, and Buchloh, "From Faktura to Factography," 82–119.

59. Warhol cited in Gene Swensen, "What is Pop Art? Answers from 8 Painters, Part 1," *Art News* 62 (November 1963): 26.

60. Andy Warhol, *The Philosophy of Andy Warhol (From A to B and Back Again)* (New York: Harcourt Brace Jovanovich, 1975), 100–101.

61. For an insightful analysis of Warhol's relation to media culture and his representations of mass subjectivity, see Hal Foster, "Death in America," *October*, no. 75 (Winter 1996): 53–58.

62. Warhol, *Philosophy*, 154.

63. For a discussion of Warhol's two versions of *The Crowd*, see Schnapp, "Mass Panorama," 276–78.

64. This version is reproduced in Schnapp, "Mass Panorama," 277.

65. As documentation of the crash, Beuys provided photographs, but their validity has been questioned. For an account of the crash, see Heiner Stachelhaus, *Joseph Beuys*, trans. David Britt (New York: Abbeville Press, 1987), 21–23. The effects of the "rebirth" must have been delayed because after Beuys had recovered sufficiently, he was redeployed and was wounded four more times, finally becoming a British prisoner of war. Regardless of the accuracy of the story of crash, however, there is no doubt that Beuys's war experience was traumatic, or that he suffered a mental breakdown and severe depression during the years 1954 to 1957.

66. Joseph Beuys, interview by Caroline Tisdall, 1978; cited in Tisdall, *Joseph Beuys*, ex. cat. (New York: Solomon R. Guggenheim Museum, 1979), 190.

67. Norbert Kricke, statement in *Die Zeit* (December 20, 1968); cited in Stachelhaus, *Joseph Beuys*, 94.

68. For a discussion of *braunkreuz* and its role as a "signature" material, see Ann Temkin, *Thinking Is Form: The Drawings of Joseph Beuys*, ex. cat. (Philadelphia and New York: The Philadelphia Museum of Art and the Museum of Modern Art, New York, 1993), 37–46.

69. Elias Canetti, *Crowds and Power*, trans. Carol Stewart (New York: Viking Press, 1962), 93–96; hereafter abbreviated as *CP*. William Trotter similarly called attention to the primitive animal herd as a prototype of social organisms, formed out of self-defense or to increase strength in pursuit or attack. Trotter emphasizes the homogeneity of the herd, which allows it to act as one, as well as the secondary associations of warmth and security provided by close crowding. See *Instincts of the Herd in Peace and War* (London: T. Fisher Unwin, 1916), 27–31.

70. Telephone interview with the artist, September 12, 2003. See also Coosje van Bruggen, *John Baldessari* (New York: Rizzoli, 1990), 163.

71. The photographic sources are reproduced in John Tagg, "A Discourse (With Shape of Reason Missing)," in *Vision and Textuality*, eds. Stephen Melville and Bill Readings (Durham, N.C.: Duke University Press, 1995), 95.

72. Tagg, "Discourse," 92. Tagg also analyses this work in the light of Canetti's *Crowds and Power*.

73. Sigmund Freud cites long passages of Le Bon's *Psychologie des foules* with approval in *Group Psychology and the Analysis of the Ego*, trans. and ed. James Strachey (1921; reprint, New York: W. W. Norton, 1959). Like Le Bon, he believes the crowd is "impulsive, changeable and irritable. It is led almost exclusively by the unconscious" (9). See also the discussion of the "Herd Instinct" (49–53). For a discussion of the crowd's desire for a direction, often issuing from a command, see *CP*, 29, 303–4, 310–11.

74. Gabriel Tarde, "The Public and the Crowd" (1901), in *On Communication and Social Influence: Selected Papers*, ed. Terry N. Clark (Chicago: University of Chicago Press, 1969), 277.

75. Tarde, "The Public and the Crowd," 278–81.

76. Tarde, "Opinion and Conversation" (1898), in *On Communication and Social Influence*, 312; hereafter abbreviated as "OC."

77. See also the discussion of smaller publics, each of which seeks to have its own newspaper: "OC," 284–87.

78. Whereas Tarde emphasized the power of the journalist to sway his readers (who have chosen which papers to read), Le Bon viewed the press as humbled before the power of the crowd, whose opinions it merely reflects. See also the discussion in Moscovici, *Age of the Crowd*, 195–215.

79. This photograph was inspired by a news photograph of the Tokyo stock exchange. Gursky saw the image while making plans for a trip to Tokyo in 1990 on the occasion of an opening of an exhibition that included his work. Peter Galassi, *Andreas Gursky*, ex. cat. (New York: Museum of Modern Art, 2001), 28.

80. Katy Siegel, "The Big Picture: The Art of Andreas Gursky—Consuming Vision," *Artforum* 39, no. 5 (January 2001): 105.

81. Holzer wrote the *Truisms* in an impersonal voice that cannot be confused with her position as an author. As she remarks: "I try to polish them so they sound as if they had been said for a hundred years, but they're mine . . . to write a quality cliché you have to come up with something new." Yet she acknowledges that the *Truisms* are based on reading a great many texts. Insofar as we recognize these views, Holzer cannot be seen as their "author" so much as their promulgator, nor are the views expressed "new" so much as rewritten in condensed form. Jenny Holzer quoted in Jeanne Siegel, "Jenny Holzer's Language Games" (interview), *Arts Magazine* 60 (December 1985): 65.

82. Kentridge explains his position in these terms: "Aware of and drawing sustenance from the anomaly of my position. At the edge of huge social upheavals, yet also removed from them. Not able to be part of these upheavals, nor to work as if they did not exist." Cited in Carolyn Christov-Bakargiev, *William Kentridge*, ex. cat. (Brussels: Palais des Beaux-Arts, 1998), 56.

83. Kentridge cited in ibid., 75.

84. Kentridge cited in Neal Benezra, "William Kentridge: Drawings for Projection," in *William Kentridge*, Neal Benezra, Staci Boris and Dan Cameron, curators, ex. cat. (New York: Abrams, 2001), 15.

85. Dan Cameron, "A Procession of the Dispossessed," in *William Kentridge* (London: Phaidon Press, 1999), 56–57.

86. Rosalind Krauss, "'The Rock': William Kentridge's Drawing for Projection," *October*, no. 92 (Spring 2000): 4–9, and passim.

87. William Kentridge, "'Fortuna': Neither Programme nor Chance in the Making of Images" (extract, 1993), in *William Kentridge* (London: Phaidon Press, 1999), 117.

88. According to Kentridge, the megaphone derives from "a photograph of Lenin speaking into a megaphone I had seen in John Willet's *The New Sobriety*. Also one often sees that horn in Max Beckmann paintings." Cited in Benezra, "William Kentridge," 15.

CHAPTER 8A

1. All Latin definitions are taken from the *Oxford Latin Dictionary*, ed. P. G. W. Glare (Oxford: Oxford University Press, 1997). All English definitions are taken from the *Oxford English Dictionary*, ed. J. A. Simpson and E. S. C. Weiner, 2nd ed. (Oxford: Clarendon Press, 1989); and the OED online (http://www.oed.com/).

CHAPTER 8B

1. The first citation is from D. Cantimori, *Galileo e la crisi della Controriforma*, in *Storici e storia* (Turin: Einaudi, 1971), 637 ff.; those from E. Canetti in *Masse e potere* (Milan, Rizzoli, 1972), 27–41. In general, cf. A. Petrucci, *La scrittura: Ideologia e rappresentazione* (Turin, Einaudi, 1986); A. Pinelli, *Feste e trionfi: Continuità e metamorfosi di un tema*, in *Memoria dell'antico nell'arte italiana: II. I generi e i temi ritrovati* (with further bibliography), ed. S. Settis (Turin: Einaudi, 1984–1986). For Italian sports writings, cf. A. Ricci, *Graffiti: Scritte di scritti: Dalle epigrafi fasciste alla bomboletta spray* (Manziana: Vecchiarelli, 2003).

CHAPTER 9

I am grateful to Linda Schlossberg, Sean McCann, Alex Star, David Cunningham, Peter Knight, Jeffrey Schnapp, and Matthew Tiews for conversations and insightful critiques of an earlier draft of this article.

1. David Riesman with Nathan Glazer and Reuel Denney, *The Lonely Crowd* (1950; abridged and revised 1961; New Haven, Conn.: Yale University Press, 1989), 307; hereafter abbreviated as *LC*.

2. Hannah Pitkin, *The Attack of the Blob: Hannah Arendt's Concept of the Social* (Chicago: University of Chicago Press, 1998).

3. Habermas's *The Structural Transformation of the Public Sphere* is far more indebted to Arendt's work on "the social" and "the public" than it acknowledges, and surprisingly ready to align itself with John Stuart Mill's fear of "the social" as invidious internal enemy.

4. Richard H. Pells, *The Liberal Mind in a Conservative Age* (Middletown, Conn.: Wesleyan University Press, 1985, 1989), 247.

5. William H. Whyte, *The Organization Man* (New York: Simon and Schuster, 1956), 397; italics in original; hereafter abbreviated as *OM*.

6. As I discuss below, the functionalism that dominated midcentury academic sociology produced fascinating value-neutral-oriented responses like that of Erving Goffman, as well as the resolutely microstructural "ethnomethodology" of Harold Garfinckel, usefully summarized in Anne Rawls, "Harold Garfinckel," in *The Blackwell Companion to Major Contemporary Social Theorists*, ed. George Ritzer (Oxford: Blackwell, 2003), 122–53. I do not mean to underestimate the sway that Parsons held, merely to suggest that our account of the 1950s in social science is radically incomplete if we neglect the historicist, agent-oriented, and resolutely preachy sociology of writers like Arendt and Riesman, for whom the problem of social forces destroying individual autonomy oozed through every intellectual crack.

7. Todd Stillman, "Introduction: Metatheorizing Contemporary Social Theorists," in Ritzer, *Blackwell Companion,* 1–11.

8. Michael Schudson, *The Good Citizen: A History of American Civic Life* (New York: Free Press, 1998).

9. Zygmunt Baumann, "On Glocalization: Or Globalization for Some, Localization for Some Others," *Thesis Eleven* 54 (1988): 37–49.

10. D. J. Waldie, *Holy Land: A Suburban Memoir* (New York: Norton, 1996).

11. M. P. Baumgartner, *The Moral Order of a Suburb* (New York: Oxford University Press, 1988).

12. In fact, the latter-day descendant of *The Stepford Wives,* the 1996 television movie *Stepford Husbands,* effectively inverts the logic of the original because it presumes that women are horrifying precisely because they want to make their husbands into emasculated lock-ins. In other words, the horror of suburbia is that it removes men from their ordinary round of social activities; it traps them at home. In the original, the horror resided in the idea that men were robotizing women precisely to make them into nothing more than reliable social beings, members of golf and sewing clubs.

13. Robert Putnam, *Bowling Alone: The Collapse and Revival of American Community* (New York: Simon and Schuster, 2000); hereafter abbreviated as *BA.* Putnam's 2003 *Better Together,* written with Lewis Feldstein and Don Cohen (New York: Simon and Schuster), continues the logic of *Bowling Alone* by way of twelve case studies of "restored American communities" ranging from UPS to CraigsList.org to a Boston union. In each case, the laudation is reserved for those who decide to agglomerate for the pure sake of agglomerating—the UPS vans that meet for lunch, the church that offers a coffee bar as well as a service. Cohesion for its own sake is king.

14. Pells, *Liberal Mind,* 232.

15. Todd Gitlin, in a moving memoir appended as preface to the 2001 Yale edition of *The Lonely Crowd* (xi–xx), insists that Riesman's later life was dedicated to nurturing just such forms of opposition group. But the language of *The Lonely Crowd* is clear in its distrust of any organizing against organization.

16. Riesman also laments that Ayn Rand's *The Fountainhead* didn't go far enough in praising individuals. In any case, he believes it exaggerates the freedom an architect would actually have in the oversocialized present: "to be admired perhaps by the reader but too stagey to be imitated" (*LC,* 156).

17. Clinton Rossiter's *Constitutional Tyranny: Crisis Government in the Modern Democracies* (Princeton, N.J.: Princeton University Press, 1948) is typical of the age in its fear of "the social" run amok, whether in communist countries or here at home.

18. Riesman quoted in Kim Phillips-Fein, "The Lonely Crowd," *Dissent* 49, no. 4 (Fall 2002): 88.

19. Nor is it social science alone that manifests this fear. As a number of recent histories, among them Timothy Melley's *Empire of Conspiracy* (Ithaca, N.Y.: Cornell University Press, 2000) have argued, the popular culture of the 1950s and 1960s was bombarded with images of alien infiltration and mental cooptation. Compared with the paranoid heights of some utterly mainstream science fiction writing and films of the era, the feverish ravings of Philip K. Dick sound anodyne.

20. Jason Kaufman, *For the Common Good: American Civic Life and the Golden Age of Fraternity* (Oxford: Oxford University Press, 2002).

21. Examples drawn from various chapters in *The Lonely Crowd,* including 3:2, 4:3, 6:1.

22. There is a fascinating analogy here to Erving Goffman's accounts of city walking as the ultimate form of "face-to-face interaction." Goffman's empirical contention is that walkers in a city virtually never collide with each other because they are constantly making microscopic adjustments to avoid what otherwise would be statistically inevitable bumps. For Goffman, this demonstrates how implicitly we rely on our social radar, even when we think of ourselves as "abstracted" or "alone." To Riesman, it might seem another germ of corruption.

23. Randall Jarrell, *Pictures from an Institution* (1952; reprint, Chicago: University of Chicago Press, 1986), 11.

24. Phillips-Fein, "Lonely Crowd," 88.

25. Sloane Wilson, *The Man in the Gray Flannel Suit* (New York: Simon and Schuster, 1955), 204–5.

26. Ibid, 210.

27. Gary Alan Fine and Philip Manning, "Erving Goffmann," in Ritzer, *Blackwell Companion,* 34.

28. Adam Kendon, "Goffman's Approach to Face to Face Interaction" in *Erving Goffman: Exploring the Interaction Order,* ed. Paul Drew and Anthony Wooton (Oxford: Polity Press, 1988), 14–

40. See also Drew and Wooton, introduction, 1–13, and "Goffman as a Systematic Social Theorist," 250–79.

29. Goffman quoted in Kendon, "Goffman's Approach," 36.

30. Frederic Jameson, "On Goffman's Frame Analysis," *Theory and Society* 3 (Spring 1976): 119–33.

31. Goffman, *Interaction Ritual* (Garden City, N.J.: Anchor Books, 1967), 3.

32. Ibid., 120.

33. In one odd moment, Goffman goes out of his way to explain that different social modalities around one's intrusion of self into a conversation (saying "I," speaking of oneself, and so on) will lead to awkward breaks in conversation when members of different cultures meet. Goffman then moves quickly to gloss such moments of cultural confusion by urging that we treat such interactions not as representative of the personality of the member of a foreign culture but instead as determined entirely by cultural practices: "It is to these differences in expressive customs that we ought to look first in trying to account for the improper behavior of those with whom we happen to be participating and not try, initially at least, to find some source of blame within the personalities of the offenders" (*Interaction Ritual,* 125). This odd passage perfectly typifies some of Goffman's tics. He presumes that a discovery of difference will inevitably lead to the judgment that the other's behavior is "improper" because it is not the same as one's own—an implicitly ethical valence that Goffman then moves to neutralize by saying that the culture, not the person, is to blame.

34. Erving Goffman, *Asylums: Essays on the Social Situation of Mental Patients and Other Inmates* (Chicago: Aldine, 1961).

35. Or, as he puts it in *City,* "What attracts people most is other people. Many urban spaces are being designed as though the opposite were true, and what people like best are the places they stay away from." William Whyte, *City: Rediscovering the Center* (New York: Doubleday, 1988), 9.

36. Jane Jacobs, *The Death and Life of Great American Cities* (New York: Random House, 1961), 14, 135, 150.

37. Excepting perhaps Marx and Engels's *The Communist Manifesto*—if it counts as sociology, and if sales figures were available for it.

38. The phrase has been variously attributed, most reputably to Glenn Loury, and the concept certainly has a substantial intellectual life among economists. Gary Becker and James Coleman,

among others, have made independent use of it.

39. All numbers are derived from LexisNexis. Interestingly, "lonely crowd" had 212 recorded usages in journals and newspapers over the last ten years, still a fairly respectable showing for a fifty-year-old phrase.

40. I am grateful to Alex Star for the reference to Barber's memoir; the most famous European flap involves a junior minister in Tony Blair's Labour government reportedly demoted for criticizing Putnam openly during one of his high-profile visits to 10 Downing Street.

41. There also seem to be a sizable number of venture firms and young entrepreneurial organizations with variations on the phrase "social capital" in their title: Googling the phrase yields, for example, SocialCapitalPartners.ca, a Canadian "social venture" firm, and a range of other quasi-commercial undertakings above the link to Putnam's own site, BowlingAlone.com.

42. See the special issue of *American Prospect* (Winter 1996).

43. James Surowiecki, *The Wisdom of Crowds* (New York: Doubleday, 2004).

44. Putnam finesses the difference between the 1950s and the 1890s, which were, according to Jason Kaufman, the true highwater mark of such associations. By Kaufman's account, in the 1890s, virtually all such organizations were explicitly ethnically segregated. As associationism declined in the early twentieth century and mutual insurance became a less important reason to join a club, memberships became more segregated by class than by ethnicity. Hence what Putnam sees in the 1950s is by Kaufman's logic only a feeble trickle-down from the great flood of fifty years earlier—and in fact a trickle that is certainly segregated by class, a fact that is disguised because class and neighborhood correspond so perfectly. Putnam can call it neighborhood assortment of a common nationwide phenomenon, but by another reading, the numbers reveal associations still devoted to assorting people by class status.

45. William Schambra endorses Edmund Burke's notion of local legions of decency in "All Community Is Local," in *Community Works: The Revival of Civic Life in America* (Washington, D.C.: Brookings Institution, 1998). Only in loyalty to our nearby platoon, writes Burke, do we understand our loyalty to the world—a line of reasoning that resonates well with Putnam's account of a social life mediated by small groups but ultimately potentially uniform on the national level.

46. Thus, for example, Putnam lauds Baumgartner's *The Moral Order of a Suburb,* which criticizes suburbs for having an "avoidance" mechanism for resolving conflict, instead of fights or legal remediation, which are the admirable alternatives practiced by small towns or well-functioning city neighborhoods.

47. Putnam may want to take warning from an Internet experiment that attempts to overcome the medium's inherent permissiveness and potentially free access and exit. Judith Donath of the MIT Media Labs, who introduced something called Chat Circles (http://chatcircles.media.mit.edu/about.html), a Web site that is open uniformly to everyone on the Web; avoids mandating any kind of conversational topic or avatar; and tries in small, technical ways to replicate the human crowdedness of a real conversational space, like a kitchen at a party or a meeting hall. Chat Circles, however, has been unsuccessful, perhaps because it makes physical movement through its "circles" deliberately difficult, and perhaps because it does not offer a topic like BMWs for members to discuss. Conversely, however, one of the most clearly successful features of the Internet has been instant messaging among teenagers, whose conversations are voluntarily restricted—with no technical assistance from Internet modalities—to the chat circles they have chosen to form with their own classmates at school.

48. Richard Hoggart, *The Uses of Literacy* (London: Chatto and Windus, 1957).

49. Robert Allen, "Frequently Asked Questions," in *The Television Studies Reader,* ed. Robert Allen and Annette Hill (Routledge: London, 2004), 7. Cf. *Television Studies,* ed. Toby Miller (London: BFI, 2002).

50. McCarthy's *Ambient Television: Visual Culture and Public Space* (Durham, N.C.: Duke University Press, 2001) is a deft discussion of the phenomenon of attending mass televised spectacles, such as going to a stadium to watch, on giant screens, a game being played elsewhere.

51. Whether the effect of the Internet is to balkanize viewership is a topic of much current debate.

52. Philip Larkin, "Vers de Societe" (1974, in *High Windows*), reprinted in *Collected Poems* (London: Faber and Faber, 2003), 147. To be fair, the poem does go on to muse, "funny, how hard it is to be alone" and it ends by almost seeming to accept the awful invitation: "Beyond the light stand failure and remorse/Whispering *Dear Warlock Williams: Why, of course—*"

53. I am indebted to Philip Joseph's forthcoming book, *Local Grounds,* for one compelling account of such important voices in the civil society debate as Michael Walzer; Michael Schudson; Benjamin Barber, *A Place for Us* (New York: Hill and Wang, 1998); Michael J. Sandel, *Democracy's Discontent: America in Search of a Public Philosophy* (Cambridge, Mass.: Harvard University Press, 1996); and Andrew Arato and Jean Cohen, *Civil Society and Social Theory* (Cambridge, Mass.: MIT Press, 1997).

54. Eric Klineberg, *Heat Wave: A Social Autopsy of Disaster in Chicago* (Chicago: University of Chicago Press, 2002); Mitch Dunier, *Sidewalk* (New York: Farrar Straus Giroux, 1999).

55. In a suggestive set of essays translated as *Solidarity, Solitude* (trans. Lillian Vallee [New York: Ecco, 1990]), the Polish poet Adam Zagajewski argues that even the most socially conscious and collectively minded thinker is obliged to retreat into solitude in order best to serve the forces of solidarity. Zagajewski's formulation is slightly different from Arendt's but equally provocative. For Arendt, it is in the very act of seeking solitary thought that we can best "represent others" to ourselves, through a proper understanding of their words and thoughts. For Zagajewski, "the collectivity doesn't have to be the subject or the severe and immediate judge of emotions or visions. It does after all consist of single, solitary (in using this word I want to deprive it of the perverse poeticalness existentialism has lent it) individuals who, if they are consumed by a spiritual quest, need not check every minute to see if there is a leash tying them to the rest of society" (88). To Zagajewski, then, it is only our reports back to the "collectivity" that bespeak our solidarity. For both thinkers, however, the social is redeemed not by sacrificing to it the individual impulse, but by finding a framework within which what the individual does and thinks best can be returned, after suitable hiatus, to social play.

56. Florence Nightingale, "Cassandra," in *Cassandra and Other Selections from Suggestions for Thought,* ed. Mary Poovey (New York: NYU Press, 1992), 210.

57. Marcel Proust, *Swann's Way*, trans. C. K. Scott Moncrieff (New York: Random House, 1934), 3. Apropos of the question of whether the Internet can perform the same kind of mental transport that a book does, it is intriguing to note that there are recent accounts of schizophrenic patients reporting that they are convinced that their thoughts or their mind are being "surfed" from one Web page to another. They describe that motion as being controlled not by themselves, but by someone else's Internet browser. This paranoid fantasy of long-distance manipulation

showcases in extremis the sort of imaginary mental travel that can occur via the World Wide Web.

CHAPTER 10

1. Salvador Giner, "Mass Society: History of the Concept," *International Encyclopedia of the Social and Behavioral Sciences,* ed. Neil J. Smelser and Paul B. Baltes (Amsterdam: Elsevier, 2001), 14:9370.

2. Paul Reiwald, for instance, calls Theodor Geiger's book, *Die Masse und ihre Aktion* (1926), "der erste durchgeführte Versuch einer Soziologie der Masse." *Vom Geist der Massen. Handbuch der Massenpsychologie* (Zürich: Pan-Verlag Zürich, 1946), 306. Unless otherwise indicated, all translations are mine.

3. José Ortega y Gasset, *La rebelión de las masas,* in *Obras completas* (Madrid: Revista de Occidente, 1957), 4:141–310. Translated anonymously as *The Revolt of the Masses* (New York: W. W. Norton, 1932), 13; hereafter abbreviated as *RM.*

4. Werner Sombart, *Der proletarische Sozialismus* (Jena: G. Fischer, 1924), 2:99.

5. Sighele cited in Helmut König, *Zivilisation und Leidenschaften: Die Masse im bürgerlichen Zeitalter* (Reinbek bei Hamburg: Rowohlt, 1992), 145.

6. Gustave Le Bon, *The Crowd: A Study of the Popular Mind* (New York: Viking Press, 1960), 18; hereafter abbreviated as *C.*

7. Le Bon cited in König, *Zivilisation,* 147.

8. Peter Sloterdijk, *Die Verachtung der Massen: Versuch über Kulturkämpfe in der modernen Gesellschaft* (Frankfurt am Main: Suhrkamp, 2000), 9–10.

9. Suzanne R. Stewart-Steinberg, "The Secret Power of Suggestion: Scipio Sighele and the Post-Liberal Subject," *Diacritics* 33, no. 1 (Spring 2003): 60–79.

10. Ibid.

11. Ortega y Gasset, *España invertebrada,* in *Obras completas* (Madrid: Revista de Occidente, 1957), 3:105; hereafter abbreviated as *EI.* Translated by Mildred Adams as *Invertebrate Spain* (New York: W. W. Norton, 1937); hereafter abbreviated as *IS.* I occasionally modify the American translation of *España Invertebrada,* or avoid it altogether when it deletes passages or is otherwise wide off the original. On such occasions, I indicate my recourse to the original by referencing the Spanish version.

12. Ortega, *Rebelión,* 179n1.

13. Paul Connerton, "Freud and the Crowd," in *Visions and Blueprints: Avant-Garde Culture and Radical Politics in Early Twentieth-Century Europe,* ed. Edward Timms and Peter Collier (Manchester: Manchester University Press, 1988), 202.

14. Ortega repeatedly insists that his use of the words *aristocracy* and *masses* does not necessarily connote class distinctions. What he has in mind is something far less mobile than the unstable modern categories of class. His mass men and elite men are innate qualities, which predestine their members to leadership or obedience according to immutable cosmic laws. The distance between them is unbridgeable and social malaise the result of the perverse disavowal of that distance.

15. Werner Sombart, *Der Bourgeois: Zur Geistesgeschichte des modernen Wirtschaftsmenschen* (Munich: Duncker and Humblot, 1913), 461.

16. Werner Sombart, *Händler und Helden* (Munich: Duncker and Humblot, 1915), 107, 120.

17. Ibid., 99.

18. König, *Zivilisation,* 186.

19. Paul Preston, *Franco* (New York: Basic Books, 1994), 418.

20. Ortega y Gasset, "Los escaparates Mandan," in *Obras completas* (Madrid: Revista de Occidente, 1957), 3:461.

21. Laquer cited in Till Bastian, *Furchtbare Ärzte: Medizinische Verbrechen im Dritten Reich* (Munich: C. H. Beck, 1995), 24; emphasis mine.

22. Ploetz cited in ibid., 22–23.

23. Schallmayer cited in ibid., 23.

24. *Medizin in Berlin an der Wende vom 19. zum 20. Jahrhundert: theoretische Fachgebiete,* ed. Peter Schneck (Husum: Matthiessen, 1999), 121.

25. Christiane Rothmaler, "Zwangssterilisationen nach dem 'Gesetz zur Verhütung erbkranken Nachwuchses,'" in *Medizin im "Dritten Reich,"* ed. Johanna Bleker and Norbert Jachertz, 2nd ed. (Cologne: Deutscher Ärzte-Verlag, 1993), 137.

26. Ibid., 143.

27. Hans-Henning Scharsach, *Die Ärzte der Nazis* (Vienna: Orac, 2000), 16.

28. Ibid., 18.

29. Johann Gottlieb Fichte, *Addresses to the German Nation,* trans. R. F. Jones and G. H. Turnbull (New York: Harper and Row, 1968), 12.

30. Antonio Vallejo Nágera, *Higiene de la raza: La asexuación de los psicópatas* (Madrid: Ediciones "Medicina," 1934), 8; hereafter abbreviated as *HR.*

31. Ibid., 60.

32. Hans Grimm, *Volk ohne Raum* (Munich: Albert Langen, 1926).

33. Antonio Vallejo Nágera, *Eugenesia de la Hispanidad y Regeneración de la raza* (Burgos: Editorial Española, 1937), 114; hereafter abbreviated as *EH*.

34. Antonio Vallejo Nágera, *Sinfonía Retaguardista* (Valladolid: Talleres "Cuesta," 1938), 13; hereafter abbreviated as *SR*.

35. Antonio de la Granda and Eduardo Isla, *Biopolítica: Esquema dialéctico de la historia* (Madrid: Ediciones Patria Hispana, 1942), 434–35; hereafter abbreviated as *B*.

36. Américo Castro, *La realidad histórica de España* (México: Porrúa, 1982), 63.

37. Angel Ganivet, *"Idearium español" y "El porvernir de España"* (Madrid: Espasa-Calpe, 1957), 30.

38. Antonio Vallejo Nágera, *Psicopatología de la conducta antisocial* (San Sebastián: Editorial Española, 1937), 52; hereafter abbreviated as *PCA*. See Ramiro de Maeztu, *Defensa de la Hispanidad* (Madrid: Editorial Fax, 1934).

39. Ortega, "Prologue for French Readers," *Rebelión*, 137–38; not included in the English translation.

40. Antonio Vallejo Nágera, "Ilicitud científica de la esterilización eugénica," *Acción Española* 1, no. 3 (1932): 262.

41. Antonio Vallejo Nágera, *Política racial del Nuevo Estado* (San Sebastián: Editorial Española, 1938), 11–12; hereafter abbreviated as *PR.*.

42. Samuel S. Epstein, "Critique of the Nazi War on Cancer," *International Journal of Health Services* 33, no. 1 (2003): 172.

43. Antonio Vallejo Nágera, "Maran-Atha," in *Divagaciones intrascendentes* (Valladolid: Talleres Tipográficos Cuesta, 1938), 96–97.

44. Antonio Vallejo Nágera, *La locura y la guerra* (Valladolid: Librería Santarén, 1939), 51, 52.

45. Ibid.

46. Ricard Vinyes, Montse Armengou, and Ricard Belis, *Los niños perdidos del franquismo* (Barcelona: Plaza y Janés, 2002).

47. Antonio Vallejo Nágera, "Psiquismo del fanatismo marxista," *Semana Médica Española* 1, no. 6 (1938); reprinted in Vinyes et al., *Niños perdidos*, 236.

48. Tomás Carreras y Artau, *Estudios sobre Médicos-Filósofos Españoles del siglo XIX* (Barcelona: Consejo Superior de Investigaciones Científicas, Instituto Luis Vives de Filosofía, 1952), 305.

49. Antonio Vallejo Nágera, "La ley del talión," in *Divagaciones intrascendentes*, 70.

50. Vinyes et al., *Niños perdidos,* 42.

51. Antonio Vallejo Nágera, "Psiquismo del fanatismo marxista: Investigaciones psicológicas en marxistas femeninos delincuentes," *Revista Española de Medicina y Cirugía Guerra* 2, no. 9 (1939), 399; reprinted in Vinyes et al., *Niños perdidos,* 257.

52. Gabriel Tarde, "Foules et Sectes au point de vue criminal," *Revue des deux mondes* 120 (1893): 369.

53. Sighele (1898) cited in König, *Zivilisation*, 165.

54. Fernando Enríquez de Salamanca, "La limitación de la natalidad," *Acción Española* 2, no. 8 (1932): 136.

CHAPTER 10A

1. Sources: Anonymous, *El Abencerraje* (Madrid: Cátedra, 2002); Anonymous, *Cantar del Mío Cid* (Barcelona: Crítica, 2000); Roque Barcia, *Primer diccionario general etimológico de la lengua española* (Barcelona: Seix, 1902); Miguel Alonso Baquer, *Generación de la conquista* (Madrid: MAPFRE, 1992); Simón Bolívar, *Fundamental* (Caracas: Monte Avila Editores, 1993); Sebastián de Covarrubias Horozco, *Tesoro de la lengua española* (Madrid: Turner, 1979); Christopher Columbus, *The Diary of Christopher Columbus's First Voyage to America*, ed. Oliver Dunn and James E. Kelly Jr. (Norman: University of Oklahoma Press, 1989); *Diccionario de la lengua* (Real Academia Espanola) (Madrid: Espasa Calpe, 2000); Sergio Moratiel Villa, *Filosofía del derecho internacional: Suárez, Grocio y epígonos*, http://www.icrc.org.

CHAPTER 11

1. For some recent mereological tractates, see Barry Smith, "Les objets sociaux," *Philosophiques* 26 (1999): 315–47; Roberto Casati and Achille C. Varzi, *Parts and Places: The Structures of Spatial Representation* (Cambridge, Mass.: MIT Press, 1999).

2. For a survey, see Steven Johnson, *Emergence: The Connected Lives of Ants, Brains, Cities, and Software* (New York: Touchstone Books, 2001).

3. See, e.g., Daniel C. Dennett, *Consciousness Explained* (Boston: Little, Brown, 1991).

4. Geoffrey Hartman, *André Malraux* (London: Bowes & Bowes, 1960), 95.

5. See Charles de Secondat, baron de Montesquieu, *L'Esprit des Lois*, in his *Oeuvres complètes* (Paris: Seuil, 1964); Johann Gottfried Herder, *Ideen zur Philosophie der Geschichte der Menschheit* (Wiesbaden: Fourier, 1966); Georg Wilhelm Friedrich Hegel, *Philosophie der Geschichte*, in *Werke* (Frankfurt am Main: Suhrkamp, 1980), vol. 12; Karl Marx, "The British Rule in India" (1854), in Karl Marx and Friedrich Engels, *On Colonialism* (New York: International Publishers, 1972), 35–41.

6. Hegel, *Philosophie der Geschichte*, 152; emphases added. On the long history of Asia's role as a foil for subjectivity, see Haun Saussy, *Great Walls of Discourse* (Cambridge, Mass.: Harvard East Asia Publications, 2001).

7. On the forms and determinants of early "populism" in China, see E. Bruce Brooks, "Intellectual Dynamics of the Warring States Period," *Studies in Chinese History* 7 (1997): 1–32; also "Evolution Towards Citizenship in Warring States China" (1998) and "Competing Systems in Pre-Imperial State Formation" (2000), both available at http://www.umass.edu/wsp/publications.

8. Sima Tan and Sima Qian, *Shiji*, "Qin Shihuang ben ji," 6, in *Shiki kaichū kōshō*, ed. Takigawa Kametarō (1934; reprint, Taipei: Hongshi chubanshe, 1982), 129. Translation adapted from Burton Watson, trans., *Records of the Grand Historian: Qin Dynasty* (New York: Columbia University Press, 1993), 64–66; and William Nienhauser, ed., *The Grand Scribe's Records* (Bloomington: Indiana University Press, 1994), 1:156–57.

9. Takigawa, *Shiki*, 129; Watson, *Records*, 67; Nienhauser, *Grand Scribe*, 158.

10. Ban Gu, *Han shu*, "Wang Mang zhuan," part 1, in *Han shu* (Beijing: Zhonghua shuju, 1962), 4052; English from Homer H. Dubs, trans., *The History of the Former Han Dynasty* (Baltimore, Md.: Waverly Press, 1938–1955), 3:156.

11. Ban Gu, *Han shu*, 4066.

12. Ibid., 4089.

13. Ibid., 4070–71; Dubs, *Former Han Dynasty*, 3:197–201.

14. On this Freudian consideration (for which the pattern is given by chapter 6.D of *The Interpretation of Dreams*), see Etienne Balibar, "Fascism, Psychoanalysis, Freudo-Marxism," in *Masses, Classes, Ideas*, trans. James Swenson (New York: Routledge, 1994), 177–89.

15. Howard Rheingold, *Smart Mobs: The Next Social Revolution* (New York: Perseus, 2002).

16. Walter Benjamin, "On Some Motifs in Baudelaire," in *Illuminations: Essays and Reflections*, trans. Harry Zohn, ed. Hannah Arendt (New York: Schocken, 1969), 166.

17. John Fryer, "Qiu zhu shixin xiaoshuo qi" (1895), translated in anonymous, "The New Novel Before the New Novel: John Fryer's Fiction Contest," in *Writing and Materiality in China*, ed. Judith T. Zeitlin and Lydia H. Liu (Cambridge, Mass.: Harvard University Asia Center, 2003), 324; emphasis added. In the first part of his statement, Fryer plays on a sentence of the ancient *Book of Filial Piety* (*Xiao jing*): "For changing customs and modifying habits, nothing is equal to music."

18. Thus Chinese thinking about mass literary genres rejoins another facet of French crowd psychology, the theory of contagious behavior. See Gabriel Tarde, *Les Lois de l'imitation* (Paris: Alcan, 1890).

19. Gek Nai Cheng, trans., "On the Relationship Between Fiction and the Government of the People," in *Modern Chinese Literary Thought: Writings on Literature, 1893–1945*, ed. Kirk A. Denton (Stanford, Calif.: Stanford University Press, 1996), 80–81. Original text: Liang Qichao, "Lun xiaoshuo yu qunzhi zhi guanxi" (1902), in Guo Shaoyu and Wang Wensheng, comps., *Zhongguo lidai wenlun xuan* (Shanghai: Guji, 1976), 3:405–9.

20. Wu Jianren, *Ershinian mudu zhi guai xianzhuang* (Hong Kong: Guangzhi, n.d.), 1:55–56.

21. See David D. W. Wang, *Fin-de-siècle Splendor: Repressed Modernities of Late Qing Fiction, 1849–1911* (Stanford, Calif.: Stanford University Press, 1997); Eileen Chow, *Spectacular Novelties: Urban Entertainments, Zhang Henshui, and "News" Culture in Republican China* (forthcoming). In narrating the emergence of May Fourth writing, it is almost obligatory to retell Lu Xun's narrative of an episode during his studies in Japan, when he watched a slide show of Chinese prisoners being decapitated at the siege of Port Arthur. What struck Lu Xun was the indifference and passivity of the Chinese crowd that stood watching the event: this sight, he said, turned him from medicine toward writing. Lu Xun, preface to *Nahan* (A call to arms, 1921; Beijing: Renmin wenxue, 1973), 4–5. The question of spectatorship thus divides the generations of modern Chinese literature (late-imperial versus the May Fourth generation) as well as its genres (writing for popular consumption versus writing for a serious, academic, or international audience).

22. Li Boyuan (=Li Baojia), *Wenming xiaoshi* (Beijing: Tongsu wenyi, 1955), 11–13. My translation, but see the fine version by

Douglas Lancashire, *Modern Times: A Brief History of Enlightenment* (Hong Kong: Renditions/Research Centre for Translation, 1996), 25–27.

23. Jean-Jacques Rousseau, "Lettre à d'Alembert," in *Oeuvres complètes* (Paris: Gallimard, 1995), 5:115.

CHAPTER IIA

1. Sources: D. C. Lau and Chen Fong Ching, eds., *A Concordance of the Guoyu* (Hong Kong: Commercial Press, 1999); D. C. Lau and Chen Fong Ching, eds. *A Concordance of the Li ji* (Hong Kong: Commercial Press, 1992); Wang Tongyi et al., eds., *A New Dictionary of Modern Chinese Language* (Haikou, China: Hainan chubanshe, 1992); Chuang-tzu (Zhuangzi), *Chuang-tzu: The Seven Inner Chapters and Other Writings from the book "Chuang-tzu,"* trans. A. C. Graham (London: George Allen and Unwin, 1981); *Ci yuan*, rev. ed., vol. 3 (Hong Kong: Shangwu yinshu guan, 1979); Confucius, *The Analects*, trans. David Hinton (Washington, D.C.: Counterpoint, 1998); *Dacheng yi zhang* (Chapters of the Mahayana Doctrines), http://www.bya.org.hk/html/T44/1851_013.htm; *Hanyu da zidian* (The dictionary of the Chinese language), vol. 5 (Wuhan: hubei cishu chubanshe and sichuan cishu chubanshe, 1986); David Hawkes, *A Little Primer of Tu Fu* (Oxford: Oxford University Press, 1967); Lu Xun, "A Warning to the People," in *Diary of a Madman and Other Stories,* trans. William A. Lyell (Honolulu: University of Hawaii Press, 1990); *Oxford English Dictionary*, http://www.oed.com; Xu Shen, *Shuowen jiezi zhu*, annotated by Duan Yucai (Shanghai: Shanghai guji chubanshe, 1981); *Zhongwen da cidian* (The encyclopedic dictionary of the Chinese language) (Taipei: The Institute for Advanced Chinese Studies, 1962).

CHAPTER 12

1. Adam Smith (pseud.), *The Money Game* (New York: Random House, 1967), 23; hereafter abbreviated as *MG*.

2. Charles D. Ellis and James R. Vertin, *The Investor's Anthology: Original Ideas from the Industry's Greatest Minds* (New York: Wiley, 1997).

3. Robert Menschel, ed., *Markets, Mobs, and Mayhem: A Modern Look at the Madness of Crowds* (New York: Wiley, 2002).

4. Robert Shiller, *Irrational Exuberance* (Princeton, N.J.: Princeton University Press, 2000); Richard Thaler, *The Winner's Curse: Paradoxes and Anomalies of Economic Life* (New York: Free Press, 1992).

5. See, e.g., James Dines, *How Investors Can Make Money Using Mass Psychology* (Belvedere, Calif.: James Dines, 1996); Laurence A. Conors and Blake E. Hayward, *Investment Secrets of Hedge Fund Managers: Exploiting the Herd Mentality of the Financial Markets* (New York: McGraw-Hill, 1995); Charles D. Ellis, *Winning the Loser's Game* (New York: McGraw-Hill, 2002).

6. Whitney cited in John Steele Gordon, *The Great Game: The Emergence of Wall Street as a World Power, 1653–2000* (New York: Scribner, 1999), 238.

7. Gregor Sidis, *The Psychology of Suggestion* (New York: Appleton, 1898).

8. Gustave Le Bon, *The Crowd: A Study of the Popular Mind* (1895; reprint, New York: Macmillan, 1896), xv. Cf. Don DeLillo, whose novel *Mao II* (London: Jonathan Cape, 1991) understands the crowd as a figure of the future: "The future belongs to crowds" (16).

9. Charles Mackay, *Extraordinary Popular Delusions, and the Madness of Crowds* (1841, rev. 1852; reprint, New York: Three Rivers Press, 1980); hereafter abbreviated as *EPD*.

10. All chapters dealing with financial speculation are part of the first volume.

11. Gustave Le Bon's eclectic crowd psychology also uses this argument, when he refers to *Völkerpsychologie* (the psychology of peoples) to explain why certain "races" fall victim to crowd phenomena more often than others (*Crowd*, 4).

12. See, e.g., John Carey, *The Intellectuals and the Mass* (London: Faber and Faber, 1992).

13. Niklas Luhmann, *Social Systems,* trans. John Bednarz Jr. (1984; reprint, Stanford, Calif.: Stanford University Press, 1995), 75 ff.

14. Urs Stäheli, "Financial Noise: The Popularity of Noise," *Soziale Systeme* 9, no. 2 (2003): 244–56.

15. This is an important difference from Le Bon's crowd psychology, where the figure of the leader becomes crucial. Mackay also uses figures of the leader such as John Law, but it is important to understand that it is the collective delusion of easy money that unifies the crowd, and only secondarily the identification with John Law.

16. Thus the speculative imagination links spatial distance (colonialism) and temporal distance (future profit).

17. Niklas Luhmann, *Die Gesellschaft der Gesellschaft,* 2 vols. (Frankfurt am Main: Suhrkamp, 1997).

18. I use problematization in the Foucauldian sense as showing the contingency of discursive constructions in order to develop techniques for dealing with these problems: "This development of a given into a question, this transformation of a group of obstacles and difficulties into problems to which the diverse solutions will attempt to produce a response, this is what constitutes the point of problematization and the specific work of thought." Michel Foucault, "Polemics, Politics, and Problematizations," interview in *Ethics: Subjectivity and Truth: Essential Works of Foucault, 1954–1984,* vol. 1 (1984; reprint, New York: New Press, 1997).

19. Henry Clews, *Fifty Years in Wall Street* (1908; reprint, New York: New York Times Company, 1973), 35.

20. Brush cited in James Alexander Ross, *Speculation, Stock Prices, and Industrial Fluctuations* (New York: Ronald Press, 1938), 59.

21. Henry Crosby Emery, *Speculation on the Stock and Product Exchanges in the United States* (1896; reprint, New York: Greenwood, 1969), 191.

22. *Business Week,* January 2001.

23. Justin Fox, "Bubbles, Delusions, and the 'New Economy,'" *Trends in Futures* 10, no. 40 (2001).

24. Bernard Baruch, introduction to *Extraordinary Popular Delusions and the Madness of Crowds* by Charles Mackay (1932), in Menschel, *Markets, Mobs, and Mayhem,* 37–8.

25. Other authors influenced by contrarianism include Fred Kelly, James Fraser, "Adam Smith," and John Maggee.

26. Cf. notably Shiller, *Irrational Exuberance,* and Thaler, *Winner's Curse.*

27. *The Collected Writings of John Maynard Keynes,* vol. 7, *The General Theory of Employment, Interest, and Money* (1935; reprint, London: Macmillan, 1973), 155.

28. *The Collected Writings of John Maynard Keynes,* vol. 6, *The Applied Theory of Money* (1930; reprint, London: Macmillan, 1971), 323.

29. Fred C. Kelly, *Why You Win or Lose: The Psychology of Speculation* (New York: Houghton Mifflin, 1930), 21; hereafter abbreviated as *WYWL.*

30. Humphrey Neill, *Tape Reading and Market Tactics* (1931; reprint, New York: Fraser, 1960), 2; hereafter abbreviated as *TR.*

31. William C. Moore, *Wall Street: Its Mysteries Revealed, Its Secrets Exposed* (New York: Moore William, 1921), 113. In very similar words, James Fraser notes that "crowds are wrong in themselves simply because they behave normally" (cited in *WYWL,* vii).

32. Humphrey Neill, *The Art of Contrary Thinking* (1954; reprint, Caldwell, Idaho: Caxton Printers, 1967), 5; hereafter abbreviated as *ACT.*

33. It is interesting to see that one of the key papers of new economic sociology also emphasizes that markets are basically arrangements of mutual observations. Harrison White, "Where Do Markets Come From?" *American Journal of Sociology* 87, no. 3 (1981): 517–47.

34. Safire cited in Menschel, *Markets, Mobs, and Mayhem,* xi.

35. Cf. Jean-Pierre Dupuy, *La Panique* (Paris: Delagrange, 1991).

36. Frederick Drew Bond, *Stock Movements and Speculation* (New York: Appleton, 1928). Cf. *WYWL,* 60.

37. Neil A. Costa, "The Temple of Boom" (presentation at the Australian Technical Analysts Association, Sydney, 2000), http://www.ataa.com.au/a_nc_boom_a.htm.

38. Karin D. Knorr Cetina and Urs Bruegger, "The Market as an Object of Attachment: Exploring Postsocial Relations in Financial Markets," *Canadian Journal of Sociology* 25, no. 2 (2000): 141–68.

39. Costa, "Temple of Boom."

40. This is precisely the logic of the "noise trader" in more recent finance theory. Fischer Black, "Noise," *Journal of Finance* 41 (1986): 529–43.

41. Niklas Luhmann, *Die Wirtschaft der Gesellschaft* (Frankfurt am Main: Suhrkamp, 1987), 72 ff.

42. This opposition of the heroic individual against the crowd implicitly draws from American individualism, notably Ralph W. Emerson. In his often-quoted essay on self-reliance, Emerson discusses how to maintain one's individual identity. The ultimate test for Emerson is to remain oneself "in the midst of the crowd." "Self-Reliance," in *Essays and English Traits,* vol. 5 (1841; reprint, New York: Collier, 1909–1914).

43. The discourse on the investor and the market crowd is a highly sexualized discourse, firmly embedded within a heterosex-

ual matrix, drawing from the discursive articulation between the crowd and femininity. See Urs Stäheli, *Spektakuläre Spekulation. Das Populäre der Ökonomie* (Weilerswist: Velbrück, forthcoming).

44. H. J. Wolf, *Studies in Stock Speculation* (1924; reprint, Wells, Vt.: Fraser, 1966), 71.

45. Sloan J. Wilson, *The Speculator and the Stock Market* (Palisades Park, N.J.: Investor's Library, 1963), 125; hereafter abbreviated as *SSM*.

46. Cf. *Collected Writings of Keynes*, 7:155.

47. Cf. David A. Zimmerman, "Frank Norris, Market Panic, and the Mesmeric Sublime," *American Literature* 75, no. 1 (2003): 61–90, for his discussion of mesmerism, suggestion, and market psychology.

48. Bond, *Stock Movements*, 13.

49. Henry Howard Harper, *The Psychology of Speculation: The Human Element in Stock Market Transactions* (1926; reprint, Wells, Vt.: Fraser, 1966), 106. Neill presents the aim of the contrarian in similar words: "attaining a mastery of himself: of his temperament, emotions, and the other variables that go to make human nature" (*TR*, 1).

50. Michel Foucault, *Discipline and Punish: The Birth of the Prison* (London: Allen Lane, 1977).

51. Charles Dow, cited in *SSM*, 122.

52. S. A. Nelson, *The ABC of Stock Speculation* (1903; reprint, Wells, Vt.: Fraser, 1964), 66–67.

53. Urs Stäheli, "Der Takt der Börse. Inklusionseffekte von Verbreitungsmedien am Fallbeispiel des Börsen-Tickers," *Zeitschrift für Soziologie* 33, no. 3 (2004): 245–63.

54. Andreas Huyssen, "Mass Culture as Woman: Modernism's Other," in *Studies in Entertainment: Critical Approaches to Mass Culture*, ed. Tania Modleski (Bloomington: Indiana University Press, 1986), 188–208.

CHAPTER 13

This essay was adapted from Charles Tilly, *Social Movements, 1768–2004* (Boulder, Colo.: Paradigm Publishers, 2004).

1. "War Prompts Street Demonstrations," http://HomerNews.com, April 3, 2003, spacing and punctuation edited.

2. "Pro-troops Demonstrators to Rally Again This Week," http://HomerNews.com, April 3, 2003.

3. As it happens, French scholars have done by far the most extensive work on the demonstration's history. See especially Pierre Favre, ed., *La Manifestation* (Paris: Presses de la Fondation Nationale des Sciences Politiques, 1990); Olivier Fillieule, *Stratégies de la rue. Les manifestations en France* (Paris: Presses de la Fondation Nationale des Sciences Politiques, 1997); Michel Pigenet and Danielle Tartakowsky, eds., "Les marches," *Le mouvement social* 202 (January–March 2003), entire issue; Vincent Robert, *Les chemins de la manifestation, 1848–1914* (Lyon: Presses Universitaires de Lyon, 1996); and Danielle Tartakowsky, *Les Manifestations de rue en France, 1918–1968* (Paris: Publications de la Sorbonne, 1997).

4. Francesca Polletta, *Freedom is an Endless Meeting: Democracy in American Social Movements* (Chicago: University of Chicago Press, 2002).

5. George Rudé, *Wilkes and Liberty* (Oxford: Clarendon Press, 1962), 22.

6. John Brewer, *Party Ideology and Popular Politics at the Accession of George III* (Cambridge: Cambridge University Press, 1976), 168.

7. Ibid., 177.

8. George Rudé, *Hanoverian London, 1714–1808* (London: Secker and Warburg, 1971), 125.

9. *Annual Register* 1768, 86.

10. Charles Tilly, "Speaking Your Mind Without Elections, Surveys, or Social Movements," *Public Opinion Quarterly* 47 (1983): 461–78.

11. Rudé, *Wilkes and Liberty*, 19.

12. *Annual Register* 1768, 68.

13. *Annual Register* 1768, 71; for details, see Dirk Hoerder, *Crowd Action in Revolutionary Massachusetts, 1765–1780* (New York: Academic Press, 1977), 166–68.

14. *South Carolina Gazette*, June 6, 1768, 3.

15. *South Carolina Gazette*, October 3, 1768, 2.

16. Pauline Maier, *From Resistance to Revolution: Colonial Radicals and the Development of American Opposition to Britain, 1765–1776* (New York: Vintage, 1972), 85.

17. Ibid., 116.

18. John Brewer, *The Sinews of Power: War, Money and the English State, 1688–1783* (New York: Knopf, 1989); Michael Mann, *States, War and Capitalism: Studies in Political Sociology* (Oxford: Blackwell, 1988), 106.

19. Charles Tilly, "Parliamentarization of Popular Contention in Great Britain, 1758–1834," *Theory and Society* 26 (1997): 245–73.

20. Brewer, *Sinews of Power*, 132.

21. Rudé, *Hanoverian London*, 172–77.

22. Ibid., 226.

23. Robert Glen, *Urban Workers in the Early Industrial Revolution* (London: Croom Helm, 1984), 245.

24. John Belchem, *Industrialization and the Working Class: The English Experience, 1750–1900* (Aldershot: Scolar, 1990), 73–144; Charles Tilly, *Popular Contention in Great Britain, 1758–1834* (Cambridge, Mass.: Harvard University Press, 1995), 240–319.

25. Wendy Hinde, *Catholic Emancipation: A Shake to Men's Minds* (Oxford: Blackwell, 1992); Fergus O'Ferrall, *Catholic Emancipation: Daniel O'Connell and the Birth of Irish Democracy, 1820–30* (Dublin: Gill and Macmillan, 1985); Charles Tilly, *Contention and Democracy in Europe, 1650–2000* (Cambridge: Cambridge University Press, 2004), 149–56.

26. J. Franklin Jameson, *The American Revolution Considered as a Social Movement* (Boston: Beacon, 1956), 9.

27. Ibid., 100.

28. Sidney Tarrow, *Power in Movement* (Cambridge: Cambridge University Press, 1998), 38.

29. Seymour Drescher, *Capitalism and Antislavery: British Mobilization in Comparative Perspective* (London: Macmillan, 1986), 70.

30. Ibid., 79.

31. Lynn Hunt, *Revolution and Urban Politics in Provincial France: Troyes and Reims, 1786–1790* (Stanford, Calif.: Stanford University Press, 1978); Hunt, *Politics, Culture, and Class in the French Revolution* (Berkeley: University of California Press, 1984); John Markoff, *The Abolition of Feudalism: Peasants, Lords, and Legislators in the French Revolution* (University Park: Pennsylvania State University Press, 1996); Peter McPhee, "Les formes d'intervention populaire en Roussillon: L'exemple de Collioure, 1789–1815," in *Les pratiques politiques en province à l'époque de la Révolution française, Centre d'Histoire Contemporaine du Languedoc Méditerranéen et du Roussillon* (Montpellier: Publications de la Recherche, Université de Montpellier, 1988); Isser Woloch, *Jacobin Legacy: The Democratic Movement Under the Directory* (Princeton: Princeton University Press, 1970); Woloch, *The New Regime: Transformations of the French Civic Order, 1789–1820s* (New York: Norton, 1994).

32. Charles Tilly, *The Contentious French* (Cambridge, Mass.: Harvard University Press, 1986), chap. 9.

33. Rudolf Dekker, *Holland in beroering: Oproeren in de 17de en 18de Eeuw* (Baarn: Amboeken, 1982); Dekker, "Women in Revolt: Popular Protest and Its Social Basis in Holland in the 17th and 18th Centuries," *Theory and Society* 16 (1987): 337–62; Karin van Honacker, *Lokaal Verzet en Oproer in de 17de en 18de Eeuw: Collectieve Acties tegen het centraal gezag in Brussel, Antwerpen en Leuven* (Heule: UGA, 1994); von Honacker, "Résistance locale et émeutes dans les chef-villes brabançonnes aux XVIIe et XVIIIe siècles," *Revue d'Histoire Moderne et Contemporaine* 47 (2000): 37–68.

34. Wayne te Brake, *Regents and Rebels: The Revolutionary World of the 18th Century Dutch City* (Oxford: Blackwell, 1989); te Brake, "How Much in How Little? Dutch Revolution in Comparative Perspective," *Tijdschrift voor Sociale Geschiedenis* 16 (1990): 349–63.

CHAPTER 13A

1. Sources: Ady Endre, *Összes Költeménye,* http://www.mek.iif.hu; Benkő Loránd, ed., *A Magyar Nyelv Történeti-Etimológiai Szótára* (Budapest: Akadémiai, 1967–1978); Ballagi Mór, *A Magyar Nyelv Teljes Szótára* (Pest: Heckenast Gusztáv, 1873); *Hungarian Historical Corpus,* http://www.nytud.hu/hhc; *Petőfi-Szótár* (Budapest: Akadémiai, 1973–1987); *Révai Nagylexikona* (Budapest: Révai Testvérek, 1925); *Új Idők Lexikona* (Budapest: Singer és Wolfner, 1942).

CHAPTER 14

1. Austin Binn, "Them Against the World," *New York Times Magazine,* November 16, 2003. Bunn puts the number at six to ten million, but estimates have varied widely.

2. Of course, at least the *Chronicle* covered the demonstrations. Most American news outlets provided scant if any coverage of the mass protests, domestically or internationally. In so doing, they played an active and crucial role in dissociating those on the street from those at home, as well as those in the United States form those abroad. Any questioning concerning the "representation" of the crowd necessarily involves the larger issues of media consolidation and deregulation.

3. "The number of people (in a crowd) is a mythical number, and now you're going to turn it into a fact, and that won't be welcomed. . . . There's an old saying in journalism: people only see what they believe. This is an emotional issue, not a factual issue as far as most people are concerned." Alex Jones, director of the Joan Shorenstein Center on the Press, Politics and Public Policy, Harvard University, quoted in the *Chronicle,* A6.

4. The *Chronicle's* project, despite its predilection for new solutions grounded in advanced technology, presents itself in the garb of the old-fashioned and hence the trustworthy. Although entirely computerized solutions could likely have been used, they opted rather for midcentury methods of human analysis. This "human touch" might seem to serve no purpose because the analysis was nothing more than the accurate counting of dots, which could be done more effectively by computer scanning. Yet its rhetorical purpose was clear: it fostered a sense of human subjectivity that served to mitigate the "cold rationality" of the machine.

5. This fantasy of the "long view" is increasingly, in the new millennium, tied to economics and the perception of a "healthy national economy." As I am writing, some twenty-four hundred protesters are scheduled to go to trial in San Francisco for disturbing the normal flow of traffic—many articles highlight the dramatically increased cost to the city for the "police overtime" due to the demonstration, and imply that the demonstrators should remunerate the city, in this time of economic downturn, for their actions. Abstracting from the cause of the demonstration, or even the rights of free association, the media coverage has tended to use a "massive" dollar amount without any context, thus implying that public demonstrations are too costly for America to sustain.

6. Cited in Albert Grimm, *120 Jahre Photogrammetrie in Deutschland: Das Tagebuch von Albrecht Meydenbauer* (Munich: Oldenbourg, 1978); reproduced in Harun Farocki, "Reality Would Have to Begin," in *Imprint: Writings* (New York: Lukas and Sternberg, 2001), 188.

7. For the seminal elaborations of this idea, see Siegfried Kracauer, "Photography," in *The Mass Ornament*, ed. and trans. Thomas Y. Levin (Cambridge, Mass.: Harvard University Press, 1995); and André Bazin, "The Ontology of the Photographic Image," in *What Is Cinema (1945–1957)* (Berkeley: University of California Press, 1970).

8. Leo Steinberg, *Other Criteria: Confrontations with Twentieth-Century Art* (New York: Oxford University Press, 1972), 82.

9. Kracauer, *Mass Ornament*.

10. In implying that the aerial perspective is not an embodied, human perspective, I am well aware of the extent to which we, in the twenty-first century, may nevertheless feel this type of vision to be a natural, everyday state of affairs. It is this very "naturalization" that I seek to describe and diagnose in this essay, a naturalization that has been effected through the massive proliferation of photographic representations in print, television, and the Internet media we regularly consume. Yet what troubles me is how the naturalization of the aerial perspective brings with it a situation in which the visual reciprocity inherent in our perceptual encounter with other beings in the world is negated, and this *lack* of reciprocity becomes increasingly naturalized and familiar. One of Merleau-Ponty's central claims in the *Phenomenology of Perception* is that the phenomenal world presents itself to us as "needing to be clarified." What seems most troubling to me is how this *naturalization* of the aerial perspective seems to be related to a world that *no longer presents itself as needing to be clarified*, a world that is increasingly encountered as data, as information that is already clear unto itself and that needs no further "investigation." When the reduction of human beings to bits of data no longer strikes us as a terrifying, liminal experience, but rather as a familiar and useful state of affairs, we may be on the verge of losing something ethically foundational as regards *human* perception. Maurice Merleau-Ponty, *The Phenomenology of Perception*, trans. Colin Smith (London: Routledge, 1962).

11. Cited in Lev Manovich, "Modern Surveillance Machines: Perspective, Radar, 3-D Computer Graphics, and Computer Vision," in *CTRL [Space]: Rhetorics of Surveillance from Bentham to Big Brother*, ed. Thomas Levin et al. (Cambridge, Mass.: MIT Press, 2002); and Michael de Landa, *War in the Age of Intelligent Machines* (New York: Zone Books, 1991). Surveillance balloons were also used by both sides in the American Civil War, though photographic equipment was not yet employed.

12. A slightly modified formulation can be found in Farocki, "Reality," 190.

13. See in particular Paul Virilio, *War and Cinema: A Logistics of Perception* (New York: Verso, 1989); de Landa, *War in the Age of Intelligent Machines*; and Farocki, "Reality."

14. The basic question of who owns satellites—what might almost seem a puerile game of "who's got the highest view"—nevertheless is what enables U.S. government and business interests unparalleled military and economic dominance over much of the world they survey.

15. Manovich, "Modern Surveillance Machines," 385.

16. Ibid., 386.

17. Jacques Lacan, *The Four Fundamental Concepts of Psychoanalysis* (New York: Norton, 1978), 86, 94.

18. Martin Heidegger, *The Question Concerning Technology,*

trans. William Lovitt (New York: Harper and Row, 1977). I am here translating the German *Bild* with "representation," rather than the traditional "picture," in order to bring out what Heidegger terms its manner of "setting-before."

19. In perhaps the decisive moment of his *Question Concerning Technology,* Heidegger writes, "Man stands so decisively in attendance on the challenging-forth of Enframing that he does not apprehend Enframing as a claim, he fails to see himself as the one spoken to." Heidegger is clear that "what is dangerous is not technology," or even, I would claim, the "enframing" of the natural world as such, so much as the *totalizing* regime of representational thought that this regime tends to bring about. Heidegger claims that where this ordering "holds sway" the "regulating and securing of the standing-reserve mark all revealing." Because this particular mode of revealing works to drive out "every other possibility," the supreme danger lies in that it might no longer allow its own "fundamental characteristic [to] appear, namely, this revealing as such." Man would thus lose the ability to hear this "question concerning technology" amid the spectacle of technological accomplishments, and the very naturalization of the increasing regulation of the mental landscape it tends to effect. Heidegger, *Question Concerning Technology,* 27–28. Farocki's film also is in dialogue with Heidegger's earlier essay, "The Age of the World Picture," in the same volume.

20. Leon Battista Alberti, *On Painting* (New Haven, Conn.: Yale University Press, 1956), 40.

21. Farocki, "Reality," 198.

22. This is why, in the philosophy of Lacan and Merleau-Ponty, the gaze can be placed not only in another person, but at the site of the world as such. This is a complex point that exceeds the bounds of this essay. The primary texts would be Sartre's *Being and Nothingness,* Lacan's *The Four Fundamental Concepts of Psychoanalysis,* and Merleau-Ponty's *The Visible and the Invisible,* as well as Kaja Silverman's *World Spectators* (Stanford, Calif.: Stanford University Press, 2001).

23. Adjusted for inflation to preserve the feeling of the scene. The original figure, £20,000, would today be well over $250,000.

24. Steinberg, *Other Criteria,* 90; my emphasis. So as to forestall any confusion, I need to clarify that although I accept Steinberg's analysis, I will be reversing his terminology of the vertical and horizontal. This is because Steinberg describes this "shift" in terms of the spatial position of the canvas as object, rather than in terms of modality of spectatorship that an object produces. He describes the traditional "picture window" as hanging "vertically" on the wall, as opposed to the "flatbed picture plane" which (theoretically) lies flat and horizontal along the floor. Because I am discussing the modality of spectatorship produced by this new orientation, I will be discussing the shift from the perspective of the viewer. Hence, the terms will be inverted—the spectator looks in front of herself, across the room, towards the horizon of the traditional "picture window," while she must stand directly above, and look down vertically at the "flatbed picture plane."

25. See Christopher Phillips, ed., *The New Vision: Photography Between the World Wars: Ford Motor Company Collection at the Metropolitan Museum of Art* (New York: Metropolitan Museum of Art, 1989).

26. Ironically, the established practice of architectural photography distorts the perspectival optics through the use of tilt and shift in a view camera in order to keep parallel lines from converging. Such representation does not correspond to our phenomenological experience of such sites, but nevertheless strikes us as more comfortable and "realistic" as a photographic representation.

27. Raoul Haussman, "Die Neue Kunst," *Die Aktion* 11, nos. 19–20 (May 12, 1921), cited in Phillips, *New Vision,* 80–81 and n46.

28. El Lissitzky's review of Erich Mendelsohn's *Amerika: Bilderbuch eines Architekten* was originally published in *Stroitel naja promyslennost* (Moscow) and is cited in Phillips, *New Vision,* 58.

29. Kracauer's text is chiefly concerned with what might be called the "seriality" of modern, capitalist production and the uncanny repetition of its structures within the "ornamental" patterns of bodies in the spectacles of Busby Berkeley and the Tiller Girls. Yet throughout his essay, Kracauer calls attention not simply to objectification of human beings with the newly Talyorized workplace, but to the way in which the masses are represented to themselves spatially. He writes that the "ornament resembles *aerial photographs* of landscapes and cities in that it does not emerge out of the interior of the given circumstances, but rather appears above them." The mass ornament can thus be understood as obstructing not simply transparency, but identification. The mass, from up in the bleachers, does not see itself in what is out there on the field; in fact, the ornamental structure—by which I am

now referring not simply to those popular revues of geometric figures but any mass representation within this particular spatial logic—would seem to produce a concomitant disidentification. For Kracauer, the "tragic misrecognition" consists in the fact that the mass can only see itself as ornament, whereas beneath, it is beginning to reveal itself, historically, as subject. See Kracauer, *Mass Ornament.*

30. Scott Bukatman, *Bladerunner* (London: BFI, 1997), 61.

31. Michel de Certeau, *The Practice of Everyday Life* (Berkeley: University of California Press, 1984), 92.

32. Ibid. The relation between spirituality, emotional investment, knowledge, and the "distanced perspective" is the complex subject of Wim Wenders's rich and beautiful *Wings of Desire* (1988), an adequate discussion of which unfortunately lies beyond the scope of this essay.

33. That Vidor's protagonist is not destined for distinction can be seen already within his name. Not only is John metaphoric for "nobody" (John Doe), but "Sims" is linked to both the Latin *similis,* "similar," and *simia,* "apelike" (the two are conjoined in the English expression, "to ape"). John Sims is Everyman, simply one of the crowd or, as Vidor's working title had it, "One of the Mob."

34. The Superman comics of a few years later would explicitly vocalize this fantasy of "leaping tall buildings in a single bound."

35. "In an apartment building comprising stack after stack of 'boxes for living in', for example, the spectators-cum-tenants grasp the relationship between part and whole directly; furthermore, they recognize themselves in that relationship. By constantly expanding the scale of things, this movement serves to compensate for the pathetically small size of each set of living-quarters." Henri Lefebvre, *The Production of Space,* trans. Donald Nicholson-Smith (Oxford: Basil Blackwell, 1991), 98. Lefebvre speaks of the ways in which we represent a building as a solid, monumental structure, thereby ignoring the ways such a supposedly "sealed" structure is permeated, pierced by myriad forces—electricity, radio signals, water, sewage, communication, windows, doorways. Benjamin thought the perfectly revolutionary house would be transparent, and I think he means in the way Buck-Morss describes the neural system in her commentary on Benjamin—as something opening out to the world, stretching out in all directions, in the way the nervous system is not self-contained, but stretches out into the world as experienced.

36. It is also the logic Freud would use to develop both the myth of the primal horde in *Moses and Monotheism* and his overall argument in *Group Psychology.*

37. Although Vidor, beginning the film with the death of John's father and his final injunction that his son will grow up to "be somebody important," anchors the film in a Freudian narrative about *individual* subjectification, Miriam Hansen has usefully linked John's personal situation to the larger socioeconomic conditions of class identification and disidentification in the 1920s. She correctly sees John as an example of the new species of "white collar office worker" with which Siegfried Kracauer's novel *Die Angestellten* was concerned. See her "Ambivalence and the Mass Ornament," *Qui Parle* 5, no. 2 (1992): 102–19.

38. Significantly, this is not just the only time John is seen *with*, rather than *against,* the crowd, it is also the only time we see him "from the street"—that is, from the position of the crowd.

39. Thus unconsciously identifying with the clown, because John's own father had made similarly improbable prophesies about him.

40. Unfortunately, this effect simply cannot be demonstrated in prose. The sequence is approximately ten seconds from end of the film. Additionally, there seems to be a kind of disjunction between the fifth and sixth images of this series that critics have not previously mentioned. The final image of "crowd as ornament" before the final fade to black seems to involve an additional camera farther above, or perhaps a different image altogether. It is curious, in the terms of the argument I am developing, because this mechanical "disjuncture" occurs at the precise moment in which we would expect the disjuncture of recognition to occur naturally. It was as if the crowd, in this penultimate shot, was still not small enough for Vidor, that he wanted to be absolutely certain we could no longer recognize people in these flickering specks of light.

41. See his "Little Shopgirls Go to the Movies," in *Mass Ornament.* This would correspond to Godard's distinction between "making political films" and "making films politically."

42. Siegfried Kracauer, *Theory of Film* (Princeton, N.J.: Princeton University Press, 1997), 51.

43. Pudovkin, *Film Technique and Film Acting,* 53–54, cited in Kracauer, *Theory of Film.*

44. Nearly contemporary with Vertov's film, Siegfried Kra-

cauer would claim that "for the first time in history, photography brings to light the entire natural cocoon . . . the photographic archive assembles in effigy the last elements of a nature alienated from meaning. . . . The images of the stock of nature disintegrated into its elements are offered up for consciousness' free disposal. Their original order is lost . . . the order they assume is necessarily provisional. It is therefore incumbent on consciousness to establish the provisional status of all given configurations." "Photography," in *Mass Ornament*, 59.

45. Garrett Stewart, *Between Film and Screen: Modernism's Photo-Synthesis* (Chicago: University of Chicago Press, 1999), 13–15.

46. Compare this to the image of the fairground from Carol Reed's *The Third Man* (fig. 14.7), in which the shadows are more visible than the people from whom they emerge.

47. The etymology of *mass* is unclear. Gertrud Koch has recently suggested derivation from the Hebrew *mazza*, as in *matzoh*, or unleavened bread. See *Siegfried Kracauer*, trans. Jeremy Gaines (Princeton, N.J.: Princeton University Press, 2000), 27. Incidentally, after starting production on *The Crowd*, Vidor begin to understand and reject the rhetorically agitational implications of his working title: "One of the Mob." With good reason—John Sims is certainly not part of a "mob," insofar as a "mob" is predicated on group cohesion and direction, and these are precisely the things that John will spend the film fighting against.

48. Samuel Weber, *Mass Mediauras: Form, Technics, Media* (Stanford, Calif.: Stanford University Press, 1996), 84. For three different translations of the same German word, see Freud's "Group Psychology and the Analysis of the Ego" ("Massenpsychologie und Ich-Analyse"), Kracauer's *Mass Ornament* (Die Ornament der Masse), and Harry Zohn's rather fluid translation, within Benjamin's artwork essay, of *massenweise* (literally, "masslike") by the English "a plurality of copies."

49. See "The Work of Art in the Age of Its Mechanical Reproducibility," in Walter Benjamin, *Selected Writings*, vols. 3 and 4 (Cambridge, Mass.: Harvard University Press, 2002–2003).

50. Ibid., 97.

51. Of the many accounts currently available, perhaps the best starting place is William J. Mitchell's *City of Bits* (Cambridge, Mass.: MIT Press, 1996).

CHAPTER 14A

1. Sources: Vladimir Dal, *Tolkovyi slovar' zhivago velikorusskago iazyka* (Saint Petersburg: M. O. Vol'fa, 1882); Maks Fasmer, *Etimologicheskii slovar' russkogo iazyka* (Moscow: Progress, 1973); Ipat'evskaia letopis', *Polnoe sobranie russkikh letopisei*, vol. 2 (Moscow: Iazyki Russkoi Kul'tury, 1998); N. M. Karamzin, *Istoriia gosudarstva rossiiskogo* (Moscow: Kniga, 1988); A. S. Pushkin, "Poet i tolpa," *Sobranie Sochinenii v piati tomakh* (Saint Petersburg: Bibliopolis, 1995); *Slovar' iazyka Pushkina* (Moscow: Gosudarstvennoe Izdatel'stvo Inostrannykh i Natsional'nykh Slovarei, 1961); *Slovar' sinonimov russkogo iazyka* (Leningrad: Izdatel'stvo Nauka, 1971); *Slovar' sovremennogo russkogo iazyka* (Moscow: Izdatel'stvo Akademii Nauk SSSR, 1963); I. I. Sreznevskii, *Materialy dlia slovaria drevne-russkago iazyka po pis'mennym pamiatnikam* (Saint Petersburg: Tipografiia Imperatorskoi Akademii Nauk, 1903); D. N. Ushakov, ed., *Tolkovyj slovar' russkogo jazyka*, 4 vols. (Cambridge, Mass.: Slavica Publishers, 1974).

CHAPTER 15

1. J. W. Goethe, *Faust*, trans. Walter Kaufmann (New York: Anchor Books, 1990), 71.

2. Georg Lukács, *Die Theorie des Romans: Ein geschichtsphilosophischer Versuch über die Form der großen Epik* (Frankfurt am Main: Luchterhand, 1977).

3. Francesco Petrarca, *De vita solitaria*, ed. Antonietta Bufano (Turin: Einaudi, 1977); 1.6, 76; hereafter abbreviated as *DVS*. Unless otherwise indicated, all translations are mine.

4. Timothy J. Reiss, *Mirages of the Selfe: Patterns of Personhood in Ancient and Early Modern Europe* (Stanford, Calif.: Stanford University Press, 2003), 326; "The debate between contemplative and social, eternal and worldly—terms more exact than the now-familiar oppositions inner/outer, private/public—was Augustinian, with *The City of God* perhaps its exemplary text" (327).

5. Paul Oskar Kristeller, "The Active and the Contemplative Life in Renaissance Humanism," in *Arbeit, Musse, Meditation: Betrachtungen zur "Vita activa" und "Vita contemplativa,"* ed. Brian Vickers (Zürich: Verlag der Fachvereine, 1985), 133–52.

6. Cf. Ugo Dotti, *Vita di Petrarca* (Roma-Bari: Laterza, 1978), 141.

7. The classic statement of this genetic argument is Michael Seidlmayer, "Petrarca: Das Urbild des Humanisten," in *Wege und Wandlungen des Humanismus* (Göttingen: Vandenhoeck und

Ruprecht, 1965), 125–77.

8. Constance Jordan, "Montaigne on Property, Public Service, and Political Servitude," *Renaissance Quarterly* 56, no. 2 (2003): 408–35. In Jordan's view, Montaigne anticipates a modern rhetoric of "possessive individualism" and dispenses with older modes of feudal or patriarchal obligation.

9. *Les Essais de Michel de Montaigne*, 2 vols., ed. Pierre Villey, rev. ed. V.-L. Saulnier (Paris: Presses universitaires de France, 1924, 1965), 1:26; hereafter abbreviated as *E*. English translation by Donald M. Frame, *Complete Essays of Montaigne* (Stanford, Calif.: Stanford University Press, 1976); hereafter abbreviated as *CE*.

10. The original reads, "ce n'est pas assez de s'estre escarté du people; ce n'est pas assez de changer de place, il se faut escarter des conditions populaires qui sont en nous: il se faut sequestrer et r'avoir de soy." *E*, 1:39, 239.

11. Francesco Guicciardini, *Maxims and Reflections: Ricordi*, trans. Mario Domandi (Philadelphia: University of Pennsylvania Press, 1992), 76n140.

12. Jean-Jacques Rousseau, *Reveries of the Solitary Walker, Botanical Writings, and Letter to Franquières*, in *Collected Writings* (Hanover, N.H.: University Press of New England, 2000), 8:3; hereafter abbreviated as *RSW*.

13. Tzvetan Todorov, *Imperfect Garden: The Legacy of Humanism*, trans. Carol Cosman (Princeton, N.J.: Princeton University Press, 2002), 99.

14. But see the discussion in Heinz Brüggemann, "Aber schickt keinen Poeten nach London!" *Großstadt und literarische Wahrnehmung im 18. und 19. Jahrhundert* (Hamburg: Rowohlt, 1985), chap. 3.

15. Goethe, *Italienische Reise* (Frankfurt am Main: Insel, 1976), 87; hereafter abbreviated as *IR*.

16. Of particular interest is an early description of the spectacle of the assembled people in the ancient amphitheatre of Verona: "When [the people] saw itself thus gathered together, it had to be astonished about itself. Since usually it is only used to crossing each other's path chaotically; to finding itself in a swarming [*Gewühle*] without order or any regiment; here the many-headed, plurivocal, wavering, stumbling animal sees itself unified into a noble body, destined for unity, united into one mass and solidified, as *one* form, animated by *one* spirit" (sich in einem Gewühle ohne Ordnung und sonderliche Zucht zu finden, so sieht das vielköpfige, vielsinnige, schwankende, hin und her irrende Tier

sich zu einem edlen Körper vereinigt, zu einer Einheit bestimmt, in eine Masse verbunden und befestigt, als *eine* Gestalt, von *einem* Geiste belebt). *IR*, 55–56.

17. As Joseph Luzzi remarks: "Anthropological inquiry never escapes the shadow of aesthetic vision in Goethe's portrait of contemporary Italy." "Italy without Italians: Literary Origins of a Romantic Myth," *Modern Language Notes* 117 (2002): 48–83.

18. Goethe's contemporary Alessandro Manzoni was extremely critical of the French Revolution, and his portrayal of the (revolutionary) masses in his historical novel *Promessi Sposi* (1827–1840) must be understood in this light. For instance, in a prominent scene concerning the bread riots in seventeenth-century Milan, the phenomenon of the crowd is defined as the spontaneous, accidental, or manipulated emergence of a general will, a unity without essence, or unified intent, which readily gives way to violence or chaos. See Wido Hempel, *Manzoni und die Darstellung der Menschenmenge als erzähltechnisches Problem in den 'Promessi Sposi,' bei Scott und in den historischen Romanen der französischen Romantik* (Krefeld: Scherpe, 1974).

19. E. T. A. Hoffmann, "My Cousin's Corner Window" (1822), in *The Golden Pot and Other Tales*, trans. Ritchie Robertson (Oxford: Oxford University Press, 1992), 337; hereafter abbreviated as *CCW*." For the original, see Hoffmann, "Des Vetters Eckfenster," in *Späte Werke* (Munich: Winkler, 1965), 595–622.

20. David Darby, "The Unfettered Eye: Glimpsing Modernity from E. T. A. Hoffmann's 'Corner Window,'" *Deutsche Vierteljahrsschrift für Geistesgeschichte und Literaturwissenschaft* 77 (June 2003): 274–94; see also the remarks in Wolfgang Kemp, "Das Bild der Menge (1780–1830)," *Städel-Jahrbuch* 4 (1973): 249–70.

21. See Helmut Lethen, "Eckfenster der Moderne. Wahrnehmungsexperimente bei Musil und E. T. A. Hoffmann," in *Robert Musils "Kakanien"—Subjekt und Geschichte: Festschrift für Karl Dinklage zum 80. Geburtstag*, ed. Josef Strutz (Munich: Fink, 1987), 195–229.

22. Walter Benjamin, *Charles Baudelaire: Ein Lyriker im Zeitalter des Hochkapitalismus*, in *Gesammelte Schriften*, ed. Rolf Tiedemann et al., 7 vols. (Frankfurt am Main: Suhrkamp, 1972–1989), 1:628. Translated as *Charles Baudelaire: A Lyric Poet in the Era of High Capitalism*, trans. Harry Zohn (London: New Left Books, 1973); hereafter abbreviated as *CB*. In the first version of the essay, in the section on the flaneur, Benjamin writes: "Dem deutschen Kleinbürger sind seine Grenzen eng gesteckt . . . Und

doch war Hoffmann nach seiner Veranlagung von der Familie der Poe und der Baudelaire" (1:551).

23. As Darby notes, "The continued application of such models to the representation of human crowds in the nineteenth century, as a modern, industrial economic and social order began to develop in Germany in the decades following the Congress of Vienna, has the potential only of nostalgic anachronism." "Unfettered Eye," 285.

24. Hoffmann was clearly familiar with J. C. Lavater's theories of physiognomy and, even more pertinently, G. C. Lichtenberg's physiognomic reading of Hogarth. See Darby, "Unfettered Eye," 283.

25. Walter Benjamin, "Über einige Motive bei Baudelaire," in *Illuminationen: Ausgewählte Schriften* (Frankfurt am Main: Suhrkamp, 1977), 1:196, 199; hereafter abbreviated as "UMB": "Die Masse war der bewegte Schleier; durch ihn hindurch sah Baudelaire Paris." See also *CB*; Richard Lehan, *The City in Literature: An Intellectual and Cultural History* (Berkeley: University of California Press, 1998), chap. 5; Marc E. Blanchard, *In Search of the City: Engels, Baudelaire, Rimbaud* (Saratoga, Calif.: Anima Libri, 1985).

26. Charles Baudelaire, *The Complete Verse*, trans. Francis Scarfe (London: Anvil Press, 1986), 186; hereafter abbreviated as *CV*.

27. Charles Baudelaire, *Petits Poèmes en Prose (Le Spleen de Paris)* (Paris: Flammarion, 1967). Translated as Charles Baudelaire, *The Poems in Prose*, trans. Francis Scarfe (London: Anvil Press, 1989), 58–59; hereafter abbreviated as *PP*.

28. Charles Baudelaire, "Le Peintre de la vie moderne," in *Oeuvres complètes*, ed. Marcel A. Ruff (Paris, 1968), 553. Translated as *The Painter of Modern Life and Other Essays*, trans. Jonathan Mayne (New York: Phaidon, 1964), 9; hereafter abbreviated as *PML*.

29. For a more detailed analysis along these lines, see Barbara Spackman, *Decadent Genealogies: The Rhetoric of Sickness from Baudelaire to D'Annunzio* (Ithaca, N.Y.: Cornell University Press, 1989), 42–58.

30. Edgar Allan Poe, "The Man of the Crowd," in *The Fall of the House of Usher and Other Writings* (London: Penguin, 2003), 132; hereafter abbreviated as "MC."

31. The same quote from La Bruyère appears in Baudelaire's "Solitude," in *Poems in Prose,* 100–101.

32. See Hinrich C. Seeba, "'Keine Systematie': Heine in Berlin and the Origin of the Urban Gaze," in *Heinrich Heine's Contested Identities*, ed. Jost Hermand and Robert C. Holub (New York: Peter Lang, 1999), 89–108.

33. Heinrich Heine, *Reisebilder* (Frankfurt am Main: Suhrkamp/Insel, 1980), 507.

34. Wolfgang Preisendanz, *Heinrich Heine: Werkstrukturen und Epochenbezüge* (Munich: Fink, 1973), 23, 66. As Preisendanz points out, in his writings from Paris, Heine repeatedly calls himself a flaneur (86).

35. Cf. Jost Hermand, "Tribune of the People or Aristocrat of the Spirit? Heine's Ambivalence Toward the Masses," in *Heinrich Heine's Contested Identities*, 155–74.

36. Russell A. Berman, *The Rise of the Modern German Novel: Crisis and Charisma* (Cambridge, Mass.: Harvard University Press, 1986), 232–33; hereafter abbreviated as *RMGN*.

37. John Plotz, *The Crowd: British Literature and Public Politics* (Berkeley: University of California Press, 2000), 103; hereafter abbreviated as *BLPP*.

38. The original reads: "Endlich allein! Man hört nur noch das Rollen einiger verspaeteter, abgehetzter Droschken. Fuer einige Stunden werden wir Schweigen haben, wenn nicht mehr. Endlich! Die Tyrannei des menschlichen Gesichtes (De Quincey!) hat aufgehoert, kein anderer kann mich noch quälen als ich selber. Endlich! Es ist mir also jetzt erlaubt, in einem Bad von Finsternis mich zu erquicken! Zuerst verschliess' ich alle Tueren. Mir ist, als vergrössere dieser doppelte Verschluss meine Einsamkeit, als verstärke er die Barrikade, die mich nun von der Welt abscheidet." Rainer Maria Rilke, *Die Aufzeichnungen des Malte Laurids Brigge* (Frankfurt am Main: Insel, 1982); hereafter abbreviated as *MLB*.

39. Hansgeorg Schmidt-Bergmann, *Die Anfänge der literarischen Avantgarde in Deutschland—Über Anverwandlung und Abwehr des italienischen Futurismus* (Stuttgart: Metzler, 1991), 27–28.

40. The original reads: "Ihr wisst nicht, was das ist, ein Dichter?—Verlaine . . . Nichts? Keine Erinnerung? Nein. Ihr habt ihn nicht unterschieden unter denen, die ihr kanntet? Unterschiede macht ihr keine, ich weiss. Aber es ist ein anderer Dichter, den ich lese, einer, der nicht in Paris wohnt, ein ganz anderer. Einer, der ein stilles Haus hat im Gebirge. Der klingt wie eine Glocke in reiner Luft. Ein glücklicher Dichter, der von seinem Fenster

erzählt und von den Glastüren seines Bücherschrankes, die eine liebe, einsame Weite nachdenklich spiegeln. Gerade der Dichter ist es, der ich hätte werden wollen." *MLB*, 482.

41. Fernando Pessoa, *The Book of Disquiet*, trans. Richard Zenith (Harmondsworth: Penguin, 2001), 165, 146.

42. Søren Kierkegaard, *Two Ages: The Age of Revolution and the Present Age: A Literary Review*, ed. Howard and Edna H. Long (Princeton, N.J.: Princeton University Press, 1978), 84; hereafter abbreviated as *TA*.

43. Howard N. Tuttle, *The Crowd Is Untruth: The Existential Critique of Mass Society in the Thought of Kierkegaard, Nietzsche, Heidegger, and Ortega y Gasset* (Peter Lang: New York, 1996).

44. Friedrich Nietzsche, "Vom Nutzen und Nachteil der Historie für das Leben," Unzeitgemässe Betrachtungen II, in *Kritische Studienausgabe*, ed. G. Colli and M. Montinari (Munich: dtv, 1999), 317; hereafter abbreviated as *HL*. The original reads: "Die Massen scheinen mir nur in dreierlei Hinsicht einen Blick zu verdienen: einmal als verschwimmende Copien der grossen Männer, auf schlechtem Papier und mit abgenutzten Platten hergestellt, sodann als Widerstand gegen die Grossen und endlich als Werkzeug der Grossen; im Übrigen hole sie der Teufel uns die Statistik." *HL*, 320.

45. C8, 22 in Friedrich Nietzsche, *Also sprach Zarathustra* (Frankfurt am Main: Suhrkamp/Insel, 1976).

46. Friedrich Nietzsche, *Thus Spoke Zarathustra*, trans. R. J. Hollingdale (London: Penguin, 1969), 78; hereafter abbreviated as *TSZ*. The original reads: "Wo die Einsamkeit aufhört, da beginnt der Markt; und wo der Markt beginnt, da beginnt auch der Lärm der großen Schauspieler und das Geschwirr der giftigen Fliegen./In der Welt taugen die besten Dinge noch nichts, ohne einen, der sie erst aufführt: große Männer heißt das Volk diese Aufführer./Wenig begreift das Volk das Große, das ist: das Schaffende." *Also sprach Zarathustra*, 54.

47. Thomas Mann, *Nietzsches Philosophie im Lichte unserer Erfahrung* (1947; Basel: Schwabe, 2005).

48. The original reads: "Er will und verkündet eine Zeit, in der man sich, unhistorisch-überhistorisch, aller Konstruktionen des Weltprozesses oder auch der Menschheitsgeschichte weislich enthält, überhaupt nicht mehr die Massen betrachtet, sondern die Großen, Zeitlos-Gleichzeitigen, die über das historische Gewimmel hinweg, ihr Geistergespräch führen." Mann, "Nietzsche's Philosophie," 347.

49. Friedrich Nietzsche, *The Will to Power*, ed. and trans. Walter Kaufmann (New York: Vintage, 1968), 4; hereafter abbreviated as *WP*.

50. For a detailed discussion, see Fredrick Appel, *Nietzsche contra Democracy* (Ithaca, N.Y.: Cornell University Press, 1999), 85–87.

51. On the coding of the crowd as female, see Spackman, *Decadent Genealogies*.

52. The original reads: "Nietzsches unauslotbare Provokation besteht darin, daß er die Verachtung der Menge für alles, was ihre Einrichtung im Horizont überschreitet, zum Material und zur Widerstandsmasse macht für eine korrektive, eine potenzierende Verachtung." Mann, "Nietzsches Philosophie," 5.

53. The original reads: "denn die Persönlichkeit, nicht die Masse, ist die eigentliche Trägerin des Allgemeinen." Thomas Mann, *Betrachtungen eines Unpolitischen* (Frankfurt am Main: Fischer, 2002), 262; hereafter abbreviated as *BU*.

54. The original reads: "Wir haben da den Unterschied zwischen Masse und Volk,—welcher dem Unterschied entspricht von Individuum und Persönlichkeit, Zivilisation und Kultur, sozialem und metaphysischem Leben. Die individualistische Masse ist demokratisch, das Volk aristokratisch. Jene ist international, diese eine mythische Persönlichkeit von eigentümlichsten Gepräge. Es ist falsch, das Überindividuelle in die Summe der Individuen, das Nationale *und* Menschheitliche in die soziale Masse zu verlegen. Träger des Allgemeinen ist das metaphysische Volk. Es ist darum geistig falsch, Politik im Geist und Sinn der Masse zu treiben." *BU*, 263.

55. Hannah Arendt, *The Origins of Totalitarianism* (New York: Harcourt, Brace, 1951).

56. The original reads: "der literarischen Publizität, welche geistig und gesellschaftlich zugleich ist (wie das Theater), und in der das Einsamkeitspathos gesellschaftsfähig, bürgerlich möglich, sogar bürgerlich-verdienstlich wird." *BU*, 38.

57. The original reads: "Diese Schrift, die die Hemmungslosigkeit privat-brieflicher Mitteilung besitzt, bietet in der Tat, nach meinem besten Wissen und Gewissen, die geistigen Grundlagen dessen, was ich als Künstler zu geben hatte, und was der Öffentlichkeit gehört." *BU*, 39.

58. Thomas Mann, "Achtung, Europa!," in *Gesammelte Werke*, ed. Peter de Mendelssohn (Frankfurt am Main: S. Fischer, 1986), 127–40; hereafter abbreviated as "AE."

59. José Ortega y Gasset, *The Revolt of the Masses* (New York: Norton, 1991), 73, 74, 92.

60. Bernhard Weyergraf and Helmut Lethen, "Der Einzelne in der Massengesellschaft," in *Literatur der Weimarer Republik 1918–1933: Hansers Sozialgeschichte der deutschen Literatur vom 16. Jahrhundert bis zur Gegenwart*, ed. Bernhard Weyergraf (Munich: Carl Hanser, 1995), 8:639.

61. Thomas Mann, "Mario und der Zauberer," in *Sämtliche Erzählungen* (Stockholm: Fischer, 1959). Translated as "Mario and the Magician," in *"Death in Venice" and Seven Other Stories*, trans. H. T. Lowe-Porter (New York: Vintage, 1989); hereafter abbreviated as "MM."

62. See Alan Bance, "The Political Becomes Personal: *Disorder and Early Sorrow* and *Mario and the Magician*," in *The Cambridge Companion to Thomas Mann*, ed. Ritchie Robertson (Cambridge: Cambridge University Press, 2002), 107–18; "The infection of nationalism or xenophobia in the air of Torre di Venere and of Mussolini's Italy attacks the liberal cosmopolitan narrator himself, so that he experiences a 'nordic' distaste for the superficiality of the Italian population and the brazenness of the southern climate, and develops a most illiberal impatience with Italian culture as a whole. A kind of infection is discernible in the way that the 'disease' of fascism spread to Germany from Italy" (115).

63. See Bernd Widdig, *Männerbünde und Massen: Zur Krise männlicher Identität in der Literatur der Moderne* (Opladen: Westdeutscher Verlag, 1992), chap. 5, "Thomas Manns *Mario und der Zauberer* aus massenpsychologischer Sicht."

64. Gustave Le Bon, *The Crowd: A Study of the Popular Mind* (Dunwoody, Ga.: N. S. Berg, 1968), 54; hereafter abbreviated as *C*.

65. Thomas Mann, *Doktor Faustus: Das Leben des deutschen Tonsetzers Adrian Leverkühn, erzählt von einem Freunde* (Frankfurt am Main: Fischer, 1975), 484; hereafter abbreviated as DF.

66. Peter Sloterdijk, *Die Verachtung der Massen: Versuch über Kulturkämpfe in der modernen Gesellschaft* (Frankfurt am Main: Suhrkamp, 2000), 21; hereafter abbreviated as *VM*. Cf. Robert Michels, *Masse, Führer, Intellektuelle: Politisch-soziologische Aufsätze 1906–1933* (Frankfurt am Main: Campus, 1987).

67. Although *Crowds and Power* was published only in 1960, it unmistakably bears the traces of a key experience in the young Canetti's life, the 1927 workers' revolt in Vienna that culminated in the burning of the palace of justice. For a detailed historical re-construction, as well as the repercussion of this event in the works of various Viennese writers, see Stefan Jonsson, "Masses, Mind, Matter: Political Passions and Collective Violence in Post-Imperial Austria," in *Representing the Passions: Histories, Bodies, Visions*, ed. Richard Meyer (Los Angeles: Getty Institute, 2003), 69–102.

CHAPTER 15A

1. Cicero, *Brutus*, 183.
2. Cicero, *Pro Q. Rosico*, 29.
3. Sources: John Henry Freese, *Cicero: The Speeches* (Cambridge, Mass: Harvard University Press, 1930); P. G. W. Glare, *Oxford Latin Dictionary* (Oxford: Clarendon Press, 1982); Richard Gummere, ed., *Seneca, Moral Essays*, vol. 1 (Cambridge, Mass: Harvard University Press, 1917); G. L. Hendrickson, *Cicero, Brutus* (Cambridge, Mass: Harvard University Press, 1930).

CHAPTER 16

This project was completed in part with the support of the Center for Advanced Research Technology in the Arts and Humanities (CARTAH) at the University of Washington.

1. Walter Benjamin, "The Interior, the Trace," in *The Arcades Project*, trans. Howard Eiland and Kevin MacLaughlin (Cambridge, Mass.: Harvard University Press, 1999), 216.

2. Gagosian Gallery, press release, "Damien Hirst: Theories, Models, Methods, Approaches, Assumptions, Results and Findings," August 9, 2000.

3. Gordon Burn, "The Hay Smells Different to the Lovers than to the Horses," in *Theories, Models, Methods, Approaches, Assumptions, Results and Findings*, vol. 1, exhibition catalog to Damien Hirst exhibit of the same name, 11.

4. Peter Galassi, "Gursky's World," in *Andreas Gursky* (New York: Museum of Modern Art, 2001), 38.

5. Nancy Spector, quoted from http://www.guggenheim collection.org/site/artist_work_md_59A_1.html.

6. Galassi, "Gursky's World," 38.

7. Adam Phillips, *Monogamy* (New York: Vintage Books, 1999), n.p., part 7.

8. National Gay and Lesbian Association Stylebook, Addenda: Gay/Lesbian Terminology, http://www.nlgja.org/pubs/style.html.

9. Tom Vanderbilt, "Doomsday Rooms," photographs by Richard Barnes, *Nest: A Quarterly of Interiors* 11 (Winter 2000–2001): 207.

10. Sigmund Freud, *The Letters of Sigmund Freud,* ed. Ernst L. Freud, trans. Tania and James Stern (New York: Basic Books, 1975); quoted in Jonathan Crary, *Suspensions of Perception: Attention, Spectacle, and Modern Culture* (Cambridge, Mass.: MIT Press, 1999), 363.

11. "People," lyrics by Bob Merrill, from *Funny Girl* (1964).

12. Rex Stout, *The Red Box* (1937; reprint, Pyramid, 1964), 7.

13. Rex Stout, *The Second Confession* (1949; reprint, Bantam, 1975), 1.

14. Rex Stout, *The Doorbell Rang* (1965; reprint, Bantam, 1971), 4.

Index

Aachen, 145
Abraham, 142
Adams, John, 306
Addison, Joseph, 6, 189
Adorno, Theodor W., 91, 204, 219
Ady, Endre, 302
Aemilius Scaurus, Marcus (ancient Roman politician), 91
Agnes (early Christian martyr), 143
agoraphobia, 359, 360
Agni (god from the *Rigveda*), 151
Alberti, Leon Battista, 311, 313–315, 343
Alcuin, 89
Al-Hakim (Fatimid caliph,) 137–138
Ali, Tariq, 109
Allahabad, 133
Allen, Robert, 219
Altamont Speedway, 128, 360
Al-Vista (camera), 14
Alypius, 114
American Revolution, x, 2, 79, 81, 293, 298, 301, 303–305, 380, 387
Amsterdam, 306
Anchor Point, Alaska 290–292
Anne Boleyn, 105
Angrand, Charles, 169
Anthony (early Christian martyr), 145
anti-crowd attitudes, ix–x, xiv, xx, 105, 203–207, 211, 214, 335, 351
anti-Iraq war protests, xvi, 93, 109, 221, 289–290, 374
antislavery movement, 303–305
antiwar and student protests of the 1960s and 1970s, xi, 44, 92, 107–108, 303, 305, 332, 361–374

Aparecida (Virgin of), 134
Apollinaire, Guillaume, 172
Apollo, 113
architecture, and human multitudes, 1, 16, 18, 20, 96, 99, 113, 151, 214–215
Arendt, Hannah, 79–80, 82, 85, 88, 90, 94–95, 203–205, 207, 214, 222, 354, 358
Aristotle, 2, 128, 279, 382
Arnold, Benedict, 116
Atget, Eugène, 360
Athens, 4, 81–83, 229, 279, 388, 400
Attis, 143
Auerbach, Erich, 369
Augustine of Hippo, 114, 337
Augustus Caesar, 81–83, 85, 114, 388
Auschwitz, 311, 315
Austen, Jane, 188–189
average man, and Everyman, 4, 50–51, 204, 276, 322, 420
Azaña, Miguel, 241

Babel, 152–153
Bach, Johann Sebastian, 182
Bailly, Jean Sylvain, 47, 54
Baldessari, John, xviii, 193–196
Balla, Giacomo, 170, 176–178, 183, 404
Ballard, J. G., 360, 374
Balzac, Honoré de, 59
Ban Gu (scribe), 251–252
Bapst, Germain, 162
Barber, Benjamin, 216
Baron, Ron, 277
Barker, Robert, 12, 14, 161–162, 403